Yellowstone Trail and Backcountry Field Manual

Thomas P. Bohannan

HAYDEN PUBLISHING
Orlando, Florida

First Edition, Version 1.00

Published by: Hayden Publishing
Orlando, Florida

Library of Congress Control Number: 20189323539
ISBN: 978-0-9854072-4-7 Paperback

Front Cover Photo: Solitary Geyser Trail, taken May 15, 2016. Photo courtesy Rhonda Tucker. Used with permission.

Back Cover Photo: Fairy Creek Trail near Upper Geyser Basin Overlook, taken September 28, 2014. Photo courtesy Rhonda Tucker. Used with permission.

Disclaimer: The mileage figures and other information contained within this book are believed to be accurate as of the publication date. Trail construction is a fact of life within Yellowstone, and at any time, trails may be realigned or modified such that the specific measurements and GPS locations provided herein may become out of date. Therefore, the author assumes no liability for inaccuracies and/or any hardship or financial impacts caused by the information contained within this book. Similarly, many of the trails described in this book are either abandoned or itinerantly closed to public use. As such, the author assumes no liability for your safety or any legal ramifications associated with the reader's use of any trail inside the park. You must check with the park's Backcountry Offices for the status of all trails and campsites prior to setting out to explore the park's vast backcountry. Please be safe.

Dedicated to Kimberly Craig Bohannan

July 19, 1966 - August 6, 2016

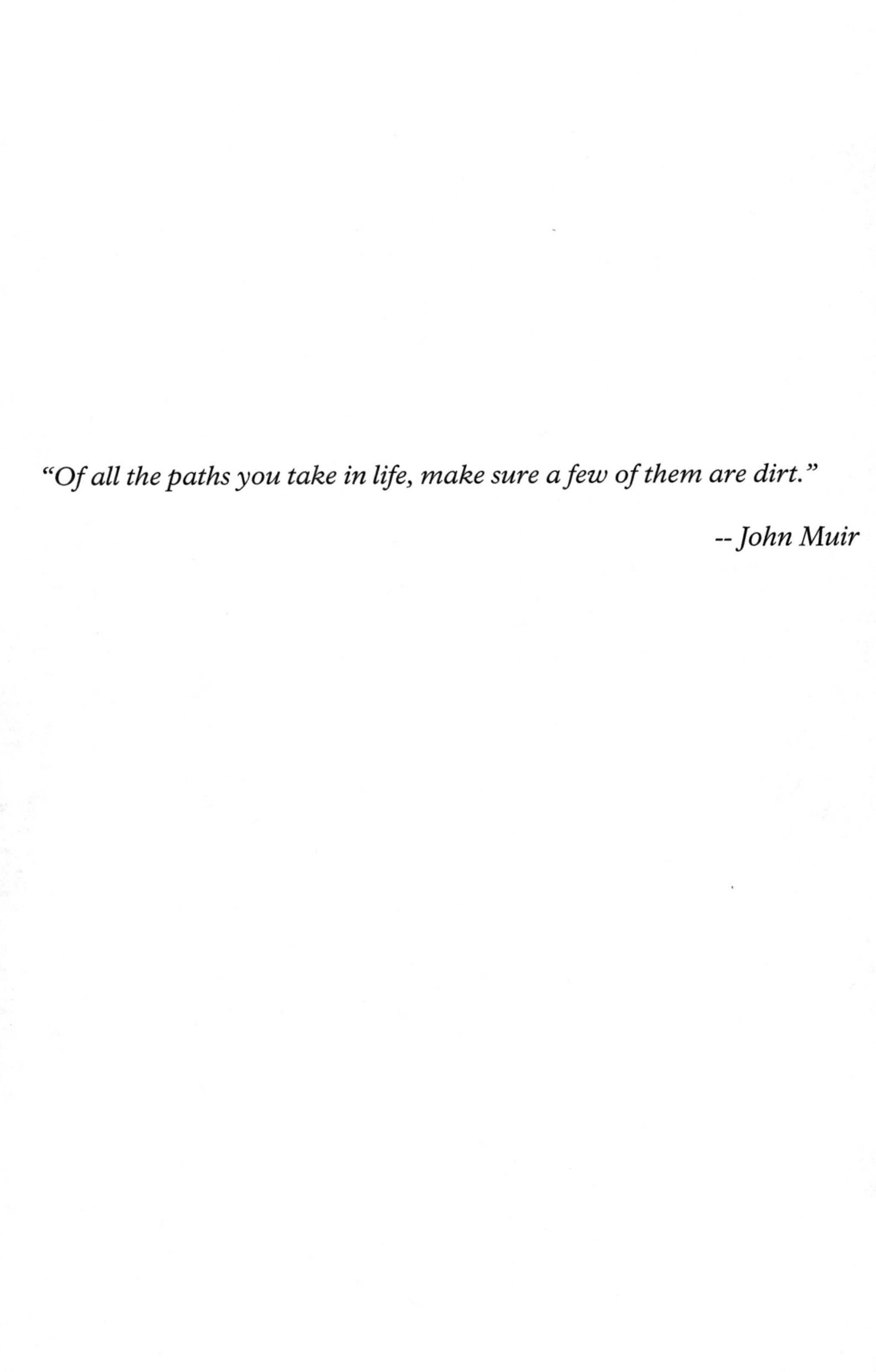

"Of all the paths you take in life, make sure a few of them are dirt."

-- John Muir

Preface

This is not your typical Yellowstone hiking book. It is much more of a technical and logistical book rather than one that vividly describes what you'll experience on the park's trails. Whereas all of the other trail books only reference about half of Yellowstone's trails (albeit the more popular ones), there's never been a book that provided information about every trail in the park. Now there is. You'll find details of literally every trail that exists within Yellowstone, as well as more than four dozen others that are no longer maintained.

This process began some four years ago. I had many of the trail paths in my own GPS devices. The park's Geographic Information System (GIS) had all of the trails in it, but they had been entered using timed GPS readings. That meant a waypoint every five to ten minutes. As a result, the trail data looked like a series of straight lines, not exactly the path that most trails travel.

So I spent close to a year with the GIS data (provided to me by the park's Spatial Analysis Center) overlaid on top of Google Earth satellite imagery. I went mile by mile for the entire trail system and rectified the data with the trail paths worn into the ground (and easily visible for the most part on the imagery). That, combined with random bits of my personal GPS data allowed me to produce the most accurate maps available of the trails in the park. While doing this, I was able to ascertain the latitude and longitude of many reference points along many of those trails (such as creek crossings, trail junctions, lakes, campsites, etc.).

I then spent another year creating the tables you will see in this book — they provide useful information about each trail as well as a list of those reference points (more than 2,000 of them). That was followed by the organizing of the data into districts and chapters, and then writing the material that explains a bit of detail about each of those trails.

All of the electronic work I have done on the trail system in the park has been consolidated into a GIS system (ESRI's ArcMap) and converted into files suitable for use with Google Earth. If you would like a copy of the KML file for the trails, e-mail me at yellowstonetrailbook@gmail.com.

Let me also state that I spend a considerable amount of time throughout this book pointing out and discussing situations where people have been injured or killed in Yellowstone. My intent is not to be dire or to make it sound as if everyone who comes to the park gets killed. But I do want to impress upon you that Yellowstone is a wild place and operates by a set of rules and conditions that exist apart from the "safe" environment you are perhaps used to at home in your local community. For avid hikers, this will not be a new thing, but I know many people cut their hiking teeth in Yellowstone, and I want you to be prepared.

Yellowstone is one of those places where it is a really good idea to heed the regulations and safety information that rangers and the signage around the park offer to you. Relatively speaking, given the number of people who visit this place every year, very few people experience any injury or lose their lives. But it does happen. Enjoy your hiking and camping in this magnificent place, but do not be lulled into a sense of false security. Do it, but be safe doing it is the takeaway message here.

Finally, this book is a "field guide," even though it is quite large. I realize for some people its size will preclude them from taking it out into the field with them, but once you've been through it, you will understand why it is so big. Providing even the most basic information about 250 trails is no small task and does not lend itself to creating a small book. I apologize for not getting it small enough to make it easy to carry, but it was important to provide you with as much information as possible to give you a robust appreciation for the vastness of Yellowstone's trail and backcountry system.

The Bannock Indian and Nez Perce Historic Trails

A quick note about two primarily historic trails that traversed the park, the Bannock Indian Trail and the Nez Perce Historic Trail. They are not discussed in any great detail in this book, except for the random occasion where an existing park trail intersects or travels along the path of one of them. There are plenty of other materials on those two trails and each is worthy of a book unto themselves, and it seemed overly duplicative to discuss those here.

Acknowledgments

In 2011, at the behest and recommendation of my wife, Kimberly, I spent my first summer working in Yellowstone National Park. We had gotten married in 1988, and from that time, at least once every year (and sometimes multiple times) we would spend a couple of weeks in the greater Yellowstone area. I can still very vividly recall the look of astonishment and excitement on her face as we drove through Hayden Valley on her first visit. It was in the middle of the annual rut in August, and we immediately got stuck in one of the largest bison jams we would ever experience. There were literally hundreds of them crowding the road and the valley. The next day we made our way up to the summit of Mt. Washburn, our first hike in Yellowstone together. She was taken with the incredible beauty of this magnificent place, as much as I had been on my first visit some ten years earlier

We would return time and time again to celebrate birthdays, our anniversary, her graduation from college, Christmas, and sometimes in celebration of nothing. One year we went three times within the space of six weeks. Yellowstone became a spiritual place for us—a place where we'd go each year to cleanse our minds and hearts of the world around us, our work, etc. We'd always have trouble picking out which trails we'd want to hike; it was always a competition between the ones we loved and wanting to experience new ones.

When the opportunity arose for me to work in Yellowstone, we were mature enough in our relationship that we felt like we could live apart for the five months I'd be away. I came out to do research for a book I wanted to write, what would become *Yellowstone Mileposts*, published in 2014. I went to work for the Yellowstone Association (since merged with the Yellowstone Foundation to form Yellowstone Forever). I ended up writing another book first (*Benchmark Hunting in Yellowstone*) because of that job. I later went to work for Xanterra, the company that operates the hotels and restaurants in Yellowstone, the next year.

In 2015 I got my dream job. I was incredibly humbled and honored to become a U.S. Park Ranger to help protect the park, educate its visitors, greet people coming to Yellowstone for their very first time, and prepare people for their first trip into the park's backcountry. Many of those people showed up with that same look of amazement and excitement I saw in Kim's face on her first trip, and that always put a smile on my face. I returned to the same position in 2016.

On August 6, 2016, though, my world changed forever. After working that day, I was notified that my lovely wife, my best friend, my soulmate, and my Yellowstone exploring buddy had been killed in an automobile accident back home in Maryland. Some guy had fallen asleep at the wheel after having visited family in Washington, D.C., crossed the centerline and hit her vehicle head on, killing her instantly. She had just celebrated her 50th birthday and in three more weeks was coming out to visit me in Yellowstone for several days.

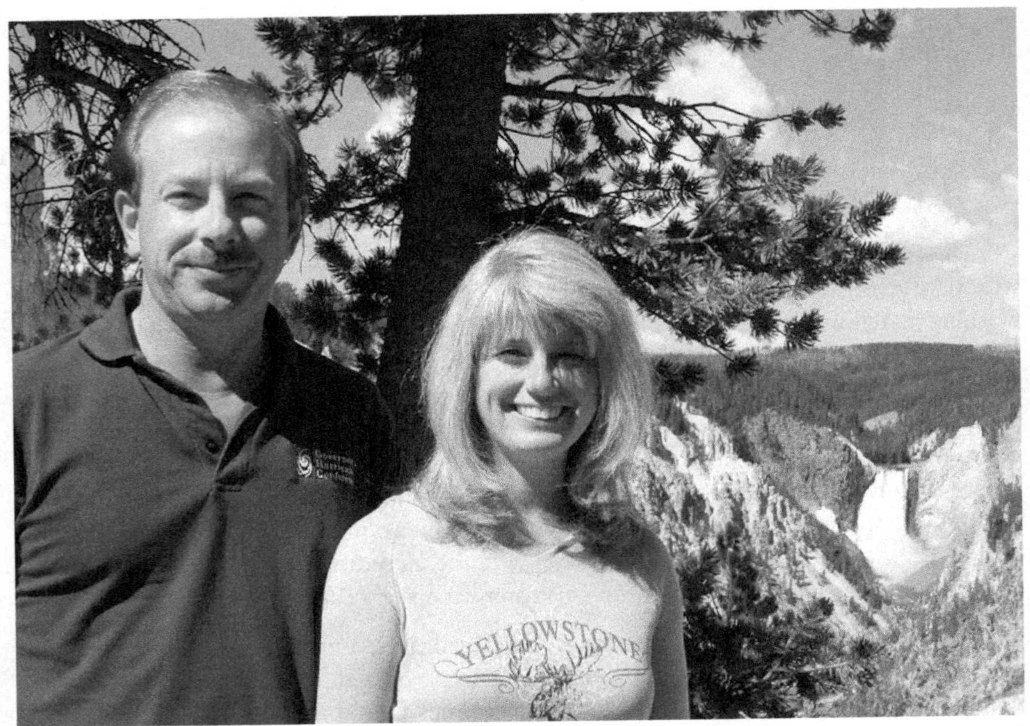

Kim and I had always had discussions about what one of us would need to do if something happened to the other, and we always had our legal paperwork in order. Just in case. This always took place in the context of me working and living in what is, in reality, a fairly dangerous place. It literally never once occurred to me that I'd have to deal with it the other way around.

I had begun work on this book in 2014, shortly after *Mileposts* was published, and had started the actual writing process while I was in Yellowstone in 2015. I was about halfway done with the initial draft when Kim was taken from me. Once that happened, I couldn't even bring myself to open the book up again for a year and a half. I managed to get back to writing on it in February of 2018. She would have wanted me to finish it.

And so to Kim's spirit and her love of hiking in Yellowstone, I dedicate this book. Her ashes are spread on the north face of Mt. Washburn, just off the parking area at the top of Chittenden Road. We had picnicked there a few times over the years, and the view of Amphitheater Valley from that point was one of her most favorite places in the world. She'd always told me that's where she wanted to rest when she passed, and so I honored that request. And now she's supporting a tree and the wildflowers there.

I received an outpouring of support from followers on Twitter and Facebook, from Kim's extended family and coworkers, and from my coworkers and friends from Yellowstone. I was incredibly touched by the offers of assistance in a variety of ways, as well as the thoughts and prayers offered by everyone. Two of her sisters, Kelly Morton and Millie Smith, graciously came up to our home for several days to help me deal with the fallout and all of the arrangements that had to take place.

There are a great many people who, in one way or another, helped make this book possible. I'd like to extend my appreciation to the staff at the Yellowstone Heritage and Research Center (HRC) and the park's library. I spent almost every off day during my 2015 and 2016 seasons there doing research for this book. I am also grateful to Ann Rodman, Carrie Guiles, and Julie Rose at the park's Spatial Analysis Center for assisting me with the data I requested related to this project (as well as all sorts of other odd little projects I've worked on for the past several years).

One of the really neat things about working for the NPS is that the overwhelming majority of rangers who work in the parks are there because they absolutely love what they do. So it was an incredible honor to work with so many people excited to be doing what they do. There were far too many rangers to mention by name, but I will call out Rob Giles. Rob and I had the unique experience of being the only two full-time staff for the South Entrance gate in my first season in the park. We were supposed to have seven full-timers there, but a variety of issues conspired to make it just the two of us. We filled in with temporary help from other gates, Interpretive rangers from the Grant Visitor Center, and staff from all sorts of other places over the course of the five months of that season. Rob and I worked really well together and working with him that summer (and the following summer) was one of my most favorite experiences in my life.

I also had the incredible fortune to work for an outstanding supervisor, Denise Altherr. She got hired on as the gate supervisor at the same time Rob and I were hired. She'd worked at the gate for several years, but had just taken a position in Yosemite National Park, so she had to pack all her stuff up and drive all the way back to Yellowstone. As you move through life and work different jobs and whatnot, you invariably have good and not-so-good people to work for. Denise was one of those people who respected her employees, listened to them, accepted input from them, wouldn't ask you to do anything she wouldn't also do, etc. She was a class act in so many ways and I hated to leave her after Kim's death.

I'd also like to thank Cynthia Garcia. Coming out of a depression after having lost someone so close to you is tough to do, and it takes a special someone to help get you out of that funk. She did it without even being aware that she was doing it through the sheer awesomeness of her personality. That meant more to me than she'll ever know.

And finally, I'd like to acknowledge the assistance I got from a handful of people in reviewing the drafts of this book before it went to press. I had several experienced Yellowstone hikers and fans read through the information here to ensure it made sense, was organized in a legitimate manner, and contained as few grammatical errors as possible. Those people include Paul Rubinstein (co-author of the book on the park's waterfalls), David Jennys, Rob Brown, and Kenneth Carrothers. And I am incredibly grateful to my editors, Susan Jennys and Vong Hamilton for helping make the end result as polished as possible. Thank you all for your time and assistance.

Table of Contents

Introduction

Yellowstone National Park is the flagship park of the U.S. National Park system. It was created by an act of Congress that was signed by President Ulysses S. Grant on March 1, 1872. It is the second largest park in terms of area in the lower 48 states, surpassed in size only by Death Valley National Park. Its footprint occupies 2.2 million square acres (3,452 square miles), an area larger than the combined sizes of Delaware and Rhode Island. In 2017, it saw over 4.5 million visitors, a record, though visitation levels are expected to continue to increase over the coming years.

Of those millions of visitors, however, only a small handful get far enough off the "beaten path" into what we refer to as the park's "backcountry." Literally millions of people see Old Faithful every summer, but just a few hundred see Union Falls, one of the most spectacular waterfalls in the lower 48. The main difference is that you have to want to go see Union Falls; you have to make an effort to get there. And many people either just don't want to exert the effort to do it, or don't have the time or wherewithal to do it. But the park's backcountry and trail system is unrivaled in this part of the world.

Yellowstone has over 220 maintained trails covering more than 1,100 miles, and well over a hundred miles of other trails that have been abandoned but are still navigable to one degree or another. Some of these trails are so busy you're often standing shoulder to shoulder with other people when hiking, while others will take you into literally the most remote places in the lower 48 where it's possible (indeed, likely) you won't see another soul for days at a time.

Yellowstone is unparalleled in terms of what kinds of hikes you can avail yourself of. You can hike to thermal features, you can hike to mountains, you can hike to valleys, you can hike to rivers, you can hike to waterfalls, you can hike to lakes, you can hike to...well, you get the idea. And on some of the trails, you can hike to all of those.

Yellowstone has over 300 known waterfalls, more than a hundred of which would easily qualify them as state parks. Yellowstone is one of the few places on the planet (less than a half dozen) where you can hike to see thermal features in their natural state. It truly is one of the most magnificent places on the planet.

I have been coming to this park for more than thirty years and still have yet to see many areas of the park. For many of those years I came as a visitor, but I have several of the last few summers working in this spectacular place. During two of those summers, I had the incredible honor of working as a U.S. Park Ranger, helping protect the park and educate people from all over the world about its incredible wonders.

Frontcountry vs. Backcountry

This book spends a lot of time talking about frontcountry vs. backcountry. What is the difference? There are no specific delineations of when the frontcountry becomes the backcountry. In Yellowstone, rangers typically refer to anything more than a couple hundred yards off the roads or developed areas as "backcountry." To many, the term denotes any area away from development, and if you have ever been in the park and been more than a hundred yards off the pavement, you can attest that, even at that relatively short distance, it feels remote. People have gotten lost in Yellowstone when they were only a few dozen yards off the beaten path; it is much easier than you might think.

This book describes all of the trails in the park. Some of these are listed as "frontcountry" trails and others as "backcountry" trails. The primary difference is that the frontcountry trails are pretty much entirely in or around the developed areas (the boardwalk trails through the thermal basin at Old Faithful, for example).

And then there are what are known as "threshold" trails. These are short trails that kind of skirt the line between frontcountry and backcountry—mostly the short "out and back" trails that take you to interesting features but not into areas where camping is available.

There will be more discussion of this issue in the trail description section of the book.

Reasons to Hike

The reasons people hike are as varied as the people who hike. But they generally fall into the following broad categories.

Exploration. One of the primary draws of Yellowstone is its vast array of unique features, everything from unique mountains to wildlife to thermal features. And being able to get out and see things that not only do many visitors to the park not see, but most people in the world never get to see. At least, not in person.

Exercise. This is a big one for me. When I am working in the park, I love to get out and get my exercise by hiking a trail. It not only serves as physical exercise, but as exercise for the mind as well.

Escape. Many people like to get out into the backcountry to get away from it all—the hustle and bustle of daily life. As is noted above, one of the most remote places in the country is in Yellowstone. There literally is no better place to escape.

Connect with Nature. As John Muir once said, "Climb the mountains and get their good tidings. Nature's peace will flow into you as sunshine flows into trees. The winds will blow their own freshness into you, and the storms their energy, while cares will drop off like autumn leaves." Many people use this country's wild places to reconnect with the earth, and there is no better place to do that than Yellowstone; you will literally be able to see nature in its wildest form just a few yards from a busy highway.

Hiking is one of those activities that does not cost anything to do. Aside from the suggested bear spray that we recommend everyone carry in the park, you can go out on a day hike with nothing but what you have on you and have a great time. There are others, though, who not only wish to camp out in the woods, but they expend considerable amounts of money on the finest equipment to do it.

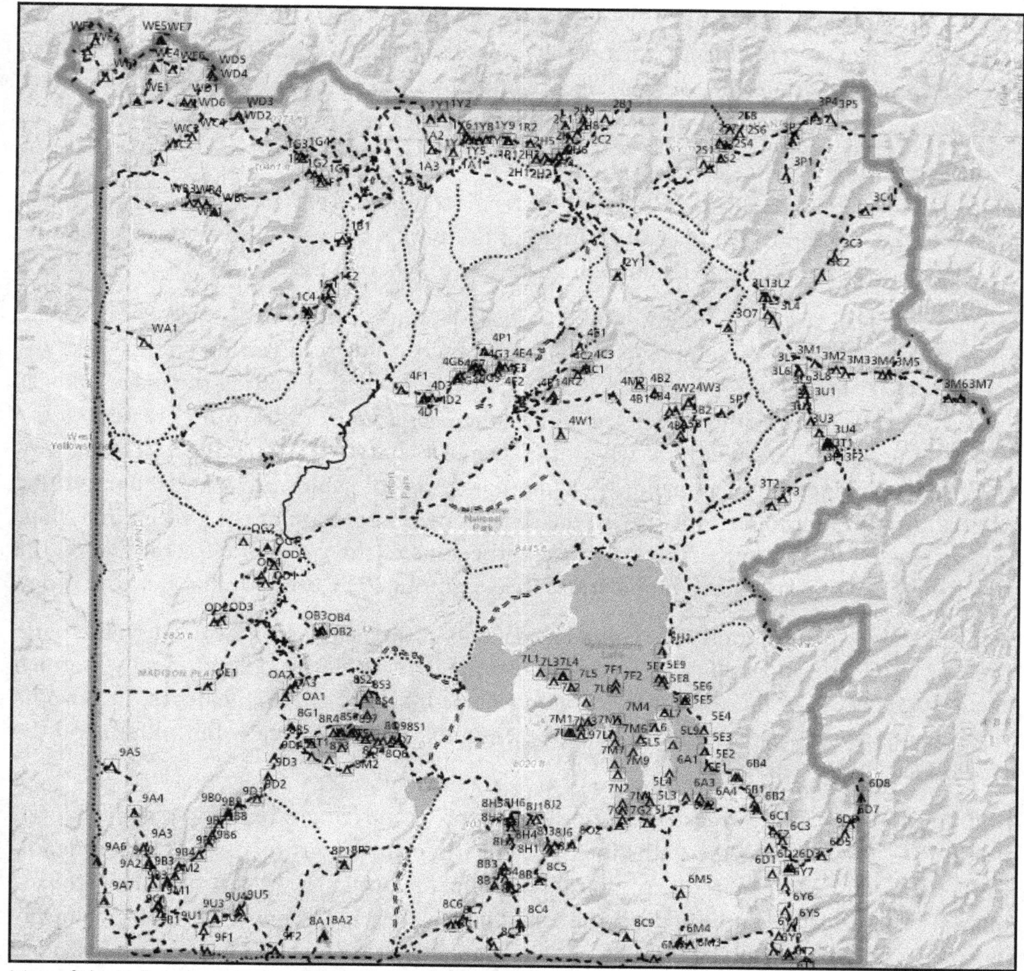

Map of the Yellowstone trail and backcountry campsite system. Produced by the author.

You can go as big or as small as you wish. And you can go as far as you wish. The park has trails as short as a third of a mile (0.5km), but there are also those that are more than two dozen miles long. You can string several trails together to create hikes of over 100 miles (161km) if that is your heart's desire.

Day Hikes vs. Overnight Hikes

Day hikes are, as the name would suggest, those where a hiker does not spend the night in the backcountry. The overwhelming majority of casual hiking in the park is day hiking. It is free and requires no permits so long as you do not enter areas that are posted as being off-limits, and there are plenty of things you can see and experience without having to spend the night out in the woods.

Overnight hikes, those where hikers camp in a backcountry campsite, do require a permit, however. This requires a visit to one of the park's backcountry offices to watch an orientation video and to secure your permit for a particular campsite or set of campsites. This is done to ensure your safety and to ensure campsites are not overloaded. Between Memorial Day and

Labor Day, camping permits are $3 per person, per night if you're on foot, or $5 per person, per night if you're traveling in with stock (horses, llamas, etc.). The money generated through these fees are used to offset the cost of maintaining the backcountry program and for trail maintenance, and it is still much cheaper than a hotel.

Historical Context

In order to understand why the park's trail system is so vast and expansive, and why so many trails have been abandoned over the course of the park's 145-year+ existence, it might be beneficial and enlightening to examine how we got to where we are today.[1]

Much of the trail system in Yellowstone has its roots in time before the park even existed. The Thorofare Trail, for example, is a well-worn path used by migrating animals and the trappers who pursued them long before anyone even thought of setting the place aside as a national park. Many others, especially the longer boundary trails, were created by the U.S. Army for patrolling the park when they were in charge of protecting it. This is why, seemingly coincidentally, the majority of the park's patrol cabins are located along these longer trails. When the National Park Service took over operation of the park in 1916, their rangers elected to continue using the trails and cabins as the backbone for protecting the park from poachers and other vandals, and they continue to be used for that purpose today.

Many of the remaining trails are remnants of some of the original roads through the park. The Spring Creek and Solfatara Trails are examples of these. And then, finally, a much smaller percentage of the trails were created to take hikers to specific features, such as the Monument Geyser Basin Trail (the first created in the park specifically for hiking) and the Riddle Lake Trail.

Trail development in the park began under its second superintendent. Philetus W. Norris didn't distinguish among the paths intended for use primarily as roads, paths intended as bridle paths, and paths intended primarily as foot paths until 1881. At that time, he listed 213 miles of trails as bridle paths and another eight listed simply as "trails."[2] He had specifically constructed these paths to be used by people who had gotten off their horses and intended to walk to view a specific feature or group of features. Bridle paths were to be used by visitors in horse-drawn wagons, and the roads (of which he listed 153 miles) were for wagons ferrying visitors en masse from one point to another.

When the U.S. Army took over in 1886, their focus was on protecting the park and, within a few years, improving the roads throughout the park (via the Army Corps of Engineers). They exerted no effort to build trails for purposes related to recreation, but did, as an adjunct to their mandate to patrol the park for poachers and other vandals, create many horse paths used by their soldiers in the conduct of those patrols. Many of those along the park's boundaries and in the outer reaches of the park still exist as trails to this day. Many of the trails they used to move from one part of the park to another within the interior of the park have long since been abandoned, however.

Though there was the occasional, random mention of the fact that the trails (specifically) were in a poor state of disrepair, the U.S. Army did little actual trail construction or maintenance anywhere in the park until 1910 when a concentrated effort was made to clear the years of downed trees across those trails that did exist and to improve access to areas of the park for fire control operations in the aftermath of a deadly and extensive wildfire season in the west that year. The trails along the southern border from the Snake River Ranger Station were built to the east in 1910 and the west (to Bechler) and north from there in 1911, in both cases to facilitate patrol work of the Army. It would not be until the National Park Service was formed in 1916 that additional work would be undertaken on improving the recreational trail system in Yellowstone.

Much of the early trail work under NPS was done to facilitate access to areas of the park by people on horseback. In 1915, the first automobiles were allowed into the park, and it was quickly discovered that horses and autos could not use the same road system (for a variety of reasons, but mostly because it spooked the horses when the noisy vehicles of the day drove past them).

A wealthy socialite by the name of Alice Morris spent a considerable amount of time visiting Yellowstone and grew to love the park's trail system. She would speak of this to the park's first NPS superintendent, Chester Lindsley. He would go on to ask her for recommendations on how to improve the trails in the park and she spent the spring and summer of 1917 riding through Yellowstone cataloging and marking the trails, and studying areas for new trails. The NPS developed the first actual map of the park's trail system based on her work (see the following page). This was the beginning of the formalized management of trails in Yellowstone. Many of the trails she proposed would go on to be built. Others never quite made it into the inventory, but would appear over and over again on the various master plans the park developed over the subsequent 60 years.

One of her recommendations, a "circular trail" that connected the hotels and places of interest was completed in 1923 and named in honor of Howard Eaton, a popular guide who'd taken many people through the park on horseback. Eaton passed away in 1922 before he was able to make use of his namesake trail, however. See the chapter on Lost and Forgotten Trails for more information about this storied trail.

By the end of the 1920s, more than 900 miles (1448km) of trail existed in Yellowstone. As the country went through the Great Depression and FDR enacted the New Deal with programs like the Emergency Conservation Work Act (ECW) and created agencies such as the Civilian Conservation Corps (CCC), another 150 miles of trail would be developed (as well as the almost complete rehabilitation of the existing trails throughout the park). And although a handful of short trails have been built since the CCC completed its work, the vast majority of today's trail system exists much as it did prior to the onset of World War II.

In the early 1970s, the park began a much more focused program of backcountry management and implemented the current campsite system. Over the succeeding 20+ years, park planners went through the process of developing a formal Backcountry Management Plan. It outlined how the trail system would be managed, how individuals would be permitted to interact with the wild spaces of the park, etc. The plan went through a variety of hearings and approval processes over the course of several months.

Despite his predecessor's approval of the document, however, Mike Finley, the park's new superintendent in 1994, had several issues with the new plan and refused to approve it. And even though today the system is managed in accordance with many of the principles outlined

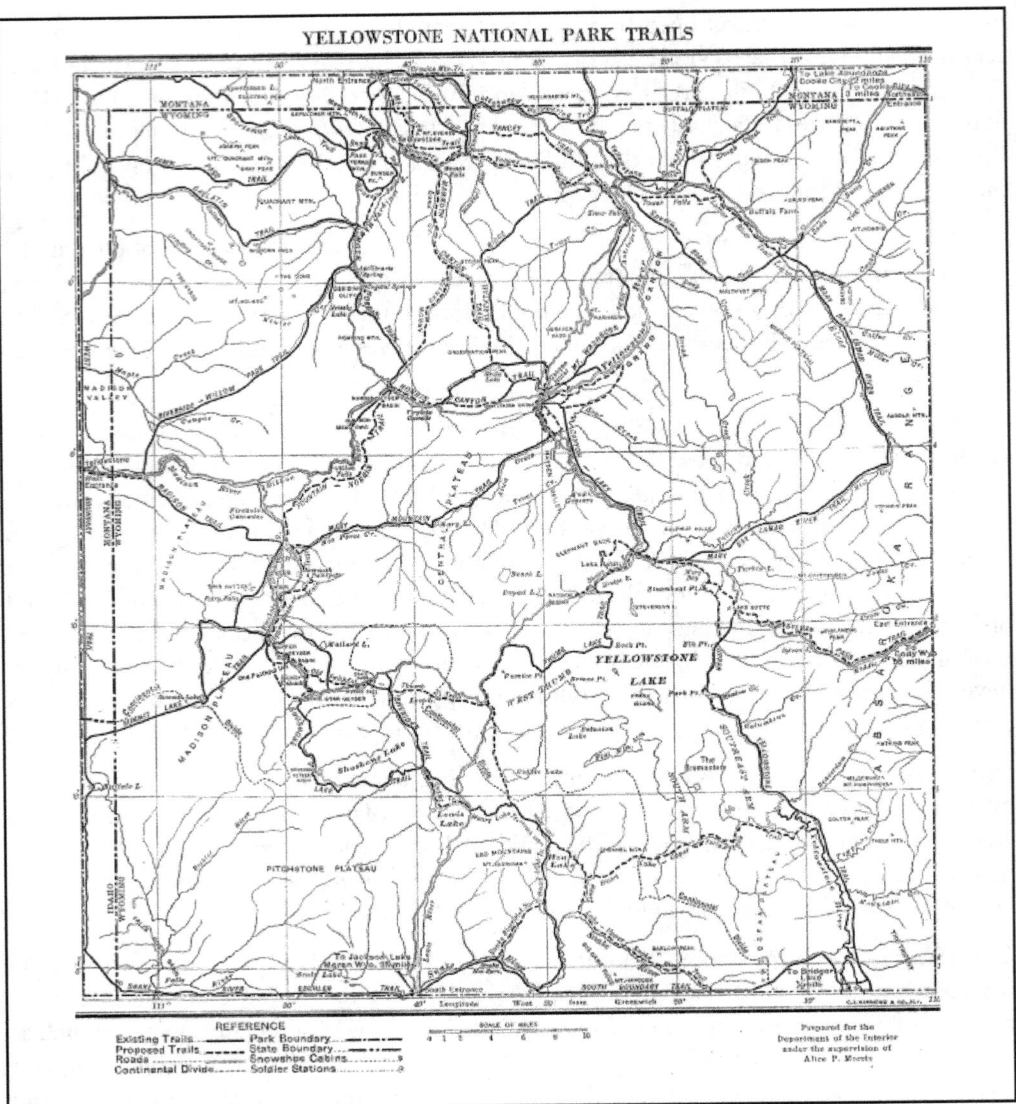

Map of the existing and proposed trails by Alice Morris, 1917. Map courtesy YNP Archives.

in that document, there remains no "official" plan for managing the park's wilderness backcountry. Despite that, the park's law enforcement, backcountry, and maintenance staff work tirelessly to ensure that hikers have a robust and meaningful experience exploring the park via its trail system.

Hiking in Yellowstone

Yellowstone is visited by over four million people each year. As I mentioned before, only a small handful (relatively speaking) of those people will venture more than a few feet away from the main highways and developments. Those who do, however, are rewarded many times over with unique views, access to points of interest that others do not get to see, and the opportunity to commune with nature in ways that the non-hikers don't. The desire to do that, in Yellowstone specifically, is, presumably, why you have acquired this book.

The Park's Trail System

The park's trail system is comprised of a little over 1,400 miles of various types of trails. These include frontcountry boardwalked paths, threshold trails that go deeper into the woods or away from the frontcountry but not so far that you could get lost, and 1,000 miles of maintained trails that will take you, literally, miles from the nearest road or occupied place. The park has something for everyone, regardless of hiking skills, how far you wish to be away from the main road, etc.

Hike According to Your Skill Level

You will want to fairly and honestly evaluate your hiking skills before you commit to taking any major hike into the park's backcountry. If you live at or near sea level, you are probably not going to want to start off with a multi-day adventure in Yellowstone, where the average elevation is around 8,000 feet (2,438m), without spending some time in the area acclimating to the thinner air and drier climate. Most of the park's trails are accessible to hikers with minimal skills, but there are a handful that demand you have some experience hiking in unstable or unforgiving terrain.

Hiking Alone or with a Group

The rangers in Yellowstone generally recommend hiking in groups of three or four or more. That is largely because there is safety in numbers. It is extremely rare for bears to attack larger groups of people. So any time you are going to be hiking into some of the more bear-dense areas such as Pelican Valley, Hayden Valley (especially on its northern end and along the Mary Mountain Trail), and the Gallatin Mountain Range, you will find signs that recommend hiking in a larger group.

Having said that, thousands of people hike alone all the time in the park. Most of my hikes are alone, largely because of my work schedule. Some people just prefer the solitude of hiking alone, and there is nothing wrong with that. You just need to be aware that hiking alone puts you at a significantly greater risk for having problems. It does not even have to be about bears. If you fall and break a leg while you are hiking alone and do not have any way to call for help, things will get difficult for you.[1]

It is not illegal to hike alone, but generally speaking it is not a good idea. Unfortunately, there is not really a system in the park that allows you to find others to hike with. Sometimes you can get lucky by hanging out at a trailhead and waiting for others to show up, and then asking if they mind if you tag along. That is a good way to make lifelong friends, in fact.

There is also a Facebook Group set up to discuss hiking in Yellowstone. Its name, oddly enough, is *Yellowstone Hiking*. Any topic related to hiking in the Greater Yellowstone Ecosystem is appropriate, and it is possible to set up "events" for individual hikes and solicit others to join you. It is also a great place to get hiking or trail recommendations for your given set of circumstances. If you are on Facebook, feel free to join and participate.

Technical Hiking/Climbing in the Park

Unfortunately, there is not a lot of technical climbing in the park, not so much because it is illegal, but primarily because the rock found in many of the park's mountains, canyons, etc., is not suitable for climbing. There are a handful of places where you can hone your skills, however. Contact the park's Central Backcountry Office for details. Technical hiking, that is, hiking for athletic enjoyment and/or physical challenge, is fairly popular, however.

Running/Trail Running in the Park

Running in an area where there are predatory animals is not a good idea. So park rangers generally do not recommend trail running in Yellowstone. If you are an employee or a visitor and need to run, please do so in the developed areas.

Trails Summary

There are basically three types of trails within Yellowstone. The first is the frontcountry trails. Many of these consist of boardwalks, paved paths, or other surfaces designed for high-volume use. These are the "everyday" trails you find around the Upper Geyser Basin, Mammoth Hot Springs, and the like.

The second type of trail is known as a "threshold" trail. These are short dirt or paved trails that usually lead to a specific feature. Examples include those that take you to Wraith Falls, Monument Geyser Basin, and the summit of Purple Mountain. These trails take you away from the frontcountry, but no so far out that you would consider camping along them.

The third type is the backcountry trail. These are the (often) miles-long trails that take you into the heart of the park's wilderness, and where you will find campsites in which to pitch a tent and spend the night. These trails are divided into several different classes depending upon their purpose. This is explained in more detail in the introduction to the park's trails in the second half of this book.

In all cases, the trails are maintained by a variety of personnel who work for the National Park Service in one capacity or another.

Trailheads

Each trail begins at a trailhead. In many cases, the trailhead is a spot alongside one of the park's roads, but they may also be at junctions with other trails or located on the park's boundary. There are almost 120 roadside or boundary trailheads scattered around the

Trail information board at the Cascade Creek Trailhead. Photo by author.

park. Many serve multiple trails. Each major trailhead has a trail information board that contains a map of the trails in that area (as well as showing the location of any backcountry campsites) along with precautionary information about hiking in bear country, the necessity of securing your food, and other important trail status information. If there have been reports of significant bear activity along the trail, this will be posted here as well. Be sure and check these boards for important information before you set out on your hike.

Trail Marking

Most of the park's trails are marked with orange "blazes," or square/rectangular strips of metal stapled to trees, posts, or other appurtenances along their length. These will typically be found 6-8 feet above the ground, though in some cases they may be attached to downed trees. Many of these blazes have been in place so long that they have become bleached and may appear a sort of beige, gray, or even solid white color. In some spots where the trails cross large expanses of grassland or barren area (such as the Pitchstone Plateau Trail), the trails may be marked with cairns, or small man-made rock piles, and in many cases, these may be augmented by a post with an orange blaze on it. In still other places there may be simple metal or wooden posts planted in the ground with an orange marker attached to them. You may occasionally run across an old tree with the letter "I" carved into its trunk. This was the original way trails were marked in the park in the 1920s and 1930s and can still be found in random places today (see photo on the next page).

On the longer trails, where you cross expansive sections of open land, you may have to strain to see the trail marker on the other side of the space. You may find a small pair of

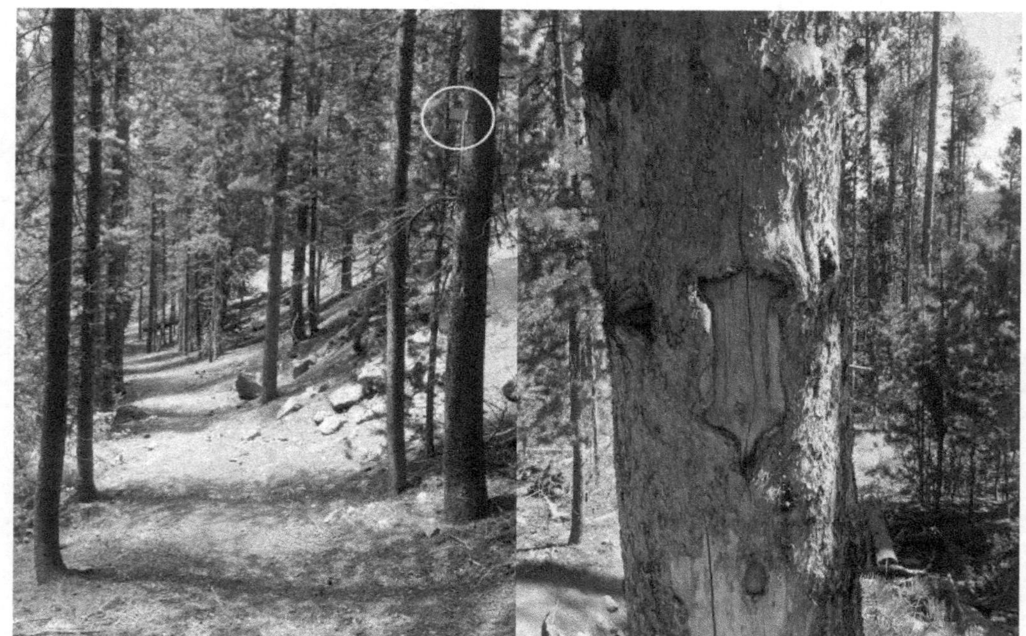

Trail marker (blaze) on tree above the Spring Creek Trail (left, note the circle), and a tree with the old "I" trail marker found on a tree on the Ribbon Lake Trail (right). Photos by the author.

binoculars to be of use in such cases. There are trails where so much open space is present that it may be difficult to follow in the absence of markers or cairns. The Pitchstone Plateau Trail is a perfect example. This is why it is good to have a working knowledge of maps, compasses, and/or GPS devices and have them available to you when you are hiking the park's backcountry.

Where two or more trails come together, there are usually signs that provide mileage figures from that point to other trail junctions or trailheads (see image on facing page). Most of the signs these days are the newer laser-etched metal plates, but there are a handful of the old wooden ones left around as well. Early in the season in many places, these signs will have been knocked down. As a result it may be hard to determine which trail you should be on unless, of course, you have your handy maps or trail guides with you. Some of the older signs may have older trail names on them as well, especially the older wooden ones. You will see references to the old Howard Eaton Trail on signs in areas where the trail has been renamed or abandoned, for example. I try to point those out in the trail information chapters in the second part of this book. And finally, it is not uncommon for the distances on these signs to be less than accurate for a variety of reasons. You should rely on the mileage figures listed in the trail information here because it is based on super-accurate measurements taken from satellite imagery overlaid by GIS mapping information.

When park managers decide to abandon trails, backcountry rangers often remove the first one or two markers from the trail's origin in an attempt to prevent people from wandering into the old trail space. For those who love to explore these old trails, a few minutes spent wandering into the woods to find where the markers pick up can be a lot of fun (be sure to keep track of the path you are taking so you can follow it back if you elect to do this).

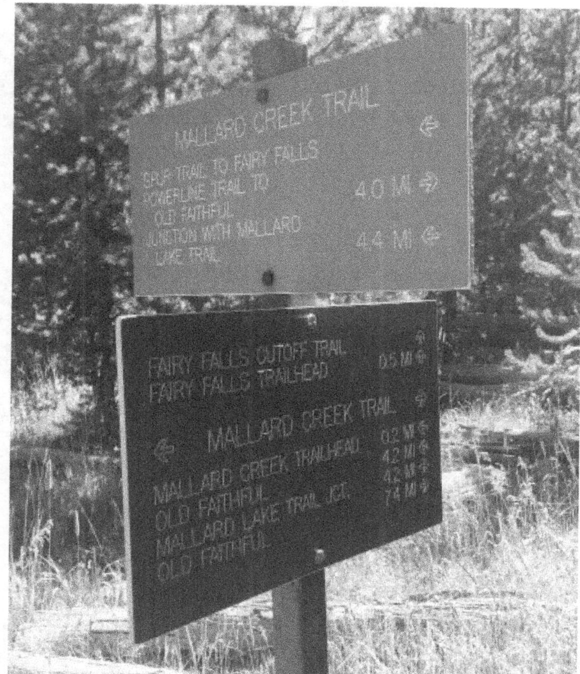

Typical mileage sign found at trail junctions. Photo by author.

Trail Designation

The park's trail system is maintained by a collection of different groups within the park hierarchy. The park has Trail Maintenance Supervisors (one for frontcountry and one for backcountry trails) whose job it is to oversee maintenance of the entire trail system. Trail maintenance crews build and maintain many parts of the system, while backcountry law enforcement rangers usually handle the minor maintenance issues and take care of clearing the trails in the early part of the season before they open up to the public. The trails are monitored for use and those that fall into disuse are often abandoned, especially if they do not take hikers along any specific points of interest or have any laudable aesthetic beauty associated with them. Trails that create resource management issues (such as resource damage, erosion, situations where recurring animal conflicts are taking place, etc.) may also force the closure or rerouting of a park trail.

Dozens of trails that have existed in the past are no longer maintained, though remnants of them remain in place for the adventurous explorer to find. Some remain visible on satellite imagery if you know where to look. In the trail descriptions that form the second part of this book, you will find descriptions of a small handful of these that still hold some interest for hikers and are, or are believed to be, still hikable to one extent or another.

Park managers are always open to the idea of creating new trails, but the process for doing so can be complex and convoluted. Anyone, including civilians, can suggest a new trail. This is presented to a committee that will evaluate the proposal, and then submit it through a planning process for the requisite approvals. Proposals for trails to the park's remote thermal areas will be rejected outright, as will any that involve encroachment upon the park's sensitive wildlife habitats, natural and cultural resources, and/or historical sites.

Social Trails

Social trails are unofficial trails that are created by continuous or repetitive use by people who hiked off official trails. Many of these take hikers to some rather popular vantage points. The paths to the top of Prismatic Point, the hill behind Grand Prismatic, were perfect examples of this until 2016. Up until the NPS built the new overlook trail, there were several different worn paths to the top of this hill. These were all social trails.

Social trails are, for the most part, considered resource damage, and are not looked upon favorably by the NPS. In fact, in many cases, the creation and use of such paths is actively discouraged by park staff. In the case of those up to Prismatic Point, many of these trails were actually dangerous. People climbed up rocky slopes on the side of the hill, and many fell each day because of the instability of the dirt and rocks that formed the trails themselves. In 2014, a park visitor was killed when a snag (a dead tree) fell on him as he climbed up one of these trails.

Animal Trails

In many areas of the park, the human trails will intersect with and/or parallel trails used by the park's wildlife as they move about the park and migrate into and out of certain areas. This is especially true in areas like Lamar Valley, Hayden Valley, and Pelican Valley. As a result, it is important that you pay attention to the trail markers and/or your maps, especially when it comes to open fields and meadows. Following an animal trail is not necessarily dangerous, but you could travel for miles before you realize you are nowhere near where you need to be to get back to a trailhead, campsite, etc. Even if you are able to hike back to where you need to be, you can end up losing valuable time and energy doing so.

Shuttles and Intrapark Transportation

At the present time, there are no organized shuttle services within Yellowstone, with the exception of a service offered by Xanterra to transport hikers into and out of a handful of sites located along the shore of Yellowstone Lake (at a significant cost). A variety of different services have been offered in the past, but they have never proven to be tenable.

The park's size and the organization of its road system make such a system rather difficult to conduct. One of the major problems associated with these kinds of operations is timing. All kinds of factors can delay hikers along their route, making an exact pickup time difficult to determine on the front end. Having to wait several hours for someone to arrive at a destination trailhead is not something most shuttle operators would want to do.

There are basically two options when it comes to traveling from Point A to Point B. First, there is hitchhiking. This is actually fairly common among park employees; you will often see them standing along the roadside near the park's major attractions with a homemade cardboard sign seeking a ride. Many tourists, in addition to other sympathetic park employees, pick them up all the time and there has never been a problem. Given how busy the roads are during a typical summer, you should have no problem getting a small group picked up and transported to at least some point closer to your destination.

Your second option is to arrange your own shuttle. This involves dropping off a vehicle at your destination trailhead the day of or the night before your hike. You then commence your hike at the other trailhead and when you arrive at your destination trailhead, your vehicle will be waiting for you. You can then transport someone back to your beginning trailhead to pick up the vehicle you left there when you began.

If you are hiking out to a trailhead that has cellular service then you can simply call someone once you are out of the woods. As a general rule, the trailheads closer to the developed areas such as Old Faithful, Canyon, Mammoth, etc., will have decent cellular signal, whereas those in more remote areas will not. There are exceptions to both. And whether or not you have signal will be determined in large part by which carrier you're using (Verizon and those that roam on Verizon's system will have much better coverage on average, generally speaking).

Compasses, Maps, and GPS

It is absolutely amazing how easy it is to get lost when you wander just a few feet from the trail. Once you lose sight of the trail itself, if you get turned around, you may never find it again. There have been rescue calls in the park where people were found literally within a dozen yards of the trail.

Anyone planning to hike in Yellowstone is *highly* encouraged to obtain and learn how to use a GPS device. They can be lifesavers and they can be used to mark spots of interest so when you want to go back to some of your favorite places, you can find your way to them. If you are one who posts on social media about your hikes, it is always a good idea to include the GPS coordinates of those points of interest as well.

At a minimum, however, you must understand how to use a map and compass. If you are going to use maps in the park's backcountry, use topographic maps either from the U.S. Geological Survey (found at www.usgs.gov) or maps that are based on the USGS maps. A variety of companies make these maps, and you will have to decide which ones have the best feature set for you. But you need to be familiar with and understand how to read these maps and understand how to use a compass in concert with the maps. Most GPS units have a compass built into them, so you could also use the GPS device in lieu of that. The downside to using a GPS device, of course, is that they rely on batteries. So you will need to carry a backup supply with you (or a way to recharge batteries if you have the rechargeable type). But it is also good to know how to use a basic compass in case all your electronics die for whatever reason.

And even if you use an electronic device with a set of these maps in them, it is always a good idea to carry hard copies of the maps as well. Again, if your electronics die, then you may have a problem if you get lost and do not have the backups. Always carry them in a plastic bag or have them laminated so they will survive a long, damp trip.

Food, Waste, Weed and Other Illegal Stuff

Most hikers carry food of some type with them into the backcountry. Avoid aromatic foods such as tuna fish, peanut butter, etc. The smell of tuna will travel for great distances and will draw bears and other animals to your location from miles around if the winds are right. There is a list of some of the better food types in the chapter on hiking and camping equipment.

You need to be prepared to pack out your waste when in Yellowstone. You can pretty much pee anywhere you want, and you can defecate anywhere, so long as you dig a hole 6-8" deep to bury it in, and then cover it appropriately when you are done. Some backcountry campsites have pit toilets located near them (especially highly used sites). If you use one of those, you can leave your waste paper in the toilet. Otherwise, you will need to pack it in plastic bags and bring it out with you. Do not dispose of any other personal hygiene items in either the pit toilets or the waste holes you dig in the backcountry. Pack it in, pack it out!

Though marijuana has been "legalized" in a handful of states, the territory of Yellowstone National Park is under federal jurisdiction and does not recognize any such legalization. Many people have assumed that since you are so far away from civilization, a little bit of recreational use would not be discovered. But backcountry rangers travel around the entire park on a daily basis, and if they catch you, you may find yourself on the way to the Mammoth Hilton (the jail at the park's headquarters), and before the park's magistrate facing a federal drug possession charge. And of course, it goes without saying that possession of any other illegal drug is similarly forbidden.

Firearms and Weapons

Most weapons are prohibited within park boundaries. The only exception to this is a legally owned firearm that is carried in compliance with the laws of the state in which you are located. In Yellowstone, that means Wyoming, Montana, or Idaho, depending on where you are physically located. See the chapter on The Yellowstone Backcountry for specifics on the rules about carrying handguns within Yellowstone.

Camping

Day use of the park's trail system does not require any permits or other intervention from NPS or anyone else. You can hike any trail (or off trail in most places) and return at your discretion. However, if you wish to camp along the trails in the park's backcountry, you must generally obtain a permit to do so from one of the park's Backcountry Offices.[2] Yellowstone has approximately 300 designated campsites for those who wish to spend a night or more in the vast backcountry spaces away from civilization. Those caught camping without the appropriate permits are subject to some pretty hefty fines.

Employees; YCERP

Park employees have it a bit easier when it comes to hiking in the park. It is often fairly easy to organize a group to go hiking, and if you ensure at least one of those going has a vehicle, then so much the better.

Another option for employees is the organized hikes offered by the Yellowstone Co-op Employee Recreation Program, known within the park as YCERP. YCERP offers a variety of hikes throughout the summer season, all of which are available to any of the park's employers (including NPS). Some of these may involve a small fee, but most are free. They even do midnight or "moonlight" hikes from time to time. They publish their schedule in the lobby of the major dorms and recreation halls, and it is available online as well. Note that these services are not available to park visitors or "friends" of park employees due to insurance issues.

All of the park's concession operators and the NPS provide some funding to YCERP to offer these hikes and a variety of other programs to park employees, and access to this service is one of the better benefits of working in the park. YCERP also offers rentals of camping and backpacking supplies to employees for a nominal fee. See the Recreation Office located at one of the major developments for more details.

Commercial Tours and Outfitters

There are a variety of different organizations and commercial concerns that offer guided hikes and outings for park visitors. This includes boating excursions as well. Anyone or any group offering commercial tour or outfitter services in the park has to be licensed by the NPS to conduct business in the park. Yellowstone maintains a list of approved vendors in the park on their website. Be sure you check it prior to making any financial commitments to anyone who offers to guide you through the park.

Accessibility

Being a wilderness area, it should come as no surprise that much of the park's trail system is not suitable for use by those with mobility issues. Many of the frontcountry boardwalk trails are accessible by those using wheelchairs and other mobility-assistance devices, however. And there are a couple of threshold trails that are somewhat suitable for wheelchairs. Details on the regulations related to the use of wheelchairs and other devices can be found in the next chapter.

You may borrow wheelchairs from the visitor centers at Mammoth, Old Faithful and Canyon, or you may rent them from the clinics at Mammoth, Old Faithful, and Lake (cost is $10 per day at the time this was written). The park's hotels also have wheelchairs for you to borrow while you are staying at each facility.

Service Animals

Service animals must generally follow the same guidelines as any other pet within the park. Appropriately trained dogs are the only type of service animal recognized under the Americans with Disabilities Act, and therefore are the only service animals that may be taken into facilities and on the trails.

All other animals (including "therapy animals" and "emotional support animals") are subject to the park's pet regulations and are prohibited on all of the park's trail system. Details on these regulations can also be found in the following chapter.

Having said that, it is generally not a good idea to take any animal into the park's backcountry, for a variety of reasons. Dogs can transmit and/or become infected by diseases that impact other animals. Both dogs and their food are attractants for other carnivores, including wolves, coyotes, and bears. Animal waste must be disposed of in the same manner as human waste (pack it out, put it in a pit toilet, or bury it more than six inches deep).

Trail Conditions by Month

There is an old saying in Yellowstone generally meant to reflect the way employees view the weather in the park: "We only have three seasons: July, August, and Winter." There is a very similar precept regarding the trails. There are four months that are really good for hiking: July, August, September, and usually most of October. At other times, a significant number of trails are impassable to foot and stock traffic due to snow or marshy conditions.

The park does begin opening for the summer season on April 15. For the avid hiker, though, the trail choices will be limited for a couple of months after that. Once the new seasonal rangers arrive in May, they go through a couple of weeks of orientation, and then are deployed out into the field to begin trail work. This includes clearing deadfall, repairing minor washouts, reposting trail markers, repairing footbridges and creating safe spots for creek and river crossings. Within a couple of months the entire system is cleared.

Here's a look at what the trail conditions will be like in a typical year. Special conditions could change this. For example, a heavy snow season will mean later trail openings.

January to early April: Almost all the trails in the park will be snowbound, except for those at the lower elevations in the Mammoth area. The Rescue Creek and Lava Creek trails may be passable on foot but are still likely to be marshy in areas.

April to mid-June: Most of the trails parkwide will slowly lose their snow, but the vast majority of these are going to be extremely marshy, and any trail that lies in a valley or low elevation area will likely be underwater. This is particularly true of the Bechler area. For trails that are mostly free of snow, you can still expect to encounter places where you will be postholing through snowfields. And do not forget many trails will be closed due to bear management regulations. By the beginning of June, backcountry rangers will begin clearing trails and campsites of debris, etc. This process starts with the Class A trails and works its way to the Class B and Class C trails.

Mid-June to mid-July: Most of the trails, with the exception of those at the elevations above 8,000-9,000 feet, will be snow-free, but will generally still have marshy areas in them that may make them all but impassable. Most of the creek and river crossings on open trails will be deep and very cold, especially in the Lamar, Thorofare and Bechler areas.

Mid-July through September: All of the park's trails should be open and passable and in good shape. Fire season starts in August, however, and conditions within the park may necessitate restrictions on the use of fires in the backcountry. Any wildfires that do start may close the occasional trail or section of the park. September is peak season for color changes in the park's foliage.

October through the first weekend in November: Trails will generally still be open and in good condition, but rangers are no longer actively clearing trails and heavier snowstorms can occur, rendering some sections of trails (especially at the higher elevations) once again impassable.

First weekend in November through December: Most of the park will be closed until December 15. The Northern Range and Mammoth areas will remain open and those trails should remain passable and in good condition until the serious snow starts falling in mid-December. By the time the park opens for the winter season on the 15th, most trails will be completely snowbound and passable only with skis or snowshoes. Rangers will have marked ski trails by the time the park opens for winter as well.

The Continental Divide Trail

The Continental Divide Trail passes through Yellowstone in the form of pieces of several of the park's existing trails (see map on the next page). From south to north:

- Enters the park at the Fox Creek Trailhead 6K3
- West on the South Boundary - Lynx Creek segment
- North on the Fox Creek Trail
- North on the Heart River Trail
- West on the Trail Creek Trail
- West on the Heart Lake Trail, exit at trailhead 8N1 (Heart Lake)
- Cross the road and re-enter at trailhead 8K1 (Lewis Channel/Dogshead)
- West on the Dogshead Trail
- South and west on the Shoshone Lake - South Shore Trail
- North on the Shoshone Lake Trail
- West on the Howard Eaton Trail to Old Faithful
- Cross the road into the Upper Geyser Basin

- West on the paved part of the Upper Geyser Basin Trail
- Continue on the Artemisia - Biscuit Basin Trail
- Cross the road into the Biscuit Basin parking lot
- Left-hand boardwalk in Biscuit Basin
- West on the Mystic Falls Trail
- West on the Summit Lake Trail
- Exit the park at trailhead 9K9 (Summit Lake)

The exit on the west side used to go straight out to the West Boundary Trail. You can still use the old trail to get to the USFS road that leads north to West Yellowstone that comprises the path outside the park. Using a trail map or a GPS with the trail data in it, just as the Summit Lake Trail starts to make its almost 90-degree left-hand turn, you will see an old path through the forest leading off to your right (GPS: 44.406636, -111.090355). Even though this old trail has been abandoned, it is still passable. Travel about 4/10 of a mile (0.6km) until you come to the point where this old trail is closest to the USFS fire road. The fire road is the northbound CDT at this point and you should cross over to it and follow it from there.

Specific details on these individual segments can be found in the district trail chapters found in the second part of this book.

If you are passing through the park using the CDT, there are special rules that apply to you regarding camping and needing permits and whatnot. Prior to departing on your trip, contact the park's Backcountry Office at 307-344-2160 or via e-mail at YELL_Backcountry_Office@nps.gov.

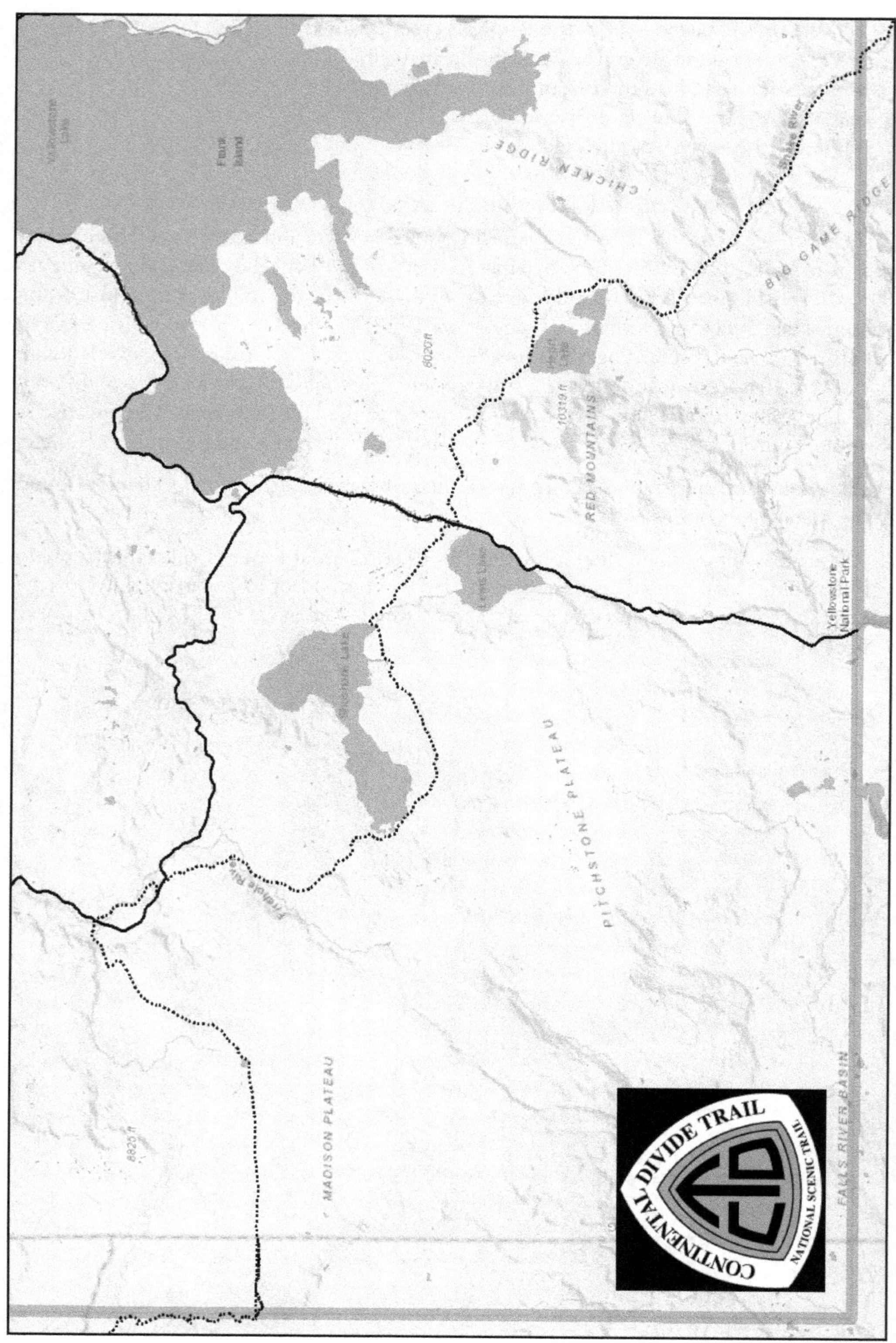
CHICKEN RIDGE
BIG GAME RIDGE
RED MOUNTAINS
10319 ft
8020 ft
PITCHSTONE PLATEAU
MADISON PLATEAU
8825 ft
Yellowstone National Park
FALLS RIVER BASIN
CONTINENTAL DIVIDE TRAIL
NATIONAL SCENIC TRAIL

The Yellowstone Backcountry

So you have decided that you want to set out on a hike in Yellowstone. Before you head out into the wilderness, however, it is a good idea to do some basic research so that you ensure your safety and understand the rules and regulations governing your trip. It therefore helps to have a bit of an understanding about how the backcountry process works in Yellowstone.

The Backcountry Offices

The Backcountry Office (BCO) is the primary point of contact the hiker will have with rangers and staff who know what's going on along the park's expansive trail system. Most of the personnel working in these offices have significant experience in the park's wilderness and are familiar with many of the trails and the conditions you will find off the beaten path. They will also have access to the very latest information about trail conditions, campsite availability, area closures, fire danger conditions, and so forth.

If you are doing simple day hikes with no plans to stay overnight in the park's backcountry, you do not *need* to visit a BCO. However, it is always a good idea to stop in and find out if anything unusual is going on where you are headed. Occasionally trails are closed for management reasons, for example. If you are in the south end of the park and are planning to drive up to the north end to hike a specific trail, you might like to know if that particular trail has been closed. Many people will visit the Visitor Centers around the park to get this information, but while the staff there may know about some of the trail closures or restrictions, they often will not have a complete picture of the status of the trails, campsites, areas with dangerous bear warnings, etc.

If you are planning on spending the night at one of the park's backcountry campsites, you are *required* to stop in at a BCO, however. You are required to receive an orientation, get updated information about your hike, obtain a parking permit for your vehicle(s), and obtain your permit to camp. Camping without this permit in Yellowstone is illegal.

The BCOs are the mechanism through which the park implements its backcountry management system. The chart on the following page shows where the park's nine backcountry offices are located. During the summer season, their hours are typically from 8:00 a.m. to 4:30 p.m., though some offices close at lunch time. During the early and late part of the summer season, staffing levels may be reduced and the offices may be available in an "on call" mode where you might have to wait a bit for a ranger to show up to assist you.

You can get information about any of the trails and campsites, and you can obtain permits for any hike-in or stock party sites at any of the BCOs. However, if you are boating into a

BACKCOUNTRY OFFICE	PHONE	NOTES
Mammoth Visitor Center	307-344-2176	Open year round (special hours or on-call in winter)
Tower Ranger Station	307-344-2817	Summer only - Closed in late summer
Canyon Visitor Center	307-242-2553	Summer only - Late summer staffing on-call
Bridge Bay Ranger Station	307-242-2413	Summer only - Boating inspections/trip permits available
Grant Visitor Center	307-344-2609	Summer only - Boating inspections/trip permits available
Snake River Ranger Station	307-242-7209	Summer & Winter - Boating insp/trip permits available
Bechler Ranger Station	406-581-7071	Summer only
Old Faithful Ranger Station	307-344-2703	Summer & Winter
West Yellowstone Visitor Center	307-344-2878	Summer & Winter (May be on-call staffing)

site on one of the park's lakes, you will need to pick up your permit at either the Bridge Bay Ranger Station, the Grant Village Backcountry Office (at the Visitor Center), or the Snake River Ranger Station. This is because you must obtain a boat inspection and license, and the inspections are available only at those three locations. If you are putting in at Lewis Lake for a Shoshone campsite and an inspector is not available at the time you show up at the Snake River location, they can arrange to have an inspector from Grant meet you at Lewis Lake.

The Purpose of the Backcountry Management System

The purpose of the backcountry management system the park has implemented is to ensure that the park's resources (e.g., its trails, campsites, etc.) are used and maintained appropriately within the context of the National Park Service's dual mandate.[1] This mandate requires the park service to allow for public use of the park's resources while at the same time ensuring those resources are not overtaxed and remain available for use by future generations.

As mentioned in the introduction to this book, the park has developed a backcountry management plan, though once it was finalized the superintendent at the time (Mike Finley) refused to sign it (for several reasons). However, many of the basic principles outlined in the document are still used today to manage the park's trail and backcountry campsite system.

Backcountry Campsite Reservations

A portion of the park's campsites are reservable in advance. Up to two-thirds of any given section's sites may be reserved at any one time, with the balance made available only on a walk-up basis. This is to ensure that those who show up wanting to camp in any certain area have access to some campsites in all areas of the park.

You may reserve a backcountry campsite via one of two methods. The park's Central Backcountry Office (CBO) begins accepting advance reservations on January 1 for the approaching summer season. You can download the form from the park's website, complete it and submit it via mail or fax, or you may bring it by in person (they do not accept e-mail requests or requests via the telephone because they do not have the staff in place to process those that early in the year).

The CBO is not fully staffed until April 1, so the actual processing of applications will not begin before that date. All of the applications that have accumulated prior to that date will be processed in random order (by lottery, basically). Any applications received on April 1 or later will be processed in the order they are received after those received before April 1 have been processed.

The fee for the reservation application is $25, regardless of the number of nights the reservation is for or the number of people/stock included in the request. If an application is for more people than can be accommodated at a given site (the limits are spelled out in the backcountry campsite descriptions before the appendices at the end of this book), you will need to submit two separate applications, each with its own processing fee. Though there's no guarantee that multiple reservations will be accepted for the same area, if you submit them together in the same envelope, they should be processed at the same time.

Once the number of reservations for a given section for any given date is reached, no more reservations will be accepted for that area. This is why it is important that you specify appropriate alternative dates or campsites you would like on your request. If sufficient space is not available for your first date, you may get it for your alternative date(s). Once your reservation request has been processed, you will receive a confirmation via e-mail (if you provided a legitimate address) or via postal mail. If the CBO is unable to fulfill your request, you will receive a note to that effect as well, and your credit card will not be charged.

When you arrive in the park and are ready to go on your hike, bring your confirmation letter to one of the backcountry offices and exchange it for your camping permit. Your reservation form is NOT valid for camping—it must be exchanged for the permit at one of the BCOs no more than 48 hours prior to your trip.

It is important to note that the $25 is simply a fee for the reservation, and you will still have to pay the per person camping fees appropriate for the type of party you have and how many people are in it once you show up to pick up the actual permit (described below).

You may also reserve a campsite more than 48 hours out by stopping in at any of the park's BCOs during the summer season. The same $25 fee applies, as does the requirement that you return to a BCO and exchange it for the appropriate permit when you are ready to begin your hike.

If you wish to reserve a campsite less than 48 hours before your hike is scheduled to start, you simply show up at one of the BCOs and work with one of the rangers to find an appropriate, available site, and you pay the appropriate camp fees—there is no $25 reservation fee for those.

If you reserve a site and find that you are unable to make your scheduled hike, please contact the park's Central Backcountry Office at 307-344-2160 or stop by one of the park's BCOs to let them know so they can release the reservation in case someone else wishes to use the site on the day(s) you have it reserved. There is no refund of your $25 if you cancel or if you simply do not show up, however.

You can use the list of backcountry campsites found near the end of this book to determine which sites are the most popular, and decide whether you need to make a reservation or not. Historically, sites along Slough Creek, around Shoshone Lake, and some of the sites in the Bechler area are the most popular, and you should probably give some serious thought to making a reservation, especially if the timing of your hike is critical.

Undesignated Area Camping

There are areas of the park that are largely devoid of trails and campsites, but that are otherwise outside of the bear management areas and open to public access. You may camp in those areas after you have obtained approval from the District Ranger with jurisdiction over that area. You can be approved for any legitimate reason, such as wanting to visit a particular mountain peak, a thermal area, or any other area that interests you. You cannot seek approval simply because all of the other campsites in an area are full, however.

In addition, a handful of permits are issued on an ad hoc basis for areas that are not included within these zones and are not in bear management areas (or have other conflicts with wildlife or resource management restrictions), but are otherwise outside existing trail or camping areas. The map on the facing page shows the undesignated zones where this type of camping is permitted. To be approved, you must meet the following requirements.

1. All requests for camping in these areas must be approved by the District Ranger (DR) in whose district the area you wish to camp in exists. This process typically takes several days. You can contact the DR yourself (through one of the backcountry offices, if you wish), or you can contact the Central Backcountry Office and have them coordinate it for you. You will need to be able to provide an explanation as to why you wish to camp in this area, why you are entering the area, your itinerary, and verify that you understand the concepts of Leave No Trace camping, etc.
2. While you are camping in these areas, you must follow the Leave No Trace camping principles (see the following chapter for an in-depth discussion of this). You must also abide by the following rules:
   - Wood fires are not permitted
   - Maximum party size is 6 people
   - Stock is not permitted, except in unique circumstances (discuss this with the DR)
   - You may not stay at any one site more than two nights.
   - You must abide by food storage regulations, even though there will be no food poles or cabinets.
   - Your campsite must be more than ½ mile (0.8km) from any trail, one mile from any existing (official) campsite, and a ¼ mile (0.4km) or more from any thermal area/feature.
   - Your campsite must be more than 100 feet from any water source (stream, creek, lake, etc.).
3. You must supply a complete itinerary and complete the trip planning worksheet at a backcountry office. If possible, you should be prepared to provide GPS coordinates for your anticipated campsites, or as close as you can get. You may not have a specific site selected, but you need to be able to provide some idea of where you are headed and where you plan to camp, so in case something happens, it will be possible to have a starting point for rangers to begin their search for you if you do not return.
4. You must watch the backcountry/bear safety video.
5. At least one person in your group should know how to use a map and compass, and everyone in the group should have experience hiking off-trail.
6. When you return from your trip, you must report back to the Central Backcountry Office or the District Ranger(s) who approved your trip request so that the park will know that you are out safely.

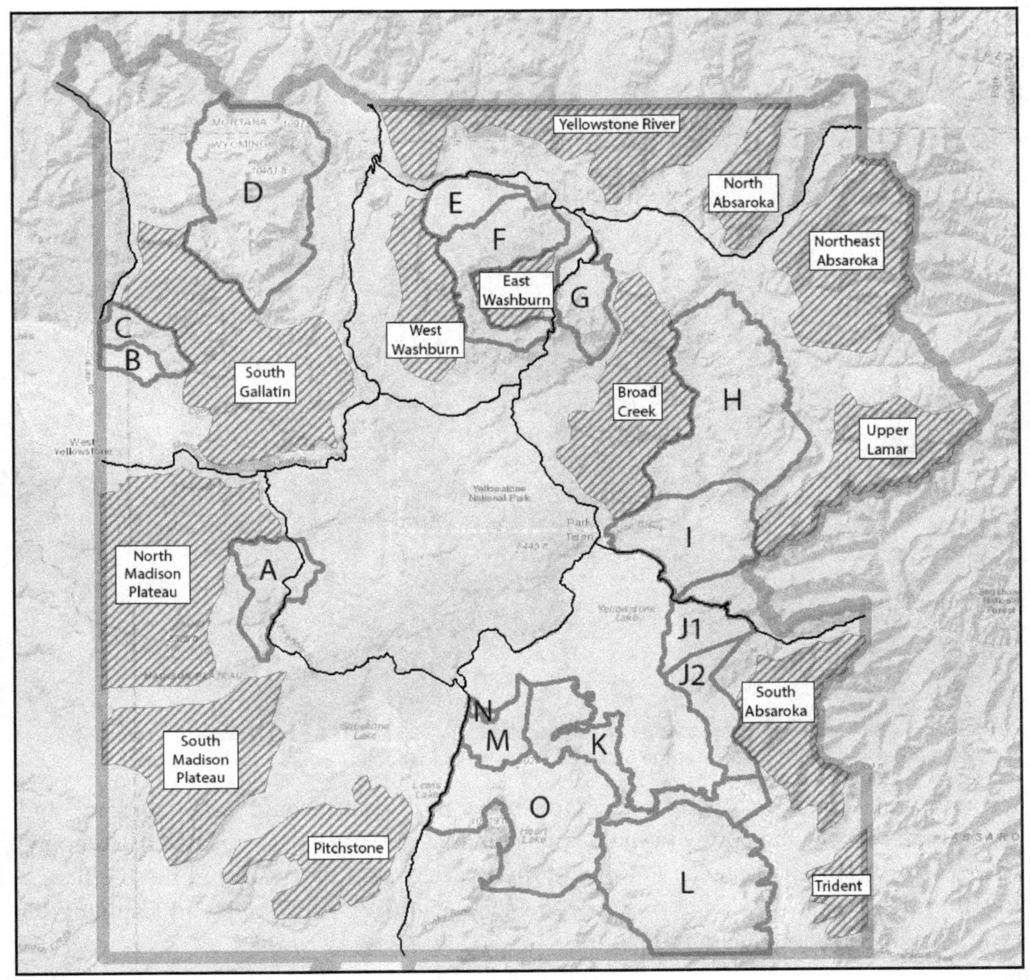

Undesignated camping areas in Yellowstone (hashed areas). Map by author.

Being approved for camping in undesignated areas is a privilege, and you should take care that you obey all the regulations and do not do any damage while you are in these areas. Failure to do so will result in problems for you and may result in the closure of some areas for future use.

Winter Camping

During winter, the park's trails and backcountry are open, though travel on the vast majority of them will require snow shoes or skis. You may also camp anywhere there is sufficient snowpack to protect vegetation. Generally speaking, you do not need to camp at a designated campsite. You must camp in a place where you are out of sight of those moving along the roadways and at least 100 feet from water or thermal features.

There are a variety of undesignated campsites located around the park in the winter. These are typically in closed picnic areas or closed parking lots. There is also limited primitive winter camping in the Old Faithful area. Check with the ranger station at Old Faithful for availability.

The Snake River Backcountry Office at the South Entrance. Photo by author.

You must check in at an open backcountry office just as you would in the summer, and provide the office with an itinerary and approximate locations where you will be camping. You can check on the availability of one of the undesignated sites at any of these offices if you are interested in staying at one. See the chapter on Winter Hiking and Camping for additional information and details.

Visiting the Backcountry Office

The Backcountry Offices are where you go to get current information on trail and campsite conditions, closures, updated animal reports, etc., and where you go to get your permit to camp in the backcountry. You can also pick up fishing licenses at the BCOs. And at three of the BCOs you can get your boat inspected and your boat permits (unless it is a float tube, in which case you can get that done at any BCO).

Most people come to the BCO with an idea of where they wish to camp—many even know the specific site(s) they want. But if you have no idea where you want to go or where you want to camp, you can stop by and the staff there will be happy to help you plan your trip.

The BCO has a large map on the wall that shows all the trails and backcountry campsites. You can use it to plan out a trip, or you can use the park's free Backcountry Trip Planner newspaper (available in hard copy from the park or electronically from their website).

Once you have an idea where you want to stay and which nights you want to stay there, you will complete a Backcountry Campsite Request Form and provide it to the ranger. The ranger can look up the status of the campsites in the computer system, and if the ones you need are available when you need them, s/he will reserve them for you. If they are not available, they will work with you to find nearby sites or find alternative dates for the sites you do want. You can do this for trips that you will be taking that start two days or less from the time you are in the office. For trips more than two days, you will have to make a reservation for the site (which involves paying a $25 fee).

You will be asked to provide some information on this form, such as your name, contact information, etc. You will also be asked to provide a name and phone number for an emergency contact. This is in case something happens to you and the NPS needs to get a hold of someone who can access your medical information, contact your family, etc. If you are attacked by a bear or are otherwise injured and have to be transported to the hospital, for example, they will want to notify your family somehow, and these forms are often the only means available for the NPS to make that happen.

You will also need your vehicle information (make and model of your car, license plate number, and its color). You will be issued a parking permit as a part of getting your camping permit. When you leave your car at the trailhead, if it does not have this permit on the dashboard, it may be towed. The permit is the way the rangers know that it belongs to someone who is out on the trail and has not just been abandoned. It also helps if a vehicle is broken into—they can make contact with the owner via a backcountry ranger because they will know where you are going to be on which days.

Before you receive your permit, you will have to watch a 20-minute video on backcountry and bear safety, and the ranger will go over a series of regulations and concerns with you that are related to the kind of trip you will be taking. The ranger will double check the Backcountry Situation Report for updated information on trail conditions and any pertinent information about your campsite and go over this with you as well. You will be asked if you plan to do any fishing and if so, you can buy your fishing license as a part of this process. The same is true if you will be taking a boat to your campsite or to a dropping-off point.

From Memorial Day through the week after Labor Day, you must pay a per-night, per-person fee for camping, and then you will be issued your permit and you may go on your way. The entire process will take from 30-45 minutes, depending on whether you walk in knowing which campsite(s) you want or not.

Backcountry Situation Reports

The Central Backcountry Office issues periodic Situation Reports on the status of the park's trail system, the backcountry campsites, and issues related to those (such as fire conditions, restrictions, etc.). Up until 2017, these reports were only available to the rangers in the park's BCOs. But in 2017 they decided to post these online, and you can now check them yourself before you head out. You can find the report at https://www.nps.gov/yell/planyourvisit/situationreport.htm.

These reports are compiled from information forwarded to the Central Backcountry Office (CBO) by backcountry rangers, the remote BCO staff, staff at the Visitor Centers, park employees, and from reports brought in by hikers and backcountry users.

These reports will include the conditions of the trails (especially important in the early part of the season as the trails start to clear), the conditions of the campsites, any animal activity reports that would be of concern to hikers, updated fire conditions, the status of the park's rivers, creeks, and streams (especially those at locations where hikers must cross them to continue on a trail), water availability at campsites, any restrictions on use of trails, and so forth. And though these reports are typically updated daily, the BCOs may have more current information that has been sent out via e-mail regarding emergency closures and whatnot.

Bear/Backcountry Safety Video

To get your permit, you will have to watch a 20-minute video that has some important information about safety in the backcountry. It includes a good deal about safety around bears, but it also has a lot of other information as well. Even if you have watched this video online (it is on the park's website), you will have to watch it in the office before they will give you your permit. If you buy one of the Annual Backcountry Passes (see below), you watch the video when you buy the pass and then do not have to watch it again on future trips. And so long as one person in the group has watched the video, the others are not required to.

For more on the safety aspects of your hikes and stays in the backcountry, please see the safety chapter.

Backcountry Fees

As mentioned previously, there are now fees for camping in the park's backcountry. There are no usage fees of any kind associated with hiking, but if you wish to stay in the backcountry, there is a small per-day, per-person fee that is used to offset the cost of maintaining the trails and campsites.

From Memorial Day to September 10, you pay a $3 per-person, per-night fee for your camping permit if you are hiking in on foot or using a boat. If you are going in with stock, the fee is $5 per person. For hikers/boaters, there is no charge for more than 5 people, so the maximum per-night charge would be $15. There is no limit to the fees for stock parties.

The fees are waived for those under 9 years of age. If you are coming in with a commercial tour guide (as a hiking party or a stock party), the tour company will typically handle your fees (though some might require you to pay the fees when you check in at the BCO prior to your departure).

If you plan to camp several times in the backcountry in a single season, you may wish to consider buying an Annual Backcountry Pass. This pass costs $25 and is good for one person (the person to whom it was issued) for the entire season from Memorial Day to September 10. You can watch the safety video when you buy the pass and then not be required to view it again for the remainder of the season so long as you have the pass with you (and your photo ID) when you show up at the BCO to get your permits. The pass is not transferable and is not shareable. If you allow someone else to try to use your pass, it will be confiscated and you will have to buy another one. If you spend more than eight nights camping, the pass pays for itself.

The park implemented these fees to help cover the cost of operating the backcountry system, maintaining trails and campsites, and paying for the staff who oversees the operation of these processes. It is only a small fee and it is capped at a minimal price, but it helps the park pay for things it would not otherwise be able to afford.

Trip Planning

It is best if you do your pre-trip planning prior to arriving at the backcountry office. While rangers are happy to help you with your planning, on most days during the summer there is a line of people waiting. And if a ranger has to help you plan a week-long trip for an area you are unfamiliar with, you are going to delay others who have arrived with their itinerary ready to go and who are anxious to get out into the woods.

The park provides a wealth of information about hiking opportunities on its website, along with some very detailed information about being in the backcountry. There are maps and descriptions of the backcountry campsites, updates on the status of the trails and campsites, videos about how to get around and remain safe in the park, and so forth. There are also a number of books available (including this one, obviously) that provide a good bit of information that can be valuable to your planning efforts.

It is always a good idea to carry with you maps of the areas you will be hiking in, even if you are just going out for the day. The USGS topographic maps are available for free online and can be ordered from the USGS or other outlets. Hikers are encouraged to use these maps or comparable maps with the park's topography shown on them. It is important to understand the terrain you will be hiking through, especially if you end up getting off your planned path. Do note that, in the majority of cases, the trails shown on these maps are general paths and they are not accurate enough to be used for detailed movement planning.

Another useful tool for trip planning is Google Earth (or Google Maps online). With its satellite imagery you can zoom in to the point where you can see the trail path on the ground and you can get a good idea of what your campsite will look like, how it is situated in the trees, etc. You can use the GPS coordinates in the trail descriptions in this book to zoom into the specific reference points to see what you will be dealing with once you arrive at that location. This book is the only one that provides that level of detail for your planning.

Do keep in mind that, given the minor variations in GPS readings from one receiver to the next, the GPS coordinates provided in this book are for reference purposes only. The readings on your receiver may differ from those herein to one extent or another based on a variety of technical issues associated with the way the GPS system functions.

Backcountry Regulations

Since you are dealing with the federal government, as you might imagine, there are a variety of regulations in place regarding how you can use the backcountry. And though some of these might seem pedestrian and/or burdensome, they exist primarily to protect the park's resources from overuse and damage, and to ensure you are as safe as possible while you are out on the trail.

Pets and Service Animals

Pets are not allowed in the Yellowstone backcountry for a variety of reasons. Aside from the risk of the animal getting loose and becoming a meal for one of the park's predators, there's also the concern of the transmission of diseases back and forth between domestic and wild animals and even the introduction of exotic plant species into the park (via fecal droppings). Having a pet with you will also make you more noticeable to the park's predators.

All pets must be on a leash or otherwise under your control, and cannot be taken onto the trails and boardwalks. You also may not leave a pet inside an enclosed vehicle while you are out, so traveling with a pet in the park is not recommended unless you are in an RV. You may allow your pet to urinate or defecate just off roadways and parking lots, but you are required to clean up after them as appropriate.

Service animals, as defined by National Park Service policy, are allowed on boardwalks and trails and in park buildings, unless a given area has been closed off to them for resource management or protection issues. The ADA defines "service animal" as a "dog that has been individually trained to do work or perform tasks for the benefit of an individual with a disability, including a physical, sensory, psychiatric, intellectual, or other mental disability." All other animals, including those recognized as "companion animals" or "emotional support animals" are treated as pets within the park. Passing an unqualified animal off as a service animal is a federal crime in Yellowstone.

If you plan to hike on any park trail with a service animal, including those in the frontcountry, you are required to obtain a (free) permit from one of the backcountry offices to do so. You basically complete a short form, the ranger on duty will discuss with you the rules for taking animals onto the trail system, and you will receive your permit. You need to keep this with you any place you take your animal in the park.

Keep in mind that, while you are in the backcountry, your service animal must be leashed or under control at all times. You must treat its food as you would your own, in that it must be hung more than 10 feet high or stored securely as you would store human food. And you must treat your animal's waste just as you would yours, disposing of it properly.

If you take your service animal into thermal areas, keep them away from the heated waters. Dogs often like to jump into puddles, and doing so in a thermal area could prove fatal for the animal. Do not allow animals to drink water in thermal areas (either in the pools themselves or the runoff from them). Many of the park's thermal features are very hot and/or highly acidic and allowing the dog to drink the water might result in catastrophic damage to his/her mouth or digestive system. Purify its water just as you would your own.

Accessibility

Unfortunately, by its very nature, hiking into the backcountry is not easily done for those who have mobility impairment issues. Most of the park's frontcountry hiking trails, however, are either boardwalked or graded such that use by wheelchairs and similar mobility devices are possible. You may use any wheelchair or similar mobility device within the park, consistent with the Americans with Disabilities Act (ADA), as amended. The wheelchairs may be manually-operated or electrically-assisted. Other types of assistance devices, such as golf carts, ATVs, etc., are not permitted anywhere in the park. Segways are permitted and regulated as bicycles (see the section below on bicycle use in the park).

There are two backcountry campsites that are available for use by those in wheelchairs. 4D3, located at Ice Lake, is approximately ½ mile (0.8km) from the trailhead, and OD5 is located at Goose Lake, approximately 1½ miles (2.4km) from the Fountain Freight trailhead. Note that 4D3 has an accessible pit toilet, but OD5 does not. Both of these campsites are held until 4 p.m. each day in the event someone with mobility impairment issues shows up and wants a site for the evening. After 4, the site is opened up to anyone who wishes to reserve it. Note that, especially early in the season, the trails to these sites may still be cluttered with debris and those in wheelchairs may need considerable assistance getting to the sites.

There are approximately a dozen trails in the park's threshold spaces that can accommodate wheelchairs. In the trail information sections in the second half of this book, each trail has an indicator that shows which ones are handicap-friendly.

Bicycles and Motorized Vehicles

Bicycles, regardless of type, and motorized vehicles are not permitted in the park's backcountry at all. Bicycles and Segway-type devices are allowed on some park roads and trails. Trails authorized for bicycle use (as of the winter of 2018):

- The old railroad bed between what used to be Cinnabar and the town of Gardiner (not a trail, per se)
- The Old Gardiner Road (and the Elk Plaza Service Road out to the radio tower running off of it at the top of the hill behind the hotel)
- The YCC Trail (from the YACC Camp down to Mammoth)
- The Swan Lake Gravel Pit Service Road (just north of Sheepeater Cliff)
- The Old Golden Gate Stagecoach Road (also known as the Golden Gate Service Road)
- The Bunsen Peak Trail (up to the point where it begins to climb the hill) and the Bunsen Peak Service Road Trail that takes you down to the YACC Camp
- The Goose Lake/Feather Lake Trail from the Fountain Freight Trailhead to its junction with the Fairy Falls Trail at the turnoff to head into the woods, and then the Fairy Falls Trail south to its trailhead (the paved portion)
- The bricked and paved trail/road from in front of the Old Faithful Lodge to Morning Glory Pool
- The Upper Geyser Basin - Biscuit Basin Bike Trail
- The Lone Star Geyser Trail (to just before you reach the geyser)
- The Natural Bridge Trail from the main trailhead south of the entrance to Bridge Bay.
- The Old Lake Road Trail
- The Chittenden Road (from its intersection at Dunraven Pass up to the summit); Bikes are not permitted on the Dunraven Pass Trail
- The old Riverside trail system between the West Entrance and Barns Hole Road
- Several of the park's entrance roads are open to bicycles early in the season before the park opens to vehicles, and after the park closes to vehicles. See the park's website for specific dates/details

Fires

Having a campfire is one of the most fun experiences many people associate with hiking, and campfires are allowed at most of the park's backcountry campsites. However, fire mishandled can result in catastrophic damage to the environment, and in the expenditure of millions of dollars to fight it if it gets out of hand.

It is a violation of federal law to leave your campfire in any condition other than fully extinguished when you leave. All of the campsites that allow wood fires have fire rings in the camp's cooking area. You are only allowed to build fires inside these rings. Note that a good many of the campsites do not allow wood fires at all. This is typically because of the lack of suitable downed material in the area for use in building fires or because conditions are not favorable for using wood fires. When you get your camping permit, the ranger will discuss with you the fact that wood fires are not allowed when you are scheduled to be staying at one of those sites. They are also indicated by a "NWF" notation on the site designators on your camping permit. The Backcountry Campsites section located after the trail descriptions section of this book also indicates which sites do not allow wood fires.

Where wood fires are permitted, you are allowed to gather *downed* wood for your fires in the general area of your campsite. You may not cut down trees (even if they are dead), nor may you cut limbs or branches off of trees (dead or alive) to build a fire. You may, however, use portable stoves/grills unless fire restrictions are in place prohibiting all open fires.

Weapons

It is illegal in Yellowstone to carry any weapon into the backcountry, with the exception of legally-permitted firearms. BB guns, bows and arrows, slingshots, stun-guns, shotguns and rifles, etc., are all illegal to possess or transport into the backcountry.

With respect to handguns, you are required to follow state law in the state you are in. For most of the park that will be Wyoming. As of this writing, it is legal to open carry a handgun in Wyoming without a permit, regardless of whether you are a resident of the state or not. Additionally, if you are a Wyoming resident, you do not need a permit to carry a concealed weapon. However, if you are from out of state, you must have a valid permit issued by a state with which Wyoming has a reciprocity agreement in order to carry a concealed weapon. Since these agreements and laws change from time to time, you are encouraged to check the state's website to ensure you comply with their laws. You can find the current information at http://wyomingdci.wyo.gov/dci-criminal-justice-information-systems-section/concealed-firearms-permits.

In the Montana section of the park, the rules are basically the same, except that Montana residents must possess a Montana concealed carry permit to carry a concealed weapon, or one issued by a state that has a reciprocity agreement with Montana. Open carry is also legal regardless of residency status. You may find out more about Montana's requirements at https://dojmt.gov/enforcement/concealed-weapons.

For the Idaho section of the park, there is no requirement for a permit to open carry, regardless of residency status, and Idaho residents are not required to have a permit for concealed carry. If you are not an Idaho resident, however, you must possess a valid permit from a state with which Idaho has a reciprocity agreement. You can find out more about Idaho's requirements at https://www.idaho.gov/laws-public-safety/gun-weapon-law.

Notwithstanding the laws of any of these states, you may not carry your weapon (openly or concealed) in any of the buildings inside the park, regardless of whether they're operated by the federal government of one or the park's concession operators.

As a general rule, the rangers are not going to harass you about carrying a handgun in the park unless you are acting irresponsibly with it. If you are approached by a ranger and you are openly carrying, s/he may direct you to keep your hands away from your gun, or s/he may ask you to hand over your weapon during the interaction for their own safety. They will return it when their contact with you is over.

If you are approached by a ranger while openly carrying, please keep your hands away from your weapon unless you are asked to hand it over. If you are carrying concealed, there is no need for you to notify the ranger you are armed unless s/he asks you if you are armed, or if the ranger is going to make physical contact with you. At that point, you should inform the ranger that you are armed and the location of your weapon. The ranger will advise you on how to proceed at that point.

You may transport your weapon in your vehicle in accordance with the states' laws as outlined above. The same general guidance applies with respect to notification to the ranger about your weapon. You should keep your weapon locked and/or secured in a safe location when you do not have it on your person. This is especially important if you have children with you. In 2013, at Grant Village, a three-year old child found a loaded handgun in an ice cooler and managed to fatally shoot herself in the head. This was a traumatic experience not only for the parents and family of the child, but for the rangers and staff who responded to that incident as well. Park rangers do not object to people having their handguns with them so much as them not handling the weapons safely. Please do your part to ensure you and those around you are safe when you are handling or carrying a weapon.

Note that, even though carrying a handgun may be legal in the park, discharging it is not, even in self-defense. This is a blip in the way the federal law allowing people to carry was written. You can carry it, but technically you cannot use it. Having said that, in 2014 a man was charged with illegal discharge of a weapon in Glacier National Park after he shot at a bear that was attacking him. NPS rangers cited him for the offense, but the prosecutor asked to have the charges dismissed before it went to trial.

Patrol Cabins

There are approximately three dozen patrol cabins located at various points around the park's backcountry. These cabins are used by rangers and researchers for official activities and are not for use by civilians. It is unlawful to break into or damage the cabins or to relieve them of any firewood or other supplies that may have been stockpiled around them. Yellowstone does not rent patrol cabins like other federal agencies do. You may, however, use the vault toilets located at these cabins if you wish.

Only a handful of these cabins are staffed consistently throughout the summer. Though the more remote cabins are only itinerantly staffed, you can usually find rangers at cabins near the more popular trails, such as Heart Lake, Shoshone Lake, Thorofare, Hellroaring, etc. If you run into trouble in these areas and are unable to get cell signal or lack a personal emergency device, it would be a good idea to check at the nearest patrol cabin if one is close by before hiking out to one of the trailheads. These cabins are shown on most trail maps (including those in this book), and they are listed as reference points in the trail information tables later in this book. Appendix 9 also provides a complete list of patrol cabins along with their GPS coordinates. If you get lost or are in need of assistance, you can use this information to try to find your way to one.

Thermal Areas

In addition to the park's flora and fauna, one of the things that attracts many visitors specifically to Yellowstone is its thermal features. There are, by most accounts, well over 10,000 unique thermal features in the park—by far the most intense concentration of such features anywhere on the planet. More than half the world's geysers are in Yellowstone, including the world's largest one—Steamboat (located in the Norris Geyser Basin).

But while many of the thermal features are located at the main developments or along the park's road system and therefore within reach of the typical day visitor to the park, a significant majority of them are located in thermal fields that lie well within the park's backcountry. Some of them have trails that either lead directly to them or that pass right by them, while others are much more remote and require some significant bushwhacking and off-trail travel to reach.

There are 101 named thermal fields in the park, plus an untold number of random collections of hot springs, mudpots and other features that lie outside the boundaries of the "official" groupings.[2] So even if you are not intending to travel to a thermal area, keep in mind that you can come across hot pools and other dangerous thermal areas just about anywhere in the park, especially if you are traveling off the beaten path. See the chapter on safety for more information about how you should hike in and around these areas.

Federal law (36 CFR 7.13.j) makes it a federal crime to travel off trail or off the boardwalks in thermal areas where those trails and boardwalks are provided. This is pretty clear guidance for those areas where there are actually trails built and maintained for such purposes. However, it gets a bit murkier in the backcountry areas where there are no maintained trails to remain on. Some contend that, because backcountry areas are open unless they're specifically closed by local edict (via a posted sign at the area or codified in the park's Superintendent's Compendium), travel into and through these areas is permitted *since no trails are provided.* Others have interpreted the regulation to mean that all areas are closed *unless* there are trails permitted.

Over the past few years, the law enforcement rangers have written increasingly large numbers of citations for people being in closed areas and/or in thermal areas where they shouldn't be. Some of the people they've cited have been caught red-handed doing damage to the park's fragile thermal features. The NPS does, of course, have the responsibility to protect these areas, and the fact that some irresponsible nitwits do these kinds of things makes that much harder to accomplish. The park has reacted by closing off more and more areas to public access, however, which defeats its other mandate to provide access to the people.

If you wish to explore these areas, please check in with one of the park's backcountry offices prior to setting out to ensure that entering these areas remains legal, and to check up on any dangers that might be present in the specific area(s) that you wish to visit. Getting caught in the closed area can result in a $150 fine (as of the end of 2018). Damaging the features will get you additional fines and will usually result in you being banned from the park. I have to assume that, by reading this book, you are one of those people who wishes to explore safely and legally, and I implore you to not only treat the park's resources with the utmost respect, but encourage you to report anyone you observe failing to do so (and, if possible, also provide photographic evidence of the illegal activities).

Trail & Backcountry Etiquette

Like within society itself, there are certain rules of etiquette that you are expected to adhere to when you are in Yellowstone's backcountry. Some are common sense, but others may not necessarily be so obvious, especially to those new to hiking and/or new to Yellowstone.

Trail Registers

Though they used to be more common, you will no longer find many trail registers within the park these days. Back in the days before cell phones and social media were ubiquitous, each trail had a trail register where you would sign your name and the date/time you entered the trail. When you came back out, you would mark that you had come back out. It was supposed to be a way of allowing the park to keep track of who was using the trails, ensuring everyone who went in came out, etc.

Of course, most people did not bother to sign the registers and the weather (and the occasional vandal) would often take its toll on the books themselves. There are a small handful of registers in unique places in the park (Lone Star Geyser, for example), but as a general rule, it is no longer necessary to use these. Be sure and give someone your itinerary, however, so if you do not return, a search and rescue operation can be undertaken sooner rather than later.

Trash and Waste

Park regulations require you to carry out your trash. There are no trash containers in the backcountry so you must bring out any trash or waste you produce (other than human waste—see below). Do not throw trash into the pit toilets that may be found at some of the backcountry campsites. Do not burn waste food or trash, with the exceptions described below. Leave the trails and campsites in as pristine a condition as you can so that those who follow you may also enjoy them.

Off-Trail Hiking

As a general rule, it is legal to hike anywhere in the park, trail or no trail, unless posted otherwise or unless otherwise restricted by park regulations. An example of the latter can be found in the Gallatin Bear Management Area. From May 1 to November 10, off trail travel is prohibited in this area to prevent incursion into sensitive bear habitat. But otherwise, you may explore to your heart's content. This includes service roads, abandoned roads, wildland and wilderness areas, thermal areas, and any other areas that do not have some type of closure notice posted. If you are unsure about whether a given area is closed, check with the nearest backcountry office.

Hiking/Camping in Wilderness Areas

Though vast swaths of the park are covered by trails, there are huge areas that have no trails or campsites whatsoever. You do not need permission to day hike into these areas (unless they are closed, of course). You will, however, need to get special permission to camp in these areas. This is done at one of the park's backcountry offices, and requires the permission from the District Ranger, the Superintendent's regional representative for the area. The DRs can be found at the ranger station located at each development.

You do not need a "good reason" to hike into or camp within a wilderness area, but you do need to demonstrate an understanding of what you are getting yourself into. When you request the permit, you will be asked about your plans for being in the area and may be asked about your hiking experience (as well as your familiarity with the use of a compass and maps). The park wants to prevent you from getting lost, getting injured, etc., and possibly having to expend large sums of money and manpower to find you and bring you out. You will also need to demonstrate a knowledge and understanding of "Leave No Trace" principles (see below). See the previous chapter for more details.

Who Goes First?

It's always a touchy subject about who goes first when you meet other parties on the trail. There's certainly no law dictating specifics about who should allow others to pass with priority, but there are some widely accepted rules of thumb in the hiking community:

- Parties/Groups going uphill have the right of way.
- The larger party of the two who meet has the right of way on flat surfaces.
- If you are hiking with a group, the group should hike either single file or side-by-side in numbers that take up no more than half the trail width.
- Stock parties always have the right of way, regardless of the surface or the incline.
- Persons who are mobility-impaired or have other disabilities have the right of way, regardless of surface or incline.
- If in doubt, or if you just want to be the courteous one, let the other party/group have the right of way. It's never wrong to be courteous.
- There are a small number of trails that allow bicycles in the park. Stock parties and hikers always have priority over bicyclists.
- All traffic should move in a pattern similar to what vehicular traffic does in the U.S.—you always travel to the right and oncoming traffic moves left.
- If you need to pass someone else, pass on their left and if you are not sure they are aware of your presence, make them aware of you before you do, especially if it is a stock party.

Meeting Stock Parties

When meeting a stock party in Yellowstone, common etiquette requires you to allow them to proceed while you step off to the side and allow them to pass. Given how large the animals are and how much of a logistical challenge it would be to get them off of a trail, it is probably easy to see why this would be the case. If two stock parties meet on flat ground, the smaller of the two parties should get off the trail and allow the other to pass. If a stock party is traveling up an incline, they will have the right of way regardless of the size of the party. If you are on a narrow trail and have the option of stepping downslope or upslope, always step downslope. Moving up makes the horse believe you are larger than it and that may startle or spook the horse.

Winter Hiking

All of the park's trails are technically open in the winter, though there are a handful that are specifically maintained for winter use. You may hike on foot, or travel on snowshoes or skis, or whatever works for you given the trail conditions. If you hike on snowshoes or on foot, please hike outside the trail made by skiers. Footprints and snowshoe prints interfere with the safe travel of skiers. If you are a skier and end up falling, take a moment to repair the tracks for future skiers.

Crimes: Do Not Damage or Destroy Stuff

For some unknown reason, there has been a recent spate of people who seek to damage or destroy the treasures they come across in our country's national parks. Yellowstone is not immune to that, sadly. The park's law enforcement rangers cite dozens of people over the course of each summer for damaging, destroying, or stealing things within the park.

Keep in mind that it is a federal crime to do any of the following:

- Damage, throw objects into, or enter any thermal pool, geyser, mudpot, fumarole, or other thermal feature. This includes writing your name in the bacterial or algal carpets surrounding such features.
- Damage or deface any of the park's features. This includes etching your name in trees, spraying graffiti on rocks or anything else, etc.
- Damage, deface, move, or remove trail signs, trail markers, campsite features, etc.
- Take or remove any object from the park. This includes archaeological features, antlers and bones, wildflowers, petrified wood specimens, etc. You can pick up things to look at them, but place them back as you found them so future visitors can enjoy them as well.
- Cut down or remove branches from any standing tree, whether dead or alive. You may only use deadfall for firewood where fires are permitted.
- Camp in any campsite or non-campsite location without a permit specifically authorizing you to be there, except in emergency situations.
- Leave campfires unattended. All fires must be completely extinguished before you depart your campsite.
- Leaving trash at your campsite.
- Entering any area that is closed.
- Using drones or any other unmanned aerial device, for any reason, without a permit.

If you encounter visitors damaging the park, or any situation or condition you believe to be unsafe or hazardous, please report this to the nearest ranger station or backcountry office as soon as practical. This includes downed food poles at campsites, situations where a bear or bears have entered and prowled around your campsite, unattended campfires, discarded trash, large animal carcasses at or very near your campsite or on the trails, etc. If you encounter a bear that charges you, whether you are forced to rely on protective measures or not, please report this to the nearest ranger station, visitor center, or backcountry office. You do NOT need to report every bear or animal sighting, however.

Leave No Trace

Leave No Trace is a philosophy that promotes respect for the land and the environment while hiking and camping. The intent is for you to enjoy your time in the outdoorsand not leave any trace of your visit behind. That way, the next person or people who come along can enjoy the space in the same undisturbed manner that you did. And the people who come after them will enjoy the same benefit, and so forth.

And while it is important that you try to live up to these principles on any foray off the asphalt in Yellowstone, it is even more critical when you venture out into the backcountry, either on trail or off the trails. The basic precepts of Leave No Trace include:

- Plan Ahead and Prepare
  - ◊ Know the regulations and special concerns for the area you will visit.
  - ◊ Prepare for extreme weather, hazards, and emergencies.
  - ◊ Schedule your trip to avoid times of high use.
  - ◊ Visit in small groups when possible. Consider splitting larger groups into smaller groups.
  - ◊ Repackage food to minimize waste.
  - ◊ Use a map and compass to eliminate the use of marking paint, rock cairns or flagging.
- Travel and Camp on Durable Surfaces
  - ◊ Durable surfaces include established trails and campsites, rock, gravel, dry grasses or snow.
  - ◊ Protect riparian areas by camping at least 200 feet from lakes and streams.
  - ◊ Good campsites are found, not made. Altering a site is not necessary.
  - ◊ Concentrate use on existing trails and campsites.
  - ◊ Walk single file in the middle of the trail, even when wet or muddy.
  - ◊ Keep campsites small. Focus activity in areas where vegetation is absent.
  - ◊ Disperse use to prevent the creation of campsites and trails.
  - ◊ Avoid places where impacts are just beginning
- Dispose of Waste Properly
  - ◊ Pack it in, pack it out. Inspect your campsite and rest areas for trash or spilled foods. Pack out all trash, leftover food and litter.
  - ◊ Deposit solid human waste in catholes dug 6 to 8 inches deep, at least 200 feet from water, camp and trails. Cover and disguise the cathole when finished.
  - ◊ Pack out toilet paper and hygiene products.
  - ◊ To wash yourself or your dishes, carry water 200 feet away from streams or lakes and use small amounts of biodegradable soap. Scatter strained dishwater.
- Leave What You Find
  - ◊ Preserve the past: examine, but do not touch cultural or historic structures and artifacts.
  - ◊ Leave rocks, plants and other natural objects as you find them.
  - ◊ Avoid introducing or transporting non-native species.
  - ◊ Do not build structures, furniture, or dig trenches.
- Minimize Campfire Impacts
  - ◊ Campfires can cause lasting impacts to the environment. Use a lightweight stove for cooking and enjoy a candle lantern for light.
  - ◊ Where fires are permitted, use established fire rings, fire pans, or mound fires.
  - ◊ Keep fires small. Only use sticks from the ground that can be broken by hand.
  - ◊ Burn all wood and coals to ash, put out campfires completely, then scatter cool ashes.
- Respect Wildlife
  - ◊ Observe wildlife from a distance. Do not follow or approach the animals.

- ◊ Never feed animals. Feeding wildlife damages their health, alters natural behaviors, and exposes them to predators and other dangers.
- ◊ Protect wildlife and your food by storing rations and trash securely.
- ◊ Avoid wildlife during sensitive times: mating, nesting, raising young, or winter.

- Be Considerate of Other Visitors
  - ◊ Respect other visitors and protect the quality of their experience.
  - ◊ Be courteous. Yield to other users on the trail.
  - ◊ Step to the downhill side of the trail when encountering pack stock.
  - ◊ Take breaks and camp away from trails and other visitors.
  - ◊ Let nature's sounds prevail. Avoid loud voices and noises.

This list is courtesy of the Leave No Trace Center for Outdoor Ethics. It is also important to note that many of these bullet points are enshrined in federal law in Yellowstone.

Swimming, Bathing, & Soaking in Park Waters

As a general rule, you may soak or swim in any park waters that are not purely of thermal origin. For example, you can swim in any of the park's lakes (many of them have leeches, in case you weren't aware of that) and rivers, and any waters that are warmed by *runoff* from thermal features. Mr. Bubbles, in the park's Bechler area, is one popular such feature.[1] However, it is illegal to enter any of the park's thermal features for any reason. In addition to being illegal, it is also highly unsafe, given that the water in these pools is often at or near boiling and may be acidic. Many of the thermal pools fluctuate wildly with respect to their temperature such that they may be cool to the touch at one moment and then will rapidly rise to boiling without notice. It's never a good thing to be cooked alive.

In the summer of 2016, two people (a brother and sister) left the boardwalk in the Norris Geyser Basin with the intention of hotpotting in one of the area's thermal pools. As they approached one that was several hundred yards off the trail, the guy fell through the crust into a pool. His sister witnessed him falling and ran to get help from the ranger based at the museum, and when she tried to direct the ranger to her brother, she could not find the specific location where he had gone in. The park had called in a LifeFlight helicopter to transport the guy out if he had survived, and the helicopter had to hover over the area for several minutes before the crew was able to locate the pool he'd fallen into. They found his shoes floating in the water, and that was literally the only thing that survived—the guy and his clothing had dissolved in the acidic pool in the space of thirty minutes. This is no joke.

The exception to this general rule is any waters that are posted as closed to swimming or that are in areas that are otherwise closed for any reason. The area around, above, and below Moose Falls is one such example. After a park employee was injured there several years ago, the Chief Ranger closed that area to people entering the waters of Crawfish Creek for public safety reasons.

You're not allowed to use soap, shampoo, conditioner, etc., or other noxious substances in park waters. Remember the old Wendell Berry axiom, "Do unto those downstream as you would have those upstream do unto you."

Stock in the Backcountry

Many people love to enjoy the park's backcountry on horseback. There are even outfitters who specialize in providing horseback tours of Yellowstone. You are also free to bring your own stock into the park. Keep in mind that only certain types of stock are allowed on trails and in the park's backcountry. This includes:

- Horses/Ponies
- Mules
- Burros
- Llamas

So...no zebra or alpacas in Yellowstone. You may only bring enough stock to accommodate your party—you can't bring extra (this is primarily to reduce the impact on the land and reduce the amount of food and supplies you are required to carry). Stock may not use the park's roadways, except when crossing at designated locations. As with hiking, day use of stock does not require a permit, but overnight camping does.

You may only camp the certain campsites that allow stock (the campsite list at the end of the book indicates which sites allow stock). You must have a negative Coggins Test certificate for all equine stock. All such animals entering Yellowstone (even those just passing through) are required to have a certificate from a veterinarian stating they are free of equine infectious anemia (EIA). This certificate must have been issued within the past 12 months.

There are many trails in the park where the use of stock is prohibited altogether. These will usually be marked at the trailheads with the "No Stock" sign (a person on a horse with a red circle & line drawn through it). The park's online Backcountry Situation Report also lists trails not suitable for stock use, and the trail charts in the second part of this book also indicate which trails are suitable for stock.

There are several other guidelines/regulations you should be aware of with regard to the use of stock in Yellowstone's backcountry:

- Stock cannot be left at trailheads and may not be kept in the park's frontcountry campgrounds.
- Before you depart the trailhead (entering or leaving) you must either remove any manure or scatter it.
- All trail travel must be in single file and you must remain on the trail itself. You may travel off-trail with your stock for day trips, though only with a single pack animal if necessary (pack strings are not allowed off-trail). Any pack animal must be led and may not be allowed to travel loose.
- All feed (including hay) provided to the horses must be certified weed-free or be processed feed. Feed must be stored securely in camp just as with human food.
- While in camp, your stock should be kept out of the core camp except for packing or unpacking. Any manure dropped in the core camp areas must be completely removed.
- Stock may graze outside the core camp area, but must do so more than 100 feet from bodies of water, trails, and the core camp area. Grazing areas should be rotated to minimize damage to the grass.
- You may use any method you wish to restrain stock while in camp, to include electric fences, highlines, pickets, etc.
- You must rotate where you keep your stock over the course of your stay to minimize damage to the area, and you must remove all of your equipment when you leave. Any methods you use to manage your stock while in camp must be done to prevent damage to park resources.

Children in the Backcountry

Consider the health and stamina of your child(ren) before taking them off into the park's backcountry. Older kids often do quite well, but younger ones may present some logistic challenges for you, especially on overnight and longer treks. If you take a child still in diapers, for example, you will not only need to take extra supplies with you, you will have to pack out the dirty ones.

Hiking/Camping Naked

Naked hiking, or "free hiking" as it is commonly known, is not terribly popular in the park, primarily because it tends to get cold later in the day and during the night and early mornings (even in July and August). And though most people would never even consider doing such a thing, there is an international day for naked hiking: June 21 (the first day of summer). There is no reason you cannot celebrate that day in Yellowstone.

Federal law does not prohibit nudity on federal lands, leaving the decisions about where to regulate that sort of thing to local units. Yellowstone regulations state that "nude swimming, nude bathing, and nude sunbathing is prohibited in areas frequented by or in the presence of park visitors."[2] There is no prohibition regarding nude hiking. Having said that, it is of course not a good idea to hike on any of the more popular trails without suitable clothing covering your important bits. While it is not a crime to be naked in most places, if you cause a disturbance, you can be cited under the federal law regarding disorderly conduct (36 CFR 2.34).

The majority of the park's trails are popular enough that they would not be suitable for hiking without clothing. The best way to figure out if a particular trail is a potentially suitable one, examine the trail guides that follow in this book. If the trail "TRAF" (traffic) rating is a "1," then it is not a very popular trail and you might wish to consider this.

Potential trails might include:

- Old South Road Trail
- Beula Lake Trail
- Terraced Falls Trail
- Turbid Lake Trail from east trailhead
- Summit Lake Trail from the west
- Pitchstone Plateau Trail
- Boundary Creek Trail
- Some of the longer, multi-day trips into the Mirror Plateau/Mist Creek Pass, the Thorofare, or the South Boundary Trail areas are conducive to naked hiking once you get into your second or third days out into the more remote areas
- Just about any of the abandoned trails or old roadways would be suitable, though the bushwhacking and climbing over trees, etc., might be problematic

The Beula Lake and Terraced Falls trails are out and back trails, and I'm not aware of anyone having hiked the old South Road Trail from the north end (it is too difficult to find). If there's no one parked at their trailheads, there's an excellent chance there's no one on the trail. So hiking to the lake or the falls naked would be safe. Coming back, be prepared, however, in case someone else has decided to use that trail as well. You should, of course, be paying complete attention to your surroundings while hiking in Yellowstone anyway, but obviously this is an even better idea if you are going to be hiking without clothing.

Follow good naked hiking etiquette. If you do elect to use one of the park's trails *au naturale*, there are some basic rules you should follow. These rules are outlined in just about every other naked hiking guide and website you will find, so I'll not reiterate them here.

Do your research. Figure out which trails will be the most conducive to encountering the fewest number of people. Do not use shorter trails that originate from the main park roads. These are often frequented by families with children (and some people think it harms their children to see naked people). It is extremely rare to come across younger children on the longer backcountry trails, however.

Keep in mind the weather and the bugs. Even at the height of summer, in July and August, temperatures in the higher elevations often do not make it out of the 60s, and everywhere in the park, the nighttime temperatures will get down into the 30s and 40s. In late May through about the first week or two of August, the park is a breeding ground for mosquitoes and biting flies of wide variety. Bring and use your insect repellent. Also keep in mind that, since you are at a much higher elevation than usual, the sun will be brighter and you will burn much easier. Therefore, you will also want to ensure you have a healthy supply of sunscreen.

Practice appropriate courtesy. It is a good idea to have something handy to cover your crotch when you are approaching other hikers. You do not need to worry about saying anything to them about your state of dress—a simple "hello" or other greeting will suffice, and then go on about your business.

Campsite nudity: It is also perfectly acceptable to be naked at your campsite. In fact, it is not terribly uncommon for rangers on patrol to come upon campers in a less than fully clothed state. In the charts for the backcountry campsites, there's a "Privacy" rating listed. You should be fine walking around naked in those with complete or partial privacy, while for those with no privacy, it may not be a good idea to be running around naked if you are averse to others seeing you nude.

If you are not hiking naked and encounter a naked hiker (or hikers), just continue on your hike as if you had encountered a clothed hiker. Exchange pleasantries just as you would with anyone else. There is no need to report a naked hiker to law enforcement unless s/he is doing something patently illegal. Rangers are not going to go out looking for someone merely hiking without any clothes on. If you have children with you, use it as an educational moment to explain there is nothing "wrong" with a naked human body, etc.

Weather in Yellowstone

As I have mentioned in other parts of the book, there is a running joke among the park staff in Yellowstone regarding the weather: *We only have three seasons in the park: July, August, and Winter.* And while that may not be wholly reflective of reality, it is much closer to it than many might believe. It literally snows well into June each season, and then after a couple of months of relative snow-freeness, it picks up again in earnest in mid to late September. So even though technically there may be a calendar-based spring and fall, to those who are used to well-defined seasons, it may indeed seem like the park gets shortchanged.

It can snow rather robustly at any time of the year in Yellowstone. On August 25 each summer, the park employees celebrate Christmas in August. The tradition has been around since at least the 1930s, and is supposedly based upon a major snowstorm blasting the park with many inches of snow around that date one year in that decade. As the story goes, the park was snowed in and people were unable to go anywhere. The employees did what they always do—got creative. So they decided since it looked like Christmas and it was August 25, why not celebrate Christmas? For many decades after that, they even went out to a specific boulder in the Firehole River (just south of Firehole Canyon) to decorate a tree. There is a boulder in the middle of the river there that has a single pine tree growing out of it. Although these days the tree is less robust than it was in the past, the tree is still growing out of that rock, and many longtime employees of the park know it as Christmas Tree Rock.[1]

The law enforcement rangers take umbrage at people decorating that tree these days, but the tradition of exchanging gifts among employees, dorm door decorating contests, decorating the inns and stores, and baking cookies for the park's guests continues to this day. To the employees who spend their summers here taking care of the visitors, it is one of the little things that makes working in this magnificent place all the more special.

Understanding the park's weather is essential to planning any hike anywhere in the park, but it becomes even more critical when you are going to be undertaking a multi-day sojourn into some of the more remote areas of Yellowstone. This chapter is designed to acquaint you with the kind of weather you are likely to encounter on your visit to the park.

Weather summary

Though you will occasionally see charts that purport to show "averages" for "the park," the reality is that Yellowstone has different weather in different places throughout its 3,471 square mile (8,990 sq km) territory. Mammoth, which sits at an elevation of roughly 6,000 feet (1,829m) above sea level (ASL), has an entirely different climate than does Canyon Village, which sits at about 8,000 feet (2,438m) ASL. The park has over a dozen weather-monitoring stations spread across the various villages and entrances, and examining the data from those stations shows that, while it may be 80F/27C in Mammoth, it can be 20 degrees cooler just a few dozen miles away at Old Faithful or Lake Village (see the temperature charts at the end of this chapter for a comparison). This is true even in the winter. The snowfall differences around the park can also be extreme, with some places receiving less than a few feet over the course of the season, while other places can get literally dozens of feet.

Rain and Snow

During the spring season, May and June tend to be the rainiest months in Yellowstone. The park does not typically get long, torrential rains, but there are times when people who live in the park wonder if there will ever be sunshine again. The chart on the next page shows the average number of days it precipitates in the park. Notice that May and June are by far the wettest months. Add this on top of all of the snow melt that is taking place throughout the park and the majority of the trails are often wet, muddy, and marshy during this period.

Once July arrives, though, the monsoon season comes to an end and things start to get drier throughout most of the park. By the time August and September roll around, the area is often so dry that the fire danger increases substantially. This is the time of year when late afternoon thunderstorms become more common, and many of them will contain cloud-to-ground lightning and hail. And though these can be irritating and dangerous in many places in the park (though they seem to be more prevalent in the southern half of the park), they can be especially dangerous around Yellowstone Lake, Lewis Lake, and Shoshone Lake where boaters may be in the water. These storms often have high winds that kick up the waves on the lakes, resulting in dangerous conditions for the boaters (and swimmers who are brave enough to be in the water).

Yellowstone tends to get snows into June each spring, and though it is somewhat uncommon, it is not unheard of to experience some light snows in July and August, especially at the higher elevations. In a typical season, though, the serious snows do not begin again until mid to late September. In October the snowstorms can often get serious enough that the park has to shut down entire stretches of road until they can be plowed.

The bulk of the snowfall occurs in the November to early March time frame, however. The park closes for the summer season on the first Monday in November, and for the next three weeks, they will keep the roads plowed for administrative use so employees can leave, the concession operators can get the park hotels and stores winterized, and the winter staff can get in and get settled and Yellowstone can prepare for a long, hard winter. After Thanksgiving, road plowing ceases and NPS allows the snow to build up on the roadways so that the snowcoaches and snowmobiles can start coming in when the park re-opens for the winter season on December 15.

Then, on March 15, the park closes in preparation for spring opening somewhere around April 15-20. The NPS begins plowing the roads and opens the park back up in phases through Memorial Day. During this time, the majority of the precipitation will still be snow. So if you come into the park this early in the season and plan to hike or camp in the backcountry, you are generally going to be limited to areas in the Northern Range.

	JAN	FEB	MAR	APR	MAY	JUN	JUL	AUG	SEP	OCT	NOV	DEC
Daylight Hours	9	10	12	14	15	16	15	14	12	11	10	9
Average UV Index	1	2	4	6	8	9	10	8	6	4	2	1

Precipitation	JAN	FEB	MAR	APR	MAY	JUN	JUL	AUG	SEP	OCT	NOV	DEC	AVG	TOTAL
Avg # Days w/ Precipitation	17	14	13.7	11.6	11.5	14.4	11	10.8	9.7	8.8	13.1	15.6	12.6	
Avg Rainfall Total (inches)	1.7	1.6	1.8	1.8	2.5	2.3	1.6	1.6	1.5	1.2	1.9	1.6	1.8	21.1
Average # of Days w/ Snowfall	16.2	13.4	12.6	9.5	4.4	0.9	0	0	1.1	5.8	12.6	14.9	7.6	
Avg Snowfall Total (inches)	34.3	30.4	25.6	21.4	8.1	1.3	0	0	1.3	9.9	30.9	30.5	16.1	193.7

Clothing Choices

Given those realities, you can see why most experts suggest you dress in layers in Yellowstone, regardless of the time of year. When you go out in the mornings, it is almost invariably going to be too cold for shorts and a T-shirt, but in the summer afternoons it will be too warm for jeans and jackets, especially when you are out on the trail.

If you are going to be hiking prior to July, ensure you have shoes or boots that are suitable for getting wet and dirty. As stated before, most of the trails in the park at this time of year are going to be marshy or muddy, and some will have sections that are literally underwater. If you are on a point-to-point hike and come across a section of trail like this and are not prepared for it, you may end up having to turn around and hike all the way back to the start.

Sunscreen

The average elevation of the park is around 8,000 feet (2,438m), and as a result, the air is much thinner. This means that much more ultraviolet radiation makes it to your skin when you are in the park. As a general rule, for every 1,000-foot (305m) increase in elevation, there is a corresponding 5%–7% increase in UV radiation over what you would experience at sea level.[2] Thus, in mid-July in Yellowstone, the time of year when UV ratings of 10 are common, you can expect to receive about 40%–50% more UV exposure on any given day than you would if you were in Bangor, Maine, which sits on roughly the same latitude as the park.

So to placate your dermatologist, it is important that you use sunscreen to protect your skin, especially if you are not used to sun exposure. And you will want to ensure you re-apply it several times throughout the course of your hike, especially if you are doing a lot of sweating. Alternatively, you can keep much of your skin covered with clothing, but once hikers get out into the open and out of the forest canopy, they often start shedding clothes and/or switch to shorts so they do not overheat (and if you are hiking naked, well...). You will also want to include good quality sunglasses in your preparations; the UV exposure will damage your eyes just as easily as it will your skin. And don't forget the lip balm!

One really cool thing about being in Yellowstone in the summer is that the park experiences very long days. In fact, at the height of the summer, daylight can last as long as 16 hours. This makes for excellent hiking experiences because you can do much longer hikes before it gets too dark to be on the trail. The chart at the top of this page shows the average number of daylight hours per month along with the average UV index.

Lightning

Yellowstone is not quite Florida when it comes to lightning, but there is lightning in many of the storms that roll through the park (most of the park's wildfires are caused by this, in fact). In 2005, a group of people on the boardwalk at Old Faithful were injured when lightning struck the area. A 12-year-old boy went into cardiac arrest. He was later resuscitated, but this demonstrates the dangers present when these kinds of storms pass through. Throughout the park's history, some half dozen people have been killed by lightning.[3]

If you are out on the trail during a storm, stay off ridgelines and mountain summits, do not find yourself under a tree out in the open, and get out of wide open spaces. If you are on a boat, get off the water. It is best to be in a tent or under a large stand of trees if possible. If you are out in open space, find a low-lying gully and lie down. If you are with a group of people, spread out so that if lightning does strike, it will not take out the entire crew.

Winter Weather

Winter activities are a very popular part of Yellowstone from December through March. And if there is one word that can characterize the park during this time of the year, it is *white*. The park is one of the coldest and snowiest places in the lower 48 states during the winter. Being in the park during this time of year is so incredibly different and involves its own set of unique circumstances, so there is an entire chapter on it.

Fire Season

One other factor that hikers need to be concerned about in the Yellowstone area is fire season. Fire season in the park generally lasts from mid to late July to the end of September or whenever the first serious snowfall occurs. Fires can impact hikers because park management will close off trails, campsites, and even entire sections of the park if a wildfire is threatening in any way. Additionally, increased fire danger typically results in restrictions on certain human behaviors in the backcountry, most notably the use of campfires.

The NPS has a dual strategy for dealing with fires that impact its wild areas. Fires caused by Mother Nature, such as those from lightning strikes, are generally allowed to burn unchecked so long as they do not threaten developed areas, humans, or park structures. A wildfire that starts in the Thorofare area, for example, will be allowed to burn, but they will take protective measures to keep the Thorofare Ranger Station from being damaged. A lightning-caused wildfire that starts burning close to Grant Village, however, would be fought as it encroached upon the developed area.[4]

Fires that are human-caused, even those deep in the backcountry, are extinguished if possible. These are "unnatural" fires and therefore they represent a human impact upon the wilderness. The most common example of this is a wildfire that starts from an unattended campfire. This is why park regulations require you to ensure your fires are fully extinguished before you depart your campsite.

Yellowstone's ecosystem is fire-dependent, in that many of its forested areas require fire to regenerate. The ubiquitous lodgepole pines you see throughout the park have what are known as serotinous cones. The cones, of course, contain the seeds for new trees, and their scales ("leaves") are closed together with a resin that requires a high temperature in order to melt so that their seeds can be released, thereby launching a new generation of trees that will eventually replace the old, existing trees. There are also species of wildflowers that live in a kind of state of subsistence until the forest canopy is removed due a fire, and once that happens, they bloom and thrive. Yellowstone cannot survive without the occasional wildfire.

One of the most incredible things about hiking through areas of the park that burned in the massive wildfire season of 1988 is seeing how far along the new growth of trees has come. You can hike through these areas at the lower elevations and see that those trees have grown at a much faster rate than those that were birthed in the higher elevations. So this need for fire for the park's ecosystems to flourish is why you will often see park firefighters simply monitoring wildfires as opposed to actively working to put them out.

As the fire season begins to get serious in late July and the fire dangers are elevated, the park implements various restrictions in order to prevent human caused wildfires from starting. Having to dedicate fire crews and resources to fighting human-caused fires is not only expensive, but it puts the firefighters in danger and prevents them from monitoring and working on other fires that might be burning.

It can be expensive for you as well. If it is determined that you failed to extinguish a campfire, and that campfire led to a wildfire that required significant manpower and resources to extinguish, the National Park Service will send you a bill. That bill that could easily total in the millions of dollars if your negligence resulted in a large fire. And, of course, that would be on top of the criminal charges you would face.

Once the fire danger reaches the EXTREME level in portions of the park, the park's wildfire management team assembles and begins evaluating the situation to determine what steps need to be taken to lessen the risk of unnatural wildfires in the park. For those who use the park's backcountry, this often includes implementing certain restrictions based on how severe the danger is perceived to be. These are known as "staged" restrictions. You will be informed of these via park press releases and via the backcountry offices when you check in to get information or to receive your camping permit.

Stage 1 Backcountry Restrictions

- Charcoal or wood fires of any sort are prohibited at backcountry campsites.
- There are no fire restrictions in park campgrounds, day-use picnic areas, and employee residential areas within provided fire rings.
- Portable stoves and lanterns which use pressurized liquid, jellied petroleum, or gas fuel and fully enclosed, sheep-herder type stoves with a ¼-inch spark-arrestor screen are permitted park-wide in areas where ground cover and overhead vegetation is cleared within three feet of the device.
- Smoking is permitted only inside vehicles, on sidewalks, in gravel or paved parking areas, in developed campgrounds, immediately adjacent to backcountry fire rings, and in designated smoking areas inside buildings. Smoking is prohibited on all trails.

Stage 2 Backcountry Restrictions

- Charcoal or wood fires of any sort that may produce ash or embers are prohibited at the park's backcountry campsites, 11 developed campgrounds, day-use picnic areas, and employee residential areas.

Wildfire approaching the Old Faithful area, September 7, 1988. Image courtesy NPS.

- Smoking is not permitted except in an enclosed vehicle, single-family dwelling, developed campground, day-use picnic area, or within a three-foot diameter area that is barren or cleared of all flammable material. Smoking is prohibited in the backcountry, except immediately adjacent to the provided fire ring or in the aforementioned barren or cleared area.
- Employees, concessionaires, permittees, contractors, and persons operating within the park who are engaging in spark-producing activities, including but not limited to, roadside mowing, welding, grinding, blasting, power saw, or heavy equipment operation in any area that is not barren or cleared at least 10 feet in diameter of all burnable vegetation, shall consult with the Fire Management Office prior to starting their project to ensure adequate wildfire prevention measures are being taken. One round-point shovel with an overall length of at least 36 inches, a chemical pressurized fire extinguisher with a minimum rating of at least 2A, and a patrol of the work area for one hour after activities have ceased are recommended wildfire prevention measures.
- All internal and external combustion engines must have a spark-arresting device in effective working order.
- Stoves and lanterns that use pressurized liquid, jellied petroleum, or gas fuel, and fully enclosed, sheep-herder type stoves with a ¼-inch spark-arrestor screen are permitted parkwide in areas which are barren or cleared of all overhead and surrounding flammable materials within three feet of the device.

Additionally, the park may close some trails and/or entire areas of the backcountry due to the potential for rapid progression of fires that are burning within the park or outside the park. For example, in late August of 2016, the Berry Fire, which had started several miles west of the John D. Rockefeller Parkway, began to track northeast toward the South Entrance and the Snake River Ranger Station. So park fire managers closed the southern portion of the backcountry from roughly Beula Lake eastward to the area southwest of Big Game Ridge and south of campsite 8B1. Within a few days the fire raced several miles, overrunning the south entrance and making its way into those closed areas. So they don't make the decision to close these trails and areas lightly. Please respect the danger fire represents to the park and to you, and remain out of closed areas and adhere to the restrictions put in place to prevent the accidental spread of wildfires.

YELLOWSTONE MONTHLY MAXIMUM TEMPERATURE AVERAGES - FAHRENHEIT (F)

STATION	ELEV F	ELEV M	JAN	FEB	MAR	APR	MAY	JUN	JUL	AUG	SEP	OCT	NOV	DEC	AVG
Mammoth	6300	1920	31	33	43	49	60	73	81	78	67	53	39	28	**53**
Tower Ranger Sta	6266	1909	26	30	42	50	59	72	80	78	71	55	34	25	**52**
Lamar Ranger Sta	6555	1998	25	31	38	49	61	69	79	77	68	56	38	27	**52**
Northeast Ent	7460	2274	29	29	38	45	54	65	73	72	61	48	35	24	**48**
Quadrant(Gallatin)	7925	2415	24	27	36	42	53	64	72	70	60	46	31	21	**46**
Canyon Village	7900	2408	27	29	38	43	53	64	72	70	60	47	34	23	**47**
West Yellowstone	6673	2034	24	31	38	48	59	69	79	77	66	53	35	25	**50**
Lake Village	7871	2399	23	28	35	43	52	61	72	71	61	49	34	25	**46**
East Entrance	8419	2566	19	19	27	34	43	58	66	64	57	39	23	17	**39**
Old Faithful	7360	2243	28	31	40	46	56	70	77	75	66	50	34	26	**50**
Bechler Ranger Sta	6400	1951	32	35	44	50	61	73	81	78	67	53	39	28	**53**
Thorofare	7910	2411	30	33	43	50	56	66	78	75	62	49	35	28	**50**
South Entrance	6883	2098	26	31	38	47	57	67	78	76	66	53	37	27	**50**
Parkwide Mean	**7225**	**2202**	**26**	**30**	**38**	**46**	**56**	**67**	**76**	**74**	**64**	**50**	**34**	**25**	**49**

YELLOWSTONE MONTHLY MINIMUM TEMPERATURE AVERAGES - FAHRENHEIT (F)

STATION	ELEV F	ELEV M	JAN	FEB	MAR	APR	MAY	JUN	JUL	AUG	SEP	OCT	NOV	DEC	AVG
Mammoth	6300	1920	16	16	25	29	37	45	51	49	43	34	22	13	**32**
Tower Ranger Sta	6266	1909	6	7	17	24	31	37	42	40	34	26	13	6	**24**
Lamar Ranger Sta	6555	1998	0	4	9	21	28	34	37	35	28	21	11	2	**19**
Northeast Ent	7460	2274	12	16	21	21	27	41	47	46	40	30	19	9	**27**
Quadrant(Gallatin)	7925	2415	12	12	19	23	33	41	48	47	40	30	18	9	**28**
Canyon Village	7900	2408	5	7	14	19	29	36	40	38	33	24	12	3	**22**
West Yellowstone	6673	2034	0	3	9	20	29	35	40	37	29	22	10	2	**20**
Lake Village	7871	2399	-1	0	5	16	25	33	39	37	30	23	12	1	**18**
East Entrance	8419	2566	9	8	15	19	28	39	47	45	40	26	13	7	**25**
Old Faithful	7360	2243	4	6	12	19	29	33	41	39	32	26	11	2	**21**
Bechler Ranger Sta	6400	1951	9	14	18	23	33	39	43	41	36	27	17	7	**26**
Thorofare	7910	2411	12	9	18	24	31	38	49	44	36	28	15	12	**26**
South Entrance	6883	2098	0	2	9	19	27	34	38	36	28	21	10	2	**19**
Parkwide Mean	**7225**	**2202**	**6**	**8**	**15**	**21**	**30**	**37**	**43**	**41**	**35**	**26**	**14**	**6**	**24**

YELLOWSTONE MONTHLY MAXIMUM TEMPERATURE AVERAGES - CELSIUS (C)															
STATION	**ELEV F**	**ELEV M**	**JAN**	**FEB**	**MAR**	**APR**	**MAY**	**JUN**	**JUL**	**AUG**	**SEP**	**OCT**	**NOV**	**DEC**	**AVG**
Mammoth	6300	1920	-1	1	6	9	16	23	27	26	19	12	4	-2	**12**
Tower Ranger Sta	6266	1909	-3	-1	6	10	15	22	27	26	22	13	1	-4	**11**
Lamar Ranger Sta	6555	1998	-4	-1	3	9	16	21	26	25	20	13	3	-3	**11**
Northeast Ent	7460	2274	-2	-2	3	7	12	18	23	22	16	9	2	-4	**9**
Quadrant(Gallatin)	7925	2415	-4	-3	2	6	12	18	22	21	16	8	-1	-6	**8**
Canyon Village	7900	2408	-3	-2	3	6	12	18	22	21	16	8	1	-5	**8**
West Yellowstone	6673	2034	-4	-1	3	9	15	21	26	25	19	12	2	-4	**10**
Lake Village	7871	2399	-5	-2	2	6	11	16	22	22	16	9	1	-4	**8**
East Entrance	8419	2566	-7	-7	-3	1	6	14	19	18	14	4	-5	-8	**4**
Old Faithful	7360	2243	-2	-1	4	8	13	21	25	24	19	10	1	-3	**10**
Bechler Ranger Sta	6400	1951	0	2	7	10	16	23	27	26	19	12	4	-2	**12**
Thorofare	7910	2411	-1	1	6	10	13	19	26	24	17	9	2	-2	**10**
South Entrance	6883	2098	-3	-1	3	8	14	19	26	24	19	12	3	-3	**10**
Parkwide Mean	**7225**	**2202**	**-3**	**-1**	**4**	**8**	**13**	**19**	**24**	**23**	**18**	**10**	**1**	**-4**	**9**

YELLOWSTONE MONTHLY MINIMUM TEMPERATURE AVERAGES - CELSIUS (C)															
STATION	**ELEV F**	**ELEV M**	**JAN**	**FEB**	**MAR**	**APR**	**MAY**	**JUN**	**JUL**	**AUG**	**SEP**	**OCT**	**NOV**	**DEC**	**AVG**
Mammoth	6300	1920	-9	-9	-4	-2	3	7	11	9	6	1	-6	-11	**0**
Tower Ranger Sta	6266	1909	-14	-14	-8	-4	-1	3	6	4	1	-3	-11	-14	**-5**
Lamar Ranger Sta	6555	1998	-18	-16	-13	-6	-2	1	3	2	-2	-6	-12	-17	**-7**
Northeast Ent	7460	2274	-11	-9	-6	-6	-3	5	8	8	4	-1	-7	-13	**-3**
Quadrant(Gallatin)	7925	2415	-11	-11	-7	-5	1	5	9	8	4	-1	-8	-13	**-2**
Canyon Village	7900	2408	-15	-14	-10	-7	-2	2	4	3	1	-4	-11	-16	**-6**
West Yellowstone	6673	2034	-18	-16	-13	-7	-2	2	4	3	-2	-6	-12	-17	**-7**
Lake Village	7871	2399	-18	-18	-15	-9	-4	1	4	3	-1	-5	-11	-17	**-8**
East Entrance	8419	2566	-13	-13	-9	-7	-2	4	8	7	4	-3	-11	-14	**-4**
Old Faithful	7360	2243	-16	-14	-11	-7	-2	1	5	4	0	-3	-12	-17	**-6**
Bechler Ranger Sta	6400	1951	-13	-10	-8	-5	1	4	6	5	2	-3	-8	-14	**-4**
Thorofare	7910	2411	-11	-13	-8	-4	-1	3	9	7	2	-2	-9	-11	**-3**
South Entrance	6883	2098	-18	-17	-13	-7	-3	1	3	2	-2	-6	-12	-17	**-7**
Parkwide Mean	**7225**	**2202**	**-14**	**-13**	**-10**	**-6**	**-1**	**3**	**6**	**5**	**1**	**-3**	**-10**	**-15**	**-5**

Fishing, Boating, and Hunting

Hunting

The hunting portion of this chapter is short and sweet: Hunting is illegal in Yellowstone. As a hunter, you can pass through the park in certain areas, but you cannot hunt or take game inside the park, even if you shot it outside the park. Once it wanders inside Yellowstone territory, it is protected.

Hunting is allowed to some extent in Grand Teton National Park to the south, and on USFS property and in the states that border the park. Each of these has their own rules and regulations governing when hunting can take place, what kinds of animals may be taken, and so forth. If this is something you are interested in, you are encouraged to avail yourself of their respective websites to find out more.

Fishing

Yellowstone is recognized the world over for its fishing opportunities. As you might imagine, though, there are a few rules regarding where you can fish, what you can use to fish, and what you can do with the fish you catch.

Fishing Licenses

If you are over the age of 15, you are required to purchase a fishing permit in order to fish in Yellowstone. This is a separate permit specifically for the park, irrespective of whether you have permits in Wyoming, Montana, or Idaho. Grand Teton allows people to fish with a Wyoming permit, but in Yellowstone you have to have one issued by the park. The reason for this is the fact that Yellowstone has its own unique set of issues regarding its fish populations and how the park's aquatic ecosystems are managed in order to maintain an appropriate balance among the species that live here. Note that a Yellowstone fishing permit does not allow you to fish in Wyoming or Grand Teton National Park. You will need a Wyoming state permit for that.

The permits are sold in three versions. Which one you need to get depends upon how long you wish it to be valid. A 3-day permit costs $18; a 7-day permit costs $25; and a season permit (good until the close of the fishing season in the year you purchase it) is $40. You can buy these at any of the park's visitor centers, backcountry offices, general stores, and the Northeast Entrance Station. Several vendors outside the park in each of the gateway cities also sell these permits. When you purchase the permit, the ranger (or salesperson) will go over the basic rules and provide you with a copy of the current regulation booklet, along with your permit and a postage-paid card you can use to record what you catch, what you did with it, etc. The NPS asks fishermen to return the card with this information because it allows them to monitor the health of the park's fish populations. You are not required to send it back, but it is very helpful to the park's fisheries staff if you do so.

Note that even if you plan to just fish at a small lake or river while you are camping in the backcountry, you are still required to have a permit. You must have your permit on you while you are actively fishing. The law enforcement rangers, both frontcountry and backcountry, routinely check people they see fishing for permits during the summer. Getting caught without one on your person may result in a citation and hefty fine.

For children 15 and under, there are two options. If the child will be fishing with an adult who has a park-issued fishing permit, they do not need to get their own. If they will be fishing either by themselves or under the supervision of an adult who does not have a park-issued permit, they must obtain a free permit from the park (or one of the vendors outside the park). The intent of this is so that they will be familiar with the regulations as well. If they are fishing with an adult with a permit, it is presumed that adult will help the child abide by the park's fishing regulations. If the adult does not have a permit, then rangers provide guidance to the child and issue him/her their own permit.

In addition to selling fishing permits, the park's General Stores sell a wide variety of fishing tackle and equipment (and many of the employees are avid Yellowstone fishermen).

Fishing Regulations

The park's fishing regulations vary from place to place in the park, based on which watershed you are in. There are three rules that remain constant throughout the park, however:

- You cannot use any lead anywhere in the park (no lead sinkers, etc.).
- The use of live bait is prohibited.
- The use of barbed hooks is prohibited. You can use barbed hooks if you pinch the barbs down or clip them off, however.

There are also a handful of guidelines you must observe:

- Dispose of fish entrails properly by throwing them back into the water or in a trash receptacle. Do not just throw them on the shore, near your campsite, etc. This will attract bears and other predators to the area.
- You may not fish from the park's roadways, bridges (to include the infamous Fishing Bridge), or boat docks.
- You may not fish in any of the park's thermal areas.
- You may only fish from sunrise to sunset. Night fishing is prohibited.
- Any fish you catch must remain identifiable to rangers. This generally means leaving the skin on.

Fishing Season

Fishing season in most areas of the park runs from the Saturday of Memorial Day weekend to the first Sunday in November (which is typically the day before the interior of the park closes at the end of the summer season). There are some areas where the season opens later (for example, the Yellowstone River opens July 15). The regulation guide you will be given when you get your permit will have further details on this.

Regional Regulations

Although there are the general regulations listed above, the specifics regarding what you can catch, what you must release, what you must kill, etc., varies depending upon which area of the park you are in. There are four regions:

- Northwest: Includes the Gallatin River and Madison River drainages (including the Gibbon River and Firehole River)
- Northeast: Includes the Lamar River, Soda Butte Creek, and the Yellowstone River below the Canyon area.
- Southeast: Includes the upper Yellowstone River (from the Canyon area back to the Lake and then back to the park's boundary), Yellowstone Lake, Middle Creek, and their tributaries.
- Southwest: Includes the Bechler River, Falls River, Snake River, and Lewis River and their tributaries, as well as Lewis Lake, Heart Lake, and Shoshone Lake.

When you get your permit, the small handbook you are provided explains the regulations for each of these regions. It will also have photographs showing those fish species that are native to Yellowstone and those that can be found in its waters that are invasive (not native). It is important that you be able to identify the fish you catch because the regulations regarding what you can do with them varies from species to species.

Since those regulations tend to vary a bit from one season to another, they're not enumerated here. The park's website will have the latest version of this handbook as a PDF, and will also explain in detail all of the park's regulations regarding fishing. You can also find out which species of fish you might find in the park in general terms. Appendix 1 to this book provides a list of the park's named lakes along with which species of fish you might expect to find in each. Appendix 2 is a detailed listing of the park's rivers and streams, and it, too, includes the relevant list of fish that you can expect to find in those bodies of water.

Boating

Boating is another popular activity within Yellowstone. Boating season is identical to that of fishing season, from the Saturday of Memorial Day weekend to the first Sunday in November.

Boat Permits

All boats and float tubes must have a Yellowstone-issued permit to be launched into the park's waters. The permits are available in two forms: one for seven days and one for the entire season. As of late 2018, the costs are as follows:

- Non-Motorized Boats/Float Tubes: $5 for 7 days; $10 for the season
- Motorized Boats: $10 for 7 days; $20 for the season

The permits for motorized and non-motorized boats can only be obtained at the Bridge Bay Ranger Station, the Grant Village Backcountry Office, or the Snake River Ranger Station. Permits for float tubes (only) may be obtained at any of the park's other Backcountry Offices.

The reason for the disparity is because boats require a much more complex Aquatic Invasive Species (AIS) inspection. These are performed by specially-trained rangers that are only available at the three locations referenced above. Floats also require an inspection, but these can be done visually quickly by any ranger, whereas those required by the boats are much more involved. Note that on some days AIS inspectors may not be available at the Snake River Ranger Station. If that is the case, you will need to travel to Grant Village or Bridge Bay for your inspection. If you wish to put in at Lewis Lake and do not wish to travel to Grant, the ranger at the Snake River Backcountry Office can contact the team at Grant Village and have an inspector meet you at the Lewis Lake Boat Dock.

Note that all boats must also be legally registered in the state where it is principally used, and the registration numbers must be visible as required by U.S. Coast Guard regulations.

When you get your permit, you will be issued a copy of the park's boating regulations pamphlet. It is critical that you read and understand the information contained within it so you do not run afoul of the park's rules on boat use.

Jet skis, airboats, and submersible watercraft are not permitted in Yellowstone waters. Also not permitted is water-skiing, kite-surfing, or any other activity that involves persons being in the water and towed from the craft.

Aquatic Invasive Species

The aquatic ecosystems in Yellowstone are as pristine as they can be, and the NPS expends considerable effort to ensure they remain as free from non-native species of fish, snails, fleas, and disease as possible. Part of this is the requirement that every boat put into the waters in the park be free from any of these invasive species. This is confirmed through an Aquatic Invasive Species (AIS) inspection performed on your boat and equipment as a condition for issuing you a boating permit.

When you apply for your permit, you will complete a form with basic information about your boat. You will need to provide information about where and when it was last in the water (the body of water and its location). The inspector will follow you out to your boat and check the entire craft, trailer, motorworks, anchors, and the wells to ensure they are free of any species that does not exist in Yellowstone's waters.

If you had your boat in another body of water prior to coming to Yellowstone, there are steps you can take to minimize the likelihood of bringing non-native species into the park. These include:

- Removing all visible mud, plants, fish, and other animals from your boat, trailer and equipment (including your clothing, nets, fish storage containers, etc.)
- Draining your boat hull and live well outside the park
- Cleaning and drying any part of your boat and equipment that has come into contact with another body of water prior to entering Yellowstone

If the inspector finds problems with your boat, you will have to clean it or rectify the issues before you can get your permit. Note that if you come into Yellowstone via Grand Teton National Park, you likely will have been required to have an inspection there prior to coming into Yellowstone (and perhaps it may be inspected by Wyoming state inspectors as well). Regardless, you will need to have your boat re-inspected once you are in Yellowstone.

The inspector will help you affix your permit and the AIS inspection sticker to your boat in the appropriate location. These stickers need to remain on the craft as long as you are in the park. If you leave the park with the boat, it will need to be re-inspected upon re-entry.

Required Equipment

As a condition of receiving your permit, you are required to have certain pieces of equipment on your boat. These include appropriate personal flotation devices (PFDs) for everyone who will be on board, a fire extinguisher (if you have engines, on-board fuel storage, or enclosed compartments), a sound-producing device such as a whistle or airhorn, appropriate lighting that is in working condition, and, if you have an inboard motor, flame arrestors.

In addition to the required equipment, you should also consider having the following:

- Oars or paddles if you are on a motorized boat
- A visual warning device of some type (flares, etc.)
- A bailing device
- Anchor (required if you are going to be headed out to one of the lakeside campsites)
- A Marine-band radio
- Cold-water survival gear (the average temperature of Yellowstone Lake's water is in the 40s much of the season)
- Compass, maps, and/or GPS device or other navigational aids

Boating Locations

There are only two lakes where motorized boats are permitted in Yellowstone. One is Yellowstone Lake and the other is Lewis Lake. Motorized boats may not be used on any other bodies of water inside the park, and are subject to restrictions on where they are allowed on Yellowstone Lake (see below). You may use either the Bridge Bay Marina or the Grant Village Marina to launch into Yellowstone Lake. There is only one boat dock at Lewis Lake.

Non-motorized boats (including paddleboards and float tubes) are permitted on any of the park's lakes except for Sylvan Lake, Eleanor Lake, Twin Lakes, and Beach Springs. You may launch a non-motorized boat into Yellowstone Lake from either of the locations mentioned above, as well as Sedge Bay and the beach areas along Gull Point Drive. Note that if you are in a sailboat, getting into Yellowstone Lake from the Bridge Bay Marina requires going under a low bridge. You will not be able to pass under the bridge with a raised mast.

Boats are not allowed on any of the park's rivers, streams, and creeks, except that non-motorized boats may be used on the Lewis Channel to access Shoshone Lake. If your boat has a motor, it must be removed from the craft and stowed on the beach at the entrance to the channel.

Boating Restrictions on Yellowstone Lake

There are a number of restrictions on the use of boats on Yellowstone Lake, specifically in the South, Southeast, and Flat Mountain Arms of the lake. This is due in large part to the fact that these areas are sensitive wildlife habitat, and park managers want to keep the human impact on these populations to an absolute minimum.

In all of these areas, travel is limited to 5 mph. In the South and Southeast Arms, the lower third (roughly) of these areas are restricted to non-motorized boats or boats designed for hand-propulsion with disabled motors only. These areas are typically marked with buoys by the middle of June.

The various islands in the lake also have restrictions regarding approach and access. Frank Island is closed to public access until August 15 each summer to protect nesting birds. You may access the picnic area on the southeast side of the island (there is a dock there, as well as a vault toilet). The southern end of Stevenson Island is similarly closed until August 15 each summer, but the north side remains accessible to the public (though there are no facilities here). The Molly Islands are closed to public access year-round and it is illegal to approach them in a boat within ½ mile of their shorelines (except traveling to campsites 6A1 and 6A2).

You may generally land a boat on the shore of Yellowstone Lake at any location, except between Little Thumb Creek and at the south end of the West Thumb Geyser Basin. You may not overnight on the lake except at one of the established campsites, and then only with the appropriate permit issued by one of the Backcountry Offices.

There are a variety of other regulations governing the operation of watercraft on the park's bodies of water. When you get your permit, the little guidebook you will receive will contain an explanation of all of those regulations, along with a variety of other pertinent information.

Weather on the Lakes

The weather in Yellowstone can be rather temperamental, and that is especially true on its lakes. Strong storms pop up with little or no warning, especially in the late afternoon. The park has a NOAA Weather Radio transmitter located at Grant Village that can be received across Yellowstone Lake (162.450MHz), and during the day, rangers based at Bridge Bay Marina will issue emergency information over Marine Band radio.

In order to prevent getting into trouble, it is highly recommended that you operate your boat close to shore, especially if you are in a non-motorized craft. If possible, remain closer to the western shores of the lake and avoid the northeastern shores as this is where the strongest winds will be a problem. If you capsize in one of the park's lakes, you will be in cold water and hypothermia will become your immediate concern.

Camping on the Lakes

For those who wish to remain overnight on the lakes, there are a number of backcountry campsites located along the shores of both Yellowstone and Shoshone Lakes. Keep in mind that access to Shoshone Lake is only possible by taking your boat up Lewis Channel, and that usually involves pulling it up the channel for at least a mile before reaching the lake. Typical travel time from the Lewis Lake dock is 3-4 hours on a good day.

Though Shoshone Lake is typically ice-free by the latter part of June, most of the campsites along its shore are not reservable until July 1 or July 15 because of the likelihood of high water preventing them from being opened. They are available on a walk-up basis if they have been deemed safe prior to that, however. If you are making a quick trip to the park and want to check, you can contact the park's Central Backcountry Office to ascertain their status.

Shoshone Lake is also subject to the high winds of the afternoons on most days. As a result, rangers recommend you remain on the west side of the lake and only cross at the Narrows in the middle of the lake when necessary. You can access Shoshone Geyser Basin from boat if you wish. There is a landing area clearly marked for arriving boaters.

Yellowstone Lake is typically ice-free in early June, and most of the campsites will be open by that time. Given the prevalence of storms and high winds on the lake, it is best to get an early start if possible. The sites on the eastern shores are usually more subject to the winds than the other sites.

Many of the campsites on the shore of the lake have their own unique restrictions. The current (as of late 2018) restrictions are provided in the campsite list near the end of this book, but you should check the park's website for the latest information.

Some sites (mainly multi-party sites) require at least one hiking party to be "self-sufficient." What that means is that you must cook, eat, and sleep on your boat. You can go ashore to explore and to use the toilet, but all other activities must be undertaken on the boat itself.

If you do not have your own boat and/or want to put into the Thorofare or Trail Creek areas without having to worry about dealing with a boat, Xanterra operates a shuttle service that takes hikers to a handful of spots on the shore of Yellowstone Lake, specifically 7L5, 7L6, 7M4, 5L8, and just south of 5E6. You will need to contact their operation at the Marina for schedules and associated costs (307-242-3893).

Safety in Yellowstone

Safety is—or should be—the foremost thing on your mind as you hike in Yellowstone. There are a variety of things that can injure or kill you in this park that you just do not find at most other places, including bears and the park's thermal features. You must have a healthy respect for the park in order to enjoy it safely. So this chapter will spend some time going over safety information that is critical for you to understand. In addition to the material you find here, be sure you review the safety information found in the newspaper you get as you enter the park as well as the various signs that can be found in the thermal areas.

Bear Safety

One of the things that makes Yellowstone such a unique place is that all of the wildlife here is just that—wild! Yellowstone is not a zoo, and the animals are not domesticated in any way. There have been a number of times when people have driven up to the entrance gates and asked the rangers, "What time do you let the animals out of their cages?" as if this were Walt Disney World. The National Park Service does not keep the animals in cages—they are all every bit as wild as Mother Nature can make them.

And while it is rare, it is not unheard of for animals, bears especially, to injure or kill people inside the park. So when you're out hiking and camping, you need to understand what these animals are capable of, how to interpret their behavior, how to prevent yourself from being attacked, and how to defend yourself if you are the unfortunate victim of such an attack.

Yellowstone Bear Basics

Yellowstone is home to two kinds of bears: black bears and grizzly bears. Either is capable of injuring and killing a human being, but the grizzly is by far the most dangerous of the two in the park. Black bears tend to avoid humans at all costs and will go out of their way to avoid them unless it is a mother protecting her cubs. Grizzlies often see humans as food or threats to their safety or food supply and will attack them (to include attacks to defend their cubs). Either will attack if caught off-guard and surprised, however. Therefore, you should work to avoid them where possible.

Bears come out of hibernation in the spring and their basic function throughout the summer is food consumer and, for many of the females, raising their young. They are always on the hunt for food. As the season progresses and fall sets in, this drive to feed becomes even more intense as they try to pack on as many calories as they can so they can hibernate through the winter. So bears will actively defend their food supplies to the maximum extent possible.

Bear Management Areas

Yellowstone uses bear management areas, or BMAs, to carve some sections of the park up into spaces where restrictions are implemented in order to prevent bear-human conflicts and to give bears space and time to roam free from human interference. These are typically spaces where there is a high presence of bears and/or a sufficient presence of bison and elk carcasses following a typical winter. These restrictions exist as much for the protection of humans as they do for the bears—a heavy presence of bears in a given area will increase the likelihood of an encounter with a hungry bear, and that will not bode well for either the human or the bear if an injury or death occurs.

The restrictions implemented in these areas will directly impact you as a hiker. During closures, all trails in a given BMA will be closed to public use. And, in some cases, even when the trails are open, off-trail travel is prohibited. This prohibition is seasonal in some areas while in others it is year-round. In the trail descriptions that constitute the bulk of this book, each trail is identified as to whether or not it is in a bear management area (and if so, which one(s). When you see that a trail is in a certain BMA, check the BMA outline in this section for specifics on travel restrictions in that area. It is not unheard of for BMA restrictions to be continued for some areas past the stated time frames due to continuing activity that wasn't anticipated. So be sure to check with your nearest backcountry office prior to setting out on your hike for any last minute details.

Bear Differentiation

As is indicated at the outset of this section, there are two types of bears in Yellowstone. One is the black bear, the other is its larger cousin, the grizzly. Trying to tell which is which is often difficult without getting an up-close look at each bear, but the chart on the following page provides some basic details. The easiest way to tell is to look at the bear's back. Grizzlies have a hump behind their shoulders (muscle mass used for digging), whereas the black bears do not. A grizzly's rump is also typically lower than its shoulders, whereas a black bear's rump will either be on the same level as its shoulders or slightly higher. The snout can also be a reliable indicator—a black bear will have a straight snout while the grizzly will have a snout that is concave (often referred to as being "saucer-shaped" or "dish-shaped").

You cannot use the color of the bear's hair to determine what kind of bear it is. Many black bears are cinnamon or brown in color, and grizzlies can be black, light brown, dark brown, cinnamon, or even silver in color. Contrary to popular belief, it is next to impossible for the average person to tell the difference between black bear scat and that of a grizzly bear (all jokes aside). Bear scat is bear scat, and if you come across fresh bear scat, you should be that much more alert.

Why is it important to know which kind of bear you are dealing with? How you react to an attack is based upon which kind of bear you are dealing with. It literally could make the difference between life and death.

Avoiding Bears

The best way to handle an encounter with a bear is to avoid one altogether. And the best way to do that is to ensure you are paying attention to where you are hiking and taking appropriate precautions to allow the bears to know you are coming. Generally speaking, bears prefer to avoid humans altogether. So if you let them know you are coming, they will

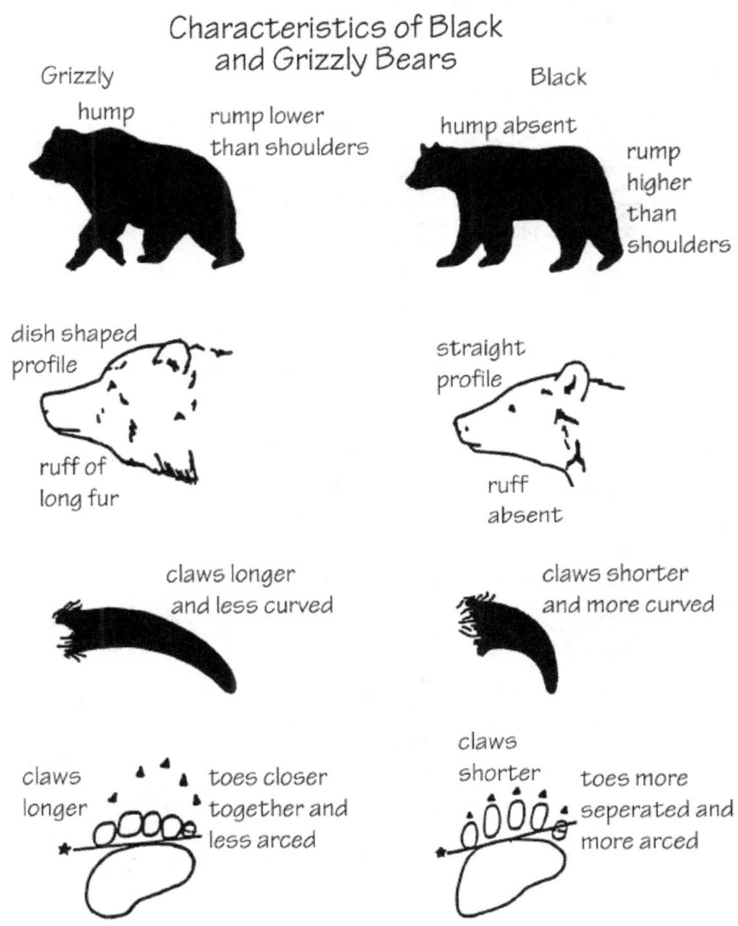

actively work to avoid coming into contact with you. The best way to do this is to make noise as you hike. Most professionals recommend you sing, clap your hands, talk loudly, holler, etc., to let bears know you are coming. If you do not want to do this continually, you need to at least do it as you go around corners, come up hills, or move through thicker underbrush. Surprising a bear is one of the best ways to get attacked.

And contrary to popular myth, bear bells are all but useless. Bells are not loud enough for bears to notice over the wind, birds chirping, and the other background noise typically present in the great outdoors. A small study done in Katmai National Park a number of years ago indicated that bears paid no attention to bells jingled by the researchers. Of course, you are welcome to use the bells if you wish, but please do not rely on them to make enough noise to suffice without adding something else to it.

Yellowstone Bear Management Areas

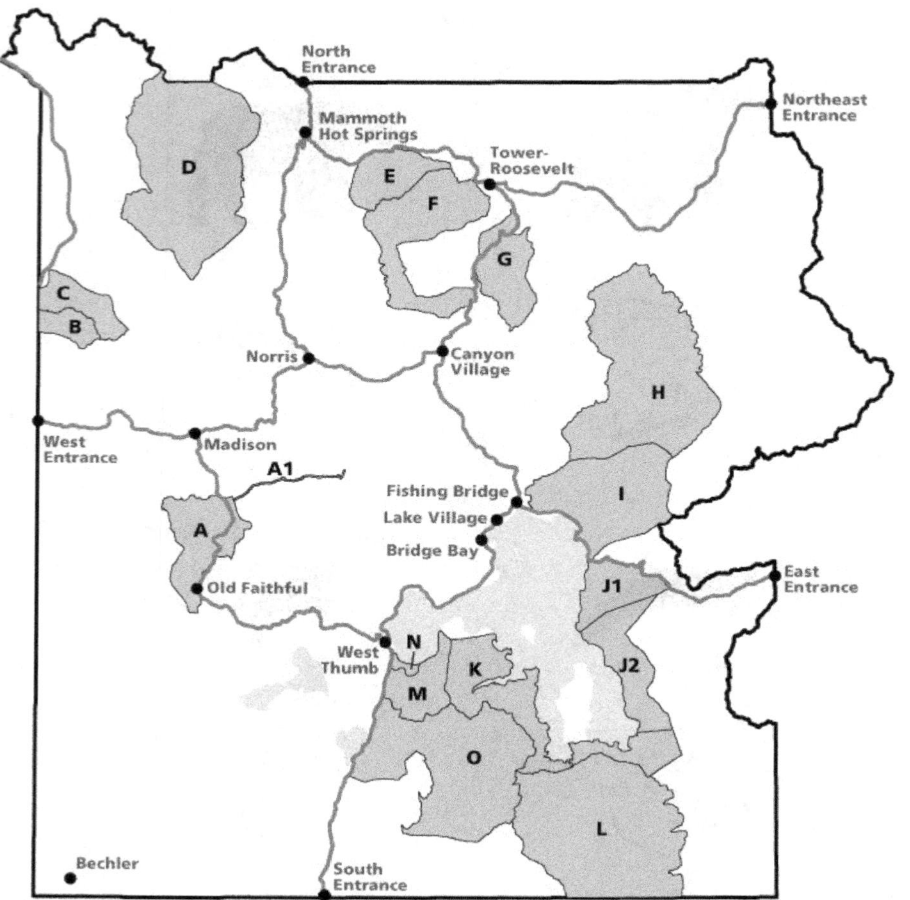

A. Firehole: Closed March 10 through the Friday of Memorial Day weekend. Area includes Firehole Freight Road, Firehole Lake Drive, and the Fairy Falls and Mystic Falls trails.

A1. Mary Mountain Trail: Closed March 10 through June 15. Closure extends from the Nez Perce trailhead to Mary Lake. Through travel from the Canyon trailhead is not allowed. However, travel is permitted between the Canyon trailhead and Mary Lake. Streamside use is allowed from the point where Nez Perce Creek crosses the main road to a point one mile upstream along Nez Perce Creek.

B. Richard's Pond: Closed March 10 through the Friday of Memorial Day weekend. From the Saturday of Memorial Day weekend through September 30, Duck Creek, from the park boundary upstream to the Campanula Creek/Richard's Creek fork, is open to streamside travel. The area upstream from Campanula Creek/Richard's Creek fork is closed from March 10 through September 30.

C. Gneiss Creek: Closed March 10 through June 30. From July 1 through November 10, travel is allowed only on designated trails: off-trail travel is prohibited.

D. Gallatin: From May 1 through November 10, travel is allowed only on designated trails: off-trail travel is prohibited. A minimum group size of four or more is recommended for hiking and camping.

E. Blacktail: Closed March 10 through June 30.

F. Washburn: Closed August 1 through November 10. From March 10 through July 31, the area is open by special permit only: contact the Tower Ranger Station for more information.

G. Antelope: Closed March 10 through November 10. The Dunraven Road and related turnouts are open. From May 25 through November 10, foot travel is allowed on the old Road Trail from Tower Campground to the Buffalo Picnic Area.

H. Mirror Plateau: From May 15 through November 10, the area is open to day use only except for overnight camping between July 1 and August 14 (for a combined total of 14 nights per summer at the 301 and 5P7 campsites).

I. Pelican Valley: Closed April 1 through July 3. From July 4 through November 10, the area is open to day use only between the hours of 9 a.m. and 7 p.m.

J1. Clear Creek North: From April 1 through August 10, travel is only allowed on the east shore from Nine-mile Trailhead to Park Point. All other trails are closed and off-trail travel is prohibited. Campsite 5H1 is open (no travel from site). On August 11, all the campsites are open and off-trail travel is permitted.

J2. Clear Creek South: From April 1 through July 14, travel is only allowed on the east shore trail from Park Point to Beaverdam Creek. All other trails are closed and off-trail travel is prohibited. Open campsites are 5E2, 5E3, 5E4, and 5E6 (no travel away from campsite). All other campsites are closed. On July 15, all campsites open and off-trail travel is permitted.

K. Lake Spawn: From May 15 through July 14, no off-trail travel allowed and the trail between Cabin Creek and Outlet Creek is closed. Open campsites are 7L5, 7L6, 7L8, 7L7, 7M3, 7M4, 7M5, 6A3, 6A4 and 6B1 (no travel away from campsite). Only July 15 all campsites open and off-trail travel is permitted.

L. Two Ocean: From March 10 through July 14 and August 22 through November 10, travel is allowed only on designated trails (off-trail travel is prohibited). From July 15 through August 21, a permit is required for persons wishing to travel away from designated trails. Contact the South Entrance Ranger Station for more information.

M. Riddle/Solution: Closed April 30 through July 14.

N. Grant Village: The Grant Campground will not open prior to June 20; actual opening dates may vary annually. If bears are still frequenting the spawning streams after opening, the campground loops adjacent to the streams will remain closed until bear activity ceases. Campground opening and closure dates are determined annually and can also be located in the park newspaper.

O. Heart Lake: Closed April 1 through June 30.

NOTE: The BMAs are subject to change at any given point, so be sure to check with your nearest Backcountry Office before entering any area subject to a BMA closure/restriction.

Hikers do a variety of things to make noise. This includes using cowbells, loud stereos (please do not do that in the wild), radio white noise (turning off the squelch), compressed air noise makers, and so forth.

Another way to avoid a bear encounter is to not use materials or food that has strong odors or scents associated with them. For example, avoid sweet-smelling perfumes, deodorant, shampoos/conditioners, etc. You will also want to avoid strong-smelling food such as tuna fish, peanut butter, etc. The park stores sell single-meal tuna kits and it makes me cringe. Tuna has a very strong odor and bears can smell something like this up to 20 miles (30km) away. Seems to me that would be a great way to bring a bear right to you.

Hike during the day. Bears know humans use the trails during the day and tend to avoid them where they can. Plus, both you and the bears can see better when it is daylight out. And while it is legal to hike anywhere in the park that is not specifically off-limits (marked or not), most bear attacks occur off trail. So while it can be fun to go exploring areas of the park that others do not see, it can also be less safe to do so.

If you do spot a bear on the trail you are traveling,or a bear sign such as fresh scat, it is a good idea to turn around and try your hike another day. Even if the bear is moving ahead of you rather quickly, bears tend to move randomly in search of food and may stop and linger for hours in any given spot. If you are on a multi-day hike and/or cannot afford to turn around due to scheduling or meeting up with other hikers, etc., find a safe place to hang out for a half hour or so and allow the bear to move along at its own pace. When you do leave, be sure to remain alert in case you come upon it again.

How to Handle a Bear Encounter

Any time you hike in Yellowstone, there is always the possibility of an up-close and personal encounter with a bear. Many people have hiked for years in the park and never encountered a bear up close, but there are also people who have encountered bears on their very first hike. You just never know when one of these creatures is going to show up in front of you. How you react to it could, again, literally mean the difference between life and death.

There are four basic bear encounter scenarios:

- You come upon a bear just digging or foraging for food. These bears generally pose no threat to you unless you make some threatening move toward it.
- Sows with cubs. In the bear's mind, you pose a threat to her cubs and she just wants to eliminate the threat, not make a meal out of you.
- Bears eating a carcass. These bears see you as a threat to their food and they just want to eliminate that threat. They likewise do not wish to turn you into a meal.
- Stalking bears—bears that follow you and are literally hunting you. These are the most dangerous type of bears to run across.

The first thing to keep in mind when you encounter a bear in any of these scenarios is **DO NOT RUN!!!** Try to back slowly away from the animal until you can no longer see it, then exit the area as expeditiously as possible. Running triggers the predatory instinct in bears and quite often the bear will chase you down and treat you as another meal. Bears can run upwards of 30 miles (48km) per hour or more, so you stand literally zero chance of outrunning one. In July, 2011, a visitor to the park (along with his wife) surprised a mother and her cubs along the Wapiti Lake Trail. They immediately turned and ran, and the mother pursued them, reaching the gentleman first. She attacked him and he was killed. If they had just slowly backed away from the animals, the chances are good he would have survived.[1]

If the bear notices you, it may ignore you altogether or it may charge at you. In the vast majority of cases, these are bluff charges—the bear is simply trying to scare you. Again, DO NOT RUN. You will want to resist the urge to try to climb a tree, especially if the bear is a black bear. Black bears are excellent tree climbers, and if it follows you up the tree, you are cornered with no place else to go. This is never a good idea.

If you are dealing with a black bear, act aggressive toward the bear. Swing stuff in its direction, holler at it, make yourself appear larger (spread your arms out, etc.), throw rocks at it if you can get one. Do not throw your pack at it, however, especially if it contains food.

If you are dealing with a grizzly bear, you want to do the exact opposite of this. Instead of acting aggressive toward the bear, do what you can to let the bear know you are not a threat. Avoid eye contact, talk calmly to the bear, make yourself smaller, continue to back slowly away. If the bear charges, hold your ground.

In both cases, ready your bear spray—pull it out of its holster if you haven't already, remove the safety and put your finger on the trigger. If the bear does continue to charge at you, you will need to deploy it when the bear is between 20 and 30 feet from you. Discharge the spray toward the ground in front of the bear for one to two seconds. The bear will run through it and, hopefully, the strong pepper in it will cause the bear's nostrils to become irritated and it may temporarily blind him. When this happens, bears generally tend to run away rather than continue an attack. Try not to discharge the entire contents of your can if possible. If the bear returns and you don't have a second can, you could be in trouble. Some hikers prefer to carry at least two cans of bear spray with them in case they do have to use one; you still have to hike out and there's no guarantee you will not see another bear on the way out!

If the spray does not deter the bear and he makes contact with you, your reaction once again must be determined by the type of bear you are dealing with. If it is a black bear, fight back! Attack the bear's nose, eyes, and other sensitive areas with anything at your disposal (rocks, sticks, knife, etc.).

If the bear is a grizzly, you will want to do the exact opposite—play dead. Roll over onto your tummy to protect your vital organs, put your hands over your neck to protect it, spread your feet to keep yourself from being rolled over. Try to remain in this position as best you can. Hopefully, you will have a day pack or backpack on that will help protect your back. The bear will likely paw at you and try to roll you over. If he does, continue rolling over until you are back on your tummy and can once again protect your vital organs.

The bear will also likely bite your limbs - your legs and arms. As tough as it will be, you must resist the urge to fight back. This will only make the bear more aggressive and you will likely sustain more serious wounds. Since bears bite each other's faces when they fight, it is possible the bear might go for your face during the attack. Keep your face covered with your hands and forearms and/or keep it buried in the dirt. Unless the bear has been stalking you, in all likelihood, once s/he believes you to no longer remain a threat, the bear will leave you alone and wander off. Remain in place for a few minutes until you are sure the bear is out of visual range of you before you move or get up. Assess your injuries and, if possible, hike out to the nearest trailhead and seek assistance. If you are unable to evacuate on your own, send someone for help, use your cell phone to call the park's Communications Center (using 9-1-1) if you have service, or use your Personal Locator Beacon (PLB) or other safety notification device (SPOT, InReach, etc.).

Bear Spray Purchase and Rental

You can buy bear spray just about everywhere in and around the Yellowstone ecosystem. It will usually cost you between $40 and $50 depending on where you get it. It is important to note that, if you are flying into or out of the Yellowstone area, you will not be able to transport bear spray with you. FAA regulations prohibit you from taking it onto aircraft either in carry-on baggage or checked luggage. If you do buy it and cannot travel home with it, you have two options. You can drop it off at one of the park's recycling centers (Mammoth or Old Faithful), or you can drop it off at one of the park's ranger stations. The NPS uses donated canisters for training and for equipping its personnel who are deployed to the backcountry. It is one way to help the NPS save some money.

There is also another option. Since 2015 it has been possible to rent bear spray in the park. As of the printing of this book, you can only rent it at the kiosk outside the Canyon Visitor Education Center. You can rent it for one day or several days (they also sell it), and when you are done with it, you can drop it off at any of the park's YPSS service stations, the Madison Campground, or the Cooke City Visitor Center. For the summer of 2018, rental prices were $9.50 per day, $18.50 for two days, $28.00 for 3-7 days, or $32.00 for 8-14 days. When you rent the spray from the kiosk you will be required to watch a short video on bear safety and how to use the spray if necessary.

Guns vs. Bear Spray

As of 2010, it is legal for civilians to carry personal firearms in the park, consistent with state law in whatever state they happen to be in. For Yellowstone, this means Wyoming for the most part. In Wyoming, it is legal to open carry a handgun without a permit. Carrying concealed requires a permit issued by the state of Wyoming or one of the states that has a reciprocity agreement with Wyoming. You will need to check Wyoming's website to determine specifically what states those are because they change from time to time. But while it is legal to carry a handgun in the park, it is technically not legal to discharge that firearm, even in self-defense.

Many people believe they can shoot a bear that attacks them. Legal ramifications aside, it is almost impossible to hit a charging grizzly bear in the right place with the right ammunition in the heat of the moment without just pissing it off further. Most people overestimate how accurate they would be under the duress of a charging grizzly. First off, grizzlies can move as fast as lightning. You are quite liable to be unable to remove your weapon from its holster, let alone draw a bead on the animal and fire it. Second, even police officers, who are trained to react under pressure, are able to hit a moving target with a handgun less than one-third of the time. Someone like you, who is (presumably) untrained in tactical handgun use, is not likely to be more accurate than police officers are.

That said, to dissuade a grizzly from attacking you, you are going to have to get a head shot in to kill it. You will need a .357 magnum or larger round that is solid (not hollow points or other expanding rounds). The bullet will need to pierce the grizzly's skull, so you will need

This sign on the left means bears have been reported on this trail recently (within the past week or so). The one on the right is used when an area is closed due to heightened bear activity, a bear attack, etc. Photos courtesy NPS.

to hit it right between the eyes (or at the bottom of the ear canal if you are shooting from the side). With a black bear, all you need to do (typically) is wound it a couple of times to let it know you mean business and it will run away.

So the question becomes, do you think you are skilled and steady enough to draw a handgun, get a bead on the small area of a moving grizzly's face, and get off a round that hits at the right angle to penetrate the skull to disable the bear? And assuming the bullet does hit the right place, will it act quickly enough to disable the bear before it gets to you and mangles your body into a pulp?

Several studies (by the USFS and civilian researchers) have shown that bear spray works at deterring attacks far more effectively than the use of firearms. In the USFS study, half of those who were able to shoot an attacking bear still suffered significant injuries, whereas the vast majority of those who deployed bear spray sustained no injuries (and those who did suffered shorter attacks and less significant injuries).[2]

So even if you do elect to carry a firearm with you while out hiking, please carry and be prepared to use bear spray as well. You will not only likely save your own life, but that of the bear, and you will save yourself a whole lot of legal trouble as well.[3]

Other Animals

Of course, there are a variety of other animals in Yellowstone that can injure or kill you. In fact, some of these have actually caused more injuries than the bears everyone fears. Let's take a look at some of the other animals you might encounter in the park.

Bison

Believe it or not, bison account for more injuries in the park in a typical year than any other animal, including the bear. In 2015, bison gored or head-butted five visitors. There was a video of another visitor early in that season where she walked right up to a lounging bull bison and tried to pet him. Fortunately for her, the bison was not in a foul mood.

People vastly underestimate how quickly these huge animals can move. Despite their size, they run as fast as 40 mph (64kph), and can turn on a dime. And though the males tend to be the more aggressive of the species, the females can become rather serious if they believe you are a threat to their young.

If you encounter a bison while hiking in the park, the best thing to do is to back away and take a few moments to rest until the bison decides to move on. If a bison is lying in your path, you can attempt to go around it with a wide berth. However, if the trail is too narrow and there is no way around it, you will need to just hang back until it decides to move. Remember that it is a violation of federal law to approach any wild animal in the park closer than 25 yards (100 yards for bears and wolves).

You can tell an irritated bison by observing its behavior. An upset one will grunt, snort, and bellow, and may start pawing the ground. It will raise its tail. There is an old saying around the park: If you see a bison with its tail raised, it is either getting ready to charge or discharge. Either way, it is not pleasant to be around one when that happens.

It is generally not a good idea to try to use bear spray to counter an attack by a bison. When bears are hit with the spray, they tend to run away. When a bison is hit with it, they are temporarily blinded and start bucking wildly. If you are close enough to the bison to spray it, you are close enough to be kicked. That can be fatal.

Wolves and Coyotes

As of 1995, Yellowstone is once again the home of the gray wolf. That year its presence was restored to the park after being hunted to extinction in the mid-1920s. Wolves have helped re-establish the natural order to the ecosystem in many ways. But despite its portrayal in stories and myth, there are few actual attacks of humans by wolves, and none inside the park. Having said that, they are wild dogs, and will hunt in packs like wild dogs do. If you encounter a wolf (or wolves) along the trail, back away slowly and leave them alone. If you are approached by wolves, act aggressively, make yourself appear larger (spread your arms or your jacket if you are wearing one), holler at it, throw stuff at it (except food), and if necessary, you can use bear spray to stop or prevent an attack.

Coyotes are much smaller than wolves, typically, and do not tend to congregate in packs as wolves do. Still, there have been situations where they have bitten humans (usually while being fed by them). Although coyotes tend to avoid people, those who have become habituated to human contact or human food will often wander into a campsite looking for groceries. An aggressive or sick animal can and will bite people if they get too close, so try to scare it away as you would any other dog.

Elk

Elk are by far the most populous large animal in the park. And, unlike bears, bison, and a few other animals, they tend to be very skittish and will run away from a threat rather than turning and attacking. The only exceptions to this are females defending their young and the males during rutting season.

Elk will hide their young in small patches of grass where they are born until the little calves can get up on their own and sprint. They are scentless and as long as they remain hidden in the grass, they are generally safe from predators such as coyotes, wolves, and bears. The mother will forage several hundred yards away from where she has sequestered her baby so that any predators will chase her rather than find the little fawn. However, if she notices a hiker approaching her calf, she will run over and physically intervene. This may include kicking you with her hooves. This can be very painful and if she were to hit you in the right place, it can be potentially fatal.

If you come across a little calf hidden alongside the trail (not uncommon at all in the park), please leave it alone and just continue on your path. Do not stop to photograph it, lest the mother think you are a danger and react accordingly. You may not even be aware of her presence, but she will be watching you from the woods somewhere.

During mating season, the males work to gather harems of females and get extremely aggressive toward anything that comes close to them—other males, people, vehicles, etc. If you come across males bugling at one another while out on the trail, watch from a safe distance. Quite often this will degenerate into a physical confrontation between the bulls. One excellent way to see this in action is to spend some time in Mammoth at the park's headquarters during the rut (September–October). There's always one or two males sparring for the right to breed the harem of females that lives there during the summer. They will run at and attack people and vehicles that get too close, and have even chased law enforcement rangers up onto the tops of vehicles.

If you encounter an aggressive elk, try to back away and remove yourself from the area. Wait until the animal has departed the area and then proceed. If you are physically attacked, try to shield your face and neck with your arms and hands, as blows from their hooves striking you in these areas will present the most significant danger. You can use bear spray on elk as well.

Moose

Though somewhat rarer in the park than they used to be, there are still 200 or so in Yellowstone. A kick from one of these animals can be fatal as well. They will often charge and mean it if you surprise them, especially when protecting their young. Bear spray may work to fend them off in an emergency.

Mountain Lions

Many people are surprised to learn that there are mountain lions (cougars) inside Yellowstone. The population is estimated to be around three dozen or so, and they're rarely seen, but they are present. There are no documented cases of cougars attacking humans in Yellowstone, but they have chased and killed humans in other parts of the country.

If you encounter an aggressive mountain lion, act like another cat would toward it—make yourself appear larger (spread your arms, jacket, etc.), snarl, bare your teeth, hiss, holler at it, etc. You can also throw stuff at it, such as large sticks, rocks, etc. Do not run from it. Bear spray has been used to deter a mountain lion attack, so use that as a last resort.[4]

Snakes

Yellowstone is home to six species of snake, only one of which is venomous. The prairie rattlesnake lives in the arid environment around the north central area of the park, from Reese Creek over to a small hill known ironically enough as Rattlesnake Butte (due north of Mt. Everts). So you are generally only likely to encounter these along some of the Mammoth area trails. There are only two recorded instances of rattlesnake bites in Yellowstone (neither of which was fatal). The other five snake species are non-venomous (though the bullsnake resembles a rattle snake, it is not venomous). They can be found in just about all areas of the park, though they are much less common in the higher elevations due to the colder climate. The Mammoth and Bechler areas seem to be home to most.

Smaller Animals and Little Critters

In addition to the larger, more well-known animals, Yellowstone is home to a huge variety of smaller animals that can bite or otherwise harm humans. This includes beaver, badgers, wolverines, otters, marmots, bobcats, lynx, foxes, weasels, pine martens, bighorn sheep, and a wide variety of little squirrels, chipmunks, and other tiny animals with teeth.

The best way to avoid being injured by any of these animals is to not get near them. Most will simply run away from humans to begin with, but while you are out hiking, you may accidentally surprise one, resulting in the animal turning on you and biting or otherwise attacking you. Your best course of action is to simply stay alert and avoid any of these creatures where possible.

Mosquitoes and Ticks

Unfortunately, like many other places where water is around, Yellowstone is home to a seemingly infinite number of mosquitoes, especially in the late June to early August time frame. You will want to invest in shares of any company that makes bug spray after a visit here in the spring. Be sure to bring spray that has DEET in it, and cover all exposed skin and areas covered by thin clothing.

There are also ticks in Yellowstone, especially from early spring through July. These are most often found in the lower elevations in the northern areas of the park, but it is increasingly common to find them in the more southern and western areas as well. DEET also repels ticks, so it is doubly important that you use the stuff out on the trail. Once you've completed your hike, or each evening before you turn in if you are on a multi-day hike, do a quick check of yourself to ensure you have not picked up any little hitchhikers along the way.

Report Serious Encounters to Rangers

If you are physically attacked by or observe otherwise unusual behavior by any animal in Yellowstone, you should report it to the nearest ranger station. You can make these reports to any of the park's Backcountry Offices, law enforcement ranger stations, or can even flag down a ranger on patrol to pass along the information. Animal attacks are something the park takes very seriously, and when a report is made, it will be investigated, especially if an injury is involved. If you are bitten or otherwise injured, you should seek medical assistance at one of the park's three clinics. Some species of animals in Yellowstone can carry diseases that affect humans and/or could lead to a dangerous infection, so it is important that you allow a medical professional to examine you to ensure you do not become sick as a result of being bitten or attacked.

Personal Safety

The most important thing you can do to enjoy your hiking experience in Yellowstone is to ensure you are prepared to hike safely. An injury at the outset of a hike can be a huge disappointment if it prevents you from completing your journey. But a serious injury or illness after you are halfway into a multi-day hike can jeopardize your life and cause a considerable amount of effort and expense to get you evacuated safely. There are no ambulances or hospitals in the backcountry; you come out by someone carrying you or on a helicopter. Both involve a lot of time, effort, and expense.

First Aid, Courses, and Equipment

Unless you are just planning on doing localized, short hikes, it is always a good idea to have some basic knowledge of first aid and how to care for the kinds of wounds and injuries that are common to hikers. This is doubly important for anyone planning to go on long-distance hikes in the backcountry where you cannot just run over to the store and buy a package of medicine or a roll of moleskin.

If you have never had any basic first aid training, you are encouraged to sign up for and take a wilderness first-aid course. Not a standard course, but one oriented specifically toward treatment of wounds and minor medical situations you are likely to encounter out on the trail. These courses are taught all over the western United States, but they are admittedly harder to find as you get into the lower elevations of the eastern part of the country. Many scouting organizations offer these in areas where wilderness rescue is not a daily occurrence. If you are in the Yellowstone area, Yellowstone Forever, the park's fundraising and educational partner, offers these courses several times each year.

Dealing with specific injuries is outside the scope of this book. There are a variety of books that are written specifically to that topic, and if you do not wish to take a course, I would highly recommend you get one of the better books and read through it. Digest the information so you will know how to handle the basic types of injuries you might encounter while you are on the trail.

Rangers working in the backcountry office occasionally get questions regarding what they think is good to have in a first aid kit in a backpack. I have provided a list of what I carry in my personal pack when I am out on longer hikes on the next page. As a former EMT myself, I tend to carry stuff to be able to treat other people's injuries in addition to anything I might have to deal with. So your pack might end up being considerably different than mine. The important point is that you should be prepared to deal with any issues you might face.

Some notes about my kit. First, I am on prescription medications. I take enough of those for the time I am planning on being out on the trail. However, there is always a chance I could either forget to do that or something comes up that requires me to be out longer than I had anticipated. So I carry an additional backup supply just in case. I label the bag with the expiration date that is the closest away, and replace all of them when that date hits.

Second, I carry an EpiPen (epinephrine). This requires me to get a prescription from my doctor, and even though I am not allergic to anything (that I know of), a dose of epinephrine can literally save someone's life in the backcountry if they are stung by something or have an

SAM Splint	Tweezers
QuikClot Bandage	Safety Pins
Tactical Tourniquet	Parachute Rope
Hand Warmers	Waterproof Matches/Firestarter
Cold Pack	Small Scissors
Moleskin	
Bandaid Assortment	MEDS (Ind baggies w/ date)
Anti-Bac/Alcohol Wipes	Aspirin/Tylenol
Neosporin/Anti-Bac Ointment	Pepto Bismol
Butterfly Bandages (Mult Sizes)	Ibuprofen
Triangular Bandage	Antihistimine (Benadryl)
Liquid Bandaid	Immodium/Anti-Diarrheal
Sunscreen	Antacid
Gauze Pads	Ducolax/Laxative
Bandage Wrap	Backup supply of prescription meds
Medical Adhesive Tape	Cortisone Cream
Emergency Blanket	Sting-Eze
Ammonia Inhalants (x2)	EpiPen* (Prescription required)
Duct Tape	

allergic reaction to food or plants they eat while on the trail, etc. My doctor writes the script for me because she knows I know how/when to use this and is familiar with my training. If you are allergic to stinging insects or some types of food, consider getting your doctor to write you a prescription for an EpiPen and carry it with you.

Finally, I also carry what are known as QuikClot bandages. These are sold under a variety of names, but they are basically bandages infused with kaolin or some other hemostatic agent. If someone experiences a severe tear of a blood vessel, stuffing it with these bandages can stop the bleeding and literally prevent a person from bleeding out (thereby saving their life). You do not see these listed on hiker first aid kit lists too often, but you face two risks in Yellowstone that make it worthwhile to have. First, if you fall and tear a large hole in your skin, you are going to need something to stop the bleeding in a hurry. Second, if you or someone is attacked by a bear, they are quite likely to tear one of your major vessels (think femoral artery). Stuffing this bandage into that hole will usually stop the bleeding.

I believe pretty much everything else on my list is common sense and speaks for itself. Do not carry the medications in the large bottles they come in. Put a small number of the pills in a plastic sandwich baggie, label it with permanent marker (including the expiration date), and then put them all in a larger plastic baggie. The total kit weighs just a few ounces.

Sunscreen

Yellowstone sits at an average elevation of 8,000 feet (2,438m) above sea level. As such, there is not as much atmosphere between you and the sun to help protect you. You get 40%–50% more UV exposure at this elevation than you would at the same latitude at sea level. It is therefore much easier to get sunburn in the park. Consequently, you need to use sunscreen and a lip balm containing sunscreen when you are out hiking in Yellowstone.

You can also further reduce your risk by wearing a hat that provides shade for your face, wearing long-sleeve shirts and long pants, and taking lunch breaks in the shade rather than out in the sun.

And believe it or not, you can even get sunburned in the winter in Yellowstone. The park is typically covered with ivory white snow for almost the entire winter. Even though the sun is low in the sky, UV rays reflecting off the snow can give you a "snowburn." So while most of your skin is going to be covered because of the cold, do not forget to put some sunscreen on your face and any other exposed skin.

And, in all seasons, sunglasses are a must. They help protect your eyes from the UV radiation as well as making it easier for you to see without all the glare. Sunglasses also prevent snow blindness in the winter.

Communications

While most of the developed areas in the park have cellular service, most of the backcountry does not. There are a small number of backcountry sites that can get cell signal, but even on the more popular hikes, you should not count on having access to a strong enough signal to be able to make an emergency call should the need arise. That's why many rangers recommend using one of the variety of "Personal Locator Beacon" (PLB) devices available these days.

There are a variety of devices on the market these days that allow you to initiate emergency communications of some type with a centralized communications center or friends or relatives. Devices such as the SPOT Satellite Messenger, the Garmin InReach devices, and the ACR ResQLink devices all allow, in some way, communication with the outside world in the event of an emergency. In the vast wilderness of the Yellowstone backcountry, this could be a lifesaver.

Each of these devices functions in a different way, but all have the basic capability of triggering a signal to an emergency monitoring center that lets them know you are injured or have some kind of emergency and are in need of assistance. Those centers then coordinate with the park's Communications Center to get assistance to you.

With the ResQLink device, you basically initiate an SOS signal to a center monitored by the National Oceanic and Atmospheric Administration (NOAA). It does not have the capability of sending messages, however, so there's no way of letting NOAA know specifically what your problem is. The upside to this is that there are no recurring service fees. You pay for the device and you own it. If you have an emergency, you send the SOS, NOAA receives your GPS coordinates, and they will contact the park's Comm Center with that information.

The SPOT Device also lacks any two-way messaging capability, but you can send a pre-configured message to let relatives or friends know you are okay. You can trigger SOS or "Assistance Needed" (non-emergency) messages, and your friends can track you as you proceed on your hike. There is a recurring service fee associated with this device, and its coverage area is not as robust as InReach is.

The Garmin (formerly DeLorme) InReach comes in two different varieties depending on whether you want built-in navigation capabilities. The SE+, which lacks this feature, is considerably less expensive, but the Explorer doubles as a typical GPS device as well. If you prefer to carry just one device, then the Explorer might be worth your consideration. The InReaches have two-way messaging capabilities (to include pre-configured messages or text on the go), and synchronize with your smart phone. As with the SPOT device, friends and relatives can track you if you allow them to do so.

There are a variety of websites out there that contrast and compare these devices and the services they offer. If you are going to be spending some serious time hiking in Yellowstone, it is a good idea to have one of these devices, simply because of the wide variety of dangers that you face combined with the fact that, if you do get injured on a remote section of trail, it may be days before anyone realizes you are missing and the park is able to get rangers out to find you. And when they go out, they have to actually locate you. These devices have saved literally hundreds of lives since they first hit the market.

You could also consider the option of a satellite telephone. These are expensive devices and they incur a steep monthly or per-minute usage charge, and they are fairly bulky for hikers to have to deal with. However, the distinct advantage they have is that they allow two-way voice communication. This could come in handy for someone with medical training who can be patched into a doctor for field treatment if the situation arose.

Hypothermia

Even at the height of summer in the park, the ambient air temperature in the park will still get down into the 20s and 30s at night in many cases. And in July and August, the temperature of the water usually does not get out of the 60s except in those areas where the water is heated by runoff from thermal features. As a result, hypothermia is a constant threat in Yellowstone. Be sure you recognize the signs of hypothermia and understand how to treat it.

Thermal Burns

Hiking in Yellowstone has one danger that is fairly unique to the park—the presence of thermal pools and other features where boiling or near-boiling water is present. Many of the park's trails pass near or through thermal areas where the crust can be very thin and fragile. In areas where trails pass through thermal fields, there will be signs telling you to stay on the trail. It is illegal to go off trail in these areas.

When you are hiking off trail into some of the more remote thermal areas, pay close attention to where you are putting your feet. There will usually be some semblance of a trail in these areas (you will not have been the first to hike into any of these areas), so try to follow the paths used by those who have been there before you.

As mentioned earlier, in the summer of 2016, a young man and his sister went off trail illegally in the Norris Geyser Basin, the hottest and most acidic thermal field in all of Yellowstone. The man got too close to one of the pools and fell through the thin crust into the boiling, acidic water. Within 30 minutes there was literally nothing left of his body except his shoes. Some two dozen people have been killed from falling or jumping into thermal pools over the course of Yellowstone's history - three times as many as have been killed by bears.[5] There are thousands of thermal features you can see from boardwalks around the park. Do not risk your life to get close to some random pool you encounter in the park's backcountry.

Water Purification and Dehydration

Another thing you will need to be concerned about as you hike in the park is dehydration. The humidity levels in Yellowstone hover in the middle teens most of the summer. That means the air will draw water from anything, including your body. So while it appears as though to you that you are not sweating, in reality your sweat is evaporating as soon as it reaches the surface of the skin. As a result, you can dehydrate rather quickly without even realizing it. By the time you feel dehydrated, you are already in a critical state. Failure to hydrate can lead to heat exhaustion and, eventually, heat stroke.

That is why it is important to drink water continuously while you are hiking in Yellowstone. On short day hikes you can usually transport enough water with you to keep yourself hydrated. However, on longer and multi-day hikes, you will need to have some kind of water purification method with you. Water purification equipment and methods are discussed in the chapter on Hiking and Camping Equipment. But the point that needs to be made here is that, just because you do not feel like you are sweating that much, you still need to maintain an appropriate level of water intake.

Altitude Sickness and Acclimation

Yellowstone sits at an average elevation of around 8,000 feet (2,438m). The available oxygen level at this altitude is roughly ¾ of what it is at sea level. If you come to the park from a much lower altitude and do not allow yourself time to acclimate, you can experience what is known as altitude sickness. Not everyone is affected by it, and those who are may not always be affected in the same way. For some people, it can be debilitating, resulting in extreme cases of them having to leave the park for lower elevations. A small percentage of people who come to work in the park every summer find themselves with severe cases of altitude sickness and have to give up their dream job, in fact.

Altitude sickness, at its most basic level may manifest itself with headaches, dizziness, nausea, fatigue, a decrease in appetite, and disruptions in sleeping patterns. Typically, just self-medicating and giving yourself a day or two to acclimate resolves the problem.

It is always a good idea to give yourself a couple of days to get adjusted to the park's environment before attempting any serious hikes at the higher altitudes. This is especially true if you fly in and have not driven up through a gradual elevation change as a way to acclimate. Start out with the level hikes, or shorter hikes that do not require too much exertion, and build up your stamina. Then set out on the longer or more extreme hikes.

In some cases, altitude sickness can progress to the point of a condition known as high-altitude pulmonary edema, which is a buildup of fluid in the lungs. Your lungs will fill with fluid and your breathing will become more labored, in addition to the other symptoms becoming more extreme. In some rare cases, it may progress to a buildup of fluid in the brain, known as high-altitude cerebral edema.

Both of these are life-threatening conditions, and if you suspect this in someone, the park's paramedics should be notified immediately so that they can get the victim to treatment. The sickness may take a couple of days to progress to this point, so if you set out on a long hike into the backcountry feeling a bit ill and it turns out to be an extreme case of altitude sickness, it is going to create a variety of problems.

Preparing to Hike in Yellowstone

While many of the hikes in Yellowstone are on flat or relatively level surfaces and do not require too much in the way of physical exertion, there are some hikes that involve significant elevation changes (up and down), crossing through scree fields or snow fields, jumping across creeks, fording rapidly-moving, deep rivers or creeks, and long, long days of walking. If you are new to hiking, or at least new to hiking in more extreme environments, you do not want to show up to Yellowstone unprepared.

There are a variety of websites out there that provide you with some good ideas for exercises that can help prepare you for serious hiking. Your preparatory work should include lunges, mountain climbers, squats, and skater jumps. Spending some time walking long distances on an incline trainer/treadmill would also be of invaluable assistance. The important point is that you should prepare yourself physically before just showing up in Yellowstone expecting to knock out 10- or 20-mile days, especially if they involve hiking to mountain summits like Mt. Washburn, Mt. Sheridan, or Mt. Holmes.

Trail Safety

Snags & Trees

Believe it or not, one of the most common causes of injuries in Yellowstone is falling trees, especially snags, the standing dead/dying trees left over following a fire or other major die-off. They have even caused a small handful of deaths. Former park historian Lee Whittlesey, in his incredibly popular book, *Death in Yellowstone: Accidents and Foolhardiness in the First National Park*, details no less than a half dozen fatalities in or immediately outside the park as the result of falling timber.

Much of the park has been subjected to wildfires that have killed literally thousands of trees. When these dead trees, now known as snags, are too close to a roadway or to a backcountry campsite, they are cut down to prevent damage or injuries. That is simply not possible or even desirable along the park's endless trail system, however. So if you spend any time at all hiking in Yellowstone's backcountry, you will hike through areas of dead trees. This can be one of the most haunting, eerie experiences you can have. The wind blowing through these dead forests often sounds like the voices of those who have come before you, according to many people. It is important that you pay attention to the condition of the trees as you are hiking through these areas. A sudden gust of wind can blow down a snag that has been standing for years. And while many of these old tree carcasses are rather small in stature, some are the remains of trees that are (or were) literally hundreds of years old and would crush you in an instant.

Rocks

A second unique facet of danger present in Yellowstone is falling rock. According to Whittlesey, three or four people have died from rocks from above. Many of the most scenic places in the park involve collections of fallen rock in one form or another (think of The Hoodoos along the Mammoth to Norris Road, or the rocks that have fallen from the walls of Spring Creek Canyon). But these rock falls can also be dangerous. Always pay particular attention to the walls of canyons you are hiking through, and listen for the crackling sounds that often precede the cleaving of a rock off of one of these walls.

You should also avoid throwing rocks into canyons and other crevices. You never know who is going to be exploring the area below. And even if you toss a small rock down into the canyon, it picks up speed and basically becomes a missile by the time it gets to the bottom of its fall. In 1972, an 11-year old girl was killed at the Brink of the Lower Falls by a football-sized rock that was thrown off a cliff by a 14-year old boy.

Fording Rivers & Streams

Many of the trails in Yellowstone require you to ford bodies of water, usually streams or creeks, but occasionally even one of its rivers. This can be disconcerting for someone who has never done it before or who does not know how to do it safely. A small number of creeks and rivers will have footbridges over them, but this is the exception rather than the rule.

Most of the park's major waterways are difficult and unsafe to cross in the early parts of the season, typically before the first to middle of July in most areas. This is because the runoff from the melting snow makes the waters run deeper and faster than they do later in the season. In most cases, in the trail descriptions, there will be mention of specific streams and rivers where you need to be careful.

Being prepared to ford running water involves the following:

- Bring the appropriate footwear. You do not want to get your enclosed hiking shoes wet, lest you end up with blisters. Similarly, you do not want to cross barefoot, as there are often sharp pointy things beneath the water that can cut your feet. Feet do not grip well, either, so crossing on rocks or other surfaces that are covered with algae, bacterial mats, etc., will be much more dangerous in bare feet. The best footwear is a sandal or other type of shoe that dries quickly. Alternatively, crossing in any shoe or boot is better than doing so barefoot.
- Survey the area where you need to cross. If trail maintenance has been done, there are typically approaches cleared out for you to cross or there are logs, rocks, or other surfaces you can use to cross the streams successfully. However, if you have to cross in the water, finding an area that is safe for you to do this is key to not falling in and getting wet, being washed downstream, or drowning.
- Find areas that have slower water movement. Rushing water is never a good place to cross, even if the depth is minimal. Rushing water can wash you off your feet, and even if you do not end up downstream, you might fall and hit your head or break a bone. Slow and deep water is better for crossing than rushing, shallow water.
- Always secure your other foot before releasing your previous one. Make sure the foot you are planting for your next step is secure before you move your last foot. You can also use hiking poles to help stabilize yourself if you have them.
- If the water is more than knee deep, face upstream and side step across the stream. Do not cross your legs as you move, and if possible, use a hiking pole or stick to provide additional support.
- If you have a heavy pack, unbuckle the waist straps before you get in the water. If you do fall over and your pack is strapped to you, it will weigh you down and might cause additional problems for you (getting snagged underwater preventing you from surfacing, for example). If it is unbuckled, it is easier to jettison the pack and let it go (which is much more preferable than allowing it to drown you).
- DO NOT cross above waterfalls, regardless of how safe it appears. Travel upstream or downstream a suitable distance and cross there.

- If you are traveling with multiple people, cross in teams, holding each other and moving one person at a time. Use the triangle method if you are in a group of three, or if in a group of more, cross as a group in a line, holding onto one another. One person should call the moves.
- If you get dumped and start to head downstream, assume a defensive swimming position (face up, feet downstream). You should be able to see where you are going and use your feet to prevent yourself from hitting anything with your head.
- If you are going to cross individually, ensure not everyone is in the water at the same time. If one person does get washed away, someone will need to call for or seek help from the rangers. Once the first person gets across the stream, they should move downstream a bit so that if a subsequent crosser falls in s/he can offer a hand or a rope to assist.
- Ensure you are familiar with the signs and symptoms of hypothermia, which is an ever present danger in Yellowstone. Even in the dead of summer, much of the park's waters remain very cold and immersion can cause hypothermia in very short order.

Carcasses

The Yellowstone ecosystem is full of predatory animals and scavengers, including wolves, mountain lions, bobcats, coyotes, and, most critically, bears. A full-size elk or bison carcass will attract predators and scavengers of all kinds from miles away. And many predators, especially grizzly bears, will defend these carcasses from anyone or anything they consider a threat. This includes humans.

If you stumble across a carcass along a trail in the park, assume it is being claimed by a bear and act accordingly. Note its location and get the hell away from it as soon as possible. Warn anyone else hiking toward the carcass of its presence so they can be alert for predators that might be in the area. When you return from the hike, stop by the nearest ranger station and notify them of what you found. Typically, rangers will close a section of trail if a carcass is near it and they can not remove it, specifically to prevent hikers from coming upon a situation where a bear or other predator feels the need to defend its food.

Running

Yellowstone is not a suitable environment for trail running. Bears and other predators will see running humans as prey and act accordingly. This is the reason why rangers tell hikers not to run when they encounter a bear in the first place. There's absolutely no way you can outrun a bear or any of the park's other major predators. In fact, the last person to be killed by a bear (summer of 2015 as of this writing) was killed while he was running off-trail. It is believed he ran into a mother and her cubs and surprised them, and he became their meal.

If you need to run, do so in the park's developed areas, such as around the commercial or housing areas at Old Faithful, Mammoth, Lake Village, Canyon Village, etc. These areas have people all over the place and bears do not typically hang out in those areas. However, do not run with headphones or earphones in place. You will not be able to hear what is going on around you.

Winter Hiking/Skiing/Snowshoeing

Winter trail travel carries with it a few risks that are not present during the summer. This includes, most importantly, avalanche danger. There are a couple of areas along the main

Proper food storage technique using food pole. Image courtesy NPS.

roads that are susceptible to avalanches (most notably Sylvan Pass on the East Entrance Road and a short section of the South Entrance Road just south of Lewis Falls). Dunraven Road is closed during the winter primarily because of avalanche hazards.

Trail markings may not be visible during the winter, as they may have been knocked down or covered by snow. Those that have worn to the point of becoming white may be all but invisible. It is therefore recommended that you do not use unmaintained trails in the winter unless you have become familiar with them in the summer and know how they pass over the terrain.

Be sure you have with you appropriate maps and know how to use them. Though you should also have and know how to use a compass, a GPS device may be more helpful to you in whiteout or other poor conditions.

Special Note for Yellowstone NPS Employees

If you are an NPS employee who is assigned a park radio, always, *always* carry it with you when you go out hiking, even on day hikes (most offices have spares you can check out if you are not permanently assigned one). You just never know when you are going to run into some situation that is going to require immediate assistance from on-duty rangers, and there are a whole lot of places in the park where cell phones do not get signal. There are very few spots where the radios do not reach, however. So even though it adds a bit of weight to your pack, it is essential that you have it with you just in case. And do not forget that, per park policy (ROP 2-07), if you are going on an overnight or multi-day hike, you are required to submit your itinerary to the Comm Center and check in at least twice a day—once in the morning and once in the evening (even for off-duty, personal travel). If you are unsure how to do this, have your supervisor show you.

Camp Safety

Food

The single most important thing you can do to help keep yourself safe from bear attacks in a campsite is to store your food safely. In Yellowstone, every backcountry campsite is equipped with a food pole located at least 100 yards away from the area where your tent is supposed to be set up (see photo on previous page). Some campsites are also now equipped with food storage bins (often called "bear boxes"), heavy-duty, lockable cabinets for your food and other items that have some kind of scent to them.

There are a handful of bear-proof food containers that may be used in Yellowstone's backcountry. These have been tested by the Interagency Grizzly Bear Committee (IGBC) and have been found to be sufficiently difficult for bears to get into that they have been approved for use in lieu of hanging food or storing it in one of the vaults. See the park's website for a list of these (the list changes from time to time). These units must be secured to the tree where the food pole is located or to a tree at the food prep area. Anything that does not fit into the container must be secured on the food pole or in a provided food locker.

Sleep in a Tent

There is often discussion about whether or not it is safe (or safer) to sleep outside in the park vs. sleeping in a tent. For some people, one of the draws of being in the backcountry is the crystal clear skies at night—you can literally see the Milky Way in all its glory at night in Yellowstone. But given the presence and the nature of bears in the region, is it safe to do so? There will probably always be some debate about this subject, but Steven Herrero, noted biologist and longtime studier of bear behavior and author of the book, *Bear Attacks: Their Causes and Avoidance*, seems to believe that being in a tent offers at least some small added measure of safety.

> *"I have mentioned that another technique for minimizing risk while backcountry camping around bears is to sleep in a tent rather than without shelter. Sleeping under the stars is one of my favorite things to do while camping, but I choose areas in which to do this carefully. My data strongly suggest that people sleeping without tents were more likely to be injured, even killed, than were people who slept in tents."*

And to be honest, for much of the summer, there will be enough mosquitoes and biting flies around to make you want to sleep in your tent anyway. A discussion about the kinds of tents that are recommended for use in Yellowstone can be found in the next chapter.

Speaking of tents and bear safety, it is important to point out that you should not coat your tent with bear spray. Some people believe that, if bear spray repels bears, let's spray it on the tent to keep the bears away at night. Unfortunately, it does not work that way. When the bear spray dries, it smells like spicy food to bears and actually *attracts* them. You should keep your bear spray in the tent with you, but do not spray anything (including clothes, the ground, etc.) with it.

Fires

Few people who visit the park are unaware that wildfires have played a significant role in the park's ecology, if for no other reason than the incredible amount of coverage of the

1988 wildfire season wherein more than one third of the park was burned. But despite the warnings people receive about fires getting out of hand and causing catastrophes, in most seasons, there are several people who leave campfires burning when they depart camp.

When you get ready to depart your campsite, whether it is just for the day or if you are moving on, you must completely extinguish your fire by using water from a nearby water source or by using dirt. You must ensure the fire is out. If a ranger comes by and discovers your fire is not completely extinguished, they will look up your permit information and you will end up with a citation.

If you are unfortunate enough to leave a fire burning, and it gets out of hand and starts a fire, you may receive a bill from the National Park Service for any efforts it undertakes to extinguish your fire, as well as a bill for any damages it causes. Do not be that person!

Scented vs. Unscented Personal Items

One way you can minimize your exposure to danger is by avoiding using scented toiletry items such as deodorants, shampoos, body washes, perfumes, etc. All of these things smell sweet to animals, including bears and other carnivores. And guess what bears and other carnivores like to do with sweet stuff? They make unscented versions of all of these (except the perfume, of course), so if you wish to use these kinds of things while you are on the trail, use the unscented one.

And, speaking of scents, another subject that often comes up in the backcountry offices is whether or not bears can smell menstruating women. While this subject has not been definitively studied, in the analysis of the sizable number of bear attacks that have occurred over the past 50 or so years, there is no evidence to suggest that bears can smell menstruating women or that they pay attention to them if they do.

Again, Steven Herrero notes in his book that, in the vast number of cases he's studied, he has observed no evidence linking menstruation to any of the attacks. And in a 1991 study, a number of black bears were studied for their reaction to used tampons and to the presence of menstruating women. The bears showed absolutely no interest in any of them.[6]

Given the tens of thousands of women who've camped in the park's backcountry over the years, a good number of them must have been menstruating at one point or another, and none of them were attacked. So there is no basis whatsoever for believing that bears will react to women at that point in their cycle any differently than they would any other woman.

One obvious recommendation is to use unscented personal hygiene products, and to carry out your used tampons in a sealed plastic baggie like you would any other waste product. You certainly do not want to bury them, though you may burn them if they burn completely up and leave no residue.

Snags and Dangerous Trees

One of the most dangerous things about being out in the backcountry is the potential for snags (dead trees) to fall on you. When the backcountry rangers and trail maintenance crews get out early in the season, one thing they do is clear the backcountry campsites of any potential snags or other trees that are precariously perched, specifically to avoid having one of them fall on you while you are in the camp.

If you arrive at a campsite and the space where you're supposed to set up your tent (if one exists) seems threatened by a precariously-perched tree, dead or otherwise, find an alternate spot to set up your tent. When you get back to civilization, stop by one of the backcountry offices and report the dangerous tree so NPS can get someone out to remedy the situation.

Animals in the Camp

What are you supposed to do if a dangerous animal comes wandering through your campsite? While you are eating? While you are sleeping? How you set your campsite up will go a long way toward preventing a lot of problems.

When you first arrive in camp and begin setting up, go ahead and hang anything with a scent to it up on the food pole or put it in the cabinet if the campsite is equipped with one (after removing the items necessary for setting up camp, of course). Be sure and set your tent up as far away from the food prep area as possible, preferably 100 yards (though the design of many campsites may not allow for that).

Once you are done setting up camp, then you can break out your food, prepare your meal, eat, and then clean up. Try to minimize the amount of time you have smelly stuff out in the open. Wash your utensils and dishes, repack your stuff, including any clothes that you were wearing while you cooked, and rehang it before turning in. Any clothes you wear to bed should be clean and/or scent-free to the extent possible. The only things you should have in your tent are your sleeping things, yourself, a flashlight, and your bear spray. If you have any legally-permitted firearms with you, you should keep them in the tent as well.

If you have a bear or other large carnivore enter your campsite while you are setting up and preparing your food, try to avoid allowing them to have your food—certainly do not offer it to them as a way to distract them. You would be teaching the bear that humans = food, and that will cause problems for all future campers that bear encounters, and may end up causing the bear to be put down because it becomes a threat to humans.

Try to back away from the bear and let it wander through, remembering the information provided earlier about being prepared for an encounter with one of the creatures. Hopefully, the bear will just walk through your campsite and go on about its business—that is what the overwhelming majority of them do.

If you are asleep in your tent in the middle of the night and believe an animal is moving through your campsite, remain quiet and motionless until the animal leaves, even if it paws at your tent. If it is a bear and you fight back at the slightest provocation, you are going to end up with some serious damage to you and your tent. Unless the bear makes a serious attempt to enter your tent, remain calm and still until it leaves.

Do not fire a weapon at the animal through your tent. It's not unheard of for park rangers to do night patrols and to stop by tents to check your permit. If you shoot without verifying an actual threat exists, you could be in a world of trouble in more ways than one.

If a bear does make contact with you while you are in your tent, holler at it and make as much noise as you can. You want to startle the bear so it will run away. If you have a noisemaker (such as a compressed air horn or a whistle) use it. DO NOT discharge your bear spray while you are in an enclosed tent. Not only will it not affect the bear, it will incapacitate you.

If a bear attacks your tent and tries to claw or tear its way in, you can safely assume the bear intends to make a meal out of you and you need to fight back with everything you have at your disposal. Fight back with fists, gouge the eyes, and deploy your bear spray. This is one of those situations where, if you have a weapon of any kind in your tent with you, I would recommend using it if you can get to it. At this point, it is too serious not to use everything at your disposal to get the bear to leave you alone.

Once you are able to get out and back to civilization, be sure to report the incident to the nearest ranger station or backcountry office so they can attempt to track the bear down. This is the kind of bear that will have to be removed from the park so that it does not injure or kill anyone else.

Boating Safety

Boating is a very popular activity in Yellowstone. Motorized boats are allowed only on Yellowstone Lake and Lewis Lake, while self-propelled boats are allowed on Shoshone Lake. Non-motorized boats are permitted on most other lakes within the park, except of Sylvan, Eleanor, and Twin Lakes, and in the Beach Springs Lagoon. Boats are not permitted on any river or stream inside the park (including Yellowstone River) except for Lewis Channel between Lewis Lake and Shoshone Lake. See the section on Boating in Yellowstone for further guidance on how and where boats can be used and additional requirements for their use in the park.

While boating is allowed in these areas, it is extremely critical that you take the appropriate safety precautions. Drowning is one of the most common cause of accidental deaths in Yellowstone. And the park's cold waters make hypothermia an ever-present concern even if you are a strong swimmer (several park rangers have lost their lives by drowning, in fact). The park's waters are typically in the 40s in the early season, and do not even make it out of the 60s at the very height of the summer.

If you are in a small craft (kayak, canoe, john boat, etc.), keep in mind that sudden winds may produce waves in excess of three to five feet, especially during the storms that often pop up with little to no warning in the summer. You want to avoid being out on the open water in the afternoon when these kinds of storms are more likely.

PFD and Other Requirements for Boaters

All boating activities inside the park are subject to the same U.S. Coast Guard regulations as boating on any other federal waters. Everyone on board must have a USCG-approved personal flotation device (PFD) available to them, and anyone 12 or younger MUST wear their PFD at all times while on the water.

All boats should also have on board a bailing device, such as a bucket. And all boats must have a USCG-approved fire extinguisher on board. You are also required to have a sound-producing device (such as a whistle) on board for use in an emergency. And while much of Yellowstone Lake has cellular service, Lewis Lake and Shoshone Lake have no coverage whatsoever. You will not be able to call for help. The Bridge Bay Ranger Station monitors Marine Channel 16 during hours it is staffed, and rangers on boat patrol on both Yellowstone and Lewis Lakes monitor that channel while they are out on their boats.

Rangers & Rescue in Yellowstone

Yellowstone has park rangers who are trained in a wide variety of rescue techniques and has access to specialized technical rescue teams in nearby parks and other jurisdictions. However, mounting a rescue operation is a time-consuming (and expensive) process. If you get into a situation where you need to be rescued, it may be several hours before a sufficient cadre of personnel can assemble and get to you. A simple rescue on the lake, for example, can be done rather quickly by rangers who patrol the lake on boats. However, if you fall into a deep canyon and get into a situation where you have to be airlifted out, it may be several hours to a full day before you are on your way out. That is why it is important for you to work to ensure your own safety while out hiking, boating, or otherwise enjoying Yellowstone National Park.

A typical backcountry rescue might look like this. Say you and a group of your friends are hiking along the Heart Lake Trail when you slip and fall into a thermal pool in one of the thermal areas near the lake. You sustain very serious burns to your legs, to the point where you are unable to hike back out. One of your friends (preferably a fast one) will need to hike back out to the trailhead or to the Heart Lake Patrol Cabin to seek help. This could take several hours.

Once the park's Communications Center (Comm Center) is notified of your situation, they will begin notifying a series of personnel to get mobilized to come to your rescue. This will include the dispatch of an initial ranger or two to come to you to assess your injuries. The rangers have to assemble their gear and hike in to you. At least one of them will be a paramedic or EMT. Once they arrive (this will take another one to two hours), they will assess your injuries and determine the best course of action for getting you out of there. Specifically how that will be done will be determined by a variety of factors, such as the time of day, the weather, the extent of your injuries, how well they are able to treat those injuries on site, how well you respond to their treatment, the terrain you are in, whether you are able to hike out on your own, how close they can find a landing zone for a LifeFlight helicopter, etc.

If it is impossible to get a helicopter in to you, the Comm Center will have started assembling an extrication team to load you onto a stretcher and hike you out of there. This, too, will take several hours. If you are fortunate, you will be in a location close enough to a landing zone to get a helicopter in to you. The Comm Center will notify the nearest LifeFlight, and it will take between 30-45 minutes to get to you. So, in a best case scenario, it might be 4-6 hours before you are out of there (and a very hefty 5-figure helicopter bill to show for your trouble). In a worst-case scenario, you will likely be relocated to the nearest patrol cabin where the rangers can stabilize you, and you will be evacuated the next morning by a team of rangers. Typically, the NPS does not bill victims for being rescued unless it is the result of negligence or unauthorized behavior. But those bills are not inexpensive, either.

Hiking & Camping Equipment

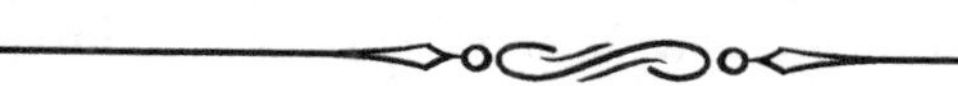

One of the most important decisions you will need to make about hiking into the backcountry of Yellowstone is what equipment you will take with you and what you will want to wear. And while this chapter is not designed to be a treatise on equipment selection for hiking (there are literally tons of books that have already been written on that subject), it is perhaps a good idea to discuss some peculiarities associated with hiking in the park that you will want to factor into your selection.[1]

Essential Tools

One of the most basic tools you will want to carry with you is **navigation material**, especially if you are going on anything other than an out-and-back day hike. Even then you are encouraged to carry at least a compass or some kind of device that includes a compass. Regardless of what you use, be sure you understand how to use it correctly. You would not believe how easy it is to wander a few feet off of a trail in Yellowstone and get completely lost. I have done it myself, and without my GPS device, I would have been up a creek. There have been numerous search and rescue calls for people who have been "lost" in Yellowstone and yet they were just a few dozen feet off the main trail.

Many newer GPS devices include not only a compass feature but also allow you to upload a variety of different electronic maps that make navigation much easier. Some people prefer to use paper copies of maps, while others prefer to have paper copies as backups in case their electronics fail or the batteries die. You can obtain hard copies and electronic copies of the USGS 24000-series topographic maps that are excellent for use in Yellowstone. There are a variety of vendors who publish specialized maps for the park, however. Be certain that any you buy includes the topographical contours and trails. It is important to note that the USGS maps do not include some of the newer trails (most of the current versions can be as old as 20+ years) and the trail paths on those maps are generally not terribly accurate.

You will want to carry a good quality **pocket knife** with you. This can come in handy for a variety of things. A good **fire starter** is also an essential, even if you are just going out on a day hike. You never know when you might become injured and have to spend a night in the woods. Without a fire to keep you warm, you risk suffering from hypothermia. And speaking of being cold, you may also wish to carry the little **hand and/or foot warmer packs**.

Sunglasses and sunscreen are also a must. As is discussed in the safety section of this book, you are at a much higher elevation and therefore get much more robust exposure to the sun in Yellowstone. Keep your exposed skin covered with sunscreen and re-apply it every so often (as is recommended on the bottle/tube). You should also do this if you are hiking or skiing in the winter as well. The entire park is covered in thick, white snow the entire winter and you will sustain snow blindness without sunglasses and can also be sunburned by the sunlight reflecting off the snow.

If you hike between early June and late August, you will want to carry **bug spray** with you or some kind of combination of clothing and equipment that protects you from the park's official bird, the mosquito. Bug spray will also help repel ticks, which can be found in the lower elevations in the northern half of the park.

A **flashlight** is another necessity, especially for those late-night bathroom runs. It literally gets so dark in Yellowstone that you cannot see your hand right in front of your face. The upside to this is that you can easily see the Milky Way and all of the stars on a clear night.

You will want to carry a basic **first aid kit** and any critical medications you might need while you are out on the trail. Be sure and include a couple of extra doses of any critical medications, just in case you get stuck out longer than you anticipated. If you are asthmatic, do not forget your inhaler, and if you are allergic to insect stings or anything else you might find out in the wilderness, you will want to carry an EpiPen with you (preferably a pair of them).

See the previous chapter for information on items recommended for your personal first aid kit.

Water & Purification

Water is also a very critical thing to have out on the trail with you. While you are out on a day hike, the water bladder you can fit into most backpacks will work just fine for most people. For multi-day hikes, however, it is unlikely you would be able to carry sufficient water to keep you hydrated (assuming you are following recommendations on how much water you should be drinking). In that case, it is necessary to have some sort of water purification method with you so that you can collect water from the park's vast water resources.

Many people like to believe that in Yellowstone's "pristine" wilderness, the water is as pure as the driven snow. Nothing could be further from the truth. In just about every body of water in the park (rivers, streams, lakes, etc.), bison, bears, and other animals bathe, defecate, urinate, and track a variety of other contaminants into the water. Sometimes even other humans do this. And in other places, sulfurous or acidic runoff from the park's thermal features will make the water undrinkable.

So while the water may appear crystal clear, it may be carrying traces of bison poop or nice big doses of chemicals that you would prefer not to ingest. It is therefore a good idea to bring with you some method of water purification. There are several types of portable water purification processes available to hikers.

Chemical Purification: Chemical purification can be done with either iodine or chlorine, and while it may be effective against many forms of bacteria and whatnot, it may not kill everything. Additionally, it won't rid the water of chemical contaminants.

UV Light: Ultraviolet light can be used to deal with bacterial contamination as well, but like chemical treatment, it doesn't deal with the possible chemical contamination of the water.

Boiling: Boiling will remove the bacteria in the water, but it will not generally do much for the chemical contamination, either. It can also take quite a while because you will need to wait until the water is cool enough to drink before ingesting it.

Filtration: Filtration is the process of passing water through a filter that can remove various organisms from your water. There are different sizes of filters, some of which are capable of removing tiny viruses from water. And some filters are combined with an activated carbon or charcoal layer that will also remove many chemicals that can be found in water.

Each of these processes has its own pros and cons, and within each group there are a variety of options as to types, mechanisms of operation, cost, etc. Do your research and figure out what kind of purification you wish to use and obtain some kind that you can use out on the trail.

During the winter, you will be surrounded by snow, and fresh snow is presumed to be contaminant-free (biologically and chemically). So there is generally no need to purify snow—you will just need to melt it. Do not eat snow for water. You would have to eat roughly 10 quarts of snow to get one quart of water. Consuming that much snow can lead to hypothermia. The best way to convert the snow into drinkable water is through heating it up in a cooking pot over a fire.

If you are carrying water bottles or a bladder of water in the winter in Yellowstone, you will need to find a way to prevent it from freezing. With a bottle, you can carry it in a pocket next to your body so as to allow your body heat to prevent freezing. With a bladder, you can place the little chemical hand/foot warmer packs next to it, especially at the bottom where the outlet hose is connected. Continuously take little sips of water from it throughout the day to keep water moving through the system to help prevent the hose and mouthpiece from freezing up. Keep your water bladder or bottles in your sleeping bag to prevent freezing at night.

Cooking Equipment and Food

Food falls into two categories: Meals and snacks. Food is, perhaps after water, the most important thing that a hiker needs to consider before undertaking a multi-day hike in the park. A hungry hiker is an unhappy hiker.

Snacks can be anything you feel like munching on as you hike along the trail. Some people use trail mix, while others carry things like gorp, gummy bears, candy bars, protein bars, potato chips, raisins, peanuts, etc. Keep these in a small baggie in one of your backpack pockets within easy reach for day use, and a master supply of them in your pack to refill the baggie each morning before you set out again.

Meal planning is essential to ensure that you get enough calories to provide the energy for your hikes and to ensure that you do not carry a bunch of useless weight (food that ends up not being eaten). There is an entire cottage industry these days surrounding pre-packaged meals for hikers. The upside to that is it makes planning easy and since they are neatly packaged, you do not have to worry about making a mess in your backpack. The downside is that they are typically quite expensive. Some people prefer to prepare their own meals while others prefer to take the easier route with the prepackaged stuff. This is totally a personal call, of course. In some cases, a group of hikers may elect to have each individual bring one or two different parts of meals and they prepare meals together. This allows for more flexibility (especially for larger groups).

Some things you will want to consider when meal planning are how many calories you need, the weight of the food you select, how easy it will be to prepare your food, and how long you will be out. The longer your hike, the more critical meal planning becomes, for obvious reasons. Fresher foods will spoil after a few days, so if you plan to take any of those, you will want to eat them early on in your hike. The freeze-dried and dehydrated stuff can be eaten in the latter stages of the trip.

A day-long hike will result in your needing an additional 1,000 or so calories (roughly) in the spring and summer, and as much as an additional 3,000–4,000 calories for a full day's hike in the winter cold. If you are hiking trails that involve serious elevation gains, especially at steeper angles, you will need even more. You also need to consider your own personal metabolism. Those with higher metabolisms will need more calories than those who have lower metabolisms.

The weight of your food will be added to the weight of all your other gear and equipment. Some things are just not worth the added weight. For example, a fresh apple would be a nice snack on the trail, but since it is laden with water, it is going to weigh a lot more relative to other snacks with higher caloric content. So you would probably want to opt for a bag of trail mix over the apple to reduce the amount of weight you are carrying. And while one apple might not seem like much of a difference, the cumulative effect of all the extra weight may indeed make a difference in how tired you are after hiking all day. Package snacks and meal items in plastic bags where possible, or plastic bottles rather than glass ones. Glass is heavy and will not compress when you put it back in your bag to pack it out.

This is another advantage that the freeze-dried foods have—they are very lightweight. But then you need to ensure you have a sufficient amount of water to make them edible. So this is why planning is so important to the overall success of your hike. They are very easy to prepare, however. You want to try to avoid planning meals that are complicated and take a lot of time to prepare, especially if you are going to be hiking long distances during the day. Taking an hour to make breakfast in the morning cuts a lot of time off your distances. And after you have hiked 15-20 miles in a day, the last thing you are going to want to do is have to take a long time preparing dinner in the evening, especially given all the other work you will have to do setting up camp, putting up your tent, etc.

You should also avoid pungent foods such as tuna. These will attract animals from all over the place. They sell the individual single-serving size tuna kits in the park's stores, for example, and even though buying something like this might make meal planning much easier, it is best to avoid those kinds of foods if possible.

Note that food caches are not allowed in Yellowstone. You cannot have someone drop food at a campsite to await your arrival, for example, nor can you pre-stage food. So you will have to carry all your food for your entire trip with you.

As a part of your meal-planning process, you need to decide what type of cooking process you are going to use. Some people take just a pot and a pan and cook over a campfire, and that is perfectly fine unless you are going to be camping at a site that does not allow wood fires (and a considerable number of them do not), or where it has rained and the available firewood is wet. So you may wish to consider carrying a small cooking stove. There are three basic types, based on the fuel they use:

- Solid Fuel: These use pellets or wood and are easy to use and maintain. The downside is that they are either on or off (there is often no way to control the cooking temperature) and the fuel can be messy.
- Compressed Gas: These burn propane or butane, are easy to maintain, and you can adjust the temperature. The downside is that they often do not work well at higher elevations (above 7,000ft/2,134m). Since most of the park sits at these elevations, your food may take longer to cook.
- Liquid Fuel: These burn kerosene, alcohol, or white gas. The advantage these have is that it is a lot easier to find fuel for them (the park stores sell it). The potential downsides are that they are more difficult to use and require more maintenance. Alcohol does not burn well at the higher elevations, either, so opt for kerosene or white gas if you are going to be using this kind of stove in Yellowstone (though most of these stoves can use any of the fuels listed).

As is the case with most other equipment, there are a variety of manufacturers who make a range of stoves for campers. Do your research; figure out which type of fuel you want to use and how much stove you want to carry, then make your own selections accordingly. Be sure your planning includes enough fuel to make it through your entire trip.

You will also want to carry any necessary pots, pans, and utensils you will need based on the meals you have planned. For most people, one or two smaller pots, a frying pan, and a small set of utensils is all they will need. If you are hiking with a group, each person can carry a portion of the equipment.

Though they are more expensive, you may wish to consider titanium pots, pans, and utensils. They are considerably lighter than those made of other materials.

Tents

Tent selection is a highly personal thing, just behind the clothing you wear in terms of personal preference holding sway over your selections. Consequently, you will need to do some research and figure out what kind of design you prefer, what kind of material you want, what kind of configuration you want, etc. You will also want to consider how many people will be sleeping in it (on any of your future trips, not just the one you are planning right now).

Generally speaking, unless you are planning on hiking and camping in the winter in the park, a decent quality three-season tent will suffice for camping in Yellowstone. Lightweight or screen tents are generally not warm enough for the colder temperatures experienced in the nighttime. If you plan on camping in the earlier parts of the season (i.e., May or June), ensure your tent includes some form of protection from the rain (both in terms of the fabric and the drainage around the tent).

Many sporting goods stores have tents set up where you can go in and look at them and get a feel for how they would suit your needs. If they do not, you can always ask the sales staff if they would allow you to set one up if they have the space to do so. Tents are like clothing in that you want something that will be comfortable for you, so you should take the time to ensure the one you pick will be one that keeps you comfortable out in the woods.

Backpacks

Like tents, the type and style of backpack you choose is a personal matter. Many hikers have at least two backpacks, a smaller one for day or overnight hikes and a larger one for multi-day trips. Again, entire books and websites are devoted to helping people pick out backpacks, so there is no need to recreate that here. You do need to keep a couple of important points in mind, however.

Select packs that allow you to organize your stuff like you want and that distribute the weight of what you are carrying appropriately. Many sporting good stores have professionals that can help you pick out a backpack that fits your body frame and will help you set it up so that the straps and other weight-bearing components are properly configured. Many pack manufacturers offer different configurations for females, males, and children (largely because of the differences in the center of gravity of the different body types).

As a general rule, you should carry no more than 15%–25% of your total body weight in your pack on multi-day hikes. And you should pack your stuff so that about half of the weight inside your pack is in the top third of it. So for most people, that means the bulkier, lighter stuff like clothing is in the bottom, your sleeping bag is on top of that, your food is in the top middle, and your heavier equipment such as your stoves, fuel, etc., are at the top.

Pack your clothing in stuff sacks or ziplocks, any items that are water sensitive in ziplocks, and carry extra plastic baggies to use to carry out waste, wet clothing, etc. Carry a large, green garbage bag to cover your pack with in the event it starts raining (unless you buy a pack that includes a rain cover like many do these days). Make sure your toiletries, quick snacks, lip balm, sunscreen, and other items you will want quick access to are stored at the top or in the pockets on the sides and/or straps. Some people also like to carry "pre-configured" baggies containing toilet paper and a wet wipe for bathroom use. When they are done, all the waste goes back into the baggie and is transported out.

Ensure the horizontal weight distribution is even so you do not get off balance when you are carrying it.

Sleeping Bags

When it comes to picking out a sleeping bag for use in Yellowstone, it is important to remember that during much of the year, the temperatures at night can dip down into the 30s and 40s in July and August, and even lower in the other months. If you are going to be hiking in the winter months, the temperatures will get below zero quite often. You want to avoid using a summer-rated bag here, unless, of course, you are just hot-natured to begin with. A good quality three-season bag should suffice for most hikers. If you are going to be here in the winter, you will want one that is rated for very cold temperatures.

Again, there are so many options for this kind of equipment it is virtually impossible to recommend specifics to anyone. You need to go to your local sporting goods store and evaluate what they have available and find one that suits your needs in terms of its temperature rating, what it is made out of, and its design.

You will also want to invest in a good quality sleeping pad, as the ground in the park is often rocky, damp, and cold. Having a pad will prevent heat loss into the ground and will make sleeping on the ground just a little more comfortable.

Clothing

In probably just about every hiking book you have read, the author refers to the principle of layering when it comes to selecting the clothing you will be hiking in. This one will be no different. In fact, given that it is common to have a 50- or 60-degree temperature swing between mid-day and the middle of the night in Yellowstone, that principle is perhaps more important here than just about any other place you will hike.

Most people use the 5-layer approach to selecting clothing for their hikes.

Base Layer: This layer is the one that rests next to the skin and is designed to wick moisture (i.e., perspiration) away from your body. There are a variety of newer technical materials available these days that serve this purpose. Many people combine this with a compression fabric to help with muscle fatigue during their hikes.

Clothing Layer: This is your typical hiking clothing, a shirt and pants of some type. The specifics of your hike in terms of the type of weather and temperatures you are expecting will dictate what you wear here. Some people wear just a standard button-down shirt and cargo pants/shorts, while others wear something a bit more substantial. You do want this to be something you can shed easily if you become too warm.

Warming Layer: This layer is lightweight clothing designed to keep you warm early in the day and later in the evening. A light jacket, fleece pullover, hoodie, sweatpants, etc.

Cold Weather Layer: These are your heavy coats and jackets and pants with some sort of insulating material in them for when it gets seriously cold. Much of the park is subject to random, itinerant storms during the summer, so you will want to include light rain gear or clothing that can get wet.

Protection Layer: This is lightweight, breathable material to keep you dry if it is raining or to protect you from the wind.

As is the case with tents, sleeping bags, backpacks, etc., the selection of what you wear is a personal choice. There are tons of different materials from which you can choose, different styles, different colors, different temperature ratings, etc. So do your research, figure out what you wish to wear based on what you have access to and what the weather is anticipated to be on your hike, and go from there.

You certainly want to avoid wearing cotton clothing. Even if it does not rain, you will likely perspire to an extent and your clothes will get damp and will stay that way for some time if they are not designed to shed water. This can contribute to rapid onset of hypothermia in the evenings once the air temperature begins to cool (which occurs quickly once the sun starts going down).

You do not want to forget your head, face, hands, and feet. Since you lose most of your body heat through your head, you want to wear some type of hat that retains the heat but also protects you from the sun and rain. You will be hiking in areas where the mosquito population exceeds that of the population of the planet's humans, so you may wish to invest in a mosquito head net that drapes over your hat and has an elastic band that collapses around your neck. This netting will protect your face from the little buggers, making hiking in those areas a lot less stressful.

You may also wish to invest in a good pair of gloves or mittens. While gloves allow for more manual dexterity, they also make your hands colder as a result of there being more surface area exposed to the elements. Mittens, on the other hand, allow the fingers to exchange heat with one another and as a result are warmer overall.

And finally, at the bottom of your body, your feet need to be taken care of. Most experts recommend you wear an inner liner sock made out of a synthetic material that wicks moisture away from your skin, with a wool or wool-nylon blend outer sock. This not only helps keep your feet dryer, but also helps prevent blisters from forming. As with the rest of your clothing, avoid cotton socks altogether (it retains moisture, potentially leading to several problems). You will want to bring multiple pairs of liners and socks with you on multi-day hikes (at least two pairs of each).

And as a final note on this subject, either bring clothing specifically to prepare food in or plan to change clothes each night before you go to bed. You never want to sleep in anything you cook in because it holds scents and will attract predators (especially bears). Any items of clothing you wear during food prep should be hung up with your food and other odorous items.

Shoes and Boots (and Barefoot Hiking)

Perhaps the single most important clothing decision you make about hiking in Yellowstone will be the shoes you wear, especially if you are on a multi-day hike. You can get away with hiking in flip-flops if necessary for a very short day hike, but for hikes that last several hours or days, you are going to need something that provides support to your feet. If your footwear is not good quality stuff that allows your feet to breathe, you are going to be in for a harrowing few days once you get far enough out that you can't go back and swap them out.

Hiking in Yellowstone requires you to be prepared for a variety of traveling conditions, including dry trail, river and creek fords, marshy and muddy fields and meadows (especially in the first half of the season), and, if you are going to be hiking above the tree line, scree and perhaps even snow.

Many people hike in waterproof ankle boots and carry good quality sandals (such as Tevas) for crossing bodies of water. The boots allow them to hike in soggy areas and in snow without getting their feet wet. The trick is to find a boot that is lightweight enough for you and comfortable enough to wear all day. You do not want your shoes weighing your feet down at the end of a long day. If you are going to be hiking in the higher elevations and/or climbing through scree, you may wish to consider a heavier boot with more substantial ankle protection. Otherwise, lighter boots should be perfectly fine for general trail use in Yellowstone. Many people will also carry a pair of lighter shoes for use around camp, while others just use their water crossing sandals for this purpose.

Tennis shoes, running shoes, or trail shoes are all fine for short, single-day hikes, and for longer hikes without marshy areas and/or elevation gains that take you into rock fields or snow fields. Do not hike in flip-flops, cheap sandals, or anything with a high heel (I have seen people hiking in all of these).

Regardless of what type of boot or shoe you elect to use, be sure to break them in before you undertake any long hikes in them. You want to ensure your feet have gotten comfortable in them and that they do not abnormally wear any places on your foot before you are committed to them for an entire trip. Getting blisters is not conducive to happy hiking (be sure your first aid kit includes blister care items!).

If you are one of those people who loves to hike in bare feet, doing so in Yellowstone is tough because of all the rock found in the soil. This includes obsidian, a glass-like rock that can cut your feet to shreds. It is present in the sands and dirts in many areas of the park. Having said that, I know a guy who hiked from the Heart Lake trailhead to the summit of Mt. Sheridan and back in a single day barefoot, a round trip of 23 miles.

Special Note for Park Employees

If you are a park employee, whether it be for the NPS or one of the authorized concession operators (Yellowstone Forever, YPSS, Xanterra, Medcor, Delaware North, etc.), you can rent a variety of hiking and camping equipment from your local YCERP Recreation Office. Each development within the park has a local YCERP representative on site (typically they are co-located with Xanterra in one of their facilities), and they have a cache of such equipment available to you (with your employee ID) for a very small fee. So you do not have to worry about bringing a whole boatload of equipment with you when you show up for your summer in the park.

Winter Hiking and Camping

Yellowstone in the Winter

As beautiful as Yellowstone is in the summer, it takes on a whole new aura in the winter. It is still just as magical, but it is a different kind of magical. And while the park sees literally millions of people in the summer, only slightly more than 100,000 people make it to the interior of the park in the winter. But while having so few people in the park might seem to make exploration much easier, you are limited in the kinds of transportation you can use.

Yellowstone's winter season begins just before Christmas each year. The park closes most of its roads the Monday following the first weekend in November to begin its preparation for the transition. For the next three weeks, the park begins to draw down its summer seasonal staff and to prepare the roads and facilities for the upcoming winter season.

By Thanksgiving, all park employees who are staying for the winter are required to have their personal vehicles out of the park. That weekend road crews will allow snow to begin accumulating on the roads. On December 15, the roads on the west side of the park open for the winter. Over the succeeding weeks, other areas of the park also open to oversnow travel.

During this time, the main roads are groomed for use by snowcoaches and snowmobiles rather than cars, buses, and other wheeled vehicles. Everything moves by skis, tracked vehicles, or vehicles equipped with low-pressure "flotation" tires made specifically for snow travel. This continues until March 15. On that day, the park closes and the massive plowing operation commences to get the park's roads open for the spring and summer season starting on April 15. That process will not conclude until around Memorial Day.

The only exception to all of this is the road from the North Entrance to Mammoth, on to Tower Junction and out the Northeast Entrance Road to Cooke City. This road is kept plowed for wheeled vehicles year-round, primarily because people who live outside the Northeast Entrance only have one way to get out to do their shopping and whatnot—through the park. All the roads east of that area are snowed in and will not re-open until April or May of the following year.

During this time of the year, the park is full of tourists enjoying winter activities such as skiing, snowmobiling, snowshoeing, etc. This brings with it a whole different kind of experience, both for employees and visitors alike. As a result, there are some unique issues that one must be prepared to deal with as a result of the extreme cold and the hundreds of inches of snow they will experience over the four months of winter operations.

Everything and everyone has to adapt to the winters in Yellowstone. Image courtesy NPS.

Winter Weather

As has been mentioned a couple of times now, Yellowstone basically has three seasons: July, August, and winter. The truth is that it can snow at just about any time of the year in the park. And though it is rare for it to do so in July and August, it does happen from time to time. In all the other months, though, snow is not uncommon. And of course, in the calendar winter (December to March), the park gets snow measured in dozens of feet.

Skiing, Snowshoeing, etc.

Yellowstone is a winter wonderland for cross-country skiers. Dozens of miles of trails are groomed specifically for skiing and/or snowshoeing, some specifically used only for winter travel. Generally, you can ski on any road that is groomed for oversnow travel and on any trail that is groomed for skis. You should stay on the left-hand shoulder of the road, skiing against the direction traffic flows, and you must yield to any oncoming oversnow vehicles, plows, etc. You may not ski on roads that are closed for plowing, though you can ski on closed roads that the NPS has not begun plowing or is not actively plowing.

In many areas, separate trails or paths on the same trail are cut for those on skis, snowshoes, and/or regular shoes/boots. It is illegal (and rude) for someone to walk in the ski trails with anything other than skis.

Skiing on Frozen Water

You may ski anywhere you like so long as it is not a closed area. This includes skiing over the frozen surfaces of lakes, rivers and streams. Kite skiing is permitted on Yellowstone Lake and Lewis Lake once they have *completely* frozen over. You must use extreme caution when hiking over frozen lake surfaces as the thickness of the ice can sometimes be deceiving.

Ice Climbing

Generally speaking, ice climbing is legal in Yellowstone, with the notable exception of in the Grand Canyon of the Yellowstone between Chittenden Bridge and Silver Cord Cascade (the very tall waterfall a couple of miles downstream from the Lower Falls). In May, 2010, two men were killed while trying to (illegally) climb Silver Cord. The ice had become weakened by the spring melting and it gave way, sending both men plummeting to their death some 300 feet (91m) below.

The two most popular areas for ice climbing are Baronnette Peak and Abiathar Peak in the northeast part of the park.

Trails

Most of the trails people use in the summer are not maintained during the winter. Those around the park's thermal areas such as Old Faithful and Mammoth are cleared to the extent possible, and a handful of ski trails are groomed for skiers. But the rest of the 1,100+ miles of trails in the park just sit and accumulate snow. Technically, most of these trails remain open. You are welcome to try to ski or snowshoe on them as your inclination compels you. Of course, you need to ensure you stay safe and don't do anything that will cause you any harm or cause any damage to park resources. If you get injured in the park's backcountry, it is an astronomically complex operation to rescue you (much more so than during the summer).

Maps that show the trails groomed for skiers in the Mammoth, Tower, Northeast, Canyon, and Old Faithful areas can be found at the end of this chapter (courtesy of NPS). Keep in mind that the specific trails maintained each year is subject to change, so please check the park's website or the Visitor Centers in the park for specifics.

Winter Safety

Rangers always counsel people to hike in groups in the summer due to the potential for encountering bears and other predators. They similarly counsel people to hike in groups in winter so that if one hiker gets into trouble, becomes hypothermic, gets sick, etc., they have someone who can reach out and get help. Winter in Yellowstone is very unforgiving, much more so than summer.

Avalanches

Like many other places in the mountainous west, Yellowstone has several areas where you need to be concerned about avalanches.

Avalanche areas you are likely to encounter in Yellowstone include:

- Sylvan Pass on the East Entrance Road
- Dunraven Pass on the road between Tower and Canyon. Though this road is not groomed for oversnow vehicles, hikers, skiers, and snowshoers are allowed through at their own risk.
- South Entrance Road between the Pitchstone Plateau and Lewis Falls.
- Any of the trails that pass by the base of the park's mountains just about anywhere in the park.

NPS is pretty good about closing areas that are known to be dangerous, to include those with a significant potential for avalanches. On Sylvan Pass, they expend a great deal of effort to keep it open by using military artillery to preempt extended road closures that can occur when the snow slides down Hoyt Peak and (the aptly-named) Avalanche Peak.

Temperature (°F)

Wind (mph) / Calm	40	35	30	25	20	15	10	5	0	-5	-10	-15	-20	-25	-30	-35	-40	-45
5	36	31	25	19	13	7	1	-5	-11	-16	-22	-28	-34	-40	-46	-52	-57	-63
10	34	27	21	15	9	3	-4	-10	-16	-22	-28	-35	-41	-47	-53	-59	-66	-72
15	32	25	19	13	6	0	-7	-13	-19	-26	-32	-39	-45	-51	-58	-64	-71	-77
20	30	24	17	11	4	-2	-9	-15	-22	-29	-35	-42	-48	-55	-61	-68	-74	-81
25	29	23	16	9	3	-4	-11	-17	-24	-31	-37	-44	-51	-58	-64	-71	-78	-84
30	28	22	15	8	1	-5	-12	-19	-26	-33	-39	-46	-53	-60	-67	-73	-80	-87
35	28	21	14	7	0	-7	-14	-21	-27	-34	-41	-48	-55	-62	-69	-76	-82	-89
40	27	20	13	6	-1	-8	-15	-22	-29	-36	-43	-50	-57	-64	-71	-78	-84	-91
45	26	19	12	5	-2	-9	-16	-23	-30	-37	-44	-51	-58	-65	-72	-79	-86	-93
50	26	19	12	4	-3	-10	-17	-24	-31	-38	-45	-52	-60	-67	-74	-81	-88	-95
55	25	18	11	4	-3	-11	-18	-25	-32	-39	-46	-54	-61	-68	-75	-82	-89	-97
60	25	17	10	3	-4	-11	-19	-26	-33	-40	-48	-55	-62	-69	-76	-84	-91	-98

Frostbite Times 30 minutes 10 minutes 5 minutes

If you are picking up a camping permit, the ranger will discuss the current avalanche danger with you. However, if you are just going out for a day hike, check in with the nearest visitor center or one of the two avalanche centers responsible for Yellowstone. Managed by Gallatin National Forest and Bridger-Teton National Forest, both have online avalanche advisory websites as well as recorded hotlines you can call to get updates. Keep in mind that these advisories are only guidelines and may not necessarily reflect the specific conditions inside the park. Learn how to determine avalanche-prone areas and how to deal with being caught in an avalanche. There are numerous websites and videos on YouTube that explain these concepts. In 1997, one of the park's geologists and a friend were killed by an avalanche in the park's backcountry. If it can happen to them, it can happen to you. If you are going to be hiking in the park's backcountry, consider getting an avalanche beacon.

Winter Weather

The two words that basically summarize the weather during the December to March time frame in Yellowstone are *cold* and *snow*. The park is one of the snowiest places in the lower 48, getting as much as 40–50 feet (12–15m) of snow in some areas over the course of the season. Once it gets white in those areas of the park south of Mammoth to Tower, you often will not see vegetation (except for the trees, obviously) or pavement again until April or May. You will notice that, in the interior of the park, every single building that is not being used has its first floor windows boarded up. That is to protect them breaking under the force of the snow that will build up around them.

Many people do not realize that fresh snow reflects more UV radiation than water does (90% of the UV reaching it), and as a result, on sunny days in the park, you can still get sunburn in the winter. If you are going to be out on a sunny day in the park, you will want to use sunscreen on your exposed skin. Bring sunglasses with you to protect your eyes from the ultraviolet radiation and from snow blindness.

The temperatures in the park typically range from 10 to 30 degrees during the day and between -20 and +10 at night. It is not uncommon to have temps occasionally drop into the -30 or even -40 range from time to time. Given that, you will want to understand how to recognize and treat hypothermia and frostbite.

NPS patrol truck caught up in an avalanche on Sylvan Pass, May, 2011. Image courtesy NPS.

Hypothermia/Frostbite

Perhaps the single biggest concern about hiking in Yellowstone during the winter is the extreme cold and the potential for hypothermia and frostbite to occur. Both can be deadly. It gets *extremely* cold in the park. In fact, it is not uncommon at all for a location inside or adjacent to the park to have the lowest recorded temperature in the lower 48 states on any given day in the winter. It is not unheard of for it to get into the -30s and even -40s occasionally during especially cold spells. As you can see in the chart on the preceding page, it does not take long at all for exposure to those kinds of temperatures to become extremely dangerous.

If you are going to be hiking and/or camping out in the park during the winter, ensure you are prepared both in terms of appropriate clothing and appropriate shelter. Wear multiple layers of good quality synthetic clothing, invest in good quality boots and gloves, keep a supply of hand and foot warmers with you, stay hydrated (and fed!), keep extra clothing with you, and have the appropriately-rated tent/shelter and sleeping bag for the park's cold environment. Learn how to construct a snow shelter in case you need it. Educate yourself about the signs of hypothermia. They include:

- Uncontrollable shivering
- Drowsiness
- Slurred speech
- Confusion and incoherence
- Impaired movement

The only way to treat hypothermia is by getting the victim into a warm, dry environment and get them to ingest warm food and drink if they're capable of doing so. In especially bad cases, getting a person naked into a sleeping bag and having another person snuggle next to them (also naked) will work. If it gets to that point, you should seek help.

Dehydration

One of the biggest concerns in the winter is dehydration. The dry air in the park and the lack of sweating may make the need for hydration seem less apparent, but do not be fooled. Carry a sufficient amount of water with you and the tools to thaw snow and frozen water, as well as the necessary equipment to purify water. Generally speaking, fresh snow does not need to be purified, but water from any of the park's lakes, rivers, and streams should be treated before consumption.

Thermal Areas

The trails and boardwalks in the park's frontcountry thermal areas (Mammoth, Old Faithful, Fountain Paint Pots, etc.) are open and maintained during the winter. You can walk or snowshoe through them without any problems. However, those off the beaten path, including those in the backcountry, do not receive any attention at all with respect to the trails passing near or through them. So any attempt to hike into or through these areas should be done with extreme caution.

Though most of the injuries and fatalities involving the park's hot springs occurs in the summer, there are occasionally people who fall into pools and are burned in the winter. Perhaps the most notable cautionary tale along these lines involved a park employee in February, 1988. A group of park employees skied out to Shoshone Geyser Basin, several miles from the Old Faithful area. One of them struck out on his own to explore the geyser basin just as a storm rolled in. In the blinding snow, he fell into one of the pools and received burns over much of his body. He managed to get back to his camp, but the effort to reach help and the subsequent rescue operation took many hours. He would pass away just before rangers reached him.[1] You should never underestimate the dangers associated with the thermal areas at any time of the year, but in the winter, getting to and having help reach you will take exponentially longer than it would in the summer as a rule.[2]

Winter Backcountry Camping

Generally speaking, you can camp along any of the park's major roadways so long as you do it on snow (no bare pavement/ground) more than ¼ mile from the roadway (i.e., out of sight of travelers), and out of sight of the developed areas, roads, parking lots, thermal features, and other backcountry campers. You should also be at least 100 feet from water (lakes, ponds, rivers, streams, etc.) and trails. You cannot camp in areas of high avalanche danger, such as along Sylvan Pass, in certain areas on Dunraven Road, and in certain areas of the South Entrance Road. There is a list of acceptable frontcountry camping sites at the end of this chapter, along with an explanation of areas in the backcountry where you can and cannot camp.

You are required to obtain a permit to camp! You will need to check in at one of the permitting sites listed on the next page. There will likely be a wait, since a law enforcement ranger will need to be called in to issue you the permit and to go over its details. There is no cost for the permit, but you can be cited for camping without one. And unlike in the summer, they do not take reservations. Permits are not required to go out on day hikes and return if you are not camping overnight.

You must follow the appropriate regulations regarding food storage and waste disposal while camping. This includes storing your food just as you would when camping during the summer. You must hang food or use food boxes that can be found in some locations (specified in the list on the following pages). One good option if you are staying at a location that has a vault toilet is to use a rope tied to the outside handle of the toilet with the food hanging inside the bathroom high enough off the ground to keep rodents from getting to it. Although bears are generally not around in the winter, there are still other animals to worry about, including ravens, coyotes, and wolves.

Proper waste disposal is also required. If you camp in one of the areas included in the list below, most of them have vault toilets available for your use (though you may have to dig them out and they certainly do not have heat!). Otherwise, bury any solid waste beneath the snow at the base of a tree. All waste paper and other products must be packed out just as you would do during the summer.

Generally, you are limited to single night stays at each camping location. The exceptions to these are Old Faithful parking lot, the Slough Creek Campground, the Tower Campground, and the Canyon Campground. Multiple night stays may be approved at other sites under certain circumstances.

Winter camping is allowed anywhere snow still covers the landscape at any time of the year. So once the park's roads begin opening in April, you may camp (with a permit) in any area that remains covered in snow. Once a given area's snowpack has melted to the point where bare ground is becoming visible, however, the park's spring/summer camping rules go into effect (i.e., you are required to camp in a designated site).

Winter Camping Permit Locations

You can pick up a winter camping permit at the following locations:

- Mammoth Ranger Station or Mammoth Visitor Center
- Northeast Entrance Station
- Old Faithful Visitor Education Center (they will arrange to get a ranger to meet you at the Ranger Station to get your permit)
- East Entrance Station
- Snake River Ranger Station at the South Entrance. You can also call to have a ranger meet you at Flagg Ranch out of normal hours (307-543-2559).
- West Yellowstone Visitor Information Center outside the West Entrance gate. You can call to make an appointment if desired (307-344-2880).
- You will NOT be able to get permits at Canyon, Tower, or the Lake area.

Most of these places will be staffed from around 8 a.m. to around 4 p.m. Because of the nature of winter operations in Yellowstone, there may be times when no one is immediately available to provide you with a permit and you may need to wait.

You will meet with one of the park's law enforcement rangers (typically) who will go over the winter regulations and help you with any questions you might have. You will be required to watch the park's Winter Safety Video, and you will be provided with any important information relevant to your trip (i.e., impending storms, avalanche dangers, etc.).

Winter Camping Locations

The following are the frontcountry camping locations and basic guidance concerning backcountry campsite selection for winter in Yellowstone.

- Frontcountry: Mammoth to Norris Junction
  - ◊ Sheepeater Cliff Parking Area (vault toilet)
  - ◊ Indian Creek Campground (vault toilet)
  - ◊ Apollinaris Picnic Area (vault toilet)
  - ◊ Beaver Lake Picnic Area (vault toilet)
  - ◊ Norris Campground (no toilet, though hikers can use vault toilets at the Norris Geyser Basin parking lot; you cannot camp in the Geyser Basin lot, however)
- Frontcountry: Norris Junction to Canyon Junction
  - ◊ Norris Meadow Picnic Area (vault toilet)
  - ◊ Ice Lake Campsite 4D3 (pit toilet, but you will need to dig it out of the snow to find it)
  - ◊ Cygnet Lakes Trailhead (no toilets & must be ¼ mile from roadway)
  - ◊ Grebe Lake Trailhead (no toilet)
  - ◊ Canyon Campground (restrooms and running water available at Canyon VC; no camping permitted in the Canyon Village parking lot)
- Frontcountry: Norris Junction to Madison Junction
  - ◊ Gibbon Meadow Picnic Area (vault toilet)
  - ◊ Caldera Picnic Area (vault toilet)
  - ◊ Iron Spring Picnic Area (vault toilet)
  - ◊ Gibbon Falls Picnic Area (no toilet)
- Frontcountry: West Entrance to Madison Junction
  - ◊ Madison River Picnic Area (vault toilet)
- Frontcountry: Madison Junction to Old Faithful
  - ◊ Madison Junction Picnic Area ((behind warming hut; restrooms and running water available; may store food in restroom lobby)
  - ◊ Firehole Picnic Area (vault toilet)
  - ◊ Nez Perce Picnic Area (vault toilet)
  - ◊ Whiskey Flat Picnic Area (vault toilet)
  - ◊ Campsite OD5 at Goose Lake (no toilet)
  - ◊ East Lot Picnic Area at Old Faithful (between Upper Service Station and Lodge; restrooms nearby at VC & Snow Lodge)
  - ◊ Camping along ski trails not permitted generally, but may be approved with valid reason. Must camp out of sight of trail.
- Frontcountry: Old Faithful to West Thumb
  - ◊ Spring Creek Picnic Area (vault toilet)
  - ◊ DeLacy Creek Picnic Area (vault toilet)
  - ◊ Divide Picnic Area (vault toilet)
- Frontcountry: South Entrance Road
  - ◊ Lewis Channel/Dogshead Trailhead (vault toilet)
  - ◊ Heart Lake Trailhead (vault toilet)
  - ◊ Lewis Lake Campground (vault toilet)
  - ◊ No camping at Grant Campground or within Grant Village
  - ◊ No camping in West Thumb parking lot
- Frontcountry: West Thumb to Fishing Bridge
  - ◊ Bridge Bay Picnic Area & Campground (no toilets)
  - ◊ Gull Point Picnic Area (vault toilet)

- ◊ Sand Point Picnic Area (vault toilet)
  - ◊ Fisherman's Access Picnic Area (vault toilet)
  - ◊ No camping in West Thumb parking lot
- Frontcountry: East Entrance Road
  - ◊ Sedge Bay Picnic Area (vault toilet)
  - ◊ Lake Butte Overlook (no toilet)
  - ◊ Sylvan Lake Picnic Area (vault toilet)
  - ◊ No camping between Sylvan Pass and one mile west of East Entrance due to avalanche danger. Camping within one mile limited to those who cannot reach Sylvan Lake Picnic Area by nightfall
- Frontcountry: Fishing Bridge to Canyon Junction
  - ◊ Cascade Picnic Area (vault toilet)
  - ◊ Nez Perce Picnic Area (vault toilet)
  - ◊ Chittenden Bridge Picnic Area (no toilet)
  - ◊ No camping allowed in Hayden Valley or in the Canyon Rim areas
- Frontcountry: Canyon Junction to Tower Junction
  - ◊ Tower Campground (vault toilet, food storage boxes available)
  - ◊ No camping allowed along route from Tower Junction to Tower Campground
  - ◊ Area between Tower Campground and Washburn Hot Springs Overlook is not groomed and area is subject to avalanches. Camping permits may be granted under appropriate circumstances.
- Frontcountry: Northeast Entrance Road
  - ◊ Slough Creek Campground (vault toilets, food storage boxes available; camping not allowed on the entrance road to the campground)
  - ◊ Pebble Creek Campground (vault toilet)
  - ◊ Camping between Pebble Creek CG and Northeast Entrance Road only approved under certain conditions (i.e., for those ice climbing Barronette Peak). No camping along either of the ski trails.
- Frontcountry: Mammoth to Tower Junction
  - ◊ Camping in any spot must be 1/4 mile from the road, including along the Blacktail Ski Trail. No camping at Lava Creek Picnic Area.
- Backcountry: Tower Area
  - ◊ Hellroaring Trail: The Hellroaring trailhead is not plowed in the winter and will be inaccessible to vehicles. You should park in the first pullout to the west of the main trailhead. Camping is not permitted in the parking areas. All camping should take place north of the Yellowstone River, preferably in designated sites.
  - ◊ Slough Creek Campground: Camping must be in the campground itself, and not along the access road. There are food storage boxes and vault toilets in the campground.
  - ◊ Camping is not permitted in Pleasant Valley, in the Garnet Hill Loop, or in the Little America Flats area along the Northeast Entrance Road.
- Backcountry: Lamar Valley/Northeast Entrance Area
  - ◊ Lamar River Trail: Camping is permitted only in the designated sites 3L1 through 3L4. Other restrictions may apply to this area. They'll be discussed with you when you appear for your permit.
  - ◊ Specimen Ridge Trail: Camping is permitted only west of the Lamar River and out of view of the roadway.
  - ◊ Pebble Creek Campground: Camping is only allowed in the campground and not along the access road. Vault toilets are available.
  - ◊ Pebble Creek Trail: Camping is not permitted between the trailhead and campsite 3P1. You may camp anywhere north of 3P1, though designated sites are recommended.
  - ◊ Base of Barronette Peak or Abiathar Peak: Camping permits are generally not issued for overnight stays in these areas because the unattended vehicles obstruct snow plows. Exceptions are made on a case-by-case basis. Camping is not permitted along the Barronette and Bannock ski trails.
  - ◊ Camping is not permitted along the Northeast Entrance Road between Lamar River Canyon and the Pebble Creek Campground due to potential wildlife conflicts. This includes Round Prairie, Mt. Norris, Druid Peak, Trout Lake, and the Lamar Valley.

- Backcountry: Canyon Area
  - ◊ Camping is not allowed in Hayden Valley within sight of the road or where wildlife is congregating
- Backcountry: Pelican Valley Area
  - ◊ Camping is not permitted within Pelican Valley itself, and all camping in the areas around it must be done in the trees and away from any locations where wildlife are congregating.
- Backcountry: Bechler Area
  - ◊ Camping is not allowed at the Ranger Station or in the developed area surrounding it.
- Backcountry: Gallatin Highway (US191) Area
  - ◊ Camping permitted along the trails in this area and campsites must be out of view of the road.
  - ◊ Several of the trails in this area have an associated avalanche potential.
  - ◊ Camping is not permitted along the Riverside Ski trails near West Yellowstone.
  - ◊ Camping is not permitted in Madison Valley (south and east of the Gneiss Creek Trail) due to potential wildlife conflicts.

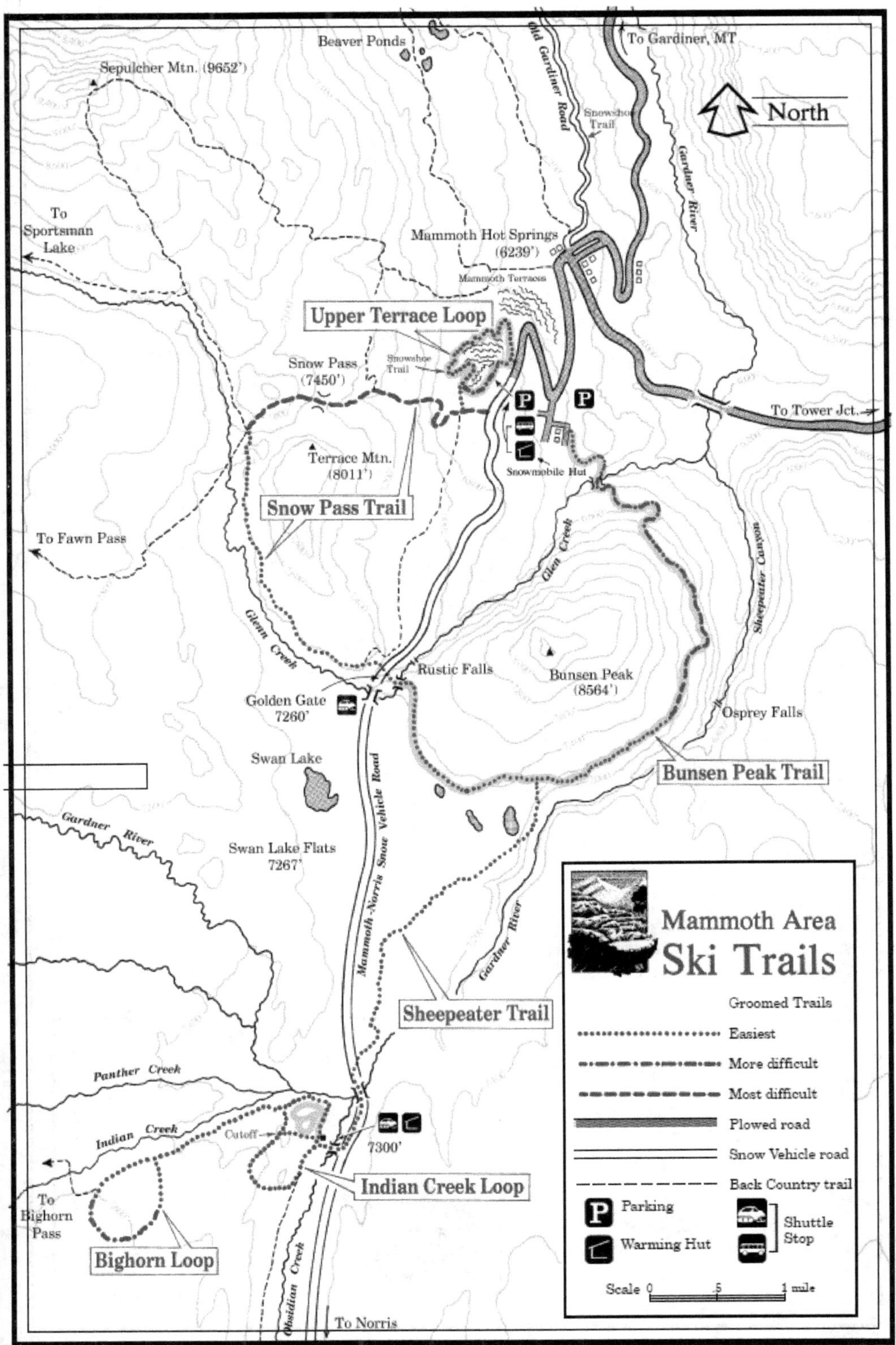

Beaver Ponds
Old Gardiner Road
To Gardiner, MT
Sepulcher Mtn. (9652')
Snowshoe Trail
North
Gardner River
To Sportsman Lake
Mammoth Hot Springs (6239')
Mammoth Terraces
Upper Terrace Loop
Snow Pass (7450')
Snowshoe Trail
To Tower Jct.
Terrace Mtn. (8011')
Snowmobile Hut
Snow Pass Trail
To Fawn Pass
Glen Creek
Sheepeater Canyon
Glenn Creek
Rustic Falls
Bunsen Peak (8564')
Golden Gate 7260'
Osprey Falls
Swan Lake
Bunsen Peak Trail
Mammoth-Norris Snow Vehicle Road
Gardner River
Swan Lake Flats 7267'
Gardner River
Mammoth Area
Ski Trails
Sheepeater Trail
Panther Creek
Indian Creek
Cutoff
7300'
Indian Creek Loop
To Bighorn Pass
Bighorn Loop
Obsidian Creek
To Norris
Groomed Trails
Easiest
More difficult
Most difficult
Plowed road
Snow Vehicle road
Back Country trail
Parking
Warming Hut
Shuttle Stop
Scale 0 .5 1 mile

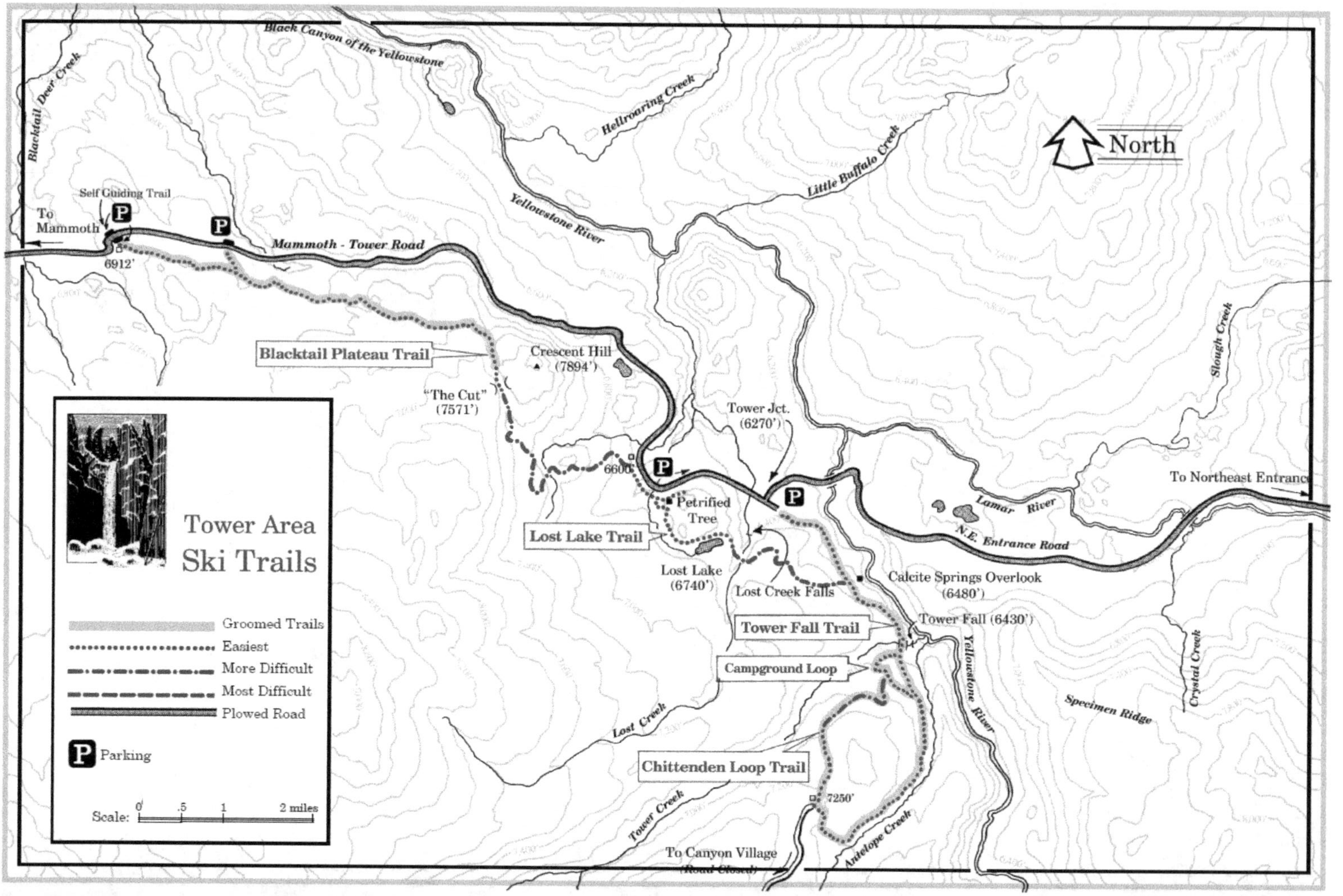

North
Black Canyon of the Yellowstone
Blacktail Deer Creek
Hellroaring Creek
Little Buffalo Creek
Yellowstone River
Self Guiding Trail
To Mammoth
6912'
Mammoth - Tower Road
Blacktail Plateau Trail
Crescent Hill (7894')
"The Cut" (7571')
6600'
Tower Jct. (6270')
Slough Creek
To Northeast Entrance
Petrified Tree
Lost Lake Trail
Lamar River
N.E. Entrance Road
Lost Lake (6740')
Lost Creek Falls
Calcite Springs Overlook (6480')
Tower Fall Trail
Tower Fall (6430')
Campground Loop
Yellowstone River
Specimen Ridge
Crystal Creek
Lost Creek
Chittenden Loop Trail
7250'
Tower Creek
Antelope Creek
To Canyon Village
(Road Closed)
Tower Area
Ski Trails
Groomed Trails
Easiest
More Difficult
Most Difficult
Plowed Road
Parking
Scale: 0 .5 1 2 miles

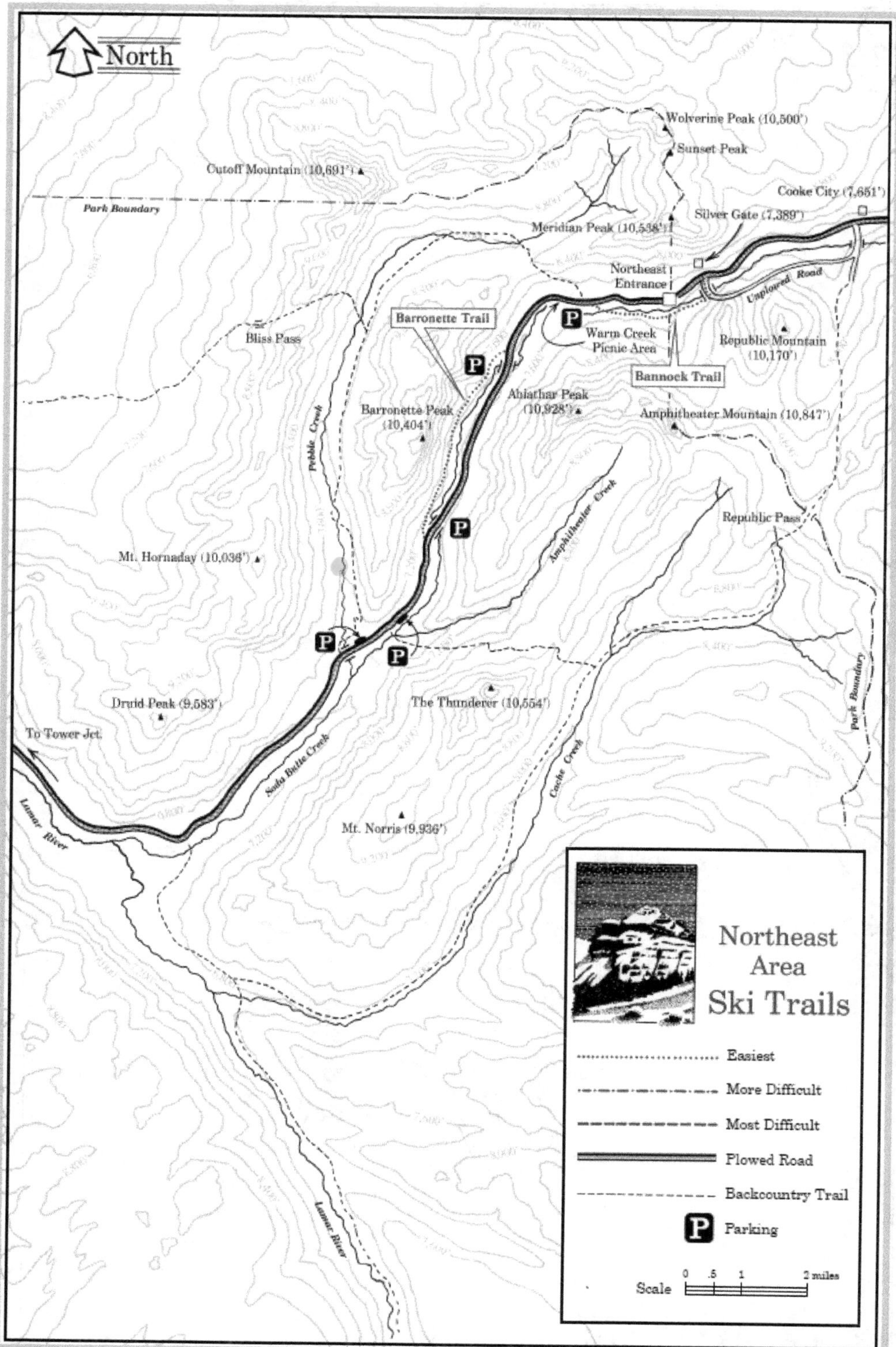
North
Wolverine Peak (10,500')
Sunset Peak
Cutoff Mountain (10,691')
Park Boundary
Cooke City (7,651')
Silver Gate (7,389')
Meridian Peak (10,538')
Northeast Entrance
Unplowed Road
Barronette Trail
Warm Creek Picnic Area
Bliss Pass
Republic Mountain (10,170')
Bannock Trail
Abiathar Peak (10,928')
Barronette Peak (10,404')
Amphitheater Mountain (10,847')
Pebble Creek
Amphitheater Creek
Republic Pass
Mt. Hornaday (10,036')
Park Boundary
Druid Peak (9,583')
The Thunderer (10,554')
To Tower Jct.
Soda Butte Creek
Cache Creek
Lamar River
Mt. Norris (9,936')
Northeast Area Ski Trails
Easiest
More Difficult
Most Difficult
Plowed Road
Backcountry Trail
Parking
Scale 0 .5 1 2 miles
Lamar River

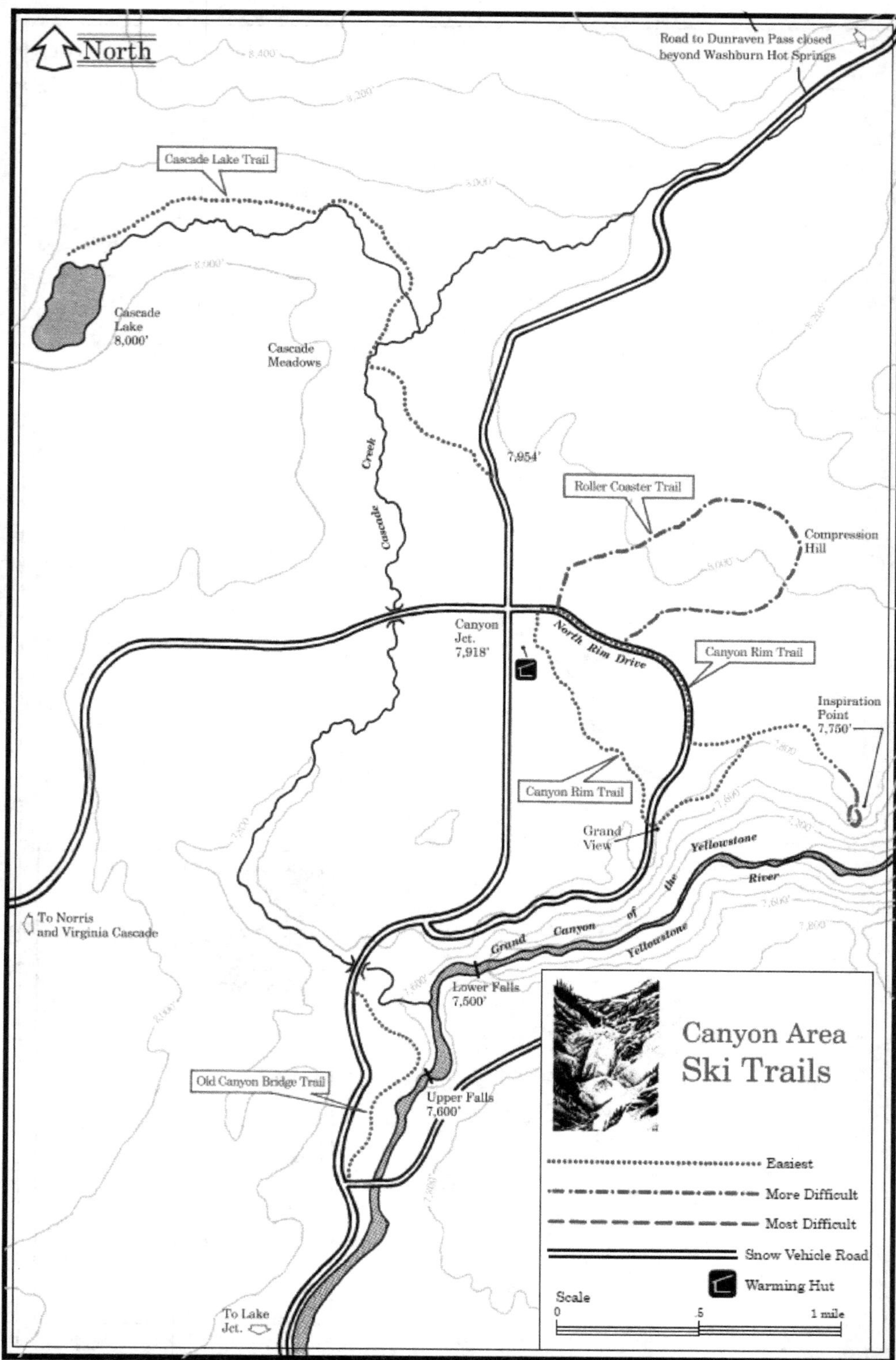
North
Road to Dunraven Pass closed beyond Washburn Hot Springs
Cascade Lake Trail
Cascade Lake 8,000'
Cascade Meadows
Cascade Creek
7,954'
Roller Coaster Trail
Compression Hill
Canyon Jct. 7,918'
North Rim Drive
Canyon Rim Trail
Inspiration Point 7,750'
Canyon Rim Trail
Grand View
Yellowstone River
Grand Canyon of the Yellowstone
To Norris and Virginia Cascade
Lower Falls 7,500'
Upper Falls 7,600'
Old Canyon Bridge Trail
To Lake Jct.
Canyon Area Ski Trails
Easiest
More Difficult
Most Difficult
Snow Vehicle Road
Warming Hut
Scale
0
.5
1 mile

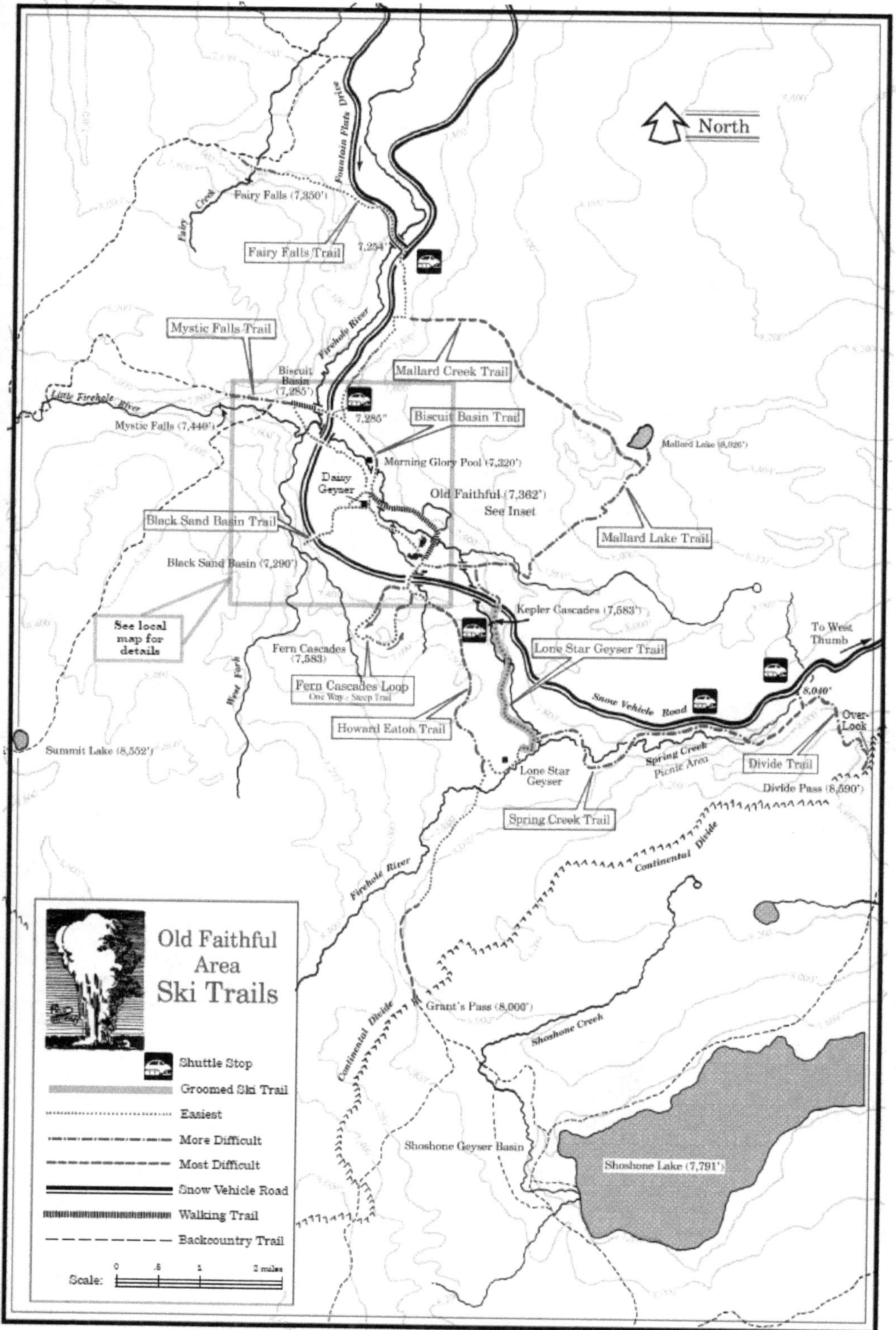

North
Fountain Flats Drive
Fairy Creek
Fairy Falls (7,350')
Fairy Falls Trail
7,254'
Firehole River
Mystic Falls Trail
Mallard Creek Trail
Biscuit Basin (7,285')
7,285"
Little Firehole River
Mystic Falls (7,440')
Biscuit Basin Trail
Morning Glory Pool (7,320')
Mallard Lake (8,026')
Daisy Geyser
Old Faithful (7,362')
See Inset
Black Sand Basin Trail
Mallard Lake Trail
Black Sand Basin (7,290')
Kepler Cascades (7,583')
See local map for details
Fern Cascades (7,583)
Lone Star Geyser Trail
To West Thumb
West Fork
Fern Cascades Loop
One Way - Steep Trail
Snow Vehicle Road
8,040'
Howard Eaton Trail
Over-Look
Summit Lake (8,552')
Lone Star Geyser
Spring Creek Picnic Area
Divide Trail
Divide Pass (8,590')
Spring Creek Trail
Continental Divide
Firehole River
Old Faithful Area Ski Trails
Grant's Pass (8,000')
Continental Divide
Shoshone Creek
Shuttle Stop
Groomed Ski Trail
Easiest
More Difficult
Most Difficult
Snow Vehicle Road
Walking Trail
Backcountry Trail
Shoshone Geyser Basin
Shoshone Lake (7,791')
Scale: 0 .5 1 2 miles

Trails: Introduction

This section of the book is organized a bit differently from what you may have seen in other hiking guidebooks; it is written for Yellowstone hiking purists. Rather than prescribing specific routes, for example, every trail in the park is included in a standalone mode. The reason for this is simple: Not everyone uses the identical route to get to the various features and areas of the park. In some cases, there may only be one route (Wraith Falls, for example), but in most others, it is possible to configure any number of paths to get to a specific point. For example, it is possible to get to Fairy Falls via any one of three different paths. Therefore, prescribing any single route and providing distance information for that route alone would not be helpful to many hikers.

By providing maps and technical information for every trail, you are allowed (encouraged, really) to configure your own route to any given point and to determine the distances involved. Hopefully, this will lead to exploration beyond what the "typical" hiker accomplishes in the park.

Lack of detail on what you'll see on the trail is also intentional, as is a lack of any substantive photos of the trails. In my view, describing what a hiker will see along a trail takes away some of the mystery. This book provides you with the technical and logistical information you need to help you decide if a trail is within your capabilities, and leaves the exploration of the viewscape to you. It's kind of like Google doing their "trailview" photography of the trails. While this can have some utility, if you are able to go in and take the trail virtually, many people would not be inclined to go out and explore for themselves. Some, of course, would be fine with that, but that's not the intent of this book. You won't generally find lists of what animals you are likely or not likely to see, because the reality is that you can see just about any given animal on any given trail at one point or another. Telling hikers they're likely to see X, Y, or Z on a trail and then them not seeing any of those often leads to disappointment.

Trail Organization

The trails are organized into 12 different chapters or book sections. The first eleven are reflective of the trail management districts within the park, while the twelfth is a section on trails of note that have been abandoned. Within each section you will find a detailed matrix and reference point list for each trail in that district (except the spur trails to campsites, patrol cabins, etc.). There are 227 maintained trails included, along with 51 abandoned trails/segments, 12 old roadbeds, and 17 unmaintained trails that are still relatively accessible. This represents over 1,450 miles (2,334km) of trails throughout Yellowstone National Park. What follows is an explanation of how to use the table for each trail.

Trail Data Matrix Cheat Sheet

① Trail Type
PTP: Point to Point
O&B: Out and Back
Loop: Loop Trail

② Trail Category
FC: Frontcountry
BC: Backcountry
TH: Threshhold

③ Trail Class
A: Backbone/Thoroughfare Trails
B: Major/Connector/Point of Interest Trails
C: Lightly Used/Utility Trails
N: No Longer Maintained Trails
U: Unofficial/Never Designated Trails

④ Trail Surface
TRAIL: Std groomed trail/dirt
PAVE: Asphalt/Pavement
BDWLK: Boardwalk
GRAVEL: Crushed rock

⑤ Trail District
1: Mammoth
2: Tower
3: Lamar
4: Canyon
5: Lake
6: Thorofare
7: Grant
8: South
9: Bechler
O: Old Faithful
W: West/Gallatin

Ⓓ Difficulty
Measure of difficulty of hike from A to B on a scale of 1-5.
1 = Easy Hike
5 = Very Difficult Hike

Ⓣ Traffic
Measure of how busy the trail is on average, using scale of 1-5.
1 = Very Few People
5 = Very Crowded

Ⓒ Children
Is trail good for smaller children?
Y = YES, N = NO

Ⓗ Handicap
Is trail suitable for those with mobility issues?
Y = YES, N = NO

Ⓤ Approved Trail Use
H: Hikers on Foot
S: Stock Use
B: Approved for Bicycle Use
K: Ski Use
R: Service Roads

EXAMPLE: Beaver Ponds Trail

Type:	①	PTP	Cat:	②	TH	Class:	③	B	Surf:	④	Trail	Dist:	⑤	1	Status:	⑥	E
Diff:	Ⓓ	3	Traf:	Ⓣ	2	Child:	Ⓒ	N	HAcc:	Ⓗ	N	Use:	Ⓤ	H	Length:	⑦	4.59
Elev A:	Ⓐ	6251	Elev B:	Ⓑ	6739	Elev G:	Ⓖ	1150	Elev L:	Ⓛ	-662	Net:	Ⓝ	488	BMA:	⑧	N
Min:	Ⓜ	6251	Max:	Ⓧ	6769	Avg:	Ⓥ	6510	Avg +:	⊕	7.4%	Avg -:	⊖	6.1%	Open:	⑨	YR

⑥ Trail Status
E: Existing Trail
A: Abandoned Trail
U: Unmaintained Trail
R: Old Road Bed (Hikeable)

⑦ Trail Length
Length of trail from Point A to Point B in U.S. Miles

⑧ Trail in BMA?
Is the trail in a Bear Management Area, and if so, which ones?
"- -" = trail is not in a BMA

⑨ Opening Date
Some trails are closed early in the season.
Opening date provided here
YR = Open year round

Ⓐ A Elevation
Elevation of the trail at the A Trailhead

Ⓑ B Elevation
Elevation of the trail at the B Trailhead

Ⓖ Elevation Gain
Total gain in elevation measured across the entire trail (how much ascent you'll do on a full-length hike)

Ⓛ Elevation Loss
Total loss in elevation measured across the entire trail (how much descent you'll do on a full-length hike)

Ⓝ Net Gain/Loss
Net gain or loss of elevation experienced across a full-length hike of the trail
(G - L = N)

Ⓜ Min Elevation
Minimum elevation encountered along the trail. May or may not be the same as Point A or Point B

Ⓧ Max Elevation
Maximum elevation encountered along the trail. May or may not be the same as Point A or Point B

Ⓥ Avg Elevation
Average elevation experienced across the length of the entire trail from Point A to Point B

⊕ Avg Incline
Average upward incline you'll experience hiking this trail (% = feet in elev gain per 100 feet of travel)

⊖ Avg Decline
Average downward incline you'll experience hiking this trail (% = feet in elev loss per 100 feet of travel)

EXAMPLE: Beaver Ponds Trail											MAP 1-1
Type:	PTP	**Cat:**	TH	**Class:**	B	**Surf:**	Trail	**Dist:**	1	**Status:**	E
Diff:	3	**Traf:**	2	**Child:**	N	**HAcc:**	N	**Use:**	H	**Length:**	4.59
Elev A:	6251	**Elev B:**	6739	**Elev G:**	1150	**Elev L:**	-662	**Net:**	488	**BMA:**	- -
Min:	6251	**Max:**	6769	**Avg:**	6510	**Avg +:**	7.4%	**Avg -:**	6.1%	**Open:**	YR

Reference Point	A-B Mi	A-B Km	B-A Mi	B-A Km	Latitude	Longitude
Trailhead 1N4 (behind Mammoth Hotel)	0.00	0.00	4.59	7.39	44.97744	-110.70135
Cross Elk Plaza Service Rd	0.12	0.19	4.47	7.19	44.97911	-110.70104
Power line crossing	1.27	2.04	3.32	5.34	44.99303	-110.70841
Unnamed creek crossing (footbridge)/Beaver Ponds	2.00	3.22	2.59	4.17	44.99789	-110.71649
Cross Elk Plaza Service Rd	3.70	5.95	0.89	1.43	44.98666	-110.71425
Power line crossing	4.15	6.68	0.44	0.71	44.98040	-110.71381
Trailhead @ jct w/ Sepulcher Mountain Trail	4.59	7.39	0.00	0.00	44.97523	-110.71405

Each trail will have a matrix such as this that provides detailed information on what you can expect to encounter on a hike. It provides the starting and ending points (Point A and Point B, respectively) which, typically, start on the west for trails that run west and east, and start on the south for trails that run north and south. You can always tell by the latitude and longitude which location is the beginning and which is the end. Note that the "MAP" designator at the right of the trail name header indicates on which maps the trail can be found. The main body of the table includes four rows of information you should use to decide if the trail is one you wish to attempt. The specific information included is as follows.

Trail Type (TYPE)

There are three basic types of trails within Yellowstone:

- PTP (Point to Point): These are trails that begin at one trailhead and end at another. To return to your starting point, you will need to arrange for a shuttle service or leave a second vehicle at the end point so you can drive back to the beginning (or hike back if you are so-inclined).
- LOOP: These are loop trails where you return back to the same place you started without doubling back on your path.
- O&B: These are "out and back" trails where you basically hike from Point A to Point B and then must return via the same path to the point where you began.

Trail Category (CAT)

Trail categories are used to designate the type of trail you are on in terms of it being a frontcountry or backcountry trail, or a trail that is known as a "threshold" trail—one that straddles the two.

The "frontcountry" (FC) in Yellowstone includes the roadways and developed areas such as Old Faithful, Canyon Village, etc. A frontcountry trail is one that does not venture too far away from civilization. The popular trails through the park's geyser basins are examples of this kind of trail.

A "backcountry" (BC) trail, conversely, is one that takes you into the woods more than, say, 200 yards or so and gets you away from the developments, roads, and other appurtenances of civilized life. These typically have backcountry campsites located along them, or connect with trails that do.

A "threshold" (TH) trail is a trail that straddles the line between being a frontcountry trail and a backcountry trail. They are usually trails that get you a ways out of the developed areas, but do not go so far back into the woods that you could find yourself needing to camp out for the night. The Monument Geyser Basin Trail is a perfect example of this kind of trail.

Trail Class (CLASS)

There are three different classes of trails in the park, plus a designator for abandoned or non-maintained trails.

Class A trails are those that are major thoroughfares or heavily used trails (also known as "backbone" trails). This includes trails such as the Heart Lake Trail, from which several other trails emanate. These trails receive priority when it comes to clearing and maintaining them, and are they typically the first to open once the backcountry rangers get into the field each spring.

Class B trails are those that are frequently used, major trails, or trails that lead to points of interest. These trails receive middle level of priority for maintenance and clearing.

Class C trails are those trails which are rarely or lightly used. They receive the lowest level of priority for clearing and maintenance.

Classes N & U trails are those that are no longer maintained by the NPS for public use.

Trail Surface (SURF)

The trail surface tells you what kind of hiking surface you will be walking on.

TRAIL means that this surface is carved out dirt or gravel trail surface (i.e., what you would expect a typical trail to be like).

PAVE means the trail surface is pavement or asphalt (typically service roads/old roadbeds).

BDWLK is an artificially-prepared wooden (or composite) boardwalk surface, usually found in the thermal areas or areas where marshiness is a problem.

DIRT means that the surface is raw dirt and is not maintained as a trail, per se. These are usually abandoned roads that may also be used as hiking trails.

In some cases, trail surfaces may show something akin to "TL/PV," which would indicate that part of the trail is paved and part of it is standard trail surface.

Trail District (DIST)

The park is divided administratively in a variety of different ways. The trails are overseen by the Resource and Visitor Protection Division (the public safety and law enforcement ranger staff) of the NPS, and maintained by the trail crews of the Maintenance Division. Therefore, the trail system is numbered and identified by a designator that reflects which ranger district each trail belongs to.

All of the trailhead and campsite designators will begin with the number or letter of the ranger district to which it belongs. For example, all of the trailheads in the Mammoth District (District 1) will begin with a "1". So the Rescue Creek trailhead is 1N2, while some of the campsites within this district include 1A1, 1Y2, 1C3, etc. Campsite 9D1 is located in the Bechler District (District 9), etc.

Yellowstone Trail Districts

The district boundaries are as follows (see the map above):

- Mammoth District (1): Generally between the summits of the Gallatin Range on the western side, north of Roaring Mountain on the south, and west of the summits of the Washburn Range on the east.
- Tower District (2): Generally east of the Washburn Range, north of Mt. Washburn and Amethyst Mountain, and the Slough Creek drainage westward.
- Lamar District (3): Basically the northeast corner of the park down through the Miller Creek and Lamar River headwaters.
- Canyon District (4): South of Mt. Washburn and Amethyst Mountain, west of the Mirror Plateau, Hayden Valley, Mud Volcano, the Central Plateau, and the Norris Geyser Basin area (south of Roaring Mountain to Artist Paint Pots on the south).
- Lake District (5): All of the areas around Fishing Bridge, Yellowstone Lake, east to the park boundary, Pelican Valley to Mist Creek Pass, and south to Beaverdam Creek.
- Thorofare District (6): The southeast corner of the park, from Beaverdam Creek to Two Ocean Plateau.

- Grant District (7): Southwest corner of Yellowstone Lake, including the South Arm and West Thumb, up to Pumice Point, north to Beach Lake, then west to Craig Pass, and south along the Continental Divide to the south tip of the South Arm of Yellowstone Lake.
- South District (8): West of Two Ocean Plateau, south of the Continental Divide, and Pitchstone Plateau eastward (everything east of the various drainages that flow through the Bechler area).
- Bechler District (9): The southwest corner of the park, south of Summit Lake and its trail.
- Old Faithful District (O): The Upper, Lower, and Midway Geyser Basins and their drainages, south to Grants Pass and Madison Lake, west along the Madison Plateau to Cougar Creek, the Madison Junction area and north to Artist Paint Pots.
- West/Gallatin District (W): Everything west of the summits of the Gallatin Range, Cougar Creek, and north of Summit Lake and its trail to the park boundaries.

This is only important in that it helps you locate which section of the book the trails can be found in, and it serves to organize the information you need to plan multi-day trips. The trail descriptions are organized into chapters based on these districts.

Trail Status (STATUS)

Within the context of this book, there are four types of trails in Yellowstone:

- E: Existing. These are trails that are maintained for public use by the park's maintenance and backcountry rangers. These show up on most trail maps of the park.
- U: Unmaintained. These are trails that exist (or existed) formally or informally, but are not maintained by the park's trail staff for use by the general public. Many of these started their lives as social trails and have gone on to become trails that are somewhat well known at least within the local hiking community, and may occasionally appear on commercially-produced maps and books.
- A: Abandoned. These are trails that have officially been abandoned by the park and are no longer actively maintained. They can be found on older maps of the park, but the newer maps will not generally show these trails. Some have been abandoned for decades, others have been abandoned for only a handful of years. Many will be overgrown and hiking through them will usually require considerable bushwhacking. They may or may not be marked once you get further out into the trail.
- R: Old roadways: These are "trails" that consist of abandoned segments of old roads that used to carry either horse-drawn or vehicular traffic. They were never designed as hiking trails, but they remain open enough that they can be hiked without too much effort today. These are not maintained by the park's trail staff.

Difficulty (DIFF)

This is a (purely subjective) measure of how difficult a hike would be from Point A to Point B as described in the chart. There are several things that are considered when coming up with this rating, including how much incline is involved, the average incline over lengths of distance, the nature of the trail surface (scree would be harder to hike through than a standard dirt trail, for example), and so forth. Difficulty ratings are on a scale of 1 to 5, with 1 being the easiest and 5 being the most difficult. Generally speaking, trails rated as a 1 would be sufficient for beginning hikers, whereas those that are rated with a 5 should be attempted only by those who have gotten considerable hiking experience under their belts and are prepared for arduous hiking conditions.

Traffic Level (TRAF)

This is a measure of how busy the trail is in terms of hiker traffic. These trails are also rated from 1 to 5, with 1 being the least used trails to 5 being trails that are so populated during the busy summer months that you are likely to be standing shoulder to shoulder with other hikers in places.

It is important to note that the NPS does not generally collect usage statistics for the park's trails (largely due to staffing shortfalls). These ratings are based on personal experience (both experientially and in dealing with hikers visiting the backcountry offices) and reading and listening to the experience of others over the years.

Child Friendliness (CHILD)

This is a measure of whether or not a particular trail is suitable for hiking with small children. There are not a lot of these in the park, but there are a handful that are specifically designed with smaller children in mind. The "Y" indicates a trail is suitable for hiking with a small child. The final decision about taking a child out onto a trail is yours, of course. You may have a child that takes to hiking longer trails rather well and could easily do a trail that is not listed as child-friendly herein.

Handicap Accessibility (HAcc)

This is a measure of whether or not a particular trail is suitable for use by those with mobility impairments, specifically those in wheelchairs or other assistive devices. Again, there are not a lot of trails that are suitable for use by those in wheelchairs. Those that are will almost invariably be boardwalk trails. There is one "backcountry" trail that is designed with wheelchair users in mind: the Ice Lake Trail.

Use (USE)

This indicates the type of use for which the trail was designed and is maintained.

- Hiking trails (H) are those that are maintained for hikers on foot.
- Stock trails (S) are those that are maintained for use by stock parties (parties with horses, llamas, etc.).
- Ski trails (K) are trails that are designed/suitable for use by skiers, and may not be signed or maintained for use by foot hikers or stock parties during the summer season (though you can still hike them if you can follow them).
- Bicycle trails (B) are trails that are designed for use by foot traffic and bicyclists. There are very few of these in the park.
- Service Roads (R) are paved or gravel roads that allow for administrative vehicle use, but may also be hiked or used by other groups as designated.

So a trail that is marked for use as "H S K" would be one that is suitable and approved for use by foot hikers, stock parties, and skiers. Trails marked with an "H" only but no "S" are for use only by foot travelers and not stock parties.

Length (LENGTH)

This is the length of the trail from Point A to Point B as measured in U.S. miles. The length is very precisely determined using GPS devices and GIS technologies.

Elevation at Point A (ELEV A)

This is the elevation of the point marked as the beginning of the trail in the table (Point A), measured in feet above mean sea level (ASL).

Elevation at Point B (ELEV B)

This is the elevation of the point marked as the end of the trail (Point B) in the table.

Elevation Gain (ELEV G)

This is the total amount of elevation gain experienced over the length of the trail (i.e., total amount of climbing). This figure does not necessarily reflect the elevation difference between Point A and Point B. This is the total accumulated elevation gain you will experience over the course of your hike. The "Net Elevation Change" (see below) reflects the difference between the two points.

Elevation Loss (ELEV L)

This is the total amount of elevation loss (downhill hiking) experienced over the length of the trail. The same caveat applies as described in the previous metric.

Net Elevation Change (NET)

This is the total net gain or loss of elevation experienced over the length of the trail. This should be the same figure you arrive at if you subtract the smaller of Point A or Point B from the other, and the same figure you arrive at if you subtract loss in elevation (ELEV L) from the elevation gain (ELEV G). So, in the example case, if you hike from Point A to Point B, you will have gained 488 feet in elevation.

Bear Management Areas (BMA)

Is the trail in a Bear Management Area (BMA)? If so, this will list which area(s) it is in. You can then refer to the BMA information found in the Safety section of this book (pages 62-63) to gain an understanding of the restrictions in place for the particular trail you are considering. A pair of dashes (--) will indicate the trail is not in any BMA.

Minimum Elevation (MIN)

This is the lowest elevation you will experience while hiking on the trail (expressed in feet ASL).

Maximum Elevation (MAX)

This is the highest elevation you will experience while hiking on this trail (likewise expressed in feet ASL).

Average Elevation (AVG)

This is the average elevation (feet ASL) you'll experience across the length of the entire trail.

Average Incline (AVG+)

This is the average upward incline you will experience while hiking this trail, expressed in degrees above the horizon. So a figure of 6.7% would indicate that the *average* incline along this trail would be 6.7 feet for every 100 feet of forward progress.

Average Decline (AVG-)

This is the average downward incline you will experience while hiking this trail, expressed in degrees below the horizon.

Opening Date (OPEN)

A handful of trails are closed until certain times of the year each season. This box will provide the opening date for those trails. Otherwise, you will see "YR," which indicates the trail is technically open year-round. The word "technically" is used because quite often access to most trails in the park is limited by snowfall, high water, or other conditions. So, technically, the trail is open, but you just cannot get to it. But it is not closed due to any administrative or regulatory action.

Reference Point Table

Underneath the statistical table is a table of reference points for each trail. There will generally be at least two points for every trail—a beginning and an end. Most trails will also have additional points of reference (PORs) included between Point A and Point B. The exceptions to these are the short trails into the canyon along its walls.

Each reference point is provided with its respective GPS location (latitude and longitude, measured in decimal degrees), as well as its specific distance from both the beginning and the end of the trail, measured in U.S. miles and kilometers. If you begin your hike at the A end, use the first two distance columns, and if you start your hike at the B end, use the second two.

It is important to note that GPS coordinates and distance measurements may be off by a few points compared to what you might see on your GPS unit as you hike on the ground in the park. This will vary depending on the type of device and its accuracy as well as how dense the forest canopy is, and so forth. The GPS system itself is only accurate to within a few feet, but you should be able to get a reading very close to what is provided in the book.

Note that it is not uncommon at all for rangers to realign trails or to relocate sections of trails. It is also possible for there to be multiple parallel paths to get from any given point to another on many of these trails. Therefore, you should use the GPS coordinates and the distances as guides rather than hard-coded information. These figures are provided to help you locate yourself as you move along the trails.

And though most hikers do not need the kind of accuracy you will find in the tables that follow, if you do, be sure to check in with your local Backcountry Office before setting out. They will always have the most accurate GPS coordinates for things like the campsites, trailheads, etc.

For trail spurs that lead to campsites, you are provided the distance (in U.S. miles) to the campsite unless it is less than one tenth of a mile. Where significant creek or river crossings are indicated, the width of the crossing is provided in feet. An indication that a bridge/footbridge is in place is provided where appropriate.

Maps

Finally, at the end of each district chapter you will find a set of maps that show the trails in context—that is, they show you all of the trails (including the abandoned ones) that exist inside the given frame. These maps should make it easier for you to decide which paths to take and to help you calculate distances. These maps also show the locations of the park's backcountry campsites and the patrol cabins. In order to reduce clutter on the maps, locations of lakes, waterfalls, thermal features/areas, etc., are not displayed, however.

Mammoth District Trails

Beaver Ponds Trail — MAP 1-1

Type:	PTP	**Cat:**	TH	**Class:**	B	**Surf:**	Trail	**Dist:**	1	**Status:**	E
Diff:	3	**Traf:**	2	**Child:**	N	**HAcc:**	N	**Use:**	H	**Length:**	4.59
Elev A:	6251	**Elev B:**	6739	**Elev G:**	1150	**Elev L:**	-662	**Net:**	488	**BMA:**	- -
Min:	6251	**Max:**	6769	**Avg:**	6510	**Avg +:**	7.4%	**Avg -:**	6.1%	**Open:**	YR

Reference Point	A-B Mi	A-B Km	B-A Mi	B-A Km	Latitude	Longitude
Trailhead 1N4 (behind Mammoth Hotel)	0.00	0.00	4.59	7.39	44.97744	-110.70135
Cross Elk Plaza Service Rd	0.12	0.19	4.47	7.19	44.97911	-110.70104
Power line crossing	1.27	2.04	3.32	5.34	44.99303	-110.70841
Unnamed creek crossing (footbridge)/Beaver Ponds	2.00	3.22	2.59	4.17	44.99789	-110.71649
Cross Elk Plaza Service Rd	3.70	5.95	0.89	1.43	44.98666	-110.71425
Power line crossing	4.15	6.68	0.44	0.71	44.98040	-110.71381
Trailhead @ jct w/ Sepulcher Mountain Trail	4.59	7.39	0.00	0.00	44.97523	-110.71405

The Beaver Ponds Trail takes you out to a series of small ponds formed when beavers dammed up an unnamed tributary of the Gardner River. If you are looking for the ponds' namesake animal, you will want to take this trail early in the morning or late in the evening, as they tend to stay indoors during most of the daylight hours. The trail itself takes you across a large expanse of land above Mammoth known as Elk Plaza, so-named because of the almost continuous presence of the ungulates (as well as pronghorn, mule deer, and the occasional bison).

The direction you take does not matter. Most day visitors to the park will start at the Sepulcher Mountain trailhead near the Commissioner's House, while those staying at the hotel or who want to find an easier place to park will start at the Old Gardiner Road behind the hotel. Starting at either end involves a relatively steep hike for a few hundred feet, but starting at the hotel end allows most of the rest of the hike to be on a gradual downhill slope.

This trail covers a lot of open land, so take plenty of water with you, especially during the summer. The Mammoth area is at a much lower elevation than the rest of the park, so it gets hotter here. This also means that the trail tends to be open year round rather than being snowbound throughout the entire winter. Consequently, the trail is very popular in the early spring.

Bighorn Ski Loop — MAP 1-2

Type:	Loop	**Cat:**	TH	**Class:**	C	**Surf:**	Trail	**Dist:**	1	**Status:**	E
Diff:	2	**Traf:**	1	**Child:**	N	**HAcc:**	N	**Use:**	H K	**Length:**	1.92
Elev A:	7414	**Elev B:**	7434	**Elev G:**	258	**Elev L:**	-237	**Net:**	20	**BMA:**	- -
Min:	7414	**Max:**	7662	**Avg:**	7537	**Avg +:**	4.6%	**Avg -:**	5.1%	**Open:**	YR

Reference Point	A-B Mi	A-B Km	B-A Mi	B-A Km	Latitude	Longitude
East jct w/ Bighorn Pass Trail	0.00	0.00	1.92	3.09	44.88590	-110.75696
West jct w/ Bighorn Pass Trail	1.92	3.09	0.00	0.00	44.88589	-110.75971

This is primarily a ski trail and generally is not maintained (marked) in the summer. The loop itself is just shy of two miles in length, but you will have to ski from the Indian Creek Warming Hut, which adds about three and a half miles of additional skiing to the distance. The trail itself is unremarkable, even in the winter, but it does afford some great views of the Gallatin mountain range.

Blacktail Deer Creek Trail — MAP 1-6,1-7

TYPE:	PTP	CAT:	BC	CLASS:	B	SURF:	TRAIL	DIST:	1	STATUS:	E
DIFF:	3	TRAF:	3	CHILD:	N	HACC:	N	USE:	H S	LENGTH:	4.00
ELEV A:	6622	ELEV B:	5534	ELEV G:	445	ELEV L:	-1415	NET:	-1088	BMA:	- -
MIN:	5534	MAX:	6754	AVG:	6286	AVG +:	6.4%	AVG -:	8.8%	OPEN:	YR

Reference Point	A-B Mi	A-B Km	B-A Mi	B-A Km	Latitude	Longitude
Trailhead 1N5 (6.7 mi E of Mammoth Junction)	0.00	0.00	4.00	6.44	44.95566	-110.59385
Jct w/ Blacktail Ponds Stock Spur Trail	0.03	0.05	3.97	6.39	44.95607	-110.59409
Unnamed Creek draining Blacktail Ponds	0.26	0.42	3.74	6.02	44.95889	-110.59563
Jct w/ abandoned Howard Eaton Trail	0.32	0.51	3.68	5.92	44.95965	-110.59619
Jct w/ Blacktail Ponds Spur/Lava Creek Cutoff Trail	0.42	0.68	3.58	5.76	44.96095	-110.59715
Jct w/ Rescue Creek Trail	0.69	1.11	3.31	5.33	44.96452	-110.59773
Rescue Creek crossing	1.25	2.01	2.75	4.43	44.97104	-110.59451
Spur trail to Campsite 1A1 (0.14 mi)	1.82	2.93	2.18	3.51	44.97862	-110.59484
Social trail to Hidden Falls	2.78	4.47	1.22	1.96	44.98754	-110.58405
Spur trail to Lower Blacktail Cabin/1Y6/1Y8 (0.82 mi)	3.76	6.05	0.24	0.39	44.99649	-110.57896
Suspension bridge over Yellowstone River	3.79	6.10	0.21	0.34	44.99686	-110.57876
Trailhead @ jct w/ Yellowstone River Trail	4.00	6.44	0.00	0.00	44.99812	-110.57433

Also known as the Lower Blacktail Creek Trail, it is primarily used as an out and back trail by day hikers, though many use it to access overnight campsites along the Yellowstone River Trail. It affords access to the lower end of the Black Canyon of the Yellowstone, and provides a breathtaking view of the Yellowstone River via a suspension bridge. You can also hike about a half hour further to get to Crevice Lake (just west of the junction of this trail with the Yellowstone River Trail).

The primary attraction of this hike is the river and the canyon (though the 20-foot Hidden Falls is worth the quick side trip). Most of the hike itself is through sagebrush and open land. You will see a couple of fenced-in enclosures as you approach the Rescue Creek Trail. These are used to study the effects of the ungulate populations on the flora in the area. This is an athletic trail, especially on the return; be sure to take plenty of water.

Blacktail Ponds - Lava Creek Cutoff Trail — MAP 1-6,1-7

TYPE:	PTP	CAT:	BC	CLASS:	B	SURF:	TRAIL	DIST:	1	STATUS:	E
DIFF:	1	TRAF:	1	CHILD:	Y	HACC:	N	USE:	H S	LENGTH:	2.29
ELEV A:	6591	ELEV B:	6622	ELEV G:	170	ELEV L:	-143	NET:	31	BMA:	- -
MIN:	6592	MAX:	6687	AVG:	6629	AVG +:	2.5%	AVG -:	2.5%	OPEN:	7/4

Reference Point	A-B Mi	A-B Km	B-A Mi	B-A Km	Latitude	Longitude
Trailhead @ jct w/ Lava Creek Trail	0.00	0.00	2.29	3.69	44.94211	-110.63254
Trailhead @ jct w/ Blacktail Ponds Trail	2.29	3.69	0.00	0.00	44.96095	-110.59715

Part of the old Howard Eaton Trail system, this is now primarily a connector trail to facilitate travel between the Lava Creek and Blacktail Ponds trails (largely for those wishing to hike the loop around Mt. Everts). The eastern half of it, however, affords excellent overviews of the Blacktail Ponds. This trail is lightly used so it may be hard to find at times, especially early in the season. Note that this trail is closed each year until July 4 because the ponds area is closed. It may also be closed intermittently at various times during the summer due to the occasional carcass in one of the ponds (which tends to attract bears).

Blacktail Ponds Stock Spur Trail — MAP 1-6

TYPE:	PTP	CAT:	BC	CLASS:	B	SURF:	TRAIL	DIST:	1	STATUS:	E
DIFF:	1	TRAF:	1	CHILD:	Y	HACC:	N	USE:	H S	LENGTH:	0.15
ELEV A:	6629	ELEV B:	6611	ELEV G:	27	ELEV L:	-45	NET:	-18	BMA:	- -
MIN:	6607	MAX:	6629	AVG:	6621	AVG +:	30.0%	AVG -:	3.8%	OPEN:	YR

Reference Point	A-B Mi	A-B Km	B-A Mi	B-A Km	Latitude	Longitude
Trailhead @ Upper Blacktail Cabin parking area	0.00	0.00	0.15	0.24	44.95505	-110.59151
Mammoth to Tower Road crossing	0.09	0.14	0.06	0.10	44.95529	-110.59242
Jct w/ Blacktail Deer Creek Trail	0.15	0.24	0.00	0.00	44.95607	-110.59409

This is a short trail from the stock parking area for the Blacktail Deer Creek Trail to the main trail itself. During the summer, oftentimes the main parking area will become full and even non-stock users may park here to access the main trail.

Boiling River Trail (Main) — MAP 1-1,1-7

TYPE:	O&B	CAT:	FC	CLASS:	A	SURF:	TRAIL	DIST:	1	STATUS:	E
DIFF:	1	TRAF:	5	CHILD:	Y	HACC:	Y	USE:	H S	LENGTH:	1.10
ELEV A:	5627	ELEV B:	5796	ELEV G:	245	ELEV L:	-76	NET:	169	BMA:	- -
MIN:	5627	MAX:	5792	AVG:	5682	AVG +:	6.2%	AVG -:	3.7%	OPEN:	YR

Reference Point	A-B Mi	A-B Km	B-A Mi	B-A Km	Latitude	Longitude
Trailhead 1N3 (Boiling River Parking Lot)	0.00	0.00	1.10	1.77	44.99236	-110.69133
Over mouth of Boiling River outlet	0.55	0.89	0.55	0.89	44.98501	-110.68919
Junction: Turn L for soaking area, R for Lava Creek Tr	0.57	0.92	0.53	0.85	44.98525	-110.68894
Jct w/ trail to Mammoth Campground (keep left)	0.67	1.08	0.43	0.69	44.98394	-110.68823
Jct w/ social trail; keep left	0.89	1.43	0.21	0.34	44.98108	-110.68674
Jct w/ social trail; keep left	0.99	1.59	0.11	0.18	44.98027	-110.68581
Trailhead @ jct w/ Lava Creek Trail	1.10	1.77	0.00	0.00	44.97935	-110.68713

For a great many years, Boiling River was a secret place known only to park employees. However, over the past couple of decades, this has become one of the most popular places in the park for everyone on the warmer summer days. It is one of only two officially-sanctioned swimming areas in the park; it is often closed until late June due to high water.[1]

Boiling River is a spot in the Gardner River where hot runoff from the terraces at Mammoth bubbles up from underground passageways and heats the water to a point where it is relaxing to soak. The river itself is not actually "boiling," but the water bubbling up from under the river makes it appear as though it is, and thus its name. The soaking area is open from 9 a.m. to 6 p.m. each day. Note the sign at the trailhead that warns you not to put your head underwater due to the presence of certain disease-causing bacteria.

There is no place to change here aside from the vault toilets (which get filthy with the high use), so show up in your swimsuit. Note that nudity is not permitted. This area gets very busy and congested during the summer, and parking is at a premium. Once the parking lots fill up, there is no parking allowed along the road. If you park there, you create a traffic hazard for motorists and you are likely to find a citation on your vehicle when you return. This trail lists a length of a little over one mile. That's because it connects into the Lava Creek Trail a fair distance away from the parking area. The soaking area itself is only a half mile up the trail from the parking lot.

Boiling River - Mammoth Campground Trail **MAP 1-1**

Type:	PTP	Cat:	FC	Class:	C	Surf:	Trail	Dist:	1	Status:	U
Diff:	1	Traf:	2	Child:	Y	HAcc:	N	Use:	H S	Length:	0.41
Elev A:	5945	Elev B:	5684	Elev G:	39	Elev L:	-301	Net:	-261	BMA:	- -
Min:	5676	Max:	5945	Avg:	5762	Avg +:	2.7%	Avg -:	14.6%	Open:	YR

Reference Point	A-B Mi	A-B Km	B-A Mi	B-A Km	Latitude	Longitude
Trailhead @ jct w/ Lava Creek Trail	0.00	0.00	0.41	0.66	44.97892	-110.68965
Trailhead @ jct w/ Boiling River Trail	0.41	0.66	0.00	0.00	44.98394	-110.68823

This is a short connector trail (from the Lava Creek Trail to the Boiling River Trail east of the soaking area) that facilitates access to the soaking area from the Mammoth Campground so guests do not have to drive down to the parking area to get to the river. Combine the 0.41 miles of this trail with the 0.12 miles of the Lava Creek Trail that you use to get to it and your total hiking distance to the Boiling River Trail is 0.53 miles.

Bunsen Peak Trail **MAP 1-3**

Type:	Loop	Cat:	TH	Class:	B	Surf:	Trail	Dist:	1	Status:	E
Diff:	2	Traf:	3	Child:	N	HAcc:	N	Use:	HSBK	Length:	7.33
Elev A:	7275	Elev B:	7275	Elev G:	1652	Elev L:	-1652	Net:	0	BMA:	- -
Min:	7202	Max:	8569	Avg:	7643	Avg +:	9.1%	Avg -:	7.8%	Open:	YR

Reference Point	A-B Mi	A-B Km	B-A Mi	B-A Km	Latitude	Longitude
Trailhead 1K4 (4.8 miles S of Mammoth Junction)	0.00	0.00	7.33	11.80	44.93216	-110.72784
Jct with Incoming Trail (turn here for short route up)	0.01	0.02	7.32	11.78	44.93199	-110.72755
Unnamed Lake (seasonal)	0.90	1.45	6.43	10.35	44.92236	-110.72018
Jct with Sheepeater Ski Trail	1.85	2.98	5.48	8.82	44.92287	-110.70238
Jct with Bunsen Peak Svc Road Trail (to Osprey Falls)	3.10	4.99	4.23	6.81	44.93447	-110.68573
Turn right at junction (old social trail to the left)	3.18	5.12	4.15	6.68	44.93444	-110.68717
Radio Building on Peak	5.25	8.45	2.08	3.35	44.93321	-110.70748
Rustic Falls/Golden Gate Canyon Overlook	7.00	11.27	0.33	0.53	44.93395	-110.72360
Jct w/ outgoing trail	7.32	11.78	0.01	0.02	44.93199	-110.72755
Trailhead 1K4	7.33	11.80	0.00	0.00	44.93216	-110.72784

The Bunsen Peak Trail is one of the most popular trails in the park, and makes an excellent day hike for those staying in the Mammoth area. The trail is open year-round, but the summit of the peak will often be snow-covered until early May, and snow will remain in places into June.

The peak is probably the remnant of an ancient volcanic bulge (scientists are actually unsure about the history of it), and it is named after physicist Robert Wilhelm Eberhard von Bunsen. In addition to his many other scientific pursuits, Bunsen (for whom the Bunsen Burner is named) also studied geysers in Iceland. Dr. Ferdinand Hayden, who led scientific explorations of Yellowstone, named the peak in Bunsen's honor because of the vast number of geysers in the park. Bunsen never actually visited the area, however.

There are two approaches you can take for this trail. The full seven-mile, round-trip takes you around to the east side of the peak (along an old service road) before you begin your ascent. This affords a gentler climb up to the top. You can also add in a side trip to Osprey Falls if you take this route. You can also opt to take the quicker, slightly more strenuous hike up the west side of the peak if you turn left just past the swing gate and little bridge over Glen Creek. This route is only two miles to the top, but again, has a much more significant incline. There is no water source on the peak, so be sure to take plenty with you. If you are planning on doing this hike in the July/August time frame, it is best to get started earlier in the day since the majority of the trail is across open land.

The view from the top is one of the best in this part of the park, affording a 360-degree panoramic view of this area. You will be able to see Electric Peak and the rest of the Gallatin Range to the west, the Washburn Range to the east, and you will have an incredible view of Mammoth Hot Springs, Gardner's Hole, Swan Lake Flat, Sheepeater Canyon, and Golden Gate Canyon (along with Cathedral Rock above it). Once you are on the summit, you will notice a small outbuilding. This houses radio communication equipment.

Bunsen Peak Service Road Trail — MAP 1-6,1-7

TYPE:	PTP	CAT:	TH	CLASS:	C	SURF:	TRAIL	DIST:	1	STATUS:	E
DIFF:	2	TRAF:	1	CHILD:	N	HACC:	N	USE:	HSKB	LENGTH:	2.77
ELEV A:	6416	ELEV B:	7119	ELEV G:	1006	ELEV L:	-303	NET:	703	BMA:	- -
MIN:	6268	MAX:	7125	AVG:	6659	AVG +:	10.7%	AVG -:	5.7%	OPEN:	YR

Reference Point	A-B Mi	A-B Km	B-A Mi	B-A Km	Latitude	Longitude
Trailhead @ YACC Camp Housing Area	0.00	0.00	2.77	4.46	44.95633	-110.70161
Glen Creek Crossing (bridge)	0.63	1.01	2.14	3.44	44.95047	-110.69651
Sheepeater Canyon Overlook	2.45	3.94	0.32	0.51	44.93579	-110.68161
Jct w/ Osprey Falls Trail	2.67	4.30	0.10	0.16	44.93498	-110.68426
Termination @ jct w/ Bunsen Peak Trail	2.77	4.46	0.00	0.00	44.93447	-110.68573

This trail takes you along an old service road, a road that was the original path to get up to the Swan Lake Flat area in the days before U.S. Army Engineer Lt. Dan Kingman built the first bridge and road through Golden Gate Canyon in the mid-1880s (the current road). There is nothing spectacular to see along this route, and it exists primarily to provide a route to the Bunsen Peak Trail from the YACC (Young Adult Conservation Corps) Camp complex, which is primarily a housing area for park employees and home to a youth program in the summer. It does provide a decent overlook into Sheepeater Canyon just before it connects to the Bunsen Peak/Osprey Falls Trails near its south end.

If you elect to take this trail from the YACC Camp side, enter the area via the driveway in the hairpin turn south of Mammoth Hot Springs, take the left fork, and drive around the housing area until you see the swing gate just north of the fuel pumps. Be sure to park out of the way and do not block access to any of the buildings or facilities.

Children's Fire Trail — MAP 1-6,1-8

TYPE:	LOOP	CAT:	FC	CLASS:	B	SURF:	BDWLK	DIST:	1	STATUS:	E
DIFF:	1	TRAF:	1	CHILD:	Y	HACC:	Y	USE:	H	LENGTH:	0.44
ELEV A:	6922	ELEV B:	6922	ELEV G:	29	ELEV L:	-29	NET:	0	BMA:	- -
MIN:	6911	MAX:	6934	AVG:	6921	AVG +:	2.6%	AVG -:	3.0%	OPEN:	YR

Reference Point	A-B Mi	A-B Km	B-A Mi	B-A Km	Latitude	Longitude
Trailhead @ parking lot	0.00	0.00	0.35	0.56	44.95941	-110.56664
Loop split	0.09	0.14	0.26	0.42	44.96009	-110.56682
Return to loop split	0.35	0.56	0.00	0.00	44.96009	-110.56682

This trail is listed on the approach signs as "Self-Guiding Trail" without any indication of what it is about. It was originally designed to acquaint children with the effects of fire upon the landscape of the Northern Range of Yellowstone. The interpretive panels have been updated to discuss a broader range of forces that impact the park, however, and the trail is known these days as the Forces of the Northern Range Trail. The trail is primarily boardwalk and is suitable for small children and those who have mobility issues.

Clagett Butte Trail — MAP 1-4,1-5

TYPE:	PTP	CAT:	BC	CLASS:	B	SURF:	TRAIL	DIST:	1	STATUS:	E
DIFF:	2	TRAF:	1	CHILD:	N	HACC:	N	USE:	H S	LENGTH:	1.12
ELEV A:	7271	ELEV B:	7280	ELEV G:	332	ELEV L:	-322	NET:	9	BMA:	- -
MIN:	7239	MAX:	7495	AVG:	7379	AVG +:	11.6%	AVG -:	8.0%	OPEN:	YR

Reference Point	A-B Mi	A-B Km	B-A Mi	B-A Km	Latitude	Longitude
South Trailhead @ Jct w/ Snow Pass Trail	0.00	0.00	1.12	1.80	44.96080	-110.72789
NWE Service Road	0.33	0.53	0.79	1.27	44.96411	-110.72684
Power Lines	0.49	0.79	0.63	1.01	44.96639	-110.72683
Clematis Creek Crossing	1.00	1.61	0.12	0.19	44.97173	-110.72738
North Trailhead @ jct w/ Sepulcher Mtn Trail	1.12	1.80	0.00	0.00	44.97310	-110.72799

Though this trail is only a mile long, you will need to take a significant hike in on either the Snow Pass Trail or the Sepulcher Mountain Trail to get to it. It exists primarily to create a loop connecting those two trails to one another, and is otherwise unremarkable.

The trail, built in 1923 concurrently with the Sepulcher Mountain Trail, skirts the east side of Clagett Butte. It is named after William H. Clagett, the delegate from the Montana Territory who introduced the bill in Congress that would go on to make Yellowstone the nation's first national park.

Grizzly Lake Trail — MAP 1-10

TYPE:	PTP	CAT:	BC	CLASS:	C	SURF:	TRAIL	DIST:	1	STATUS:	E
DIFF:	2	TRAF:	2	CHILD:	N	HACC:	N	USE:	H S	LENGTH:	4.15
ELEV A:	7443	ELEV B:	7582	ELEV G:	793	ELEV L:	-654	NET:	139	BMA:	- -
MIN:	7422	MAX:	7851	AVG:	7591	AVG +:	6.5%	AVG -:	6.2%	OPEN:	YR

Reference Point	A-B Mi	A-B Km	B-A Mi	B-A Km	Latitude	Longitude
Trailhead 1K8 (6.3 mi N of Norris Junction)	0.00	0.00	4.15	6.68	44.79903	-110.74532
Bridge over Obsidian Creek	0.10	0.16	4.05	6.52	44.80041	-110.74586
Grizzly Lake	2.13	3.43	2.02	3.25	44.81690	-110.76836
Straight Creek Crossing (25 to 75')	2.23	3.59	1.92	3.09	44.81823	-110.76900
Spur trail to campsite 1C1	2.99	4.81	1.16	1.87	44.82581	-110.77004
Spur trail to campsite 1C2 & Unnamed Lake	3.65	5.87	0.50	0.80	44.83446	-110.76672
Winter Creek crossing (25 to 75')	3.83	6.16	0.32	0.51	44.83697	-110.76686
Termination @ jct w/ Mt Holmes Trail	4.15	6.68	0.00	0.00	44.84126	-110.76555

This is a nice, fairly short hike (four miles round trip if you go to the lake and back) to a gorgeous backcountry lake. It takes you through some areas that were heavily burned in the 1988 fires, and affords great views of Mt. Holmes along the way. Grizzly Lake is the 9th largest lake in the park, and contains a population of brook trout. It is more than 30 feet deep in places. If you hike around the perimeter of the lake itself, it will add three miles to your travels.

If you go on to the end of this trail, you will connect to the Mt. Holmes Trail. Just before you reach that point, you will have to ford Winter Creek. During the spring runoff, the creek can be quite high and it may not be safe to do so, but later in the season the creek is typically running at 1-2 feet.

At about three and three and a half miles, there are two backcountry campsites, both of which are easily accessible for those wanting to spend the night in the woods without too great a hike. Of the two, 1C1 is about a half mile north of the lake. It is important that you set up your tent(s) at this site and not camp near the water due to the possibility that bears might show up and wish to enjoy the lake with you.

Grizzly Lake was named after the grizzly bear, of course, as a part of the practice of naming park features after local flora and fauna. It was not named because there is an increased likelihood of seeing the bears at the lake, but of course, that is possible at any point inside Yellowstone, so take the appropriate precautions.

Howard Eaton Trail: Mammoth - Golden Gate MAP 1-6,1-4

Type:	PTP	**Cat:**	BC	**Class:**	B	**Surf:**	Trail	**Dist:**	1	**Status:**	E
Diff:	2	**Traf:**	3	**Child:**	N	**HAcc:**	N	**Use:**	H S K	**Length:**	4.10
Elev A:	6413	**Elev B:**	7277	**Elev G:**	1542	**Elev L:**	-679	**Net:**	864	**BMA:**	- -
Min:	6413	**Max:**	7459	**Avg:**	7064	**Avg +:**	10.8%	**Avg -:**	7.1%	**Open:**	YR

Reference Point	A-B Mi	A-B Km	B-A Mi	B-A Km	Latitude	Longitude
Trailhead @ jct w/ Sepulcher Mountain Trail	0.00	0.00	4.10	6.60	44.97325	-110.70843
Above Narrow Gauge Spring/Terrace	0.33	0.53	3.77	6.07	44.96987	-110.71026
Old Snow Pass Road bed	0.78	1.26	3.32	5.34	44.96633	-110.71560
Dedolph Springs (A, B, & C)	0.89	1.43	3.21	5.17	44.96480	-110.71629
Area of Unnamed Springs	0.91	1.46	3.19	5.13	44.96451	-110.71627
Social Trail to Squirrel Spring	1.00	1.61	3.10	4.99	44.96320	-110.71521
River Styx Spring	1.00	1.61	3.10	4.99	44.96296	-110.71521
Jct w/ White Elephant Back Spur Trail	1.10	1.77	3.00	4.83	44.96236	-110.71509
Jct w/ Snow Pass Trail - Left to Trailhead	1.32	2.12	2.78	4.47	44.95946	-110.71487
Jct w/ Snow Pass Trail - Right to Snow Pass	1.35	2.17	2.75	4.43	44.95916	-110.71509
Jct w/ Fawn Pass Trail	3.87	6.23	0.23	0.37	44.93358	-110.73181
Trailhead 1K3 (4.8 mi S of Mammoth Junction)	4.10	6.60	0.00	0.00	44.93295	-110.72764

This trail is one of the more unique trails in the Mammoth district, and was once a part of the famed Howard Eaton Trail system throughout the park (see the chapter on Lost Trails near the end of this book for more details).

You will need to hike about a quarter mile up the Sepulcher Mountain Trail and turn left, then you will head along the western edge of the Upper Terraces thermal area. You won't really be able to see much of it until you get to Orange Spring Mound, however. As you pass that, you will enter a small, unnamed thermal area (be sure to stay on the trail for safety reasons), cross through a forested area, and then you will enter a large rock field. This is part of The Hoodoos, a large rockfall from the edge of Terrace Mountain above you to your west.

To make a day-length loop hike out of this, when you get to the end of the trail, turn right onto the Fawn Pass Trail, take it approximately two miles north to the Snow Pass Trail, take that trail another one and a half miles back to the Howard Eaton Trail, and then north back to your original starting point (for a total of about nine miles).

Indian Creek Ski Loop Trail — MAP 1-2

TYPE:	LOOP	CAT:	TH	CLASS:	C	SURF:	TRAIL	DIST:	1	STATUS:	E
DIFF:	2	TRAF:	1	CHILD:	N	HACC:	N	USE:	H K	LENGTH:	1.48
ELEV A:	7322	ELEV B:	7322	ELEV G:	227	ELEV L:	-227	NET:	0	BMA:	- -
MIN:	7295	MAX:	7480	AVG:	7378	AVG +:	6.9%	AVG -:	4.9%	OPEN:	YR

Reference Point	A-B Mi	A-B Km	B-A Mi	B-A Km	Latitude	Longitude
Trailhead @ Big Horn Pass Turn/HET	0.00	0.00	1.48	2.38	44.88268	-110.73527
Power line crossing south	0.48	0.77	1.00	1.61	44.87876	-110.74334
Power line crossing north	1.00	1.61	0.48	0.77	44.88389	-110.74523
Jct w/ spur to Big Horn Trail NW of campground	1.19	1.92	0.29	0.47	44.88552	-110.74264
Trailhead @ Big Horn Pass Turn/HET	1.48	2.38	0.00	0.00	44.88268	-110.73527

The Indian Creek Ski Loop is a gentle, easy ski trail you can pick up from the Indian Creek Warming Hut located just outside the Indian Creek Campground in the winter. It is not marked for use during the summer (though the route is somewhat visible). Xanterra provides a shuttle service to and from the warming hut during the winter season (for a fee).

The main trail is a little under two miles from the hut and back, but there is a second loop that connects up to the Bighorn Pass Trail and loops back to the hut as well. If you ski/hike the outer loop of this trail, it is approximately 2.5 miles total distance. Regardless of which loop you take, you basically hike through thick forest with some glimpses of the Gallatin Range off to the east.

Lava Creek Trail — MAP 1-7

TYPE:	PTP	CAT:	BC	CLASS:	B	SURF:	TRAIL	DIST:	1	STATUS:	E
DIFF:	2	TRAF:	1	CHILD:	N	HACC:	N	USE:	H S	LENGTH:	4.62
ELEV A:	5967	ELEV B:	6564	ELEV G:	1177	ELEV L:	-580	NET:	597	BMA:	- -
MIN:	5744	MAX:	6599	AVG:	6044	AVG +:	6.9%	AVG -:	6.2%	OPEN:	YR

Reference Point	A-B Mi	A-B Km	B-A Mi	B-A Km	Latitude	Longitude
North Trailhead 1N3 (1.2 mi N of Mammoth Jct)	0.00	0.00	4.62	7.44	44.97858	-110.69203
Trail to Boiling River (shortcut)	0.12	0.19	4.50	7.24	44.97892	-110.68965
Jct with Boiling River Trail	0.29	0.47	4.33	6.97	44.97934	-110.68714
Jct with trail to Mammoth Boneyard	0.76	1.22	3.86	6.21	44.97369	-110.68369
Bridge over Gardiner River	0.78	1.26	3.84	6.18	44.97375	-110.68328
Confluence of the Gardiner River and Lava Creek	1.98	3.19	2.64	4.25	44.95936	-110.67399
Spur trail to campsite 1A3	3.12	5.02	1.50	2.41	44.95060	-110.65527
Social trails to Undine Falls Overlook	4.19	6.74	0.43	0.69	44.94425	-110.63830
Jct with Blacktail Ponds Cutoff Trail/Mt. Everts Trail	4.52	7.27	0.10	0.16	44.94211	-110.63254
South Trailhead 1N6 (4.4 mi E of Mammoth Jct)	4.62	7.44	0.00	0.00	44.94089	-110.63220

The Lava Creek Trail takes you along the base of Mt. Everts, first alongside the Gardner River and then Lava Creek (assuming west to east travel). Though most people just hike this trail from one end to the other, some use this as the first leg of a loop around Mt. Everts (connecting to the Blacktail Deer Creek Trail and then the Rescue Creek Trail). It is a reasonable hike for most people and is one of the prettier ones in this part of the park.

Though you can do the trip in either direction, going from west to east involves altitude gain, whereas going the other direction is mostly downhill. There is a single overnight campsite along the trail that is fairly easy to get to.

Probably the highlight of this trip is the ability to see Undine Falls from the opposite side most people see it. The view is much prettier on the north side. Be careful, though, there are no rails to keep you from falling into the canyon here. Watch your footing. In 1980 a tourist fell into the canyon while trying to get a better photograph of the falls and died from injuries sustained in the fall.[2]

Note that on maps and in books produced prior to 1990, the north trailhead for this might show a different location (the Mammoth Boneyard maintenance area). In 1990, the current 1N3 trailhead was established just north of the entrance to the Mammoth Campground, and this is the appropriate trailhead to use for trip planning purposes.

Mammoth Hot Springs Lower Trail — MAP 1-4

TYPE:	LOOP	CAT:	FC	CLASS:	C	SURF:	BDWLK	DIST:	1	STATUS:	E
DIFF:	2	TRAF:	5	CHILD:	N	HACC:	N	USE:	H	LENGTH:	0.97
ELEV A:	6289	ELEV B:	6357	ELEV G:	289	ELEV L:	-221	NET:	68	BMA:	- -
MIN:	6289	MAX:	6512	AVG:	6398	AVG +:	11.5%	AVG -:	10.4%	OPEN:	YR

Reference Point	A-B Mi	A-B Km	B-A Mi	B-A Km	Latitude	Longitude
Trailhead @ lower parking lot	0.00	0.00	0.84	1.35	44.97265	-110.70937
Liberty Cap/Spur to Palette Spring, Devil's Thumb	0.02	0.03	0.82	1.32	44.97261	-110.70435
Base of New Palette Spring	0.06	0.10	0.78	1.26	44.97204	-110.70384
Sidewalk Spring	0.10	0.16	0.74	1.19	44.97161	-110.70351
Cavern Terrace, Middle Parking Lot	0.13	0.21	0.71	1.14	44.97130	-110.70329
Loop Split - Keep straight	0.16	0.26	0.68	1.09	44.97095	-110.70377
Jct w/ lower cutoff	0.22	0.35	0.62	1.00	44.97029	-110.70350
Jct w/ spur trail to upper parking lot (take right fork)	0.25	0.40	0.59	0.95	44.97003	-110.70291
Base of Jupiter Terrace	0.32	0.51	0.52	0.84	44.96953	-110.70379
Base of Mound Terrace, jct w/ upper cutoff	0.38	0.61	0.46	0.74	44.97013	-110.70462
Naiad Spring	0.42	0.68	0.42	0.68	44.97014	-110.70554
Jct w/ Mammoth Hot Springs Upper Trail	0.47	0.76	0.37	0.60	44.97011	-110.70637
Cleopatra Spring	0.54	0.87	0.30	0.48	44.97096	-110.70718
Palette Spring Overlook	0.67	1.08	0.17	0.27	44.97193	-110.70571
Minerva Terrace Spur	0.76	1.22	0.08	0.13	44.97101	-110.70457
Jct w/ upper cutoff	0.79	1.27	0.05	0.08	44.97062	-110.70435
Jct w/ lower cutoff	0.81	1.30	0.03	0.05	44.97049	-110.70407
Return to loop split	0.84	1.35	0.00	0.00	44.97029	-110.70350

The Lower Mammoth Trail is a boardwalk trail that provides access to the lower areas of the travertine Mammoth Terraces. And while you can travel across the boardwalks and paths any direction you wish, this is the most efficient way of doing it. Though this is listed as not favorable for children, they may enjoy the areas that do not require a lot of stair-climbing.

Pick up a copy of the NPS/Yellowstone Forever pamphlet on Mammoth Terraces at the Mammoth Visitor Center or one of the pedestals located at the terraces for in-depth discussion of the specific features you will encounter as you move around this area.

Mammoth Hot Springs Upper Trail — MAP 1-4

TYPE:	PTP	CAT:	FC	CLASS:	A	SURF:	BDWLK	DIST:	1	STATUS:	E
DIFF:	2	TRAF:	5	CHILD:	N	HACC:	N	USE:	H	LENGTH:	0.42
ELEV A:	6620	ELEV B:	6452	ELEV G:	82	ELEV L:	-250	NET:	-168	BMA:	- -
MIN:	6452	MAX:	6620	AVG:	6552	AVG +:	6.0%	AVG -:	13.5%	OPEN:	YR

Reference Point	A-B Mi	A-B Km	B-A Mi	B-A Km	Latitude	Longitude
Trailhead @ entrance to Upper Terrace Drive	0.00	0.00	0.42	0.68	44.96539	-110.70788
Grassy Spring, spur to Canary Spring, Dryad Springs	0.14	0.23	0.28	0.45	44.96719	-110.70729
Spur to Cupid Spring	0.23	0.37	0.19	0.31	44.96797	-110.70748
Cupid Spring parking lot	0.25	0.40	0.17	0.27	44.96819	-110.70764
Spur to New Blue Spring	0.30	0.48	0.12	0.19	44.96890	-110.70761
Jct w/ Mammoth Hot Springs Lower Trail	0.42	0.68	0.00	0.00	44.97011	-110.70637

Similar to the Lower Trail, this trail takes you across the upper areas of the Mammoth Terraces. To reach this trail's starting point, park in the lot outside the entrance to the Upper Terrace Drive, and then walk down toward that entrance. You will see a sign pointing you to the walking trail.

Mount Everts Trail — MAP 1-7

TYPE:	PTP	CAT:	BC	CLASS:	N	SURF:	TRAIL	DIST:	1	STATUS:	U
DIFF:	3	TRAF:	1	CHILD:	N	HACC:	N	USE:	H	LENGTH:	6.89
ELEV A:	5362	ELEV B:	6587	ELEV G:	3213	ELEV L:	1990	NET:	1225	BMA:	- -
MIN:	5362	MAX:	7756	AVG:	7017	AVG +:	13.6%	AVG -:	11.85	OPEN:	YR

Reference Point	A-B Mi	A-B Km	B-A Mi	B-A Km	Latitude	Longitude
Trailhead @ jct w/ Rescue Creek Trail	0.00	0.00	6.89	11.09	45.01807	-110.69280
Cross unnamed creek	0.17	0.27	6.72	10.81	45.01609	-110.69074
Trailhead @ jct w/Lava Creek Trail	6.89	11.09	0.00	0.00	44.94211	-110.63253

The trail over Mt. Everts, originally built in 1922, was abandoned by NPS in the 1970s, but is still hikable today (and is rather popular with Mammoth-based park employees). The view of the park's headquarters and the terraces from the summit make the trip worthwhile. On the western end, just before you get to the ridgeline, you can look down on McMinn Bench, which was the site of a coal mining operation during the early days of the park (mid-1880s).

Mount Holmes-Winter Creek Trail — MAP 1-7

TYPE:	O&B	CAT:	BC	CLASS:	B	SURF:	TRAIL	DIST:	1	STATUS:	E
DIFF:	4	TRAF:	1	CHILD:	N	HACC:	N	USE:	H S	LENGTH:	10.95
ELEV A:	7348	ELEV B:	10330	ELEV G:	3499	ELEV L:	-518	NET:	2982	BMA:	- -
MIN:	7323	MAX:	10330	AVG:	8098	AVG +:	7.7%	AVG -:	3.4%	OPEN:	YR

Reference Point	A-B Mi	A-B Km	B-A Mi	B-A Km	Latitude	Longitude
Trailhead 1K6 (9.5 mi N of Norris Junction)	0.00	0.00	10.95	17.62	44.83825	-110.73273
Cross power lines	0.39	0.63	10.56	16.99	44.84038	-110.73914
Winter Creek crossing (50')	1.10	1.77	9.85	15.85	44.84902	-110.74172
Jct with Grizzly Lake Trail	2.56	4.12	8.39	13.50	44.84126	-110.76555
Spur trail to campsite 1C4	5.46	8.79	5.49	8.84	44.81230	-110.79708
Jct with Trilobite Lake Trail/Winter Creek Patrol Cabin	5.67	9.12	5.28	8.50	44.81127	-110.80115
Spur trail to campsite 1C5 (0.26 mi)	5.72	9.21	5.23	8.42	44.81095	-110.80202
Tree Line	10.40	16.74	0.55	0.89	44.81612	-110.86080
Summit/Fire Lookout	10.95	17.62	0.00	0.00	44.81890	-110.85554

Though it is possible to hike to the summit of Mt. Holmes and back in a single day, it is an exhausting trip for all but the most in-shape people. Typically, hikers will travel to one of the two excellent backcountry campsites on day one, get up early the next morning and hike to the summit of the mountain and back to the campsite on day 2, and then hike out on day 3 (sometimes adding in side trips to either Grizzly Lake or Trilobite Lake).

This hike requires fording Winter Creek. During the early season (up until the end of June), the water can be quite high and cold. From July on, the water is typically one to two feet deep and the crossing is very easy. The summit of Mt. Holmes will have some snow on it until well into July in most years, but ensure you have sufficient water to get you to the top and back to your campsite (or to the trailhead if you are doing it in a single day).

Built in 1930, the first 7.5 miles of this trail is a gradual climb, but the last 3.5 is where the hike gets really serious. You will climb over 2,000 feet (610m) in that short distance. Once you get to the summit, you will find one of the park's fire lookouts. This is one of three that used to be staffed during the summer, but thanks to the camera array you will find there, it is no longer staffed unless the park is experiencing severe fire conditions. Please do not interfere with the cameras or the weather station on your visit. At the summit, you will have incredible views of the Gallatin Range to the north and south, the Washburn and Absaroka ranges to the east, and on a clear day, the Teton Range south of Yellowstone. You will easily understand why this site was selected for a fire lookout.

Old Gardiner Road Trail — MAP 1-7

TYPE:	PTP	CAT:	FC	CLASS:	B	SURF:	TRAIL	DIST:	1	STATUS:	E
DIFF:	1	TRAF:	2	CHILD:	N	HACC:	N	USE:	HSBR	LENGTH:	3.98
ELEV A:	6251	ELEV B:	5354	ELEV G:	259	ELEV L:	-1157	NET:	-897	BMA:	- -
MIN:	5354	MAX:	6333	AVG:	5890	AVG +:	5.5%	AVG -:	6.8%	OPEN:	YR

Reference Point	A-B Mi	A-B Km	B-A Mi	B-A Km	Latitude	Longitude
Trailhead 1N4 (behind Mammoth Hotel)	0.00	0.00	3.98	6.41	44.97743	-110.70135
Jct with Elk Plaza Service Road	0.20	0.32	3.78	6.08	44.97947	-110.69932
Trailhead @ North Entrance Kiosks	3.98	6.41	0.00	0.00	45.02520	-110.70083

This trail is an old service road, and was the second road constructed for visitors to get into the park. Today, it is used primarily as a scenic side road, and a service road for work vehicles to get to the water reservoir for Mammoth and the cell and radio tower located on Elk Plaza.

Though usually open to the public for vehicular travel during the summer, it is often closed following heavy rain storms until the mud dries out. However, when it is closed to automobiles, it usually remains open to hikers and bicyclists.

The trail itself is unremarkable, but does facilitate hiking and biking access to the park's North Entrance Station and the Town of Gardiner, Montana, in lieu of taking the North Entrance Road (and it is much safer than taking that road if you are on foot or bicycle).

Old Golden Gate Stagecoach Road — MAP 1-3

TYPE:	PTP	CAT:	TH	CLASS:	N	SURF:	TRAIL	DIST:	1	STATUS:	R
DIFF:	2	TRAF:	1	CHILD:	N	HACC:	N	USE:	H B R	LENGTH:	1.84
ELEV A:	7136	ELEV B:	6480	ELEV G:	73	ELEV L:	-729	NET:	-656	BMA:	- -
MIN:	6480	MAX:	7136	AVG:	6797	AVG +:	3.7%	AVG -:	9.1%	OPEN:	YR

Reference Point	A-B Mi	A-B Km	B-A Mi	B-A Km	Latitude	Longitude
Trailhead @ Golden Gate (4.3 mi S of Mammoth Jct)	0.00	0.00	1.84	2.96	44.93686	-110.72114
Trail split to Reservoir & Joffe Lake (keep left)	1.10	1.77	0.74	1.19	44.94733	-110.70888
Trailhead on north side of YCC Dorms	1.84	2.96	0.00	0.00	44.95707	-110.70447

This trail follows an old service road that was once the original road to get up to the Golden Gate Viaduct prior to construction of the existing road. It was used originally by stage coaches, and then went into service as a road for park maintenance workers to access the old Mammoth water supply system. Most of the road is largely unused today. You will see why as you hike along it—the road is unsuitable for use by vehicles. Though it is open to bicyclists, if you decide to ride through here, note that it is very difficult to navigate with all of the gravel, potholes, washouts, etc.

The primary attraction of this hike is the fact you are experiencing a part of the park's history. You also pass through the lower reaches of The Hoodoos, the large boulders of limestone that have dislodged and fallen from the shoulder of Terrace Mountain. At the lower end of this hike, you will come across a service road that leads down to the park's current water aeration reservoir and the water treatment plant. You can also get to Joffe Lake via this service road (which is open to public fishing). The trail itself ends at the YACC Camp parking lot.

Old Hoodoo Road Segment — MAP 1-3

TYPE:	PTP	**CAT:**	TH	**CLASS:**	N	**SURF:**	TRAIL	**DIST:**	1	**STATUS:**	R
DIFF:	3	**TRAF:**	1	**CHILD:**	N	**HACC:**	N	**USE:**	H	**LENGTH:**	0.46
ELEV A:	7109	**ELEV B:**	7086	**ELEV G:**	128	**ELEV L:**	-151	**NET:**	-23	**BMA:**	- -
MIN:	7047	**MAX:**	7119	**AVG:**	7075	**AVG +:**	10.4%	**AVG -:**	10.0%	**OPEN:**	YR

Reference Point	A-B Mi	A-B Km	B-A Mi	B-A Km	Latitude	Longitude
Trailhead near Golden Gate	0.00	0.00	0.46	0.74	44.93827	-110.72019
Trailhead at Hoodoos	0.46	0.74	0.00	0.00	44.94336	-110.71756

This short segment of the original road through The Hoodoos is largely unknown and invisible today. But, like many of the other abandoned road segments throughout the park, it is often quite enlightening to travel along a largely forgotten part of the park's history.

The north end of this trail travels through The Hoodoos, the large limestone boulders that have fallen from the shoulder of Terrace Mountain above you. The south end is largely forested and may require some bushwhacking. There is no suitable parking at the north end of this trail, so you will need to find a pulloff and walk a bit to get to it. The best way to do it is to park on the shoulder just south of the south end of the trail, and then walk alongside the road (be careful—the road is narrow through here).

Finding the south end is tough, so use your GPS to locate it. You can walk north and then return via the same path.

Old Undine Falls Road Segment — MAP 1-6

TYPE:	PTP	**CAT:**	TH	**CLASS:**	N	**SURF:**	TRAIL	**DIST:**	1	**STATUS:**	R
DIFF:	3	**TRAF:**	1	**CHILD:**	N	**HACC:**	N	**USE:**	H	**LENGTH:**	1.23
ELEV A:	6571	**ELEV B:**	6397	**ELEV G:**	202	**ELEV L:**	-376	**NET:**	-174	**BMA:**	- -
MIN:	6397	**MAX:**	6693	**AVG:**	6599	**AVG +:**	7.1%	**AVG -:**	9.6%	**OPEN:**	YR

Reference Point	A-B Mi	A-B Km	B-A Mi	B-A Km	Latitude	Longitude
Trailhead @ Lava Creek Picnic Area	0.00	0.00	1.23	1.98	44.94067	-110.63315
Site of old Undine Ski Area (to 1992)	0.44	0.71	0.79	1.27	44.94267	-110.64061
Trailhead east of High Bridge	1.23	1.98	0.00	0.00	44.94596	-110.65468

This trail is part of the original Mammoth to Tower Road that existed before the current road was constructed in the mid-1930s. The best way to approach this is to park at the Lava Creek Picnic Area, and then try to follow the old road footprint west from that location. It will be tough to find in some locations, and much of the east and west ends of this trail will require some bushwhacking.

In the middle section of it, however, you will find the most interesting part. Almost a half mile in, you will come across the site of the old Undine Ski Area, which existed from 1942 until 1992. The ski area was not generally open to the public; it was used by park employees and residents for recreation and for students in Gardiner to learn how to ski. In 1990, the park service decided they wanted to put in an actual ski lift to get skiers to the top of the hill. That was going to require cutting down some huge trees, however, and when environmentalists got wind of what was going on, they made a big fuss about it. The superintendent at the time (Bob Barbee) decided that the ski area was unsuitable to have in the park, and it was removed. All of the structures here were razed in 1994.

If you continue further west about 650 yards (594m), you will come across an interesting remnant of the old road system—a brick wall. This was part of the retaining wall that kept vehicles from running off the road and down the hill.

Osprey Falls Trail — MAP 1-3

Type:	O&B	**Cat:**	TH	**Class:**	B	**Surf:**	Trail	**Dist:**	1	**Status:**	E
Diff:	3	**Traf:**	2	**Child:**	N	**HAcc:**	N	**Use:**	H	**Length:**	1.24
Elev A:	7117	**Elev B:**	6445	**Elev G:**	245	**Elev L:**	-916	**Net:**	-672	**BMA:**	- -
Min:	6437	**Max:**	7142	**Avg:**	6930	**Avg +:**	10.7%	**Avg -:**	17.7%	**Open:**	YR

Reference Point	A-B Mi	A-B Km	B-A Mi	B-A Km	Latitude	Longitude
Jct with Bunsen Peak Service Road Trail	0.00	0.00	1.24	2.00	44.93498	-110.68426
Termination near Osprey Falls	1.24	2.00	0.00	0.00	44.93045	-110.68062

Osprey Falls is one of the most impressive waterfalls in the park—a 150-foot drop of the Gardner River into the Sheepeater Canyon. It is the 29th highest waterfall in the park. This is a great hike to take early in the morning. You will arrive at the falls in time to have lunch with one of the most incredible views in the park.

The trail itself is somewhat strenuous, with an elevation loss of around 800 feet (244m) across the one and a quarter mile trip. Going to the falls is the easy part, of course. It gets tough coming back up, though the switchbacks make it somewhat easier. It is well worth the trip if you want to see a waterfall that not many others get to see, however.

If you come in from the main Bunsen Peak trailhead (the way 99% of those who hike it do), it will add three miles to your trip in (and out). You can ride a bicycle along the Bunsen Peak road, though, and just hike down this trail if you wish.

Rescue Creek Trail — MAP 1-7

Type:	PTP	**Cat:**	BC	**Class:**	B	**Surf:**	Trail	**Dist:**	1	**Status:**	E
Diff:	3	**Traf:**	2	**Child:**	N	**HAcc:**	N	**Use:**	H S	**Length:**	7.34
Elev A:	5361	**Elev B:**	6725	**Elev G:**	1782	**Elev L:**	-419	**Net:**	1364	**BMA:**	- -
Min:	5359	**Max:**	6870	**Avg:**	6271	**Avg +:**	6.8%	**Avg -:**	3.0%	**Open:**	YR

Reference Point	A-B Mi	A-B Km	B-A Mi	B-A Km	Latitude	Longitude
Trailhead 1N2 (1.1 miles N of Roosevelt Arch)	0.00	0.00	7.34	11.81	45.01780	-110.69366
Gardiner River crossing (footbridge)	0.06	0.10	7.28	11.72	45.01828	-110.69288
Jct w/ Mt. Everts Trail	0.08	0.13	7.26	11.68	45.01807	-110.69280
Old US Army Artillery training sites	0.54	0.87	6.80	10.94	45.02263	-110.68631
West spur trail to campsite 1A2 (0.10 mi)/Rescue Crk	5.41	8.71	1.93	3.11	44.98306	-110.62301
East spur trail to campsite 1A2 (0.24 mi)	5.61	9.03	1.73	2.78	44.98184	-110.61917
Termination @ jct w/ Blacktail Deer Trail	7.34	11.81	0.00	0.00	44.96452	-110.59773

The Rescue Creek Trail is one of the most interesting trails in the park. You cross over the Gardner River on a footbridge, and then travel across a large expanse of flat land that was used by the U.S. Army in the park's early days for gunnery and artillery training. To this day, park employees and locals refer to this area as Shooting Range Flat. As you hike out, you can still see the trenches and revetments where the training took place.

As you continue down the trail you will pass a couple of points of interest with unique names: Turkey Pen Peak and Rattlesnake Butte. The peak got its name from an old prospector's cabin that was in the area at one time. Someone thought the dilapidated thing looked like a turkey pen, and so that gave rise to the name of the hill and the creek that flows by it (as well as the pass through which you travel as you hike). In the early summer of 2017, a man fell to his death on the peak as he was searching for a treasure supposedly hidden somewhere in the Rocky Mountains by an eccentric millionaire. Rattlesnake Butte gets its name from the presence of the snakes in the area (the only part of the park where they live).

Despite its name, this trail does not actually meet Rescue Creek until about five and half miles in. So of its more than seven mile length, less than a third of it actually parallels the creek. The creek actually got its name through a misunderstanding. It was the mistaken belief of Ferdinand Hayden that Truman Everts had been found along this creek, when in actuality he was found just off the Blacktail Plateau Drive over in the Tower area. Everts became lost on one of the early expeditions through the park, and wandered in the wilderness for 37 days before being found. His story is told in the book, *Lost In Yellowstone: Truman Everts' Thirty-Seven Days of Peril.*

Though this trail is hiked out and back by many hikers, you can make a loop around Mt. Everts by following it to its termination at the Blacktail Deer Creek Trail, then heading south to the connector that takes you to the Lava Creek Trail, and then following the Lava Creek Trail back to its northern trailhead about three miles south of where you began (or to the Boiling River parking lot about one mile closer to where you started).

There is one campsite along this trail, but it is much easier reached from the Blacktail Deer Creek side (and with a lot less of a climb). Note that Rescue Creek is often dry in the latter parts of the summer, as are all the other creeks along this route (with the obvious exception of the river), so take plenty of water with you.

Sepulcher Mountain Trail — MAP 1-5

Type:	PTP	**Cat:**	BC	**Class:**	B	**Surf:**	Trail	**Dist:**	1	**Status:**	E
Diff:	4	**Traf:**	3	**Child:**	N	**HAcc:**	N	**Use:**	H S	**Length:**	7.66
Elev A:	6276	**Elev B:**	7586	**Elev G:**	3516	**Elev L:**	-2206	**Net:**	1310	**BMA:**	- -
Min:	6276	**Max:**	9632	**Avg:**	8138	**Avg +:**	14.2%	**Avg -:**	13.4%	**Open:**	YR

Reference Point	A-B Mi	A-B Km	B-A Mi	B-A Km	Latitude	Longitude
Trailhead 1K1 (@ Mammoth Terraces)	0.00	0.00	7.66	12.33	44.97379	-110.70432
Site of old McCartney Hotel	0.11	0.18	7.55	12.15	44.97331	-110.70632
Jct with Howard Eaton Trail	0.22	0.35	7.44	11.97	44.97325	-110.70843
Clematis Creek crossing	0.23	0.37	7.43	11.96	44.97338	-110.70841
Jct with Beaver Ponds Trail	0.77	1.24	6.89	11.09	44.97523	-110.71405
Cross power lines	0.99	1.59	6.67	10.73	44.97538	-110.71798
Jct with Clagett Butte Trail	1.59	2.56	6.07	9.77	44.97310	-110.72799
Turn right here - do not continue straight	4.38	7.05	3.28	5.28	44.99307	-110.75868
Sepulcher Overlook Trail	4.79	7.71	2.87	4.62	44.99173	-110.76588
Trailhead @ jct w/ Sportsman Lake Trail	7.66	12.33	0.00	0.00	44.96755	-110.75577

The summit of Sepulcher Mountain can be reached a few different ways. The most popular is to begin at the trailhead near the terraces, but you can also approach it from the Glen Creek trailhead (by way of the Fawn Pass and Sportsman Lake trails or the Snow Pass and Sportsman Lake trails). Many people make a loop out of it by taking the trail to the Sportsman Lake Trail, then the Snow Pass Trail, the Clagett Butte Trail, and back to the trailhead at the terraces. Regardless of which route you use, be sure to take a map with you as this trail intersects with several other trails and it is easy to end up going down the wrong path (especially if the sign posts have not been reset in the early spring).

The mountain is named after the rock formations that appear near the summit. Apparently, someone thought they resembled sepulchers, or grave markers, and the name stuck.

This is a difficult trail. You will climb over 3,500 feet (1,067m) over the course of five miles—a continuous climb with little respite. In many places, the incline will exceed 10%. Alternatively, you can begin at the Glen Creek trailhead. It will add a couple of (relatively flat) miles to your hike, but you will start out more than 1,500 feet (457m) higher in elevation and thus have less incline. When you reach the top, you are rewarded with incredible views of Paradise Valley to the north of the park, the Washburn and Absaroka ranges to the east, and Gardner's Hole to the south, etc. From the main trail, there is a short side trail that takes you out to an overlook of the rock formations that gave the mountain its name.

It is possible to get to the summit and back in a day, but many include this hike at the beginning of a hike into the Gallatin area trails. The trail was constructed in 1923.

Sheepeater Ski Trail — MAP 1-2

TYPE:	PTP	CAT:	TH	CLASS:	B	SURF:	TRAIL	DIST:	1	STATUS:	E
DIFF:	2	TRAF:	1	CHILD:	N	HACC:	N	USE:	H K	LENGTH:	2.98
ELEV A:	7269	ELEV B:	7244	ELEV G:	147	ELEV L:	-173	NET:	-25	BMA:	- -
MIN:	7239	MAX:	7347	AVG:	7297	AVG +:	1.6%	AVG -:	2.5%	OPEN:	YR

Reference Point	A-B Mi	A-B Km	B-A Mi	B-A Km	Latitude	Longitude
Trailhead @ Sheepeater Cliff Parking Area	0.00	0.00	2.98	4.80	44.89135	-110.72974
Sheepeater Canyon Overlook	2.19	3.52	0.79	1.27	44.91371	-110.71059
Jct w/ Bunsen Peak Trail	2.98	4.80	0.00	0.00	44.92287	-110.70238

This trail is primarily a winter ski trail and is not maintained (marked) for use as a hiking trail during the summer. Still, you can take this path from the Sheepeater Cliff Picnic Area up to the Bunsen Peak Trail and beyond if you wish. During the winter, you can pick up a Xanterra shuttle (for a fee) that will drop you off at the Indian Creek Warming Hut. From there, you ski about a half mile north along the road, then into the picnic area and on to the trail. Once you connect up with the Bunsen Peak Trail, you can follow it around the east side of the peak and down into the YACC Camp and back to Mammoth. The total distance doing this is a little over nine miles (excellent cross-country skiing, though).

Snow Pass Trail — MAP 1-4,1-5

TYPE:	PTP	CAT:	BC	CLASS:	B	SURF:	TRAIL	DIST:	1	STATUS:	E
DIFF:	2	TRAF:	2	CHILD:	N	HACC:	N	USE:	H S K	LENGTH:	2.10
ELEV A:	6787	ELEV B:	7434	ELEV G:	774	ELEV L:	-127	NET:	647	BMA:	- -
MIN:	6787	MAX:	7475	AVG:	7236	AVG +:	8.9%	AVG -:	4.7%	OPEN:	YR

Reference Point	A-B Mi	A-B Km	B-A Mi	B-A Km	Latitude	Longitude
Trailhead 1K2 (2.5 mi S of Mammoth Junction)	0.00	0.00	2.10	3.38	44.95897	-110.71212
Jct with spur trail to YCC Housing Area	0.03	0.05	2.07	3.33	44.95919	-110.71259
Jct with Howard Eaton Trail (parallels trail for .03 mi)	0.15	0.24	1.95	3.14	44.95946	-110.71487
Divergence from Howard Eaton Trail. Take right fork	0.18	0.29	1.92	3.09	44.95917	-110.71508
Jct with Clagett Butte Trail	1.00	1.61	1.10	1.77	44.96079	-110.72789
Begin paralleling power lines	1.16	1.87	0.94	1.51	44.96007	-110.73063
Summit Lake	1.40	2.25	0.70	1.13	44.95946	-110.73521
Trail split. Stay R for Sportsman Lake, L for Trailhead	1.84	2.96	0.26	0.42	44.96024	-110.74361
Jct with Sportsman Lake Trail	2.10	3.38	0.00	0.00	44.95960	-110.74791

The Snow Pass Trail is rarely mentioned in most guidebooks, and then usually only in the context of making loops associated with other trails in the area. And it is not one of the most popular trails in the park (as evidenced by the small parking pullout across from the trailhead[3]).

This is another of the trails that have a historical connection to the park. In the first few years of the park's existence, the road that people used to get from the Mammoth area up onto Swan Lake Flat and into Gardner's Hole traveled through Snow Pass. This ended in 1884 when the road through Golden Gate Canyon was completed.

This trail follows a part of that old road as it climbs up the north shoulder of Terrace Mountain. The stagecoach drivers of the day absolutely hated this route because they typically had to get off their coaches and have the passengers get out and help push the rig up the steep grade. It was often referred to in the day as "Hell Gate."[4]

Of course, this trail can also be used as an alternate way into the Sportsman Lake and/or Fawn Pass trails. You can also make a good loop if you use Snow Pass to get to Clagett Butte and then the Sepulcher Mountain trails. Aside from the historical nature of the trail, the only other feature of interest is Summit Lake, which is a small, seasonal lake on the pass itself (and not to be confused with the Summit Lake west of Old Faithful). Though this trail is open year-round, it gets its name legitimately. It is not uncommon for this pass to be covered in snow until well into the late parts of June.

Solfatara Trail — MAP 1-11

TYPE:	PTP	CAT:	BC	CLASS:	B	SURF:	TRAIL	DIST:	1	STATUS:	E
DIFF:	3	TRAF:	2	CHILD:	N	HACC:	N	USE:	H S	LENGTH:	6.41
ELEV A:	7436	ELEV B:	7500	ELEV G:	833	ELEV L:	-769	NET:	64	BMA:	- -
MIN:	7427	MAX:	7895	AVG:	7616	AVG +:	6.2%	AVG -:	3.5%	OPEN:	YR

Reference Point	A-B Mi	A-B Km	B-A Mi	B-A Km	Latitude	Longitude
North Trailhead 1K7 (7.1 mi N of Norris Junction)	0.00	0.00	6.41	10.32	44.80660	-110.73471
Lemonade Creek crossing	0.07	0.11	6.34	10.20	44.80677	-110.73336
Enter the Amphitheater Springs Thermal Area	0.62	1.00	5.79	9.32	44.80182	-110.72665
Power line Crossing	0.64	1.03	5.77	9.29	44.80174	-110.72615
Trail begins following power lines	0.82	1.32	5.59	9.00	44.80064	-110.72326
Hibbard's Pass	0.94	1.51	5.47	8.80	44.80007	-110.72107
Old "Norris" Stagecoach Road	0.97	1.56	5.44	8.75	44.79993	-110.72047
Thermal drainage to Lake of the Woods	1.22	1.96	5.19	8.35	44.79710	-110.71735
Best social trail to Lake of the Woods	1.45	2.33	4.96	7.98	44.79460	-110.71453
Extinct section of Whiterock Springs Thermal Area	2.41	3.88	4.00	6.44	44.78486	-110.70091
Whiterock Springs Thermal Area	2.73	4.39	3.68	5.92	44.78085	-110.69773
Pick up Solfatara Creek	3.19	5.13	3.22	5.18	44.77691	-110.69068
Enter unnamed thermal area along Solfatara Creek	5.62	9.04	0.79	1.27	44.74547	-110.68064
Jct with Howard Eaton - Chain of Lakes Trail	5.93	9.54	0.48	0.77	44.74241	-110.68496
South Trailhead 4K1 (Norris Campground)	6.41	10.32	0.00	0.00	44.73814	-110.69214

This trail (referred to in some other guides as the Solfatara Creek Trail) is one of the more interesting ones in the park. It, too, follows one of the original roads in the park, but also takes you through a couple of interesting thermal areas that most other visitors to the park do not get to see.

A solfatara is a steam vent in which sulfur gases are the primary constituent. You will understand why this trail (and the creek it is named after) has this name as you hike through the area. This trail is not well-maintained, but the fact that much of it runs along a wide powerline easement means you should have little trouble navigating through.

You will start off by crossing Lemonade Creek, so named because of the yellow-green sulfur deposits that can be found along the stream. And though the water may look enticing, you do not want to drink it. You then face a 400-foot (122m) climb over the next mile or so as you climb through the Amphitheater Springs Thermal Area up onto the Solfatara Plateau.

From that point you will be going downhill slightly until you get to the trail's end at the Norris Campground. If you are staying in the campground and have a few hours to spare, this is a great out and back hike to occupy yourself with.

Trilobite Lake Trail — MAP 1-10

TYPE:	O&B	CAT:	BC	CLASS:	C	SURF:	TRAIL	DIST:	1	STATUS:	E
DIFF:	3	TRAF:	1	CHILD:	N	HACC:	N	USE:	H S	LENGTH:	2.35
ELEV A:	7684	ELEV B:	8362	ELEV G:	976	ELEV L:	-298	NET:	678	BMA:	- -
MIN:	7684	MAX:	8562	AVG:	8130	AVG +:	9.4%	AVG -:	12.2%	OPEN:	YR

Reference Point	A-B Mi	A-B Km	B-A Mi	B-A Km	Latitude	Longitude
Jct with Mt. Holmes Trail	0.00	0.00	2.35	3.78	44.81127	-110.80115
Trail termination at Trilobite Lake	2.35	3.78	0.00	0.00	44.82918	-110.83377

Trilobite Lake, so named because of the presence of trilobite fossils found in rocks in the area, is a small, out-of-the-way lake located on the northeastern flank of Mt. Holmes. There are actually several small lakes in the area with this name. The trail takes you to the lower (main) Trilobite Lake. Approximately 700 yards (640m) west of this is Middle Trilobite Lake, and about 500 yards (457m) southwest of that is Upper Trilobite Lake (about 900 yards (823m) west southwest of the lower lake).

There are no official trails to the other two lakes, so you will likely have to do a bit of bushwhacking to get to them. Even the main trail receives little maintenance, so it may be difficult to follow at times, especially early in the season (and then it will likely be marshy and soggy in many places). The lower lake has had a small population of (non-native) brook trout in it, but the other two are fishless. This trail makes an excellent side trip if you happen to be staying at one of the Mt. Holmes campsites for a couple of days.

I know people who have climbed to the summit of Mt. Holmes from this area, hiking up the northeast shoulder of the mountain. Doing this requires some serious climbing as you will have a 1,375-foot (419m) elevation gain over the first half mile.

Wraith Falls Trail — MAP 1-6

Type:	O&B	**Cat:**	TH	**Class:**	B	**Surf:**	Trail	**Dist:**	1	**Status:**	E
Diff:	1	**Traf:**	4	**Child:**	Y	**HAcc:**	N	**Use:**	H	**Length:**	0.39
Elev A:	6611	**Elev B:**	6748	**Elev G:**	194	**Elev L:**	-58	**Net:**	137	**BMA:**	- -
Min:	6611	**Max:**	6748	**Avg:**	6646	**Avg +:**	9.2%	**Avg -:**	5.3%	**Open:**	YR

Reference Point	A-B Mi	A-B Km	B-A Mi	B-A Km	Latitude	Longitude
Trailhead (4.9 mi E of Mammoth Junction)	0.00	0.00	0.39	0.63	44.94225	-110.62343
Lupine Creek crossing	0.30	0.48	0.09	0.14	44.93809	-110.62424
Observation Platform	0.39	0.63	0.00	0.00	44.93757	-110.62381

Wraith Falls (on Lupine Creek) is one of the prettiest waterfalls in the park in the early part of the year during the snow melt. As the season progresses, however, the waterfall gets smaller and smaller. A wraith is a ghostlike apparition, and the waterfall gets its name from early visitors who thought its appearance resembled that of a wraith.

This trail, built in 1919, is very easy and very short, with little elevation change, and is therefore great for small children.

YCC to Snow Pass Connector Trail — MAP 1-4,1-5

Type:	PTP	**Cat:**	TH	**Class:**	U	**Surf:**	Trail	**Dist:**	1	**Status:**	U
Diff:	3	**Traf:**	1	**Child:**	N	**HAcc:**	N	**Use:**	H S	**Length:**	0.57
Elev A:	6459	**Elev B:**	6798	**Elev G:**	362	**Elev L:**	-23	**Net:**	339	**BMA:**	- -
Min:	6459	**Max:**	6798	**Avg:**	6621	**Avg +:**	12.4%	**Avg -:**	8.1%	**Open:**	YR

Reference Point	A-B Mi	A-B Km	B-A Mi	B-A Km	Latitude	Longitude
Trailhead @ YCC Entrance	0.00	0.00	0.57	0.92	44.95905	-110.70344
Cross Norris to Mammoth Road	0.54	0.87	0.03	0.05	44.95941	-110.71209
Trailhead @ Snow Pass Trail	0.57	0.92	0.00	0.00	44.95919	-110.71259

This trail is used primarily by park employees who live in the YACC Camp complex to get to the Snow Pass Trail. Visitors can, of course, use it as well, but if you have a vehicle, you may as well park at the little pulloff at the trailhead rather than adding a half mile to each end of your hike.

YCC Trail — MAP 1-4

Type:	PTP	**Cat:**	FC	**Class:**	B	**Surf:**	Trail	**Dist:**	1	**Status:**	E
Diff:	1	**Traf:**	2	**Child:**	Y	**HAcc:**	N	**Use:**	H S	**Length:**	1.10
Elev A:	6463	**Elev B:**	6286	**Elev G:**	62	**Elev L:**	-239	**Net:**	-177	**BMA:**	- -
Min:	6286	**Max:**	6463	**Avg:**	6368	**Avg +:**	4.1%	**Avg -:**	5.5%	**Open:**	YR

Reference Point	A-B Mi	A-B Km	B-A Mi	B-A Km	Latitude	Longitude
South Trailhead @ YCC Camp Entrance	0.00	0.00	1.10	1.77	44.95875	-110.70319
Fort Yellowstone Cemetery/Mammoth Corrals	0.44	0.71	0.66	1.06	44.96459	-110.70091
Driveway for the Mammoth Corrals	0.55	0.89	0.55	0.89	44.96616	-110.70069
Original Walkway for Lodge to Hotel	0.60	0.97	0.50	0.80	44.96682	-110.70098
Lost Creek crossing (footbridge)	0.69	1.11	0.41	0.66	44.96809	-110.70107
Capitol Hill	0.94	1.51	0.16	0.26	44.97140	-110.70301
Little Joker Spring	0.98	1.58	0.12	0.19	44.97197	-110.70343
Terminates at the Opal Terrace Parking Lot	1.10	1.77	0.00	0.00	44.97331	-110.70332

Though primarily a trail for Mammoth employees who live in the YACC Camp complex to get to work, this trail has some utility for those who wish to get back to Mammoth from other trails further south (specifically the Bunsen Peak Service Road Trail and the Snow Pass Trail). If you arrive into the YACC Camp from either of these other trails, you can make it all the way back to Mammoth using this path.

This trail is unique in a way. Part of it (the section between the old corrals and Opal Terrace) has been designated as historic. This section of trail was constructed back when the old Mammoth Lodge and Cabins existed on the large flat space just north of the corrals. It was the path guests of the lodge used to get to the stores, the hotel, and restaurants up until the lodge operation was shut down in the late 1930s. It is considered an important part of the Mammoth Hot Springs Historic District. As you cross over Lost Creek, note the detailed rock and concrete work that provide the trail with its unique character.

If you use this trail, be sure to visit the Fort Yellowstone Cemetery. Many of the park's early visitors and employees or members of their families are buried here (including several stillborn infants). The U.S. Army also buried its soldiers here during the time they ran the park, but they've since been disinterred and relocated to military cemeteries elsewhere.

Yellowstone River Trail — MAP 1-9

TYPE:	PTP	CAT:	BC	CLASS:	A	SURF:	TRAIL	DIST:	1	STATUS:	E
DIFF:	3	TRAF:	2	CHILD:	N	HACC:	N	USE:	H S	LENGTH:	15.55
ELEV A:	6128	ELEV B:	5873	ELEV G:	2835	ELEV L:	-3090	NET:	-255	BMA:	- -
MIN:	5300	MAX:	6325	AVG:	5686	AVG +:	6.8%	AVG -:	6.3%	OPEN:	YR

Reference Point	A-B Mi	A-B Km	B-A Mi	B-A Km	Latitude	Longitude
Trailhead 1N1 (Off White Lane in Gardiner)	0.00	0.00	15.55	25.03	45.04540	-110.67801
Road crossing	0.18	0.29	15.37	24.74	45.04372	-110.67545
Begin paralleling Bear Creek	1.51	2.43	14.04	22.60	45.03612	-110.66565
Intersection with original/old Yellowstone Trail	2.00	3.22	13.55	21.81	45.03077	-110.66994
Entrance into the Bear Creek Thermal Area	2.10	3.38	13.45	21.65	45.03100	-110.66936
Footbridge crossing over Bear Creek	2.24	3.60	13.31	21.42	45.03109	-110.66599
Enter Yellowstone boundary	2.74	4.41	12.81	20.62	45.02988	-110.65777
Spur to campsite 1Y1	4.95	7.97	10.60	17.06	45.01415	-110.62608
Spur to campsite 1Y2	5.93	9.54	9.62	15.48	45.01580	-110.61064
Social trails to Knowles Falls	6.92	11.14	8.63	13.89	45.01342	-110.52389
Crevice Mountain Patrol Cabin Spur	7.35	11.83	8.20	13.20	45.01145	-110.58708
Spur to campsite 1Y4	8.00	12.87	7.55	12.15	45.00411	-110.58027
Crevice Lake	8.19	13.18	7.36	11.84	45.00216	-110.57766
Jct with Blacktail Deer Trail	8.54	13.74	7.01	11.28	44.99812	-110.57433
Spur to campsite 1Y5 (0.11 mi)	8.72	14.03	6.83	10.99	44.99634	-110.57214

Reference Point	A-B Mi	A-B Km	B-A Mi	B-A Km	Latitude	Longitude
Spur to campsite 1Y7 (0.14 mi)	9.47	15.24	6.08	9.78	44.99262	-110.55859
Spur to campsite 1Y9 (0.12 mi)	10.06	16.19	5.49	8.84	44.99456	-110.54709
Cottonwood Creek crossing (often dry)	11.68	18.80	3.87	6.23	44.99385	-110.51660
Spur to campsite 1R1	11.73	18.88	3.82	6.15	44.99369	-110.51605
Spur to campsite 1R2 (0.11 mi)	11.82	19.02	3.73	6.00	44.99370	-110.51418
Little Cottonwood Creek crossing (often dry)	13.25	21.32	2.30	3.70	44.99109	-110.48833
Spur to campsite 1R3	13.48	21.69	2.07	3.33	44.99084	-110.48311
Trail termination @ Hellroaring Creek Trail	15.55	25.03	0.00	0.00	44.97282	-110.45588

The Yellowstone River Trail (listed in many guides at the Black Canyon of the Yellowstone Trail or hike) is one of the most spectacular trails in the park, taking you along the mighty Yellowstone River and through the Black Canyon of the Yellowstone, one of the most visually stunning areas in the park. The canyon is almost 1,000 feet (304m) deep and in some places the walls are sheer. The trail was originally constructed as a "fire lane" by the U.S. Army in 1918 to allow crews to access forest fires occurring north of the Yellowstone River.

Many older guides list the western trailhead for this as being in Gardiner. When this was the case, the trail crossed a section of private land. The property owners have since disallowed public access to their land, so the NPS was forced to relocate the trailhead to USFS property in Jardine. Do not go to Gardiner thinking you can access this trail from the old location. There are no signs to the current trailhead, so follow the signs to Jardine in Gardiner, and use your GPS to get to the trailhead.

This trail has little shade on it until you get to the canyon area, so use sunscreen and ensure you have plenty of water with you. It is tough to get into the area and back out and still have time to see everything in a single day, and there are several good quality campsites along this trail. Plan to spend at least one night here and take your time. Even starting from the east side at the Hellroaring Trail trailhead, it is tough to get in and out in a single day.

There are three primary ways to hike this trail. The first, of course, is to hike from the USFS trailhead in Jardine. The second, and more popular route, is to hike north along the Blacktail Deer Creek Trail, then east on the Yellowstone River Trail, and come out on the Hellroaring Creek Trail. And last, you can go in from the east side using the Hellroaring Creek Trail and hike it "backwards."

If you elect to go in or come out via the Hellroaring Creek Trail, note that you will have to ford Hellroaring Creek. Do not let the name fool you. It is a rather large creek, and early in the season (prior to mid-July in most years), it may be unsafe to ford. In that case, you will need to hike about a mile and a half upstream and use the stock bridge, and then return along the other side to get back to the trail. At one time there was a footbridge on the main trail, but it was washed out and has not been replaced for some reason.

There are several excellent campsites along the Yellowstone River. 1Y1 and 1Y7 are particularly popular, so if you wish to stay in those, it might be a good idea to use the reservation system to grab them if you've settled on specific dates for your hike. There are four outstanding sites along the Hellroaring Creek west of the trail that make for excellent layover points on your hike. This trail (specifically the part through the Black Canyon) is considered to be one of the most scenic in the northern half of the park, and is highly recommended for a multi-day trip if you are looking for one in the Mammoth-Tower area.

Map 1-1

Mammoth District Trail Map

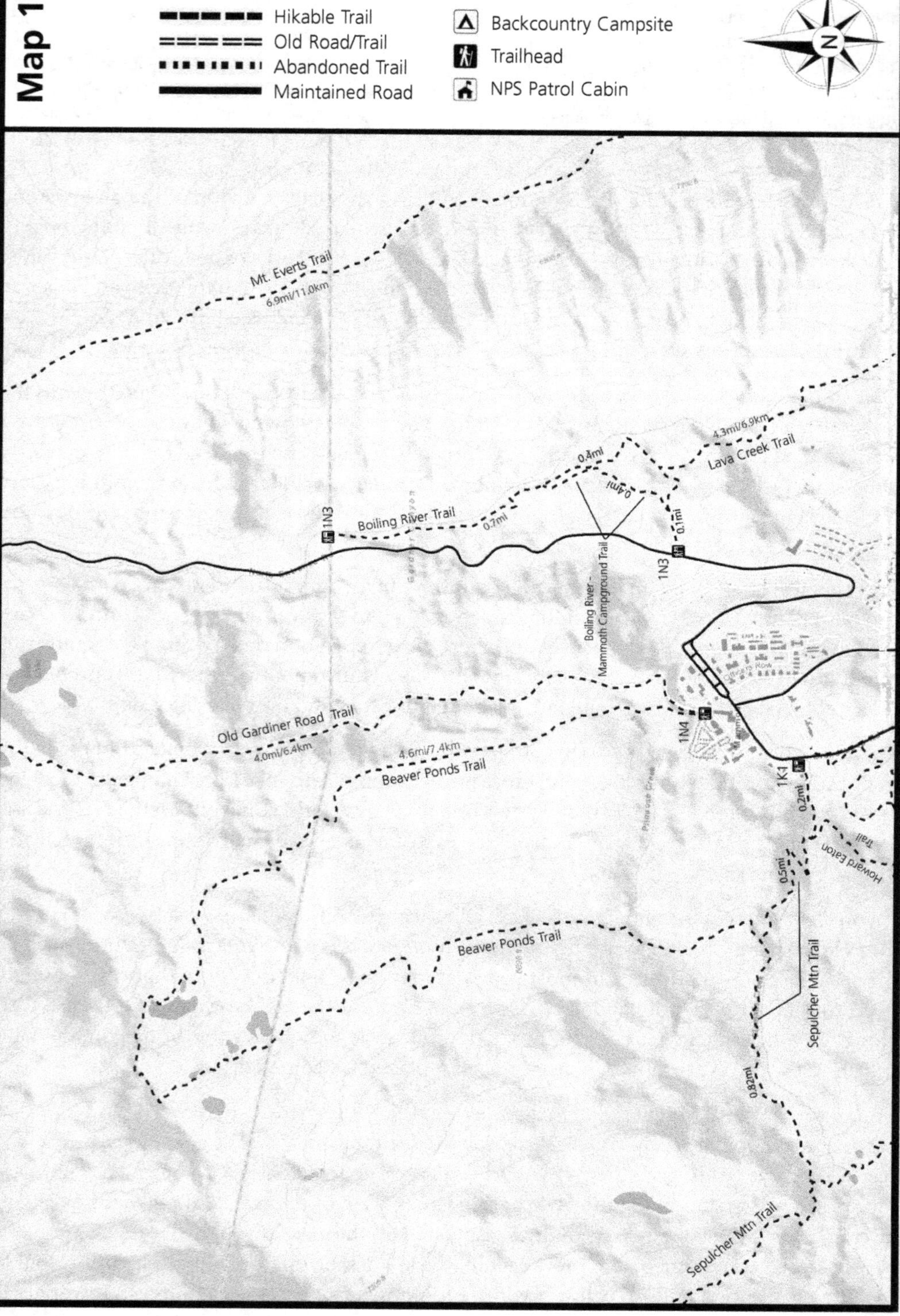

Hikable Trail
Old Road/Trail
Abandoned Trail
Maintained Road

Backcountry Campsite
Trailhead
NPS Patrol Cabin

N

Mt. Everts Trail
6.9mi/11.0km
4.3mi/6.9km
Lava Creek Trail
0.4mi
0.4mi
0.1mi
1N3
Boiling River Trail
0.7mi
1N3
Boiling River - Mammoth Campground Trail
Officers Row
Old Gardiner Road Trail
4.0mi/6.4km
4.6mi/7.4km
Beaver Ponds Trail
1N4
1K1
0.2mi
Howard Eaton Trail
0.5mi
Beaver Ponds Trail
Sepulcher Mtn Trail
0.82mi
Sepulcher Mtn Trail

Map 1-2

Mammoth District Trail Map

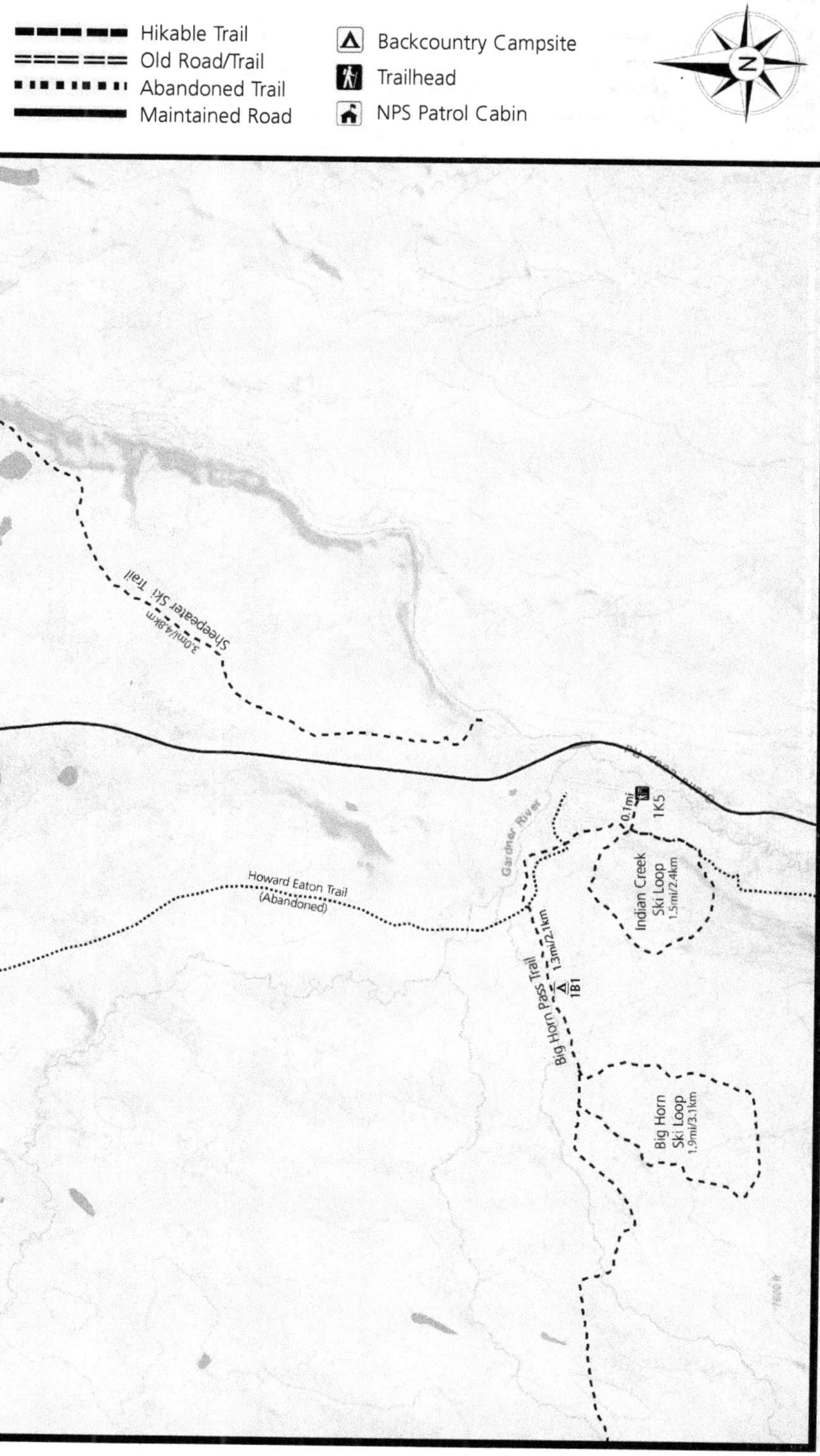

Hikable Trail
Old Road/Trail
Abandoned Trail
Maintained Road
Backcountry Campsite
Trailhead
NPS Patrol Cabin
N
Gardner River
Bunsen Peak Trail
Sheepeater Ski Trail
3.0mi/4.8km
Howard Eaton Trail
(Abandoned)
Gardner River
0.1mi
1K5
Indian Creek
Ski Loop
1.5mi/2.4km
Big Horn Pass Trail
1.3mi/2.1km
1B1
Big Horn
Ski Loop
1.9mi/3.1km

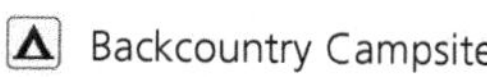

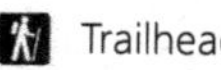

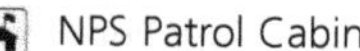

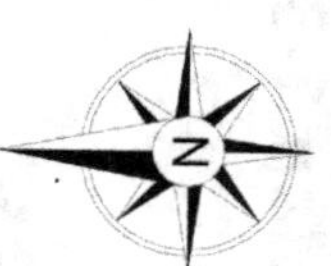

Map 1-3

Mammoth District Trail Map

Hikable Trail
Old Road/Trail
Abandoned Trail
Maintained Road
Backcountry Campsite
Trailhead
NPS Patrol Cabin

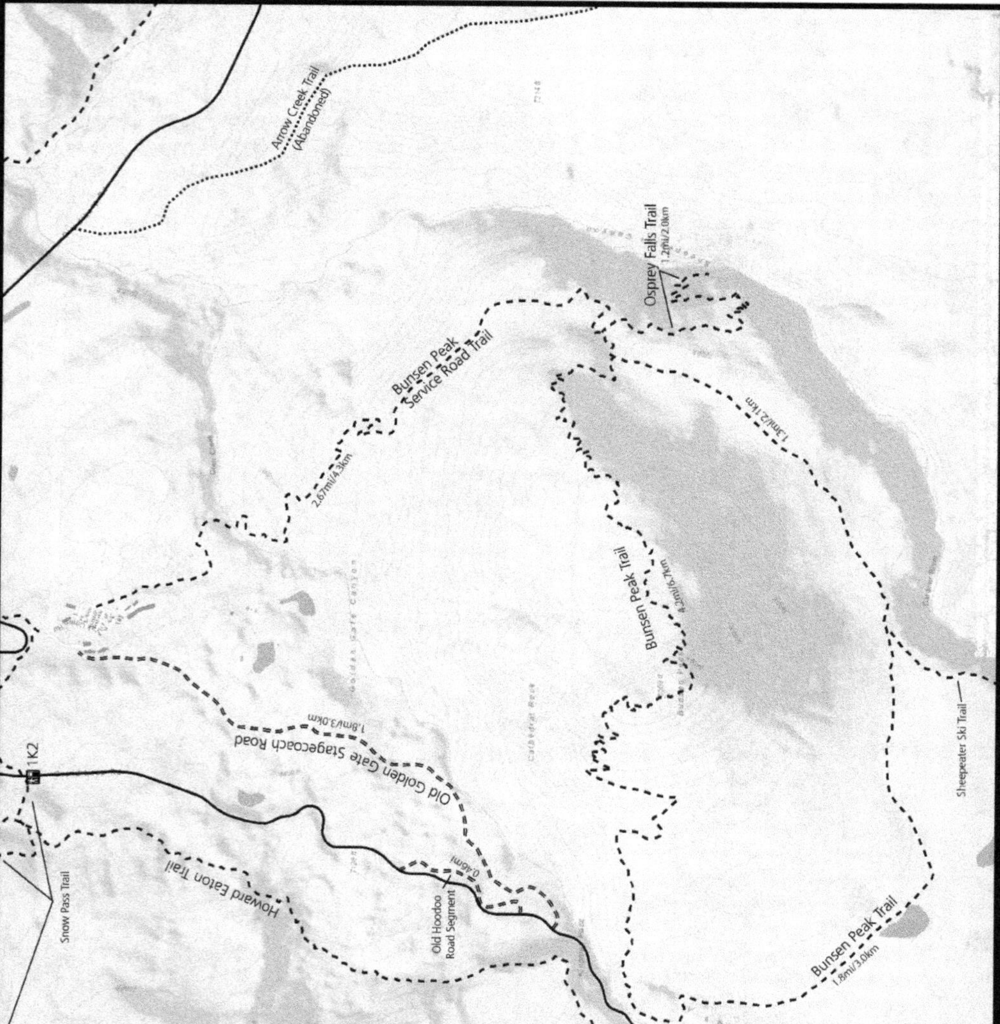

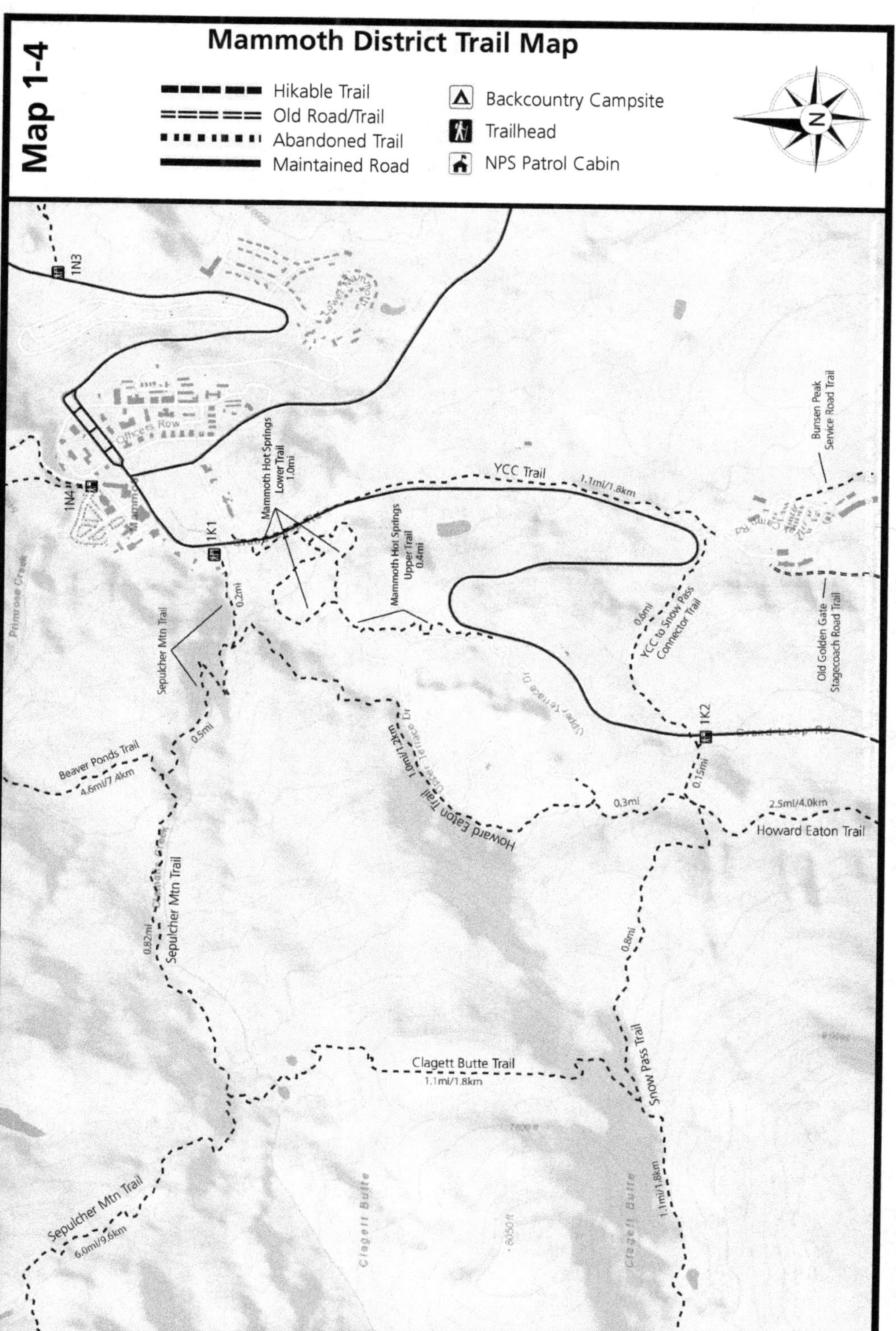
Map 1-4
Mammoth District Trail Map
Hikable Trail
Old Road/Trail
Abandoned Trail
Maintained Road
Backcountry Campsite
Trailhead
NPS Patrol Cabin
N
1N3
1N4
Officers Row
Mammoth Hot Springs Lower Trail 1.0mi
Mammoth Hot Springs Upper Trail 0.4mi
YCC Trail
1.1mi/1.8km
1K1
0.2mi
Sepulcher Mtn Trail
Primrose Creek
0.5mi
Beaver Ponds Trail
4.6mi/7.4km
Howard Eaton Trail
1.0mi/1.2km
Upper Terrace Dr
0.6mi
YCC to Snow Pass Connector Trail
1K2
Grand Loop Rd
0.15mi
0.3mi
2.5mi/4.0km
Howard Eaton Trail
Bunsen Peak Service Road Trail
Old Golden Gate Stagecoach Road Trail
0.82mi
Sepulcher Mtn Trail
0.8mi
Snow Pass Trail
Clagett Butte Trail
1.1mi/1.8km
Sepulcher Mtn Trail
6.0mi/9.6km
Clagett Butte
8050 ft
Clagett Butte
1.1mi/1.8km

Map 1-5

Mammoth District Trail Map

Hikable Trail
Old Road/Trail
Abandoned Trail
Maintained Road
Backcountry Campsite
Trailhead
NPS Patrol Cabin

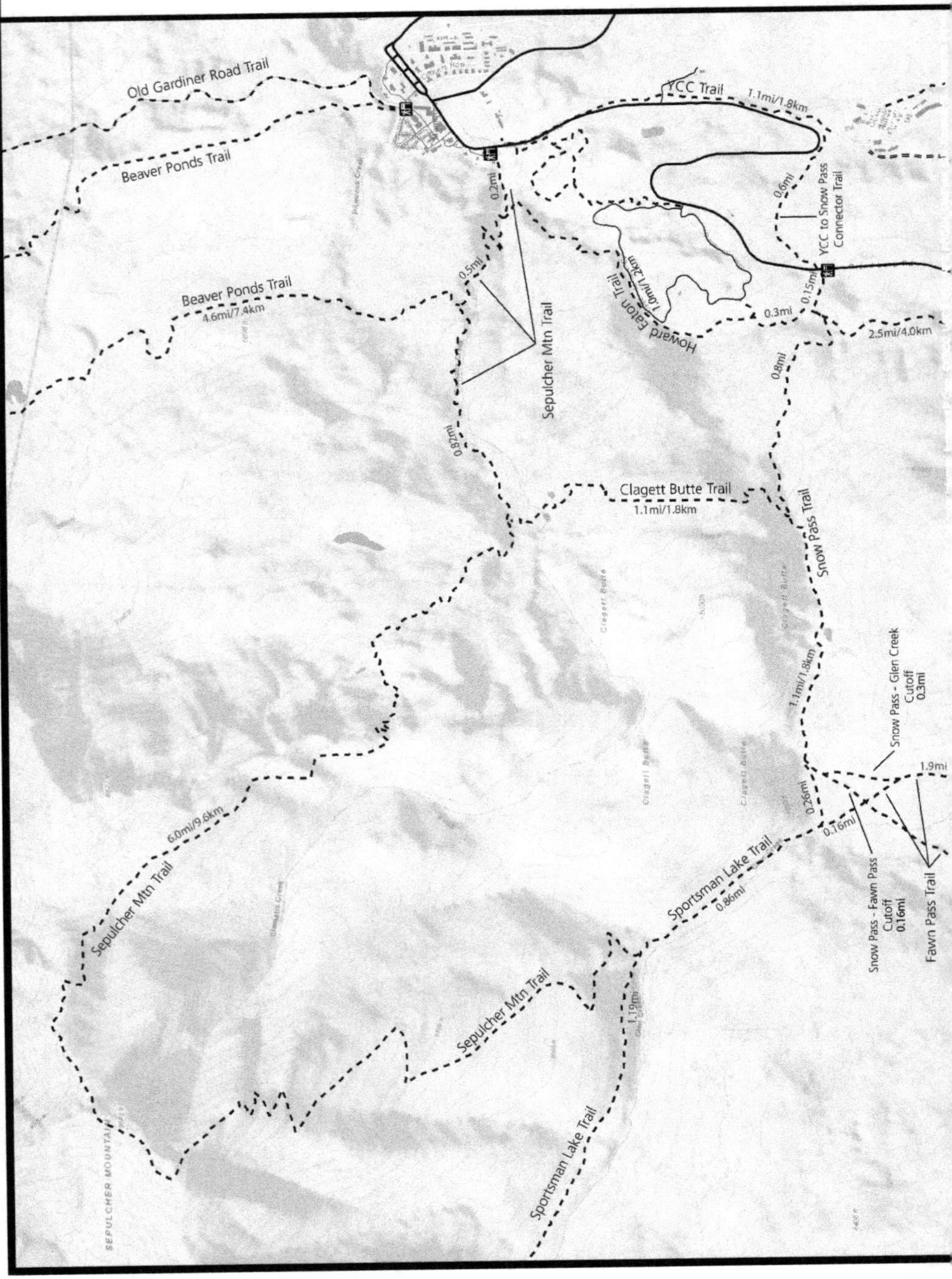

Old Gardiner Road Trail
Beaver Ponds Trail
YCC Trail
1.1mi/1.8km
0.2mi
0.6mi
YCC to Snow Pass Connector Trail
0.5mi
Beaver Ponds Trail
4.6mi/7.4km
Howard Eaton Trail
1.0mi/1.2km
0.15mi
0.3mi
2.5mi/4.0km
Sepulcher Mtn Trail
0.8mi
0.82mi
Clagett Butte Trail
1.1mi/1.8km
Snow Pass Trail
1.1mi/1.8km
Snow Pass - Glen Creek Cutoff 0.3mi
1.9mi
0.26mi
0.16mi
6.0mi/9.6km
Sepulcher Mtn Trail
Sportsman Lake Trail
0.86mi
Snow Pass - Fawn Pass Cutoff 0.16mi
Fawn Pass Trail
Sepulcher Mtn Trail
1.19mi
Sportsman Lake Trail
SEPULCHER MOUNTAIN

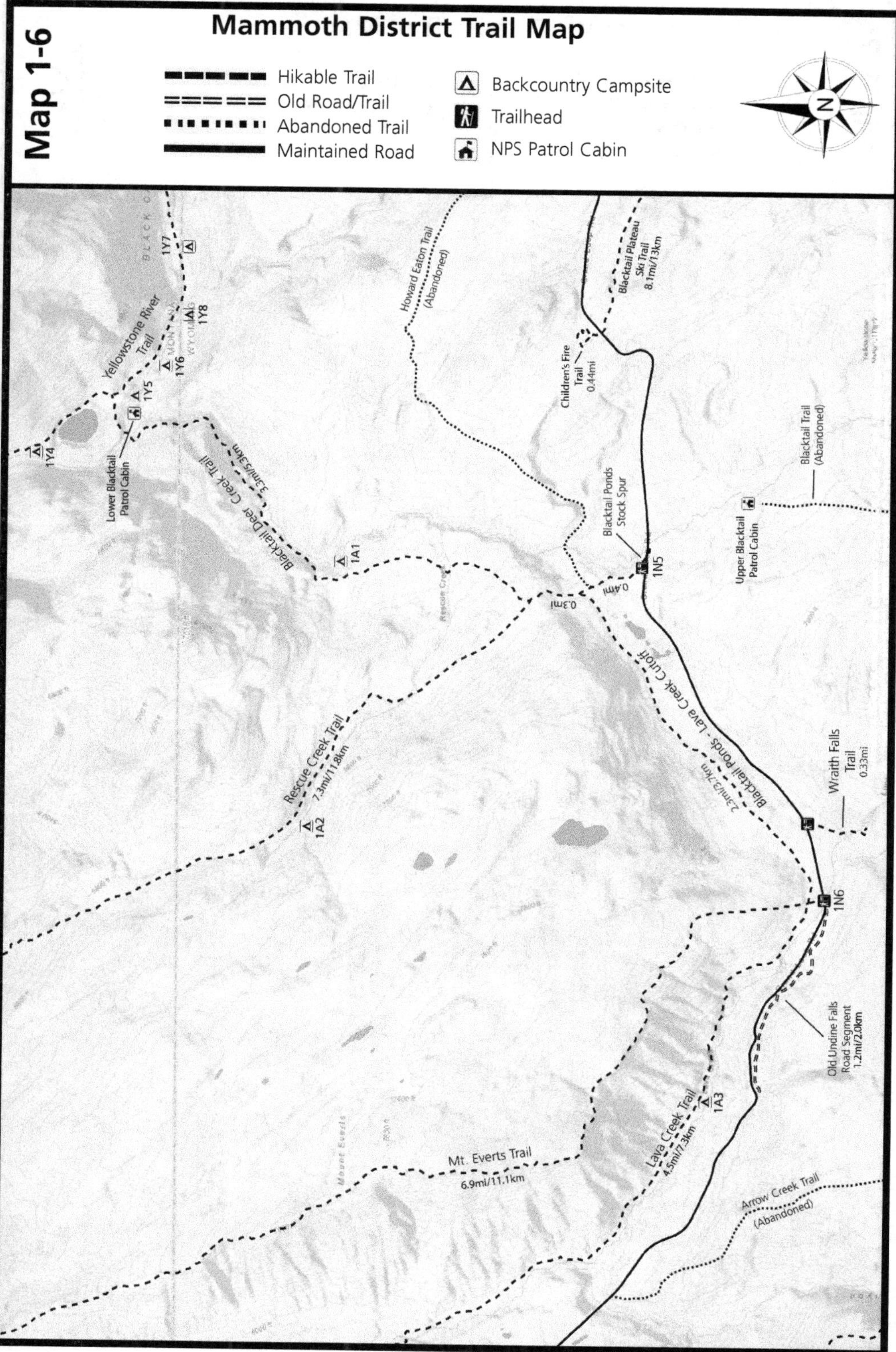

Map 1-6
Mammoth District Trail Map
Hikable Trail
Old Road/Trail
Abandoned Trail
Maintained Road
Backcountry Campsite
Trailhead
NPS Patrol Cabin
N
Yellowstone River Trail
1Y7
1Y8
1Y6
1Y5
1Y4
MONTANA
WYOMING
Lower Blacktail Patrol Cabin
Blacktail Deer Creek Trail
3.3mi/5.3km
1A1
Howard Eaton Trail (Abandoned)
Blacktail Plateau Ski Trail
8.1mi/13km
Children's Fire Trail
0.44mi
Blacktail Ponds Stock Spur
1N5
0.4mi
0.3mi
Rescue Creek
Upper Blacktail Patrol Cabin
Blacktail Trail (Abandoned)
Rescue Creek Trail
7.3mi/11.8km
1A2
Blacktail Ponds - Lava Creek Cutoff
2.3mi/3.7km
Wraith Falls Trail
0.33mi
1N6
Old Undine Falls Road Segment
1.2mi/2.0km
Lava Creek Trail
4.5mi/7.3km
1A3
Mount Everts
Mt. Everts Trail
6.9mi/11.1km
Arrow Creek Trail
(Abandoned)

Map 1-7

Mammoth District Trail Map

1Y7
1Y8
1Y6
1Y5
1Y4
Lower Blacktail Patrol Cabin
Blacktail Deer Creek Trail
3.3mi/5.3km
Howard Eaton Trail (Abandoned)
Upper Blacktail Patrol Cabin
1A1
0.3mi
0.4mi
Yellowstone River Trail
1Y2
Blacktail Ponds - Lava Creek Cutoff
2.3mi/3.7km
1Y1
1A2
Rescue Creek Trail
7.3mi/11.8km
1N6
Old Undine Falls Road Segment 1.2mi/2.0km
1A3
Lava Creek Trail
4.5mi/7.3km
Mt. Everts Trail
6.9mi/11.1km
Arrow Creek Trail (Abandoned)
Boiling River Trail
0.1mi
1N2
1N3
Old Gardiner Road Trail
4.0mi/6.4km
4.6mi/7.4km
Beaver Ponds Trail
1N4
1K1

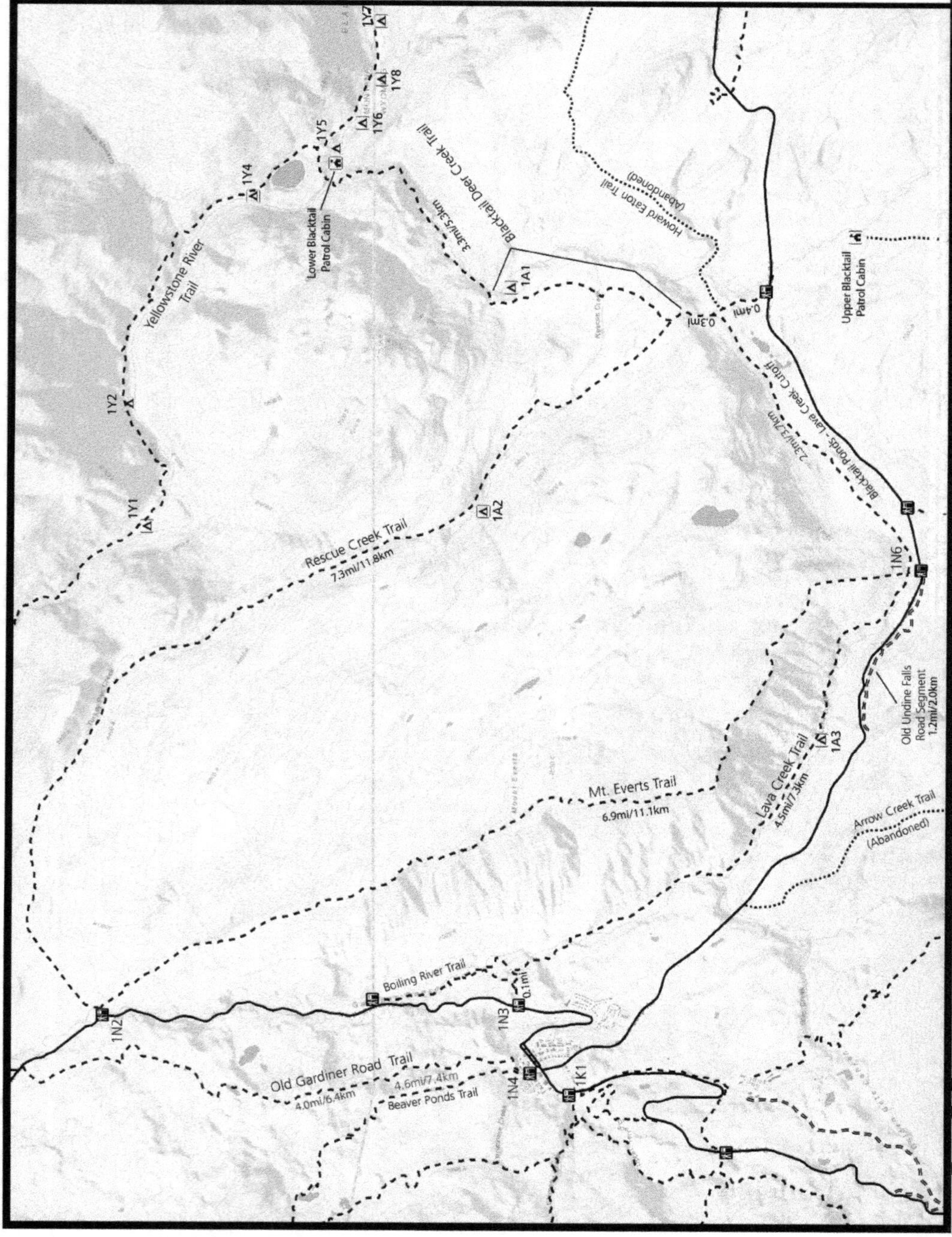

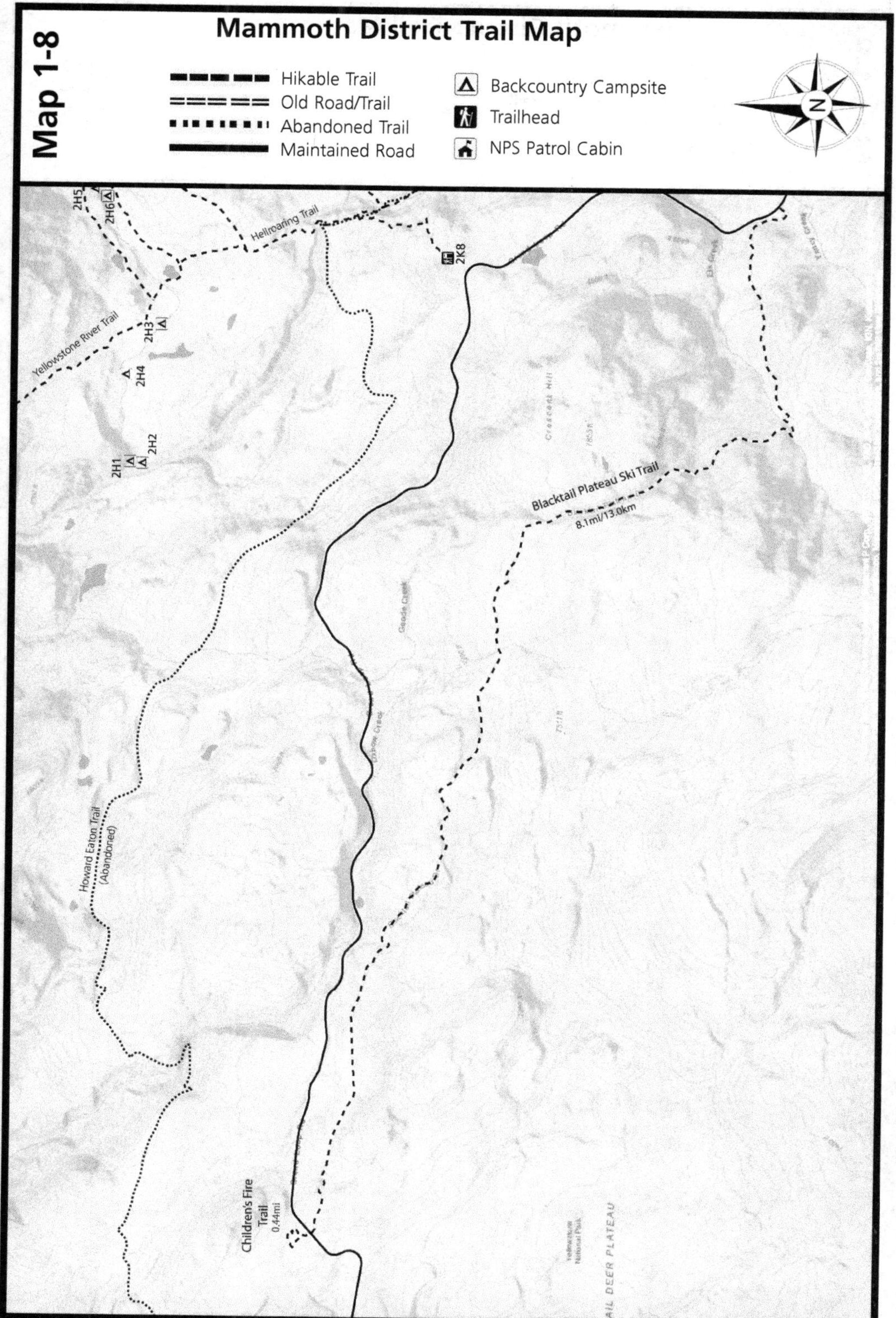

Map 1-8
Mammoth District Trail Map
Hikable Trail
Old Road/Trail
Abandoned Trail
Maintained Road
Backcountry Campsite
Trailhead
NPS Patrol Cabin
N
2H5
2H6
Hellroaring Trail
2K8
2H3
Yellowstone River Trail
2H4
2H2
2H1
Crescent Hill
Blacktail Plateau Ski Trail
8.1mi/13.0km
Geode Creek
Oxbow Creek
Howard Eaton Trail
(Abandoned)
Children's Fire Trail
0.44mi
BLACKTAIL DEER PLATEAU

Map 1-9

Mammoth District Trail Map

Hikable Trail

Old Road/Trail

Abandoned Trail

Maintained Road

2H5 2H6 2H3 2H4 2H1 2H2 1R3 1R1 1R2 1Y9 1Y7 1Y8 1Y5 1Y6 1Y4 1Y2 1Y1 1A1 1A2 1A3 1N1 1N5 1N6

Yellowstone River Trail

15.5mi/25.0km

Blacktail Plateau Ski Trail
8.1mi/13km

Howard Eaton Trail
(Abandoned)

Blacktail Trail
(Abandoned)

BLACKTAIL DEER PLATEAU

Crevice Mountain
Patrol Cabin

Lower Blacktail
Patrol Cabin

Blacktail Deer Creek Trail
3.3mi/5.3km

Upper Blacktail
Patrol Cabin

Blacktail Ponds - Lava Creek Cutoff
2.3mi/3.7km

Wraith Falls
Trail
0.33mi

Rescue Creek Trail
7.3mi/11.8km

Old Undine Falls
Road Segment
1.2mi/2.0km

Arrow Creek Trail
(Abandoned)

Mt. Everts Trail
6.9mi/11.1km

Lava Creek Trail
4.5mi/7.3km

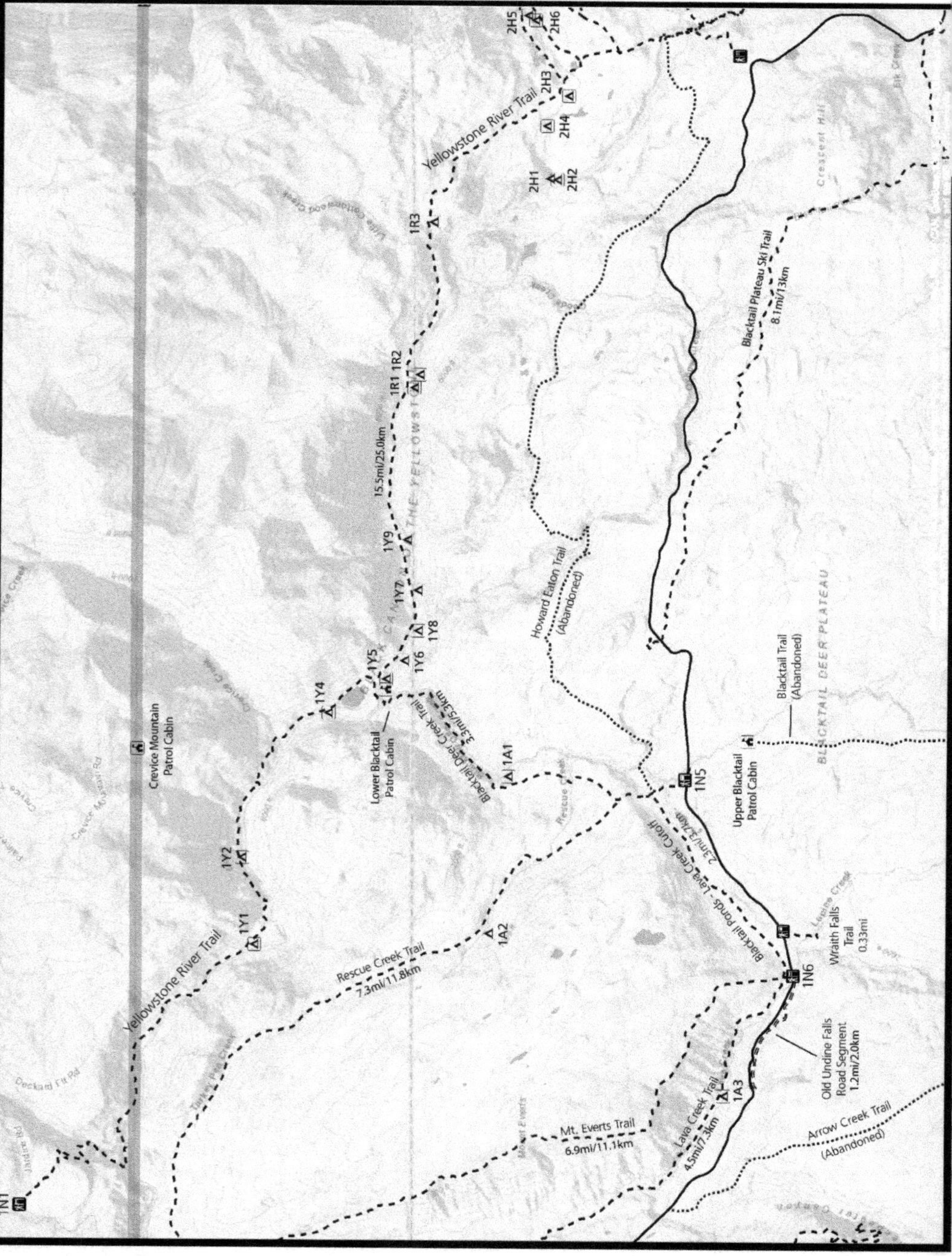

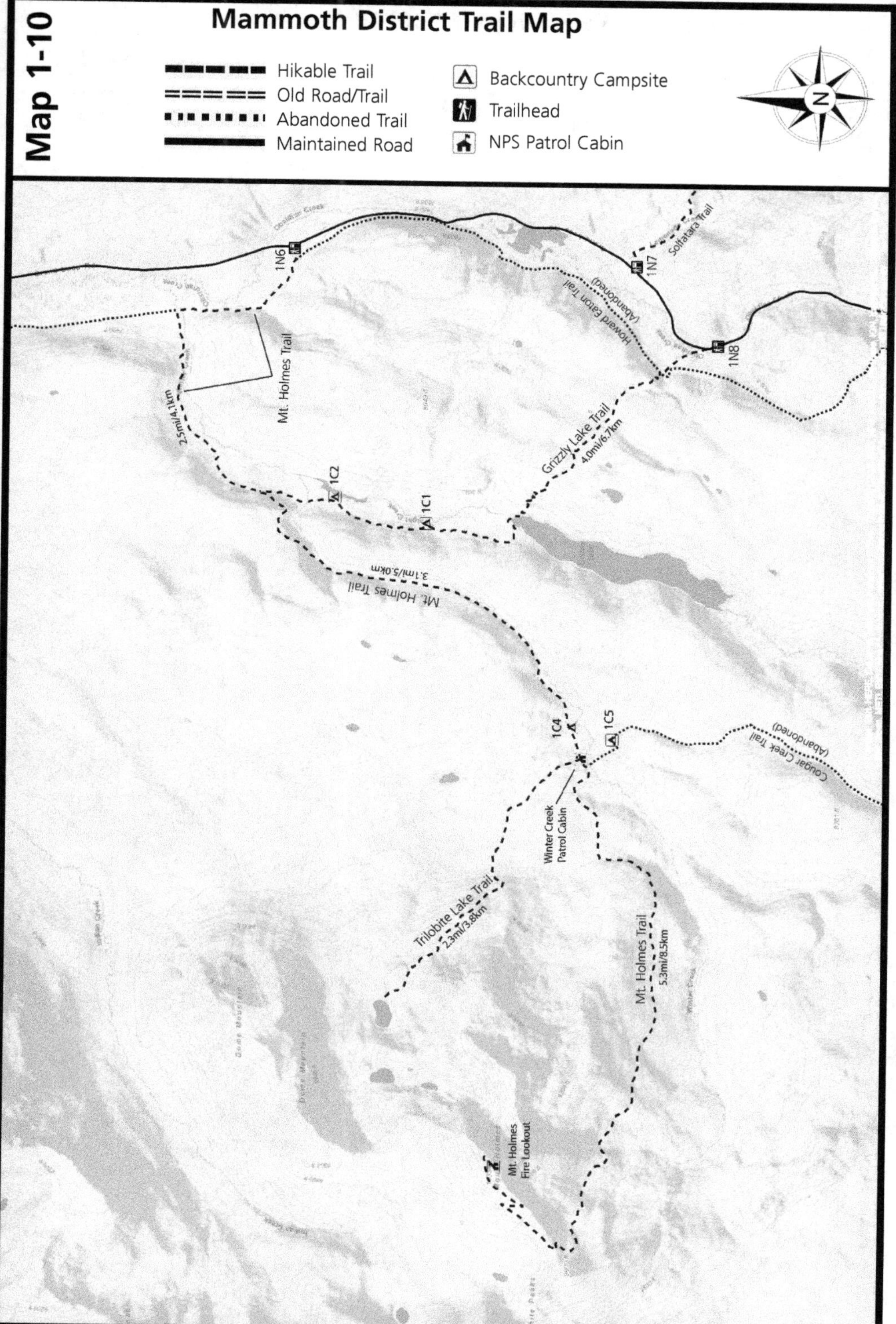

Map 1-10
Mammoth District Trail Map
Hikable Trail
Old Road/Trail
Abandoned Trail
Maintained Road
Backcountry Campsite
Trailhead
NPS Patrol Cabin
N
1N6
Mt. Holmes Trail
2.5mi/4.1km
1C2
1C1
Grizzly Lake Trail
4.0mi/6.7km
Howard Eaton Trail
(Abandoned)
1N7
Solfatara Trail
1N8
Mt. Holmes Trail
3.1mi/5.0km
1C4
1C5
Cougar Creek Trail
(Abandoned)
Winter Creek
Patrol Cabin
Trilobite Lake Trail
2.3mi/3.8km
Mt. Holmes Trail
5.3mi/8.5km
Mt. Holmes
Fire Lookout

Map 1-11

Mammoth District Trail Map

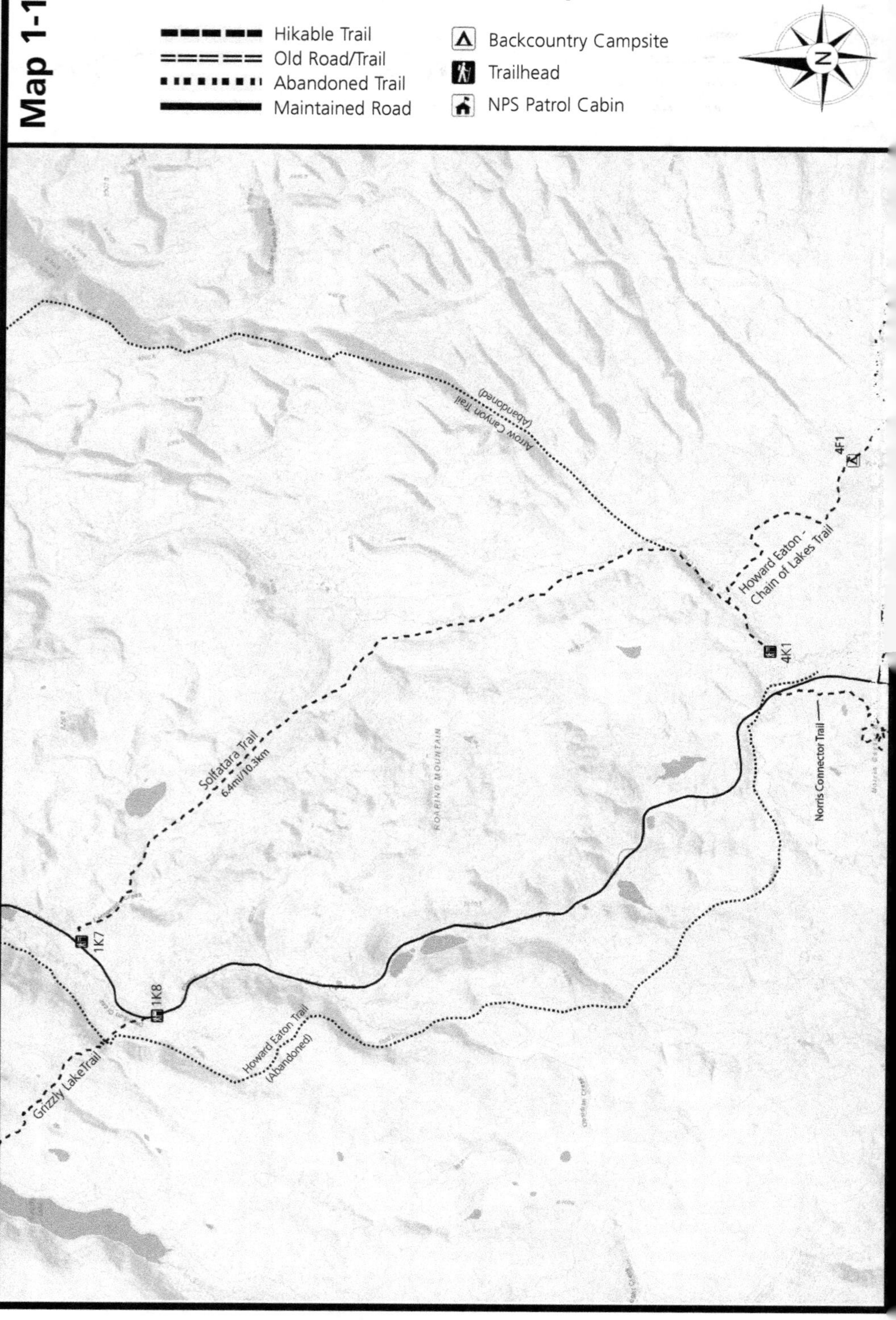

Hikable Trail
Old Road/Trail
Abandoned Trail
Maintained Road

Backcountry Campsite
Trailhead
NPS Patrol Cabin

Arrow Canyon Trail (Abandoned)

4F1

Howard Eaton - Chain of Lakes Trail

4K1

Norris Connector Trail

Solfatara Trail 6.4mi/10.3km

ROARING MOUNTAIN

1K7

1K8

Howard Eaton Trail (Abandoned)

Grizzly LakeTrail

Tower District Trails

Agate Creek Trail

MAP 2-1

TYPE:	O&B	CAT:	BC	CLASS:	C	SURF:	TRAIL	DIST:	2	STATUS:	E
DIFF:	3	TRAF:	1	CHILD:	N	HACC:	N	USE:	H S	LENGTH:	4.23
ELEV A:	7186	ELEV B:	6311	ELEV G:	715	ELEV L:	-1590	NET:	-875	BMA:	- -
MIN:	6311	MAX:	7638	AVG:	7231	AVG +:	6.5%	AVG -:	12.4%	OPEN:	YR

Reference Point	A-B Mi	A-B Km	B-A Mi	B-A Km	Latitude	Longitude
Trailhead @ jct w/ Specimen Ridge Trail	0.00	0.00	4.23	6.81	44.89261	-110.36168
Quartz Creek crossing	1.55	2.49	2.68	4.31	44.87487	-110.34486
Campsite 2Y1 and Petersen Falls	4.10	6.60	0.13	0.21	44.85216	-110.35832
Terminates at confluence of Yell River & Agate Creek	4.23	6.81	0.00	0.00	44.85032	-110.36009

The Agate Creek Trail is a fairly lightly used trail that has quite the reward at the end—a gorgeous waterfall. The campsite sits just above Petersen Falls on Agate Creek.

Most of the trail is out in the open without any water source, so be sure to pack plenty of water. There is a 1,300-foot (396m) drop over the last mile and a half (which means you climb back up on the way out, of course).

Baronett Bridge - Buffalo Ford Trail

MAP 2-4,2-

TYPE:	O&B	CAT:	TH	CLASS:	U	SURF:	TRAIL	DIST:	2	STATUS:	U
DIFF:	2	TRAF:	2	CHILD:	N	HACC:	N	USE:	H S	LENGTH:	2.26
ELEV A:	6123	ELEV B:	6023	ELEV G:	484	ELEV L:	-585	NET:	-100	BMA:	- -
MIN:	5998	MAX:	6316	AVG:	6116	AVG +:	7.5%	AVG -:	9.4%	OPEN:	YR

Reference Point	A-B Mi	A-B Km	B-A Mi	B-A Km	Latitude	Longitude
Trailhead @ Wrecker Pullout (1 mi N of Tower Jct)	0.00	0.00	2.26	3.64	44.92230	-110.40060
Spur to site of old Baronette Bridge	0.39	0.63	1.87	3.01	44.92760	-110.40071
Confluence of Lamar & Yellowstone Rivers	0.50	0.80	1.76	2.83	44.92901	-110.40147
Spur trail to old Junction Butte gravel pit	1.44	2.32	0.82	1.32	44.92538	-110.3898
Buffalo Ford (Lamar River)	2.26	3.64	0.00	0.00	44.92424	-110.3775

Also known as the Junction Butte Trail, this is not an official or maintained NPS trail, but rather a fairly popular social trail that takes you out to a historic site near the junction of the Yellowstone and Lamar Rivers—the location of the old Baronett Bridge.[1] In 187 "Yellowstone Jack" Baronett constructed a toll bridge along what was the original road through here to Cooke City (then a bustling mining town). It was burned by the Nez Perce in 1877 as they attempted to flee the U.S. Army. Baronett rebuilt it shortly thereafter and was used until 1903 when the U.S. Army Corps of Engineers built a bridge along the new route (the current route). Baronett's bridge was burned in 1905, and all that remains are little pieces of the footings along the river's edge.

If you continue along the trail past the confluence of the rivers, you will find yourself on the north side of Junction Butte, a large, practically square-shaped, basaltic butte named for its proximity to the junction of the rivers. On the north side of this is an old excavation pit.

If you continue to the trail's end at the river, you will find yourself at a historic spot known as Buffalo Ford. It is a popular river crossing for the bison in the park that dates back to the establishment of the Lamar Buffalo Ranch. There was an old trail that crossed the river here and connected to a trail known as the Little Buffalo Pack Trail (long since abandoned).

Blacktail Plateau Ski Trail — MAP 1-8

TYPE:	PTP	CAT:	TH	CLASS:	C	SURF:	TRAIL	DIST:	2	STATUS:	E
DIFF:	3	TRAF:	1	CHILD:	N	HACC:	N	USE:	H K B	LENGTH:	8.08
ELEV A:	6923	ELEV B:	6599	ELEV G:	1095	ELEV L:	-1419	NET:	-324	BMA:	- -
MIN:	6599	MAX:	7605	AVG:	7134	AVG +:	4.5%	AVG -:	6.0%	OPEN:	YR

Reference Point	A-B Mi	A-B Km	B-A Mi	B-A Km	Latitude	Longitude
West Trailhead @ Frog Rock (8.2 mi E of Mammoth)	0.00	0.00	8.08	13.00	44.95906	-110.56642
NPS Maintenance Yard	0.88	1.42	7.20	11.59	44.95579	-110.54994
Jct w/ Blacktail Plateau Drive	1.35	2.17	6.73	10.83	44.95609	-110.54034
Dirt Service Road	2.19	3.52	5.89	9.48	44.95127	-110.52653
Grizzly Bear Rock to the southeast (about 1 O'Clock)	2.65	4.26	5.43	8.74	44.94895	-110.51908
Oxbow Creek crossing (bridge)	3.87	6.23	4.21	6.78	44.94438	-110.49723
Garnett Creek/The Cut	4.80	7.72	3.28	5.28	44.94037	-110.48199
Elk Creek crossing (bridge)/Yancey Hill	6.43	10.35	1.65	2.66	44.92066	-110.47137
East Trailhead @ Elk Creek (1.5 mi W of Tower Jct)	8.08	13.00	0.00	0.00	44.92197	-110.44419

This is an easy to moderately difficult cross-country ski route in the winter. And though it is not technically a trail in the summer, many people do hike it. Much of it is a side road that was part of the original road from Mammoth to Tower. The trail begins at the Frog Rock pullout eight miles east of Mammoth. You'll ski/hike through a huge NPS maintenance yard (stay out of the area), and then continue along to meet up with the old road. From there, you will ski/hike through an area that affords outstanding views of the Northern Range. There is a slow, gentle climb along the first five miles of the trail, and the last two and a half miles are a steady 1,000-foot (304m) descent. You can bike this route as well during the summer.

One interesting feature along this trail is Grizzly Bear Rock, a colloquially-named rock that resembles a crouching grizzly according to some people. In the winter it may be covered with snow, but if you are able to see it, you will instantly see the likeness.

Buffalo Fork Trail — MAP 2-3

TYPE:	PTP	CAT:	BC	CLASS:	C	SURF:	TRAIL	DIST:	2	STATUS:	E
DIFF:	3	TRAF:	1	CHILD:	N	HACC:	N	USE:	H S	LENGTH:	6.44
ELEV A:	6542	ELEV B:	7541	ELEV G:	1676	ELEV L:	-677	NET:	999	BMA:	- -
MIN:	6487	MAX:	7740	AVG:	7253	AVG +:	6.9%	AVG -:	5.0%	OPEN:	YR

Reference Point	A-B Mi	A-B Km	B-A Mi	B-A Km	Latitude	Longitude
Trailhead @ jct w/ Slough Creek Trail	0.00	0.00	6.44	10.36	44.95175	-110.28144
Slough Creek crossing (150 to 170')	0.27	0.43	6.17	9.93	44.95224	-110.27736
Jct with Old Soldier's Trail	1.20	1.93	5.24	8.43	44.96308	-110.28133
Park boundary TH 2N3 (Trail continues into CGNF)	6.44	10.36	0.00	0.00	45.02977	-110.29316

While you can connect to this trail via the Slough Creek Trail, it is actually a bit easier to reach it via the old Soldier's Trail running north out of the Slough Creek Campground (see below). It cuts about a mile off your trip and you do not have to hike through the marshy areas of the lower Slough Creek (usually impassable during the early part of the season). This trail will take you north to the park's boundary and beyond, eventually connecting up to an old Poacher's Trail about a half mile to the north (which is maintained by the USFS). From there you can head west and connect to the Buffalo Plateau Trail and return to the Hellroaring Creek Trail trailhead, or east to connect back into the Slough Creek Trail.

Buffalo Plateau Trail — MAP 2-2

Type:	PTP	**Cat:**	BC	**Class:**	B	**Surf:**	Trail	**Dist:**	2	**Status:**	E
Diff:	4	**Traf:**	1	**Child:**	N	**HAcc:**	N	**Use:**	H S	**Length:**	8.10
Elev A:	5976	**Elev B:**	9223	**Elev G:**	3571	**Elev L:**	-324	**Net:**	3247	**BMA:**	- -
Min:	5976	**Max:**	9233	**Avg:**	7788	**Avg +:**	9.6%	**Avg -:**	3.9%	**Open:**	YR

Reference Point	A-B Mi	A-B Km	B-A Mi	B-A Km	Latitude	Longitude
Trailhead @ jct w/ Hellroaring Trail	0.00	0.00	8.10	13.04	44.96539	-110.44987
Jct with Coyote Creek Trail	0.50	0.80	7.60	12.23	44.97023	-110.44304
Jct with abandoned Buffalo Pack Trail	1.00	1.61	7.10	11.43	44.97264	-110.43289
Spur trail to campsite 2B1 (0.68 mi)	5.35	8.61	2.75	4.43	45.00817	-110.37524
Buffalo Plateau Patrol Cabin	6.95	11.18	1.15	1.85	45.02494	-110.35921
Park boundary TH 2N2 (Trail continues into CGNF)	8.10	13.04	0.00	0.00	45.02979	-110.34507

The Buffalo Plateau Trail takes you up onto, not surprisingly, Buffalo Plateau in the northern reaches of the park. It is a long and steady climb of about 3,500 feet (1067m) over the course of its eight miles. And much of it is across wide open space with little shade and few water sources, so pack accordingly.

Just after you pass the point where the Coyote Creek Trail splits off to the left, you will encounter quite a few animal trails. Be sure you follow the signs and the worn human stock trail, lest you find yourself wandering off into the wilderness. There is a lightly used campsite along this trail (with an incredible view, but limited water availability late in the season), and you will pass right by the NPS' Buffalo Plateau Patrol Cabin, an outpost used primarily to monitor for poachers.

This trail will take you to the park's boundary, and if you continue on into USFS land about a half mile, you will come across the old Poacher's Trail. This trail is maintained by USFS and if you go east two and a half miles, you will connect to the Buffalo Fork Trail.

Coyote Creek Trail — MAP 2-2

Type:	PTP	**Cat:**	BC	**Class:**	C	**Surf:**	Trail	**Dist:**	2	**Status:**	E
Diff:	3	**Traf:**	1	**Child:**	N	**HAcc:**	N	**Use:**	H S	**Length:**	5.20
Elev A:	6180	**Elev B:**	7510	**Elev G:**	1651	**Elev L:**	-321	**Net:**	1330	**BMA:**	- -
Min:	6180	**Max:**	7526	**Avg:**	6810	**Avg +:**	7.6%	**Avg -:**	3.5%	**Open:**	YR

Reference Point	A-B Mi	A-B Km	B-A Mi	B-A Km	Latitude	Longitude
Trailhead @ jct w/ Buffalo Plateau Trail	0.00	0.00	5.20	8.37	44.97023	-110.4430
Spur to campsite 2C1 (0.10 mi)	2.84	4.57	2.36	3.80	44.99987	-110.4158
Campsite 2C2	3.64	5.86	1.56	2.51	45.00882	-110.4077
Spur to campsite 2C3 (0.14 mi)	4.00	6.44	1.20	1.93	45.01448	-110.4073
Park boundary TH 2N1 (Trail continues into CGNF)	5.20	8.37	0.00	0.00	45.02984	-110.4030

The Coyote Creek Trail takes you up along the Coyote Creek drainage on the east flank of Bull Mountain. You will climb about 1,500 feet (457m) over the course of the five miles of the trail. There are three moderately used campsites along the way, one of which is just upstream of a nice waterfall. You can continue north into the Custer-Gallatin National Forest from the park boundary. About 6/10th of a mile north you can turn east on the (maintained) poacher trail and go east about three miles to the Buffalo Plateau Trail, or continue north about seven miles to the Hellroaring Trail to return to Yellowstone via the Hellroaring Creek Trail.

Garnet Hill Loop Trail — MAP 2-4

Type:	Loop	**Cat:**	BC	**Class:**	B	**Surf:**	Trail	**Dist:**	2	**Status:**	E
Diff:	3	**Traf:**	2	**Child:**	N	**HAcc:**	N	**Use:**	H S	**Length:**	8.32
Elev A:	6271	**Elev B:**	6271	**Elev G:**	1235	**Elev L:**	-1235	**Net:**	0	**BMA:**	- -
Min:	5893	**Max:**	6377	**Avg:**	6171	**Avg +:**	5.0%	**Avg -:**	4.9%	**Open:**	YR

Reference Point	A-B Mi	A-B Km	B-A Mi	B-A Km	Latitude	Longitude
Trailhead 2K2E (Roosevelt Corrals)	0.00	0.00	8.32	13.39	44.91614	-110.41608
Turn north onto main trail	0.12	0.19	8.20	13.20	44.91544	-110.41397
Cross Northeast Entrance Road	0.51	0.82	7.81	12.57	44.91971	-110.41250
Jct with concession horse trail	0.99	1.59	7.33	11.80	44.92524	-110.41739
Garnett Hill & Yellowstone River	3.50	5.63	4.82	7.76	44.95536	-110.42452
Jct with spur trail to Hellroaring Trail	4.92	7.92	3.40	5.47	44.95397	-110.44451
Elk Creek crossing (west)	6.38	10.27	1.94	3.12	44.93683	-110.43523
Elk Creek crossing (east)	6.68	10.75	1.64	2.64	44.93289	-110.43584
Yancey Split (take right fork)	6.85	11.02	1.47	2.37	44.93059	-110.43495
Yancey Creek crossing/Old Hotel Site/Pleasant Valley	6.90	11.10	1.42	2.29	44.93006	-110.43456
Trail split (take right fork)	7.10	11.43	1.22	1.96	44.92858	-110.43132
Lost Creek crossing	8.16	13.13	0.16	0.26	44.91739	-110.41896
Trailhead 2K2W (Tower Junction)	8.32	13.39	0.00	0.00	44.91614	-110.41608

Technically, this trail (built in 1926, and originally known as the Elk Creek Trail) starts and ends at the Roosevelt Corrals stagecoach crossing, but most people start and end it at the parking area next to the vault toilets adjacent to the Tower Service Station. This is an interesting half- to most of the day hike that will take you along the Yellowstone River, then along Elk Creek into Pleasant Valley. This is where "Uncle" John Yancey operated a hotel from 1884 to 1906 (when Camp Roosevelt, the predecessor of today's Roosevelt Lodge, opened).[2] You will cross Yancey Creek and Lost Creek as well on your way.

Since the northern half of this trail is entirely out in the open, it is best to start out early in the day and begin by hiking the northern half. That way, when the sun gets higher in the sky you will be in the partially-shaded portion of the trail until the last mile or so. As you come around the west side of the hill and begin to parallel Elk Creek, you enter a small canyon known as Dry Canyon (one of several places in the park with that name). While you are on the northern half of the trail, look up Anniversary Falls in Appendix 3 and if you have the time, walk down to the Yellowstone River to see if you can find it.

Garnet Hill is believed to be comprised of some of the oldest rock on the planet (roughly 4.5 billion years old). It is named for the impure garnets that can be found in its rock.

Garnett Hill - Hellroaring Cutoff — MAP 2-4,2-1

Type:	PTP	**Cat:**	BC	**Class:**	C	**Surf:**	Trail	**Dist:**	2	**Status:**	E
Diff:	3	**Traf:**	1	**Child:**	N	**HAcc:**	N	**Use:**	H S	**Length:**	0.18
Elev A:	5954	**Elev B:**	6011	**Elev G:**	162	**Elev L:**	-105	**Net:**	57	**BMA:**	- -
Min:	5939	**Max:**	6046	**Avg:**	5999	**Avg +:**	25.0%	**Avg -:**	17.6%	**Open:**	YR

Reference Point	A-B Mi	A-B Km	B-A Mi	B-A Km	Latitude	Longitude
Trailhead @ jct w/ Garnett Hill Trail	0.00	0.00	0.18	0.29	44.95397	-110.44451
Elk Creek crossing	0.04	0.06	0.14	0.23	44.95438	-110.44495
Trailhead @ jct w/ Hellroaring Trail	0.18	0.29	0.00	0.00	44.95621	-110.44549

This is merely a short trail segment that connects the Garnet Hill Loop Trail with the Hellroaring Creek Trail. If you are hiking the Garnet Hill Trail and have the time to spare, it is worth it to take a side trip over to the Hellroaring Creek Trail and down to the suspension bridge over the Yellowstone River.

Hellroaring Creek Trail — MAP 2-2

Type:	PTP	**Cat:**	BC	**Class:**	B	**Surf:**	Trail	**Dist:**	2	**Status:**	E
Diff:	3	**Traf:**	3	**Child:**	N	**HAcc:**	N	**Use:**	H S	**Length:**	7.33
Elev A:	6496	**Elev B:**	6330	**Elev G:**	1155	**Elev L:**	-1320	**Net:**	-166	**BMA:**	- -
Min:	5859	**Max:**	6496	**Avg:**	6109	**Avg +:**	4.8%	**Avg -:**	6.8%	**Open:**	YR

Reference Point	A-B Mi	A-B Km	B-A Mi	B-A Km	Latitude	Longitude
Trailhead 2K8 (3.7 mi W of Tower Junction)	0.00	0.00	7.33	11.80	44.94895	-110.45058
Jct with spur trail from Garnett Hill Trail	0.74	1.19	6.59	10.61	44.95621	-110.44549
Suspension bridge over Yellowstone River	1.00	1.61	6.33	10.19	44.95972	-110.44683
Jct with Buffalo Plateau Trail	1.51	2.43	5.82	9.37	44.96539	-110.44987
Hellroaring Trail Stock Cutoff (south)	1.91	3.07	5.42	8.72	44.97078	-110.45163
Spur trail to campsites 2H2 & 2H4 (1.33 mi)	1.96	3.15	5.37	8.64	44.97056	-110.45268
Hellroaring Creek ford (75 to 100')	2.11	3.40	5.22	8.40	44.97214	-110.45407
Jct with Yellowstone River Trail/Spur to 2H1 & 2H3	2.21	3.56	5.12	8.24	44.97282	-110.45587
Spur trail to campsite 2H5	3.00	4.83	4.33	6.97	44.97873	-110.44248
Hellroaring Patrol Cabin/Barn	3.27	5.26	4.06	6.53	44.97945	-110.43838
Spur to campsite 2H7	3.64	5.86	3.69	5.94	44.98329	-110.43389
Jct with Hellroaring Trail Stock Cutoff (north)	4.10	6.60	3.23	5.20	44.98775	-110.42884
Spur to campsite 2H9	5.67	9.12	1.66	2.67	45.00819	-110.43475
Park boundary TH 2N5 (continues into CGNF)	7.33	11.80	0.00	0.00	45.02971	-110.44023

The Hellroaring Creek Trail is one of the most heavily used trails in the northern half of Yellowstone, especially after stock season begins in earnest in July. This is because it provides access to several other trails in the district and also serves as an ingress/egress route for those who want to spend some time in the Black Canyon area.

About two miles in you will need to make a decision. The trail itself crosses Hellroaring Creek here. Early in the season (before mid- to late July) the creek may be too high to ford safely, so you may elect to turn right onto the Stock Cutoff Trail (see below) and go about two miles up to the bridge to cross the creek at that location. If you're using this trail to get to the Yellowstone River Trail, or if you're trying to get to the 2H1-2H4 campsites, you will end up adding four miles to your trip by using the stock trail. But it is better to be safe than sorry.

Once you cross the creek on the (non-stock) trail, you will turn right to remain on the Hellroaring Creek Trail and head on up into the wilderness. Continuing straight will put you onto the Yellowstone River Trail and take you into the Black Canyon of the Yellowstone.

Staying on the Hellroaring Creek Trail, you pass Hellroaring Mountain on your left and then follow the creek all the way up to the park's boundary. Once you reach the park boundary, you can continue north for three miles until you get to the USFS ranger station, and then head east to come back into Yellowstone via the Coyote Creek Trail (or further east for other trails). There are eight campsites located along Hellroaring Creek, all of which are fairly decent sites. 2H1 and 2H2 are personal favorites because they are located at the junction of the creek and the Yellowstone River. 2H2 is well-shaded and very private if no one is occupying 2H1.

Hellroaring Stock Cutoff Trail — MAP 2-2

TYPE:	PTP	CAT:	BC	CLASS:	B	SURF:	TRAIL	DIST:	2	STATUS:	E
DIFF:	2	TRAF:	2	CHILD:	N	HACC:	N	USE:	H S	LENGTH:	1.85
ELEV A:	5898	ELEV B:	6050	ELEV G:	320	ELEV L:	-168	NET:	152	BMA:	- -
MIN:	5896	MAX:	6100	AVG:	5978	AVG +:	4.4%	AVG -:	5.9%	OPEN:	YR

Reference Point	A-B Mi	A-B Km	B-A Mi	B-A Km	Latitude	Longitude
Trailhead Jct with Hellroaring Trail	0.00	0.00	1.85	2.98	44.97078	-110.45163
Spur to campsite 2H6 (0.10 mi)	0.63	1.01	1.22	1.96	44.97633	-110.44261
Spur to campsite 2H8 (0.54 mi)	1.80	2.90	0.05	0.08	44.98760	-110.42796
Hellroaring Creek crossing (bridge)	1.81	2.91	0.04	0.06	44.98765	-110.42815
Jct with Hellroaring Trail	1.85	2.98	0.00	0.00	44.98775	-110.42884

This trail is primarily a connector trail to facilitate stock access to the upper reaches of the Hellroaring Trail. During the early part of the season when it is too dangerous to ford the creek at the upper end, this trail is used primarily by hikers detouring up to use the bridge.

Lost Lake Trail — MAP 2-5

TYPE:	PTP	CAT:	TH	CLASS:	B	SURF:	TRAIL	DIST:	2	STATUS:	E
DIFF:	3	TRAF:	3	CHILD:	N	HACC:	N	USE:	H S K	LENGTH:	2.83
ELEV A:	6371	ELEV B:	6323	ELEV G:	828	ELEV L:	-876	NET:	-48	BMA:	- -
MIN:	6322	MAX:	6895	AVG:	6677	AVG +:	10.5%	AVG -:	10.6%	OPEN:	YR

Reference Point	A-B Mi	A-B Km	B-A Mi	B-A Km	Latitude	Longitude
Trailhead behind Roosevelt Lodge	0.00	0.00	2.83	4.55	44.91199	-110.41751
Lost Creek crossing (bridge)	0.06	0.10	2.77	4.46	44.91216	-110.41813
Jct with Lost Lake Horse Spur Trail from corral	0.60	0.97	2.23	3.59	44.91101	-110.42409
Footbridge over unnamed creek	0.62	1.00	2.21	3.56	44.91134	-110.42429
Lost Lake	0.91	1.46	1.92	3.09	44.90997	-110.42942
Jct with concession horse trail	1.72	2.77	1.11	1.79	44.91496	-110.43913
Trailhead at Petrified Tree Parking Lot	1.76	2.83	1.07	1.72	44.91526	-110.43832
Trailhead at Tower Administrative/Govt Area	2.83	4.55	0.00	0.00	44.91450	-110.42123

The Lost Lake Trail is one of the more popular short hikes in the Roosevelt area. And though this chart shows the full loop trail, it can be approached in any one of three different ways. You can hike from the lodge up to the lake and back (round trip would be about two miles), hike it from the Petrified Tree parking area and back (round trip would be about 1.7 miles), or you can do the full loop. Once you get to the end of the trail at the Tower Ranger Station, follow the trail markers across the parking lot and back into the lodge area.

Lost Lake is home to many waterfowl and the occasional beaver and is virtually unknown outside this little area of the park. No one knows for sure how it got its name (which dates back to at least the 1910s), but it likely has to do with the fact that it is largely hidden from anyone who does not know it is there.

Just as you begin the hike from behind the Roosevelt Lodge, there is a very short spur trail that takes you up to Lost Creek Falls, a gorgeous 40-foot (12m) plunge waterfall on Lost Creek. Contrary to popular belief, Lost Creek does not emanate from Lost Lake (though it does drain via a tributary of Lost Creek), but rather from the north face of Prospect Peak located to the southwest of the Roosevelt area.

Lost Lake Horse Spur Trail — MAP 2-5

Type:	PTP	**Cat:**	TH	**Class:**	B	**Surf:**	Trail	**Dist:**	2	**Status:**	E
Diff:	2	**Traf:**	1	**Child:**	N	**HAcc:**	N	**Use:**	H S K	**Length:**	1.73
Elev A:	6310	**Elev B:**	6740	**Elev G:**	728	**Elev L:**	-299	**Net:**	430	**BMA:**	- -
Min:	6310	**Max:**	6804	**Avg:**	6643	**Avg +:**	12.0%	**Avg -:**	8.2%	**Open:**	YR

Reference Point	A-B Mi	A-B Km	B-A Mi	B-A Km	Latitude	Longitude
Trailhead behind corral	0.00	0.00	1.73	2.78	44.91320	-110.41312
Jct with Roosevelt-Tower Fall Trail	0.56	0.90	1.17	1.88	44.91031	-110.41096
Lost Creek crossing	1.29	2.08	0.44	0.71	44.90656	-110.42245
Jct with Lost Lake Trail	1.73	2.78	0.00	0.00	44.91101	-110.42409

This trail exists primarily to allow riders on horseback to access the Lost Lake area from the Roosevelt Corrals. If you prefer a much more gentle incline as you hike up to Lost Lake, you can hike this trail as well (just watch where you are stepping).

McBride Lake Trail — MAP 2-3

Type:	O&B	**Cat:**	BC	**Class:**	U	**Surf:**	Trail	**Dist:**	2	**Status:**	U
Diff:	2	**Traf:**	1	**Child:**	N	**HAcc:**	N	**Use:**	H S	**Length:**	1.09
Elev A:	6527	**Elev B:**	6590	**Elev G:**	151	**Elev L:**	-88	**Net:**	63	**BMA:**	- -
Min:	6489	**Max:**	6593	**Avg:**	6514	**Avg +:**	4.0%	**Avg -:**	5.0%	**Open:**	YR

Reference Point	A-B Mi	A-B Km	B-A Mi	B-A Km	Latitude	Longitude
Trailhead @ jct w/ Slough Creek Trail	0.00	0.00	1.09	1.75	44.95032	-110.26818
Slough Creek crossing	0.60	0.97	0.49	0.79	44.95693	-110.26191
McBride Lake	1.09	1.75	0.00	0.00	44.96098	-110.25830

This unmaintained (and unofficial) trail takes you up to McBride Lake, a gorgeous, 27-acre backcountry lake that is popular with fishermen in the Slough Creek area. The lake is known to contain cutthroat trout and lake chub. It is named after James McBride, who was one of the park's first scouts during the U.S. Army era, and went on to become one of the park's first official rangers. He was the park's first Chief Ranger from 1920 until his retirement in 1929.[3]

Old Dunraven Service Road Trail — MAP 2-7

Type:	PTP	**Cat:**	BC	**Class:**	N	**Surf:**	Trail	**Dist:**	2	**Status:**	R
Diff:	2	**Traf:**	1	**Child:**	N	**HAcc:**	N	**Use:**	HBKR	**Length:**	1.99
Elev A:	6599	**Elev B:**	7281	**Elev G:**	766	**Elev L:**	-84	**Net:**	682	**BMA:**	G
Min:	6599	**Max:**	7281	**Avg:**	7001	**Avg +:**	8.5%	**Avg -:**	3.6%	**Open:**	YR

Reference Point	A-B Mi	A-B Km	B-A Mi	B-A Km	Latitude	Longitude
Trailhead @ Tower Campground	0.00	0.00	1.99	3.20	44.88994	-110.3896
Tower Campground Amphitheater	0.06	0.10	1.93	3.11	44.88913	-110.3896
Tower Falls Borrow Pit	0.64	1.03	1.35	2.17	44.88444	-110.3953
Trailhead @ Dunraven Road (5.4 mi N of Tower Jct)	1.99	3.20	0.00	0.00	44.86837	-110.4064

Part of the original road that took visitors from Mt. Washburn to Tower (and back), this old road is only hikable/bikable at certain times of the year. During much of the summer it is closed due to the presence of a carcass dump approximately halfway between the entry and exit. Check in with the Tower Ranger Station to see if it is possible to hike this trail.

Roosevelt Lodge-Tower Falls Trail — MAP 2-6

TYPE:	PTP	CAT:	TH	CLASS:	C	SURF:	TRAIL	DIST:	2	STATUS:	E
DIFF:	2	TRAF:	2	CHILD:	N	HACC:	N	USE:	H K	LENGTH:	1.91
ELEV A:	6649	ELEV B:	6507	ELEV G:	317	ELEV L:	-459	NET:	-142	BMA:	- -
MIN:	6480	MAX:	6811	AVG:	6696	AVG +:	5.7%	AVG -:	9.0%	OPEN:	YR

Reference Point	A-B Mi	A-B Km	B-A Mi	B-A Km	Latitude	Longitude
Trailhead @ jct w/ Lost Lake Horse Trail	0.00	0.00	1.91	3.07	44.91031	-110.41096
Tower Creek crossing (25 to 30')	1.88	3.03	0.03	0.05	44.89201	-110.38983
Trailhead @ Tower Campground	1.91	3.07	0.00	0.00	44.89168	-110.38957

To catch this trail, you will need to walk up along the horse trail from the corral about a half mile. The trail then heads east over a mile and a half with a slight incline before dropping 300 feet (91m) into Tower Creek. You will have to ford the creek (or cross on deadfall if present), whereupon you will be on the entrance road into the campground. An interesting side note: This little section of trail used to be part of the old Howard Eaton Trail system.

Slough Creek Trail — MAP 2-3

TYPE:	PTP	CAT:	BC	CLASS:	A	SURF:	TRAIL	DIST:	2	STATUS:	E
DIFF:	3	TRAF:	4	CHILD:	N	HACC:	N	USE:	H S	LENGTH:	10.20
ELEV A:	6245	ELEV B:	6662	ELEV G:	1341	ELEV L:	-924	NET:	417	BMA:	- -
MIN:	6245	MAX:	6742	AVG:	6609	AVG +:	4.0%	AVG -:	3.1%	OPEN:	YR

Reference Point	A-B Mi	A-B Km	B-A Mi	B-A Km	Latitude	Longitude
Trailhead 2K5 (5.9 mi N of Tower Junction)	0.00	0.00	10.20	16.42	44.94352	-110.30805
Jct with Buffalo Fork Trail	1.70	2.74	8.50	13.68	44.95175	-110.28144
Slough Creek Patrol Cabin	1.93	3.11	8.27	13.31	44.95065	-110.27727
Jct with trail to McBride Lake	2.38	3.83	7.82	12.59	44.95032	-110.26818
Spur to campsite 2S1 (0.60 mi)	4.27	6.87	5.93	9.54	44.96164	-110.23594
Spur to campsite 2S2 (0.10 mi)	4.78	7.69	5.42	8.72	44.96654	-110.22804
Spur to campsite 2S3 (0.14 mi)	5.83	9.38	4.37	7.03	44.97676	-110.21415
Spur to campsite 2S4 (0.11 mi)	6.84	11.01	3.36	5.41	44.98887	-110.20309
South spur to Elk Tongue Patrol Cabin/2S7/2S8	6.95	11.18	3.25	5.23	44.98983	-110.20136
North spur to ETPC/Jct with Bliss Pass Trail	7.00	11.27	3.20	5.15	44.99036	-110.20004
Spur to campsite 2S6 (0.05 mi)	8.20	13.20	2.00	3.22	45.00299	-110.18559
Trail split (N/B stay right)	9.37	15.08	0.83	1.34	45.01829	-110.17690
Trail split (S/B stay left)	9.54	15.35	0.66	1.06	45.02039	-110.17693
Park boundary TH 2N4 (Silver Tip Ranch/CGNF)	10.20	16.42	0.00	0.00	45.02941	-110.17477

The Slough (pronounced "slew") Creek Trail is one of the most popular trails in the northeast quadrant of the park for hikers, stock parties, and fishermen. It is also the only way for visitors and supplies to get to the Silver Tip Ranch, located just outside the park's north boundary. This trail begins at the big pullout just south of the campground itself, not at the campground (that's the old Soldier's Trail - see below).

All of the campsites along this trail are among the most heavily used in the park, so if you have a schedule you need to adhere to, consider trying to reserve these sites before you arrive. Note that prior to opening and after this campground closes, the swing gate at the entrance will be closed and you will have to hike from the road back to the trailhead. That will add almost two miles to your hike (each way if you are returning via the same route).

Soldier's Trail — MAP 2-3

TYPE:	PTP	CAT:	BC	CLASS:	B	SURF:	TRAIL	DIST:	2	STATUS:	E
DIFF:	2	TRAF:	2	CHILD:	N	HACC:	N	USE:	H S	LENGTH:	1.74
ELEV A:	6259	ELEV B:	6650	ELEV G:	525	ELEV L:	-134	NET:	391	BMA:	- -
MIN:	6245	MAX:	6683	AVG:	6426	AVG +:	7.8%	AVG -:	4.5%	OPEN:	YR

Reference Point	A-B Mi	A-B Km	B-A Mi	B-A Km	Latitude	Longitude
Trailhead at Slough Creek Campground	0.00	0.00	1.74	2.80	44.94888	-110.30688
Cross Slough Creek (80 to 100')	0.03	0.05	1.71	2.75	44.94927	-110.30644
Terminates at Buffalo Fork Trail	1.74	2.80	0.00	0.00	44.96308	-110.28133

The Soldier's Trail (sometimes referred to as the Old Soldier's Trail or the Buffalo Fork Creek Trail) is an alternate route that can be used to get to the Buffalo Fork Trail. The fact that this route was used by U.S. Army patrols to reach the upper Buffalo Creek area back in the day is where it gets its name. If you are looking to head up into the Buffalo Creek region, using this trail to ford Slough Creek is almost invariably a better option than using the Slough Creek Trail. Fording of the latter involves a wider expanse of the creek and takes you through an area that even later in the season remains fairly marshy in places. When you cross on the Soldiers Trail, you ford the creek and you are on dry land the rest of the way. It also reduces the distance you need to hike to get up into that area. Having said that, crossing at either location can be quite trying well into July.

Specimen Ridge Trail — MAP 2-1

TYPE:	PTP	CAT:	BC	CLASS:	C	SURF:	TRAIL	DIST:	2	STATUS:	E
DIFF:	4	TRAF:	1	CHILD:	N	HACC:	N	USE:	H S	LENGTH:	17.14
ELEV A:	6264	ELEV B:	6654	ELEV G:	4237	ELEV L:	-3848	NET:	390	BMA:	- -
MIN:	6258	MAX:	9614	AVG:	7908	AVG +:	8.2%	AVG -:	8.8%	OPEN:	YR

Reference Point	A-B Mi	A-B Km	B-A Mi	B-A Km	Latitude	Longitude
Trailhead 2K4 (2.0 mi N of Tower Junction)	0.00	0.00	17.14	27.58	44.91229	-110.38738
Jct w/ Yellowstone Picnic Area Outer Spur Trail	0.19	0.31	16.95	27.28	44.90979	-110.38633
Jct w/ Yellowstone River Overlook Trail	1.12	1.80	16.02	25.78	44.89988	-110.37871
Trail junction w/ social trail (to nowhere)	1.43	2.30	15.71	25.28	44.90182	-110.37332
Jct with Agate Creek Trail	2.32	3.73	14.82	23.85	44.89261	-110.36168
Trails to petrified forest	2.85	4.59	14.29	23.00	44.88856	-110.35268
Agate Creek crossing	5.68	9.14	11.46	18.44	44.86766	-110.31109
Jct w/ Opal Creek Trail (Access to 3O1)	11.10	17.86	6.04	9.72	44.81724	-110.23878
Access to Wild Rose Falls	14.00	22.53	3.14	5.05	44.83731	-110.19585
Lamar River Ford (100 to 150')	15.10	24.30	2.04	3.28	44.84736	-110.18525
Jct with Lamar River Trail	15.80	25.43	1.34	2.16	44.85364	-110.17717
Jct with Lamar River Stock Cutoff Trail	16.00	25.75	1.14	1.83	44.85626	-110.17583
Soda Butte Creek bridge	17.05	27.44	0.09	0.14	44.86921	-110.16473
Soda Butte Trailhead 3K1 (13.9 mi W of NE Entrance)	17.14	27.58	0.00	0.00	44.86922	-110.16622

The Specimen Ridge Trail is the second longest in the park without any campsites along the trail. So when you elect to hike this trail, you will need to be prepared for a full day's walk from one end to the other. You can, of course, elect to take the Agate Creek Trail to get to the lone campsite in this area if you wish. It should be noted that if your intent is to see the petrified trees in this area, you will not see any on this trail. You should use one of the Specimen Forest trails listed below.

Once you get up onto the ridge, the trail can be a bit difficult to follow, especially early in the season. Typically, there are posts and cairns along the way to help guide you, but early in the season, these may be knocked down and the trail may not be worn enough to allow you to figure out the correct route. If you can download a trail GPX file into a GPS unit, that would be the best way to solve this problem. However, as the season progresses and the rangers get out and reset the markers, things become much easier. Most of this trail is also above the tree line and therefore out in the open. Be sure you use sunscreen and take along enough water for your trip.

Despite the fact that I have the A-B routing for this trip from west to east (which is the standard way of doing it in this book), there is one thing that makes hiking from the other end a distinct advantage. On the east end there is a ford of the Lamar River (which is typically not crossable prior to late June or early July). If you are coming from the west and have been hiking all day, you will be tired when it comes time to cross the river. And in the middle part of the season (roughly July through August), you will find it requires a good deal of concentration and strength to cross through the river, which will often be at least thigh-depth and occasionally waist-depth depending on what the snow pack and stormy season have been like. So by starting on the east end you get that river ford out of the way while you are not tired. Having said that, hiking from the east involves a much more significant incline than doing it from west to east (2,500 foot/762-meter elevation gain in less than five miles vs. the same incline over almost ten miles coming from the west).

Regardless of which direction you take, however, this trail offers some of the most spectacular views of both the Northern Range and the Mirror Plateau.

Specimen Forest Trail - East — MAP 2-1

Type:	O&B	**Cat:**	BC	**Class:**	N	**Surf:**	Trail	**Dist:**	2	**Status:**	U
Diff:	4	**Traf:**	1	**Child:**	N	**HAcc:**	N	**Use:**	H	**Length:**	1.77
Elev A:	6202	**Elev B:**	7940	**Elev G:**	1780	**Elev L:**	-42	**Net:**	1738	**BMA:**	- -
Min:	6202	**Max:**	7940	**Avg:**	6894	**Avg +:**	17.7%	**Avg -:**	10.4%	**Open:**	YR

Reference Point	A-B Mi	A-B Km	B-A Mi	B-A Km	Latitude	Longitude
Trailhead @ unmarked pullout (5.0 mi N of Tower Jct)	0.00	0.00	1.77	2.85	44.91180	-110.32773
Trail split - take right hand fork	0.08	0.13	1.69	2.72	44.91097	-110.32657
Jct w/ Specimen Forest Trail - West Spur	1.25	2.01	0.52	0.84	44.89639	-110.33037
Social trails to petrified forests	1.50	2.41	0.27	0.43	44.89392	-110.33363
Summit of Specimen Ridge	1.77	2.85	0.00	0.00	44.89041	-110.33514

This trail is referred to in some older (really old) guidebooks as the Crystal Creek Trail. It used to be an "official" trail up to the summit of Specimen Ridge, but over time most guides are no longer mentioning it because of the sensitive nature of the forest at the upper end of the trip. This hike is from an unlabeled trailhead marked only with a sign that says "Trail Head" on it (in both directions). It is the preferred route (preferred by the rangers) for those hiking up to see the Petrified Forest trees near the summit of Specimen Ridge.

Prior to making this hike, check in with the ranger at the Tower Ranger Station for an update on the conditions and status of the trail. They have a small map they will give you to ensure you get up to the top correctly. They will likely also counsel you about not screwing around with the pieces of trees you find in the area.

Specimen Forest Trail - West — MAP 2-1

TYPE:	PTP	CAT:	BC	CLASS:	U	SURF:	TRAIL	DIST:	2	STATUS:	U
DIFF:	5	TRAF:	1	CHILD:	N	HACC:	N	USE:	H	LENGTH:	1.00
ELEV A:	6228	ELEV B:	7324	ELEV G:	1101	ELEV L:	-5	NET:	1096	BMA:	- -
MIN:	6224	MAX:	7324	AVG:	6602	AVG +:	19.2%	AVG -:	2.0%	OPEN:	YR

Reference Point	A-B Mi	A-B Km	B-A Mi	B-A Km	Latitude	Longitude
Trailhead @ unmarked pullout (4.2 mi N of Tower Jct)	0.00	0.00	1.00	1.61	44.90733	-110.34301
Jct w/ Specimen Forest Trail - East	1.00	1.61	0.00	0.00	44.89639	-110.33037

This is the western access trail for the hike up to the Specimen Ridge petrified trees. Technically, it is an unofficial and unmaintained trail, but there is an unmarked pullout here that can accommodate several vehicles. The pullout is two pullouts west of the preferred one listed for the "east" access route above. The primary (well, only) advantage to using this route vs the eastern one is that this one has a more gradual climb to it for the mile or so you are on it. After one mile, you connect into the old Crystal Creek Trail (the east access trail above) and make the rest of the climb on it. Be sure to check with the ranger at the Tower Ranger Station prior to beginning this hike.

Stagecoach Road Trail — MAP 2-4

TYPE:	O&B	CAT:	TH	CLASS:	B	SURF:	TRAIL	DIST:	2	STATUS:	E
DIFF:	1	TRAF:	2	CHILD:	N	HACC:	N	USE:	H S R	LENGTH:	1.84
ELEV A:	6278	ELEV B:	6208	ELEV G:	84	ELEV L:	-154	NET:	-70	BMA:	- -
MIN:	6199	MAX:	6278	AVG:	6230	AVG +:	2.2%	AVG -:	2.3%	OPEN:	YR

Reference Point	A-B Mi	A-B Km	B-A Mi	B-A Km	Latitude	Longitude
Trailhead at corral	0.00	0.00	1.84	2.96	44.91420	-110.41366
Cross Tower to Canyon Road	0.09	0.14	1.75	2.82	44.91541	-110.41408
Cross Northeast Entrance Road	0.21	0.34	1.63	2.62	44.91673	-110.41532
Lost Creek crossing	0.43	0.69	1.41	2.27	44.91793	-110.41843
Termination at Yancey's Hole	1.84	2.96	0.00	0.00	44.92993	-110.43578

This is technically not a "trail" per se, but rather the road that the cookout stagecoaches from Roosevelt use to get to Yancey's Hole where they have their evening programs. But it is hikable and is a nice little trip if you do not want a long hike and would like to wander out and see the site of "Uncle" John Yancey's former hotel and cabin. The old hotel served as the only place to stay in this area of the park until the predecessor to the Roosevelt Lodge opened up in 1906.

Tower Creek Trail — MAP 2-7

TYPE:	O&B	CAT:	BC	CLASS:	N	SURF:	TRAIL	DIST:	2	STATUS:	U
DIFF:	2	TRAF:	2	CHILD:	N	HACC:	N	USE:	H S	LENGTH:	3.60
ELEV A:	6580	ELEV B:	6940	ELEV G:	714	ELEV L:	-355	NET:	360	BMA:	- -
MIN:	6538	MAX:	6940	AVG:	6782	AVG +:	5.3%	AVG -:	4.5%	OPEN:	YR

Reference Point	A-B Mi	A-B Km	B-A Mi	B-A Km	Latitude	Longitude
Trailhead @ Tower Campground	0.00	0.00	3.60	5.79	44.88962	-110.39105
Tower Creek crossing (20 to 25')	0.16	0.26	3.44	5.54	44.88844	-110.39338
Trail end	3.60	5.79	0.00	0.00	44.86123	-110.44591

This trail takes you back along Tower Creek from the campground, almost back to where Carnelian Creek empties into Tower Creek at the north foot of Inside Mountain. The area is used primarily by fishermen (especially those staying in the campground), but it makes a nice hike along a mountain stream as well. You will have to ford Tower Creek about one-tenth of a mile in, and that likely will not be possible/safe until mid- to late July or even early August in some years. At one time there was a footbridge over the creek but it became unsafe and the NPS removed it. The trail is no longer maintained by the NPS. This is one of the prettier short hikes in the park and well worth a couple of hours of your time if you are staying in the Tower Campground.

Tower Fall Trail — MAP 2-7,2-6

Type:	O&B	**Cat:**	FC	**Class:**	B	**Surf:**	Trail	**Dist:**	2	**Status:**	E
Diff:	2	**Traf:**	1	**Child:**	N	**HAcc:**	N	**Use:**	H	**Length:**	0.35
Elev A:	6457	**Elev B:**	6169	**Elev G:**	187	**Elev L:**	-475	**Net:**	-288	**BMA:**	- -
Min:	6169	**Max:**	6475	**Avg:**	6300	**Avg +:**	18.3%	**Avg -:**	27.6%	**Open:**	YR

Reference Point	A-B Mi	A-B Km	B-A Mi	B-A Km	Latitude	Longitude
Trailhead @ Tower General Store	0.00	0.00	0.35	0.56	44.89219	-110.38667
Viewing Platform	0.09	0.14	0.26	0.42	44.89319	-110.38577
Current trail closure*	0.19	0.31	0.16	0.26	44.89356	-110.38394
Trail end at confluence	0.35	0.56	0.00	0.00	44.89470	-110.38364

This trail is a short, paved hike up to the Tower Fall observation platform located just beyond where the Tower General Store sits, and then down to the river if you wish.

Up until 2004, the trail continued down the side of the hill to the base of the falls. But a section of the trail washed out and it became dangerous for people to go down to that area, so the NPS closed that portion of the trail. There are currently no plans to re-open that section, but the status of that trail is always subject to change.

Yellowstone River Overlook Trail — MAP 2-6

Type:	PTP	**Cat:**	BC	**Class:**	B	**Surf:**	Trail	**Dist:**	2	**Status:**	E
Diff:	3	**Traf:**	2	**Child:**	Y	**HAcc:**	N	**Use:**	H S	**Length:**	1.93
Elev A:	6252	**Elev B:**	6620	**Elev G:**	719	**Elev L:**	-351	**Net:**	368	**BMA:**	- -
Min:	6252	**Max:**	6646	**Avg:**	6471	**Avg +:**	11.2%	**Avg -:**	8.0%	**Open:**	YR

Reference Point	A-B Mi	A-B Km	B-A Mi	B-A Km	Latitude	Longitude
Trailhead 2K7 (Picnic Area 1.2 mi N of Tower Jct)	0.00	0.00	1.93	3.11	44.91674	-110.40064
Calcite Springs overlook	0.74	1.19	1.19	1.92	44.90834	-110.39267
View down into The Narrows	1.29	2.08	0.64	1.03	44.90148	-110.38830
Termination @ jct w/ Specimen Ridge Trail	1.93	3.11	0.00	0.00	44.89988	-110.37871

Some guidebooks refer to this as the Yellowstone Picnic Area (or Picnic Area Overlook) Trail because it begins in the picnic area. This trail takes you along the wall of the lower end of the Grand Canyon of the Yellowstone, including along an area known as The Narrows (named appropriately enough because it is the narrowest part of the canyon). You also get great views of Calcite Springs and Bannock Ford, a location along the river that was once part of the Bannock Indian Trail through this area. This trail is child-friendly, but it is almost entirely out in the open. A small herd of bighorn sheep hangs out along this trail from time to time as well.

At about two miles out, the trail intersects with the Specimen Ridge Trail. You can turn around and go back the way you came, or you can take the far less scenic route back following the Specimen Ridge Trail back toward the road for about a mile until just before you reach the road. There will be an unmarked trail that leads off to the west that takes you back to the picnic area (see below).

Yellowstone River Picnic Area Outer Spur Trail — MAP 2-6

Type:	PTP	**Cat:**	TH	**Class:**	U	**Surf:**	Trail	**Dist:**	2	**Status:**	U
Diff:	1	**Traf:**	1	**Child:**	Y	**HAcc:**	N	**Use:**	H S	**Length:**	0.86
Elev A:	6266	**Elev B:**	6279	**Elev G:**	112	**Elev L:**	-99	**Net:**	13	**BMA:**	- -
Min:	6266	**Max:**	6310	**Avg:**	6279	**Avg +:**	4.7%	**Avg -:**	4.2%	**Open:**	YR

Reference Point	A-B Mi	A-B Km	B-A Mi	B-A Km	Latitude	Longitude
Trailhead @ jct w/ Specimen Ridge Trail	0.00	0.00	0.86	1.38	44.90979	-110.38633
Trailhead @ Yellowstone River Picnic Area	0.86	1.38	0.00	0.00	44.91686	-110.40025

This short spur is merely a trail to get you back to the Yellowstone River Picnic Area from either the Yellowstone River Overlook Trail or the Specimen Ridge Trail if you parked at the picnic area and used this trail to get up onto the ridge. It is unremarkable, however, and most people prefer to go back via the original trail.

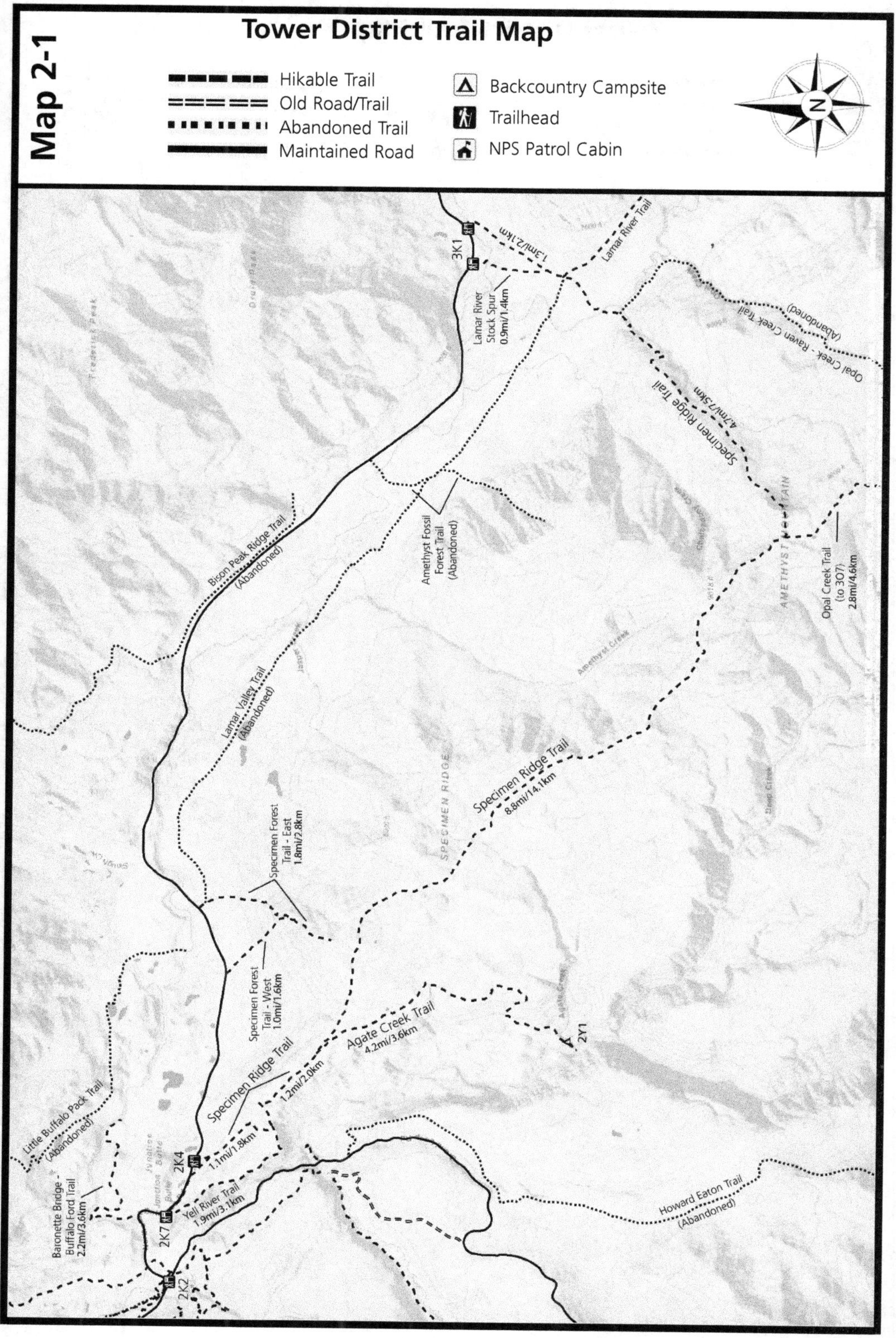

Map 2-1

Tower District Trail Map

Hikable Trail
Old Road/Trail
Abandoned Trail
Maintained Road

Backcountry Campsite
Trailhead
NPS Patrol Cabin

3K1
1.3mi/2.1km
Lamar River Trail
Lamar River Stock Spur 0.9mi/1.4km
Opal Creek - Raven Creek Trail (Abandoned)
Specimen Ridge Trail 4.7mi/7.5km
Bison Peak Ridge Trail (Abandoned)
Amethyst Fossil Forest Trail (Abandoned)
Opal Creek Trail (to 3O7) 2.8mi/4.6km
AMETHYST MOUNTAIN
Amethyst Creek
Lamar Valley Trail (Abandoned)
SPECIMEN RIDGE
Specimen Ridge Trail 8.8mi/14.1km
Specimen Forest Trail - East 1.8mi/2.8km
Specimen Forest Trail - West 1.0mi/1.6km
Agate Creek Trail 4.2mi/3.6km
2Y1
Specimen Ridge Trail
1.2mi/2.0km
1.1mi/1.8km
Little Buffalo Pack Trail (Abandoned)
2K4
Baronette Bridge - Buffalo Ford Trail 2.2mi/3.6km
2K7
Yell River Trail 1.9mi/3.1km
2K2
Howard Eaton Trail (Abandoned)

Map 2-2

Tower District Trail Map

Hikable Trail
Old Road/Trail
Abandoned Trail
Maintained Road

Backcountry Campsite

Trailhead
NPS Patrol Cabin

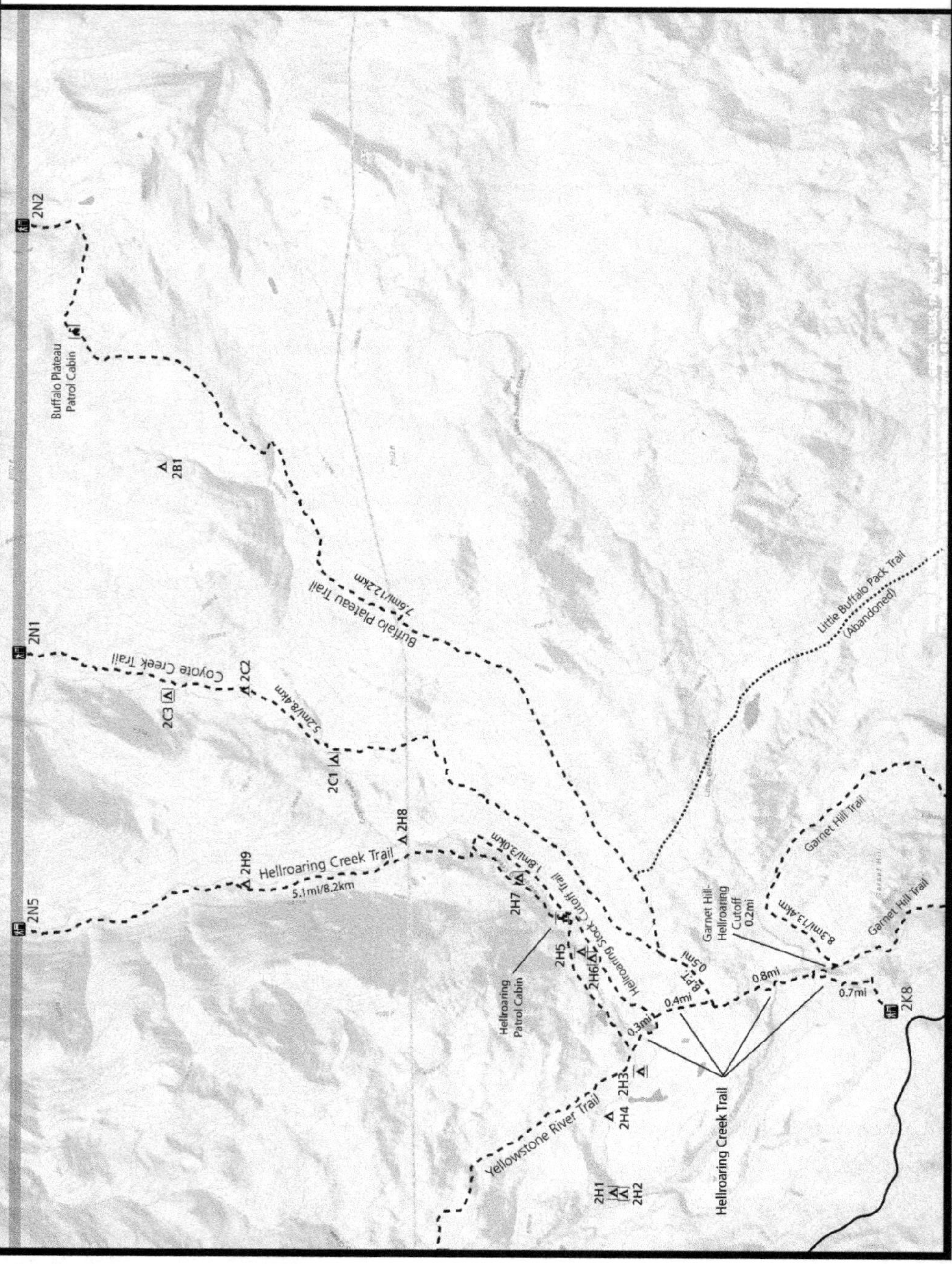

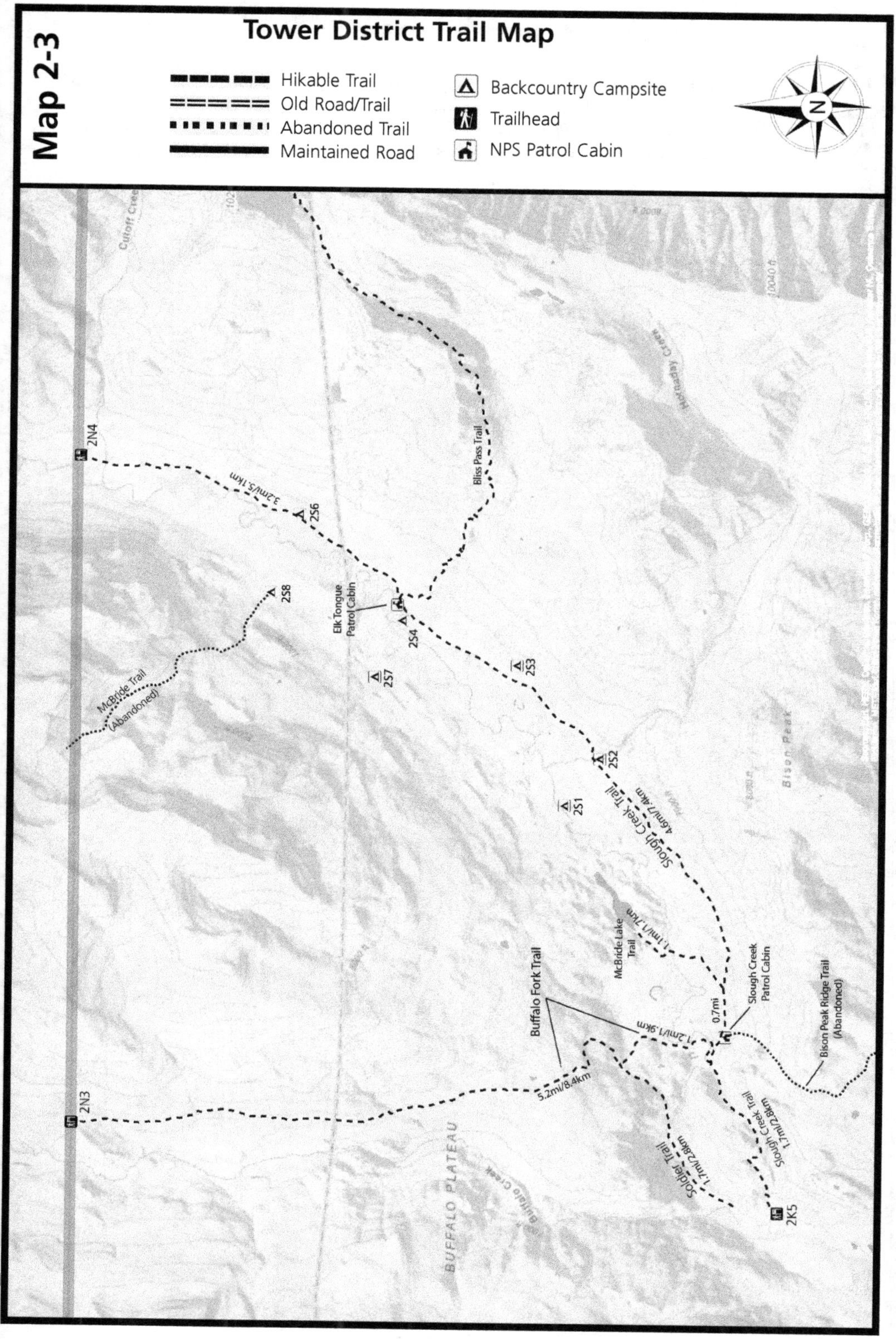

Map 2-3
Tower District Trail Map
Hikable Trail
Old Road/Trail
Abandoned Trail
Maintained Road
Backcountry Campsite
Trailhead
NPS Patrol Cabin
N
Cutoff Creek
2N4
3.2mi/5.1km
2S6
2S8
McBride Trail (Abandoned)
Elk Tongue Patrol Cabin
2S4
2S7
2S3
Bliss Pass Trail
Hornaday Creek
2S2
2S1
Slough Creek Trail
4.6mi/7.4km
Bison Peak
McBride Lake Trail
1.1mi/1.7km
Slough Creek Patrol Cabin
0.7mi
Buffalo Fork Trail
1.2mi/1.9km
5.2mi/8.4km
Bison Peak Ridge Trail (Abandoned)
2N3
Slough Creek Trail
1.7mi/2.8km
Soldier Trail
1.7mi/2.8km
2K5
BUFFALO PLATEAU
Buffalo Creek

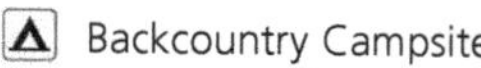

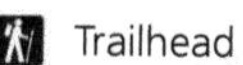

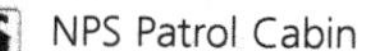

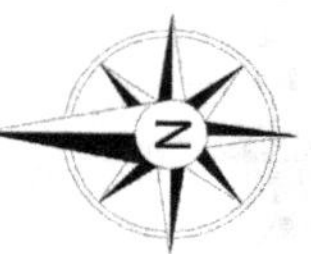

Map 2-4

Tower District Trail Map

Hikable Trail
Old Road/Trail
Abandoned Trail
Maintained Road

Backcountry Campsite
Trailhead
NPS Patrol Cabin

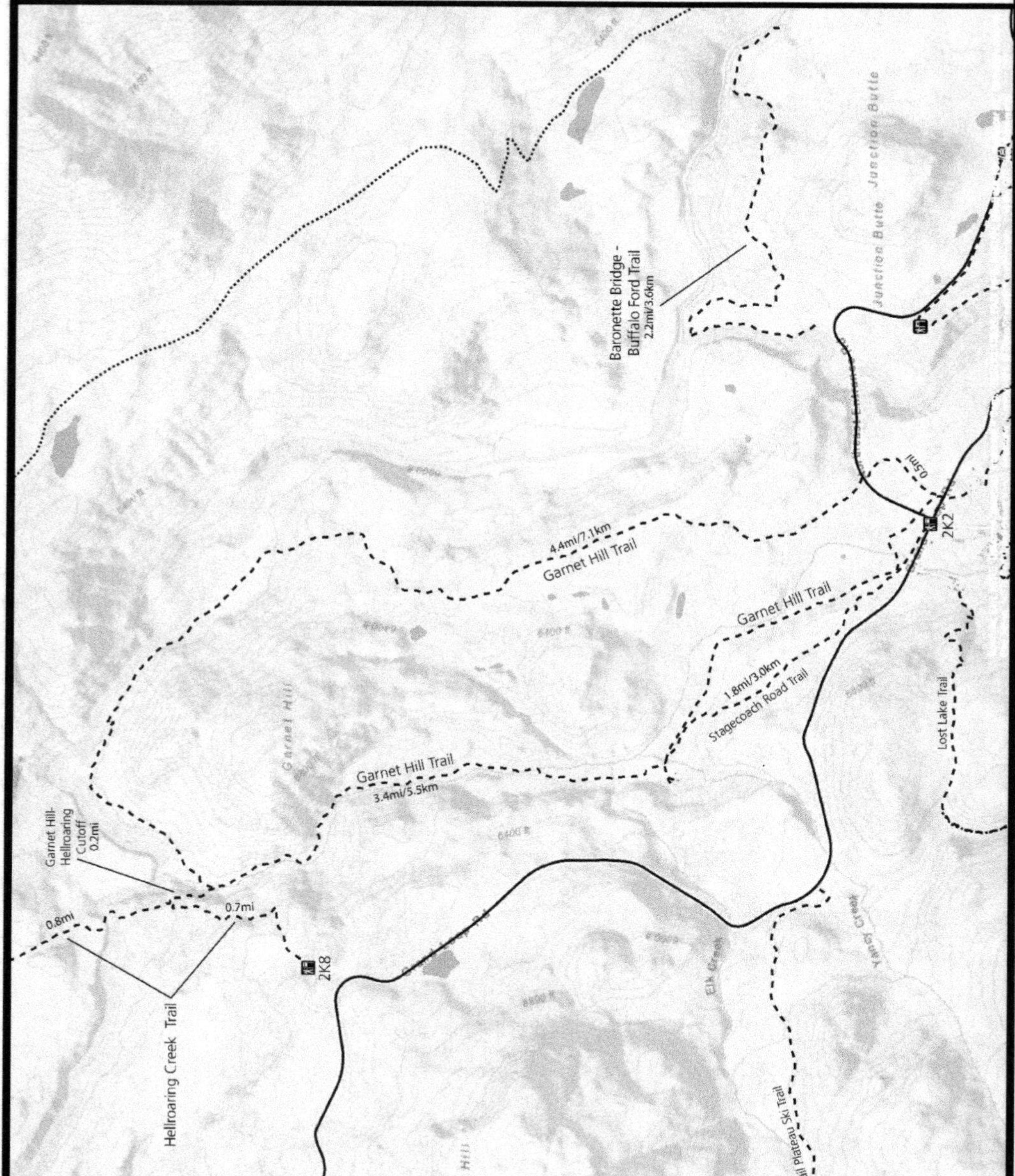

Junction Butte
Baronette Bridge - Buffalo Ford Trail
2.2mi/3.6km
0.5mi
2K2
4.4mi/7.1km
Garnet Hill Trail
Garnet Hill Trail
1.8mi/3.0km
Stagecoach Road Trail
Lost Lake Trail
Garnet Hill
Garnet Hill Trail
3.4mi/5.5km
Garnet Hill-Hellroaring Cutoff 0.2mi
0.8mi
0.7mi
2K8
Hellroaring Creek Trail
Elk Creek
Yancy Creek
Blacktail Plateau Ski Trail
Crescent Hill
7855 ft

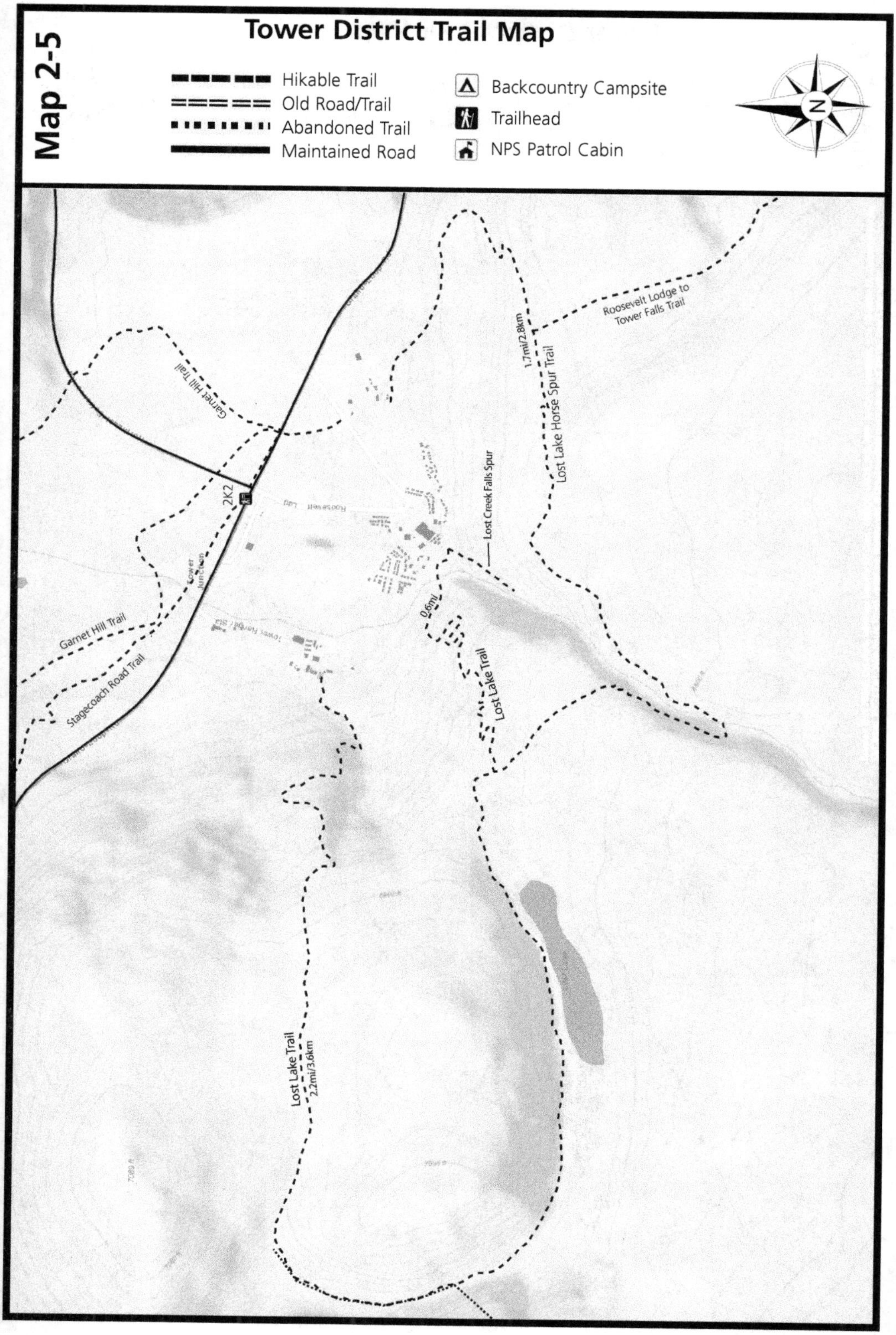

Map 2-5

Tower District Trail Map

- Hikable Trail
- Old Road/Trail
- Abandoned Trail
- Maintained Road
- Backcountry Campsite
- Trailhead
- NPS Patrol Cabin

N

Garnet Hill Trail

Roosevelt Lodge to Tower Falls Trail

1.7mi/2.8km

Lost Lake Horse Spur Trail

2K2

Lost Creek Falls Spur

Tower Junction

0.6mi

Garnet Hill Trail

Stagecoach Road Trail

Lost Lake Trail

Lost Lake Trail

2.2mi/3.6km

Map 2-6

Tower District Trail Map

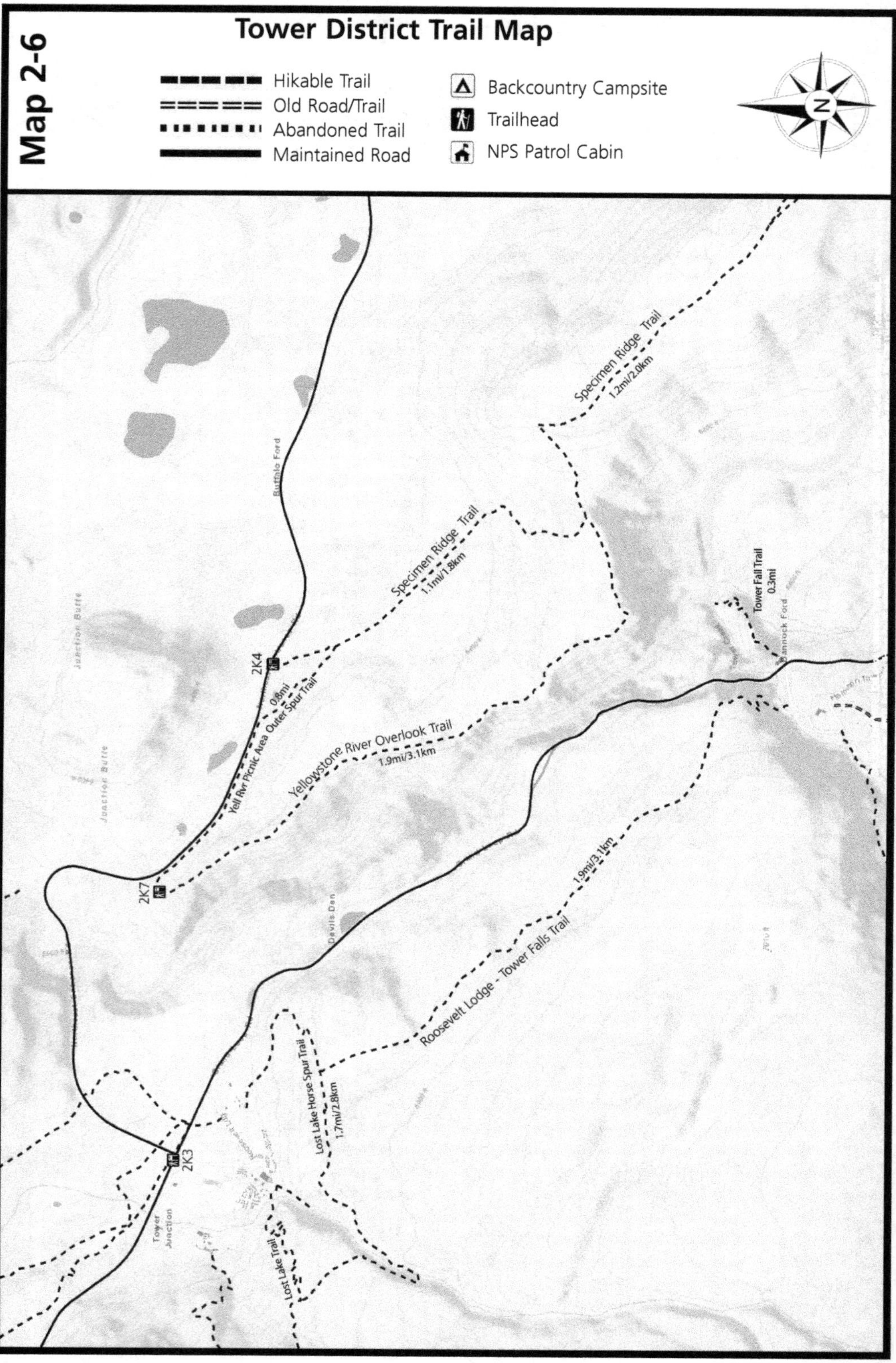

Hikable Trail
Old Road/Trail
Abandoned Trail
Maintained Road

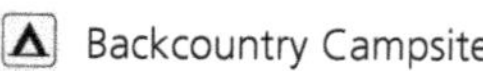
Backcountry Campsite

Trailhead

NPS Patrol Cabin

Specimen Ridge Trail
1.2mi/2.0km

Buffalo Ford

Specimen Ridge Trail
1.1mi/1.8km

Tower Fall Trail
0.3mi

Bannock Ford

Junction Butte

2K4

0.8mi
Yell Rvr Picnic Area Outer Spur Trail

Yellowstone River Overlook Trail
1.9mi/3.1km

2K7

Devils Den

1.9mi/3.1km
Roosevelt Lodge - Tower Falls Trail

Lost Lake Horse Spur Trail
1.7mi/2.8km

2K3

Tower Junction

Lost Lake Trail

Map 2-7

Tower District Trail Map

Hikable Trail
Old Road/Trail
Abandoned Trail
Maintained Road

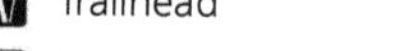

Tower Fall Trail
0.3mi

Howard Eaton Trail
(Abandoned)

Roosevelt Lodge -
Tower Falls Trail
1.9mi/3.1km

Old Dunraven Service Road Trail
2.0mi/3.2km

Tower Creek Trail
3.6mi/5.8km

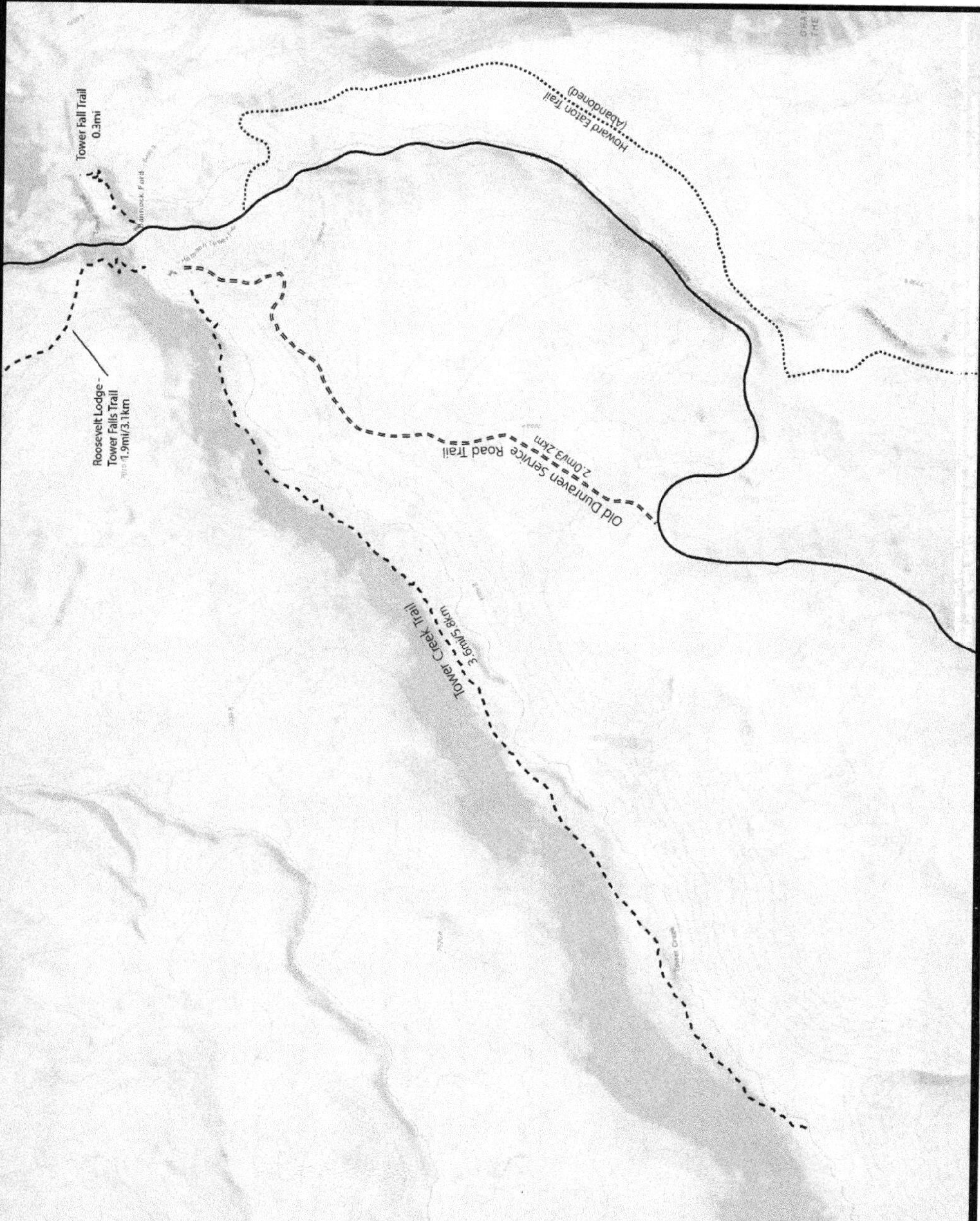

Lamar District Trails

Amethyst Fossil Forest Trail — MAP 2-1

TYPE:	O&B	CAT:	TH	CLASS:	N	SURF:	TRAIL	DIST:	3	STATUS:	A
DIFF:	5	TRAF:	1	CHILD:	N	HACC:	N	USE:	H	LENGTH:	2.40
ELEV A:	6552	ELEV B:	8037	ELEV G:	1609	ELEV L:	-125	NET:	1485	BMA:	- -
MIN:	6539	MAX:	6845	AVG:	8037	AVG +:	14.2%	AVG -:	4.2%	OPEN:	YR

Reference Point	A-B Mi	A-B Km	B-A Mi	B-A Km	Latitude	Longitude
Trailhead @ Midpoint Turnout (11.5 mi N of Tower)	0.00	0.00	2.40	3.86	44.88475	-110.22101
Lamar River crossing (70 to 200')	0.17	0.27	2.23	3.59	44.88316	-110.22365
Petrified tree area	2.40	3.86	0.00	0.00	44.85622	-110.23562

This unmaintained and (now) unofficial trail takes you up to an area of fossilized trees on the side of Amethyst Mountain. You will have to ford the Lamar River, which will be difficult until at least mid-July in most years (and possibly later in wetter years), and then climb up into the mountain through a dense forest of trees. You may need to bushwhack your way through some areas. The trail will be hard to follow in places and there will be many bison trails through this area, so use the GPS coordinates and keep your eyes on where you are headed as you hike across the valley floor.

Bannock Ski Trail — MAP 3-1

TYPE:	PTP	CAT:	BC	CLASS:	C	SURF:	TRAIL	DIST:	3	STATUS:	E
DIFF:	1	TRAF:	2	CHILD:	N	HACC:	N	USE:	H K	LENGTH:	2.52
ELEV A:	7267	ELEV B:	7407	ELEV G:	380	ELEV L:	-29	NET:	140	BMA:	- -
MIN:	7254	MAX:	7434	AVG:	7345	AVG +:	4.2%	AVG -:	4.2%	OPEN:	YR

Reference Point	A-B Mi	A-B Km	B-A Mi	B-A Km	Latitude	Longitude
Trailhead @ Warm Springs Picnic Area	0.00	0.00	2.52	4.06	44.00411	-110.03086
Park boundary	1.67	2.69	0.85	1.37	44.00149	-110.00183
Trailhead @ Monument Ave & Bannock Trail	2.52	4.06	0.00	0.00	44.00456	-109.98758

This is a fairly level ski trail that takes you from the Warm Springs Picnic Area into the little town of Silver Gate. It runs along what was the original road to Cooke City (and Bannock Trail) through the forest along Soda Butte Creek, terminating at the dead end of Monument Road. From there you can continue on the snowmobile road to Cooke City if you wish.

Baronette Ski Trail — MAP 3-1

TYPE:	PTP	CAT:	BC	CLASS:	C	SURF:	TRAIL	DIST:	3	STATUS:	E
DIFF:	1	TRAF:	1	CHILD:	N	HACC:	N	USE:	H K	LENGTH:	3.80
ELEV A:	7010	ELEV B:	7197	ELEV G:	469	ELEV L:	-283	NET:	187	BMA:	- -
MIN:	7010	MAX:	7226	AVG:	7155	AVG +:	3.3%	AVG -:	2.9%	OPEN:	YR

Reference Point	A-B Mi	A-B Km	B-A Mi	B-A Km	Latitude	Longitude
West Trailhead @ Soda Butte Creek crossing	0.00	0.00	3.80	6.12	44.94487	-110.08260
East Trailhead @ Soda Butte Creek crossing	3.80	6.12	0.00	0.00	44.99200	-110.05663

This is primarily a winter ski trail and is not maintained for summer hiking, though the path is generally visible in the summer as well. It follows what at one time was the original road between Tower and the Northeast Entrance. The ends of the trail are not usually marked in summer. It is an easy cross-country trail with minimal elevation loss/gain in either direction, and affords some outstanding views of Baronette Peak.

Bliss Pass Trail

MAP 2-3,3-1

TYPE:	PTP	CAT:	BC	CLASS:	C	SURF:	TRAIL	DIST:	3	STATUS:	E
DIFF:	3	TRAF:	2	CHILD:	N	HACC:	N	USE:	H S	LENGTH:	6.99
ELEV A:	6599	ELEV B:	7796	ELEV G:	3045	ELEV L:	-1848	NET:	1197	BMA:	- -
MIN:	6599	MAX:	9410	AVG:	8228	AVG +:	12.1%	AVG -:	14.5%	OPEN:	YR

Reference Point	A-B Mi	A-B Km	B-A Mi	B-A Km	Latitude	Longitude
Trailhead @ jct w/ Slough Creek Trail	0.00	0.00	6.99	11.25	44.99036	-110.20004
Bliss Pass (top of hill)	4.54	7.31	2.45	3.94	44.99859	-110.14152
Pebble Creek crossing (15 to 20')	6.89	11.09	0.10	0.16	45.00007	-110.10878
Trailhead @ jct w/ Pebble Creek Trail	6.99	11.25	0.00	0.00	44.99923	-110.10724

Bliss Pass is the mountain pass between Mt. Hornaday and Cutoff Mountain. This trail takes you from the Slough Creek drainage to the Pebble Creek drainage (hiking west to east). The pass itself is named for the brothers who bought the Silver Tip Ranch (just outside the park boundary on the Slough Creek Trail) after the original owner passed away.

This trail is designed to allow you to form a loop from the Slough Creek trailhead to the Warm Creek or Pebble Creek trailheads on the Pebble Creek Trail. From west to east, there is a 3,000-foot (914m) elevation gain over the course of the first five miles. Going east to west, you will have a 2,000-foot (610m) gain in just over two miles. There are no campsites along this trail, but there are on each end of it at its junction with the other trails.

This trail is often snowpacked well into June, and is steep and often muddy. It is authorized for stock, but pack strings are not recommended because of the tight set of switchbacks on the eastern half of the trail.

Bootjack Gap Trail

MAP 3-4,3-2

TYPE:	PTP	CAT:	BC	CLASS:	C	SURF:	TRAIL	DIST:	3	STATUS:	E
DIFF:	3	TRAF:	1	CHILD:	N	HACC:	N	USE:	H S	LENGTH:	4.62
ELEV A:	7614	ELEV B:	9219	ELEV G:	2198	ELEV L:	-593	NET:	1605	BMA:	- -
MIN:	7596	MAX:	9229	AVG:	8288	AVG +:	11.6%	AVG -:	7.3%	OPEN:	YR

Reference Point	A-B Mi	A-B Km	B-A Mi	B-A Km	Latitude	Longitude
Trail @ jct w/ Miller Creek, Canoe Lake Trails	0.00	0.00	4.62	7.44	44.75214	-109.96686
Spur to Upper Miller Creek Patrol Cabin	0.62	0.00	4.00	6.44	44.74992	-109.95533
Jct with Hoodoo Basin Trail	0.67	1.08	3.95	6.36	44.74998	-109.95425
Park boundary TH 3N3 (SNF: Papoose Creek Trail)	4.62	7.44	0.00	0.00	44.74819	-109.88654

Bootjack Gap was named for the shape of the pass (gap is just another name for a mountain pass). This is one of the most remote areas of the park. The trail begins at the end of the Miller Creek Trail. Approximately a half mile in, you will pass the Upper Miller Creek Patrol Cabin and the junction with the Hoodoo Basin Trail. Continue straight and begin the 1,500-foot (457m) climb over the four miles to the pass.

Once you reach the park boundary, the trail continues on into Shoshone National Forest along the Papoose Creek Trail (listed on many maps as Trail 607.2B) for 12 miles (19km) to the Sunlight Basin Road. This trail is part of the Nez Perce Historic Trail.

There's little mention of this trail in most guidebooks. It is very lightly used because most people hiking into this part of the park head down into Hoodoo Basin (see below).

Cache Creek Trail — MAP 3-3

TYPE:	PTP	CAT:	BC	CLASS:	B	SURF:	TRAIL	DIST:	3	STATUS:	E
DIFF:	4	TRAF:	1	CHILD:	N	HACC:	N	USE:	H S	LENGTH:	16.25
ELEV A:	6935	ELEV B:	10000	ELEV G:	4192	ELEV L:	-1126	NET:	3065	BMA:	- -
MIN:	6848	MAX:	10000	AVG:	7648	AVG +:	6.5%	AVG -:	3.7%	OPEN:	YR

Reference Point	A-B Mi	A-B Km	B-A Mi	B-A Km	Latitude	Longitude
Trailhead @ jct with Lamar River Trail	0.00	0.00	16.25	26.15	44.83604	-110.15291
Enter the Wahb Springs Thermal Area	2.00	3.22	14.25	22.93	44.82575	-110.11678
Death Gulch Overlook	2.22	3.57	14.03	22.58	44.82527	-110.11383
Confluence of Cache Creek & South Cache Creek	4.18	6.73	12.07	19.42	44.83885	-110.08093
Spur trail to campsite 3C2 (0.13 mi)	5.57	8.96	10.68	17.19	44.85474	-110.06874
Spur trail to campsite 3C3 (0.22 mi)	7.29	11.73	8.96	14.42	44.87538	-110.05146
Jct with Thunderer Cutoff Trail	10.65	17.14	5.60	9.01	44.91602	-110.02300
Cache Creek Patrol Cabin	10.81	17.40	5.44	8.75	44.91760	-110.02046
Cache Creek crossing	10.95	17.62	5.30	8.53	44.91917	-110.01863
Spur trail to campsite 3C4 (0.13 mi)	11.70	18.83	4.55	7.32	44.92408	-110.00631
Republic Pass/Park boundary TH 3N1 (cont into SNF)	16.25	26.15	0.00	0.00	44.95184	-109.95323

The Cache Creek Trail splits off from the Lamar River Trail about a mile and a half after crossing the river. The first couple of miles of the trail are the most popular, used by many to access the Wahb Springs Thermal Area and an area known as Death Gulch. This area got its name back in the early days of the park when explorers found the remains of a number of large animals here. The deaths were believed to be the result of noxious gases emanating from the thermal field. There have been all sorts of tales told about this place, and it has been the subject of numerous scientific studies as well as part of the storyline of at least one book.[1] This trail is often snowpacked until the middle of June.

The trail parallels Cache Creek for most of its path until it gets to the base of Republic Peak, where it climbs 1,800 feet (549m) in two miles. From the pass, it continues on into the Shoshone National Forest as the Republic Creek Trail (shown as Trail 616 on some maps), terminating at an old mine off US212 near Cooke City. Republic Pass will typically have snow on it until well into July, and the trail near the top can be difficult to find, especially early in the season before the rangers can reset the markers.

There are three campsites along this trail, all with incredible views. They all also lack any shade to speak of, however. Many hikers use the Thunderer Cutoff Trail, Cache Creek Trail, and the Lamar River Trail to create a loop, encircling The Thunderer and Mt. Norris.

Canoe Lake Trail — MAP 3-5,3-2

TYPE:	PTP	CAT:	BC	CLASS:	C	SURF:	TRAIL	DIST:	3	STATUS:	E
DIFF:	3	TRAF:	1	CHILD:	N	HACC:	N	USE:	H S	LENGTH:	3.86
ELEV A:	7578	ELEV B:	9226	ELEV G:	1874	ELEV L:	-226	NET:	1648	BMA:	- -
MIN:	7578	MAX:	9226	AVG:	8505	AVG +:	11.0%	AVG -:	5.3%	OPEN:	YR

Reference Point	A-B Mi	A-B Km	B-A Mi	B-A Km	Latitude	Longitude
Trail jct with Miller Creek, Bootjack Gap Trails	0.00	0.00	3.86	6.21	44.75214	-109.96686
Canoe Lake	3.69	5.94	0.17	0.27	44.79146	-110.93816
Park boundary TH 3N2 (Crandall/Timber Crk Tr SNF)	3.86	6.21	0.00	0.00	44.79324	-109.93584

This trail takes you up to Canoe Lake, a small, oblong-shaped lake just inside the park's east boundary. There is no documentation about how this lake got its name, but former park historian Lee Whittlesey speculates it may either be because of the shape of the lake or the fact that it lies along the old Bannock Indian Trail.[2] The lake is fishless. From the park's boundary, the trail continues on as the Crandall Trail (shown on some maps as Trail 607), taking you out to the Crandall Ranger Station (USFS) located on Chief Joseph Highway.

Frost Lake Trail

MAP 3-6,5-1

Type:	PTP	**Cat:**	BC	**Class:**	B	**Surf:**	Trail	**Dist:**	3	**Status:**	E
Diff:	3	**Traf:**	1	**Child:**	N	**HAcc:**	N	**Use:**	H S	**Length:**	5.64
Elev A:	7300	**Elev B:**	9692	**Elev G:**	2804	**Elev L:**	-413	**Net:**	2392	**BMA:**	- -
Min:	7300	**Max:**	9771	**Avg:**	8581	**Avg +:**	11.4%	**Avg -:**	6.4%	**Open:**	YR

Reference Point	A-B Mi	A-B Km	B-A Mi	B-A Km	Latitude	Longitude
Trailhead @ jct with Lamar River & Mist Creek Tr	0.00	0.00	5.64	9.08	44.67717	-110.05556
Spur trail to campsite 3F2	0.94	1.51	4.70	7.56	44.66936	-110.04198
Park boundary TH 3N5 (Red Creek Trail in SNF)	5.64	9.08	0.00	0.00	44.62387	-110.02555

This trail takes you from Cold Creek Junction up to the park's boundary near Frost Lake, not directly to the lake itself. Once you get to the boundary, you can travel south approximately one-half mile to get to the lake (to which there is no maintained trail, but it is not a difficult hike). The lake is not named for anything related to the cold, but rather for Ned Frost, an early park trail guide and author. He also helped build the original Corkscrew Bridge along the first East Entrance Road in the early 1900s.[3]

The trail is lightly used, and there is one mediocre campsite located along its path. From the park's boundary, the trail continues into Shoshone National Forest via the Red Creek Trail (shown as Trail 751.2D on many maps), and then out to a point a couple of miles east of Yellowstone's East Entrance (near Pahaska Tepee). This trail has a 2,400-foot (732m) elevation gain in 4.5 miles

Hoodoo Basin Trail

MAP 3-4,3-2

Type:	PTP	**Cat:**	BC	**Class:**	C	**Surf:**	Trail	**Dist:**	3	**Status:**	E
Diff:	3	**Traf:**	1	**Child:**	N	**HAcc:**	N	**Use:**	H S	**Length:**	9.84
Elev A:	7685	**Elev B:**	10465	**Elev G:**	3986	**Elev L:**	-1205	**Net:**	2780	**BMA:**	- -
Min:	7663	**Max:**	10465	**Avg:**	9413	**Avg +:**	10.1%	**Avg -:**	8.3%	**Open:**	YR

Reference Point	A-B Mi	A-B Km	B-A Mi	B-A Km	Latitude	Longitude
Trailhead @ jct with Bootjack Gap Trail	0.00	0.00	9.84	15.84	44.74998	-109.95425
Saddle of Parker Peak	4.68	7.53	5.16	8.30	44.72790	-109.89133
Spur trail to campsite 3M6	5.11	8.22	4.73	7.61	44.72678	-109.88479
Spur trail to campsite 3M7	6.58	10.59	3.26	5.25	44.72699	-109.86572
Park boundary TH 3N4 (Sunlight Basin Trail: SNF)	9.84	15.84	0.00	0.00	44.70052	-109.82663

Hoodoo Basin, not to be confused with The Hoodoos rock formations found along the road between Mammoth and Norris, is one of the most interesting and intriguing places in the park. Getting to it is a multi-day exercise, however.

Hoodoo Basin is an area of unique, weathered volcanic rock formations that reminded some visitors of goblins. A quote from an 1883 tour guidebook for the park perhaps sums this area up best: "Upon the southern face of the [Hoodoo] mountain...the frosts and storms of ages

The Hoodoos rock formations. Image courtesy USGS (Iddings, 1890)

have worn numberless deep, narrow, crooked channels amid the slender tottering pillars, shafts, mounds and pyramids which form this singular maze. The formations are totally unlike in shape those seen in other eroded districts. They are not symmetrical, but assume every curious and fantastic form, among which may be seen gigantic figures of beasts, birds, and reptiles. One mound is described as looking like a large altar pyre, 125 feet in height, resting on a pyramidal base, the sacrificial victim lying on top."[4]

The trail itself departs from the Miller Creek Trail at the Upper Miller Creek Patrol Cabin. You immediately cross Miller Creek (almost always crossable, but usually no more than a foot or so deep by early to mid-July), and then begin a 2,000-foot (610m) climb to the saddle of Parker Peak (with numerous switchbacks). You then descend into Hoodoo Valley. Campsite 3M6 is located here.

If you choose to continue on along the trail, you will climb another 1,000 feet (304m) over the course of three miles to and along the park boundary just below the ridge of Hoodoo Peak. There is another campsite (3M7) just west of the boundary. Both of these campsites are located in areas that have little, if any, water during the latter part of the season. So plan accordingly (fill up at Miller Creek).

It is also important to note that this area is rife with grizzly bears, especially in the latter part of the season when they are feeding on the moths that can be found among the scree. The views are spectacular, but do not forget to keep your eyes open for the more immediate concern.

The trail into Hoodoo Basin is among the oldest in the park, dating from the early 1880s. Park superintendent Philetus W. Norris was infatuated with this area and created the trail to allow visitors to view it for themselves. At the park boundary, it continues into Shoshone National Forest down the Sunlight Creek drainage (shown on some maps as Trail 606), and out to Sunlight Basin Road.

Lamar River Trail

MAP 3-2

Type:	PTP	**Cat:**	BC	**Class:**	A	**Surf:**	Trail	**Dist:**	3	**Status:**	E
Diff:	3	**Traf:**	3	**Child:**	N	**HAcc:**	N	**Use:**	H S	**Length:**	15.53
Elev A:	6656	**Elev B:**	7301	**Elev G:**	2568	**Elev L:**	-1923	**Net:**	645	**BMA:**	- -
Min:	6656	**Max:**	7323	**Avg:**	7028	**Avg +:**	4.8%	**Avg -:**	4.9%	**Open:**	YR

Reference Point	A-B Mi	A-B Km	B-A Mi	B-A Km	Latitude	Longitude
Trailhead @ jct w/ Specimen Ridge Trail	0.00	0.00	15.53	24.99	44.85364	-110.17717
Remains of Harry Yount Cabin	0.21	0.34	15.32	24.66	44.85108	-110.17494
Extinct thermal area	1.12	1.80	14.41	23.19	44.84274	-110.16123
Jct with Cache Creek Trail	1.75	2.82	13.78	22.18	44.83604	-110.15291
Spur trail to campsite 3L1 (0.17 mi)	2.17	3.49	13.36	21.50	44.83201	-110.14664
Cache Creek crossing (30 to 50')	2.19	3.52	13.34	21.47	44.83173	-110.14665
Spur trail to campsite 3L2 (0.14 mi)	2.23	3.59	13.30	21.40	44.83122	-110.14656
Spur trail to campsite 3L3 (0.10 mi)	3.58	5.76	11.95	19.23	44.81462	-110.14287
Spur trail to campsite 3L4 (0.10 mi)	4.30	6.92	11.23	18.07	44.80715	-110.13414
Spur trail to Calfee Creek Patrol Cabin	6.67	10.73	8.86	14.26	44.77991	-110.11364
Jct with Miller Creek Trail	7.74	12.46	7.79	12.54	44.76837	-110.10426
Miller Creek crossing (30 to 40')	7.86	12.65	7.67	12.34	44.76724	-110.10308
Spur trail to campsite 3L6 (0.16 mi)	8.75	14.08	6.78	10.91	44.75727	-110.09798
Spur trail to campsite 3L7 (0.10 mi)	9.10	14.64	6.43	10.35	44.75352	-110.09514
Junction w/ (abandoned) Timothy Creek Trail	10.21	16.43	5.32	8.56	44.73919	-110.09064
Spur trail to campsite 3L8 (0.14 mi)	10.70	17.22	4.83	7.77	44.73285	-110.08776
Spur trail to campsite 3L9 (0.10 mi)	10.90	17.54	4.63	7.45	44.73089	-110.08742
Spur trail to campsite 3U1 (0.27 mi)	12.17	19.59	3.36	5.41	44.71495	-110.08395
Spur trail to campsite 3U2 (0.12 mi)	13.12	21.11	2.41	3.88	44.70311	-110.07808
Spur trail to campsite 3U3 (0.16 mi)	14.19	22.84	1.34	2.16	44.69198	-110.06755
Spur trail to Cold Creek Patrol Cabin	14.93	24.03	0.60	0.97	44.68453	-110.05788
Spur trails to campsites 3U4 (0.21 mi)/3F1 (0.10 mi)	15.35	24.70	0.18	0.29	44.67935	-110.05367
Lamar River crossing north side (30 to 60')	15.42	24.82	0.11	0.18	44.67839	-110.05457
Lamar River crossing south side	15.49	24.93	0.04	0.06	44.67771	-110.05521
Jct with Frost Lake & Mist Creek Trails	15.53	24.99	0.00	0.00	44.67717	-110.05556

The Lamar River Trail is one of the busiest trails in the northeastern section of the park, largely because it is the primary path to get to many of the other trails that lead up into the Mirror Plateau, Specimen Ridge, and eastern boundary areas. Many of the park's most popular campsites lie along this trail as well.

There are two access points for the Lamar River Trail. The primary one, which is technically the Specimen Ridge Trail east trailhead, and a secondary one used mainly by stock parties (see below). If you elect to use the main foot trail, you will need to add 1.34 miles (2.16km) to the beginning of your hike. If you use the stock trailhead (known colloquially as the Hitching Post), you will need to add 1.14 miles (1.83km) to the beginning of your hike. Further adding to the confusion is the fact that both trailheads are signed as "Lamar River" trailheads.[5] The trail is usually closed south of Cache Creek until well into June due to high water.

One of the most interesting aspects of this trail is that, once you cross Cache Creek and head south, the Lamar River takes on a completely different character. You are no longer in the lush, open Lamar Valley, but rather in a wide canyon with the river at its base. It is certainly not the Lamar River you are used to seeing in most of the photos of the area.

Though a great many people hike out along this trail with the intent of staying overnight and/or proceeding on to further exploration, a popular day hike is to hike up to the Cache Creek Trail and take it to the Wahb Springs Thermal Area, and then return. This makes for a nice nine- to ten-mile round trip.

There are a number of campsites along this trail, most of which are pretty decent. Some of them allow stock use and are well worn. The 3L sites are much more heavily used than the 3U sites.

Lamar River Stock Cutoff Trail — MAP 3-2

TYPE:	PTP	CAT:	BC	CLASS:	A	SURF:	TRAIL	DIST:	3	STATUS:	E
DIFF:	1	TRAF:	3	CHILD:	N	HACC:	N	USE:	H S	LENGTH:	0.89
ELEV A:	6621	ELEV B:	6648	ELEV G:	75	ELEV L:	-49	NET:	27	BMA:	- -
MIN:	6596	MAX:	6648	AVG:	6624	AVG +:	2.4%	AVG -:	2.8%	OPEN:	YR

Reference Point	A-B Mi	A-B Km	B-A Mi	B-A Km	Latitude	Longitude
Trailhead 3K1	0.00	0.00	0.89	1.43	44.86840	-110.17449
Soda Butte Creek crossing (40' or more)	0.19	0.31	0.70	1.13	44.86595	-110.17378
Jct with Specimen Ridge Trail	0.89	1.43	0.00	0.00	44.85626	-110.17583

This trail is basically a stock trail to facilitate access to the Lamar River Trail and those that lie beyond. There is a large parking area at the trailhead to accommodate trailers and larger vehicles. The parking area pullout itself is known to locals as Hitching Post.

Unlike the foot trail a few hundred yards further east, there is no bridge over Soda Butte Creek. If you are on foot, you will have to get your feet wet crossing the creek.

Miller Creek Trail — MAP 3-5

TYPE:	PTP	CAT:	BC	CLASS:	B	SURF:	TRAIL	DIST:	3	STATUS:	E
DIFF:	3	TRAF:	1	CHILD:	N	HACC:	N	USE:	H S	LENGTH:	7.79
ELEV A:	7049	ELEV B:	7575	ELEV G:	1480	ELEV L:	-953	NET:	526	BMA:	- -
MIN:	6998	MAX:	7576	AVG:	7283	AVG +:	5.0%	AVG -:	4.2%	OPEN:	YR

Reference Point	A-B Mi	A-B Km	B-A Mi	B-A Km	Latitude	Longitude
Trailhead @ jct w/ Lamar River Trail	0.00	0.00	7.79	12.54	44.76837	-110.10426
Miller's Valley/Spur trail to campsite 3M1(0.27 mi)	1.64	2.64	6.15	9.90	44.76393	-110.07548
Spur trail to campsite 3M2 (0.18 mi)	3.46	5.57	4.33	6.97	44.75806	-110.04521
Spur trail to campsite 3M3 (0.10 mi)	4.43	7.13	3.36	5.41	44.75240	-110.03112
Spur trail to campsite 3M4 (0.10 mi)	7.18	11.56	0.61	0.98	44.75152	-109.97830
Spur trail to campsite 3M5 (0.23 mi)	7.76	12.49	0.03	0.05	44.75229	-109.96735
Jct with Canoe Lake & Bootjack Gap Trails	7.79	12.54	0.00	0.00	44.75214	-109.96686

The Miller Creek Trail is primarily a thorofare trail that facilitates access to Bootjack Gap, Canoe Lake, and the Hoodoo Basin. The creek (and the little valley known as Miller's Valley where campsite 3M1 is located) was named after Adam Miller, an associate of the park's second superintendent, Philetus W. Norris. Miller claimed to have retreated along this creek as he escaped a band of Native Americans, and so Norris named the creek after him.[6]

This trail is one of the easiest in the park's wild backcountry, gaining only about 500 feet (152m) over the course of its nearly eight-mile length. There are five lightly-used campsites along this trail, one of which (3M4) is among the least used in the entire park.

Mist Creek Trail — MAP 3-6,5-1

TYPE:	PTP	**CAT:**	BC	**CLASS:**	A	**SURF:**	TRAIL	**DIST:**	3	**STATUS:**	E
DIFF:	3	**TRAF:**	1	**CHILD:**	N	**HACC:**	N	**USE:**	H S	**LENGTH:**	10.22
ELEV A:	7300	**ELEV B:**	7911	**ELEV G:**	1963	**ELEV L:**	-1353	**NET:**	611	**BMA:**	- -
MIN:	7299	**MAX:**	8745	**AVG:**	7999	**AVG +:**	5.6%	**AVG -:**	5.6%	**OPEN:**	YR

Reference Point	A-B Mi	A-B Km	B-A Mi	B-A Km	Latitude	Longitude
Trailhead @ jct w/ Lamar River & Frost Lake Trails	0.00	0.00	10.22	16.45	44.67717	-110.05556
Cold Creek crossing (60 to 70')	0.12	0.19	10.10	16.25	44.67571	-110.05622
Spur trail to campsite 3T1 (abandoned site)	0.25	0.40	9.97	16.05	44.67509	-110.05789
Lovely Pass (to the northwest)	5.66	9.11	4.56	7.34	44.63692	-110.10139
Spur trail to campsite 3T2 (0.10 mi)	5.90	9.50	4.32	6.95	44.62233	-110.11916
Spur trail to campsite 3T3 (0.23 mi)	6.57	10.57	3.65	5.87	44.61594	-110.13484
Mist Creek Pass	8.14	13.10	2.08	3.35	44.60360	-110.16115
Pelican Springs Cabin Trail (north end)	9.70	15.61	0.52	0.84	44.59814	-110.18632
Jct with Pelican Valley Trail	10.22	16.45	0.00	0.00	44.59624	-110.19476

The Mist Creek Trail, though lightly used, is a critical trail in the park. It provides access to Pelican Valley from the park's northeast quadrant. Some other guidebooks incorrectly refer to this as either the Mist Pass Trail or the Mist Creek Pass Trail.

This trail has a couple of campsites, either of which can serve as a base for northbound travel out of Pelican Valley (it is ten miles from the Pelican Valley trailhead to campsite 3T3), or for southbound travel through the valley after staying a night along Mist Creek. Keep in mind that Pelican Valley is closed to foot travel until the July 4th weekend, so you will not be able to travel any further south than the Pelican Creek Patrol Cabin until that time. Pelican Valley is also only open during daylight hours, so there are no longer any overnight campsites on those trails. Therefore, if your plans call for overnighting on a trip from the Lamar Valley to Pelican Valley, you should reserve site 3T2 or 3T3 in advance to ensure you can stick to your schedule. If you are traveling north to south, this is a slow, fairly easy climb of about 1,500 feet (457m) over the course of eight miles to Mist Pass, and then a quick 800-foot (244m) descent into Pelican Valley.

Pebble Creek Trail — MAP 3-1

TYPE:	PTP	**CAT:**	BC	**CLASS:**	B	**SURF:**	TRAIL	**DIST:**	3	**STATUS:**	E
DIFF:	3	**TRAF:**	2	**CHILD:**	N	**HACC:**	N	**USE:**	H S K	**LENGTH:**	11.75
ELEV A:	6843	**ELEV B:**	7302	**ELEV G:**	2147	**ELEV L:**	-1688	**NET:**	459	**BMA:**	- -
MIN:	6843	**MAX:**	8309	**AVG:**	7701	**AVG +:**	4.8%	**AVG -:**	6.7%	**OPEN:**	YR

Reference Point	A-B Mi	A-B Km	B-A Mi	B-A Km	Latitude	Longitude
Trailhead 3K2 (Pebble Crk CG; 9.7 mi W of NE Ent)	0.00	0.00	11.75	18.91	44.91689	-110.11318
Jct w/ trail from roadside trailhead	0.20	0.32	11.55	18.59	44.91869	-110.11085
Spur trail to campsite 3P1	3.37	5.42	8.38	13.49	44.95923	-110.11675
Pebble Creek crossing (20')	4.53	7.29	7.22	11.62	44.97547	-110.11987
Pebble Creek crossing (35')	5.37	8.64	6.38	10.27	44.98648	-110.11528
Spur trail to campsite 3P2	6.10	9.82	5.65	9.09	44.99453	-110.10958
Jct with Bliss Pass Trail	6.43	10.35	5.32	8.56	44.99923	-110.10724
Spur trail to campsite 3P3	6.56	10.56	5.19	8.35	45.00108	-110.10676
Pebble Creek crossing (30')	8.25	13.28	3.50	5.63	45.01856	-110.08596
Spur trail to campsite 3P4	8.72	14.03	3.03	4.88	45.02044	-110.07759

Reference Point	A-B Mi	A-B Km	B-A Mi	B-A Km	Latitude	Longitude
Spur trail to campsite 3P5	9.81	15.79	1.94	3.12	45.01996	-110.05572
Pebble Creek crossing (50')	9.94	16.00	1.81	2.91	45.01919	-110.05341
Trailhead 3K4 (1.6 mi W of Northeast Entrance)	11.75	18.91	0.00	0.00	45.00539	-110.03420

There are two trail entry points for the Pebble Creek Trail. The first one, the "official" one, is from a parking area off the entrance road for the Pebble Creek Campground. The second is located almost 2/10th of a mile east of the bridge over Pebble Creek. It is a pulloff on the north side of the main road. The advantage of using the second one is that you do not have to ford Pebble Creek, which, earlier in the season when the creek is running high, can be dangerous for less-experienced hikers. The measurements in the table above are from the first entry point. If you are parking a stock trailer or long vehicle, park along the side of the campground entrance road.

Pebble Creek runs through a drainage between Baronette Peak and Mt. Hornaday on its southern end, and Baronette Peak and Cutoff Mountain and Wolverine Peak on its northern end. The trail passes through some of the most spectacular scenery in the park, and is one of the few trails where it is almost guaranteed you will see wildlife.

This trail does have a handful of creek crossings, and in the early part of the season (prior to mid-June), the creek may be rather high (up to three feet or more in heavy snow seasons) and therefore closed past the first ford north of campsite 3P1 (site 3P1 is typically open early in the season, however). You may need to spend some time moving up or downstream to find a suitable place to cross once it opens. Even later in the season, the creek will often be knee to thigh deep. There will usually be a considerable number of marshy spots along the trail as well, so plan your footwear accordingly.

There are five campsites along this trail, all of which are good sites and are moderately used. If you prefer a specific site, it is best to reserve it in advance if possible. Site 3P1 is the only site that will be available early in the season before the creek becomes fordable, however (usually around July 1). Hiking from the Warm Creek side involves an immediate 1,000-foot (309m) climb over a mile and a half, whereas doing it from the Pebble Creek side involves a 750-foot (229m) climb over about the same distance.

Thunderer Cutoff Trail — MAP 3-3,3-1

Type:	PTP	**Cat:**	BC	**Class:**	B	**Surf:**	Trail	**Dist:**	3	**Status:**	E
Diff:	4	**Traf:**	1	**Child:**	N	**HAcc:**	N	**Use:**	H S	**Length:**	5.00
Elev A:	6918	**Elev B:**	7778	**Elev G:**	2166	**Elev L:**	-1305	**Net:**	860	**BMA:**	- -
Min:	6854	**Max:**	8795	**Avg:**	7849	**Avg +:**	13.6%	**Avg -:**	11.3%	**Open:**	YR

Reference Point	A-B Mi	A-B Km	B-A Mi	B-A Km	Latitude	Longitude
Trailhead 3K3 (8.7 mi W of Northeast Entrance)	0.00	0.00	5.00	8.05	44.92144	-110.09559
Soda Butte Creek crossing (50 to 60')	0.14	0.23	4.86	7.82	44.91973	-110.09614
Chaw Pass	3.52	5.66	1.48	2.38	44.91745	-110.04337
Jct with Cache Creek Trail	5.00	8.05	0.00	0.00	44.91602	-110.02300

The Thunderer Cutoff Trail serves two purposes. The vast majority of hikers simply climb to the top of The Thunderer for the views, and then return to the trailhead. The trails gets its name from its other use, however: to provide a shorter access to the Cache Creek Trail and Republic Pass that lies on the park's eastern boundary. By using this route vs. coming in via the Lamar River trailhead, you can shave a day's travel off both ends of your trip if you are wanting to get up to the pass. This trail requires a ford of Soda Butte Creek, which is usually not possible before the middle of June.

The climb up is a little over 2,000 feet (610m) in the course of 3.5 miles, almost entirely covered by a forest canopy. While there are some occasional glimpses of the little valley through which Amphitheater Creek passes, you won't really see much more than trees on the way up. Once you get to the top, however, you are rewarded with some incredible views of many of the mountains of the Absaroka Range that make up the park's eastern boundary. If you elect to hike down to Cache Creek, it is a 1,000-foot (304m) descent over the course of 1.5 miles (almost entirely out in the open). Note that this trail does not take you to the summit of The Thunderer, but it is reachable via a ¾-mile hike along the ridge from the pass.

There are no campsites along this trail. However, site 3C4 is just a mile up the Cache Creek Trail if you wish to make an overnight stay in the area. The Thunderer gets its name from the fact that early explorers of the peak encountered numerous thunderstorms during their time in the area.

Trout Lake Trail — MAP 3-3

Type:	Loop	**Cat:**	TH	**Class:**	B	**Surf:**	Trail	**Dist:**	3	**Status:**	E
Diff:	1	**Traf:**	4	**Child:**	Y	**HAcc:**	N	**Use:**	H	**Length:**	1.18
Elev A:	6767	**Elev B:**	6767	**Elev G:**	305	**Elev L:**	-305	**Net:**	0	**BMA:**	- -
Min:	6764	**Max:**	6994	**Avg:**	6940	**Avg +:**	9.5%	**Avg -:**	5.4%	**Open:**	YR

Reference Point	A-B Mi	A-B Km	B-A Mi	B-A Km	Latitude	Longitude
Trailhead	0.00	0.00	1.18	1.90	44.89911	-110.12319
Trout Lake /Trail Split	0.30	0.48	0.88	1.42	44.89988	-110.12817
Social trail to Buck Lake	0.49	0.79	0.69	1.11	44.90175	-110.12993
Social Trail to Shrimp Lake	0.52	0.84	0.66	1.06	44.90203	-110.13036
Return to Trail Split	0.88	1.42	0.30	0.48	44.89988	-110.12817
Trailhead	1.18	1.90	0.00	0.00	44.89911	-110.12319

The Trout Lake Trail is perhaps the busiest trail in the northeast quadrant of the park. This is largely because of its short distance, the fact that a scenic (and historic) lake lies at its end, and the promise of seeing moose and otters near the lake's shore. This trail is so busy that, during the height of the summer tourist season, the parking area is full and people are parking along the side of the road.

The trail is fairly easy, even for smaller children, with a 250-foot (76m) climb over the course of the third of a mile it takes to get to the lake itself. You can hike around the lake if you wish. There are a couple of social (unmaintained, unofficial) trails to a couple of smaller lakes to the northeast of Trout Lake as well. Buck Lake is the larger of the two. Shrimp Lake was named for the large number of freshwater shrimp that are found within its waters.

Trout Lake was the site of a major fish hatchery from the early 1920s up until 1951, though you can hardly tell that today. The hatchery operation was located at the lake's outlet, a stream known as Fish Creek. The lake supplied eggs and fish that were used to populate other lakes in Yellowstone and lakes in other parts of the country. The lake still contains a healthy population of rainbow trout and a hybrid rainbow/cutthroat trout, and is quite popular with anglers during fishing season.

Upper Lamar River Trail MAP 3-2

Type:	O&B	**Cat:**	BC	**Class:**	N	**Surf:**	Trail	**Dist:**	3	**Status:**	A
Diff:	3	**Traf:**	1	**Child:**	N	**HAcc:**	N	**Use:**	H S	**Length:**	5.73
Elev A:	7328	**Elev B:**	7789	**Elev G:**	1032	**Elev L:**	-571	**Net:**	461	**BMA:**	- -
Min:	7328	**Max:**	7789	**Avg:**	7537	**Avg +:**	4.9%	**Avg -:**	4.0%	**Open:**	YR

Reference Point	A-B Mi	A-B Km	B-A Mi	B-A Km	Latitude	Longitude
Trailhead @ jct w/ Lamar River Trail @ 3F1	0.00	0.00	5.73	9.22	44.67935	-110.05367
Confluence of Lamar & Little Lamar Rivers	2.30	3.70	3.43	5.52	44.67179	-110.01177
Trail terminus/Site of old Upper Lamar Patrol Cab	5.73	9.22	0.00	0.00	44.68841	-109.95371

The Upper Lamar River Trail is an abandoned and unmaintained remnant of an old trail that paralleled the upper Lamar River, terminating at the Upper Lamar River Patrol Cabin (built here in 1934 and relocated further east some time later). The Lamar River travels along the base of Castor and Pollux Peaks on the south and Saddle Mountain on the north. The trail was abandoned decades ago so any travel along this path today would require significant bushwhacking (though it does parallel Lamar River for the entire route).

Map 3-1

Lamar District Trail Map

Hikable Trail
Old Road/Trail
Abandoned Trail
Maintained Road

Backcountry Campsite
Trailhead
NPS Patrol Cabin

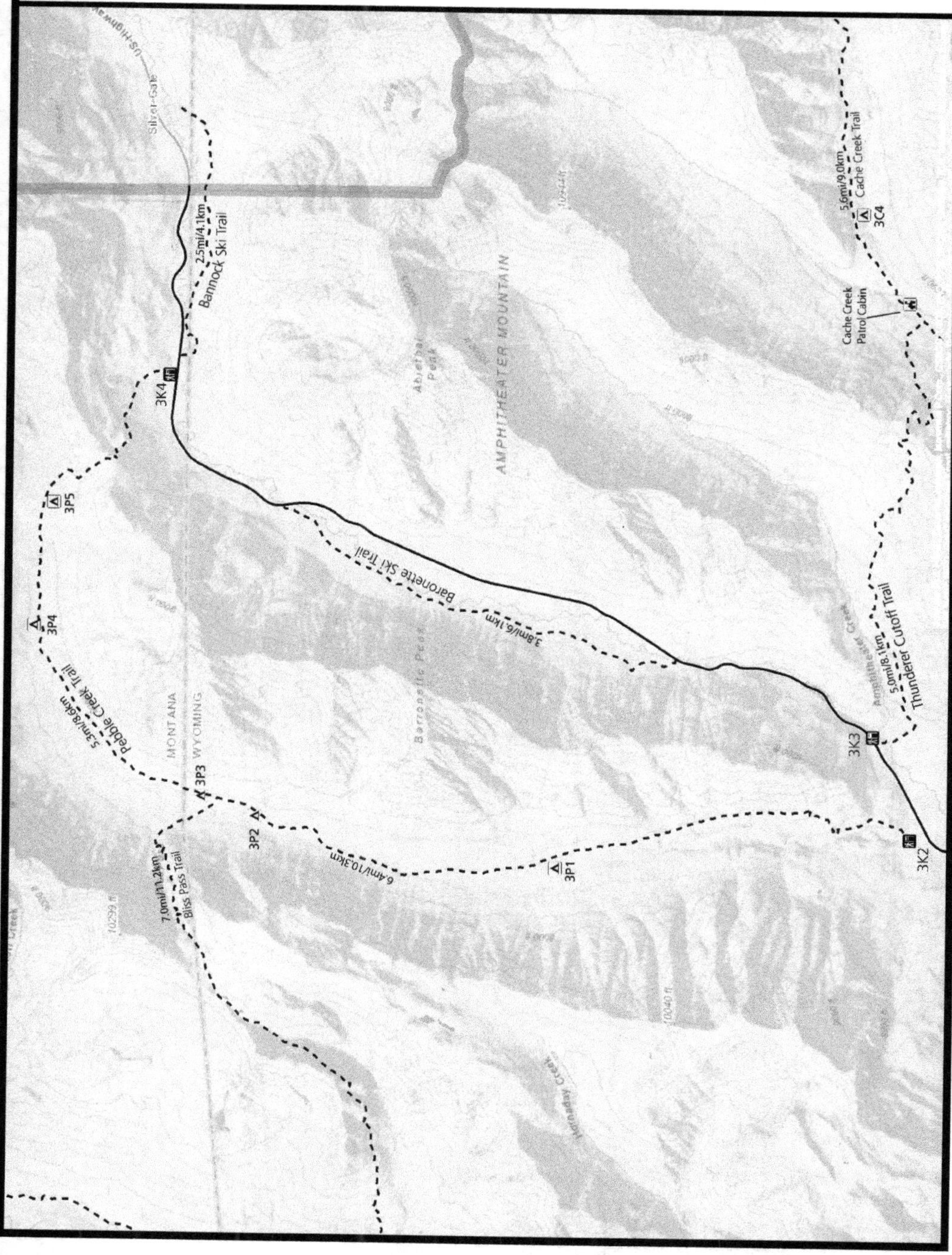

Silver Gate
2.5mi/4.1km Bannock Ski Trail
3K4
3P5
3P4
5.3mi/8.6km Pebble Creek Trail
MONTANA
WYOMING
3P3
3P2
7.0mi/11.2km Bliss Pass Trail
6.4mi/10.3km
3P1
Barronette Ski Trail
3.8mi/6.1km
Barronette Peak
Abiathar Peak
AMPHITHEATER MOUNTAIN
5.6mi/9.0km Cache Creek Trail
3C4
Cache Creek Patrol Cabin
5.0mi/8.1km Thunderer Cutoff Trail
Amphitheater Creek
3K3
3K2
Hoodoo Creek

Map 3-2

Lamar District Trail Map

Hikable Trail
Old Road/Trail
Abandoned Trail
Maintained Road

Backcountry Campsite
Trailhead
NPS Patrol Cabin

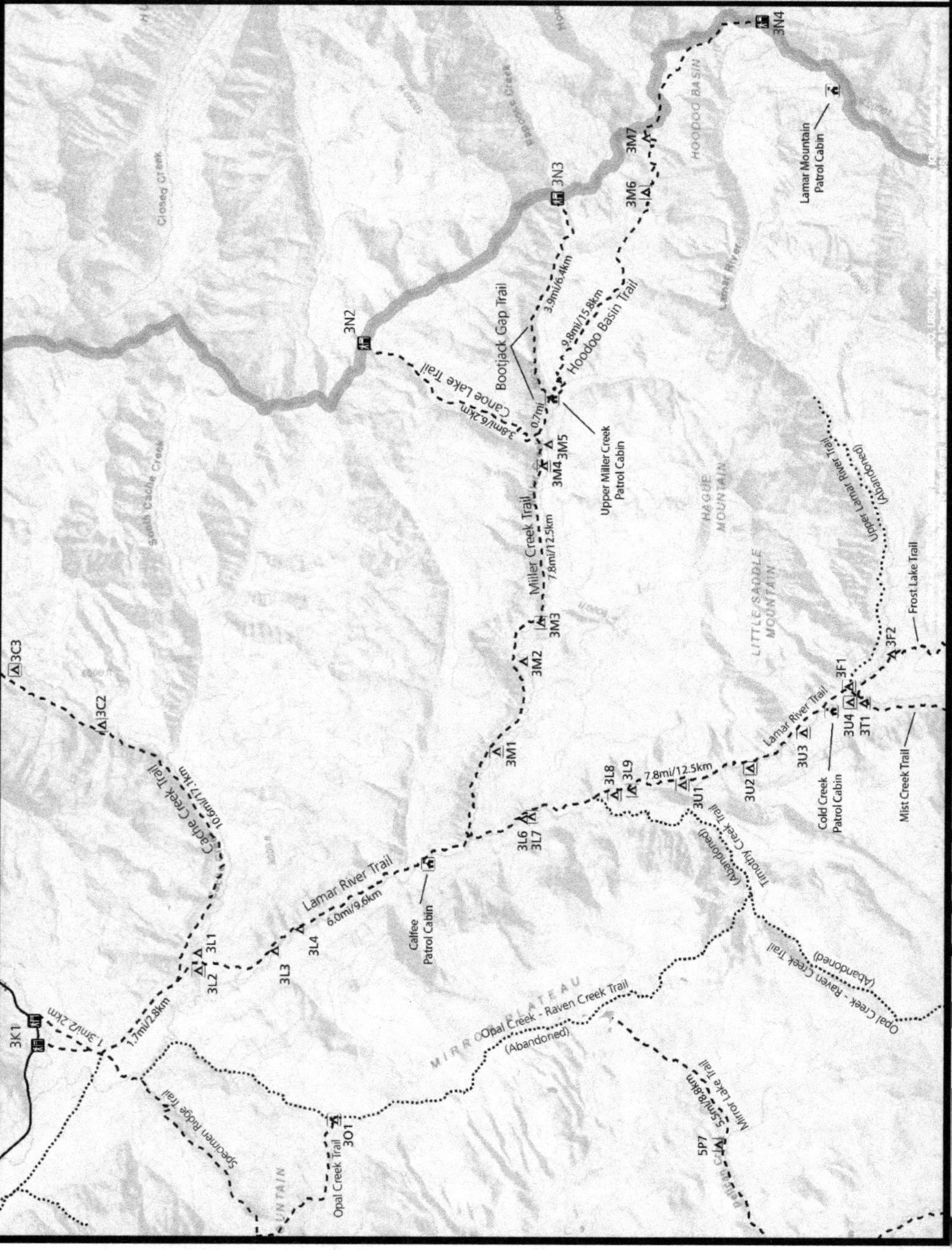

3N2
3N3
3N4
3M1
3M2
3M3
3M4
3M5
3M6
3M7
Lamar Mountain Patrol Cabin
Hoodoo Basin
Closed Creek
South Cache Creek
Bootjack Gap Trail
3.9mi/6.4km
9.8mi/15.8km
Hoodoo Basin Trail
Canoe Lake Trail
3.8mi/6.2km
0.7mi
Upper Miller Creek Patrol Cabin
Miller Creek Trail
7.8mi/12.5km
Lamar River
Hague Mountain
Little Saddle Mountain
Upper Lamar River Trail
(Abandoned)
Frost Lake Trail
3F1
3F2
3C2
3C3
Cache Creek Trail
10.6mi/17.1km
Lamar River Trail
7.8mi/12.5km
3L8
3L9
3U1
3U2
3U3
3U4
3T1
Cold Creek Patrol Cabin
Mist Creek Trail
3L6
3L7
Timothy Creek Trail
(Abandoned)
Lamar River Trail
6.0mi/9.6km
Calfee Patrol Cabin
3L1
3L2
3L3
3L4
Opal Creek - Raven Creek Trail
(Abandoned)
3K1
1.3mi/2.2km
1.7mi/2.8km
Mirror Plateau
Specimen Ridge Trail
Opal Creek Trail
3O1
Mirror Lake Trail
5.5mi/8.8km
5P7

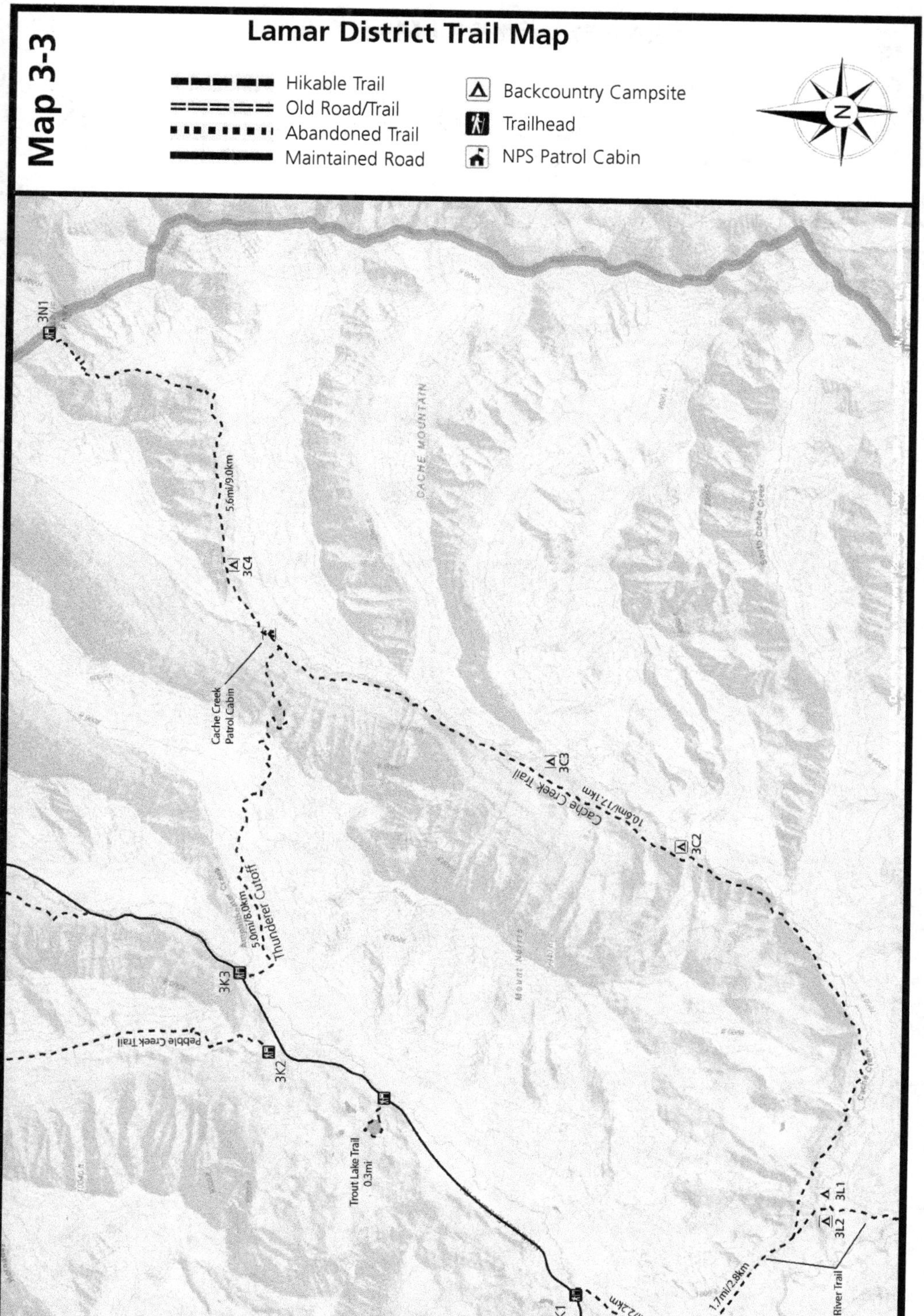

Map 3-3

Lamar District Trail Map

Hikable Trail
Old Road/Trail
Abandoned Trail
Maintained Road

Backcountry Campsite
Trailhead
NPS Patrol Cabin

3N1
5.6mi/9.0km
3C4
Cache Creek Patrol Cabin
CACHE MOUNTAIN
3C3
Cache Creek Trail
10.6mi/17.1km
3C2
South Cache Creek
Cache Creek
Amphitheater Creek
5.0mi/8.0km
Thunderer Cutoff
3K3
Mount Norris
Pebble Creek Trail
3K2
Trout Lake Trail
0.3mi
3L1
3L2
1.7mi/2.8km
Lamar River Trail
3K1
1.3mi/2.2km

Map 3-4

Lamar District Trail Map

3N4

Hoodoo Basin

Lamar Mountain Patrol Cabin

3M7

3N3

3M6

Hoodoo Basin Trail 9.8mi/15.8km

3.9mi/6.4km

Bootjack Gap Trail

Upper Miller Creek Patrol Cabin

Canoe Lake Trail

0.6mi/1.1km

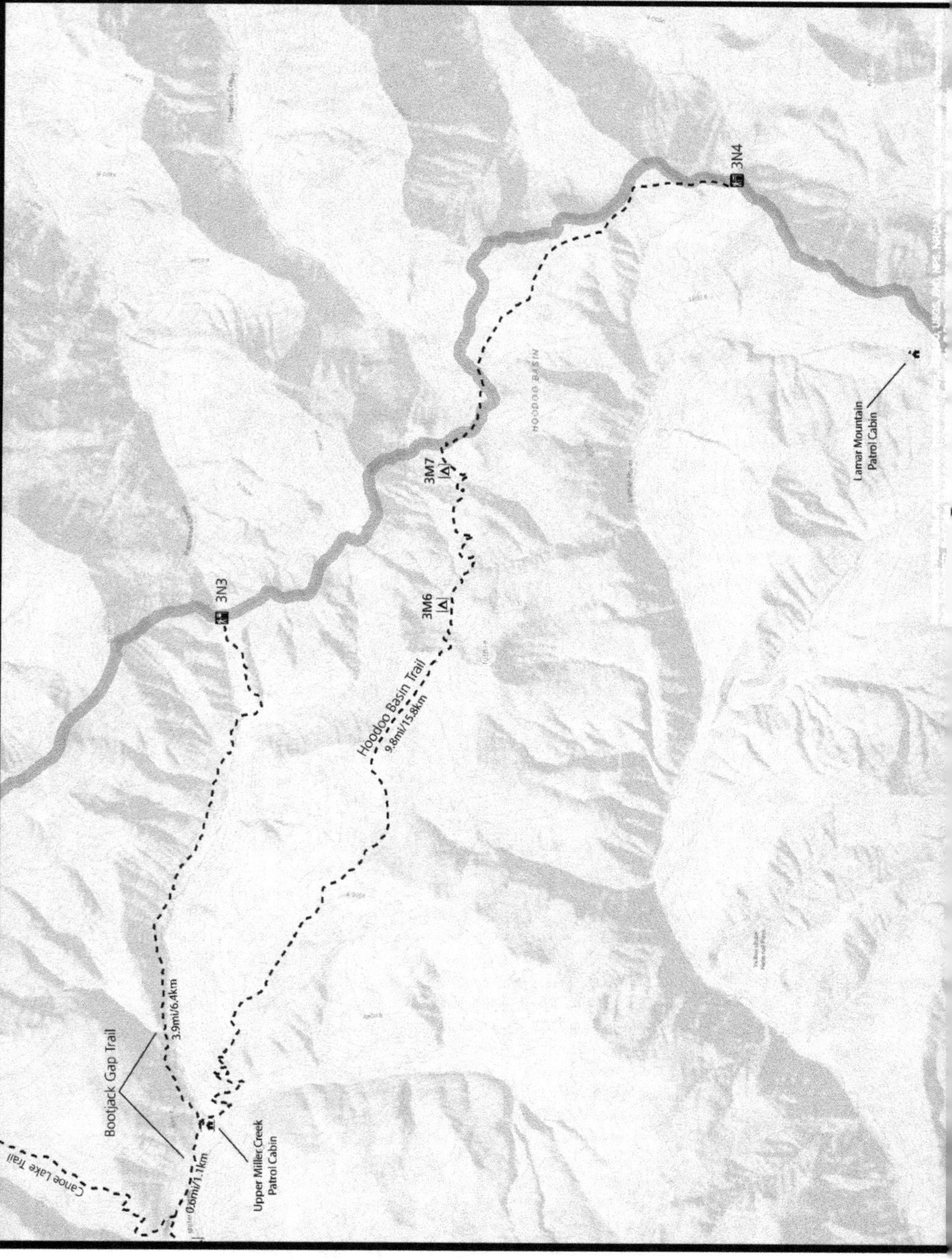

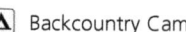

Map 3-5

Lamar District Trail Map

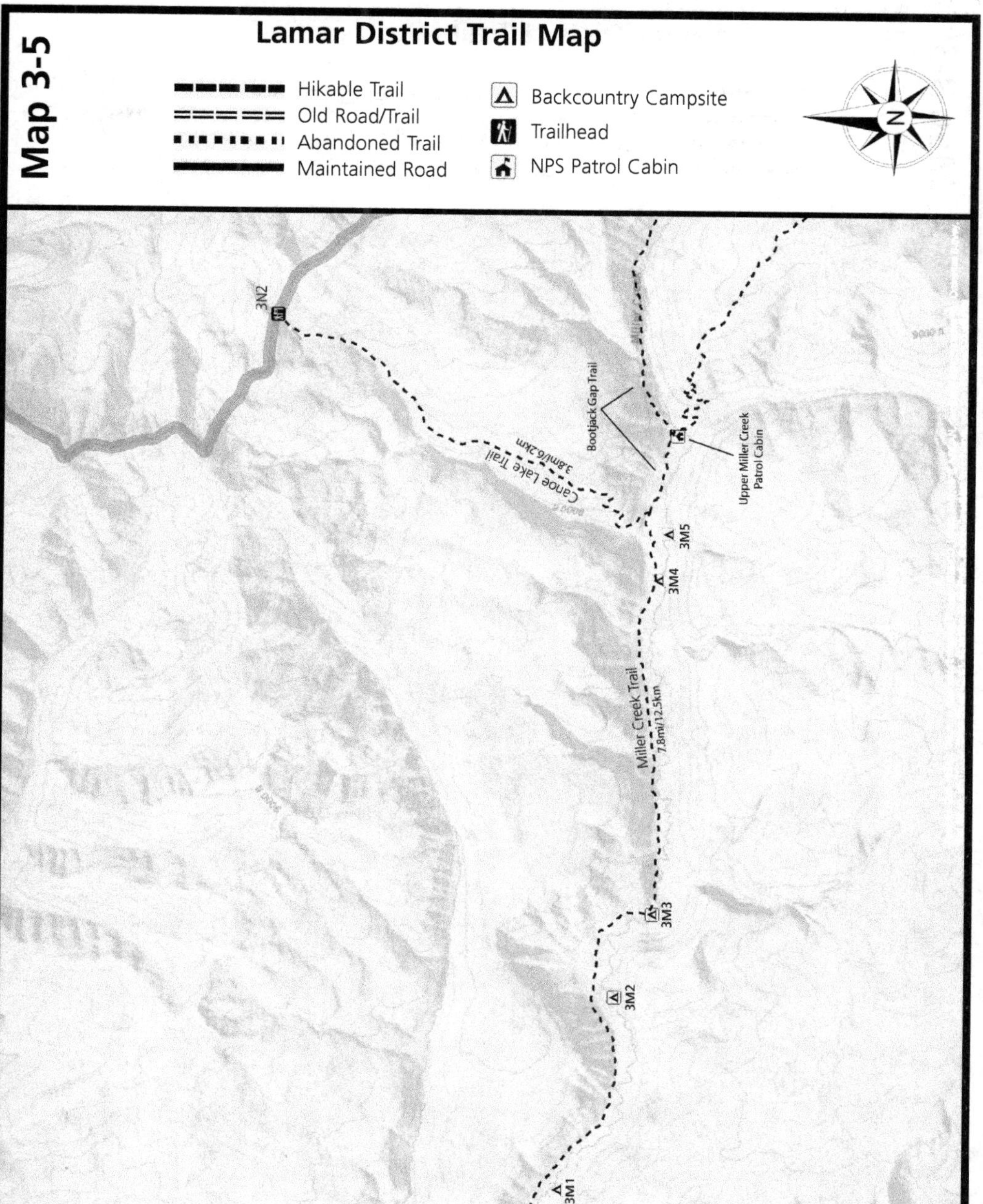

Hikable Trail
Old Road/Trail
Abandoned Trail
Maintained Road

Backcountry Campsite
Trailhead
NPS Patrol Cabin

3N2
Canoe Lake Trail
3.8mi/6.2km
Bootjack Gap Trail
Upper Miller Creek
Patrol Cabin
3M5
3M4
Miller Creek Trail
7.8mi/12.5km
3M3
3M2
3M1
Lamar River Trail
6.0mi/9.6km
3L6
3L7
3L8
3L9
3U1
Timothy Creek Trail
(Abandoned)
Calfee Creek
Calfee
Patrol Cabin
Lamar River Trail
6.0mi/9.6km

Map 3-6

Lamar District Trail Map

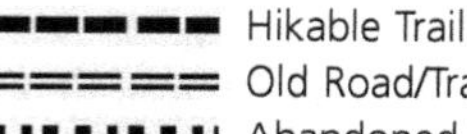

Hikable Trail
Old Road/Trail
Abandoned Trail
Maintained Road

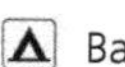 Backcountry Campsite

 Trailhead

NPS Patrol Cabin

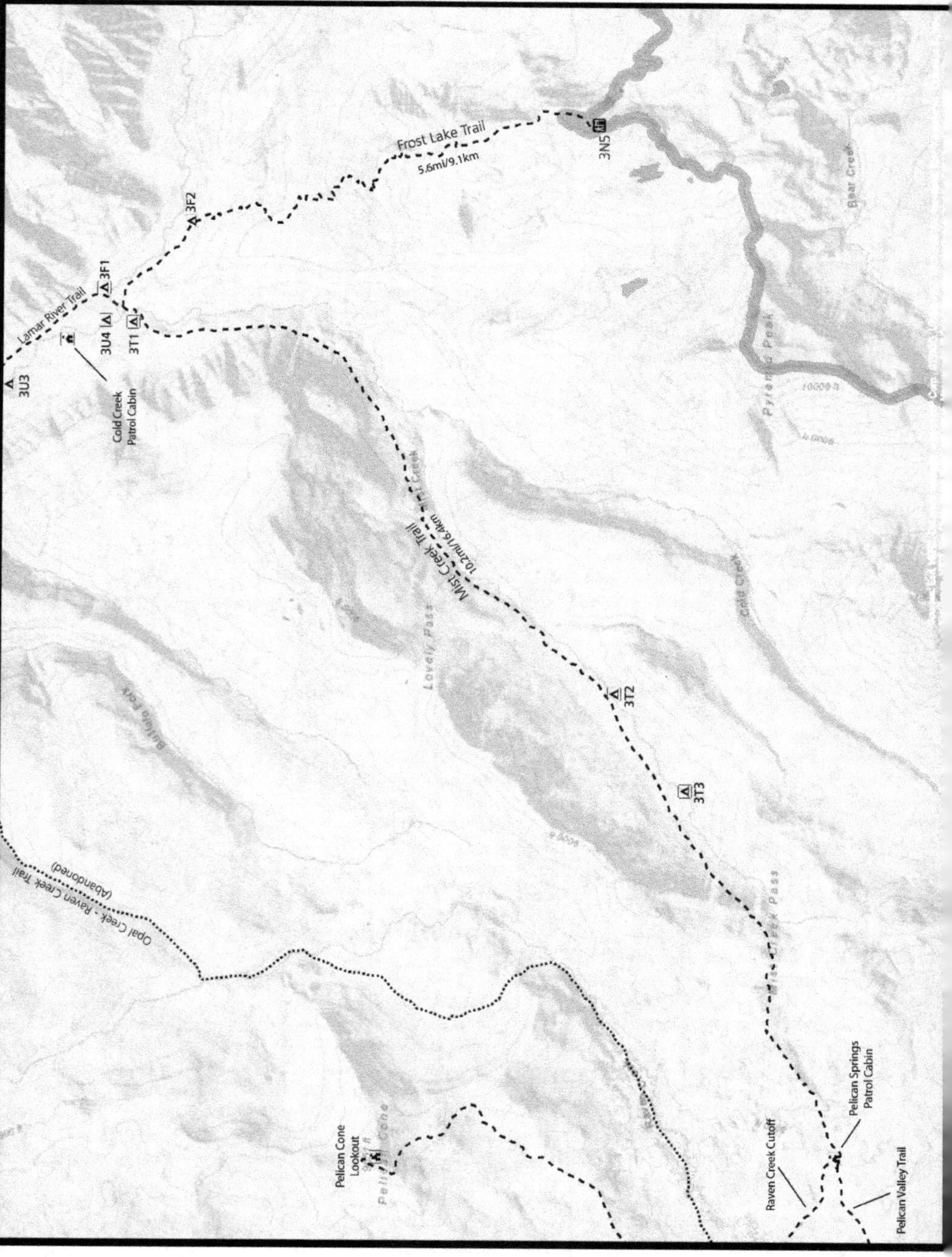

Frost Lake Trail
5.6mi/9.1km
3N5
3F2
3F1
Lamar River Trail
3U4
3T1
3U3
Cold Creek Patrol Cabin
Bear Creek
Pyramid Peak
Mist Creek Trail
10.2mi/16.4km
Lovely Pass
Cold Creek
Buffalo Fork
3T2
3T3
Opal Creek - Raven Creek Trail (Abandoned)
Mist Creek Pass
Pelican Cone Lookout
Pelican Springs Patrol Cabin
Raven Creek Cutoff
Pelican Valley Trail

Canyon District Trails

Artists' Paint Pots Trail — MAP 4-2

Type:	Loop	Cat:	FC	Class:	B	Surf:	Trail	Dist:	4	Status:	E
Diff:	1	Traf:	5	Child:	N	HAcc:	N	Use:	H	Length:	1.04
Elev A:	7349	Elev B:	7349	Elev G:	146	Elev L:	-146	Net:	0	BMA:	- -
Min:	7348	Max:	7454	Avg:	7383	Avg +:	4.2%	Avg -:	6.3%	Open:	YR

Reference Point	A-B Mi	A-B Km	B-A Mi	B-A Km	Latitude	Longitude
Trailhead APP (3.7 mi S of Norris Junction)	0.00	0.00		0.00	44.62627	-110.74105
Power line crossing	0.16	0.26		0.00	44.69455	-110.73915
Loop split	0.31	0.50		0.00	44.69285	-110.73757
Flash Spring	0.68	1.09		0.00	44.69264	-110.73667
Return to loop split	0.73	1.17		0.00	44.69285	-110.73757

Artists' Paint Pots got its name from the fact that the colorful little pots of mud and bubbling water here reminded people of an artist's palette. This area is one of the little out-of-the-way gems of the park. It is not visited by as many people as some of the more popular thermal areas, and makes a nice diversion if you are looking for a thermal field to visit without too many people crowding the trail. There is some uphill climb on this trail, but it is short-lived and nothing most people can't handle. The original trail through this area was built in 1932.

Maps and guides produced prior to 2004 will show the entrance to this area from a pullout alongside the road. That was removed in favor of the new parking lot that year.

Artist Point Trail — MAP 4-9

Type:	Loop	Cat:	FC	Class:	A	Surf:	Pave	Dist:	4	Status:	E
Diff:	1	Traf:	5	Child:	Y	HAcc:	Y	Use:	H	Length:	0.23
Elev A:	- -	Elev B:	- -	Elev G:	- -	Elev L:	- -	Net:	- -	BMA:	- -
Min:	- -	Max:	- -	Avg:	- -	Avg +:	- -	Avg -:	- -	Open:	YR

Reference Point	A-B Mi	A-B Km	B-A Mi	B-A Km	Latitude	Longitude
Trailhead @ parking lot	0.00	0.00		0.00	44.72020	-110.47978
Loop split	0.10	0.16		0.00	44.72091	-110.47892
Return to loop split	0.13	0.21		0.00	44.72091	-110.47892

Artist Point is one of the most visited spots in Yellowstone, second only to Old Faithful. The overwhelming majority of photos you see of the Lower Falls of the Yellowstone are taken from this location. The trail is just a short walk from the parking lot; it is child-friendly and wheelchair-accessible, with the exception of the upper viewing platform.

This area (including the parking lot and the bathrooms) gets extremely busy during the peak of the summer tourist season and there is often a long traffic backup, so pack your patience.

Pro tip: Try to time your visit so you are there around 9:15 on a sunny morning. For a period of about 15-30 minutes around that time, the angle of the sun causes a rainbow to appear in the downwash mist of the falls, making it one of the most moving sights in the park.

People often mistake Artist Point for Moran Point, believing that artist Thomas Moran created his famous paintings of the canyon from this location. Even park photographer Frank J. Haynes erroneously believed Moran had done his work here and bestowed the name Artist Point upon it because of that. Moran Point, from where the namesake artist actually did his work, is on the other side of the canyon, however.

Artist Point-Point Sublime Trail

MAP 4-6

Type:	O&B	**Cat:**	TH	**Class:**	B	**Surf:**	Trail	**Dist:**	4	**Status:**	E
Diff:	2	**Traf:**	2	**Child:**	N	**HAcc:**	N	**Use:**	H	**Length:**	1.24
Elev A:	7686	**Elev B:**	7658	**Elev G:**	682	**Elev L:**	-709	**Net:**	-28	**BMA:**	- -
Min:	7635	**Max:**	7837	**Avg:**	7750	**Avg +:**	2.7%	**Avg -:**	3.5%	**Open:**	YR

Reference Point	A-B Mi	A-B Km	B-A Mi	B-A Km	Latitude	Longitude
Trailhead 4K8 (Artist Point)	0.00	0.00	1.24	2.00	44.72097	-110.47884
Jct with Ribbon Lake Trail	0.57	0.92	0.67	1.08	44.72022	-110.49988
Terminus at Sublime Point	1.24	2.00	0.00	0.00	44.72443	-110.46000

This trail, constructed in 1921, takes you along the rim of the canyon east to a location known as Point Sublime (referred to erroneously by some as Sublime Point). This is the point at which the Cook-Folsom-Peterson Expedition emerged from the woods in 1869 and got their first view of the Grand Canyon of the Yellowstone. So it is easy to see how this location got its name.

This trail also serves as a path to the Ribbon Lake Trail and the east end access to the Clear Lake Trail. Note that there are no barriers along the rim of the canyon along most of this trail, so be very careful if you elect to get off the trail to get a better look at the canyon.

Cascade Creek Trail

MAP 4-3

Type:	PTP	**Cat:**	BC	**Class:**	B	**Surf:**	Trail	**Dist:**	4	**Status:**	E
Diff:	1	**Traf:**	2	**Child:**	N	**HAcc:**	N	**Use:**	H S	**Length:**	1.69
Elev A:	7889	**Elev B:**	7962	**Elev G:**	333	**Elev L:**	-260	**Net:**	73	**BMA:**	- -
Min:	7889	**Max:**	7980	**Avg:**	7939	**Avg +:**	6.3%	**Avg -:**	6.2%	**Open:**	YR

Reference Point	A-B Mi	A-B Km	B-A Mi	B-A Km	Latitude	Longitude
Trailhead 4K4 (0.5 mi W of Canyon Junction)	0.00	0.00	1.69	2.72	44.73527	-110.50339
Jct with Cascade Lake Trail	1.69	2.72	0.00	0.00	44.75572	-110.50614

This trail is often confused with the Cascade Lake Trail (which departs from near a picnic area off the Dunraven Road). And though it does serve as a sort of "south entrance" into the Cascade Lake area, its main draw is that it parallels Cascade Creek, which for many years served as the primary source of water for the development (hotels, stores, etc.) in the Canyon area prior to the creation of the current village.

This trail facilitates easy access to Cascade Lake and the Chain of Lakes Trail (see below), especially if you are staying in the Canyon Village area and would like to just walk to a trail rather than driving to one. And like most of the other trails in this area, it can be somewhat marshy in places early in the season.

In the past, the trail continued across the road and through Cascade Meadow toward the old Canyon Village area (down where the Brink of the Upper Falls area exists now).

Cascade Lake Trail

MAP 4-3

Type:	PTP	**Cat:**	BC	**Class:**	B	**Surf:**	Trail	**Dist:**	4	**Status:**	E
Diff:	2	**Traf:**	2	**Child:**	N	**HAcc:**	N	**Use:**	H S	**Length:**	2.15
Elev A:	8023	**Elev B:**	8003	**Elev G:**	238	**Elev L:**	-258	**Net:**	-20	**BMA:**	- -
Min:	7949	**Max:**	8041	**Avg:**	7983	**Avg +:**	3.9%	**Avg -:**	4.3%	**Open:**	YR

Reference Point	A-B Mi	A-B Km	B-A Mi	B-A Km	Latitude	Longitude
Trailhead 4K5 (1.0 mi N of Canyon Junction)	0.00	0.00	2.15	3.46	44.75018	-110.49197
Jct with old trail from Picnic Area	0.24	0.39	1.91	3.07	44.75251	-110.48931
Jct with Cascade Creek Trail	1.24	2.00	0.91	1.46	44.75572	-110.50614
Spur trail to campsite 4E4	1.82	2.93	0.33	0.53	44.75615	-110.51738
Cascade Lake; Jct w/ Obs Pk & Howard Eaton Trails	2.15	3.46	0.00	0.00	44.75415	-110.52341

Cascade Lake is a gorgeous, quiet lake that serves as the headwater for Cascade Creek (see above). There are two access points for this trail. This first and primary one is located in a new parking area that was constructed in 2007. It lies about a mile north of Canyon Junction. The old trailhead was located at the Cascade Lake Picnic Area about 3⁄10th of a mile north of the new parking area. The new area was created because trail users were clogging up the picnic area. The original segment of trail is no longer maintained, but is still quite passable.

Following this trail to the lake will take you through more marshy areas and across a few spring-fed creeks compared to the Cascade Creek Trail, but this route is shorter by roughly half a mile (each way).

Chittenden Road (Road to Parking Area) — MAP 4-4

Type:	PTP	**Cat:**	FC	**Class:**	C	**Surf:**	Grvl	**Dist:**	4	**Status:**	E
Diff:	2	**Traf:**	1	**Child:**	N	**HAcc:**	N	**Use:**	HSBKR	**Length:**	1.33
Elev A:	8194	**Elev B:**	8755	**Elev G:**	613	**Elev L:**	-52	**Net:**	561	**BMA:**	- -
Min:	8194	**Max:**	8777	**Avg:**	8488	**Avg +:**	9.5%	**Avg -:**	5.5%	**Open:**	YR

Reference Point	A-B Mi	A-B Km	B-A Mi	B-A Km	Latitude	Longitude
Trailhead @ intersection w/ Dunraven Pass Rd	0.00	0.00	1.33	2.14	44.84022	-110.43894
Trailhead @ parking area	1.33	2.14	0.00	0.00	44.82458	-110.44476

This is not a trail, per se, but can be hiked in the spring before the NPS opens the road up to vehicular traffic. Many people will do this prior to opening to get to the summit of Mt. Washburn. It is a slow, gradual climb up to the parking area, and will add 1⅓ miles to your hike in each direction. When the swing gate is closed, hiking is permitted so long as the "No Hiking" placard is not posted on the gate.

Once you get to the top near the parking area, there will be another swing gate just where you make your U-turn into the parking lot. In the summer, this road is used to allow vehicles up to the summit to provision the lookout as well as provide maintenance services to the large array of communications equipment located on the tower.

Chittenden Road-Mount Washburn Trail — MAP 4-4

Type:	PTP	**Cat:**	TH	**Class:**	A	**Surf:**	Trail	**Dist:**	4	**Status:**	E
Diff:	3	**Traf:**	3	**Child:**	N	**HAcc:**	N	**Use:**	HSBKR	**Length:**	2.85
Elev A:	8741	**Elev B:**	10238	**Elev G:**	1573	**Elev L:**	-76	**Net:**	1497	**BMA:**	- -
Min:	8741	**Max:**	10238	**Avg:**	9505	**Avg +:**	10.9%	**Avg -:**	7.8%	**Open:**	YR

Reference Point	A-B Mi	A-B Km	B-A Mi	B-A Km	Latitude	Longitude
Trailhead at Chittenden Road Parking Lot	0.00	0.00	2.85	4.59	44.82452	-110.44458
Jct with service road	0.18	0.29	2.67	4.30	44.82204	-110.44391
Service road to generator	2.10	3.38	0.75	1.21	44.80170	-110.43594
Jct with Dunraven Pass & Washburn Springs Trails	2.56	4.12	0.29	0.47	44.79776	-110.43249
Summit of Mt Washburn	2.85	4.59	0.00	0.00	44.79765	-110.43399

This trail is one of the two primary routes up to the summit of Mt. Washburn (the other being the Dunraven Pass Trail; see below). It is a half-mile shorter, but is a bit steeper and is entirely through open area (i.e., no shade). It actually follows the service road up to the fire lookout (the road is how crews keep the lookout stocked during the summer).

The Chittenden Road - Mount Washburn Trail is one of the most popular in the park, largely because it is well-maintained and Mt. Washburn is one of its most accessible mountain summits. Contrary to popular belief, however, Mt. Washburn is not the highest peak in the park. It is not even in the top 20, believe it or not. Washburn is the 43rd highest peak in the park (see the complete list in Appendix 4).

At the summit, you will find the largest fire lookout tower in the park, complete with a massive array of telecommunications equipment. This lookout is the only one that is continually staffed during the summers (from June until the first snows of the fall). The bottom floor of the lookout is accessible to the public and has bathrooms, running water, and an overlook with incredible views of the canyon. The top floors of the tower are the office and the residence of the lookout who is based here during the summer, however. Please respect his/her privacy and do not go climbing all over the exterior of the lookout. There is a variety of other monitoring equipment on and around the tower, so please do not interfere with this equipment in any way.

This trail is popular for many reasons, including the incredible views from up top. On the way up, especially along the south trail, you will likely find an abundance of wildflowers and wildlife. The upper elevations of this trail include some prime pika habitat (though it is much more common to see them on the other trail). There is a small herd of bighorn sheep that call the mountain home during the summers as well. If you see them, do not approach or feed them. They are wild animals.

Clear Lake Cutoff Trail — MAP 4-6

Type:	PTP	**Cat:**	BC	**Class:**	B	**Surf:**	Trail	**Dist:**	4	**Status:**	E
Diff:	1	**Traf:**	3	**Child:**	Y	**HAcc:**	N	**Use:**	H S	**Length:**	0.70
Elev A:	7779	**Elev B:**	7890	**Elev G:**	156	**Elev L:**	-45	**Net:**	111	**BMA:**	- -
Min:	7766	**Max:**	7899	**Avg:**	7839	**Avg +:**	6.3%	**Avg -:**	3.8%	**Open:**	YR

Reference Point	A-B Mi	A-B Km	B-A Mi	B-A Km	Latitude	Longitude
Trailhead 4N2 (Uncle Tom's Trail Parking Lot)	0.00	0.00	0.70	1.13	44.71458	-110.49539
Artist Point Road crossing	0.10	0.16	0.60	0.97	44.71414	-110.49359
Trail terminus at jct w/ Clear Lake Trail	0.70	1.13	0.00	0.00	44.71243	-110.48257

The Clear Lake Cutoff Trail is a short trail that provides access to the main Clear Lake Trail from the parking lot at Uncle Tom's trailhead. If you are hiking the trail specifically to see the lake or to make a loop out of the Clear Lake-Ribbon Lake trails, this is a shorter, quicker way to get into that area than taking the official trail from the Wapiti trailhead.

Clear Lake Trail — MAP 4-6

Type:	PTP	**Cat:**	BC	**Class:**	B	**Surf:**	Trail	**Dist:**	4	**Status:**	E
Diff:	1	**Traf:**	3	**Child:**	Y	**HAcc:**	N	**Use:**	H S	**Length:**	1.24
Elev A:	7872	**Elev B:**	7778	**Elev G:**	184	**Elev L:**	-278	**Net:**	-94	**BMA:**	- -
Min:	7778	**Max:**	7930	**Avg:**	7843	**Avg +:**	5.9%	**Avg -:**	7.0%	**Open:**	YR

Reference Point	A-B Mi	A-B Km	B-A Mi	B-A Km	Latitude	Longitude
Trailhead @ jct w/ Wapiti Lake Trail	0.00	0.00	1.24	2.00	44.70924	-110.49068
Jct w/ Clear Lake Cutoff Trail	0.47	0.76	0.77	1.24	44.71243	-110.48257
Clear Lake/Forest Springs Thermal Area (West)	0.63	1.01	0.61	0.98	44.71291	-110.47941
Trail terminus at Ribbon Lake Jct (FSTA East)	1.24	2.00	0.00	0.00	44.71671	-110.47036

The Clear Lake Trail is interesting for a couple of reasons. First, you will come across Clear Lake, a small, bucolic lake that is often murky or cloudy due to runoff from nearby hot springs. Then you will pass through the northern reaches of what is known as the Forest Springs Thermal Area. Along the trail you will see evidence of about a dozen unnamed thermal features. Please stay on the trail here as this is a very fragile thermal field. You can see the south end of this thermal area on the Wapiti Lake Trail (see below).

This trail terminates at the junction with the Ribbon Lake Trail, and many people proceed on to that lake, then return by heading south to connect up with the Wapiti Lake Trail and back to the trailhead they left from.

Crater Hills/Sulphur Mountain Trail MAP 4-7,4-8

TYPE:	O&B	CAT:	TH	CLASS:	U	SURF:	TRAIL	DIST:	4	STATUS:	U
DIFF:	1	TRAF:	2	CHILD:	N	HACC:	N	USE:	H	LENGTH:	1.29
ELEV A:	7701	ELEV B:	7757	ELEV G:	166	ELEV L:	-110	NET:	56	BMA:	- -
MIN:	7690	MAX:	7781	AVG:	7128	AVG +:	3.7%	AVG -:	3.4%	OPEN:	YR

Reference Point	A-B Mi	A-B Km	B-A Mi	B-A Km	Latitude	Longitude
Trailhead @ pullout south of Alum Creek	0.00	0.00	1.29	2.08	44.67527	-110.48231
Sulphur Spring Creek	0.62	1.00	0.67	1.08	44.66646	-110.48390
Crater Hills Thermal Area	1.29	2.08	0.00	0.00	44.65707	-110.48561

This is an unofficial and unmaintained trail that takes you out to one of the most interesting thermal areas in the park. Back in the park's very early days, the road from the Old Faithful area came across roughly what is today's Mary Mountain Trail. The road split a couple of miles west of the current road, with one leg heading toward the Lake area (the old Trout Creek Road; see below) and the other heading up toward the Canyon area, terminating near today's Canyon Corral location. That leg passed right by the Crater Hills Thermal Area.

So when you start this hike from the trailhead pullout (the first one north of Alum Creek on the west side of the road), you will see the remnants of that old stagecoach road from 145 years ago still gouged into the valley floor. Your hike will follow that historic path.

This area is very heavily traveled by bison and grizzly bears. You will need to keep your eyes on the ground (bison poop!) and on your surroundings as you hike. Hikers are encouraged to travel to this area in groups for safety reasons.

Once you reach the thermal area, you will see several thermal features very few visitors to the park get to see. Though most of these features are unnamed, there are a few with some unique names: Blue Mud Pot, Foamy Spring, and Turbid Blue Mud Spring. Sulphur Spring is perhaps one of the most interesting thermal features in the park. It is also known as Crater Hills Geyser, and is almost always in eruptions of up to eight feet or more in height. The pool itself is surrounded by vivid yellow deposits of pure sulfur and is absolutely stunning.

There are no official trails in this area, so be sure you watch your footing.

Cygnet Lakes Trail — MAP 4-7,4-3

Type:	O&B	**Cat:**	BC	**Class:**	C	**Surf:**	Trail	**Dist:**	4	**Status:**	E
Diff:	2	**Traf:**	1	**Child:**	N	**HAcc:**	N	**Use:**	H S	**Length:**	4.27
Elev A:	8207	**Elev B:**	8297	**Elev G:**	512	**Elev L:**	-422	**Net:**	90	**BMA:**	- -
Min:	8197	**Max:**	8416	**Avg:**	8299	**Avg +:**	3.9%	**Avg -:**	3.4%	**Open:**	YR

Reference Point	A-B Mi	A-B Km	B-A Mi	B-A Km	Latitude	Longitude
Trailhead 4N3 (6.7 mi E of Norris Junction)	0.00	0.00	4.27	6.87	44.70586	-110.57299
Jct with old (unmaintained) Plateau Trail	4.13	6.65	0.14	0.23	44.65755	-110.60313
Terminus at Cygnet Lakes	4.27	6.87	0.00	0.00	44.65833	-110.60563

Cygnet Lakes are a series of five small lakes named after the babies (cygnets) of swans. This is a good trail to take if you are interested in seeing some of the area burned in the 1988 fires and how it is recovering. The lakes themselves are rather unremarkable, and the area around them can be quite marshy, especially early in the season (up until late July). At one point, this trail continued south to the Mary Mountain Trail. It was known then as the Plateau Trail (for the Central Plateau upon which it lies). You can still pick out the old trail and follow it southward, but it is unmaintained and traversing it requires considerable bushwhacking (see page 207 for more details).

This is a day-use area only due to the heavy presence of grizzly bears. No camping is allowed, and you are encouraged to hike in groups. In 2013, two hikers (one of whom was an off-duty park ranger) were attacked and injured by a bear on this trail.

Grebe Lake Trail — MAP 4-3

Type:	PTP	**Cat:**	BC	**Class:**	B	**Surf:**	Trail	**Dist:**	4	**Status:**	E
Diff:	2	**Traf:**	3	**Child:**	N	**HAcc:**	N	**Use:**	H S	**Length:**	4.00
Elev A:	8143	**Elev B:**	8032	**Elev G:**	277	**Elev L:**	-388	**Net:**	-111	**BMA:**	- -
Min:	8028	**Max:**	8154	**Avg:**	8098	**Avg +:**	2.4%	**Avg -:**	3.0%	**Open:**	YR

Reference Point	A-B Mi	A-B Km	B-A Mi	B-A Km	Latitude	Longitude
Trailhead 4K3 (3.5 mi W of Canyon Junction)	0.00	0.00	4.00	6.44	44.71793	-110.54974
Spur trail to campsite 4G2 (0.14 mi)	3.00	4.83	1.00	1.61	44.75059	-110.55381
Spur trail to campsite 4G3/Connector to HET	3.35	5.39	0.65	1.05	44.75393	-110.55255
Back entrance to campsite 4G4	3.76	6.05	0.24	0.39	44.75522	-110.55956
Trail terminus @ Gibbon River/Back entrance to 4G5	4.00	6.44	0.00	0.00	44.75324	-110.56398

Grebe Lake is a gorgeous backcountry lake, and is the headwater for the Gibbon River. The Gibbon, of course, flows into the Madison River at Madison Junction, and is part of the fishing ecosystem on the west side of the park for which Yellowstone is world-famous. Grebe Lake is also a historic site, as it was the location of a major fish hatchery operation in Yellowstone from 1933 to 1956. The hatchery supplied grayling to many of the park's other lakes and to lakes around other parts of the United States.

Because of the lake's proximity to the roadway and its beauty, it is one of the most popular areas in the park for overnight campers. There are four campsites on the shore of the lake, all of which are fairly heavily used. If you wish to guarantee yourself a night at one of them, I encourage you to make a reservation for it. The hike to the lake itself is very easy. It follows the old service road that was used to access the hatchery, and though the road has long since been abandoned, it is still very hikable.

Howard Eaton: Chain of Lakes Trail — MAP 4-3

TYPE:	PTP	CAT:	BC	CLASS:	B	SURF:	TRAIL	DIST:	4	STATUS:	E
DIFF:	2	TRAF:	3	CHILD:	N	HACC:	N	USE:	H S	LENGTH:	11.34
ELEV A:	7550	ELEV B:	8028	ELEV G:	1533	ELEV L:	-1054	NET:	478	BMA:	- -
MIN:	7505	MAX:	8134	AVG:	7932	AVG +:	4.2%	AVG -:	3.6%	OPEN:	YR

Reference Point	A-B Mi	A-B Km	B-A Mi	B-A Km	Latitude	Longitude
Trailhead at Jct w/ Solfatara Trail (E of Norris CG)	0.00	0.00	11.34	18.25	44.74241	-110.68496
Solfatara Creek crossing (20', deadfall)	0.06	0.10	11.28	18.15	44.74219	-110.68386
Power line/small creek crossing	1.45	2.33	9.89	15.92	44.73142	-110.66937
Spur trail to campsite 4F1	1.76	2.83	9.58	15.42	44.73024	-110.66370
Jct with Ice Lake Trail	3.52	5.66	7.82	12.59	44.72343	-110.63444
Spur trail to campsite 4D1	3.67	5.91	7.67	12.34	44.72270	-110.63180
Spur trail to campsite 4D2	4.27	6.87	7.07	11.38	44.72268	-110.62035
Gibbon River crossing (15')	4.50	7.24	6.84	11.01	44.72216	-110.61647
Jct with Wolf Lake Cutoff Trail	5.00	8.05	6.34	10.20	44.72131	-110.60754
Gibbon River crossing (10')	6.53	10.51	4.81	7.74	44.73688	-110.59047
Campsite 4G7 (alongside trail)	7.16	11.52	4.18	6.73	44.74348	-110.58591
Gibbon River crossing/Wolf Lake (75+')	7.20	11.59	4.14	6.66	44.74366	-110.58527
Unnamed creek crossing (8 to 10')	7.41	11.93	3.93	6.32	44.74489	-110.58129
Spur trail to campsite 4G6	7.45	11.99	3.89	6.26	44.74523	-110.58062
Spur trail to campsite 4G5	8.52	13.71	2.82	4.54	44.75397	-110.56461
Spur trail to campsite 4G4	8.77	14.11	2.57	4.14	44.75592	-110.56083
Spur trail to campsite 4G3/Connector to Grebe Lake	9.23	14.85	2.11	3.40	44.75398	-110.55246
Spur trail to campsite 4E2	10.96	17.64	0.38	0.61	44.74963	-110.52723
Terminus at jct of Obs Peak & Cascade Lake Trails	11.34	18.25	0.00	0.00	44.75415	-110.52341

Once a part of the old Howard Eaton Trail system, this trail is now commonly referred to as the Chain of Lakes Trail by many other guides/books. It connects four of the park's small lakes in the Canyon area: Ice Lake, Wolf Lake, Grebe Lake, and Cascade Lake. You can get to each lake independently of the others, but for those looking for a more extensive experience, the entire trail is worthy of the effort.

There are a handful of campsites along this trail, all of which are fairly decent and just off the trail. But this being a damp, marshy area for much of the season, it is home to many squadrons of mosquitoes during the first half of the summer.

Trails in this area remain waterlogged and marshy until well into July, and the Gibbon River crossing just east of campsite 4G7 can be as deep at 3-4 feet until early July (sometimes later in the wetter years).

Ice Lake Trail — MAP 4-3

TYPE:	PTP	CAT:	BC	CLASS:	B	SURF:	TRAIL	DIST:	4	STATUS:	E
DIFF:	1	TRAF:	2	CHILD:	Y	HACC:	Y	USE:	H S	LENGTH:	0.56
ELEV A:	7887	ELEV B:	7910	ELEV G:	93	ELEV L:	-70	NET:	23	BMA:	- -
MIN:	7887	MAX:	7917	AVG:	7903	AVG +:	5.3%	AVG -:	5.0%	OPEN:	YR

Reference Point	A-B Mi	A-B Km	B-A Mi	B-A Km	Latitude	Longitude
Trailhead 4K2 (3.4 mi E of Norris Junction)	0.00	0.00	0.56	0.90	44.71683	-110.63397
Spur trail to campsite 4D3/East Spur to Ice Lake	0.13	0.21	0.43	0.69	44.71829	-110.63412
Jct w/ Howard Eaton Trail/Chain of Lakes Trail	0.56	0.90	0.00	0.00	44.72343	-110.63444

This is a nice, short little hike that is suitable not only for young children, but the trail is built to allow wheelchair access as well. In fact, one of the park's two handicap-accessible campsites (4D3) is located just off this trail. You can use the trail to access the campsite around the lake, or to access the Chain of Lakes (Howard Eaton) Trail to get to either the Solfatara Trail (headed west) or to Wolf, Grebe, and Cascade Lakes (heading east).

4D3 is not reservable, and is held each day until 4 p.m. in case someone who is handicapped wishes to book it. At 4 p.m. it becomes available for any other camper who wishes to use it. This lake gets its name from the fact that ice from it was used to store food and other perishable goods at the old hotels that once existed at the nearby Norris Geyser Basin area in the late 1800s and early 1900s.

Monument Geyser Basin Trail — MAP 4-2

Type:	O&B	**Cat:**	TH	**Class:**	B	**Surf:**	Trail	**Dist:**	4	**Status:**	E
Diff:	3	**Traf:**	2	**Child:**	N	**HAcc:**	N	**Use:**	H	**Length:**	1.21
Elev A:	7352	**Elev B:**	7992	**Elev G:**	724	**Elev L:**	-84	**Net:**	640	**BMA:**	- -
Min:	7349	**Max:**	7995	**Avg:**	7592	**Avg +:**	14.8%	**Avg -:**	4.8%	**Open:**	YR

Reference Point	A-B Mi	A-B Km	B-A Mi	B-A Km	Latitude	Longitude
Trailhead MGB (4.7 mi S of Norris Junction)	0.00	0.00	1.21	1.95	44.68378	-110.74466
Jct w/ Sylvan Springs Thermal Basin Trail	0.46	0.74	0.75	1.21	44.68991	-110.74656
Terminus at geyser field	1.21	1.95	0.00	0.00	44.68414	-110.75308

The Monument Geyser Basin Trail is one of the oldest in the park. It was built by the park's second superintendent, Philetus W. Norris, in 1879. He also named the area and some of its uniquely-shaped thermal features. The area is home to about three dozen mostly unnamed features. Thermos Bottle Geyser is the only remaining active geyser and it is very weak and rarely active. This trail starts out fairly flat for the first half mile or so as it travels along the Gibbon River. But you then begin a steady climb of more than 600 feet (183m) over the course of the remaining ¾ of a mile. You are rewarded at the top by the moderately-sized thermal field, as well as a view along Chromatic Canyon to the south.

Some people use the beginning of this trail to access the thermal fields on the far western side of Gibbon Meadow in lieu of crossing the Gibbon River on foot. When the trail takes a hairpin turn, keep going straight along the river to the first oxbow bend, then head in a northwest direction toward the thermal area (which will be visible by the steam and other emissions from the area). This avoids the extreme marshy areas you would have to trudge through by traveling across Gibbon Meadows. It is a little over a mile from the trail bend to the main body of the thermal area. The area is known as the Sylvan Springs Thermal Area (see below for trail information).

Mount Washburn (Dunraven Pass) Trail — MAP 4-4

Type:	PTP	**Cat:**	TH	**Class:**	A	**Surf:**	Trail	**Dist:**	4	**Status:**	E
Diff:	3	**Traf:**	3	**Child:**	N	**HAcc:**	N	**Use:**	H S	**Length:**	3.23
Elev A:	8880	**Elev B:**	10109	**Elev G:**	1572	**Elev L:**	-343	**Net:**	1229	**BMA:**	- -
Min:	8880	**Max:**	10149	**Avg:**	9487	**Avg +:**	10.8%	**Avg -:**	7.8%	**Open:**	YR

Reference Point	A-B Mi	A-B Km	B-A Mi	B-A Km	Latitude	Longitude
Trailhead 4K9 (Dunraven Pass; 4.8 mi N of Can Jct)	0.00	0.00	3.23	5.20	44.78500	-110.45344
Jct with Chittenden Rd & Washburn Springs Trails	3.23	5.20	0.00	0.00	44.79776	-110.43249

This is the second most popular way to get up to the summit of Mt. Washburn, but in my opinion, this is by far the most scenic and best route to take. One of the primary reasons it is better than the other, more popular route (the Chittenden side) is that this trail is shaded and has a wealth of small mammals that make hiking it entertaining. There are plenty of marmots and pika (near the top) always on the move or lounging on the rocks along the trail.

Much of this trail follows what was once an auto road that took passenger cars and tourist buses to the summit. In the late 1950s, they stopped letting private vehicles go up, but buses continued taking passengers to the top of the mountain until the early 1970s. You will still see some of the old asphalt along this trail on your way up.

This trail is very popular and although the parking area at the trailhead is fairly new, it is still not large enough to accommodate everyone in the peak months of the summer season. So plan to arrive early in the morning to ensure you get a spot, or be prepared to wait (without blocking traffic) until someone returns and leaves.

Mount Washburn Spur Trail — MAP 4-4

Type:	PTP	Cat:	BC	Class:	B	Surf:	Trail	Dist:	4	Status:	E
Diff:	4	Traf:	1	Child:	N	HAcc:	N	Use:	H	Length:	5.46
Elev A:	8045	Elev B:	10110	Elev G:	2600	Elev L:	-535	Net:	2065	BMA:	- -
Min:	8045	Max:	10136	Avg:	8651	Avg +:	13.0%	Avg -:	5.1%	Open:	YR

Reference Point	A-B Mi	A-B Km	B-A Mi	B-A Km	Latitude	Longitude
Trailhead at Jct with Seven Mile Hole Trail	0.00	0.00	5.46	8.79	44.74976	-110.43888
Brimstone Cascade Thermal Area	0.88	1.42	4.58	7.37	44.75946	-110.43874
Sulphur Creek	1.38	2.22	4.08	6.57	44.76371	-110.43147
Washburn Hot Springs	1.48	2.38	3.98	6.41	44.76456	-110.43020
Glade Creek crossing	2.28	3.67	3.18	5.12	44.76979	-110.41610
Spur trail to campsite 4E1	2.94	4.73	2.52	4.06	44.77784	-110.41172
Jct with Chittenden Rd and Dunraven Pass Trails	5.46	8.79	0.00	0.00	44.79776	-110.43249

This is the third and least popular route up to the summit of Mt. Washburn. Getting to this trail requires you first hike in on the Seven Mile Hole Trail, however, so that adds 2.5 miles to the front end (and coming back if you return via the same route). The climb is also much more substantial - 2,000 feet (610m) in 2.5 miles rather than half that with the other two routes, but you are rewarded on the hike with access to the Brimstone Cascade and Washburn Hot Springs Thermal Areas.

This trail does have the advantage of having a campsite located on it, so a hike into the campsite one day, and then a trip to the summit and back the next is rather popular with hikers who use this trail.

The segment from the junction at Seven Mile Hole to the campsite 4E1 was once part of the old Howard Eaton Trail system.

Mud Volcano Trail — MAP 4-8,4-7

Type:	Loop	Cat:	FC	Class:	B	Surf:	Bw/Pv	Dist:	4	Status:	E
Diff:	2	Traf:	5	Child:	Y	HAcc:	Y	Use:	H	Length:	0.72
Elev A:	7757	Elev B:	7767	Elev G:	233	Elev L:	-222	Net:	10	BMA:	- -
Min:	7756	Max:	7893	Avg:	7825	Avg +:	13.0%	Avg -:	9.5%	Open:	YR

Reference Point	A-B Mi	A-B Km	B-A Mi	B-A Km	Latitude	Longitude
North trailhead @ park. lot (9.5 mi S of Canyon Jct)	0.00	0.00	0.72	1.16	44.62489	-110.43377
Dragon's Mouth Spring	0.09	0.14	0.63	1.01	44.62519	-110.43472
Mud Volcano/Spur to Mud Caldron & parking lot	0.12	0.19	0.60	0.97	44.62432	-110.43445
Grizzly Fumarole	0.23	0.37	0.49	0.79	44.62319	-110.43561
Sour Lake/Black Dragon's Caldron	0.40	0.64	0.32	0.51	44.62085	-110.43572
Churning Caldron	0.47	0.76	0.25	0.40	44.62114	-110.43447
Sizzling Basin	0.53	0.85	0.19	0.31	44.62177	-110.43379
Mud Geyser	0.64	1.03	0.08	0.13	44.62306	-110.43295
South trailhead/Mud Cauldron	0.72	1.16	0.00	0.00	44.62418	-110.43298

The Mud Volcano area is one of the more interesting thermal fields in the park, and certainly one of the most noxious. It is also one of the most popular since it lies right along the road on the way to Hayden Valley. As a result, on busy days during the summer it can be almost impossible to get into the parking lot, let alone find a place to park your vehicle.

It is an excellent trail for young children (who will be fascinated by many of the features that lie along it), and can be used by those in wheelchairs with strong arms or with someone to assist their movement.

Most of the springs and features here are muddy, sulfur-based, and very acidic. Some of the features in this area have pHs that measure below one (roughly the equivalent of battery acid), making this area among the most acidic places on earth.

Norris Geyser Back Basin Trail — MAP 4-1

TYPE:	LOOP	CAT:	FC	CLASS:	B	SURF:	TR/PV	DIST:	4	STATUS:	E
DIFF:	2	TRAF:	4	CHILD:	N	HACC:	Y	USE:	H	LENGTH:	1.73
ELEV A:	7585	ELEV B:	7577	ELEV G:	219	ELEV L:	-228	NET:	-8	BMA:	- -
MIN:	7505	MAX:	7585	AVG:	7532	AVG +:	4.5%	AVG -:	4.7%	OPEN:	YR

Reference Point	A-B Mi	A-B Km	B-A Mi	B-A Km	Latitude	Longitude
Trailhead in front of Norris Museum	0.00	0.00	1.73	2.78	44.72637	-110.70364
Loop split	0.04	0.06	1.69	2.72	44.72593	-110.70405
Emerald Spring	0.08	0.13	1.65	2.66	44.72565	-110.70410
Dr. Allen's Paint Pots	0.10	0.16	1.63	2.62	44.72524	-110.70412
Steamboat Geyser	0.25	0.40	1.48	2.38	44.72341	-110.70344
Cistern Sprg/jct w/ c/o to Veteran & Corporal Geysers	0.35	0.56	1.38	2.22	44.72316	-110.70404
Sulphur Pot/Black Pit Spring	0.46	0.74	1.27	2.04	44.72227	-110.70223
Echinus Geyser	0.47	0.76	1.26	2.03	44.72210	-110.70226
Tantalus Creek/Trail jct	0.49	0.79	1.24	2.00	44.72189	-110.70258
Crater Spring	0.52	0.84	1.21	1.95	44.72197	-110.70308
Root Pool	0.54	0.87	1.19	1.92	44.72197	-110.70346
Arch Steam Vent	0.56	0.90	1.17	1.88	44.72173	-110.70374
Tantalus Geyser	0.59	0.95	1.14	1.83	44.72189	-110.70418
Dishwater Spring	0.63	1.01	1.10	1.77	44.72186	-110.70491
Mystic Spring	0.67	1.08	1.06	1.71	44.72148	-110.70565
Mud Spring	0.69	1.11	1.04	1.67	44.72128	-110.70599
Yellow Mud Pool	0.75	1.21	0.98	1.58	44.72046	-110.70622
Puff and Stuff Geyser	0.78	1.26	0.95	1.53	44.72014	-110.70609
Black Hermit Cauldron	0.80	1.29	0.93	1.50	44.71992	-110.70636
Green Dragon Spring	0.83	1.34	0.90	1.45	44.72016	-110.70693
Gray Lakes	0.85	1.37	0.88	1.42	44.72025	-110.70723

Reference Point	A-B Mi	A-B Km	B-A Mi	B-A Km	Latitude	Longitude
Blue Mud Steam Vent	0.88	1.42	0.85	1.37	44.72065	-110.70719
Yellow Funnel & Tangled Root Spring	0.91	1.46	0.82	1.32	44.72099	-110.70714
Son of Green Dragon Spring	0.92	1.48	0.81	1.30	44.72114	-110.70717
Porkchop Geyser	1.10	1.77	0.63	1.01	44.72237	-110.70815
Pearl Geyser	1.12	1.80	0.61	0.98	44.72232	-110.70734
Vixen Pool	1.16	1.87	0.57	0.92	44.72290	-110.70702
Rubble Geyser - c/o to Veteran & Corporal Geysers	1.21	1.95	0.52	0.84	44.72336	-110.70641
Palpitator Spring	1.25	2.01	0.48	0.77	44.72392	-110.70621
Fearless Geyser	1.26	2.03	0.47	0.76	44.72407	-110.70614
Monarch Geyser	1.29	2.08	0.44	0.71	44.72443	-110.70571
Branch Spring	1.34	2.16	0.39	0.63	44.72502	-110.70593
Minute Geyser	1.35	2.17	0.38	0.61	44.72508	-110.70602
Rediscovered Geyser	1.49	2.40	0.24	0.39	44.72703	-110.70636
Spur trail to Porcelain Basin Trail/Museum	1.63	2.62	0.10	0.16	44.72690	-110.70381
Bath Tub Spring	1.69	2.72	0.04	0.06	44.72642	-110.70450
Return to loop split	1.73	2.78	0.00	0.00	44.72593	-110.70405

Norris Geyser Basin is the hottest and one of the most active thermal basins in the park. It is divided into three major areas: Porcelain Basin (see below), the Back Basin (this trail), and One Hundred Spring Plain, which is closed to the public because of ground instability. There are a variety of interesting and unique features located along this trail, not the least of which is Steamboat Geyser, the largest active geyser in the world. In the past, its erratic eruptions (oftentimes decades apart) meant that not many people got to see this impressive natural wonder in its full glory. However, in 2018 it began erupting almost regularly throughout the summer. Who knows how long this cycle will continue?

Norris Geyser Basin is one of those areas you should dedicate a full day to exploring, especially if you enjoy learning about the thermal features themselves. Be sure to take a copy of Scott Bryan's book, *The Geysers of Yellowstone* (5th edition), so that you can read the fascinating details of each. The little pamphlet available at the head of the trail offers some basic details about some of the more popular features found throughout the basin, but Scott's book offers vivid details about over a hundred features, including detailed accounts of their eruption cycles and histories, as well as excellent descriptions of the "disturbances" that impact the area occasionally (which, in turn, affect many of the thermal features).

At almost two miles in length, this trail is probably not good for younger children with short attention spans. The trail is almost entirely boardwalk and has very little elevation change, so it is an excellent trail for those in wheelchairs.

Norris Geyser Porcelain Basin Trail — MAP 4-1

TYPE:	LOOP	**CAT:**	FC	**CLASS:**	B	**SURF:**	TR/BDW	**DIST:**	4	**STATUS:**	E
DIFF:	1	**TRAF:**	1	**CHILD:**	Y	**HACC:**	N	**USE:**	H	**LENGTH:**	0.74
ELEV A:	7475	**ELEV B:**	7502	**ELEV G:**	114	**ELEV L:**	-87	**NET:**	27	**BMA:**	- -
MIN:	7474	**MAX:**	7551	**AVG:**	7519	**AVG +:**	4.6%	**AVG -:**	5.6%	**OPEN:**	YR

Reference Point	A-B Mi	A-B Km	B-A Mi	B-A Km	Latitude	Longitude
Trailhead @ rear of Norris Museum	0.00	0.00	0.64	1.03	44.72660	-110.70360
Loop split	0.02	0.03	0.62	1.00	44.72680	-110.70351
Congress Pool/Locomotive Spring	0.14	0.23	0.50	0.80	44.72784	-110.70147
Spur trail to Incline Geyser & Connector Trail	0.17	0.27	0.47	0.76	44.72823	-110.70115

Reference Point	A-B Mi	A-B Km	B-A Mi	B-A Km	Latitude	Longitude
Swiss Cheese Pool/Primrose Springs	0.20	0.32	0.44	0.71	44.72829	-110.70159
Colloidal Pool/Hurricane Vent	0.24	0.39	0.40	0.64	44.72805	-110.70233
Spur trail to Black Growler/Ledge Geyser	0.26	0.42	0.38	0.61	44.72789	-110.70277
Scummy Pool/Sunday Geyser	0.28	0.45	0.36	0.58	44.72807	-110.70277
Whirligig, Little Whirligig, Constant Geysers	0.33	0.53	0.31	0.50	44.72866	-110.70333
Splutter Geyser	0.34	0.55	0.30	0.48	44.72882	-110.70338
Pinwheel Geyser	0.35	0.56	0.29	0.47	44.72888	-110.70344
Yellow Crown Crater	0.44	0.71	0.20	0.32	44.72888	-110.70521
Whale's Mouth	0.46	0.74	0.18	0.29	44.72859	-110.70530
Crackling Lake	0.52	0.84	0.12	0.19	44.72788	-110.70484
Cat's Eye Spring/Glacier Melt Geyser	0.54	0.87	0.10	0.16	44.72766	-110.70461
Milky Complex	0.55	0.89	0.09	0.14	44.72755	-110.70465
Teal Blue Bubbler	0.56	0.90	0.08	0.13	44.72744	-110.70458
Spur trail to Black Growler/Ledge Geyser	0.62	1.00	0.02	0.03	44.72710	-110.70347
Jct w/ spur to Back Basin Trail	0.63	1.01	0.01	0.02	44.72690	-110.70355
Return to loop split	0.64	1.03	0.00	0.00	44.72680	-110.70351

The Porcelain Basin is the most famous of the three thermal zones at Norris Geyser Basin. It is the one you always see on the news and in photos when there are stories about one of Yellowstone's thermal fields. Porcelain Basin, named for its bland color, is also the more popular for the tourists and visitors, as it is easy to see from the Norris Museum. Its features, while interesting in their own right, pale in comparison to those in the Back Basin, however (see above). This trail is fine for children, but the severe inclines would make it tough for visitors in wheelchairs or who do not get around very easily. As with the Back Basin, Scott Bryan's book details the vagaries of the various thermal features found in this area as well, including Whirligig and Little Whirligig Geysers.

If you spend much time doing research on the thermal areas of the park, you will occasionally see references to the "disturbances" that occur in the Norris Geyser Basin. These are basically fluctuations in the temperature and pH balance of the various thermal features, and they occur pretty much basin-wide. These changes are often most visible in the Porcelain Basin because they tend to result in the field switching from its bland appearance to a much more colorful one (or back). Geologists are unsure of what causes these disturbances, which occur seemingly at random.

North Rim Cutoff Trail — MAP 4-6

Type:	PTP	**Cat:**	FC	**Class:**	C	**Surf:**	Tr/Pv	**Dist:**	4	**Status:**	E
Diff:	1	**Traf:**	2	**Child:**	Y	**HAcc:**	Y	**Use:**	H	**Length:**	0.42
Elev A:	7869	**Elev B:**	7828	**Elev G:**	60	**Elev L:**	-101	**Net:**	-41	**BMA:**	- -
Min:	7825	**Max:**	7869	**Avg:**	7839	**Avg +:**	6.1%	**Avg -:**	5.6%	**Open:**	YR

Reference Point	A-B Mi	A-B Km	B-A Mi	B-A Km	Latitude	Longitude
Trailhead at Canyon Cabin P-26	0.00	0.00	0.42	0.68	44.72904	-110.48723
Trailhead at North Rim Trail	0.42	0.68	0.00	0.00	44.72420	-110.48439

This short trail is designed to facilitate quick access to the North Rim Trail from the Canyon Lodge and Cabins area. The trailhead can be found on the east side of the P-26 cabin at the southernmost section of the area's guest lodging. Though used primarily by park employees, it does provide a quick way for visitors to get to the North Rim area without having to deal with all the traffic that accumulates along that road during the busy summer months.

North Rim Trail — MAP 4-6

TYPE:	PTP	CAT:	FC	CLASS:	B	SURF:	TRAIL	DIST:	4	STATUS:	E
DIFF:	2	TRAF:	5	CHILD:	N	HACC:	N	USE:	H	LENGTH:	3.12
ELEV A:	7705	ELEV B:	7809	ELEV G:	1074	ELEV L:	-969	NET:	104	BMA:	- -
MIN:	7636	MAX:	7921	AVG:	7775	AVG +:	12.1%	AVG -:	10.2%	OPEN:	YR

Reference Point	A-B Mi	A-B Km	B-A Mi	B-A Km	Latitude	Longitude
Trailhead at Chittenden Bridge	0.00	0.00	3.12	5.02	44.70824	-110.50304
Jct with Canyon Water Intake Service Road	0.08	0.13	3.04	4.89	44.70927	-110.50353
Bridge over Jay Creek (seasonal)	0.25	0.40	2.87	4.62	44.71135	-110.50193
Brink of the Upper Falls Overlook	0.41	0.66	2.71	4.36	44.71313	-110.50013
Parking Lot/Comfort Station	0.52	0.84	2.60	4.18	44.71456	-110.50076
Spur trail to Crystal Falls overlook	0.68	1.09	2.44	3.93	44.71573	-110.50170
Cross over Cascade Creek	0.79	1.27	2.33	3.75	44.71705	-110.50149
Jct with Brink of the Lower Falls Trail	1.10	1.77	2.02	3.25	44.71907	-110.49871
Jct with Lookout Point & Red Rock Point Trails	1.68	2.70	1.44	2.32	44.72145	-110.48767
Lookout Point Overlook	1.91	3.07	1.21	1.95	44.72281	-110.48422
Trailhead at Inspiration Point	3.12	5.02	0.00	0.00	44.72551	-110.47020

This trail is another of those that have you traveling over a historic path. Much of it was once the original road between Canyon and Fishing Bridge, including the old bridge over Jay Creek. Jay Creek is a seasonal creek and is often dry, especially late in the season.

There is no parking at the A end of this trail (Chittenden Bridge). You will need to park in the lot at the Wapiti Lake trailhead and walk down to the bridge to begin the hike. After you cross over Jay Creek, you will come to the overlook of the Upper Falls of the Yellowstone, a breathtaking viewpoint if ever there was one. From there, you will pass by the restroom building and parking lot (where the original ranger station, stores, etc., were located), and then on to an overlook of Crystal Falls.

As you continue on, you will come to the trail that takes you to the Brink of the Lower Falls of the Yellowstone (see the end of this chapter). This, too, is a breathtaking sight to behold. As you walk down to the platform, you will begin to feel the ground vibrating from the force of the water rushing over the edge of the canyon. This trail is a little over a third of a mile in length and drops about 250 feet. Going down isn't too bad, but the climb back up is a bit more strenuous (there are benches to rest on). From there, you will head to Lookout Point and then Inspiration Point. There is limited parking at Inspiration Point, so the best way to do this is to start from the Chittenden Bridge end.

Observation Peak Trail — MAP 4-3

TYPE:	O&B	CAT:	BC	CLASS:	B	SURF:	TRAIL	DIST:	4	STATUS:	E
DIFF:	3	TRAF:	2	CHILD:	N	HACC:	N	USE:	H S	LENGTH:	2.59
ELEV A:	8004	ELEV B:	9391	ELEV G:	1496	ELEV L:	-109	NET:	1387	BMA:	- -
MIN:	8004	MAX:	9391	AVG:	8725	AVG +:	12.0%	AVG -:	6.3%	OPEN:	YR

Reference Point	A-B Mi	A-B Km	B-A Mi	B-A Km	Latitude	Longitude
Trailhead at jct w/ Chain of Lakes & Cascade Lake Tr	0.00	0.00	2.59	4.17	44.75415	-110.52341
Spur trail to campsite 4E3	0.14	0.23	2.45	3.94	44.75592	-110.52471
Spur trail to campsite 4P1	2.50	4.02	0.09	0.14	44.77132	-110.54650
Summit/Lookout	2.59	4.17	0.00	0.00	44.77197	-110.54768

This trail takes you up to one of the park's old fire lookout/patrol cabins. And while the trails leading to this trail are relatively flat, you will be in for a drastic change on the way up to Observation Peak (an average upward incline of 12%). The trip is well worth it, though; you can see portions of the Washburn Range and westward that you cannot see from the top of Mt. Washburn itself (which is why the lookout is here).

There are two campsites on this trail. One immediately after the trail splits from the Chain of Lakes Trail, and another just below the summit. In my opinion, this (4P1) is one of the best campsites in the park. Great privacy, outstanding views, and the campsite is in good condition. The only downside is that once the snow has melted on the peak, there is no water source near the site. You will have to hike all the way back down to Cascade Lake to get water if you run out. Wood fires are not permitted here, so it can get very chilly at night.

Old Canyon Road East Trail — MAP 4-3

Type:	O&B	**Cat:**	TH	**Class:**	N	**Surf:**	Trail	**Dist:**	4	**Status:**	R
Diff:	1	**Traf:**	1	**Child:**	N	**HAcc:**	N	**Use:**	H R	**Length:**	1.13
Elev A:	8174	**Elev B:**	8117	**Elev G:**	119	**Elev L:**	-176	**Net:**	-57	**BMA:**	- -
Min:	8117	**Max:**	8179	**Avg:**	8143	**Avg +:**	4.5%	**Avg -:**	5.0%	**Open:**	YR

Reference Point	A-B Mi	A-B Km	B-A Mi	B-A Km	Latitude	Longitude
Trailhead @ roadside (4.1 mi W of Canyon Junction)	0.00	0.00	1.13	1.82	44.71239	-110.55776
Extinct Solfatara Plateau Thermal Area	0.23	0.37	0.90	1.45	44.71361	-110.55340
Maintenance Yard/Gravel Pit	0.76	1.22	0.37	0.60	44.71391	-110.54270
Trail closure	1.13	1.82	0.00	0.00	44.71486	-110.53545

This is another of the old abandoned roads that can be found around the park. This road segment was part of the original road between Norris and the old "Canyon Village" (before the current village was born in the late 1950s). There is no real pullout at the A end of this, so you'll need to ensure you pull off the road far enough so you do not present a traffic hazard.

Once you get out of your vehicle, climb over the berm and you will see the old roadbed. Much of the asphalt remains in place in some areas. You will pass through a largely extinct thermal field (stay on the road bed), though the presence of a sulfur odor will let you know that it still has some breath in it.

Continue eastward and you will come across one of the larger maintenance yards for the NPS. Do not enter this area as it is basically an active construction zone. You will be able to travel roughly another half mile eastward until you come to a trail closure. This is in place due to the presence of a carcass dump further up the road. Proceeding past this point may result in your getting a citation if you get caught.

Old Canyon Road West Trail — MAP 4-3

Type:	PTP	**Cat:**	TH	**Class:**	N	**Surf:**	Pv/Trl	**Dist:**	4	**Status:**	R
Diff:	2	**Traf:**	1	**Child:**	N	**HAcc:**	N	**Use:**	H	**Length:**	1.77
Elev A:	7779	**Elev B:**	8133	**Elev G:**	439	**Elev L:**	-86	**Net:**	353	**BMA:**	- -
Min:	7779	**Max:**	8134	**Avg:**	7936	**Avg +:**	5.8%	**Avg -:**	3.0%	**Open:**	YR

Reference Point	A-B Mi	A-B Km	B-A Mi	B-A Km	Latitude	Longitude
Trailhead @ Virginia Meadows Pullout	0.00	0.00	1.77	2.85	44.71253	-110.63885
Trailhead @ Dunraven Pass	1.77	2.85	0.00	0.00	44.70477	-110.61041

This is the western half of the original road between Virginia Cascade and the old Canyon Village. It was abandoned in 1959 when the new (existing) road was constructed to the current village. Much of the pavement remains in place along this road and with the exception of the far western portion of it, the path is almost entirely forested. The western third of a mile is through Virginia Meadows, which can be rather marshy at times, especially early in the season.

The hill you climb (going west to east) is known as Blanding Hill, named after the foreman who was in charge of constructing the original road through this area. The road was originally designed for stagecoaches, which is why it is snakelike as it climbs up the hill.

At the west end of the trail, you will have to ford the Gibbon River unless there happens to be enough deadfall in place to permit you to cross without getting your feet wet. The eastern two-thirds of a mile parallel the power line easement until you return to the existing road.

Old Dunraven Road Trail — MAP 4-4

TYPE:	PTP	CAT:	BC	CLASS:	N	SURF:	TRAIL	DIST:	4	STATUS:	R
DIFF:	3	TRAF:	1	CHILD:	N	HACC:	N	USE:	H	LENGTH:	2.42
ELEV A:	8368	ELEV B:	8865	ELEV G:	702	ELEV L:	-205	NET:	497	BMA:	- -
MIN:	8368	MAX:	8994	AVG:	8770	AVG +:	7.7%	AVG -:	4.7%	OPEN:	YR

Reference Point	A-B Mi	A-B Km	B-A Mi	B-A Km	Latitude	Longitude
Trailhead @ rear of Dunraven Picnic Area	0.00	0.00	2.42	3.89	44.76259	-110.47179
Trailhead @ Dunraven Pass	2.42	3.89	0.00	0.00	44.78435	-110.45402

This is an old segment of the original road that took travelers from Canyon up to Mt. Washburn and Dunraven Pass. It is a bit tough to follow in a couple of locations, but the sections carved out of the side of the mountain make it easy to find in rather short order. The north end can be a bit difficult to locate, so start at the south end for best results.

Old Trout Creek Service Road Trail — MAP 4-7

TYPE:	PTP	CAT:	BC	CLASS:	N	SURF:	TRAIL	DIST:	4	STATUS:	R
DIFF:	2	TRAF:	1	CHILD:	N	HACC:	N	USE:	H S	LENGTH:	8.76
ELEV A:	7716	ELEV B:	8179	ELEV G:	1031	ELEV L:	-569	NET:	463	BMA:	- -
MIN:	7715	MAX:	8180	AVG:	7898	AVG +:	3.0%	AVG -:	2.8%	OPEN:	YR

Reference Point	A-B Mi	A-B Km	B-A Mi	B-A Km	Latitude	Longitude
Trailhead @ Hayden Valley Road (7.8 mi S of Canyon)	0.00	0.00	8.76	14.10	44.64273	-110.45683
Power line crossing	0.80	1.29	7.96	12.81	44.63550	-110.46881
Old Trout Creek Landfill	2.38	3.83	6.38	10.27	44.62118	-110.49362
Trout Creek crossing (5 to 10')	3.50	5.63	5.26	8.47	44.61608	-110.51492
Upper Alum Creek Thermal Area	7.60	12.23	1.16	1.87	44.60888	-110.58569
Social trails to Glen Africa Basin Thermal Area	7.70	12.39	1.06	1.71	44.60971	-110.58711
Jct w/ Mary Mountain Trail	8.76	14.10	0.00	0.00	44.61540	-110.60477

This old road/trail is another of the park's historic features that no longer receives much attention. Back in the very early days of the park, before the road between Canyon and Norris was constructed, travel from the west side to the east side and back was accomplished via an old wagon road that generally started on the west end where today's Mary Mountain trailhead is located. On the east side it came past Mary Lake, and then drifted in two different directions, one along Alum Creek in the north end of Hayden Valley,

Canyon Bear Feeding Area in use, ca. 1940. Photo courtesy NPS

and the other southward along Trout Creek. This old trail follows the Trout Creek segment. You can still see the ruts of the wagon wheels in some locations.

Additionally, for much of the park's history, up until the early 1970s, most of the trash generated in daily operations was buried at various places inside the park. There were a handful of dumps located around the park, one of which was along Trout Creek, about two miles west of the current main road. The eastern two miles of this old road remained in service until the dump was closed in 1972.

If you are a Yellowstone history buff, this makes for an exciting eastern half of the hike from one side of the park to the other. You can also do a loop whereby you hike in via this route, travel up to the Mary Mountain Trail, and then hike out via the trail along Alum Creek. This area is rife with grizzly bears, though, so keep your eyes peeled and your senses sharp.

Otter Creek Bear Feeding Area Trail — MAP 4-3,4-7

TYPE:	O&B	CAT:	TH	CLASS:	N	SURF:	TRAIL	DIST:	4	STATUS:	A
DIFF:	1	TRAF:	1	CHILD:	Y	HACC:	N	USE:	H K R	LENGTH:	0.56
ELEV A:	7686	ELEV B:	7743	ELEV G:	128	ELEV L:	-71	NET:	57	BMA:	- -
MIN:	7674	MAX:	7762	AVG:	7706	AVG +:	3.1%	AVG -:	2.5%	OPEN:	YR

Reference Point	A-B Mi	A-B Km	B-A Mi	B-A Km	Latitude	Longitude
Trailhead @ pullout (2.7 mi S of Canyon Junction)	0.00	0.00	0.56	0.90	44.70239	-110.50617
Otter Creek crossing (bridge)	0.22	0.35	0.34	0.55	44.70103	-110.50983
Bear feeding platform	0.56	0.90	0.00	0.00	44.69770	-110.51427

This trail takes you back to one of the most historic places in the park, yet it is hardly mentioned in any of the park's public literature. In the early 1930s, NPS constructed a large concrete platform and would feed bears each night. Tourists staying at the nearby Canyon hotel and lodge facilities would flock to the evening shows (most accounts of the spectacle discuss the long lines of traffic), during which garbage from area hotels would be emptied out onto the platform. Visitors would be seated on the hillside opposite the platform (see photo, above) and be treated to an evening's entertainment of the bears wandering out of the woods, digging through the trash, and often fighting one another for the scraps. Armed rangers were stationed around the area lest one of the bruins escaped and threatened the crowd in any way (no serious injuries were ever reported at the Canyon feeding area).

These evening festivities continued until World War II began, but once the war was over, the NPS elected not to continue the practice. However, the platform itself was never removed and still exists today (albeit in a somewhat decayed condition). This is a short hike along a nice little creek, but the area is often closed due to bear activity.

Plateau Trail — MAP 4-7

TYPE:	PTP	CAT:	BC	CLASS:	N	SURF:	TRAIL	DIST:	4	STATUS:	A
DIFF:	3	TRAF:	1	CHILD:	N	HACC:	N	USE:	H	LENGTH:	4.36
ELEV A:	8301	ELEV B:	8248	ELEV G:	761	ELEV L:	-814	NET:	-53	BMA:	- -
MIN:	8207	MAX:	8470	AVG:	8351	AVG +:	5.6%	AVG -:	6.5%	OPEN:	YR

Reference Point	A-B Mi	A-B Km	B-A Mi	B-A Km	Latitude	Longitude
Trailhead @ jct w/ Cygnet Lakes Trail	0.00	0.00	4.36	7.02	44.65755	-110.60313
Trailhead @ jct w/ Mary Mountain Trail	4.36	7.02	0.00	0.00	44.60516	-110.63774

The Plateau Trail, though officially abandoned in the late 1980s, still shows up on many trail maps, especially those produced in the 1970s-1990s. Before it was abandoned, it served as a conduit from the Norris-Canyon Road to Mary Lake (and out to either of the Mary Mountain trailheads). It was lightly used, however, and the NPS elected to forgo continuing maintenance on it. The trail remains navigable on its north and south ends, but much of the middle section is covered in downed trees. So while it is possible to make your way through, be prepared to exert some significant effort to make it happen.

Ribbon Lake Trail — MAP 4-6,4-5

TYPE:	PTP	CAT:	BC	CLASS:	B	SURF:	TRAIL	DIST:	4	STATUS:	E
DIFF:	2	TRAF:	2	CHILD:	N	HACC:	N	USE:	H S	LENGTH:	2.27
ELEV A:	7717	ELEV B:	7863	ELEV G:	489	ELEV L:	-342	NET:	146	BMA:	- -
MIN:	7717	MAX:	7971	AVG:	7854	AVG +:	6.7%	AVG -:	6.4%	OPEN:	YR

Reference Point	A-B Mi	A-B Km	B-A Mi	B-A Km	Latitude	Longitude
Trailhead @ jct w/ Artist Point-Sublime Point Trail	0.00	0.00	2.27	3.65	44.72022	-110.46989
Lilypad Lake (Unofficial name)	0.20	0.32	2.07	3.33	44.71794	-110.47036
Jct with Clear Lake Trail	0.28	0.45	1.99	3.20	44.71671	-110.47036
Spur trail to campsites 4R1/4R2, Silver Cord Cascade	1.40	2.25	0.87	1.40	44.72391	-110.45168
Terminus @ jct w/ Wapiti Lake Trail	2.27	3.65	0.00	0.00	44.71738	-110.44844

The Ribbon Lake Trail, constructed in 1921, takes you from the Clear Lake Trail to Ribbon Lake, and then south to the Wapiti Lake Trail. The trail system in this area is confusing to many people because of the different names used and which segments belong to which trails. Regardless, Ribbon Lake is a bucolic little backcountry lake that has a couple of nice campsites near it. Both campsites, however, lie right off the trail and lack any real privacy.

One of the neat things about this trail is that, at the end of it, if you double back along the wall of the canyon, you will be right at the precipice of the Silver Cord Cascade (see below).

Surface Creek drains through Ribbon Lake and together they provide the water that powers Silver Cord Cascade.

Seven Mile Hole Trail MAP 4-5

TYPE:	O&B	CAT:	BC	CLASS:	B	SURF:	TRAIL	DIST:	4	STATUS:	E
DIFF:	4	TRAF:	3	CHILD:	N	HACC:	N	USE:	H	LENGTH:	4.91
ELEV A:	7914	ELEV B:	6741	ELEV G:	998	ELEV L:	-2172	NET:	-1173	BMA:	- -
MIN:	6720	MAX:	8175	AVG:	7719	AVG +:	7.4%	AVG -:	14.8%	OPEN:	YR

Reference Point	A-B Mi	A-B Km	B-A Mi	B-A Km	Latitude	Longitude
Trailhead 4K6 (Glacial Boulder on Inspiration Pt Drive)	0.00	0.00	4.91	7.90	44.72964	-110.47277
Jct with Washburn Spur Trail	2.67	4.30	2.24	3.60	44.74976	-110.43888
Painted Cliffs Thermal Area	3.80	6.12	1.11	1.79	44.75267	-110.42067
Spur trail to Campsite 4C1 (0.27 mi)	4.12	6.63	0.79	1.27	44.75123	-110.41484
Campsite 4C2	4.68	7.53	0.23	0.37	44.75334	-110.40536
Campsite 4C3/Trail terminus	4.91	7.90	0.00	0.00	44.75505	-110.40142

The Seven Mile Hole Trail is named for the fact that it takes you down into the Grand Canyon of the Yellowstone to a location seven miles downstream from the Lower Falls (which explains how Seven Mile Hole gets its name). Along this trail is an excellent view of the Silver Cord Cascade on the opposite wall of the canyon. You can also visit a couple of small thermal areas located on the canyon walls.

The first three miles of this trail is relatively flat, but you will have a 1,300-foot (396m) descent into the canyon for the last two miles (and, of course, you will get to climb back up on the way out). The middle third of this trail was once part of the Howard Eaton Trail.

There are three campsites at the far end of this trail, each giving you the unique opportunity to camp in the canyon. All of these are moderately busy, but decent sites, and well worth the experience if you would like to say you camped in the canyon. Of the three, 4C2 has the least privacy, and 4C3 has the best fishing. Note that 4C3 may not be accessible early in the season due to high water in Sulphur Creek.

Silver Cord Cascade Spur Trail MAP 4-6

TYPE:	O&B	CAT:	BC	CLASS:	B	SURF:	TRAIL	DIST:	4	STATUS:	E
DIFF:	1	TRAF:	1	CHILD:	N	HACC:	N	USE:	H	LENGTH:	0.22
ELEV A:	- -	ELEV B:	- -	ELEV G:	- -	ELEV L:	- -	NET:	- -	BMA:	- -
MIN:	- -	MAX:	- -	AVG:	- -	AVG +:	- -	AVG -:	- -	OPEN:	YR

Reference Point	A-B Mi	A-B Km	B-A Mi	B-A Km	Latitude	Longitude
Trailhead @ jct w/ Ribbon Lake Trail	0.00	0.00	0.22	0.35	44.72391	-110.45168
Spur trail to campsite 4R1	0.10	0.16	0.12	0.19	44.72510	-110.45067
Surface Creek crossing	0.16	0.26	0.06	0.10	44.72569	-110.44995
Spur trail to campsite 4R2	0.19	0.31	0.03	0.05	44.72623	-110.44985
Silver Cord Cascade	0.22	0.35	0.00	0.00	44.72596	110.45030

This is the spur trail at the end of the Ribbon Lake Trail just where it takes a 90-degree right turn and heads south (see above). This trail leads to the Ribbon Lake campsites and the little spur that doubles back along the canyon wall to the top of Silver Cord Cascade. You cannot even tell it is a cascade from this vantage point, but you can sit right at a tiny, unnamed waterfall that exists just above where the creek flows over the edge of the canyon wall and becomes the cascade. It is an exquisite place for a few moments of solitude. For an excellent view of the cascade itself, take the Seven Mile Hole Trail on the other side of the canyon.

Sour Creek Trail — MAP 4-7,4-8

TYPE:	PTP	CAT:	BC	CLASS:	B	SURF:	TRAIL	DIST:	4	STATUS:	E
DIFF:	1	TRAF:	2	CHILD:	N	HACC:	N	USE:	H S	LENGTH:	1.71
ELEV A:	7831	ELEV B:	7700	ELEV G:	148	ELEV L:	-280	NET:	-131	BMA:	- -
MIN:	7700	MAX:	7831	AVG:	7723	AVG +:	4.1%	AVG -:	4.9%	OPEN:	YR

Reference Point	A-B Mi	A-B Km	B-A Mi	B-A Km	Latitude	Longitude
Trailhead @ jct w/ Wapiti Lake Trail	0.00	0.00	1.71	2.75	44.70859	-110.48273
Jct with Wrangler Lake Trail	0.66	1.06	1.05	1.69	44.70344	-110.47179
Sour Creek crossing (10 to 20')	1.58	2.54	0.13	0.21	44.69087	-110.46589
Jct w/ Howard Eaton Trail (Fishing Bridge to Canyon)	1.71	2.75	0.00	0.00	44.68917	-110.46512

This is a fairly short trail that takes you from the Wapiti Lake Trail to the Howard Eaton Trai that leads into Hayden Valley. It is often used to make a loop from the Wapiti Lake trailheac and back using those three sections of trail. In 2011, a couple from California was attacked by a bear on this trail near its junction with the Wapiti Lake Trail. The woman sustained minor injuries, but the man died from his wounds.[1]

Sour Creek itself lies at the south end of this trail, and there is a little secret that few people know about. When you get to the creek, hike a few hundred feet upstream to the Falls of Hayden Valley, the only waterfall in the entire valley. In the early part of the season, it is particularly robust (and the creek crossing may be more than knee-deep). Sour Creek gets its name as you might imagine from its acidic nature. For many of the past several seasons, this trail (and the Howard Eaton Trail) has been closed most or all of the season due to wolf dens in the area. The NPS prohibits people from entering into areas with active wolf dens, so check the trail's status before heading out.

South Rim Trail — MAP 4-6

TYPE:	PTP	CAT:	FC	CLASS:	B	SURF:	TRAIL	DIST:	4	STATUS:	E
DIFF:	1	TRAF:	5	CHILD:	N	HACC:	N	USE:	H	LENGTH:	1.69
ELEV A:	7702	ELEV B:	7661	ELEV G:	569	ELEV L:	-610	NET:	-41	BMA:	- -
MIN:	7657	MAX:	7803	AVG:	7741	AVG +:	11.5%	AVG -:	12.6%	OPEN:	YR

Reference Point	A-B Mi	A-B Km	B-A Mi	B-A Km	Latitude	Longitude
Trailhead at Chittenden Bridge	0.00	0.00	1.69	2.72	44.70809	-110.50217
Upper Falls Overlook	0.40	0.64	1.29	2.08	44.71239	-110.49841
Upper Falls/Crystal Falls Overlooks @ Uncle Tom's	0.64	1.03	1.05	1.69	44.71469	-110.49713
Brink of the Lower Falls Overlook	0.81	1.30	0.88	1.42	44.71682	-110.49698
Jct with trail to Uncle Tom's parking lot	0.91	1.46	0.78	1.26	44.71653	-110.49583
Jct with Uncle Tom's Trail	0.91	1.46	0.78	1.26	44.71653	-110.49583
Trailhead at Artist Point Parking Lot	1.69	2.72	0.00	0.00	44.71881	-110.48236

The South Rim Trail, like its cousin on the other side of the canyon, picks up its A point at the Chittenden Bridge, albeit on the east side. It follows along the bank of the Yellowstone River for a bit, then passes through the Uncle Tom's Trailhead parking area, and continues on to the Artist Point parking area.

This trail offers some stunning views down into the canyon once you get to the Lower Falls. Most people actually hike just a part of this trail—from Uncle Tom's to Artist Point and back. If you are going to start at the bridge, note that there is no parking there. You will need to park at the Wapiti Lake trailhead and then walk down to the bridge. Use caution when crossing the road here as people driving around the curve headed toward the trailheads are not expecting to see pedestrians.

Sylvan Springs Thermal Area Trail — MAP 4-2

Type:	O&B	**Cat:**	TH	**Class:**	U	**Surf:**	Trail	**Dist:**	4	**Status:**	U
Diff:	3	**Traf:**	1	**Child:**	N	**HAcc:**	N	**Use:**	H	**Length:**	1.27
Elev A:	7351	**Elev B:**	7444	**Elev G:**	165	**Elev L:**	-71	**Net:**	93	**BMA:**	- -
Min:	7333	**Max:**	7445	**Avg:**	7364	**Avg +:**	3.3%	**Avg -:**	3.1%	**Open:**	YR

Reference Point	A-B Mi	A-B Km	B-A Mi	B-A Km	Latitude	Longitude
Trailhead @ jct w/ Monument Geyser Basin Trail	0.00	0.00	1.27	2.04	44.68991	-110.74656
Sylvan Springs Thermal Field	1.27	2.04	0.00	0.00	44.69899	-110.76743

This unofficial and unmaintained trail takes you out to the Sylvan Springs Thermal Area on the west side of Gibbon Meadows. This is the large white thermal area you see off to the west when you are exiting the parking area at Artist Paint Pots. The area is comprised of a couple of larger fields along with several smaller ones. It is home to around 85 mostly unnamed features. Dante's Inferno, a vigorously churning pool, is here, as is Bridge Spring, named for a bridge-like structure that spans one end of the pool. Evening Primrose Spring is also located here. This spring goes through cycles where it is a pretty emerald or turquoise color at some times and a murky brown color at others (due to pH shifts).

There is no official trail out to this area, and this one is not maintained and will require you to bushwhack part of your way to the area. The only other way to get to the thermal area is by crossing the Gibbon River in Gibbon Meadows, which is often extremely marshy. As is the case in all thermal fields, be sure you watch where you step as you explore the basin.

Violet Springs Trail — MAP 4-7

Type:	O&B	**Cat:**	TH	**Class:**	U	**Surf:**	Trail	**Dist:**	4	**Status:**	U
Diff:	2	**Traf:**	1	**Child:**	N	**HAcc:**	N	**Use:**	H S	**Length:**	0.90
Elev A:	7750	**Elev B:**	7918	**Elev G:**	276	**Elev L:**	-108	**Net:**	168	**BMA:**	- -
Min:	7750	**Max:**	7940	**Avg:**	7838	**Avg +:**	7.0%	**Avg -:**	7.4%	**Open:**	YR

Reference Point	A-B Mi	A-B Km	B-A Mi	B-A Km	Latitude	Longitude
Trailhead @ jct w/ Mary Mountain Trail	0.00	0.00	0.90	1.45	44.64875	-110.55084
Violet Springs Thermal Area	0.90	1.45	0.00	0.00	44.65047	-110.56750

This is a short trail out to an old, largely quiet thermal area that consists of about two dozen rather benign, unnamed thermal features and small hot springs. The trail is not maintained, but enough people use it each season to create an actual trail to it. It runs north off the Mary Mountain Trail just west of Violet Creek (most of the water of which comes from runoff from the thermal field).

While traveling through the thermal field, be sure you pay attention to the previous tracks of others. Like any other thermal area, the ground can be thin and it can be dangerous to go wandering too close to some of the pools.

It is possible to continue your hike north, bushwhacking your way through the woods to get to another set of thermal fields known as the Central Plateau Thermal Area and the "Hot Pots" (about 200 features).

Wapiti Lake Trail — MAP 4-8

TYPE:	PTP	CAT:	BC	CLASS:	B	SURF:	TRAIL	DIST:	4	STATUS:	E
DIFF:	4	TRAF:	2	CHILD:	N	HACC:	N	USE:	H S	LENGTH:	16.44
ELEV A:	7732	ELEV B:	8468	ELEV G:	2453	ELEV L:	-1717	NET:	736	BMA:	- -
MIN:	7723	MAX:	8998	AVG:	8349	AVG +:	4.0%	AVG -:	4.7%	OPEN:	YR

Reference Point	A-B Mi	A-B Km	B-A Mi	B-A Km	Latitude	Longitude
Trailhead 4K7 (Chittenden Bridge Picnic Area)	0.00	0.00	16.44	26.46	44.70773	-110.50028
Jct with Clear Lake Trail	0.50	0.80	15.94	25.65	44.70924	-110.49068
Jct with Sour Creek Trail	0.91	1.46	15.53	24.99	44.70859	-110.48273
Forest Springs Thermal Area West	1.20	1.93	15.24	24.53	44.70778	-110.47688
Forest Springs Thermal Area East	1.48	2.38	14.96	24.08	44.70917	-110.47191
Jct with Ribbon Lake Trail	2.97	4.78	13.47	21.68	44.71738	-110.44844
Moss Creek crossing	7.81	12.57	8.63	13.89	44.72612	-110.36399
Spur trail to campsite 4M2	7.85	12.63	8.59	13.82	44.72617	-110.36319
Unnamed, small thermal area	8.23	13.24	8.21	13.21	44.72335	-110.35728
Jct with Fern Lake Trail (Unnamed pass)	12.35	19.88	4.09	6.58	44.69457	-110.30034
Broad Creek crossing (route to campsite 4B3)	14.09	22.68	2.35	3.78	44.70980	-110.27809
Spur trail to campsite 4B4	14.38	23.14	2.06	3.32	44.71124	-110.27374
Jct with Astringent Creek Trail	14.83	23.87	1.61	2.59	44.70992	-110.26543
Wapiti Lake	15.47	24.90	0.97	1.56	44.71643	-110.25925
Spur trail to campsite 4W2	15.79	25.41	0.65	1.05	44.72018	-110.25519
Spur trail to campsite 4W3	15.85	25.51	0.59	0.95	44.72089	-110.25471
Trail terminus at Pelican Creek Trail	16.44	26.46	0.00	0.00	44.72588	-110.24617

If you love hiking through forests, this is the trail for you. Once you get about a mile into the trail it is pretty much solid forest hiking until you get to its terminus at the Pelican Creek Trail. And though the trail does pass through a couple of interesting thermal areas, it is largely just...trees.

This trail passes through the Forest Springs Thermal Area on its west end. This area stretches up to the Clear Lake Trail and includes approximately 370 unnamed thermal features.

The trail is used mainly by hikers headed out to the campsites at the far end, staying there primarily to use them as a base for exploring the northern reaches of the Pelican Valley (in which there are no campsites), and the lakes in the area (Wapiti Lake, Fern Lake, the Tern Lakes, and White Lake). And this is the only trail that will get you to Pelican Valley from the Canyon area. Because it is so lightly used, this trail is one of the last to be cleared in this district each season.

Wolf Lake Cutoff/Little Gibbon Falls Trail — MAP 4-3

TYPE:	PTP	CAT:	BC	CLASS:	C	SURF:	TRAIL	DIST:	4	STATUS:	E
DIFF:	1	TRAF:	2	CHILD:	N	HACC:	N	USE:	H	LENGTH:	1.35
ELEV A:	7812	ELEV B:	7981	ELEV G:	318	ELEV L:	-149	NET:	169	BMA:	- -
MIN:	7793	MAX:	8013	AVG:	7871	AVG +:	6.8%	AVG -:	5.3%	OPEN:	YR

Reference Point	A-B Mi	A-B Km	B-A Mi	B-A Km	Latitude	Longitude
Trailhead 4N4 (3.7 mi E of Norris Junction)	0.00	0.00	1.35	2.17	44.71284	-110.62732
Little Gibbon Falls overlook	0.75	1.21	0.60	0.97	44.71655	-110.61617
Gibbon River crossing (15+')	0.79	1.27	0.56	0.90	44.71701	-110.61561
Jct with Howard Eaton Trail/Chain of Lakes Trail	1.35	2.17	0.00	0.00	44.72131	-110.60754

This little segment of trail is known as the Wolf Lake Cutoff Trail, and kind of serves as a "shorter way" to get to Wolf Lake from the Norris-Canyon Road area. But its main draw for most visitors is the Little Gibbon Falls, a small but gorgeous little cascade-type waterfall located on the upper end of the Gibbon River. It is very similar to the larger Gibbon Falls, and thus its name.

The trailhead itself is kind of hard to find if you are not familiar with the area. When you park in the pullout, the trailhead is across the street on the right-hand side of the hill you will see before you. It is generally marked with an orange blaze, but that is sometimes covered by tree growth and whatnot. Be careful crossing the road here as vehicles tend to speed through this area at a considerable pace above the posted speed limit. Note that, like most of the other trails in this area, during the first half of the season (well into July), sections of it can be rather marshy and difficult to cross.

Wrangler Lake Trail — MAP 4-7,4-8

TYPE:	O&B	CAT:	BC	CLASS:	B	SURF:	TRAIL	DIST:	4	STATUS:	E
DIFF:	3	TRAF:	2	CHILD:	N	HACC:	N	USE:	H S	LENGTH:	2.46
ELEV A:	7725	ELEV B:	7861	ELEV G:	215	ELEV L:	-79	NET:	136	BMA:	- -
MIN:	7725	MAX:	7884	AVG:	7767	AVG +:	2.5%	AVG -:	1.6%	OPEN:	YR

Reference Point	A-B Mi	A-B Km	B-A Mi	B-A Km	Latitude	Longitude
Trailhead @ jct w/ Sour Creek Trail	0.00	0.00	2.46	3.96	44.70344	-110.47179
Sour Creek crossing (25 to 30')	1.59	2.56	0.87	1.40	44.69492	-110.44238
Spur trail to campsite 4W1	2.43	3.91	0.03	0.05	44.68520	-110.43717
Wrangler Lake - Terminus	2.46	3.96	0.00	0.00	44.68484	-110.43671

This trail departs from the Sour Creek Trail (which itself departs from the Wapiti Lake Trail) and takes you to a small, fishless lake nestled in the woods. This lake, with its one, pretty decent campsite, is in a nice setting for a bit of privacy without having to hike a full day. The downside is that, early in the season, the lake may be difficult to get to because of the need to ford Sour Creek. At that time of year, the stream can be very deep (>four feet).

Canyon Wall Trails

Brink of the Lower Falls Trail MAP 4-9

Reference Point	A-B Mi	A-B Km	B-A Mi	B-A Km	Latitude	Longitude
Trailhead @ jct w/ North Rim Trail	0.00	0.00	0.35	0.56	44.71907	-110.49871

This short, dirt/gravel trail takes you down about 250 feet to a platform from which you can view the Lower Falls from right over the top as it rushes over the canyon wall. The average grade is 13%, and though the climb back up can be a bit strenuous, there are benches and places to rest along the trail.

One of the most enthralling aspects of this trail is that the closer you get to the bottom, the more you can feel the ground rumbling under your feet from the power of the water.

Red Rock Point Trail MAP 4-9

Reference Point	A-B Mi	A-B Km	B-A Mi	B-A Km	Latitude	Longitude
Trailhead @ jct w/ North Rim Trail	0.00	0.00	0.34	0.55	44.72145	-110.48767

This short trail departs to the right from the little path down to Lookout Point. Like the Brink of the Lower Falls Trail, it descends approximately 250 feet down into the canyon via a path that is part pavement and part stairs (the average grade is around 15%). The view of the falls from here is well worth the climb back up, however.

Red Rock Point was given its name from the red-colored spire below the Lower Falls visible from the lookout. The reddish tint comes from the iron oxide in the rock. It was given its name in 1886 by park photographer Frank J. Haynes.[2]

Uncle Tom's Trail MAP 4-9

Reference Point	A-B Mi	A-B Km	B-A Mi	B-A Km	Latitude	Longitude
Trailhead @ jct w/ North Rim Trail	0.00	0.00	0.16	0.26	44.71653	-110.49583

There's an old saying about Uncle Tom's Trail: "It's 328 steps going down, and 3280 steps coming back up!" (or some variant of this). And although this trail is usually listed in the "short hikes" list of other guides, when you are done, you will feel like you have taken anything but a short hike.

Despite its short length, this is one of the most strenuous hikes in the park's frontcountry, and if you have heart or breathing problems, or problems with your lower extremities, you should probably think twice before attempting it. The view at the bottom is grand, but not worth risking your health over. Having said that, there are handrails and plenty of benches to rest on as you make your way back up.

The entire "trail" is basically a long staircase to a viewpoint of the Lower Falls of the Yellowstone nestled on the side of the canyon wall. The trail gets its name from "Uncle" Tom Richardson who, in the early days of the park, took visitors down to the bottom of the canyon here via rope ladders and wooden steps, and then back up again (if you think doing it on stairs is tough, imagine having to come back up a rope ladder from that depth!).

This is one area where you want to definitely stay on the trail. Several people have been struck by falling rocks here as a result of people climbing on the canyon walls, including a 10-year old boy who was killed in 1983 by a falling 35lb (16kg) boulder.[3]

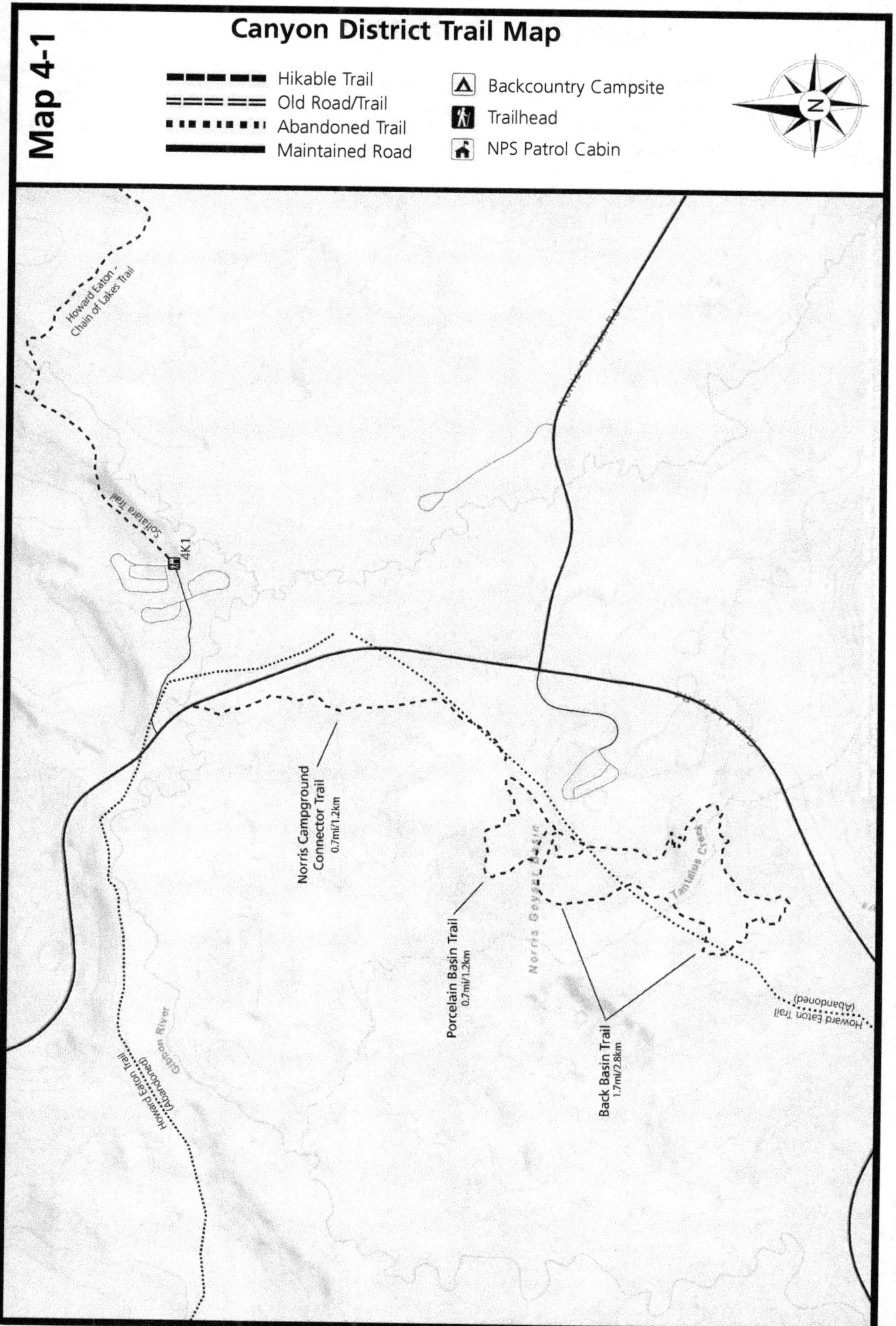
Map 4-1
Canyon District Trail Map
Hikable Trail
Old Road/Trail
Abandoned Trail
Maintained Road
Backcountry Campsite
Trailhead
NPS Patrol Cabin
N
Howard Eaton - Chain of Lakes Trail
Solfatara Trail
4K1
Norris Campground Connector Trail
0.7mi/1.2km
Porcelain Basin Trail
0.7mi/1.2km
Norris Geyser Basin
Tantalus Creek
Back Basin Trail
1.7mi/2.8km
Howard Eaton Trail (Abandoned)
Gibbon River

Map 4-2

Canyon District Trail Map

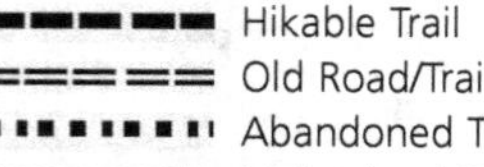

Hikable Trail
Old Road/Trail
Abandoned Trail
Maintained Road

Backcountry Campsite
Trailhead
NPS Patrol Cabin

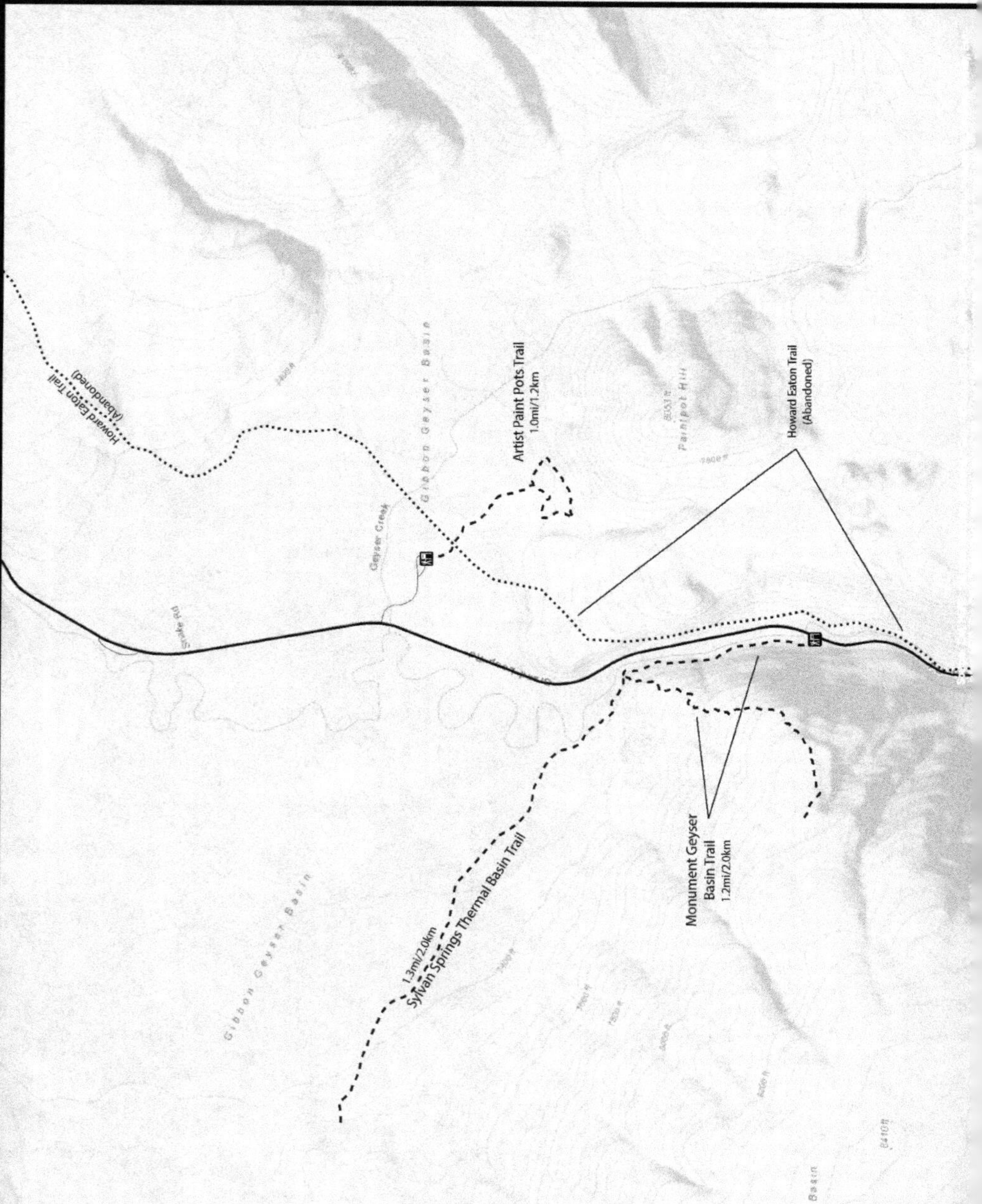

Howard Eaton Trail (Abandoned)

Gibbon Geyser Basin

Artist Paint Pots Trail 1.0mi/1.2km

Paintpot Hill

Howard Eaton Trail (Abandoned)

Geyser Creek

Sylvan Springs Thermal Basin Trail 1.3mi/2.0km

Gibbon Geyser Basin

Monument Geyser Basin Trail 1.2mi/2.0km

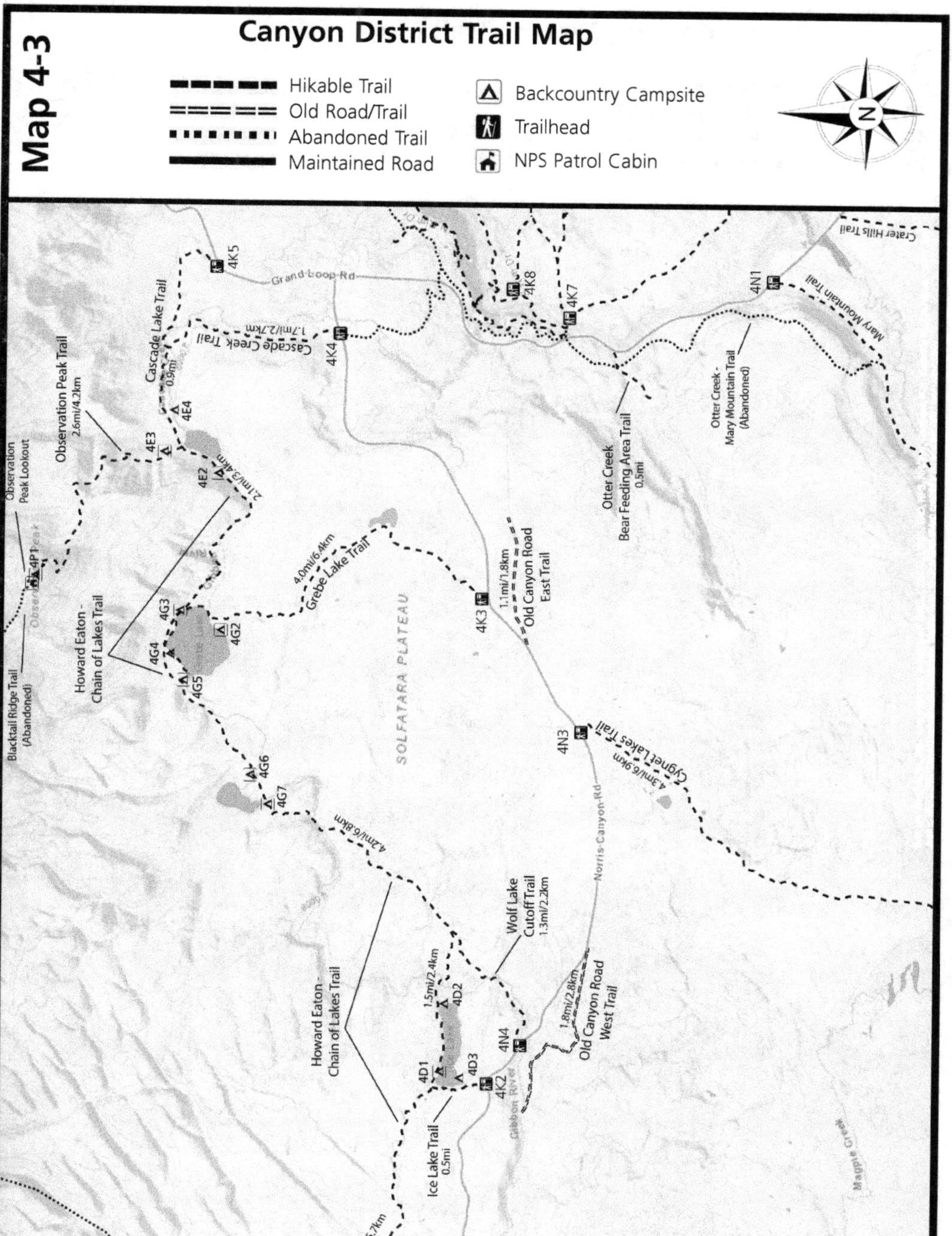

Map 4-3

Canyon District Trail Map

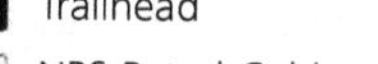

Hikable Trail
Old Road/Trail
Abandoned Trail
Maintained Road

Backcountry Campsite
Trailhead
NPS Patrol Cabin

Grand Loop Rd
4K5
Cascade Lake Trail
0.9mi
Cascade Creek Trail
1.7mi/2.7km
4K4
4K8
4K7
4N1
Crater Hills Trail
Mary Mountain Trail
Otter Creek - Mary Mountain Trail (Abandoned)
Otter Creek Bear Feeding Area Trail 0.5mi
Observation Peak Trail 2.6mi/4.2km
Observation Peak Lookout
4P1
4E4
4E3
4E2
2.1mi/3.4km
Howard Eaton - Chain of Lakes Trail
Blacktail Ridge Trail (Abandoned)
4.0mi/6.4km
Grebe Lake Trail
4G3
4G2
4G4
4G5
4K3
1.1mi/1.8km
Old Canyon Road East Trail
SOLFATARA PLATEAU
4G6
4G7
4.2mi/6.8km
4N3
Cygnet Lakes Trail
4.3mi/6.9km
Norris-Canyon Rd
Wolf Lake Cutoff Trail 1.3mi/2.2km
1.5mi/2.4km
4D2
Howard Eaton - Chain of Lakes Trail
4N4
1.8mi/2.8km
Old Canyon Road West Trail
4D1
4D3
4K2
Gibbon River
Ice Lake Trail 0.5mi
3.5mi/5.7km
4F1
Arrow Canyon Trail (Abandoned)
0.5mi
K1
Magpie Creek

Map 4-4

Canyon District Trail Map

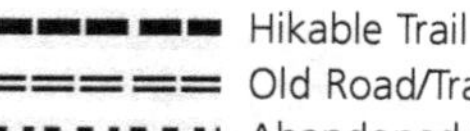

Hikable Trail
Old Road/Trail
Abandoned Trail
Maintained Road

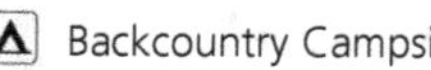

Backcountry Campsite

Trailhead

NPS Patrol Cabin

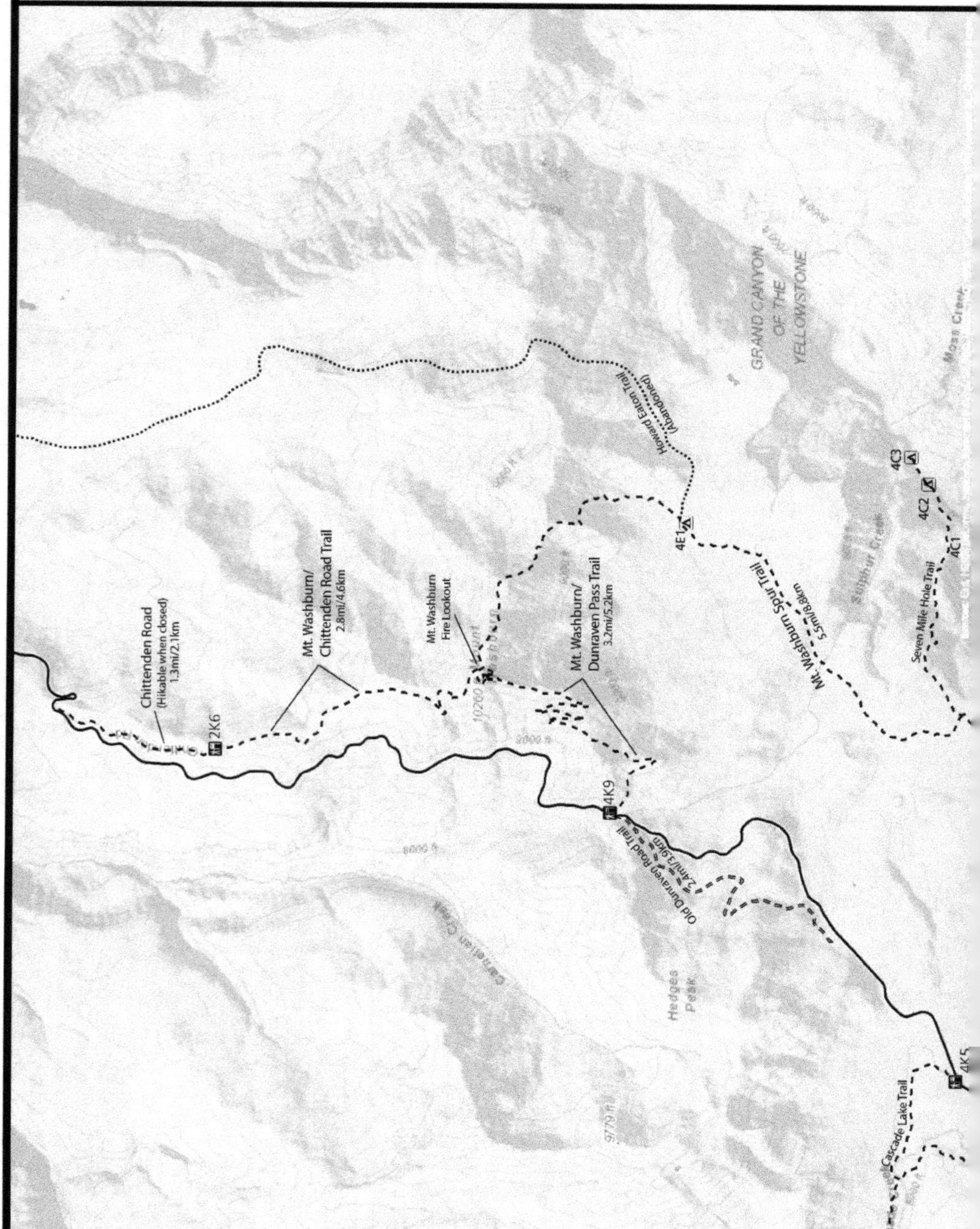

Howard Eaton Trail (Abandoned)

GRAND CANYON OF THE YELLOWSTONE

Chittenden Road (Hikable when closed) 1.3mi/2.1km

2K6

Mt. Washburn/ Chittenden Road Trail 2.8mi/4.6km

Mt. Washburn Fire Lookout

10260

Mt. Washburn/ Dunraven Pass Trail 3.2mi/5.2km

4K9

Old Dunraven Road Trail 2.4mi/3.9km

4E1

Mt. Washburn Spur Trail 5.5mi/8.8km

Sulphur Creek

4C3

4C2

4C1

Seven Mile Hole Trail

Moss Creek

Hedges Peak

Carnelian Creek

9779 ft

8000 ft

4K5

Cascade Lake Trail

4E4

Map 4-5

Canyon District Trail Map

Hikable Trail
Old Road/Trail
Abandoned Trail
Maintained Road

Backcountry Campsite
Trailhead
NPS Patrol Cabin

Moss Creek
4C3
4C2
4C1
Sulphur Creek
Seven Mile Hole Trail
2.2mi/3.6km
Washburn Spur Trail
GRAND CANYON OF THE YELLOWSTONE
Surface Creek
Washburn Lake Trail
4R2
4R1
2.7mi/4.3km
Howard Eaton Trail (Abandoned)
Seven Mile Hole Trail
Ribbon Lake Trail
Sublime Point Trail
4K6
North Rim Trail
4K8
Clear Lake Trail
8429 ft

Map 4-6

Canyon District Trail Map

Hikable Trail
Old Road/Trail
Abandoned Trail
Maintained Road

Backcountry Campsite

Trailhead

NPS Patrol Cabin

Wapiti Lake Trail
4R2
4R1
Silver Cord Cascade Spur Trail 0.2mi/0.3km
Ribbon Lake Trail 0.9mi/1.4km
Seven Mile Hole Trail
1.1mi/1.8km
0.7mi/1.1km
2.1mi/3.4km Wapiti Lake Trail
Ribbon Lake Trail
Artist Point - Point Sublime Trail
0.3mi
Wrangler Lake Trail
4K6
0.6mi/0.9km
0.8mi/1.2km
0.7mi/1.1km
Howard Eaton Trail (Abandoned)
North Rim Trail
Sour Creek Trail
4K8
3.1mi/5.0km
1.7mi/2.7km
Clear Lake Trail
0.5mi/0.8km
Clear Lake Cutoff 0.7mi/1.1km
North Rim Cutoff 0.4mi/0.6km
Canyon Village
South Rim Trail
4N2
Wapiti Lake Trail 0.5mi/0.8km
Howard Eaton Trail
4K7
Howard Eaton Trail (Abandoned)
4K4

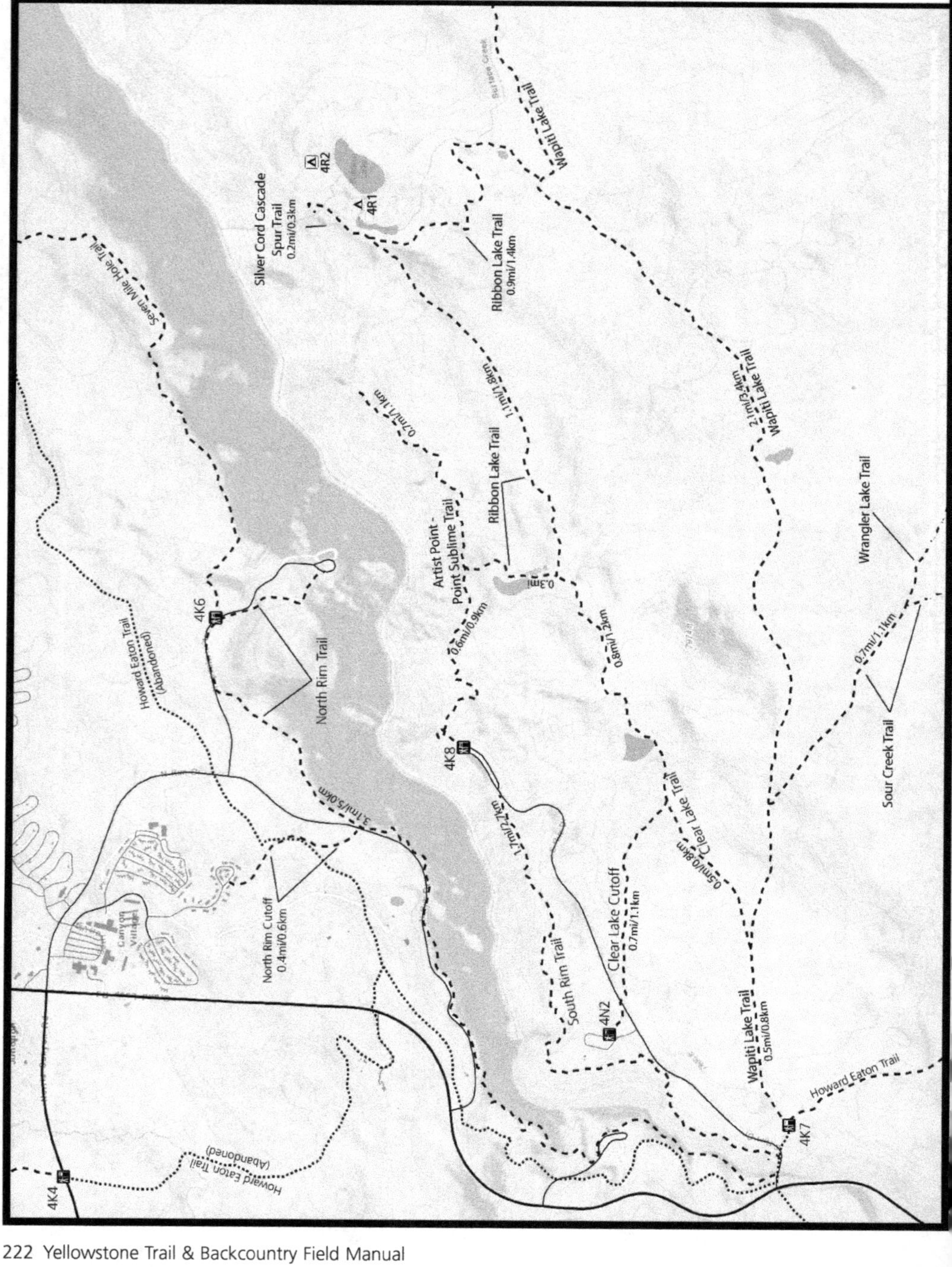

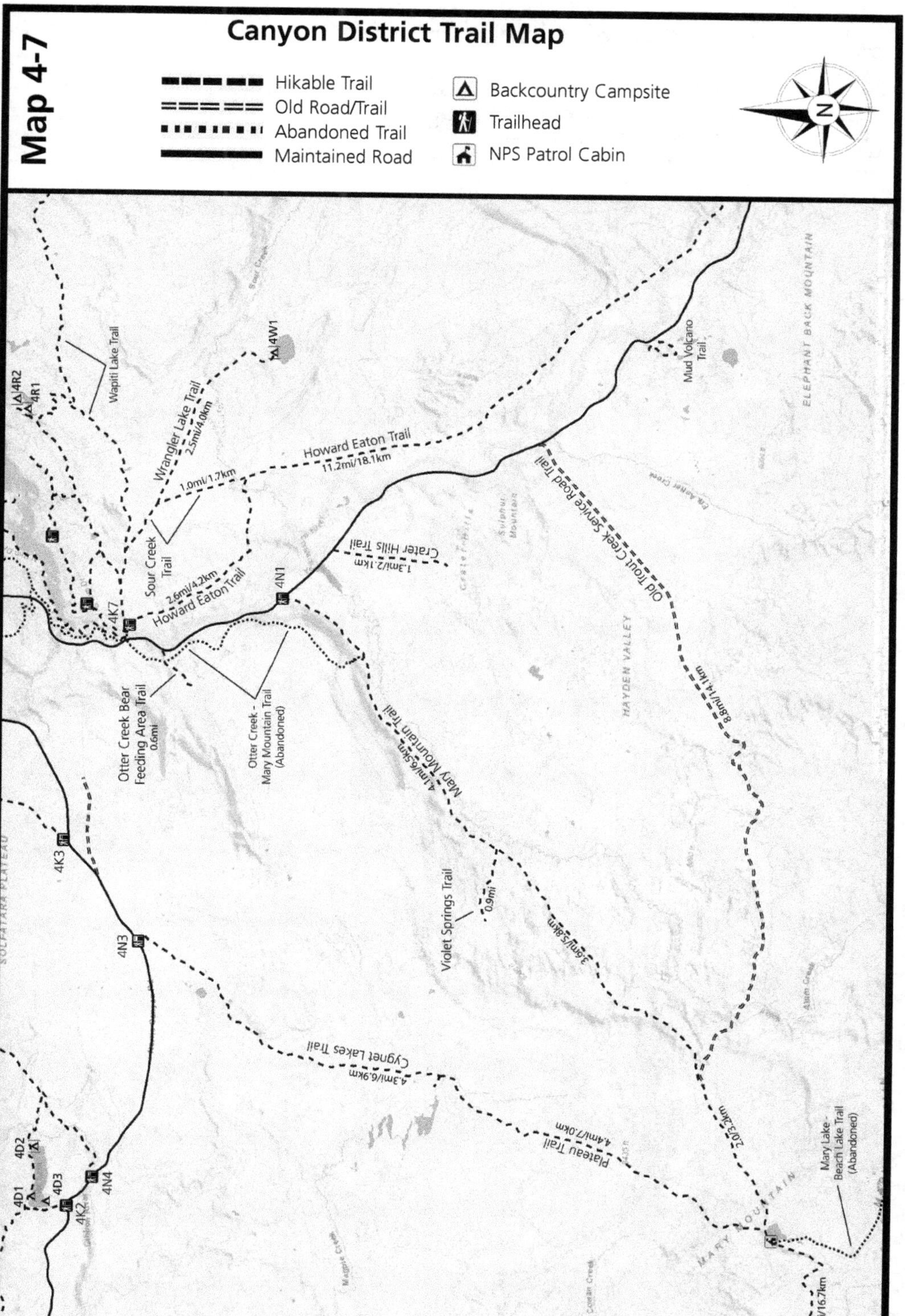

Map 4-7

Canyon District Trail Map

Hikable Trail
Old Road/Trail
Abandoned Trail
Maintained Road

Backcountry Campsite
Trailhead
NPS Patrol Cabin

N

Wapiti Lake Trail
4R2
4R1
4W1
Wrangler Lake Trail
2.5mi/4.0km
Howard Eaton Trail
11.2mi/18.1km
1.0mi/1.7km
Sour Creek Trail
2.6mi/4.2km
Howard Eaton Trail
4K7
4N1
Crater Hills Trail
1.3mi/2.1km
Mud Volcano Trail
ELEPHANT BACK MOUNTAIN
Old Trout Creek Service Road Trail
8.8mi/14.1km
HAYDEN VALLEY
Otter Creek Bear Feeding Area Trail
0.6mi
Otter Creek - Mary Mountain Trail (Abandoned)
Mary Mountain Trail
4.1mi/6.5km
4K3
SOLFATARA PLATEAU
Violet Springs Trail
0.9mi
3.6mi/5.8km
4N3
Cygnet Lakes Trail
4.3mi/6.9km
Plateau Trail
4.4m/7.0km
2.0/3.2km
4D2
4D1
4D3
4K2
4N4
MARY MOUNTAIN
Mary Lake - Beach Lake Trail (Abandoned)
10.3mi/16.7km

Map 4-8

Canyon District Trail Map

Hikable Trail
Old Road/Trail
Abandoned Trail
Maintained Road

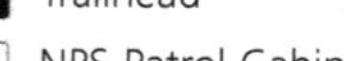

Backcountry Campsite
Trailhead
NPS Patrol Cabin

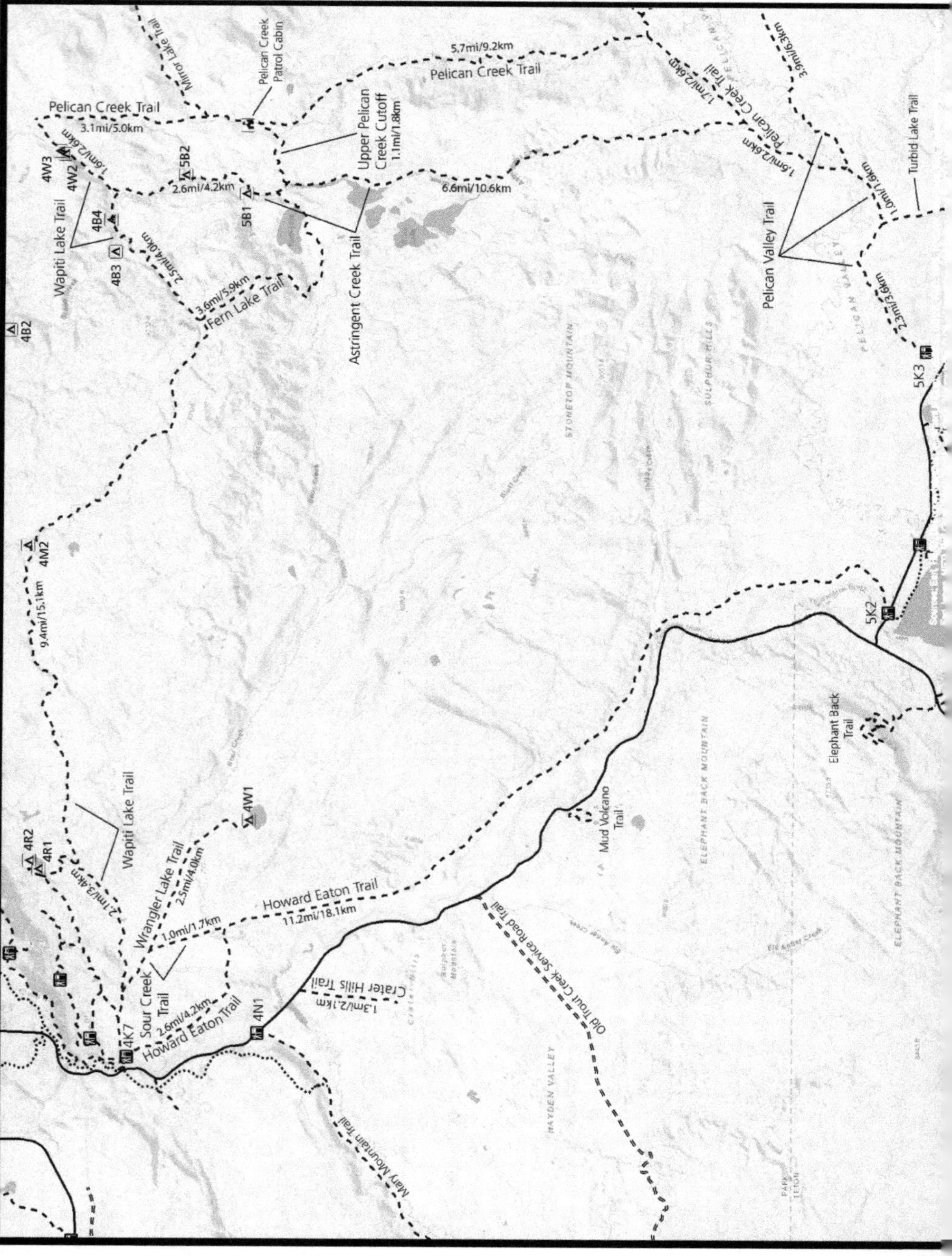

Pelican Creek Trail
3.1mi/5.0km
Mirror Lake Trail
Pelican Creek Patrol Cabin
5.7mi/9.2km
Pelican Creek Trail
Upper Pelican Creek Cutoff
1.1mi/1.8km
1.7mi/2.6km
Pelican Creek Trail
1.6mi/2.6km
3.9mi/6.3km
Turbid Lake Trail
4W3
4W2
1.6mi/2.6km
5B2
2.6mi/4.2km
5B1
6.6mi/10.6km
1.0mi/1.6km
4B4
Wapiti Lake Trail
4B3
2.5mi/4.0km
3.6mi/5.9km
Fern Lake Trail
Astringent Creek Trail
Pelican Valley Trail
2.3mi/3.6km
4B2
5K3
STONETOP MOUNTAIN
SULPHUR HILLS
PELICAN VALLEY
4M2
9.4mi/15.1km
5K2
Elephant Back Trail
ELEPHANT BACK MOUNTAIN
Mud Volcano Trail
4W1
Wapiti Lake Trail
4R2
4R1
2.1mi/3.4km
Wrangler Lake Trail
2.5mi/4.0km
Howard Eaton Trail
11.2mi/18.1km
1.0mi/1.7km
Sour Creek Trail
2.6mi/4.2km
Howard Eaton Trail
4K7
4N1
Crater Hills Trail
1.3mi/2.1km
Old Trout Creek Service Road Trail
HAYDEN VALLEY
Mary Mountain Trail

Map 4-9

Canyon District Trail Map

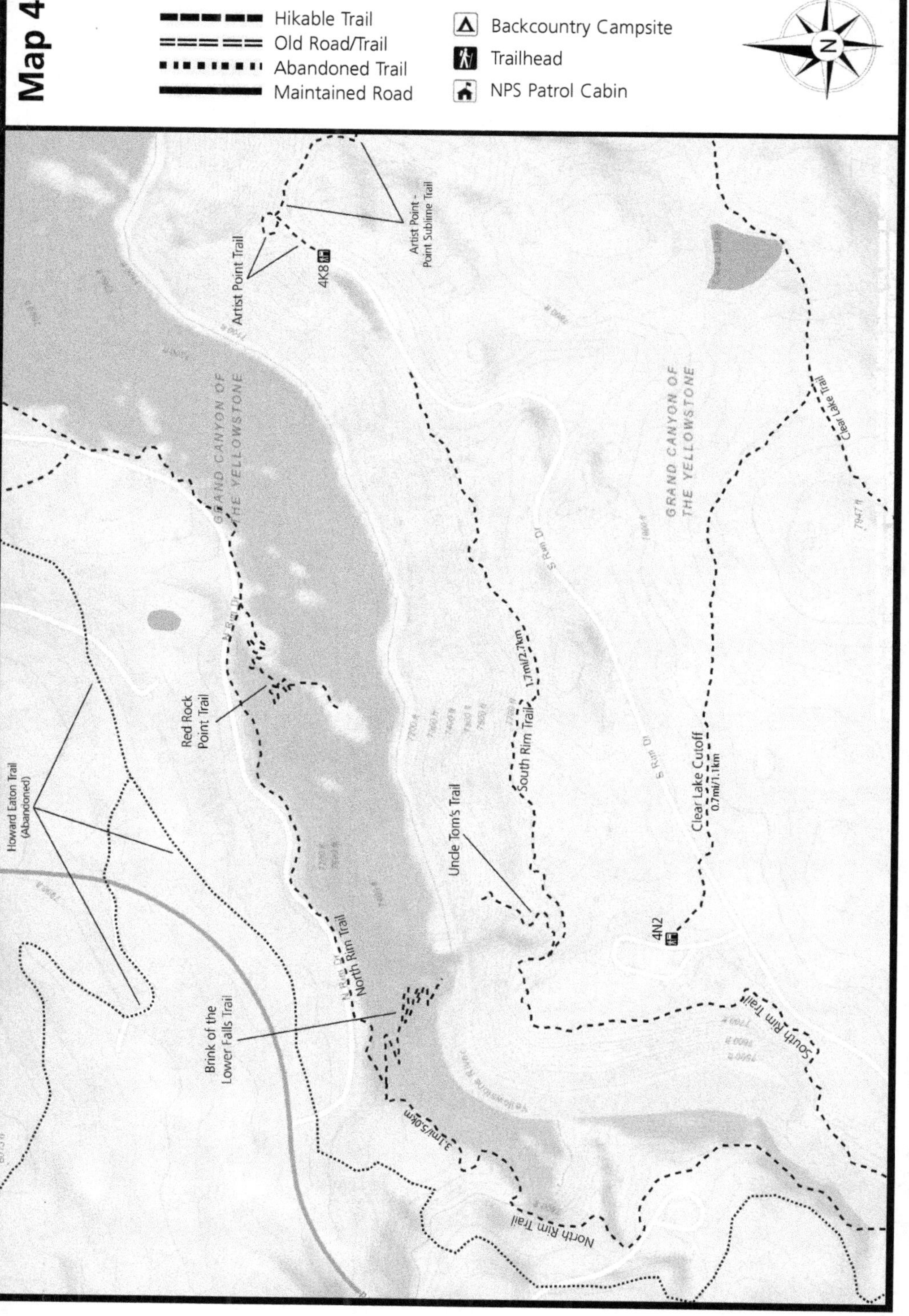

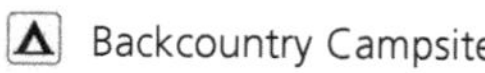

Hikable Trail
Old Road/Trail
Abandoned Trail
Maintained Road
Backcountry Campsite
Trailhead
NPS Patrol Cabin
N
Artist Point Trail
Artist Point - Point Sublime Trail
4K8
GRAND CANYON OF THE YELLOWSTONE
GRAND CANYON OF THE YELLOWSTONE
Clear Lake Trail
N Rim Dr
S Rim Dr
1.7mi/2.7km
Red Rock Point Trail
South Rim Trail
Clear Lake Cutoff
0.7mi/1.1km
Howard Eaton Trail (Abandoned)
Uncle Tom's Trail
4N2
North Rim Trail
Brink of the Lower Falls Trail
South Rim Trail
3.1mi/5.0km
North Rim Trail

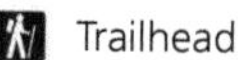

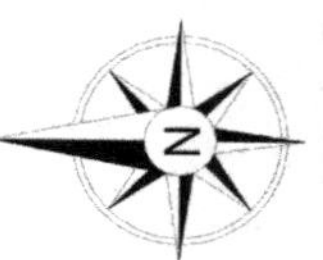

Lake District Trails

Astringent (Broad) Creek Trail

MAP 5-1,4-8

TYPE:	PTP	CAT:	BC	CLASS:	C	SURF:	TRAIL	DIST:	5	STATUS:	E
DIFF:	2	TRAF:	2	CHILD:	N	HACC:	N	USE:	H S	LENGTH:	9.19
ELEV A:	7901	ELEV B:	8202	ELEV G:	1002	ELEV L:	-701	NET:	301	BMA:	H/I
MIN:	7901	MAX:	8281	AVG:	8149	AVG +:	2.9%	AVG -:	2.7%	OPEN:	7/4

Reference Point	A-B Mi	A-B Km	B-A Mi	B-A Km	Latitude	Longitude
Trailhead @ jct w/ Pelican Creek Trail	0.00	0.00	9.19	14.79	44.59320	-110.24596
Astringent Creek crossing	0.60	0.97	8.59	13.82	44.60133	-110.24782
Astringent Creek crossing	2.18	3.51	7.01	11.28	44.62266	-110.24979
Enter the Astringent Creek Thermal Area	3.04	4.89	6.15	9.90	44.63281	-110.25406
Leave the Astringent Creek Thermal Area	3.26	5.25	5.93	9.54	44.63518	-110.25673
Tern Lake off to the west	5.22	8.40	3.97	6.39	44.66034	-110.26335
Jct with Upper Pelican Creek Cutoff Trail	6.58	10.59	2.61	4.20	44.67865	-110.26324
Jct with Fern Lake Trail	6.76	10.88	2.43	3.91	44.68049	-110.26561
Spur trail to campsite 5B1 (0.08 miles)	7.13	11.47	2.06	3.32	44.68554	-110.26551
Spur trail to campsite 5B2 (0.05 miles)	8.23	13.24	0.96	1.54	44.69750	-110.26221
Terminus @ jct w/ Wapiti Lake Trail	9.19	14.79	0.00	0.00	44.70992	-110.26543

This trail has had so many different monikers over the past decades that it is hard to keep track of them. Its most popular is the Broad Creek Trail, though it is also known as the Tern Lakes Trail, the White Lake Trail, and several others, depending upon which guidebook you get and how old it is. The trail does parallel Astringent Creek along its southern half and Broad Creek along its northern half.

Note that the southern third of the trail is in the bear management area in Pelican Valley. As a result, it does not open until July 4, and even then it is only open to travel from 9 a.m. until 7 p.m. From the Astringent Creek Thermal Area northward, however, it is open year-round and subject to itinerant closures like every other trail is.

Fortunately, along the northern part of the trail there are a couple of decent campsites from which you can base your exploration of the area (there are a variety of lakes and thermal fields within a day's hike of each). There were a couple of other campsites on this trail at one time, one of which was at White Lake. In 1984, a woman who was asleep in her tent there was attacked and killed by a bear. That was the proverbial straw that broke the camel's back, so to speak. Park wildlife managers had already been considering restricting activity in this area to allow the bears access to the area without human interference, and this pretty much sealed the deal. Since that death, overnight camping in Pelican Valley was prohibited and hiking was restricted to certain times of the day after July 4.

Avalanche Peak Trail

MAP 5-3

TYPE:	O&B	CAT:	TH	CLASS:	C	SURF:	TRAIL	DIST:	5	STATUS:	E
DIFF:	4	TRAF:	2	CHILD:	N	HACC:	N	USE:	H	LENGTH:	2.33
ELEV A:	8483	ELEV B:	10565	ELEV G:	2249	ELEV L:	-168	NET:	2082	BMA:	- -
MIN:	8483	MAX:	10566	AVG:	9627	AVG +:	19.6%	AVG -:	9.5%	OPEN:	YR

Reference Point	A-B Mi	A-B Km	B-A Mi	B-A Km	Latitude	Longitude
Trailhead 5N2 (7.8 mi W of East Entrance)	0.00	0.00	2.33	3.75	44.47072	-110.14258
Cairn shelter	2.14	3.44	0.19	0.31	44.48733	-110.14225
Summit	2.33	3.75	0.00	0.00	44.48951	-110.13998

Avalanche Peak is perhaps the most popular "extreme climb" in the park, especially among park employees. Many ascend the peak early in the season, long before the snow melts from the summit. I do not recommend this hike early in the season for anyone other than seasoned hikers who have experience climbing mountains and navigating snow fields.

The hike is a steady climb up 2,100 feet (640m) over the course of 2⅓ miles. The bottom half of the trail is in thick forest, while the top half is out in the open above the tree line. You begin the hike near Sylvan Pass, so you are already far above 8,000 feet (2438m) to start with. This is not something you want to do before you acclimate to the elevation. Much of the runoff from the snow melt cascades down the unnamed creek you will have to cross a couple of times on this hike. Again, early in the season, this water flow will be rather robust (and cold!), so exercise caution.

When you do get to the top, you are rewarded with breathtaking views of the park, Yellowstone Lake, and of the Absaroka Mountains.

Beach Lake Trail — MAP 5-2

Type:	PTP	**Cat:**	BC	**Class:**	N	**Surf:**	Trail	**Dist:**	5	**Status:**	A
Diff:	2	**Traf:**	1	**Child:**	N	**HAcc:**	N	**Use:**	H	**Length:**	5.19
Elev A:	7781	**Elev B:**	8165	**Elev G:**	909	**Elev L:**	-525	**Net:**	384	**BMA:**	- -
Min:	7781	**Max:**	8231	**Avg:**	7978	**Avg +:**	4.5%	**Avg -:**	4.7%	**Open:**	YR

Reference Point	A-B Mi	A-B Km	B-A Mi	B-A Km	Latitude	Longitude
Trailhead @ end of Arnica Creek Bypass Service Rd	0.00	0.00	5.19	8.35	44.47863	-110.54470
Beach Lake	5.19	8.35	0.00	0.00	44.54106	-110.56550

This is another trail that was lost to the round of maintenance budget cuts in the early 2000s.[1] And though this trail is no longer maintained, it is still fairly navigable in most places, though you will have to hop over (or climb under) a considerable number of trees along the way. Five miles of doing that can be tiring.

There is (was) an older trail that leads off to the east toward Dryad Lake. This trail, too, has long since been abandoned and is barely navigable any longer. Hiking it will likewise require considerable bushwhacking. At one time there was also an old (probably unmaintained) trail that led north to Mary Lake (see the Lost and Forgotten Trails chapter for both).

Bridge Bay-Natural Bridge Cutoff Trail — MAP 5-2

Type:	PTP	**Cat:**	FC	**Class:**	B	**Surf:**	Trail	**Dist:**	5	**Status:**	E
Diff:	1	**Traf:**	3	**Child:**	Y	**HAcc:**	N	**Use:**	H S	**Length:**	0.74
Elev A:	7778	**Elev B:**	7827	**Elev G:**	206	**Elev L:**	-167	**Net:**	49	**BMA:**	- -
Min:	7778	**Max:**	7848	**Avg:**	7810	**Avg +:**	0.0%	**Avg -:**	0.0%	**Open:**	YR

Reference Point	A-B Mi	A-B Km	B-A Mi	B-A Km	Latitude	Longitude
Trailhead at A-Loop in BB Campground	0.00	0.00	0.74	1.19	44.53558	-110.43806
Terminus at Jct with Natural Bridge Trail	0.74	1.19	0.00	0.00	44.52786	-110.44549

This is a short cutoff trail that allows campers at the Bridge Bay Campground to access the Natural Bridge Trail without having to drive or hike all the way around to the main trailhead. It is a short, flat, mostly forested hike that is suitable for smaller children, but may not be suitable for those in wheelchairs. If you are in a wheelchair, it is best to begin at the main trailhead on the road south of Bridge Bay.

Elephant Back Trail — MAP 5-2

Type:	O&B/L	**Cat:**	BC	**Class:**	B	**Surf:**	Trail	**Dist:**	5	**Status:**	E
Diff:	2	**Traf:**	4	**Child:**	N	**HAcc:**	N	**Use:**	H S	**Length:**	3.86
Elev A:	7822	**Elev B:**	7822	**Elev G:**	951	**Elev L:**	-951	**Net:**	0	**BMA:**	- -
Min:	7822	**Max:**	8619	**Avg:**	8263	**Avg +:**	9.3%	**Avg -:**	10.4%	**Open:**	YR

Reference Point	A-B Mi	A-B Km	B-A Mi	B-A Km	Latitude	Longitude
Trailhead @ pullout (1.1 mi S of Fishing Bridge Jct)	0.00	0.00	2.96	4.76	44.55666	-110.40207
Old waterworks in woods	0.15	0.24	2.81	4.52	44.55719	-110.40473
Powerline crossing	0.17	0.27	2.79	4.49	44.55741	-110.40505
Trail loop junction	0.90	1.45	2.06	3.32	44.56465	-110.40918
Trail loop junction	2.96	4.76	0.00	0.00	44.56465	-110.40918

The Elephant Back Trail, constructed in 1927, is one of the most popular threshold trails in the park, especially among employees. It can be hiked at the upper section as a loop, making the total hike just under four miles from the trailhead and back, or you can hike up the short side (go left at the junction) and return that way to cut the total hike to just over 3½ miles. Regardless, the view from the top of the lake, Pelican Valley, and the Absaroka Mountains is worth the trip.

If you are a park employee, check out the YCERP recreation schedules posted in the dorms and recreation halls. They occasionally offer moonlight hikes to the summit of Elephant Back during the summer. Viewing the lake with the moon reflecting off of it will be a fond memory of the park you will have with you forever. This trail tends to be fairly popular with bears, especially in the first half of the season (and one person was killed by a bear along the power line easement just off this trail in 2015), so be sure to remain alert while hiking in this area.

Fern Lake Trail — MAP 5-1,4-8

Type:	PTP	**Cat:**	BC	**Class:**	C	**Surf:**	Trail	**Dist:**	5	**Status:**	E
Diff:	3	**Traf:**	2	**Child:**	N	**HAcc:**	N	**Use:**	H S	**Length:**	3.65
Elev A:	8872	**Elev B:**	8231	**Elev G:**	398	**Elev L:**	-1039	**Net:**	-641	**BMA:**	- -
Min:	8218	**Max:**	8884	**Avg:**	8496	**Avg +:**	4.9%	**Avg -:**	8.0%	**Open:**	YR

Reference Point	A-B Mi	A-B Km	B-A Mi	B-A Km	Latitude	Longitude
Trailhead @ jct w/ Wapiti Lake Trail	0.00	0.00	3.65	5.87	44.69457	-110.30034
Ponuntpa Springs Thermal Area	2.08	3.35	1.57	2.53	44.67339	-110.29057
Fern Lake (west side)	2.93	4.72	0.72	1.16	44.67538	-110.27583
Fern Lake (east side)	3.32	5.34	0.33	0.53	44.67696	-110.26956
Trailhead @ jct w/ Astringent Creek Trail	3.65	5.87	0.00	0.00	44.68049	-110.26561

Fern Lake is believed to exist in a crater that resulted from a hydrothermal explosion several thousand years ago.[2] The trail to get to it is basically a cutoff trail between the Wapiti Lake Trail (at an unnamed pass) and the Astringent Creek Trail. Hiking to the lake from the northern terminus of the trail is much easier as it is all downhill. The lake is the 13th largest in the park and has a population of cutthroat trout.

You will hike past a small thermal area known as Ponuntpa Springs, composed of a couple of dozen small springs and other insignificant oozes. The word *Ponuntpa* is a Shoshone word meaning "the water has power."[3]

Howard Eaton: Arnica Creek to Natural Bridge — MAP 5-2

Type:	PTP	**Cat:**	BC	**Class:**	N	**Surf:**	Trail	**Dist:**	5	**Status:**	R
Diff:	3	**Traf:**	1	**Child:**	N	**HAcc:**	N	**Use:**	H R	**Length:**	6.76
Elev A:	7775	**Elev B:**	7812	**Elev G:**	1021	**Elev L:**	-984	**Net:**	37	**BMA:**	- -
Min:	7775	**Max:**	8466	**Avg:**	8094	**Avg +:**	5.0%	**Avg -:**	5.1%	**Open:**	YR

Reference Point	A-B Mi	A-B Km	B-A Mi	B-A Km	Latitude	Longitude
Trailhead @ Arnica Creek Turnout (5.8 mi N of WT)	0.00	0.00	6.76	10.88	44.47746	-110.54307
Jct with Beach Lake Trail	0.11	0.18	6.65	10.70	44.47863	-110.54470
Abandoned Bridge Bay Quarry	5.62	9.04	1.14	1.83	44.51973	-110.47287
Abandoned Natural Bridge Pit	6.10	9.82	0.66	1.06	44.52329	-110.46535
North closure gate	6.62	10.65	0.14	0.23	44.52513	-110.45495
Jct w/ Natural Bridge Trail	6.76	10.88	0.00	0.00	44.52607	-110.45238

This is another abandoned section of road that has some historic significance. It was along this road that many of the knotted trees used in the construction of the Old Faithful Inn were harvested back in 1903. There is also an old quarry where much of the rock used in constructing the existing road along the lake shore was taken. From 1905 to 1926, this segment of road was the main road between Fishing Bridge and West Thumb. In 1927, the existing road was opened and this one has been used primarily as a service road (for electrical utility crews, mainly) ever since.

This road is often closed from Arnica Creek to the junction with the Natural Bridge Trail because there is a carcass dump located at the north end of it, and there are often grizzly bear studies being conducted along its path. At other times you can hike in from the south but you will eventually reach the south closure for the carcass dump and be forced to turn around and return to the Arnica Creek end of the trail. Be sure to check in with one of the backcountry offices before making plans to hike this trail. The south end trailhead is also used to access Beach Lake and Dryad Lake.

Howard Eaton: Fishing Bridge to Canyon — MAP 4-8

Type:	PTP	**Cat:**	BC	**Class:**	A	**Surf:**	Trail	**Dist:**	5	**Status:**	E
Diff:	2	**Traf:**	2	**Child:**	N	**HAcc:**	N	**Use:**	H S	**Length:**	13.82
Elev A:	7752	**Elev B:**	7753	**Elev G:**	972	**Elev L:**	-971	**Net:**	1	**BMA:**	- -
Min:	7703	**Max:**	8003	**Avg:**	7816	**Avg +:**	2.4%	**Avg -:**	2.6%	**Open:**	YR

Reference Point	A-B Mi	A-B Km	B-A Mi	B-A Km	Latitude	Longitude
Trailhead 5K2 (East Fishing Bridge Parking Lot)	0.00	0.00	13.82	22.24	44.56579	-110.37943
Follow Fishing Bridge Wastewater Plant Service Road	0.33	0.53	13.49	21.71	44.56671	-110.37344
Old Lift Station across road	0.65	1.05	13.17	21.20	44.56970	-110.36851
Dirt road up to old bunkhouse/storage building	0.70	1.13	13.12	21.11	44.57019	-110.36786
Trail separates from roadway (take left fork)	0.73	1.17	13.09	21.07	44.57043	-110.36749
Grizzly Creek crossing	3.13	5.04	10.69	17.20	44.60105	-110.38013
LeHardy Rapids Overlook	3.70	5.95	10.12	16.29	44.60817	-110.38320
Thistle Creek crossing	3.89	6.26	9.93	15.98	44.60993	-110.38562
Hayden Valley (south end)	6.38	10.27	7.44	11.97	44.63019	-110.42326
Cottongrass Creek crossing	10.67	17.17	3.15	5.07	44.68140	-110.46226
Jct with Sour Creek Trail (Hayden Valley north end)	11.23	18.07	2.59	4.17	44.68917	-110.46512
Sour Creek crossing (10 to 30')	11.32	18.22	2.50	4.02	44.68976	-110.46729
Terminus at Wapiti Lake Trailhead	13.82	22.24	0.00	0.00	44.70777	-110.50013

This trail is a remnant of the old Howard Eaton Trail system that used to traverse much of the park. It is the only trail that takes hikers through Hayden Valley, but in several of the last few years, the northern end of the trail has been closed much (if not all) of the season because of the presence of wolf dens in the area. It would be a good idea to contact the Canyon Backcountry Office for updated status on this trail's north end before you attempt to hike if you are planning to go through, or if you are planning on hiking just the north end into the valley.

Even when the north end is closed, however, it is still a good trail to take for about four miles from its south trailhead due to an excellent overlook of LeHardy Rapids along the Yellowstone River. A couple of miles north of that is Nez Perce Ford (a narrow spot on the river where the Nez Perce Indians crossed on their flight through the park to avoid the U.S. Army) and access to the thermal features on the opposite side of the river from the Mud Volcano area.

When the trail is open all the way through, it is important to note that there is no camping along the entire 14-mile route. So it will be a long day's worth of hiking.

The actual south trailhead for this trail is at the parking area just east of the Fishing Bridge. You can shave a half mile off your hike (if you return to the trailhead you started at) by parking near the entrance to the service road that takes you back to the Fishing Bridge Wastewater Treatment Plant (park near the buildings at the back of the large vacant/softball field behind the Yellowstone General Store).

Mirror Lake Trail — MAP 5-1

TYPE:	O&B	**CAT:**	BC	**CLASS:**	U	**SURF:**	TRAIL	**DIST:**	5	**STATUS:**	U
DIFF:	3	**TRAF:**	1	**CHILD:**	N	**HACC:**	N	**USE:**	H S	**LENGTH:**	5.47
ELEV A:	8298	**ELEV B:**	8957	**ELEV G:**	1965	**ELEV L:**	-405	**NET:**	659	**BMA:**	H
MIN:	8283	**MAX:**	8966	**AVG:**	8551	**AVG +:**	5.3%	**AVG -:**	2.7%	**OPEN:**	5/15

Reference Point	A-B Mi	A-B Km	B-A Mi	B-A Km	Latitude	Longitude
Trailhead at Jct w/ Pelican Creek Trail	0.00	0.00	5.47	8.80	44.69359	-110.24522
Pelican Creek Crossing	0.48	0.77	4.99	8.03	44.69827	-110.23932
West Trail to 5P7 (0.16 mi)	2.18	3.51	3.29	5.29	44.70833	-110.21024
East Trail to 5P7 (0.26 mi)	2.55	4.10	2.92	4.70	44.70728	-110.20291
Cross Unnamed Creek	3.55	5.71	1.92	3.09	44.71728	-110.18564
Mirror Lake	5.47	8.80	0.00	0.00	44.73429	-110.16460

This unmaintained and unpublicized trail is designed to take hikers and stock parties out to backcountry campsite 5P7. On most other maps, including the park's own materials, there is no trail shown as a viable route to the campsite, but there is a decently worn path (courtesy of the park's bison population) to it from the Pelican Creek Trail.

The trail continues eastward past the campsite to Mirror Lake. The NPS does not maintain this trail, so hiking or traveling to it via horseback may require some bushwhacking.

The 5P7 campsite is one of the handful of "remote" sites where camping is allowed a small number of days each season. Using this area requires adhering to Leave No Trace principles.

The (fishless) lake gets its name from its calm and reflective surface. The plateau upon which it sits is named after the lake.

Natural Bridge Trail — MAP 5-2

Type:	O&B	**Cat:**	BC	**Class:**	B	**Surf:**	Paved	**Dist:**	5	**Status:**	E
Diff:	1	**Traf:**	4	**Child:**	Y	**HAcc:**	Y	**Use:**	HSBKR	**Length:**	1.00
Elev A:	7773	**Elev B:**	7826	**Elev G:**	232	**Elev L:**	-179	**Net:**	53	**BMA:**	- -
Min:	7773	**Max:**	7837	**Avg:**	7806	**Avg +:**	0.0%	**Avg -:**	0.0%	**Open:**	YR

Reference Point	A-B Mi	A-B Km	B-A Mi	B-A Km	Latitude	Longitude
Trailhead @ pullout (3.7 mi S of Fishing Bridge Jct)	0.00	0.00	1.00	1.61	44.53058	-110.43629
Jct with Bridge Bay Cutoff Trail	0.49	0.79	0.51	0.82	44.52786	-110.44549
Powerline crossing	0.66	1.06	0.34	0.55	44.52717	-110.44845
Jct w/ Howard Eaton Trail - Arnica Creek to Nat Brdg	0.88	1.42	0.12	0.19	44.52607	-110.45238
Natural Bridge/Bridge Creek/Cascade	1.00	1.61	0.00	0.00	44.52579	-110.45499

This trail is an easy, flat, mostly paved trail (and service road) that takes you back to one of the more unique natural features in the park. It is a natural rhyolite bridge over a creek (Bridge Creek, named for the bridge it created) that has carved out a tunnel underneath it. The cascade down the creek is known, oddly enough, as Natural Bridge Cascade.

The bridge was discovered by Ferdinand V. Hayden on one of his expeditions through the park in 1871. And though there was apparently some discussion about horses and carriages using the bridge to bypass some of the obstacles otherwise present in the area, there is no actual documentation that any such traffic actually crossed the bridge.

Today, the bridge is closed to all traffic of any kind (including foot traffic) because of its instability. This is an excellent trip for smaller children, and since it is a paved service road, it will accommodate wheelchairs as well. You can also ride a bike along this path. This trail is also the north end of the Arnica Creek to Natural Bridge section of the Howard Eaton Trail. However, that trail (an old segment of road) is usually closed during much of the summer due to the presence of a carcass dump located along its north end. So travel from the swing gate just west of Natural Bridge is not permitted during that time. Check with the Backcountry Office at Bridge Bay or Grant Village for specifics when you arrive.

Old Lake Road Trail — MAP 5-2

Type:	PTP	**Cat:**	FC	**Class:**	C	**Surf:**	Trail	**Dist:**	5	**Status:**	E
Diff:	1	**Traf:**	2	**Child:**	Y	**HAcc:**	Y	**Use:**	HBKR	**Length:**	0.69
Elev A:	7768	**Elev B:**	7754	**Elev G:**	134	**Elev L:**	-148	**Net:**	-14	**BMA:**	- -
Min:	7742	**Max:**	7818	**Avg:**	7771	**Avg +:**	3.4%	**Avg -:**	3.7%	**Open:**	7/4

Reference Point	A-B Mi	A-B Km	B-A Mi	B-A Km	Latitude	Longitude
Trailhead Lake View pullout (2.3 mi S of Fish Brg Jct)	0.00	0.00	0.69	1.11	44.54556	-110.41779
Trailhead @ gate at old Fisheries Building	0.69	1.11	0.00	0.00	44.54944	-110.40527

Also known as the Hatchery Creek-Bridge Bay Trail, this is a short segment of old roadbed that has been converted into a trail. Until the early 1970s, the original road through this area passed right in front of the Lake Hotel before the bypass that currently exists was constructed. This short piece of trail is a segment of that original road.

Though this trail is not technically located in a bear management area, the area is closed each season until July 4 because of heavy bear activity in the area. The trail is suitable for hiking and for use by bicyclists.

Old Turbid Lake Trail - West — MAP 5-3

Type:	PTP	Cat:	BC	Class:	N	Surf:	Trail	Dist:	5	Status:	A
Diff:	3	Traf:	1	Child:	N	HAcc:	N	Use:	CLOSD	Length:	2.10
Elev A:	7817	Elev B:	7913	Elev G:	446	Elev L:	-350	Net:	96	BMA:	I
Min:	7817	Max:	8017	Avg:	7923	Avg +:	7.1%	Avg -:	6.6%	Open:	YR

Reference Point	A-B Mi	A-B Km	B-A Mi	B-A Km	Latitude	Longitude
Pelican Valley Trailhead 5K3	0.00	0.00	2.10	3.38	44.55899	-110.30778
Jct w/ existing Turbid Lake Trail	2.10	3.38	0.00	0.00	44.55384	-110.26942

This is another path that used to be both an old road (the original East Entrance Road that was constructed in 1903) and an old trail. After the road was realigned in the 1930s to put it along the lake shore, this segment was used as a trail to provide access to Turbid Lake. During the rethinking and reconfiguration of access to and hiker use of Pelican Valley during the mid-1980s, however, it was decided that this trail and the area around it would be rehabilitated and closed off to public access for most of the year. It is one of the few old road segments in the park to actually have been rehabilitated back to its natural state.

It is difficult to find any time when this area is actually open. And, when it is, all of the trail markings and old roadbed has been removed and the area rehabbed. As a result, it is almost impossible to find your way through here; it would require considerable bushwhacking in some places these days.

Pelican Cone Trail — MAP 5-1

Type:	O&B	Cat:	BC	Class:	C	Surf:	Trail	Dist:	5	Status:	E
Diff:	3	Traf:	1	Child:	N	HAcc:	N	Use:	H S	Length:	3.87
Elev A:	7920	Elev B:	9652	Elev G:	1836	Elev L:	-103	Net:	1732	BMA:	H/I
Min:	7920	Max:	9652	Avg:	8670	Avg +:	9.9%	Avg -:	3.8%	Open:	7/4

Reference Point	A-B Mi	A-B Km	B-A Mi	B-A Km	Latitude	Longitude
Trailhead at jct w/ Raven Creek Cutoff Trail	0.00	0.00	3.87	6.23	44.61232	-110.21685
Summit/Lookout	3.87	6.23	0.00	0.00	44.64819	-110.19331

This trail to the top of Pelican Cone, a small peak at the north end of Pelican Valley, is lightly used these days. Since this area is only accessible for day use, you would need to depart from the Pelican Valley trailhead (the shortest route), make it to the summit (where there is an old fire lookout used primarily for monitoring bear activity in the valley), and back to the trailhead in a single day. That would be an almost 22-mile round trip, difficult even for all but the most athletically-inclined to pull off.

Pelican Creek Nature Trail — MAP 5-2,5-3

Type:	Loop	Cat:	FC	Class:	B	Surf:	Trail	Dist:	5	Status:	E
Diff:	1	Traf:	4	Child:	Y	HAcc:	N	Use:	H S	Length:	0.69
Elev A:	7761	Elev B:	7761	Elev G:	86	Elev L:	-86	Net:	0	BMA:	- -
Min:	7748	Max:	7779	Avg:	7755	Avg +:	0.0%	Avg -:	0.0%	Open:	YR

Reference Point	A-B Mi	A-B Km	B-A Mi	B-A Km	Latitude	Longitude
Trailhead PEL (1.5 mi E of Fishing Bridge Junction)	0.00	0.00	0.55	0.89	44.55998	-110.36075
Loop Junction	0.14	0.23	0.41	0.66	44.55872	-110.36280
Loop Junction	0.55	0.89	0.00	0.00	44.55872	-110.36280

This is a short hike out to the mouth of Pelican Creek where it empties into Yellowstone Lake. It is an excellent place to see a variety of waterfowl, including, of course, pelicans. The short nature of the trail makes it suitable for smaller children, but it will not accommodate wheelchairs. Rangers occasionally offer guided educational hikes along this trail during the summer (though that is certainly not necessary to enjoy the hike). Check with the park newspaper or the Fishing Bridge Museum desk for details.

Pelican Creek Trail

MAP 5-1,4-8

Type:	PTP	**Cat:**	BC	**Class:**	B	**Surf:**	Trail	**Dist:**	5	**Status:**	E
Diff:	3	**Traf:**	2	**Child:**	N	**HAcc:**	N	**Use:**	H S	**Length:**	12.20
Elev A:	7849	**Elev B:**	8534	**Elev G:**	1585	**Elev L:**	-900	**Net:**	685	**BMA:**	H/I
Min:	7845	**Max:**	8648	**Avg:**	8171	**Avg +:**	3.9%	**Avg -:**	3.3%	**Open:**	7/4

Reference Point	A-B Mi	A-B Km	B-A Mi	B-A Km	Latitude	Longitude
Trailhead @ jct w/ Pelican Valley Trail	0.00	0.00	12.20	19.63	44.57402	-110.25818
Astringent Creek crossing	1.53	2.46	10.67	17.17	44.59277	-110.24696
Jct with Astringent Creek Trail	1.60	2.57	10.60	17.06	44.59320	-110.24596
Unnamed thermal area	2.54	4.09	9.66	15.55	44.60258	-110.23274
Pelican Creek crossing (15 to 35')	3.27	5.26	8.93	14.37	44.61059	-110.22391
Jct with Raven Creek Cutoff Trail	3.35	5.39	8.85	14.24	44.61137	-110.22283
Enter the Mushpots Thermal Area (N/B)	5.10	8.21	7.10	11.43	44.63351	-110.22736
Leave the Mushpots Thermal Area (N/B)	5.47	8.80	6.73	10.83	44.63889	-110.22878
Expansive unnamed thermal area to ENE	5.70	9.17	6.50	10.46	44.64195	-110.22796
Pelican Creek crossing (25+')	5.87	9.45	6.33	10.19	44.64286	-110.23041
Pelican Creek crossing (20 to 25')	6.20	9.98	6.00	9.66	44.64732	-110.22956
Enter the Central Pelican Creek Thermal Area	6.72	10.81	5.48	8.82	44.65473	-110.22987
Leave the Central Pelican Creek Thermal Area	7.40	11.91	4.80	7.72	44.66389	-110.23235
Pelican Creek Mud Volcano area to the west	7.80	12.55	4.40	7.08	44.66881	-110.23596
Pelican Creek Mud Volcano area to the NE	8.08	13.00	4.12	6.63	44.67156	-110.23855
Jct w/ Upper Pelican Creek Cutoff Trail	9.10	14.64	3.10	4.99	44.68378	-110.24709
Jct w/ Mirror Lake Trail (U)	9.81	15.79	2.39	3.85	44.69359	-110.24522
Pelican Creek crossing	10.09	16.24	2.11	3.40	44.69751	-110.24581
Terminus @ jct w/ Wapiti Lake Trail	12.20	19.63	0.00	0.00	44.72588	-110.24617

The Pelican Creek Trail departs from the Pelican Valley Trail approximately three miles from the trailhead and takes hikers northward up along Pelican Creek itself, much of it along an old fire service road (whereas the Pelican Valley Trail continues northeast). It also facilitates access to the Astringent Creek/Broad Creek area from the south.

While the Pelican Valley itself is pretty, most hikers use this trail to access the variety of thermal areas located along the creek. Since you cannot camp in this part of the park during the summer (the lower third of this trail is in a bear management area), many users hike in and hike out the same day, making for very long days. An alternative is to hike up to the Broad Creek campsites (5B1 and 5B2) and use those for launching day-long explorations of the thermal areas, and then hiking out.

During the early part of the season (i.e., the few weeks after the trail opens at the south end on July 4), many of the signs in this area will still be down. Be sure you follow the trail markings and do not get sidetracked on the bison trails in the area. And this area is one of the most bear-dense areas of the park during the summer, so keep your eyes peeled. This is one trail where you definitely want to heed the guidance to have a party of three or more.

You pass through three thermal areas on this hike. The Mushpots (east side of the creek) and Mudkettles (west side of the creek) area is a large zone consisting of just under 200 unnamed mud pots and springs, hot pools, frying pans, and oozes. To the north, the Central Pelican Valley Creek Thermal Area is a small area consisting of about four dozen unnamed minor thermal features. And on the north end of the trail is the Pelican Valley Mud Volcano area. It contains around 80 unnamed thermal features, some of which resemble the features found at the Mud Volcano area on the road between Canyon and Fishing Bridge. Be sure to remain on the trail as you pass through these areas.

Pelican Valley Trail — MAP 5-1

Type:	PTP	**Cat:**	BC	**Class:**	A	**Surf:**	Trail	**Dist:**	5	**Status:**	E
Diff:	2	**Traf:**	3	**Child:**	N	**HAcc:**	N	**Use:**	H S	**Length:**	7.13
Elev A:	7817	**Elev B:**	7938	**Elev G:**	839	**Elev L:**	-717	**Net:**	121	**BMA:**	I
Min:	7817	**Max:**	7969	**Avg:**	7888	**Avg +:**	3.7%	**Avg -:**	3.6%	**Open:**	7/4

Reference Point	A-B Mi	A-B Km	B-A Mi	B-A Km	Latitude	Longitude
Trailhead 5K3 (3.3 mi E of Fishing Bridge Junction)[4]	0.00	0.00	7.13	11.47	44.55899	-110.30778
Jct with Turbid Lake Trail	2.26	3.64	4.87	7.84	44.56735	-110.27335
Jct with Pelican Creek Trail	3.23	5.20	3.90	6.28	44.57402	-110.25818
Sage Creek crossing	5.10	8.21	2.03	3.27	44.58484	-110.23067
Jct with Mist Creek Trail	7.10	11.43	0.03	0.05	44.59624	-110.19476
Jct with Raven Creek Cutoff & Mist Creek Pass Trails	7.13	11.47	0.00	0.00	44.59658	-110.19326

This trail is the primary route into the Pelican Valley, one of the most wildlife-rich areas in the park. As an official trail, it dates to 1880, but it was a path for wildlife (and hunters and poachers) long before that. This includes, of course, grizzly bears. As a result of the fact that this area is one of their prime habitats, the trails do not open to the public until July 4, and then are only for day use from 9 a.m. to 7 p.m. So any travel into the southern half of the valley must be completed by the evening. This can be an out-and-back trip, or it can be a trip where you travel up into the Mist Creek Pass, Astringent Creek or Pelican Creek areas.

This area is wide open space, with little to any forest cover. As a result, be sure you use sufficient sunscreen to prevent being sunburned. The trail stays on the east side of Pelican Creek, but it does cross through several areas that are marshy early in the season (until late July) and you will have to cross a couple of small creeks. Many people who are not staying in the northern campsites elect to cross to the west on the Raven Creek Cutoff and come back south on the Pelican Creek Trail to get back to the trailhead (a total of about 14 miles, which makes for a great full-day hike).

Early in the season, many of the trail signs will have been knocked down by animals or the winter snows. Combined with the substantial number of bison trails you will find it can be easy to become misdirected. Pay close attention to where you are going. The trailhead for this trail is due to be relocated in 2019, so the GPS coordinates on the A end may change.

Raven Creek Cutoff Trail — MAP 5-1

Type:	PTP	**Cat:**	BC	**Class:**	B	**Surf:**	Trail	**Dist:**	5	**Status:**	E
Diff:	2	**Traf:**	1	**Child:**	N	**HAcc:**	N	**Use:**	H S	**Length:**	2.10
Elev A:	7905	**Elev B:**	7939	**Elev G:**	247	**Elev L:**	-213	**Net:**	34	**BMA:**	I
Min:	7880	**Max:**	7973	**Avg:**	7911	**Avg +:**	4.5%	**Avg -:**	3.5%	**Open:**	7/4

Reference Point	A-B Mi	A-B Km	B-A Mi	B-A Km	Latitude	Longitude
Trailhead @ jct w/ Pelican Creek Trail	0.00	0.00	2.10	3.38	44.61137	-110.22283
Trail to Pelican Cone Lookout	0.35	0.56	1.75	2.82	44.61232	-110.21685
Raven Creek crossing (25 to 30')	1.10	1.77	1.00	1.61	44.60337	-110.20928
Cross runoff channel from extinct thermal area	1.69	2.72	0.41	0.66	44.59817	-110.20005
Cross runoff channel from extinct thermal area	1.74	2.80	0.36	0.58	44.59792	-110.19907
Trailhead @ jct w/ Pelican Valley Trail	2.10	3.38	0.00	0.00	44.59658	-110.19326

This trail serves as a crossover between the Pelican Valley Trail and the Pelican Creek Trail and facilitates access to the Pelican Cone Trail that takes you up to the old fire observation cabin. You will cross through an extinct thermal area (the Pelican Creek Thermal Area) and have to ford Raven Creek. When you get to the creek, be sure to check water depth where you are crossing. It is one of those streams where it can be one foot deep in one place and chest deep in another (especially early in the season).

Storm Point Trail

MAP 5-3,5-2

Type:	Loop	Cat:	FC	Class:	B	Surf:	Trail	Dist:	5	Status:	E
Diff:	1	Traf:	4	Child:	Y	HAcc:	N	Use:	H	Length:	2.41
Elev A:	7780	Elev B:	7780	Elev G:	346	Elev L:	-346	Net:	0	BMA:	- -
Min:	7736	Max:	7889	Avg:	7770	Avg +:	0.0%	Avg -:	0.0%	Open:	YR

Reference Point	A-B Mi	A-B Km	B-A Mi	B-A Km	Latitude	Longitude
Trailhead STM (West; 3.2 mi E of Fishing Bridge Jct)	0.00	0.00	2.10	3.38	44.55940	-110.32772
Jct with trail from East trailhead	0.06	0.10	2.04	3.28	44.55867	-110.32723
Loop junction	0.21	0.34	1.89	3.04	44.55675	-110.32831
Footbridge over unnamed creek	0.43	0.69	1.67	2.69	44.55436	-110.33021
Storm Point	0.98	1.58	1.12	1.80	44.54814	-110.33327
Dormant thermal area	1.15	1.85	0.95	1.53	44.54878	-110.33667
Loop junction	2.10	3.38	0.00	0.00	44.55675	-110.32831

This is a short little hike out to a scenic point on the lake adjacent to Mary Bay, and is popular for those looking for wildflowers and wildlife. Rangers often conduct short guided hikes on this trail. See the park newspaper or visit the Fishing Bridge Museum desk for more details. The north end of the trail also provides an excellent overlook of Indian Pond.

The east side of the loop follows the shore of Concretion Cove, the small bay on the west shore of Mary Bay, itself an old hydrothermal explosion crater. Concretions are rocks formed by the accumulation of sediment and other materials, and they were present in large numbers in the park's early days. Thus, the name.

The point is named characteristically, and it is an excellent location from which to watch the late afternoon storms move in over the lake in the latter part of the summer. Note that there is an east and a west trailhead for this trail. The easternmost one is technically a pullout for an overlook of Indian Pond, but there is a social trail leading from it that will take you to the main trail. The distance is the same regardless of which you use.

Thorofare Trail

MAP 6-1,6-2,6-3

Type:	PTP	Cat:	BC	Class:	A	Surf:	Trail	Dist:	5	Status:	E
Diff:	4	Traf:	2	Child:	N	HAcc:	N	Use:	H S	Length:	33.37
Elev A:	7846	Elev B:	8233	Elev G:	3496	Elev L:	-3109	Net:	387	BMA:	J1/J2
Min:	7778	Max:	8889	Avg:	8035	Avg +:	3.3%	Avg -:	4.1%	Open:	YR

Reference Point	A-B Mi	A-B Km	B-A Mi	B-A Km	Latitude	Longitude
Nine Mile Trailhead 5K5 (8.8 mi E of Fishing Bridge)	0.00	0.00	33.37	53.70	44.50562	-110.27556
Cub Creek crossing	1.23	1.98	32.14	51.72	44.48935	-110.27706
Clear Creek crossing (25 to 30')	2.40	3.86	30.97	49.84	44.47400	-110.27970
Spur trl campsite 5E9 (.15 mi)/N spur to 5E7 (0.05mi)	5.94	9.56	27.43	44.14	44.42867	-110.29073
Spur trail to campsite 5E8 (0.15 miles)	6.16	9.91	27.21	43.79	44.42582	-110.28914
S spur to campsite 5E7 (.26 mi)/Meadow Crk crsg	6.32	10.17	27.05	43.53	44.42633	-110.28629
Spur trail to campsite 5E6 (0.05 miles)	8.66	13.94	24.71	39.77	44.40593	-110.25490
Spur trail to old (NLE) campsite 5E5	8.74	14.07	24.63	39.64	44.40495	-110.25403
Columbine Creek crossing (20+')	9.07	14.60	24.30	39.11	44.40105	-110.25195
Brimstone Basin/Alluvium Creek crossing (5+')	10.58	17.03	22.79	36.68	44.38765	-110.23395
Spur trail to campsite 5E4 (0.10 miles)	11.59	18.65	21.78	35.05	44.37510	-110.22663
Spur trail to campsite 5E3 (0.11 miles)	13.32	21.44	20.05	32.27	44.35196	-110.22449
Spur trail to campsite 5E2 (.12 mi)/Langford Cairn E	14.79	23.80	18.58	29.90	44.33368	-110.21966
Monument Cairn	15.70	25.27	17.67	28.44	44.32849	-110.20193
Jct with abandoned section of trail (north)	16.25	26.15	17.12	27.55	44.32865	-110.19274
Spur trail to campsite 5E1 (0.02 miles)	16.96	27.29	16.41	26.41	44.32518	-110.18082
Beaverdam Creek crossing (50 to 75')	17.02	27.39	16.35	26.31	44.32427	-110.18041
Jct with abandoned section of trail (south)	17.30	27.84	16.07	25.86	44.32081	-110.18266
Spur trail to campsite 6B4 (0.33 miles)	17.42	28.03	15.95	25.67	44.31990	-110.18104
Cabin Creek Cabin Trail (north)	19.28	31.03	14.09	22.68	44.30206	-110.15574
Cabin Creek Cabin Trail (south)	19.46	31.32	13.91	22.39	44.29979	-110.15453
Jct w/ Lower Ford Trail & campsite 6B1	19.55	31.46	13.82	22.24	44.29896	-110.15348
Cabin Creek crossing	19.71	31.72	13.66	21.98	44.29702	-110.15213
Abandoned Lower Ford Trail	19.79	31.85	13.58	21.85	44.29604	-110.15145
Jct w/ Upper Ford Trail (& campsite 6B2)	20.62	33.18	12.75	20.52	44.28552	-110.14506
Spur trail to campsite 6C1 (0.04 miles)	22.05	35.49	11.32	18.22	44.26996	-110.12794
Trappers Creek crossing (130 to 250')	22.68	36.50	10.69	17.20	44.26533	-110.11882
Spur trail to campsite 6C3 (0.13 miles)	23.17	37.29	10.20	16.42	44.25869	-110.11728
Spur trail to campsite 6C2 (1.10 miles)	23.26	37.43	10.11	16.27	44.25716	-110.11684
Jct w/ Mountain Creek Trail (north)	24.88	40.04	8.49	13.66	44.23920	-110.10149
Mountain Creek crossing (70 to 100')	25.59	41.18	7.78	12.52	44.23077	-110.10690
Campsite 6D2/Spur trail to campsite 6D3 (0.30 miles)	25.63	41.25	7.74	12.46	44.23039	-110.10717
Jct w/ Mountain Creek Trail (south)	25.84	41.59	7.53	12.12	44.22757	-110.10675
Spur trail to campsite 6D1 (1.15 miles)	26.17	42.12	7.20	11.59	44.22326	-110.10969
Spur trail to campsite 6Y7 (0.03 miles)	26.98	43.42	6.39	10.28	44.21183	-110.10981
Spur trail to campsite 6Y6 (0.27 miles)	28.87	46.46	4.50	7.24	44.18626	-110.10539
Abandoned segment of trail (north end)	29.78	47.93	3.59	5.78	44.17435	-110.10153
Cliff Creek crossing	30.08	48.41	3.29	5.29	44.17139	-110.09617
Abandoned segment of trail (south end)	30.55	49.17	2.82	4.54	44.16578	-110.09706
Spur trail to campsite 6Y5 (0.31 miles)	30.56	49.18	2.81	4.52	44.16570	-110.09704
Escarpment Creek crossing	31.43	50.58	1.94	3.12	44.15443	-110.09177
Yellowstone Meadows Cutoff Trail (& to 6Y4)	31.72	51.05	1.65	2.66	44.15047	-110.08986
Jct w/ Thorofare Cabin Trail	32.25	51.90	1.12	1.80	44.14527	-110.08370
Jct w/ Thorofare-South Boundary Cutoff Trail	32.34	52.05	1.03	1.66	44.14421	-110.08308
Jct w/ Hawk's Lake Trail	32.76	52.72	0.61	0.98	44.13876	-110.08005
Park boundary TH 6K2 (continues into BTNF)	33.37	53.70	0.00	0.00	44.13264	-110.07231

The Thorofare Trail is perhaps the most storied existing trail in the park. It is famous for taking hikers out into the Thorofare in the southeast corner of the park, one of the most remote places in the lower 48 states. The Thorofare gets its name from the fact that the area was a traveling route for so many hunters, trappers, explorers, and migrating animals in the days before the park existed.

The trip along this trail is one of the most scenic and uniquely Yellowstone experiences the park has to offer. And while you can hike a few miles south to one of the lakeside campsites, the vast majority of people use this trail to get into the lower end of the park on multi-day camping trips that take them deep into the upper reaches of the Yellowstone River.

The trail starts at Nine-Mile Trailhead, which is named for the fact it is about nine miles from Fishing Bridge. The trail hugs the lake shoreline for most of the first 17 miles until just before you cross Beaverdam Creek, and then travels along the north side of Yellowstone River and Cabin Creek where you reach the Lower Ford Trail. This will take you the short way to Trail Creek Trail (which will take you westward toward the two arms of Yellowstone Lake and on to Heart Lake), but it can be a very difficult cross of the Yellowstone River most of the season. As a result, it is sometimes better to hike another mile up river to the Upper Ford Trail and cross there.

The Thorofare Trail itself continues southward from this point. You will cross Mountain Creek and be rewarded with an incredible view of The Trident, named for its three-pronged shape. You will eventually reach the Thorofare Ranger Station, one of the most remote structures in the country, and a couple of different paths to get to the park's south boundary trail system. If you continue southward, you will reach the park boundary and continue on into Bridger-Teton National Forest.

Many who elect to do week-long or other multi-day hikes into Yellowstone like to travel from Nine-Mile trailhead to the Thorofare, and then westward on the south boundary trails back to the Snake River Ranger Station. You can elect to cut a day's worth of hiking off your trip if you use Xanterra's shuttle service to drop you off at Columbine Creek (for about $200!). Note that much of this trail is in bear management areas with late opening dates.

This trip is long but not really arduous. It does involve several crossings and fords of streams, many of which can be quite high and fast early in the season (see the Reference Point list for stream widths). You will also be hiking through some very marshy areas early on. That is why my preferred hiking season for this trail is late August or early September.

Turbid Lake Trail — MAP 5-3

TYPE:	PTP	**CAT:**	BC	**CLASS:**	B	**SURF:**	TRAIL	**DIST:**	5	**STATUS:**	E
DIFF:	3	**TRAF:**	1	**CHILD:**	N	**HACC:**	N	**USE:**	H S	**LENGTH:**	6.63
ELEV A:	7846	**ELEV B:**	7864	**ELEV G:**	951	**ELEV L:**	-933	**NET:**	18	**BMA:**	I
MIN:	7843	**MAX:**	8278	**AVG:**	8005	**AVG +:**	5.2%	**AVG -:**	4.2%	**OPEN:**	7/4

Reference Point	A-B Mi	A-B Km	B-A Mi	B-A Km	Latitude	Longitude
Nine Mile Trailhead 5K5 (8.8 mi E of Fishing Bridge)	0.00	0.00	6.63	10.67	44.50617	-110.27552
Old barn debris	0.15	0.24	6.48	10.43	44.50793	-110.27707
Cross Lake Butte Road	0.95	1.53	5.68	9.14	44.50524	-110.26435
Trail diversion	1.80	2.90	4.83	7.77	44.51119	-110.25114
Pick up the abandoned roadbed	2.21	3.56	4.42	7.11	44.51455	-110.25459
Jct w/ abandoned Jones Pass Trail	3.40	5.47	3.23	5.20	44.53001	-110.24975
Turbid Springs/Bear Creek	4.62	7.44	2.01	3.23	44.54300	-110.25879
Turbid Lake	4.99	8.03	1.64	2.64	44.54529	-110.26453
Sedge Creek crossing (20 to 30')	5.20	8.37	1.43	2.30	44.54786	-110.26652
Old west approach trail (abandoned)	5.65	9.09	0.98	1.58	44.55384	-110.26942
Terminus @ jct w/ Pelican Valley Trail	6.63	10.67	0.00	0.00	44.56735	-110.27335

Turbid Lake is one of the more interesting lakes in the park, named because of its murky waters resulting from the acidic hot springs that feed and drain into it. In the park's early days, the East Entrance Road ran right along the southern end of the lake, but the road was reshaped to its present alignment along Yellowstone Lake in the 1930s.

For years, there was a direct access route to the lake from the west (along the original roadbed, in fact), but bear management concerns led to the removal of that trail some years ago. The current approach from the north side is often tough to find, especially early in the season when the signs are down and the trails haven't been worn in. Therefore it is usually best to approach from the other trailhead.

From the south side, you can start at Nine-Mile Trailhead or park your car along the road to Lake Butte and shave about a mile off your trip. From here you climb up Lake Butte and then follow the old roadbed northward to the lake. The hike to the lake itself is pretty straightforward. Once you get on the north side, however, you will need to pay close attention to the trail markers as you cross the meadows to get to the tree line. From there follow the tree line all the way to the trail's connection with the Pelican Valley Trail, and then head south to the Pelican Valley trailhead (assuming you are not returning to Nine-Mile trailhead).

Upper Pelican Creek Cutoff Trail — MAP 5-1,4-8

Type:	PTP	**Cat:**	BC	**Class:**	B	**Surf:**	Trail	**Dist:**	5	**Status:**	E
Diff:	1	**Traf:**	1	**Child:**	N	**HAcc:**	N	**Use:**	H S	**Length:**	1.10
Elev A:	8227	**Elev B:**	8222	**Elev G:**	176	**Elev L:**	-181	**Net:**	-5	**BMA:**	- -
Min:	8207	**Max:**	8271	**Avg:**	8242	**Avg +:**	5.9%	**Avg -:**	6.0%	**Open:**	YR

Reference Point	A-B Mi	A-B Km	B-A Mi	B-A Km	Latitude	Longitude
Trailhead @ jct w/ Astringent Creek Trail	0.00	0.00	1.10	1.77	44.67865	-110.26324
Jct with Fern Lake Cabin Trail	1.00	1.61	0.10	0.16	44.68309	-110.24829
Pelican Creek crossing	1.06	1.71	0.04	0.06	44.68315	-110.24795
Trailhead @ jct w/ Pelican Creek Trail	1.10	1.77	0.00	0.00	44.68378	-110.24709

This trail serves primarily to connect the upper ends of the Pelican Creek and Astringent Creek Trails, facilitating movement between the two and allowing for the creation of a loop up one side and down the other from the Pelican Valley trailhead. It can also be used to provide a shortcut from the Canyon area into the Pelican Creek area if you've come in via the Fern Lake Trail without having to head all the way north to the Wapiti Lake Trail and heading east. The trail itself is otherwise unremarkable.

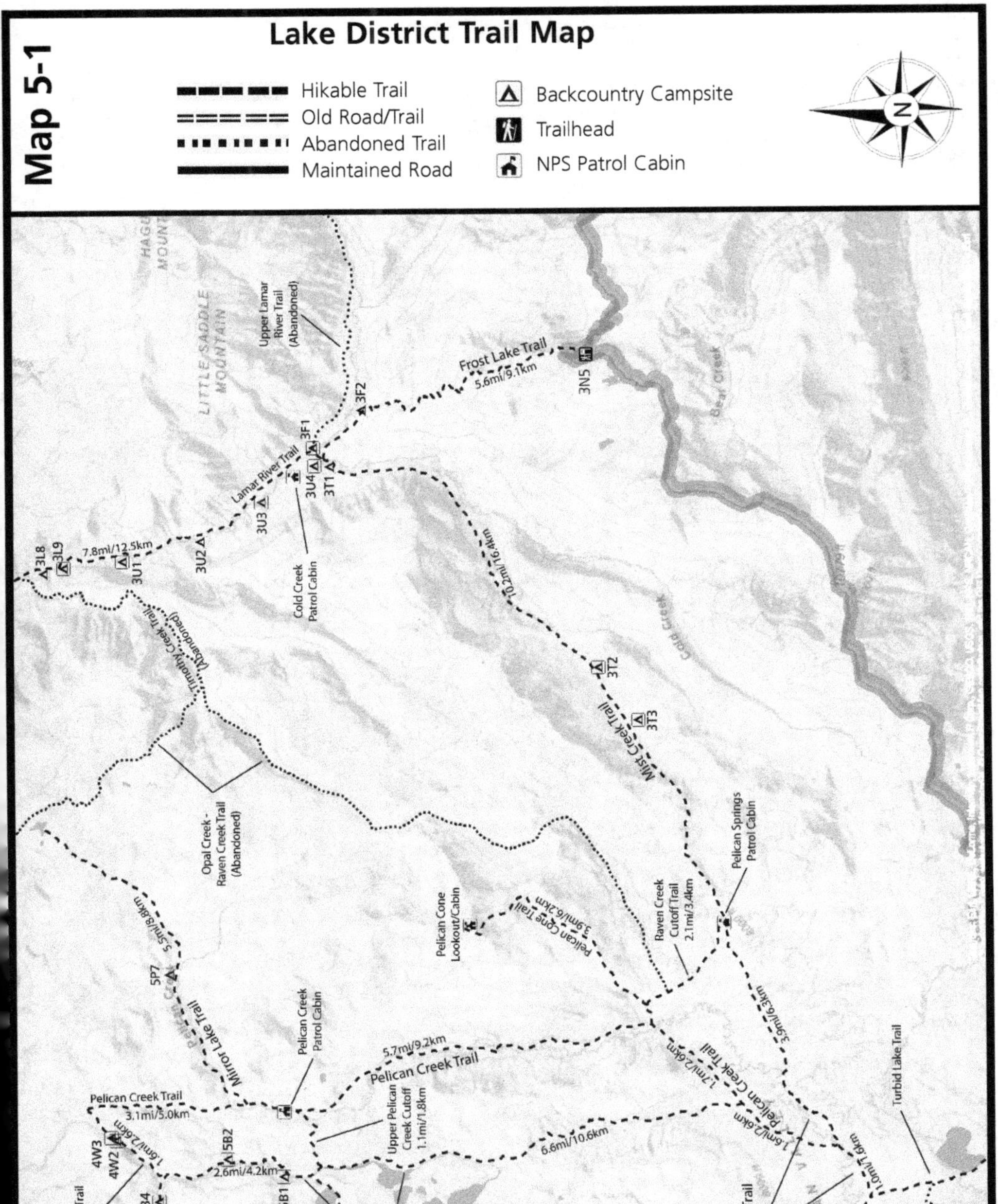

Map 5-1

Lake District Trail Map

Hikable Trail
Old Road/Trail
Abandoned Trail
Maintained Road

Backcountry Campsite
Trailhead
NPS Patrol Cabin

Upper Lamar River Trail (Abandoned)
LITTLE SADDLE MOUNTAIN
Frost Lake Trail
5.6mi/9.1km
3N5
3F2
3F1
3U4
3T1
Lamar River Trail
3U3
Cold Creek Patrol Cabin
3U2
7.8mi/12.5km
3L8
3L9
3U1
Timothy Creek Trail (Abandoned)
10.2mi/16.4km
3T2
3T3
Mist Creek Trail
Opal Creek - Raven Creek Trail (Abandoned)
Pelican Springs Patrol Cabin
Raven Creek Cutoff Trail
2.1mi/3.4km
Pelican Cone Lookout/Cabin
Pelican Cone Trail
3.9mi/6.2km
5.5mi/8.8km
5P7
Mirror Lake Trail
Pelican Creek Patrol Cabin
5.7mi/9.2km
Pelican Creek Trail
1.7mi/2.6km
3.9mi/6.3km
Pelican Creek Trail
3.1mi/5.0km
Upper Pelican Creek Cutoff
1.1mi/1.8km
6.6mi/10.6km
1.6mi/2.6km
1.0mi/1.6km
Turbid Lake Trail
4W3
4W2
1.6mi/2.6km
5B2
2.6mi/4.2km
5B1
4B4
4B3
2.5mi/4.0km
Wapiti Lake Trail
3.6mi/5.9km
Fern Lake Trail
9232 ft
4B2
Astringent Creek Trail
Pelican Valley Trail
2.3mi/3.6km
Turbid Lake West (Abandoned)
5K3
East Entrance Rd
STONETOP MOUNTAIN
SULPHUR HILLS
4B1
9.4mi/15.1km
Sour Creek
Bear Creek
Cold Creek

Map 5-2

Lake District Trail Map

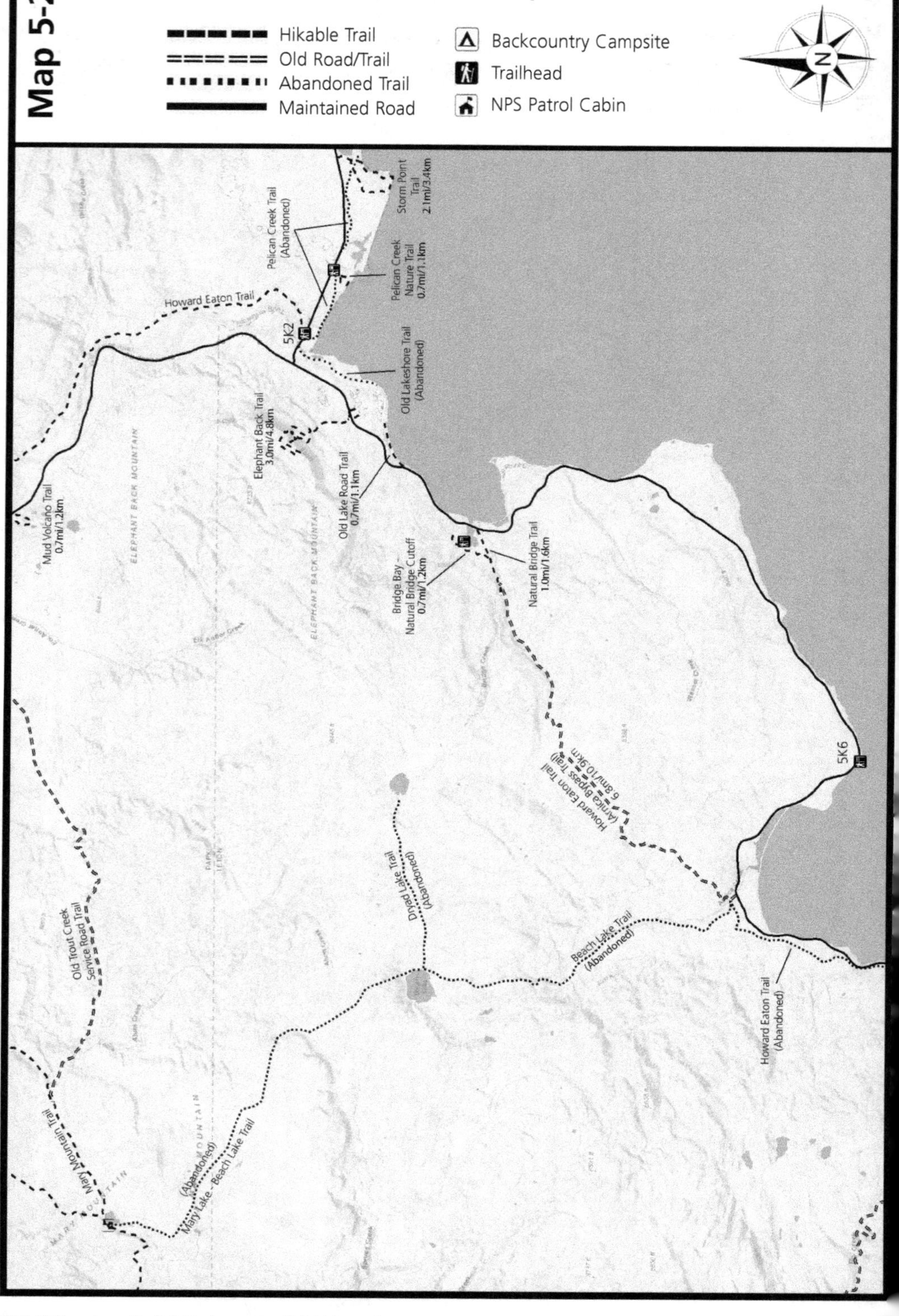

Hikable Trail
Old Road/Trail
Abandoned Trail
Maintained Road

Backcountry Campsite
Trailhead

NPS Patrol Cabin

Storm Point Trail 2.1mi/3.4km
Pelican Creek Trail (Abandoned)
Pelican Creek Nature Trail 0.7mi/1.1km
Howard Eaton Trail
5K2
Old Lakeshore Trail (Abandoned)
Elephant Back Trail 3.0mi/4.8km
Old Lake Road Trail 0.7mi/1.1km
Mud Volcano Trail 0.7mi/1.2km
ELEPHANT BACK MOUNTAIN
Bridge Bay – Natural Bridge Cutoff 0.7mi/1.2km
Natural Bridge Trail 1.0mi/1.6km
Howard Eaton Trail (Arnica Bypass Trail) 6.8mi/10.9km
5K6
Dryad Lake Trail (Abandoned)
Beach Lake Trail (Abandoned)
Howard Eaton Trail (Abandoned)
Old Trout Creek Service Road Trail
Mary Mountain Trail
Mary Lake - Beach Lake Trail (Abandoned)
MARY MOUNTAIN

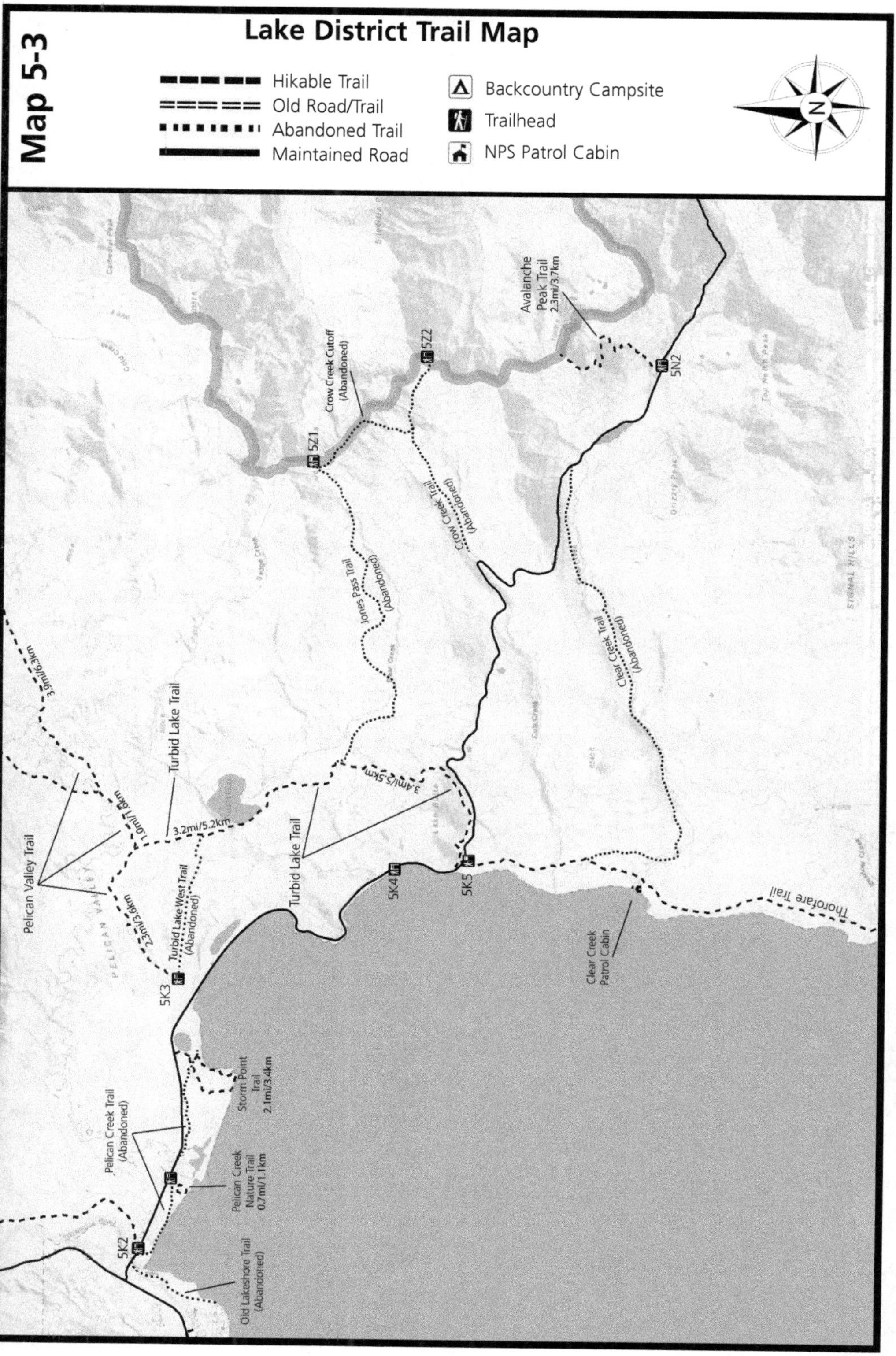

Map 5-3

Lake District Trail Map

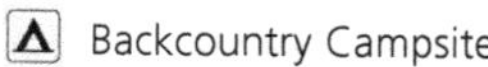

Hikable Trail
Old Road/Trail
Abandoned Trail
Maintained Road

Backcountry Campsite
Trailhead
NPS Patrol Cabin

Avalanche Peak Trail 2.3mi/3.7km
5N2
5Z2
Crow Creek Cutoff (Abandoned)
5Z1
Crow Creek Trail (Abandoned)
Jones Pass Trail (Abandoned)
Clear Creek Trail (Abandoned)
SIGNAL HILLS
3.9mi/6.3km
Turbid Lake Trail
1.0mi/1.6km
3.2mi/5.2km
3.4mi/5.5km
Turbid Lake Trail
Pelican Valley Trail
PELICAN VALLEY
2.3mi/3.6km
Turbid Lake West Trail (Abandoned)
5K3
5K4
5K5
Thorofare Trail
Clear Creek Patrol Cabin
Storm Point Trail 2.1mi/3.4km
Pelican Creek Trail (Abandoned)
Pelican Creek Nature Trail 0.7mi/1.1km
5K2
Old Lakeshore Trail (Abandoned)

Thorofare District Trails

Dike Creek Trail — MAP 6-2

TYPE:	PTP	CAT:	BC	CLASS:	C	SURF:	TRAIL	DIST:	6	STATUS:	E
DIFF:	2	TRAF:	1	CHILD:	N	HACC:	N	USE:	H S	LENGTH:	0.71
ELEV A:	8395	ELEV B:	8621	ELEV G:	305	ELEV L:	-78	NET:	226	BMA:	- -
MIN:	8381	MAX:	8621	AVG:	8455	AVG +:	10.3%	AVG -:	4.8%	OPEN:	YR

Reference Point	A-B Mi	A-B Km	B-A Mi	B-A Km	Latitude	Longitude
Trailhead @ jct w/ Mountain Creek Trail	0.00	0.00	0.71	1.14	44.28498	-110.00793
Howell Creek crossing (30 to 75')	0.12	0.19	0.59	0.95	44.28347	-110.00889
Park boundary TH 6Z1 (continues into BTNF)	0.71	1.14	0.00	0.00	44.27876	-110.00114

The Dike Creek Trail is a short trail that facilitates access to the Teton Wilderness (managed by the Bridger-Teton National Forest) via an unnamed pass. The trail goes up and over the pass and down to the Mountain Creek Trail and on into the Glacier Basin area in the USFS property.

Fox Creek Trail — MAP 6-4

TYPE:	PTP	CAT:	BC	CLASS:	B	SURF:	TRAIL	DIST:	6	STATUS:	E
DIFF:	3	TRAF:	1	CHILD:	N	HACC:	N	USE:	H S	LENGTH:	11.02
ELEV A:	8060	ELEV B:	7318	ELEV G:	1377	ELEV L:	-2119	NET:	-742	BMA:	O
MIN:	7311	MAX:	8178	AVG:	7746	AVG +:	5.0%	AVG -:	5.3%	OPEN:	7/1

Reference Point	A-B Mi	A-B Km	B-A Mi	B-A Km	Latitude	Longitude
Trailhead @ jct w/ South Boundary-Lynx Creek Trail	0.00	0.00	11.02	17.73	44.13365	-110.31269
Spur trail to campsite 8C9 (0.04 miles)	2.29	3.69	8.73	14.05	44.15680	-110.33615
Snake River crossing (50 to 70')	2.91	4.68	8.11	13.05	44.15893	-110.34710
Snake River Overlook	6.47	10.41	4.55	7.32	44.18406	-110.40035
Sickle Creek crossing	7.10	11.43	3.92	6.31	44.18544	-110.40696
Trailhead @ jct w/ Heart River Trail	11.02	17.73	0.00	0.00	44.21746	-110.46285

The Fox Creek Trail parallels the Snake River from where it enters the park at the south boundary about a half mile west of the Fox Creek Patrol Cabin, northwest up to its confluence with the Heart River. One might expect such a trail to be called the Snake River Trail, but that is not the case, despite some other guide books using that name. When hikers get into the backcountry and signs read "Fox Creek Trail," they can become disoriented if they are not expecting the disparity.

This trail is a part of the Continental Divide Trail through the park, but local hikers generally use it to facilitate access between the Heart Lake area and the Thorofare area, or to create a large loop from the Heart Lake trailhead down to the south boundary and then back to the west to come out at the Snake River Ranger Station. Along the trail there are quite a few minor creek crossings, none of which will be particularly challenging. There is a crossing of the Snake River, however, about three miles above the trail's south terminus. This is generally passable without much difficulty once access to the area is possible (generally late June to early July).

The northern quarter of this trail is located inside the Heart Lake Bear Management Area and is not open until July 1. So through hikers on the CDT who arrive prior to that date will need to take an alternate route via the South Boundary Trail westward to the Snake River Ranger Station, and then north.

Hawk's Rest Trail — MAP 6-3

TYPE:	PTP	CAT:	BC	CLASS:	C	SURF:	TRAIL	DIST:	6	STATUS:	E
DIFF:	1	TRAF:	1	CHILD:	N	HACC:	N	USE:	H S	LENGTH:	0.51
ELEV A:	7888	ELEV B:	7875	ELEV G:	41	ELEV L:	-54	NET:	-13	BMA:	- -
MIN:	7873	MAX:	7894	AVG:	7882	AVG +:	2.9%	AVG -:	3.9%	OPEN:	YR

Reference Point	A-B Mi	A-B Km	B-A Mi	B-A Km	Latitude	Longitude
Trailhead @ jct w/ Thorofare Trail	0.00	0.00	0.51	0.82	44.13876	-110.08005
Thorofare Creek crossing (150')	0.28	0.45	0.23	0.37	44.13498	-110.08167
Park Boundary TH 6K5 (continues into BTNF)	0.51	0.82	0.00	0.00	44.13263	-110.08484

The Hawk's Rest Trail is a short segment of trail that takes you from the Thorofare Trail into the Bridger-Teton National Forest, specifically down to Bridger Lake and then on to the other trails that crisscross the area around Hawk's Rest, a small peak just south of the lake. From there you can go over Phelp's Pass or Two Ocean Pass into other trails in the forest, eventually winding up at one of the trailheads along the road in Grand Teton National Park.

If you are heading into the Hawk's Rest area early in the season, the travel is likely to be through a lot of marshy areas.

Lower Ford Trail — MAP 6-2

TYPE:	PTP	CAT:	BC	CLASS:	B	SURF:	TRAIL	DIST:	6	STATUS:	E
DIFF:	1	TRAF:	2	CHILD:	N	HACC:	N	USE:	H S	LENGTH:	0.81
ELEV A:	7759	ELEV B:	7823	ELEV G:	129	ELEV L:	-65	NET:	64	BMA:	K
MIN:	7750	MAX:	7823	AVG:	7768	AVG +:	4.9%	AVG -:	3.8%	OPEN:	YR

Reference Point	A-B Mi	A-B Km	B-A Mi	B-A Km	Latitude	Longitude
Trailhead @ jct w/ Trail Creek Trail	0.00	0.00	0.81	1.30	44.28978	-110.15594
Left turn @ jct with old trail segment	0.24	0.39	0.57	0.92	44.29263	-110.15384
Yellowstone River crossing (250 to 350')	0.33	0.53	0.48	0.77	44.29349	-110.15467
Campsite 6B1	0.60	0.97	0.21	0.34	44.29664	-110.15558
Trailhead @ jct w/ Thorofare Trail	0.81	1.30	0.00	0.00	44.29896	-110.15348

The Lower Ford Trail is a short connector trail that shunts traffic from the Thorofare Trail to the Trail Creek Trail and vice versa. If you are heading south on the Thorofare Trail and want to go west on the Trail Creek Trail, for example, this would be where you would ford the Yellowstone River to do that. Approximately one mile further south is the Upper Ford.

These two crossings of the Yellowstone River are probably where you are most likely to encounter the deepest water you will have to cross in the park in a typical year. They generally are not fordable until well into August, and even in September can be waist-deep. And, generally speaking, the Lower Ford will be the deepest of the two, though either can be deep and swift in the aftermath of a heavy rain anywhere in the lower southeast portion of the park. The ford is roughly 100 yards wide. As long as you understand how to cross safely (see the chapter on Safety for details), you should be good, however.

If you make it to the Lower Ford and it appears too deep or swift to cross, consider hiking the additional distance to the south and see how the conditions look there. The rangers try to ensure that crossings are located in the safest places possible, so you are not likely to find a better place to cross between the two official fords.

Mountain Creek Trail — MAP 6-2

TYPE:	PTP	CAT:	BC	CLASS:	B	SURF:	TRAIL	DIST:	6	STATUS:	E
DIFF:	3	TRAF:	1	CHILD:	N	HACC:	N	USE:	H S	LENGTH:	10.00
ELEV A:	7890	ELEV B:	9517	ELEV G:	2310	ELEV L:	-683	NET:	1627	BMA:	- -
MIN:	7890	MAX:	9517	AVG:	8379	AVG +:	5.2%	AVG -:	3.5%	OPEN:	YR

Reference Point	A-B Mi	A-B Km	B-A Mi	B-A Km	Latitude	Longitude
Trailhead @ jct w/ Thorofare Trail	0.00	0.00	10.00	16.09	44.23920	-110.10149
Jct w/ Mountain Creek "Triangle" Trail	0.98	1.58	9.02	14.52	44.23793	-110.08316
Spur trail to campsite 6D5 (0.10 miles)	2.31	3.72	7.69	12.38	44.24405	-110.05992
Spur trail to campsite 6D6 (0.15 miles)	4.96	7.98	5.04	8.11	44.26897	-110.02636
Spur trail to campsite 6D7 (0.07 miles)	5.65	9.09	4.35	7.00	44.27653	-110.01769
Jct with Dike Creek Trail	6.48	10.43	3.52	5.66	44.28498	-110.00793
Spur trail to Howell Fork Patrol Cabin (0.07 miles)	6.63	10.67	3.37	5.42	44.28701	-110.00733
Howell Creek crossing (10 to 15')	8.05	12.96	1.95	3.14	44.30523	-110.00368
Spur trail to campsite 6D8 (0.09 miles)	8.12	13.07	1.88	3.03	44.30562	-110.00300
Eagle Pass/Park Boundary TH 6K1 (cont into BTNF)	10.00	16.09	0.00	0.00	44.32408	-110.00437

The Mountain Creek Trail, built in 1921, is perhaps one of the most spectacular trails in the park in terms of scenery. It takes you from the Thorofare up to Eagle Pass south of Eagle Peak, the highest mountain peak inside (or on the border of, in this case) the park. You will be afforded stunning views of some of the tallest peaks in the Absaroka Range as you hike up to the pass. There are a handful of excellent campsites along the trail as well, from which you can base your exploration of this area. This trail continues out into USFS property as the Eagle Creek Trail. The trailhead is on Highway 20, 17 miles from the pass.

Though many features in the park are named after wildlife that can be found within it, Eagle Peak was given its name because surveyors believed it was shaped like an eagle with spread wings.[1] Eagle Creek (outside the park on the mountain's east flank) and the similarly named pass were named for their location relative to the mountain. For many years, it was believed Electric Peak in the northern portion of the park was the park's highest peak, but a survey conducted in 1930 revealed that Eagle Peak was indeed the highest. Howell Creek, the stream the northern half of the trail follows, was named after Billy Howell, a guide who used to bring tour groups in via horseback over Eagle Pass.

Mountain Creek Triangle Trail — MAP 6-2

TYPE:	PTP	CAT:	BC	CLASS:	B	SURF:	TRAIL	DIST:	6	STATUS:	E
DIFF:	1	TRAF:	1	CHILD:	N	HACC:	N	USE:	H S	LENGTH:	1.55
ELEV A:	7865	ELEV B:	7944	ELEV G:	206	ELEV L:	-127	NET:	79	BMA:	- -
MIN:	7855	MAX:	7948	AVG:	7912	AVG +:	4.0%	AVG -:	3.4%	OPEN:	YR

Reference Point	A-B Mi	A-B Km	B-A Mi	B-A Km	Latitude	Longitude
Trailhead @ jct w/ Thorofare Trail	0.00	0.00	1.55	2.49	44.22757	-110.10675
Mountain Creek crossing (225 to 275')	1.39	2.24	0.16	0.26	44.23579	-110.08417
Trailhead @ jct w/ Mountain Creek Trail	1.55	2.49	0.00	0.00	44.23793	-110.08316

This short trail is basically a cutoff trail from the southern end of the Thorofare Trail up to the Mountain Creek Trail. Using this route prevents you from having to hike an additional mile or so northbound to reach the trail up to Eagle Pass. It does involve fording Mountain Creek, but that is generally not a problem by the time you can reach this section of the park.

South Boundary Trail: Harebell-Fox Creek — MAP 6-4,8-1

Type:	PTP	**Cat:**	BC	**Class:**	A	**Surf:**	Trail	**Dist:**	6	**Status:**	E
Diff:	4	**Traf:**	1	**Child:**	N	**HAcc:**	N	**Use:**	H S	**Length:**	10.88
Elev A:	7598	**Elev B:**	8112	**Elev G:**	3203	**Elev L:**	-2689	**Net:**	514	**BMA:**	N
Min:	7598	**Max:**	10060	**Avg:**	8919	**Avg +:**	9.8%	**Avg -:**	9.9%	**Open:**	YR

Reference Point	A-B Mi	A-B Km	B-A Mi	B-A Km	Latitude	Longitude
Trailhead @ Harebell Cabin	0.00	0.00	10.88	17.51	44.14107	-110.47766
Harebell Creek crossing	1.55	2.49	9.33	15.02	44.13536	-110.45462
Harebell Creek crossing	2.55	4.10	8.33	13.41	44.13135	-110.43965
Jct w/ Fox Creek & South Boundary-Lynx Creek Trails	10.88	17.51	0.00	0.00	44.13365	-110.31269

This is the middle segment of the hike along the south boundary eastward from the Snake River Ranger Station, between the Harebell Patrol Cabin and the Fox Creek Patrol Cabin.

This trail parallels Harebell Creek (named after the flower, which is found in the park) and climbs 2,500 feet (762m) over the course of 6.5 miles onto Big Game Ridge before descending to the Snake River where it connects with the Fox Creek Trail or into the easternmost segment of the South Boundary Trail (see below). The two crossings of Harebell Creek are shallow and should not be problematic once you can get into this area.

One unique thing about this trail is that much of it exists outside the boundary of Yellowstone and NPS jurisdiction.[2] The view from the top of Big Game Ridge is incredible, with views of the Absaroka Mountain Range to the east, the Tetons to the south, and the Red Mountains to the north.

As the peak you are climbing is known as Big Game Ridge, you can expect to see quite a few elk and deer in the area. Hunting is allowed in the areas of this trail that are outside the park boundary, so if you hike this trail during hunting season, be sure you wear the bright orange vest or other gear so that hunters do not mistake you for their prey. If you see any signs of poaching in this area, be sure to notify the nearest ranger at the earliest opportunity. This includes anyone pursuing injured/shot animals into the park after having legally hunted them in areas outside the park.

South Boundary Trail: Lynx Creek — MAP 6-3

Type:	PTP	**Cat:**	BC	**Class:**	A	**Surf:**	Trail	**Dist:**	6	**Status:**	E
Diff:	4	**Traf:**	1	**Child:**	N	**HAcc:**	N	**Use:**	H S	**Length:**	13.39
Elev A:	8060	**Elev B:**	7856	**Elev G:**	1813	**Elev L:**	-2017	**Net:**	-204	**BMA:**	L
Min:	7838	**Max:**	9296	**Avg:**	9476	**Avg +:**	4.3%	**Avg -:**	5.4%	**Open:**	YR

Reference Point	A-B Mi	A-B Km	B-A Mi	B-A Km	Latitude	Longitude
Trailhead @ jct w/ SB-Harebell & Fox Creek Trails	0.00	0.00	13.39	21.55	44.13365	-110.31269
Snake River crossing (60+')	0.18	0.29	13.21	21.26	44.13313	-110.30968
Spur trail to Fox Creek Cabin/Fox Creek Spur Trail	0.66	1.06	12.73	20.49	44.13320	-110.30035
Spur trail to campsite 6M7 (0.09 miles)	0.79	1.27	12.60	20.28	44.13334	-110.29768
Plateau Creek crossing (40')	2.59	4.17	10.80	17.38	44.14325	-110.26719
Jct w/ Two Ocean Plateau Trail/Spur to 6M4	3.30	5.31	10.09	16.24	44.15147	-110.26032
Spur trail to campsite 6M3 (0.03 miles)	4.14	6.66	9.25	14.89	44.15056	-110.24601
Mariposa Lake	4.26	6.86	9.13	14.69	44.15158	-110.24403
Trail to old campsite 6M3	4.57	7.35	8.82	14.19	44.15428	-110.23754

Reference Point	A-B Mi	A-B Km	B-A Mi	B-A Km	Latitude	Longitude
Lynx Creek crossing (10 to 20')	10.52	16.93	2.87	4.62	44.16403	-110.13205
North spur trail to campsite 6Y4 (0.62 miles)	10.80	17.38	2.59	4.17	44.16169	-110.12833
Yellowstone River crossing (75 to 90')	12.13	19.52	1.26	2.03	44.14353	-110.12707
Spur trail to campsite 6Y2 (0.01 miles)	12.26	19.73	1.13	1.82	44.14399	-110.12628
Trailhead @ jct with Yellowstone Meadows Cutoff	13.39	21.55	0.00	0.00	44.13875	-110.10504

This is the easternmost section of the South Boundary Trail. It takes you from near the Fox Creek Patrol Cabin eastward to the Yellowstone Meadows Trail (and thus, the Thorofare). If you are traveling west to east, you will have a 1,200-foot (366m) climb over the course of the first half of the trail, up onto the Two Ocean Plateau, followed by a 1,400-foot (426m) descent into the Yellowstone River Valley as you make your way to the remote, southeast corner of the park.

You do make a couple of creek crossings before you get to the Yellowstone River Valley, but both are quite shallow most of the season and should not present a problem. There is a nice little campsite at Mariposa Lake (no sign and no designated camping spot), but it has no food pole and staying there requires hikers to adhere to the Leave No Trace protocols. Additionally, there is no off-trail travel in that area without a permit (and then only between July 15 and August 21). Check with the backcountry office for specific details.

One tip rangers often mention to hikers is that, if you are heading up north into the Thorofare and/or up into the Mountain Creek area, take the spur trail to campsite 6Y4. You will cross the Yellowstone River and Thorofare Creek where they join together (known as the Confluence Ford, which tends to be slow water with a crossing of about 150 feet). Once you get to the campsite, continue heading south on that spur trail to the Yellowstone Meadows Cutoff Trail. This will be easier and will cut considerable time off your trip than if you hike the Lynx Creek segment all the way down to Yellowstone Meadows and head north from there. Doing that will add more distance (a little over two miles) to your trip, plus you will have to ford the river and the creek separately. Regardless of which river/creek crossing you use, the water will likely be waist deep early in the season, but should recede to knee-depth in late August (possibly even lower in drier years). However, if there is a heavy rainstorm in the southeastern section of the park, water levels may rise rapidly.

Thorofare - South Boundary Cutoff — MAP 6-3

Type:	PTP	**Cat:**	BC	**Class:**	B	**Surf:**	Trail	**Dist:**	6	**Status:**	E
Diff:	1	**Traf:**	1	**Child:**	N	**HAcc:**	N	**Use:**	H S	**Length:**	1.10
Elev A:	7867	**Elev B:**	7891	**Elev G:**	87	**Elev L:**	-63	**Net:**	24	**BMA:**	- -
Min:	7860	**Max:**	7892	**Avg:**	7874	**Avg +:**	2.6%	**Avg -:**	2.5%	**Open:**	YR

Reference Point	A-B Mi	A-B Km	B-A Mi	B-A Km	Latitude	Longitude
Trailhead @ jct w/ Yellowstone Meadows Cutoff	0.00	0.00	1.10	1.77	44.14165	-110.10039
Trailhead @ jct w/ Thorofare Trail	1.10	1.77	0.00	0.00	44.14421	-110.08308

This short segment of trail provides a more direct route to the Thorofare Ranger Station from the South Boundary Trail than going further north on the Yellowstone Meadows Trail and then turning south. It exists more for the rangers going out on patrols than hikers, per se, but if you need to get to the station, or if you need to head south into the Hawk's Rest area or continue south on the Thorofare Trail into the Teton Wilderness, this will shorten your hike a bit.

Trail Creek Cabin Bypass Trail — MAP 6-4

TYPE:	PTP	CAT:	BC	CLASS:	C	SURF:	TRAIL	DIST:	6	STATUS:	E
DIFF:	1	TRAF:	1	CHILD:	N	HACC:	N	USE:	H S	LENGTH:	0.37
ELEV A:	7755	ELEV B:	7749	ELEV G:	94	ELEV L:	-100	NET:	-6	BMA:	K
MIN:	7749	MAX:	7827	AVG:	7796	AVG +:	8.1%	AVG -:	8.7%	OPEN:	YR

Reference Point	A-B Mi	A-B Km	B-A Mi	B-A Km	Latitude	Longitude
Trailhead @ west jct w/ Trail Creek Trail	0.00	0.00	0.37	0.60	44.29718	-110.23438
Trailhead @ east jct w/ Trail Creek Trail	0.37	0.60	0.00	0.00	44.29503	-110.23053

This trail is designed to provide a path to bypass the main trail that runs past the cabin during the early part of the season when the main trail is particularly marshy and muddy, making travel difficult. It adds only a minimal amount of distance if you elect to use it.

Trail Creek-Two Ocean Cutoff Trail — MAP 6-4,6-3

TYPE:	PTP	CAT:	BC	CLASS:	C	SURF:	TRAIL	DIST:	6	STATUS:	E
DIFF:	1	TRAF:	1	CHILD:	N	HACC:	N	USE:	H S	LENGTH:	1.52
ELEV A:	7750	ELEV B:	7918	ELEV G:	298	ELEV L:	-130	NET:	168	BMA:	L
MIN:	7750	MAX:	7938	AVG:	7850	AVG +:	5.2%	AVG -:	4.8%	OPEN:	YR

Reference Point	A-B Mi	A-B Km	B-A Mi	B-A Km	Latitude	Longitude
North Trailhead @ jct w/ Trail Creek Trail	0.00	0.00	1.52	2.45	44.27698	-110.30189
South trailhead @ jct w/ Two Ocean Plateau Trail	1.52	2.45	0.00	0.00	44.26494	-110.27850

As the trail's name implies, this is a cutoff trail that allows you to get up onto Two Ocean Plateau and the trail on top of it if you are coming from the Heart Lake side rather than having to go all the way up to the Two Ocean Plateau's north trailhead up by the Southeast Arm of the lake. This will shave considerable distance and a lot of time off your hike if you are headed south in order to do a loop or if you are just headed into the Teton Wilderness. It is a 200-foot (61m) climb over little more than a mile.

Two Ocean Plateau Trail — MAP 6-3,6-4

TYPE:	PTP	CAT:	BC	CLASS:	B	SURF:	TRAIL	DIST:	6	STATUS:	E
DIFF:	3	TRAF:	1	CHILD:	N	HACC:	N	USE:	H S	LENGTH:	11.78
ELEV A:	8651	ELEV B:	7820	ELEV G:	1155	ELEV L:	-1987	NET:	-831	BMA:	L
MIN:	7802	MAX:	9324	AVG:	8433	AVG +:	5.6%	AVG -:	4.2%	OPEN:	YR

Reference Point	A-B Mi	A-B Km	B-A Mi	B-A Km	Latitude	Longitude
South Trailhead @ jct w/ South Boundary-Lynx Creek	0.00	0.00	11.78	18.96	44.15147	-110.26032
Spur trail to campsite 6M5 (0.10 miles)	4.37	7.03	7.41	11.93	44.20344	-110.26150
Passage Creek crossing	4.38	7.05	7.40	11.91	44.20349	-110.26153
Passage Creek crossing	7.77	12.50	4.01	6.45	44.24237	-110.27932
Jct w/ Trail Creek - Two Ocean Cutoff Trail	9.42	15.16	2.36	3.80	44.26494	-110.27850
Chipmunk Creek crossing (50 to 60')	10.44	16.80	1.34	2.16	44.27491	-110.27046
Trailhead @ jct w/ Trail Creek Trail	11.78	18.96	0.00	0.00	44.29262	-110.26376

The Two Ocean Plateau Trail takes you up and over a unique plateau sitting in the middle part of the southeastern section of the park. It basically divides the Thorofare District and the South District, and provides a route from the north to the south (or vice versa) for those who wish to create loops deeper into the backcountry. The trail is lightly used, and in some places it may be difficult to follow, especially early in the season.

If you are headed north, you will climb 700 feet (213m) over the course of two miles, and then begin a slow, steady descent toward the lake. Heading north, you will have a 1,500-foot (457m) climb over seven miles. Either way is very doable and the views are spectacular. If you are moving north, when you get near the end of the trail, it splits just before the final descent down to the lake. To remain on the Two Ocean Plateau Trail, take the right fork toward the Trail Creek Patrol Cabin. If you are going to head back to the west toward Heart Lake, take the left fork. This is the Trail Creek - Two Ocean Cutoff Trail mentioned above.

There are two crossings of Passage Creek, so named because it provides a "passage" down from the top of the plateau. It is rather unique in that it did not get its name early in park history, but rather in the 1960s.[3] Both crossings are narrow and shallow, even early in the season. There is also a very nice, lightly-used campsite sitting atop the plateau.

Upper Ford Trail — MAP 6-2

TYPE:	PTP	CAT:	BC	CLASS:	B	SURF:	TRAIL	DIST:	6	STATUS:	E
DIFF:	1	TRAF:	2	CHILD:	N	HACC:	N	USE:	H S	LENGTH:	0.75
ELEV A:	7759	ELEV B:	7838	ELEV G:	129	ELEV L:	-50	NET:	79	BMA:	K
MIN:	7755	MAX:	7838	AVG:	7766	AVG +:	5.8%	AVG -:	2.6%	OPEN:	YR

Reference Point	A-B Mi	A-B Km	B-A Mi	B-A Km	Latitude	Longitude
Trailhead @ jct w/ Trail Creek Trail	0.00	0.00	0.75	1.21	44.28978	-110.15594
Spur trail to campsite 6B2 (0.05 miles)	0.26	0.42	0.49	0.79	44.28951	-110.15082
Unnamed creek crossing (25 to 30')	0.31	0.50	0.44	0.71	44.28897	-110.15069
Yellowstone River crossing (200+')	0.64	1.03	0.11	0.18	44.28542	-110.14647
Trailhead @ jct w/ Thorofare Trail	0.75	1.21	0.00	0.00	44.28552	-110.14506

This trail provides the uppermost crossing of the Yellowstone River for those going from the Thorofare region over to the Trail Creek Trail or vice versa. Like its sister trail, the Lower Ford Trail (see above), it is designed to get people to cross the river where rangers have determined it is safest to do so. The crossing here is roughly 200 feet wide.

As with the lower trail, crossing here will be difficult in the earlier parts of the season; the water can be waist-high or deeper. If you are heading in before early August, be sure to discuss the crossing with the backcountry office for the latest conditions. Sometimes it is actually easier to cross at the Lower Ford, and you may wish to consider hiking the extra mile north to get to it.

Yellowstone Meadows Cutoff Trail — MAP 6-3

TYPE:	PTP	CAT:	BC	CLASS:	C	SURF:	TRAIL	DIST:	6	STATUS:	E
DIFF:	1	TRAF:	1	CHILD:	N	HACC:	N	USE:	H S	LENGTH:	1.67
ELEV A:	7915	ELEV B:	7865	ELEV G:	24	ELEV L:	-74	NET:	-50	BMA:	- -
MIN:	7862	MAX:	7915	AVG:	7875	AVG +:	1.1%	AVG -:	1.1%	OPEN:	YR

Reference Point	A-B Mi	A-B Km	B-A Mi	B-A Km	Latitude	Longitude
Trailhead @ jct w/ Thorofare Trail	0.00	0.00	1.67	2.69	44.15047	-110.08986
Spur trail to campsite 6Y4 (1.63 miles)	0.48	0.77	1.19	1.92	44.14552	-110.09618
Jct w/ South Boundary-Thorofare Cutoff Trail	0.83	1.34	0.84	1.35	44.14165	-110.10039
Thorofare Creek crossing (150 to 200')	1.00	1.61	0.67	1.08	44.14049	-110.10332
Spur trail to campsite 6T1 (0.03 miles)	1.09	1.75	0.58	0.93	44.14016	-110.10413
Jct w/ South Boundary-Lynx Creek Trail	1.17	1.88	0.50	0.80	44.13875	-110.10504
Park boundary TH 6K4 (Bridger Lake: BTNF)	1.67	2.69	0.00	0.00	44.13265	-110.10951

The Yellowstone Meadows Cutoff Trail is designed to provide a shorter route to the South Boundary Trail from the Thorofare Trail without having to go all the way down to the ranger station. It also takes you to the park boundary and into the Teton Wilderness to the west side of Bridger Lake, and then on down into the crisscross of trails that overlay that area.

You will have to ford Thorofare Creek on this trail, and it is typically knee-high to thigh-high once you get into August (and can be as wide as 200 feet). Like the Yellowstone River, the creek can get considerably higher on short notice if there are heavy rainstorms upstream, a fairly common occurrence during the height of the summer.

If you are looking to cross over to the South Boundary Trail and head west, consider taking the spur trail to campsite 6Y4. Once you get to the campsite, continue on the north access spur to the South Boundary Trail. This will shave a couple of miles off your trip AND you will cross the Yellowstone River and Thorofare Creek at their confluence rather than having to cross them individually.

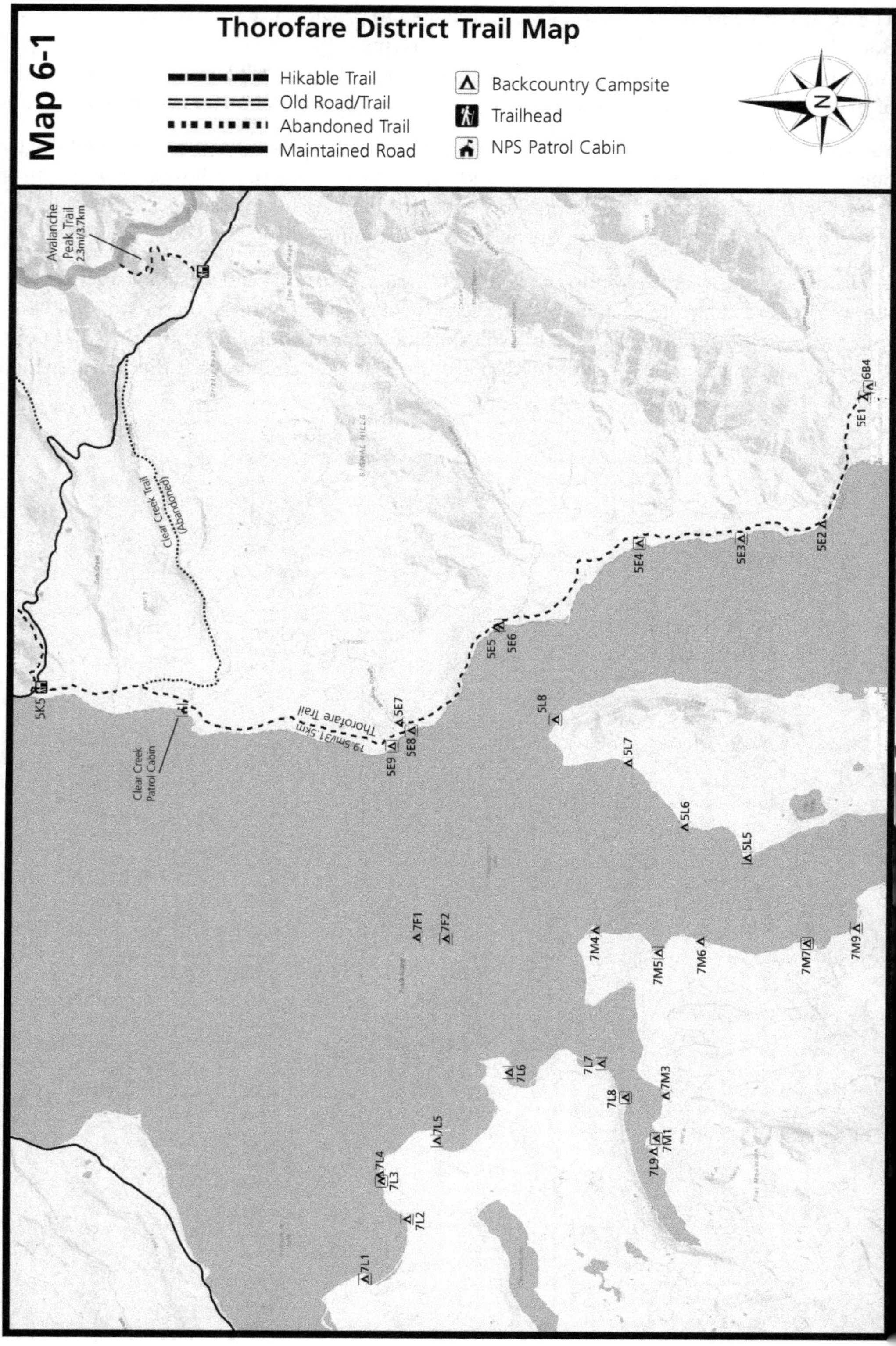

Map 6-1

Thorofare District Trail Map

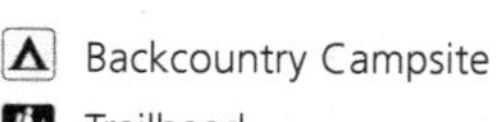

Avalanche Peak Trail 2.3mi/3.7km

Clear Creek Trail (Abandoned)

Thorofare Trail 19.5mi/31.5km

Clear Creek Patrol Cabin

5K5 5E9 5E8 5E7 5E6 5E5 5E4 5E3 5E2 5E1 6B4

5L8 5L7 5L6 5L5

7F1 7F2

7M4 7M5 7M6 7M7 7M9 7M3 7M1

7L1 7L2 7L3 7L4 7L5 7L6 7L7 7L8 7L9

Map 6-2

Thorofare District Trail Map

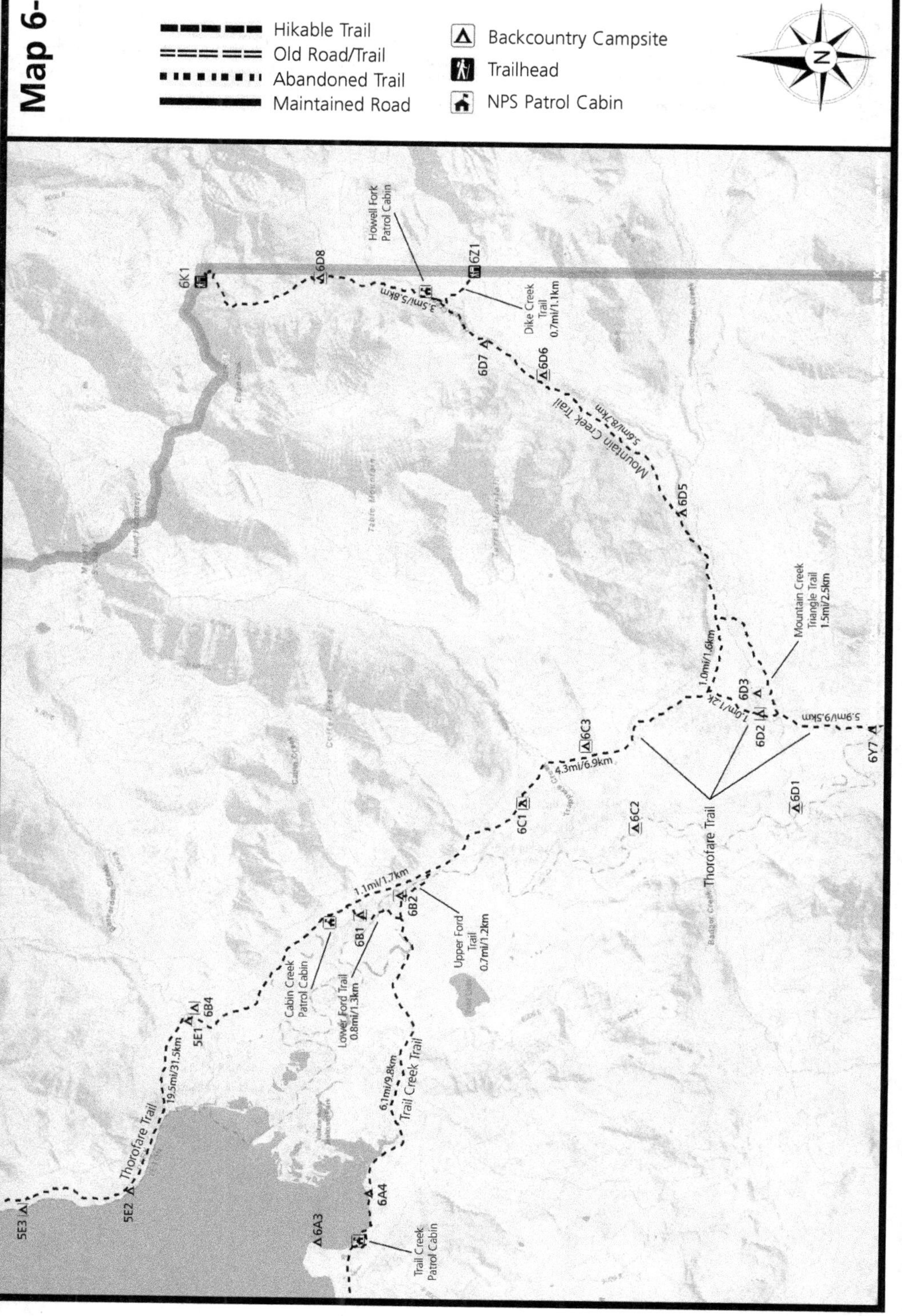

Hikable Trail
Old Road/Trail
Abandoned Trail
Maintained Road

Backcountry Campsite
Trailhead
NPS Patrol Cabin

Howell Fork Patrol Cabin
6K1
6D8
6Z1
3.5mi/5.8km
Dike Creek Trail 0.7mi/1.1km
6D7
6D6
5.6mi/8.7km
Mountain Creek Trail
6D5
Mountain Creek Triangle Trail 1.5mi/2.5km
1.0mi/1.6km
6D3
1.0m/1.2k
6D2
5.9mi/9.5km
6Y7
6C3
4.3mi/6.9km
6C1
6C2
6D1
Thorofare Trail
1.1mi/1.7km
6B2
6B1
Upper Ford Trail 0.7mi/1.2km
Cabin Creek Patrol Cabin
Lower Ford Trail 0.8mi/1.3km
6B4
5E1
19.5mi/31.5km
6.1mi/9.8km
Trail Creek Trail
Thorofare Trail
5E2
5E3
6A4
6A3
Trail Creek Patrol Cabin

Map 6-3

Thorofare District Trail Map

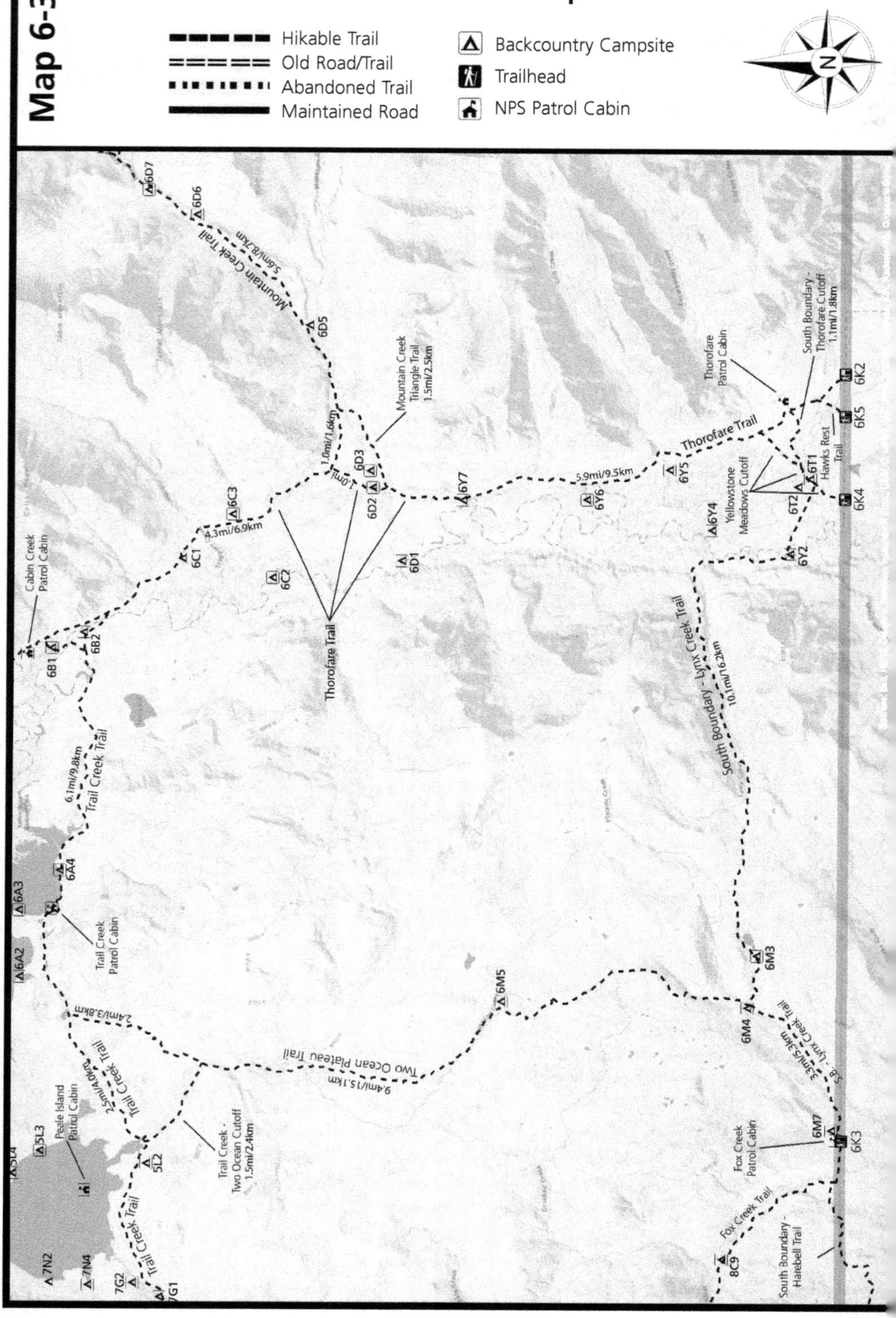

Hikable Trail
Old Road/Trail
Abandoned Trail
Maintained Road

NPS Patrol Cabin

6D7
6D6
Mountain Creek Trail
5.6mi/8.7km
6D5
Mountain Creek Triangle Trail 1.5mi/2.5km
1.0mi/1.6km
1.0mi
6D3
6D2
6C3
4.3mi/6.9km
6C1
6C2
6D1
6Y7
Thorofare Trail
5.9mi/9.5km
6Y6
6Y5
Thorofare Patrol Cabin
South Boundary - Thorofare Cutoff 1.1mi/1.8km
6K2
6K5
Hawks Rest Trail
6T1
6T2
6K4
Yellowstone Meadows Cutoff
6Y4
6Y2
Cabin Creek Patrol Cabin
6B1
6B2
Thorofare Trail
South Boundary - Lynx Creek Trail
10.1mi/16.2km
Trail Creek Trail
6.1mi/9.8km
6A4
6A3
Trail Creek Patrol Cabin
6A2
6M5
6M3
6M4
2.4mi/3.8km
Two Ocean Plateau Trail
9.4mi/15.1km
S.B. - Lynx Creek Trail
3.3mi/5.3km
5L3
5L4
Peale Island Patrol Cabin
2.5mi/4.0km
Trail Creek Trail
Trail Creek - Two Ocean Cutoff 1.5mi/2.4km
5L2
6M7
6K3
Fox Creek Patrol Cabin
Fox Creek Trail
Trail Creek Trail
7N2
7N4
7G2
7G1
8C9
South Boundary - Harebell Trail

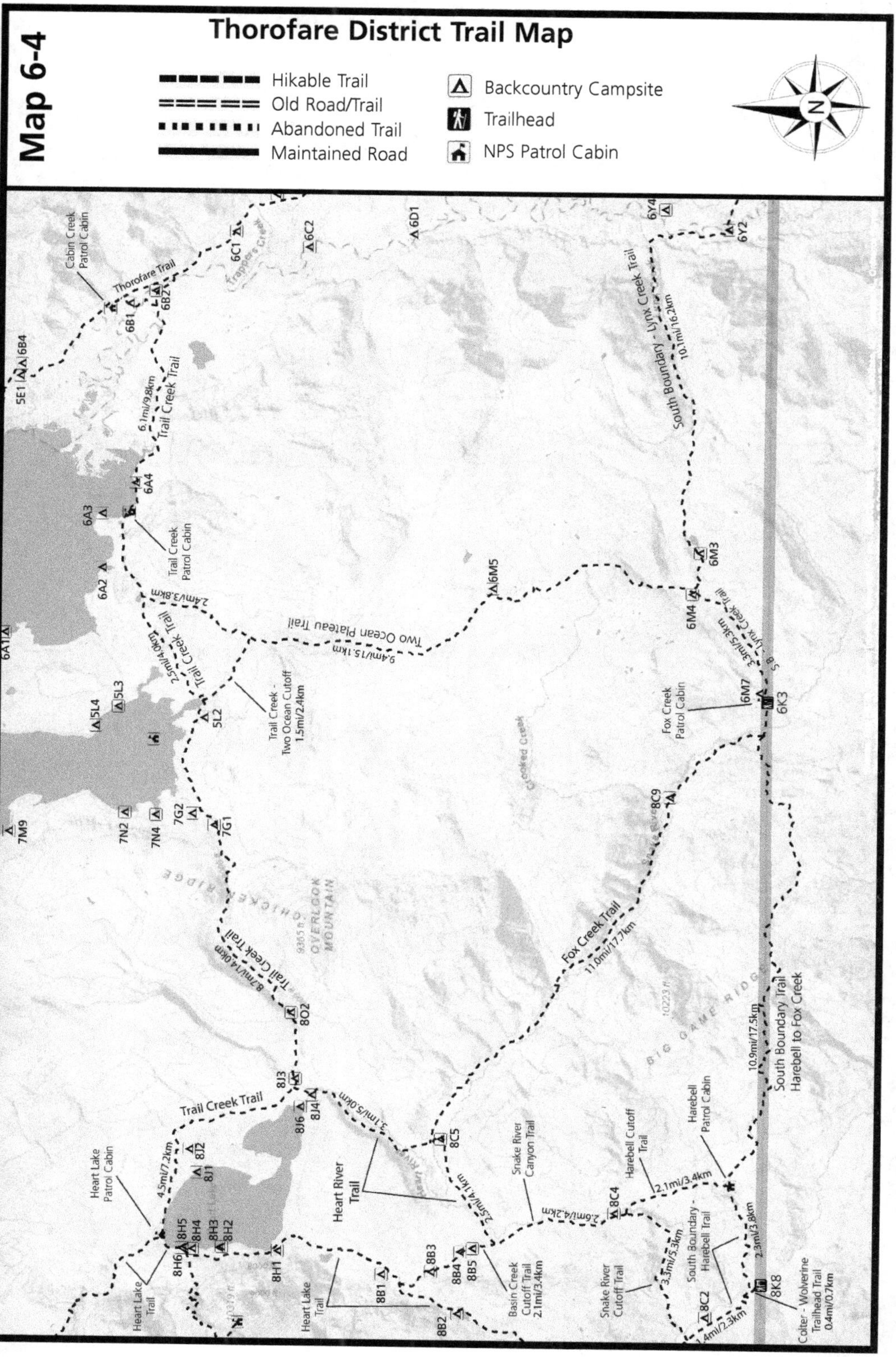

Map 6-4

Thorofare District Trail Map

- Hikable Trail
- Old Road/Trail
- Abandoned Trail
- Maintained Road
- Backcountry Campsite
- Trailhead
- NPS Patrol Cabin

Cabin Creek Patrol Cabin
Thorofare Trail
Trappers Creek
6C1 6C2 6D1 6Y4 6Y2
6B1 6B2 5E1 6B4
Trail Creek Trail
6.1mi/9.8km
South Boundary - Lynx Creek Trail
10.1mi/16.2km
6A4 6A3 6A2 6A1
Trail Creek Patrol Cabin
2.4mi/3.8km
6M5 6M3 6M4
Two Ocean Plateau Trail
9.4mi/15.1km
S. B. - Lynx Creek Trail
3.3mi/5.3km
2.5mi/4.0km
Trail Creek Trail
5L4 5L3 5L2
Trail Creek - Two Ocean Cutoff
1.5mi/2.4km
Fox Creek Patrol Cabin
6M7 6K3
Crooked Creek
8C9
7M9 7N2 7N4 7G2 7G1
Chicken Ridge
Overlook Mountain
9365 ft
Trail Creek Trail
8.7mi/14.0km
Fox Creek Trail
11.0mi/17.7km
10229 ft
Big Game Ridge
8O2
South Boundary Trail Harebell to Fox Creek
10.9mi/17.5km
8J3 8J4 8J6
Trail Creek Trail
3.1mi/5.0km
Heart Lake Patrol Cabin
4.5mi/7.2km
8J2 8J1
8C5
Heart River Trail
Snake River Canyon Trail
Harebell Cutoff Trail
Harebell Patrol Cabin
2.1mi/3.4km
2.5mi/4.1km
2.6mi/4.2km
8C4
8H5 8H4 8H3 8H2 8H6 8H1
8B3 8B4 8B5 8B1 8B2
2.3mi/3.6km
Heart Lake Trail
Heart Lake Trail
Basin Creek Cutoff Trail
2.1mi/3.4km
Snake River Cutoff Trail
3.3mi/5.3km
South Boundary - Harebell Trail
8C2
1.4mi/2.3km
8K8
Colter - Wolverine Trailhead Trail
0.4mi/0.7km

Grant District Trails

DeLacy Creek Trail — MAP 7-

Type:	PTP	Cat:	TH	Class:	B	Surf:	Trail	Dist:	7	Status:	E
Diff:	3	Traf:	2	Child:	N	HAcc:	N	Use:	H S	Length:	7.18
Elev A:	7944	Elev B:	7805	Elev G:	1271	Elev L:	-1410	Net:	-139	BMA:	- -
Min:	7794	Max:	7982	Avg:	7856	Avg +:	5.7%	Avg -:	5.8%	Open:	YR

Reference Point	A-B Mi	A-B Km	B-A Mi	B-A Km	Latitude	Longitude
Trailhead 7K2 (8.7 miles W of West Thumb Junction)	0.00	0.00	7.18	11.56	44.44678	-110.70161
Intersection w/ old Howard Eaton Trail	0.67	1.08	6.51	10.48	44.43853	-110.69729
Dry Creek crossing	0.92	1.48	6.26	10.07	44.43522	-110.69743
DeLacy Park	1.34	2.16	5.84	9.40	44.43013	-110.70099
Jct w/ Shoshone Lake North Shore Trail	2.97	4.78	4.21	6.78	44.40843	-110.69490
Jct w/ Dogshead, South Shore, & 8S1 Spur Trails	7.18	11.56	0.00	0.00	44.35932	-110.66219

The DeLacy Creek Trail is the "north" way, and the shortest way into the Shoshone Lak area. For the first mile and a half or so, you will be hiking through forest. For the next mil and a half, you will be hiking along the side of DeLacy Park, the large meadow throug which the creek runs.[1] At three miles, you will reach the shoreline and follow it around th east side of the lake until you connect to the Dogshead Trail. From this point you can hea out via that trail, continue south another few hundred yards to the Lewis Channel Trail, o you can proceed around the south side of the lake.

The parking for this trailhead is on the north side of the Craig Pass Road, while the entranc to the trail itself is across the highway. Vehicles tend to speed through this area, so exercis caution when crossing here. If you are looking for a quick way to get into a campsite o the park's second largest lake, reserve 8S2, which is just a little over a half mile west of th junction with the North Shore Trail, making the total hike to it just 3.5 miles (5.6km).

Duck Lake Trail — MAP 7-1

Type:	O&B	Cat:	FC	Class:	B	Surf:	Trail	Dist:	7	Status:	E
Diff:	2	Traf:	3	Child:	N	HAcc:	N	Use:	H S	Length:	0.44
Elev A:	7807	Elev B:	7809	Elev G:	101	Elev L:	-99	Net:	2	BMA:	- -
Min:	7807	Max:	7903	Avg:	7851	Avg +:	8.3%	Avg -:	8.8%	Open:	YR

Reference Point	A-B Mi	A-B Km	B-A Mi	B-A Km	Latitude	Longitude
Trailhead (across from West Thumb Parking Lot)	0.00	0.00	0.44	0.71	44.41664	-110.57553
Power line crossing	0.21	0.34	0.23	0.37	44.41957	-110.57610
Duck Lake	0.44	0.71	0.00	0.00	44.42173	-110.57726

The Duck Lake Trail is a quick hike up to a small lake that has a unique history to it. Though it is hard to believe today, there was once a considerable development at West Thumb— several hundred cabins, stores, dorms, post office, gas station, and a full-sized campground Duck Lake served as the water supply for that development, and some of the old parts of the pumping system can still be found in places around the lake if you know where to look.

The development was removed in the late 1970s, and the only thing remaining is the one building there now that serves as a bookstore in the summer and a warming hut in the winter. Once you get down to the shore of the lake (located in a hydrothermal explosion crater), you can hike around the lake. You may have to crawl over a considerable amount of deadfall, however. The hike around the lake itself is one mile (1.6km) in length.

Lake Overlook Trail (West Thumb Overlook) — MAP 7-1

Type:	Loop	**Cat:**	FC	**Class:**	B	**Surf:**	Trail	**Dist:**	7	**Status:**	E
Diff:	2	**Traf:**	3	**Child:**	N	**HAcc:**	N	**Use:**	H	**Length:**	1.45
Elev A:	7795	**Elev B:**	7795	**Elev G:**	300	**Elev L:**	-300	**Net:**	0	**BMA:**	- -
Min:	7785	**Max:**	8024	**Avg:**	7859	**Avg +:**	8.1%	**Avg -:**	7.0%	**Open:**	YR

Reference Point	A-B Mi	A-B Km	B-A Mi	B-A Km	Latitude	Longitude
Trailhead @ West Thumb Parking Lot	0.00	0.00	1.45	2.33	44.41555	-110.57511
South Entrance Road crossing	0.22	0.35	1.23	1.98	44.41343	-110.57791
Loop Junction	0.26	0.42	1.19	1.92	44.41317	-110.57849
Small thermal area (part of West Thumb GB)	0.93	1.50	0.52	0.84	44.41221	-110.58654
Loop Junction	1.45	2.33	0.00	0.00	44.41317	-110.57849

The Lake Overlook Trail takes you up to the top of a hill known colloquially as Savage Hill, with an incredible view of Yellowstone Lake. The hill gets its name from the fact that many park concession employees, who in the olden days were known as "savages," would use this hill for everything from drinking to courting. This was back in the days when there was a huge development at the West Thumb area. All of that was taken out, and of course, the employees are no longer present in significant numbers, but the hill maintains its old name among those who are familiar with the area's history.

When you get to the summit of the Savage Hill, there is a small thermal field that is technically part of the West Thumb Geyser Basin complex. It contains a small handful of minor thermal features. There is also a little bench at the summit that makes a nice place to sit and take in the view for a few minutes before you head back down.

The primary trailhead for this is located at the parking lot in the thermal basin, but you can park alongside the road and go in, cutting off about a half mile of hiking for the round trip. If you park in the parking lot and have to cross the road, be careful as vehicles tend to speed through this area at times. There is a crosswalk and people are supposed to stop to allow hikers to cross, but sometimes that just does not happen.

Old Dry Creek - West Thumb Road — MAP 7-1

Type:	PTP	**Cat:**	BC	**Class:**	U	**Surf:**	Trail	**Dist:**	7	**Status:**	R
Diff:	2	**Traf:**	1	**Child:**	N	**HAcc:**	N	**Use:**	H	**Length:**	7.13
Elev A:	7973	**Elev B:**	8087	**Elev G:**	1038	**Elev L:**	-923	**Net:**	114	**BMA:**	- -
Min:	7960	**Max:**	8374	**Avg:**	8244	**Avg +:**	4.0%	**Avg -:**	4.3%	**Open:**	YR

Reference Point	A-B Mi	A-B Km	B-A Mi	B-A Km	Latitude	Longitude
Trailhead @ roadside pullout on OF-WT Road	0.00	0.00	7.13	11.47	44.45225	-110.68620
Old Howard Eaton Trail crossing	5.98	9.62	1.15	1.85	44.42721	-110.61095
Trailhead @ Duck Lake Curve	7.13	11.47	0.00	0.00	44.42149	-110.59225

This is a segment of the original road that used to exist between Old Faithful and West Thumb back prior to the 1940s. In the late 1930s it was converted into a horse trail and became a part of the updated Howard Eaton Trail. It was abandoned in the 1970s.

Today, you will still be able to hike a good bit of it without any problem, though in many places there will be downed trees and other obstacles. There are no real pullouts at either end of this trail, and it is almost completely hidden on the west end.

Riddle Lake Trail — MAP 7-1

TYPE:	O&B	CAT:	BC	CLASS:	B	SURF:	TRAIL	DIST:	7	STATUS:	E
DIFF:	2	TRAF:	3	CHILD:	N	HACC:	N	USE:	H S	LENGTH:	2.39
ELEV A:	7987	ELEV B:	7917	ELEV G:	247	ELEV L:	-318	NET:	-70	BMA:	M
MIN:	7914	MAX:	7987	AVG:	7946	AVG +:	4.0%	AVG -:	4.0%	OPEN:	7/15

Reference Point	A-B Mi	A-B Km	B-A Mi	B-A Km	Latitude	Longitude
Trailhead 7K3 (4.1 miles S of West Thumb Junction)	0.00	0.00	2.39	3.85	44.35852	-110.58170
Riddle Lake	1.95	3.14	0.44	0.71	44.36180	-110.55206
Terminus	2.39	3.85	0.00	0.00	44.36069	-110.54381

Riddle Lake is a moderate-sized lake that makes for a pretty half-day hike when the trail i open. Though the trail technically is scheduled to open on July 15 each summer, for man of the past summers it has remained closed the entire season due to the presence of nestin endangered or threatened bird species. If it does open on time, the trail can be fairly marsh in places until well into August.

The trail itself begins right on the Continental Divide, but is relatively level all the way to th lake. You have a few small hills, but nothing of any consequence. This trail is a bit too lon for most smaller children, but older children should be fine.

Old South Entrance Trail: North Segment — MAP 7-1

TYPE:	PTP	CAT:	BC	CLASS:	N	SURF:	TRAIL	DIST:	8	STATUS:	R
DIFF:	2	TRAF:	1	CHILD:	N	HACC:	N	USE:	H	LENGTH:	5.83
ELEV A:	7815	ELEV B:	7818	ELEV G:	693	ELEV L:	-690	NET:	3	BMA:	- -
MIN:	7798	MAX:	7992	AVG:	7905	AVG +:	3.6%	AVG -:	4.0%	OPEN:	YR

Reference Point	A-B Mi	A-B Km	B-A Mi	B-A Km	Latitude	Longitude
Trailhead @ Entrance to Grant Incinerator Rd	0.00	0.00	5.83	9.38	44.39852	-110.57041
Grant Maintenance Storage Yard	0.40	0.64	5.43	8.74	44.39526	-110.57547
Trailhead @ jct w/ Dogshead Trail	5.83	9.38	0.00	0.00	44.33156	-110.61320

This is another trail that exists over what used to be an old road. In this case, it was part of the original South Entrance Road, specifically the northern half of it from Lewis Lake to what is now the Grant Village area. It was abandoned in the 1960s, and today can be hard to find at either end, but once you get into the woods you can see the path carved out fairly easily.

On the north end, this trail begins at an NPS maintenance yard and you will not be able to drive back to park at the beginning of the trail. You will need to park on the side of the road near the swing gate (do not block access) and walk back along the service road until you get to the yard. As soon as you get to the end of the service road, turn right and head off into the woods where you will pick up the old roadbed (use a GPS device if you have one).

This trail and its companion southern end (described in detail in the Lost Trails chapter later in this book) provided a route for horse parties to enter the park from the Flagg Ranch area. Over time the number of parties coming in via horseback dwindled and there was no longer a need for a trail to accommodate them. The southern end was abandoned and never used again. Since this section was originally a road, the path remains carved into the woods and it is possible to navigate it with a bit of effort.

West Thumb Geyser Basin Trail (Loop & Cutoff) MAP 7-1

TYPE:	LOOP	CAT:	FC	CLASS:	A	SURF:	BDWLK	DIST:	7	STATUS:	E
DIFF:	1	TRAF:	5	CHILD:	Y	HACC:	Y	USE:	H	LENGTH:	0.81
ELEV A:	7799	ELEV B:	7799	ELEV G:	73	ELEV L:	-73	NET:	0	BMA:	- -
MIN:	7745	MAX:	7801	AVG:	7779	AVG +:	3.4%	AVG -:	4.6%	OPEN:	YR

Reference Points for Outer/Main Loop	A-B Mi	A-B Km	B-A Mi	B-A Km	Latitude	Longitude
Trailhead @ YA Store/Warming Hut	0.00	0.00	0.67	1.08	44.41584	-110.57357
Loop split	0.07	0.11	0.60	0.97	44.41599	-110.57241
Jct w/ Inner cutoff trail	0.10	0.16	0.57	0.92	44.41592	-110.57183
Bluebell Pool/Seismograph Pool	0.14	0.23	0.53	0.85	44.41566	-110.57109
Lakeside Spring	0.25	0.40	0.42	0.68	44.41639	-110.56971
Venting Pool	0.26	0.42	0.41	0.66	44.41653	-110.56983
Lakeshore Geyser	0.28	0.45	0.39	0.63	44.41675	-110.56997
Vandalized Pool	0.31	0.50	0.36	0.58	44.41708	-110.57031
Fishing Cone	0.32	0.51	0.35	0.56	44.41724	-110.57041
Big Cone (East)/Little Cone (West)	0.35	0.56	0.32	0.51	44.41758	-110.57071
King Geyser (N)	0.43	0.69	0.24	0.39	44.41836	-110.57189
Black Pool	0.45	0.72	0.22	0.35	44.41820	-110.57209
Abyss Pool	0.46	0.74	0.21	0.34	44.41822	-110.57232
Spur to Abyss Pool/Roadside Steamer	0.47	0.76	0.20	0.32	44.41812	-110.57240
Jct w/ Inner cutoff trail	0.53	0.85	0.14	0.23	44.41739	-110.57299
Painted Pools	0.57	0.92	0.10	0.16	44.41691	-110.57317
Jct w/ spur trail to parking lot	0.61	0.98	0.06	0.10	44.41641	-110.57293
Mimulus Pools	0.62	1.00	0.05	0.08	44.41622	-110.57273
Return to loop split	0.67	1.08	0.00	0.00	44.41599	-110.57241

Reference Points for Cutoff Trail	A-B Mi	A-B Km	B-A Mi	B-A Km	Latitude	Longitude
North jct with West Thumb Loop Trail	0.00	0.00	0.14	0.23	44.41739	-110.57299
Twin Geysers	0.01	0.02	0.13	0.21	44.41724	-110.57284
New Twin Geyser	0.02	0.03	0.12	0.19	44.41716	-110.57265
Blue Funnel Spring	0.07	0.11	0.07	0.11	44.41675	-110.57200
Ephydra Spring, Perforated Pool	0.08	0.13	0.06	0.10	44.41671	-110.57185
Thumb Geyser	0.09	0.14	0.05	0.08	44.41661	-110.57176
Percolating Pool	0.09	0.14	0.05	0.08	44.41655	-110.57164
Ledge Spring, Collapsing Pool	0.10	0.16	0.04	0.06	44.41648	-110.57159
Surging Spring	0.11	0.18	0.03	0.05	44.41632	-110.57156
Spur trail to Thumb Paint Pots	0.13	0.21	0.01	0.02	44.41605	-110.57163
South jct w/ West Thumb Loop Trail	0.14	0.23	0.00	0.00	44.41592	-110.57183

The West Thumb Geyser Basin is one of the park's major thermal fields. As such it can be extremely busy and congested during the peak of the summer visitation season. Note that the reference point chart is divided into two segments. The first starts at the bookstore, proceeds down the trail, turns right and then takes the entire outer loop. The second is the little cutoff boardwalk in the western portion of the loop.

West Thumb is home to approximately 150 thermal features, some 30 of which have official names.[2] This does not include the features found in Potts Basin just north of here (which is closed to public access). Up until the 1970s, West Thumb was home to a major development not unlike what you see today at Old Faithful - stores, a cabin complex, a large campground, post office, cafeteria, gas station, ranger station, etc. Today, all that is left is the old ranger station that is now a bookstore during the summer and warming hut in the winter.

Map 7-1

Grant District Trail Map

Hikable Trail
Old Road/Trail
Abandoned Trail
Maintained Road

Backcountry Campsite
Trailhead
NPS Patrol Cabin

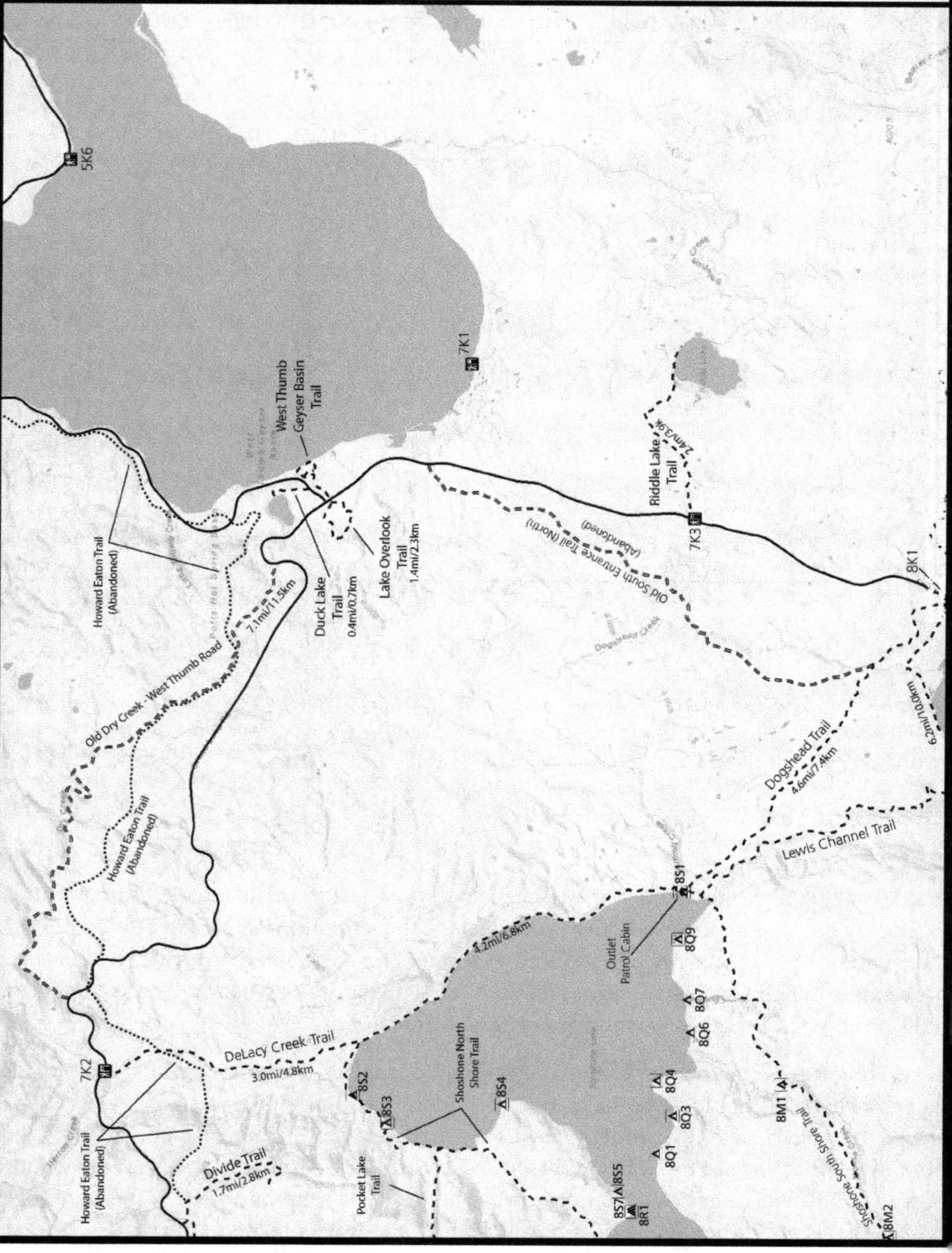

5K6
7K1
West Thumb Geyser Basin Trail
Riddle Lake Trail
2.4mi/3.9k
7K3
8K1
Old South Entrance Trail (North) (Abandoned)
Howard Eaton Trail (Abandoned)
Duck Lake Trail 0.4mi/0.7km
Lake Overlook Trail 1.4mi/2.3km
Old Dry Creek - West Thumb Road 7.1mi/11.5km
Howard Eaton Trail (Abandoned)
Dogshead Trail 4.6mi/7.4km
6.2mi/10.0km
Lewis Channel Trail
8S1
Outlet Patrol Cabin
8Q9
4.2mi/6.8km
8Q7
8Q6
DeLacy Creek Trail 3.0mi/4.8km
7K2
8S2
8S3
Shoshone North Shore Trail
8S4
8Q4
8Q3
8Q1
8M1
Shoshone South Shore Trail
Howard Eaton Trail (Abandoned)
Divide Trail 1.7mi/2.8km
Pocket Lake Trail
8S7
8S5
8R1
8M2

South District Trails

Basin Creek Cutoff Trail — MAP 8-1

Type:	PTP	**Cat:**	BC	**Class:**	B	**Surf:**	Trail	**Dist:**	8	**Status:**	E
Diff:	2	**Traf:**	2	**Child:**	N	**HAcc:**	N	**Use:**	H S	**Length:**	2.10
Elev A:	7380	**Elev B:**	7289	**Elev G:**	233	**Elev L:**	-324	**Net:**	-91	**BMA:**	O
Min:	7245	**Max:**	7380	**Avg:**	7299	**Avg +:**	4.8%	**Avg -:**	5.0%	**Open:**	7/1

Reference Point	A-B Mi	A-B Km	B-A Mi	B-A Km	Latitude	Longitude
North Trailhead @ jct w/ Heart Lake Trail	0.00	0.00	2.10	3.38	44.22483	-110.51397
Jct w/ abandoned section of Basin Creek C/O	0.30	0.48	1.80	2.90	44.22095	-110.51461
Basin Creek crossing (20 to 30')	0.71	1.14	1.39	2.24	44.21713	-110.50989
Campsite 8B3	0.72	1.16	1.38	2.22	44.21701	-110.50989
Spur trail to campsite 8B4 (0.03 miles)	1.39	2.24	0.71	1.14	44.20939	-110.50334
Spur trail to campsite 8B5 (0.02 miles)	1.62	2.61	0.48	0.77	44.20664	-110.50101
Basin Creek crossing (20 to 30')	1.68	2.70	0.42	0.68	44.20593	-110.50051
Terminus @ jct w/ Heart Rvr & Snake Rvr Canyon Trail	2.10	3.38	0.00	0.00	44.20075	-110.49960

The Basin Creek Cutoff is primarily designed as a crossover trail between the Heart Lake Trail on the west and the Snake River Canyon and Heart River Trails on the east, largely to facilitate travel between the west side of Heart Lake and the lower, middle section of the southeastern portion of the park. It is fairly heavily used by stock parties.

There are a couple of crossings of Basin Creek, but even early in the season they should not be a significant challenge.

Beula Lake Trail — MAP 8-3

Type:	O&B	**Cat:**	BC	**Class:**	B	**Surf:**	Trail	**Dist:**	8	**Status:**	E
Diff:	2	**Traf:**	1	**Child:**	N	**HAcc:**	N	**Use:**	H S	**Length:**	2.73
Elev A:	7255	**Elev B:**	7404	**Elev G:**	561	**Elev L:**	-412	**Net:**	149	**BMA:**	- -
Min:	7255	**Max:**	7648	**Avg:**	7538	**Avg +:**	6.9%	**Avg -:**	5.9%	**Open:**	YR

Reference Point	A-B Mi	A-B Km	B-A Mi	B-A Km	Latitude	Longitude
Trailhead 8K6 (Grassy Lake Rd ## mi W of Flagg Rch)	0.00	0.00	2.73	4.39	44.12561	-110.78629
Jct w/ South Boundary - Grassy Lake Trail	0.54	0.87	2.19	3.52	44.13263	-110.78835
Campsite 8A1/Beula Lake/Jct w/ Hering Lake Trail	2.58	4.15	0.15	0.24	44.15551	-110.76765
Campsite 8A2	2.67	4.30	0.06	0.10	44.15677	-110.76783
Terminus	2.73	4.39	0.00	0.00	44.15762	-110.76818

This trail takes you out to a gorgeous, remote backcountry lake that is usually teeming with waterfowl. It has been a common nesting area for loons over the past few years, and there is often an area closure to the west of the campsites due to the presence of loon nests (this trail is great for a relaxing day of bird-watching). The two campsites are nicely situated, though they are close to the trail. The trailhead is somewhat difficult to find and is not marked well, so use your GPS to locate it if possible. Once at the lake, there is a short spur trail to Hering Lake (see below).

Colter/Wolverine Trailhead Trail — MAP 8-1

Type:	PTP	**Cat:**	BC	**Class:**	C	**Surf:**	Trail	**Dist:**	8	**Status:**	E
Diff:	1	**Traf:**	1	**Child:**	N	**HAcc:**	N	**Use:**	H S	**Length:**	0.43
Elev A:	7090	**Elev B:**	7114	**Elev G:**	84	**Elev L:**	-60	**Net:**	24	**BMA:**	- -
Min:	7086	**Max:**	7137	**Avg:**	7108	**Avg +:**	5.2%	**Avg -:**	6.5%	**Open:**	YR

Reference Point	A-B Mi	A-B Km	B-A Mi	B-A Km	Latitude	Longitude
Trailhead @ jct w/ South Boundary Trail	0.00	0.00	0.43	0.69	44.13699	-110.51750
Coulter Creek crossing (30 to 40′)	0.23	0.37	0.20	0.32	44.13467	-110.51550
Park boundary TH 8K8 (continues into BTNF)	0.43	0.69	0.00	0.00	44.13260	-110.51342

This short spur trail takes you to the park boundary and into the Teton Wilderness, where you can take one of two trails depending upon where you want to go. One of these is the Coulter Creek Trail. Note that the name is spelled differently from the name of the Yellowstone trail. This comes from a mistake regarding the identity of the man for whom the trails were originally named.

Coulter Creek is named for John Merle Coulter, a gentleman who was a botanist in one of the Hayden Expeditions that explored this area in 1872. The creek bearing his name was given that after an incident in which Coulter, feeling a tap on his shoulder and believing it was one of his fellow explorers, turned to find that it was a bear that had tapped him. Coulter jumped into the water and swam across the creek to get away from the bear.

Seventeen years later, three park guides came across a tree in which the initials "J.C." were carved. Believing they must have been left by the famous explorer John Colter, they began referring to this trail by his name. So the trail bears the spelling of the explorer, but the creek bears the name of the botanist.[1]

Dogshead Trail — MAP 8-2,7-1

Type:	PTP	Cat:	BC	Class:	B	Surf:	Trail	Dist:	8	Status:	E
Diff:	2	Traf:	2	Child:	N	HAcc:	N	Use:	H S	Length:	4.62
Elev A:	7798	Elev B:	7806	Elev G:	683	Elev L:	-675	Net:	8	BMA:	- -
Min:	7795	Max:	8019	Avg:	7881	Avg +:	4.8%	Avg -:	4.8%	Open:	YR

Reference Point	A-B Mi	A-B Km	B-A Mi	B-A Km	Latitude	Longitude
Trailhead 8K1 (7.0 miles S of West Thumb Junction)	0.00	0.00	4.62	7.44	44.32009	-110.59953
Jct w/ old South Entrance Trail (North Segment)	1.26	2.03	3.36	5.41	44.33156	-110.61320
Dogshead Creek crossing	1.29	2.08	3.33	5.36	44.33160	-110.61374
Summit Creek crossing	4.43	7.13	0.19	0.31	44.35766	-110.65928
Terminus @ jct w/ DeLacy Creek & South Shore Trails	4.62	7.44	0.00	0.00	44.35932	44.35932

This is the shorter, but less scenic, of the two trails that lead from the Dogshead Trailhead to Shoshone Lake. The trail gets its name from the fact it crosses Dogshead Creek (and no one is really sure how that creek got its name). And though many people use it to get to the lake, many others use it as a part of a loop to the lake and back to the same trailhead via the other trail. So, for instance, you can take the more scenic route (the Lewis Channel Trail) to the lake, and then use this shorter trail to get back more quickly.

This is an almost flat route and the two creek crossings are tame. This is among the first trails in the southern area of the park to be cleared each season, and it is typically open by the end of May or first of June. This trail tends to be drier than the Lewis Channel Trail early in the season, however, so if you are looking to get into the lake area with the least amount of marshiness, this would be the preferred route.

The Dogshead Trail is a part of the Continental Divide Trail through Yellowstone, and was also an adjunct part of the Howard Eaton Trail system. On their longer tours, outfitters would take groups down to the Grand Teton area via the DeLacy Creek Trail and this route.

Harebell Cutoff Trail — MAP 8-1,6-4

Type:	PTP	**Cat:**	BC	**Class:**	B	**Surf:**	Trail	**Dist:**	8	**Status:**	E
Diff:	2	**Traf:**	1	**Child:**	N	**HAcc:**	N	**Use:**	H S	**Length:**	2.10
Elev A:	7187	**Elev B:**	7603	**Elev G:**	776	**Elev L:**	-360	**Net:**	416	**BMA:**	- -
Min:	7173	**Max:**	7716	**Avg:**	7425	**Avg +:**	11.1%	**Avg -:**	7.9%	**Open:**	YR

Reference Point	A-B Mi	A-B Km	B-A Mi	B-A Km	Latitude	Longitude
Trailhead @ jct w/ Snake River Canyon/SRCO Trails	0.00	0.00	2.10	3.38	44.16724	-110.48805
Snake River crossing (40 to 60')	0.11	0.18	1.99	3.20	44.16675	-110.48603
Harebell Cabin; Jct w/ South Boundary Trail	2.10	3.38	0.00	0.00	44.14107	-110.47766

This is a cutoff trail that takes you from the Snake River Cutoff to the Harebell Patrol Cabin and the South Boundary Trail. It is most often used to get people from the west side of Heart Lake down to the south boundary. There is a crossing of the Snake River immediately after entering the trail, but by the time you can get into this area (after trail clearing and the end of the bear restrictions), the crossing is usually passable on foot without much trouble.

Heart Lake Trail — MAP 8-1

Type:	PTP	**Cat:**	BC	**Class:**	A	**Surf:**	Trail	**Dist:**	8	**Status:**	E
Diff:	3	**Traf:**	3	**Child:**	N	**HAcc:**	N	**Use:**	H S	**Length:**	18.94
Elev A:	7791	**Elev B:**	6963	**Elev G:**	1864	**Elev L:**	-2692	**Net:**	-828	**BMA:**	O
Min:	6963	**Max:**	8149	**Avg:**	7557	**Avg +:**	3.1%	**Avg -:**	4.4%	**Open:**	7/1

Reference Point	A-B Mi	A-B Km	B-A Mi	B-A Km	Latitude	Longitude
Trailhead 8N1 (7.2 mi south of West Thumb Jct)	0.00	0.00	18.94	30.48	44.31744	-110.59825
West boundary - Heart Lake Geyser Basin	4.40	7.08	14.54	23.40	44.31057	-110.53301
Witch Creek crossing (north footbridge)	5.52	8.88	13.42	21.60	44.30351	-110.51973
Witch Creek crossing (south footbridge)	6.00	9.66	12.94	20.82	44.29822	-110.51642
Southeast boundary - Heart Lake Geyser Basin	6.93	11.15	12.01	19.33	44.29152	-110.50451
Heart Lake Patrol Cabin	7.47	12.02	11.47	18.46	44.28644	-110.49800
Jct with Trail Creek Trail	7.54	12.13	11.40	18.35	44.28542	-110.49776
Witch Creek crossing (Heart Lake footbridge)	7.73	12.44	11.21	18.04	44.28476	-110.50146
Heart Lake Geyser Basin - Rustic Group	7.93	12.76	11.01	17.72	44.28226	-110.50247
Spur trail to campsite 8H6 (0.05 mi)	8.07	12.99	10.87	17.49	44.28106	-110.50239
Spur trail to campsite 8H5 (0.10 mi)	8.10	13.04	10.84	17.45	44.28036	-110.50321
Jct with Mount Sheridan Trail	8.17	13.15	10.77	17.33	44.27941	-110.50390
Spur trail to campsite 8H4 (0.11 mi)	8.22	13.23	10.72	17.25	44.27885	-110.50453
Sheridan Creek crsg/Spur trail to 8H2/8H3 (0.17 mi)	8.92	14.36	10.02	16.13	44.26994	-110.50531
Extinct area of the Heart Lake Geyser Basin	9.85	15.85	9.09	14.63	44.25752	-110.50321
Spur trail to campsite 8H1 (0.10 mi)	9.89	15.92	9.05	14.56	44.25717	-110.50251
Social trail to Sheridan Lake	11.16	17.96	7.78	12.52	44.24274	-110.50267
Basin Creek Cutoff Trail	12.73	20.49	6.21	9.99	44.22483	-110.51397
Basin Creek crossing (20')	12.79	20.58	6.15	9.90	44.22483	-110.51509
Abandoned trail segment	12.87	20.71	6.07	9.77	44.22530	-110.51633
Jct w/ abandoned segment of old Basin Creek C/O	13.07	21.03	5.87	9.45	44.22247	-110.51823
Spur trail to campsite 8B2 (0.10 mi)	14.06	22.63	4.88	7.85	44.20971	-110.52375
Basin Creek Lake	14.10	22.69	4.84	7.79	44.20928	-110.52379
Red Creek crossing	16.63	26.76	2.31	3.72	44.18895	-110.55215
Spur trail to campsite 8C6	18.39	29.60	0.55	0.89	44.17481	-110.56922
Snake River crossing (60 to 120')	18.50	29.77	0.44	0.71	44.17377	-110.57096
Trailhead @ jct w/ South Boundary - Harebell Trail	18.94	30.48	0.00	0.00	44.16980	-110.57719

The Heart Lake Trail (a former road) is the most popular day-hike distance trail in the southern half of the park once it opens on July 1. A sizable number of people hike the 7.5 miles to the lake and the thermal area and then hike back out the same day. The trail is also a popular route for some people to get into the remote portions of the park's backcountry, especially those on horseback. This trail is part of the Continental Divide Trail in the park.

There is about a 400-foot (122m) climb over the first four miles, and then a 700-foot (213m) descent to the lake. That reverses on the way back, of course. If you continue south on the trail, you will continue to lose altitude very gradually, about 500 feet (152m) over the subsequent 11 miles. If you decide to travel northbound on this trail from the southern part of the park, it is a slow, steady climb until you get to the lake and begin to head back.

There are a number of good campsites along the west side of the lake, many of which are among the most popular in the park. If you need to camp in a specific area during a specific time frame, it might be best to consider reserving these sites in advance. A great many campers use the campsites as a base from which to launch a climb of Mt. Sheridan, the site of one of the park's old fire lookout towers. I know people who have hiked all the way in to the summit of Sheridan and back (a 23-mile round trip) on the same day, but it is not for the faint of heart (and you don't really get a chance to enjoy the scenery doing it that way).

On the way to the lake you will pass along and through the Heart Lake Geyser Basin, one of the park's largest with over 400 identified thermal features, and along the base of Factory Hill. Keep in mind that it is illegal and very unsafe to travel off trail into the basin itself, or to get into any of the thermal features. There are places along Witch Creek where you can soak and enjoy the warm runoff from the thermal fields, however, and this is perfectly legal. Given that this water is primarily runoff from chemically active water, you are probably not going to want to drink it. The only water source on the trail will be the lake itself (until you head south).

Factory Hill got its name from one of the expeditions in the 1880s. They felt that the steam emanating from the thermal vents along the base of it resembled factory towns in the eastern United States. It was along the east side of this hill that park geologist Rick Hutchinson and an associate geologist working with him, Diane Dustman, were killed by an avalanche in early 1997.

The Heart Lake Patrol Cabin is located at the junction of this trail and the Trail Creek Trail (which runs along the north side of the lake). This cabin is staffed most of the summer, and rangers regularly patrol the thermal areas and the campsites. If you run into some kind of emergency and can get to the cabin before hiking out or sending someone out for help, consider doing that first.

Heading south from the lake, you will get back into heavily forested areas and pass by Sheridan Lake (which has a population of cutthroats and shiners) and then to the junction with the Basin Creek Cutoff. This trail will take you down to the Heart River and Snake River Canyon trails. Continue right to remain on the Heart Lake Trail. You will pass Basin Creek Lake and then make your way along Red Creek southward to the South Boundary Trail. Just prior to that junction you will have to ford the Snake River which, by the time you can get into this part of the backcountry, should be crossable without any issues.

Heart River Trail

MAP 8-1,6-4

Type:	PTP	Cat:	BC	Class:	B	Surf:	Trail	Dist:	8	Status:	E
Diff:	2	Traf:	2	Child:	N	HAcc:	N	Use:	H S	Length:	5.66
Elev A:	7276	Elev B:	7489	Elev G:	795	Elev L:	-582	Net:	213	BMA:	O
Min:	7246	Max:	7492	Avg:	7353	Avg +:	3.9%	Avg -:	3.7%	Open:	7/1

Reference Point	A-B Mi	A-B Km	B-A Mi	B-A Km	Latitude	Longitude
Trailhead @ jct w/ Snake River Canyon & BC C/O Tr	0.00	0.00	5.66	9.11	44.20075	-110.49960
Snake River crossing (70 to 120′)	0.88	1.42	4.78	7.69	44.20740	-110.48507
Snake River crossing (50 to 60′)	2.19	3.52	3.47	5.58	44.21403	-110.46183
Spur trail to campsite 8C5 (0.05 miles)	2.24	3.60	3.42	5.50	44.21442	-110.46109
Jct w/ Fox Creek Trail	2.53	4.07	3.13	5.04	44.21746	-110.46285
Heart River crossing (25 to 40′)	2.94	4.73	2.72	4.38	44.22266	-110.46549
Heart River crossing (50′)	5.16	8.30	0.50	0.80	44.24646	-110.44351
Outlet Creek crossing (35′)	5.28	8.50	0.38	0.61	44.24760	-110.44504
Spur trail to campsite 8J4 (0.02 miles)	5.30	8.53	0.36	0.58	44.24788	-110.44514
Trailhead @ jct w/ Trail Creek Trail	5.66	9.11	0.00	0.00	44.25265	-110.44318

The Heart River Trail takes you from the Snake River Canyon Trail northward to the Trail Creek Trail, mostly along the Snake River and the Heart River. This trail is used quite frequently by people who begin their hike at the Heart Lake trailhead and want to head on down to the southern boundary trail system.

Traveling the length of this trail requires two fords of the Snake River and two of the Heart River. The Heart River crossings will not be too substantial, but the Snake River crossings could be pretty deep early in the season (thigh to waist deep until mid-July). The northern half of this trail is a part of the Continental Divide Trail (from the Fox Creek Trail to the Trail Creek Trail). However, as it is closed until July 1, through hikers will need to take an alternate route if they arrive prior to that date.

Heart River and its headwater lake are named after an infamous hunter named Hart Hunney and not the heart-shaped appearance of the lake (notwithstanding the misspelling of his name).[2]

Hering Lake Spur Trail

MAP 8-3

Type:	PTP	Cat:	BC	Class:	U	Surf:	Trail	Dist:	8	Status:	U
Diff:	1	Traf:	1	Child:	N	HAcc:	N	Use:	H S	Length:	0.40
Elev A:	7412	Elev B:	7410	Elev G:	56	Elev L:	-58	Net:	-2	BMA:	- -
Min:	7401	Max:	7414	Avg:	7406	Avg +:	5.4%	Avg -:	4.7%	Open:	YR

Reference Point	A-B Mi	A-B Km	B-A Mi	B-A Km	Latitude	Longitude
Trailhead @ jct w/ Beula Lake Trail	0.00	0.00	0.40	0.64	44.15551	-110.76765
Hering Lake	0.40	0.64	0.00	0.00	44.15078	-110.76509

Hering Lake is a small lake situated southeast of Beula Lake. It is named after Rudolph Hering, a topographer on one of the Hayden expeditions.[3] The lake is believed to contain a small population of cutthroat trout.

This trail is not an official park trail and is unmaintained by the NPS. You basically follow a small creek that drains Hering Lake into Beula Lake. The entire area can be rather marshy well into August.

Lewis Channel Trail — MAP 8-2

TYPE:	PTP	CAT:	BC	CLASS:	B	SURF:	TRAIL	DIST:	8	STATUS:	E
DIFF:	2	TRAF:	3	CHILD:	N	HACC:	N	USE:	H S	LENGTH:	6.19
ELEV A:	7798	ELEV B:	7807	ELEV G:	891	ELEV L:	-882	NET:	9	BMA:	- -
MIN:	7782	MAX:	7866	AVG:	7807	AVG +:	4.4%	AVG -:	4.4%	OPEN:	YR

Reference Point	A-B Mi	A-B Km	B-A Mi	B-A Km	Latitude	Longitude
Trailhead 8K1 (7.0 miles S of West Thumb Junction)	0.00	0.00	6.19	9.96	44.32009	-110.59953
Dogshead Creek crossing	0.87	1.40	5.32	8.56	44.32670	-110.61389
Lewis Lake	1.36	2.19	4.83	7.77	44.32281	-110.62111
Lewis Lake (from the W)	1.80	2.90	4.39	7.07	44.32012	-110.62835
Pick up the Lewis Channel (heading west)	3.17	5.10	3.02	4.86	44.32397	-110.64351
Summit Creek crossing	6.00	9.66	0.19	0.31	44.35571	-110.66089
Terminus @ jct w/ Shoshone Lake South Shore Trail	6.19	9.96	0.00	0.00	44.35718	-110.66316

The Lewis Channel Trail is one of two trails that lead from the Dogshead/Lewis Channel Trailhead to Shoshone Lake. It is the longer of the two, but it is also the more scenic, at least after the first three miles. Many hikers make a day hike loop by hiking up to the lake on this trail and then taking the shorter, quicker Dogshead Trail back to the trailhead.

This trail typically becomes snow-free around the same time as the Dogshead Trail, but in some years parts of it will remain waterlogged and/or marshy until well into July.

Moose Falls - South Entrance Trail — MAP 8-3

TYPE:	PTP	CAT:	BC	CLASS:	N	SURF:	TRAIL	DIST:	8	STATUS:	U
DIFF:	2	TRAF:	1	CHILD:	N	HACC:	N	USE:	H K	LENGTH:	1.43
ELEV A:	6890	ELEV B:	6977	ELEV G:	295	ELEV L:	-208	NET:	87	BMA:	- -
MIN:	6867	MAX:	7018	AVG:	6916	AVG +:	6.5%	AVG -:	6.0%	OPEN:	YR

Reference Point	A-B Mi	A-B Km	B-A Mi	B-A Km	Latitude	Longitude
Trailhead @ Snake River Picnic Area	0.00	0.00	1.43	2.30	44.13689	-110.66596
Confluence of Lewis River and Snake River	0.31	0.50	1.12	1.80	44.14129	-110.66357
Confluence of Crawfish Creek & Lewis River	1.19	1.92	0.24	0.39	44.15008	-110.66894
Moose Falls	1.43	2.30	0.00	0.00	44.15178	-110.67275

This is an unofficial (and therefore unmaintained) trail that leads from the Snake River Ranger Station north to Moose Falls. It is popular with the employees at the South Entrance, but is little used by the public. Since there is roadside access to the falls, there is little reason for the public to hike this route, but it is very scenic as it parallels the Snake River, the Lewis River, and Crawfish Creek for its entire path.

Mount Sheridan Trail — MAP 8-1

TYPE:	O&B	CAT:	BC	CLASS:	B	SURF:	TRAIL	DIST:	8	STATUS:	E
DIFF:	4	TRAF:	2	CHILD:	N	HACC:	N	USE:	H S	LENGTH:	3.51
ELEV A:	7496	ELEV B:	10298	ELEV G:	2834	ELEV L:	-32	NET:	2802	BMA:	O
MIN:	7496	MAX:	10298	AVG:	8841	AVG +:	15.4%	AVG -:	4.7%	OPEN:	7/1

Reference Point	A-B Mi	A-B Km	B-A Mi	B-A Km	Latitude	Longitude
Trailhead @ jct w/ Heart Lake Trail	0.00	0.00	3.51	5.65	44.27941	-110.50390
Social trail to overlook of Heart Lake GB (Rustic Grp)	0.30	0.48	3.21	5.17	44.27837	-110.50960
Summit/Fire Lookout	3.51	5.65	0.00	0.00	44.26608	-110.52924

The hike up to the summit of Mt. Sheridan is one of the most spectacular in the park, and one of the most popular for those who camp around the western side of Heart Lake. The trail does have a 2,800-foot (853m) climb over its 3.5 miles, but the trail is routed so that it is a steady, gradual climb. The trail was constructed by park crews in 1926.

Once you get to the top of the mountain, you will see the old fire lookout tower. For many years, this tower, along with those on Mt. Holmes and Mt. Washburn, were staffed during the summer to keep an eye out for wildfires. Sheridan and Holmes are no longer staffed except in periods of extreme fire danger, but the lookout does contain some of the park's important radio equipment.

Once you are on top, you can see why Mt. Sheridan was selected as a lookout. The 360-degree viewscape from the summit provides an incredible view of the Pitchstone Plateau to the west, the Tetons to the south, the Absaroka Range to the east, and Heart Lake and Yellowstone Lake to the north.

It is possible to hike to the summit from the Heart Lake trailhead and get back before dark during the height of the summer. It's a total of 23 miles for the round trip, however, and should not be attempted unless you are in good physical condition. After the snow melts in the late spring, there is no water source at all along the trail, so be sure to load up before you begin your climb.

North Shore Shoshone Lake Trail — MAP 8-2

TYPE:	PTP	CAT:	BC	CLASS:	B	SURF:	TRAIL	DIST:	8	STATUS:	E
DIFF:	3	TRAF:	2	CHILD:	N	HACC:	N	USE:	H S	LENGTH:	7.98
ELEV A:	7860	ELEV B:	7796	ELEV G:	1574	ELEV L:	-1638	NET:	-64	BMA:	- -
MIN:	7791	MAX:	8053	AVG:	7906	AVG +:	6.2%	AVG -:	6.7%	OPEN:	YR

Reference Point	A-B Mi	A-B Km	B-A Mi	B-A Km	Latitude	Longitude
Trailhead @ jct w/ Shoshone Lake Trail	0.00	0.00	7.98	12.84	44.35857	-110.79590
Spur trail to campsite 8R5 (0.40 miles)	0.22	0.35	7.76	12.49	44.35917	-110.79252
Cove Patrol Cabin Spur Trail	2.99	4.81	4.99	8.03	44.36999	-110.75028
Spur trail to campsite 8R3 (0.17 miles)	3.12	5.02	4.86	7.82	44.37026	-110.74785
Spur trail to campsite 8R2 (0.17 miles)	3.21	5.17	4.77	7.68	44.37070	-110.74614
Jct w/ Pocket Lake Trail	5.90	9.50	2.08	3.35	44.39601	-110.71796
Spur trail to campsite 8S3 (0.04 miles)	6.81	10.96	1.17	1.88	44.40495	-110.71254
Campsite 8S2	7.30	11.75	0.68	1.09	44.40951	-110.70652
DeLacy Creek crossing	7.56	12.17	0.42	0.68	44.41073	-110.70225
Jct w/ DeLacy Creek Trail	7.98	12.84	0.00	0.00	44.40843	-110.69490

The trail around the north side of Shoshone Lake is, contrary to what one might expect, not the most scenic trail in the park. The vast majority of it is forested and has little or no view of the lake, save for the easternmost one-fifth of the trail. That part of it skirts along the coast and eventually crosses over DeLacy Creek just before it connects with the trail of the same name.

There are a handful of minor stream crossings along this trail, most of which are actually dry once the snow melt has completed. This trail is also the primary way to access a handful of the campsites that lie along the shore of the lake. There is a short, fairly new trail that takes you to the small Pocket Lake, just northwest of the horn of the lake's eastern side (see below).

Old South Road Hiking/Bike Trail

MAP 8-3,8-1

TYPE:	PTP	**CAT:**	BC	**CLASS:**	N	**SURF:**	TRAIL	**DIST:**	8	**STATUS:**	R
DIFF:	2	**TRAF:**	1	**CHILD:**	N	**HACC:**	N	**USE:**	H K	**LENGTH:**	5.10
ELEV A:	7235	**ELEV B:**	7710	**ELEV G:**	885	**ELEV L:**	-409	**NET:**	475	**BMA:**	- -
MIN:	7234	**MAX:**	7888	**AVG:**	7653	**AVG +:**	4.8%	**AVG -:**	3.5%	**OPEN:**	YR

Reference Point	A-B Mi	A-B Km	B-A Mi	B-A Km	Latitude	Longitude
Unmarked trailhead @ pullout 4 miles N of South Ent	0.00	0.00	5.10	8.21	44.16478	-110.66676
Old Pulloff/Picnic Area	1.36	2.19	3.74	6.02	44.18348	-110.66347
North end of trail/terminus	5.10	8.21	0.00	0.00	44.23235	-110.65347

This is one of the true gems of park hiking - an old roadbed that is still fairly easily accessible and in good shape such that there is not a lot of bushwhacking required to get from one end to the other. This trail starts at an unmarked pullout four miles north of the South Entrance. The only way you'll know you are at the correct pullout is by finding the swing gate that is still in place to keep vehicles from traveling up the old path. As you head north from the gate, you'll still see the old bicycle placard attached to a post (though there is too much deadfall to bike on it now). No one knows for sure why this trail was abandoned, and it is likely that it was simply left to die off from general lack of use since few hikers realize it is there.

This was once a long segment of the original road built from the south entrance up to West Thumb. The new alignment was established in the mid-1930s and put the road much closer to Lewis Canyon for its scenic beauty. As you hike along the old route you will occasionally see the old asphalt and debris left over from its original use.

On the north end of this trail there is no pullout and it is almost impossible to find the end of the road. So it is pretty much a requirement that you hike from the south. The only "feature" of any kind is an old pulloff that used to be an informal picnic area. This is an excellent trail for someone looking to do some hiking simply for exercise.

Pitchstone Plateau Trail

MAP 8-3

TYPE:	PTP	**CAT:**	BC	**CLASS:**	B	**SURF:**	TRAIL	**DIST:**	8	**STATUS:**	E
DIFF:	4	**TRAF:**	1	**CHILD:**	N	**HACC:**	N	**USE:**	H S	**LENGTH:**	17.18
ELEV A:	7750	**ELEV B:**	7091	**ELEV G:**	1718	**ELEV L:**	-2377	**NET:**	-659	**BMA:**	- -
MIN:	7079	**MAX:**	8785	**AVG:**	8229	**AVG +:**	4.0%	**AVG -:**	4.6%	**OPEN:**	YR

Reference Point	A-B Mi	A-B Km	B-A Mi	B-A Km	Latitude	Longitude
Trailhead 8K4 (8.2 miles N of South Entrance)	0.00	0.00	17.18	27.65	44.24324	-110.64732
Phantom Fumarole Thermal Area	4.62	7.44	12.56	20.21	44.24198	-110.72293
Spur trails to campsites 8P1 (.03 mi) & 8P2 (.06 mi)	5.91	9.51	11.27	18.14	44.22975	-110.73902
Divert around southern aspect of plateau	14.97	24.09	2.21	3.56	44.16006	-110.81435
Proposition Creek crossing (usually dry)	15.35	24.70	1.83	2.95	44.15546	-110.81703
Spur trail to campsite 9F2 (0.04 miles)	17.02	27.39	0.16	0.26	44.14044	-110.83712
Trailhead @ jct w/ Mountain Ash Creek Trail	17.18	27.65	0.00	0.00	44.14126	-110.83969

The Pitchstone Plateau is one of the park's most interesting and least explored areas. Pitchstone is a dull black glassy volcanic rock that is similar to obsidian (also present in the Yellowstone area) formed when lava cools quickly. The plateau is the youngest lava extrusion from the park's volcanic subsurface, having issued forth only 70,000 years ago. This large, flat expanse is largely ignored by many of the park's visitors today.

This hike begins with a steep climb up onto the plateau, and then remains relatively flat fo the first ten miles of the trek. Then it begins a slow, gradual descent into the Cascade Corne region of the park.

The vast majority of hikers hike out either to Phantom Fumarole and return, or hike out t one of the two campsites to spend the night and then return. A few hardy souls continu southward and use this trail to create a loop that takes them into the southwest corner o the park to come out at some other trailhead. Because this trail is so lightly used, it does no get cleared until late in the season, and the lower half of it can be difficult to hike without compass and map or a GPS. You will also want to take plenty of water with you as there i no water source after the spring dries up each season (typically in August).

Pocket Lake Trail — MAP 8-2

TYPE:	O&B	CAT:	BC	CLASS:	C	SURF:	TRAIL	DIST:	8	STATUS:	E
DIFF:	2	TRAF:	1	CHILD:	N	HACC:	N	USE:	H	LENGTH:	1.19
ELEV A:	7841	ELEV B:	8140	ELEV G:	562	ELEV L:	-264	NET:	299	BMA:	- -
MIN:	7819	MAX:	8289	AVG:	8010	AVG +:	11.1%	AVG -:	11.3%	OPEN:	YR

Reference Point	A-B Mi	A-B Km	B-A Mi	B-A Km	Latitude	Longitude
Trailhead @ jct with Shoshone Lake North Shore	0.00	0.00	1.19	1.92	44.39601	-110.71796
Pocket Lake	1.19	1.92	0.00	0.00	44.36948	-110.74015

The trail to Pocket Lake is little used but easy to follow. This newer trail takes you back to a small lake named for the fact it is located in a little pocket in the woods. The lake does have a population of cutthroat trout, but unless you are a fisherman, there is no real reason to go

Shoshone Lake Trail — MAP 8-2

TYPE:	PTP	CAT:	BC	CLASS:	A	SURF:	TRAIL	DIST:	8	STATUS:	E
DIFF:	3	TRAF:	2	CHILD:	N	HACC:	N	USE:	H S K	LENGTH:	6.92
ELEV A:	7661	ELEV B:	7822	ELEV G:	1045	ELEV L:	-885	NET:	161	BMA:	- -
MIN:	7642	MAX:	8058	AVG:	7843	AVG +:	4.4%	AVG -:	4.3%	OPEN:	YR

Reference Point	A-B Mi	A-B Km	B-A Mi	B-A Km	Latitude	Longitude
Trailhead @ jct w/ Lone Star & HET - OF to LS	0.00	0.00	6.92	11.14	44.41948	-110.81047
Spur trail to campsite OA1	0.16	0.26	6.76	10.88	44.41792	-110.81262
Enter Lone Star Geyser Basin (North)	0.24	0.39	6.68	10.75	44.41683	-110.81331
Firehole River crossing (bridge)	0.28	0.45	6.64	10.69	44.41643	-110.81365
Spur trail to campsite OA2	0.62	1.00	6.30	10.14	44.41343	-110.81846
Spur trail to campsite OA3	1.36	2.19	5.56	8.95	44.40512	-110.82618
Boardwalk segment	1.49	2.40	5.43	8.74	44.40334	-110.82692
Enter Lone Star Geyser Basin (South)	1.72	2.77	5.20	8.37	44.40020	-110.82732
Grant's Pass	3.49	5.62	3.43	5.52	44.37881	-110.82238
Jct w/ Bechler River Trail	3.80	6.12	3.12	5.02	44.37513	-110.81948
Spur trail to campsite 8G1	3.93	6.32	2.99	4.81	44.37395	-110.81741
Shoshone Creek crossing (10-20')	4.21	6.78	2.71	4.36	44.37186	-110.81268
Shoshone Geyser Basin Stock Cutoff Trail	4.82	7.76	2.10	3.38	44.36584	-110.80631
Jct w/ Shoshone Lake North Shore Trail	5.86	9.43	1.06	1.71	44.35857	-110.79590
Jct w/ Shoshone Geyser Basin Spur Trail (SGB)	5.95	9.58	0.97	1.56	44.35772	-110.79505
Enter Shoshone Geyser Basin (South)	6.56	10.56	0.36	0.58	44.35050	-110.79796
Shoshone Creek crossing (10 to 20')	6.61	10.64	0.31	0.50	44.34988	-110.79831
Jct w/ Horse Cutoff & South Shore Trails	6.92	11.14	0.00	0.00	44.34618	-110.79539

Shoshone Lake is the largest backcountry lakes in the lower 48 states, and it is one of the most popular hiking/camping destinations in the park. This particular trail takes you to the lake and to Shoshone Geyser Basin from the Old Faithful/Lone Star Geyser area, and you can use it to get onto the North Shore or the South Shore Trails, the two trails that take you either north or south of the lake itself (respectively). The trail is also the northern access to the Bechler River Trail.

The north end of this trail has the three campsites that get listed as the "Lone Star" campsites, even though they are a ways south of the geyser itself. These sites are easy to get to for those looking for quick access to a campsite, however.

Heading south from Lone Star, you will climb 350 feet (107m) over the course of ¾ of a mile to Grants Pass (named after the U.S. President). The pass is typically snowed in until early July, though it can often be negotiated earlier than that if you don't mind a bit of postholing.

The southern half of the trail takes you into Shoshone Geyser Basin, home to about 500 or so thermal features, over 100 of which are geysers. Approximately 70 of the features have names. In the past, there were several social trails in and around the thermal field. However, visitors vandalizing the features led to the NPS closing all but the main trail through this area, so now it is impossible to get good views of many of its more interesting thermal features.

This trail is part of the Continental Divide Trail through the park.

Shoshone Geyser Basin Spur Trail — MAP 8-2

Type:	O&B	**Cat:**	BC	**Class:**	C	**Surf:**	Trail	**Dist:**	8	**Status:**	E
Diff:	1	**Traf:**	2	**Child:**	N	**HAcc:**	N	**Use:**	H	**Length:**	0.21
Elev A:	7825	**Elev B:**	7803	**Elev G:**	34	**Elev L:**	-56	**Net:**	-22	**BMA:**	- -
Min:		**Max:**		**Avg:**		**Avg +:**	0.0%	**Avg -:**	0.0%	**Open:**	YR

Reference Point	A-B Mi	A-B Km	B-A Mi	B-A Km	Latitude	Longitude
Trailhead @ jct w/ Shoshone Lake Trail	0.00	0.00	0.21	0.34	44.35772	-110.79505
Trail terminus at lakeside	0.21	0.34	0.00	0.00	44.35633	-110.79267

This is a short little spur that takes you around the north side of the thermal field at Shoshone Lake to allow you to access more thermal features. There are another two to three dozen scattered along the edges of the trail as it winds around the hill and over to the lake. Be sure to remain on the trail surface in this area (if it is still open when you arrive).

Shoshone Geyser Basin Stock Cutoff Trail — MAP 8-2,9-3

Type:	PTP	**Cat:**	BC	**Class:**	B	**Surf:**	Trail	**Dist:**	8	**Status:**	E
Diff:	1	**Traf:**	1	**Child:**	N	**HAcc:**	N	**Use:**	H S	**Length:**	2.22
Elev A:	7843	**Elev B:**	7823	**Elev G:**	543	**Elev L:**	-563	**Net:**	-20	**BMA:**	- -
Min:	7823	**Max:**	8020	**Avg:**	7911	**Avg +:**	9.4%	**Avg -:**	8.7%	**Open:**	YR

Reference Point	A-B Mi	A-B Km	B-A Mi	B-A Km	Latitude	Longitude
Trailhead @ jct w/ Shoshone Lake Trail	0.00	0.00	2.22	3.57	44.36584	-110.80631
Squirrel Creek crossing	0.60	0.97	1.62	2.61	44.35636	-110.80790
Swamp Lake to the west (over ridge)	1.41	2.27	0.81	1.30	44.34999	-110.80699
Fall Creek crossing	1.54	2.48	0.68	1.09	44.34868	-110.80617
Trailhead @ jct w/ Shoshone Lake South S Trail	2.22	3.57	0.00	0.00	44.34618	-110.79539

Stock is not permitted in the park's thermal fields, so if you are on horseback or have othe stock carrying equipment, you will need to take this trail around the western edge of th thermal area if you are headed north or south around the lake. There are a couple of minc creek crossings along this trail, but neither should be problematic for horses or humans.

Snake River Canyon Trail

MAP 8-1,6-

TYPE:	PTP	**CAT:**	BC	**CLASS:**	B	**SURF:**	TRAIL	**DIST:**	8	**STATUS:**	E
DIFF:	1	**TRAF:**	1	**CHILD:**	N	**HACC:**	N	**USE:**	H S	**LENGTH:**	2.59
ELEV A:	7187	**ELEV B:**	7274	**ELEV G:**	328	**ELEV L:**	-242	**NET:**	87	**BMA:**	- -
MIN:	7181	**MAX:**	7277	**AVG:**	7212	**AVG +:**	4.0%	**AVG -:**	3.6%	**OPEN:**	YR

Reference Point	**A-B Mi**	**A-B Km**	**B-A Mi**	**B-A Km**	**Latitude**	**Longitud**
Trailhead @ jct/ Snake River & Harebell Cutoff Trails	0.00	0.00	2.59	4.17	44.16724	-110.4880
Spur trail to campsite 8C4 (0.05 miles)	0.23	0.37	2.36	3.80	44.17026	-110.4891
Basin Creek crossing (15 to 20')	1.98	3.19	0.61	0.98	44.19357	-110.4938
Terminus @ jct w/ Basin Creek & Heart River Trails	2.59	4.17	0.00	0.00	44.20075	-110.4996

The Snake River Canyon Trail takes you north or south between two sets of trail splits. C the north end you have the two trails that come from either side of Heart Lake. On the sout end you have two trails that take you either east or west along the south boundary. A goc number of hikers make a "loop" from the Heart Lake Trail down past the lake, and the head south on this trail and the Snake River Cutoff (see below) and come out at the Snal River Ranger Station at the South Entrance. The one campsite along the trail is lightly use

Snake River Cutoff Trail

MAP 8-1,6-

TYPE:	PTP	**CAT:**	BC	**CLASS:**	B	**SURF:**	TRAIL	**DIST:**	8	**STATUS:**	E
DIFF:	2	**TRAF:**	1	**CHILD:**	N	**HACC:**	N	**USE:**	H S	**LENGTH:**	3.31
ELEV A:	7050	**ELEV B:**	7187	**ELEV G:**	718	**ELEV L:**	-581	**NET:**	137	**BMA:**	- -
MIN:	7033	**MAX:**	7461	**AVG:**	7264	**AVG +:**	7.3%	**AVG -:**	6.9%	**OPEN:**	YR

Reference Point	**A-B Mi**	**A-B Km**	**B-A Mi**	**B-A Km**	**Latitude**	**Longitud**
Trailhead @ jct with South Boundary - Harebell Trail	0.00	0.00	3.31	5.33	44.15098	-110.5337
Snake River crossing (100 to 125')	0.08	0.13	3.23	5.20	44.15159	-110.5325
Trailhead @ jct w/ Snake River Canyon Trail	3.31	5.33	0.00	0.00	44.16724	-110.4880

This trail serves as a cutoff from the Snake River Canyon Trail to the western half of t east segment of the South Boundary Trail (quite the geographic tongue-twister there, no If you are heading south from the east side of Heart Lake and would like to return to t South Entrance, or if you have come in from the South Entrance and would like to head the east side of the lake, this is the trail you would use. Being one of the lesser used trai this one may be a bit difficult to follow until later into the season.

Snake River Lookout Trail

MAP 8-3,8-

TYPE:	PTP	**CAT:**	BC	**CLASS:**	N	**SURF:**	TRAIL	**DIST:**	8	**STATUS:**	A
DIFF:	4	**TRAF:**	1	**CHILD:**	N	**HACC:**	N	**USE:**	H	**LENGTH:**	1.70
ELEV A:	6895	**ELEV B:**	8172	**ELEV G:**	1509	**ELEV L:**	-233	**NET:**	1277	**BMA:**	- -
MIN:	6895	**MAX:**	8176	**AVG:**	7376	**AVG +:**	20.6%	**AVG -:**	10.1%	**OPEN:**	YR

Reference Point	**A-B Mi**	**A-B Km**	**B-A Mi**	**B-A Km**	**Latitude**	**Longituc**
Trailhead @ jct w/ South Boundary - Harebell Trail	0.00	0.00	1.70	2.74	44.14532	-110.652
Summit/Fire Lookout	1.70	2.74	0.00	0.00	44.14120	-110.630

his short but steep unmaintained trail takes you up to the old Snake River Fire Lookout, ne of the few remaining lookouts built by the Civilian Conservation Corps throughout the ark in the 1930s. The lookout is no longer used, but remains standing.[4] It is an interesting de trip for those who wish to experience a bit of park history. The trail is not marked and an be difficult to follow at times.

outh Boundary Trail: Harebell — MAP 8-1

YPE:	PTP	CAT:	BC	CLASS:	A	SURF:	TRAIL	DIST:	8	STATUS:	E
IFF:	2	TRAF:	2	CHILD:	N	HACC:	N	USE:	H S	LENGTH:	12.26
LEV A:	6886	ELEV B:	7583	ELEV G:	1813	ELEV L:	-1116	NET:	697	BMA:	- -
IIN:	6861	MAX:	7640	AVG:	7079	AVG +:	3.9%	AVG -:	3.6%	OPEN:	YR

eference Point	A-B Mi	A-B Km	B-A Mi	B-A Km	Latitude	Longitude
ailhead 8K7 (Behind Ranger Station)	0.00	0.00	12.26	19.73	44.13644	-110.66601
nake River crossing (200')	0.12	0.19	12.14	19.54	44.13551	-110.66459
t w/ Sheffield Creek Trail to Snake River Bridge	0.62	1.00	11.64	18.73	44.13757	-110.65756
outh Boundary Thermal Area	0.94	1.51	11.32	18.22	44.14184	-110.65753
bandoned trail to fire lookout	1.32	2.12	10.94	17.61	44.14532	-110.65206
nake River Hot Springs	4.97	8.00	7.29	11.73	44.16826	-110.59127
ampsite 8C1	5.22	8.40	7.04	11.33	44.16867	-110.58664
ampsite 8C7	5.57	8.96	6.69	10.77	44.16894	-110.57990
t w/ Heart Lake Trail	5.73	9.22	6.53	10.51	44.16980	-110.57719
t w/ Snake River Cutoff Trail/9-Mile Meadow	8.49	13.66	3.77	6.07	44.15098	-110.53378
pur trail to campsite 8C2 (0.19 miles)	8.85	14.24	3.41	5.49	44.14708	-110.52934
oulter Creek crossing (40 to 60')	9.83	15.82	2.43	3.91	44.13737	-110.51899
t w/ Colter/Wolverine Trail	9.92	15.96	2.34	3.77	44.13699	-110.51750
t w/ Harebell Cutoff/South Boundary - Fox Creek Tr	12.26	19.73	0.00	0.00	44.14107	-110.47766

his is the first segment of the eastern half of the South Boundary Trail. It takes you from the outh Entrance to the Harebell Patrol Cabin. This trail scoots around the northern aspect f Huckleberry Ridge, so it does not explicitly follow the park boundary like many of the ther trail segments do. At the west end of the trail you will have to ford the Snake River. his is typically not feasible until well into July in most seasons. From then the river will be igh-calf to mid-thigh deep depending upon rainfall levels upstream.

s an alternative, if you are trying to go in when the Snake River is too high, you can use the heffield Creek trailhead located just south of the bridge over the Snake River just south of lagg Ranch. This will add three miles to the beginning of your hike.

his trail is primarily through forested area except for the very eastern third, which is mainly n open area with the occasional tree here and there. The trail is often marshy early on, argely because of runoff from snow melt off the ridge. It passes through two small thermal elds, the South Boundary Trail Thermal Area just east of the river ford, and the Snake River hermal Area just west of the Heart Lake Trail, each with two dozen unnamed features.

outh Boundary Trail: South Ent to Grassy Lake — MAP 8-3

YPE:	PTP	CAT:	BC	CLASS:	B	SURF:	TRAIL	DIST:	8	STATUS:	E
IFF:	2	TRAF:	1	CHILD:	N	HACC:	N	USE:	H S	LENGTH:	8.15
LEV A:	6943	ELEV B:	7123	ELEV G:	1030	ELEV L:	-850	NET:	180	BMA:	- -
IIN:	6943	MAX:	7714	AVG:	7298	AVG +:	5.0%	AVG -:	3.7%	OPEN:	YR

Reference Point	A-B Mi	A-B Km	B-A Mi	B-A Km	Latitude	Longitude
Trailhead 8K5 (South Entrance Gov't Housing Area)	0.00	0.00	8.15	13.12	44.13436	-110.66894
Social trail to Tanager Lake	0.63	1.01	7.52	12.10	44.13182	-110.67944
Unnamed creek - follow back to Tanager Lake	0.75	1.21	7.40	11.91	44.13038	-110.68013
Polecat Creek crossing (25')	2.48	3.99	5.67	9.12	44.13313	-110.70904
Glade Creek crossing (may be dry)	4.65	7.48	3.50	5.63	44.13272	-110.75032
South Boundary Lake	4.98	8.01	3.17	5.10	44.13242	-110.75686
Jct w/ Beula Lake Trail	6.58	10.59	1.57	2.53	44.13263	-110.78835
Trailhead @ Grassy Lake Reservoir	8.15	13.12	0.00	0.00	44.13253	-110.81957

This section of the South Boundary Trail runs westward from the Snake River Range Station to the Grassy Lake Reservoir, lying right on the boundary for much of its path. Th trail begins behind the horse corrals in the government housing area across the road fro the ranger station itself. Park in the picnic area behind the ranger station and walk across th road, paying close attention to the vehicles driving along the road here (drivers are often no paying attention to what they are doing). Walk along the little pathway in the woods righ across from the entrance kiosks and head into the housing area. You will see the corral o to your 11 o'clock position. Once you get there you will see the orange marker on the nort side of the corral and away you go.

As you head west, you will pass Tanager Lake, visible off in the distance. There is no officia trail to it, but you can hike back to it if you wish. You will ford Polecat Creek, which shoul not be a problem even early in the season. From there you spend much of the rest of you time on the trail in the forest until you get to the reservoir. From there you can pick up th Mountain Ash Creek Trail on the opposite side of the parking lot.

South Shore Shoshone Lake Trail — MAP 8-2, 9-3

Type:	PTP	**Cat:**	BC	**Class:**	A	**Surf:**	Trail	**Dist:**	8	**Status:**	E
Diff:	3	**Traf:**	2	**Child:**	N	**HAcc:**	N	**Use:**	H S	**Length:**	8.61
Elev A:	7823	**Elev B:**	7806	**Elev G:**	1665	**Elev L:**	-1682	**Net:**	-17	**BMA:**	- -
Min:	7191	**Max:**	8212	**Avg:**	7956	**Avg +:**	7.0%	**Avg -:**	5.9%	**Open:**	YR

Reference Point	A-B Mi	A-B Km	B-A Mi	B-A Km	Latitude	Longitude
Trailhead @ jct w/ Shoshone Lake Trail/Stock Cutoff	0.00	0.00	8.61	13.86	44.34618	-110.79539
Campsite 8T1	0.56	0.90	8.05	12.96	44.34235	-110.78697
Spur trail to campsite 8M2 (0.04 miles)	3.62	5.83	4.99	8.03	44.32914	-110.73754
Moose Creek crossing (20 to 25')	5.76	9.27	2.85	4.59	44.34400	-110.70386
Spur trail to campsite 8M1 (0.04 miles)	5.80	9.33	2.81	4.52	44.34450	-110.70379
Lewis River crossing (120 to 140')	8.29	13.34	0.32	0.51	44.35553	-110.66443
Jct w/ Lewis Channel Trail	8.45	13.60	0.16	0.26	44.35718	-110.66316
Trailhead @ jct w/ Dogshead Trail & 8S1 spur	8.61	13.86	0.00	0.00	44.35932	-110.66219

This trail is believed (erroneously) by many to be simply an extension of the Shoshone Lake Trail that originates near the Lone Star Geyser. The fact is, however, that it is one of the three segments of the major trail system around the lake. It is the least popular of the three, probably because there are no foot-reachable campsites along the lake on this trail. The only two hiker sites are located along Moose Creek. All of the shore-based sites that can be reached by foot are located on the North Shore Trail.

The trail itself is largely uninteresting. It involves a few minor creek crossings, including a crossing of (shallow) Moose Creek. Near the end of the trail, just before it terminates at the junction with the Dogshead Trail and the DeLacy Creek Trail, there is a crossing of the Lewis Channel. Typically, the water here will be knee-deep to almost thigh-deep by mid-July, but it can be shallower or deeper depending on how much snow and rain this area of the park has gotten over the preceding few days and weeks.

On the west end of the trail, just before arriving at campsite 8T1, you will need to cross Cold Mountain Creek. In the early part of the season, this creek can be backed up and overflowing its banks, resulting in hikers having to travel through a half mile of two-foot deep, very cold water (the creek gets its name honestly).

This trail is part of the Continental Divide Trail through Yellowstone.

Trail Creek Trail

MAP 6-4

TYPE:	PTP	CAT:	BC	CLASS:	A	SURF:	TRAIL	DIST:	8	STATUS:	E
DIFF:	3	TRAF:	2	CHILD:	N	HACC:	N	USE:	H S	LENGTH:	21.86
ELEV A:	7513	ELEV B:	7774	ELEV G:	2984	ELEV L:	-2724	NET:	261	BMA:	K/O
MIN:	7507	MAX:	8558	AVG:	7922	AVG +:	4.9%	AVG -:	4.6%	OPEN:	7/15

Reference Point	A-B Mi	A-B Km	B-A Mi	B-A Km	Latitude	Longitude
Trailhead @ jct w/ Heart Lake Trail	0.00	0.00	21.86	35.18	44.28542	-110.49776
Abandoned trail segment (old Heart Lake Trail)	0.75	1.21	21.11	33.97	44.28406	-110.48312
Spur trail to campsite 8J1 (0.43 miles)	1.37	2.20	20.49	32.98	44.28212	-110.47193
Spur trail to campsite 8J2 (0.21 miles)	1.68	2.70	20.18	32.48	44.28189	-110.46635
Abandoned trail segment (old Heart Lake Trail)	2.72	4.38	19.14	30.80	44.27479	-110.45558
Spur trail to campsite 8J6 (0.37 miles)	4.16	6.69	17.70	28.49	44.25582	-110.44815
Jct w/ Heart River Trail	4.50	7.24	17.36	27.94	44.25265	-110.44318
Outlet Creek crossing (20 to 30')	4.65	7.48	17.21	27.70	44.25193	-110.44041
Spur trail for campsite 8J3 (0.01 miles)	4.69	7.55	17.17	27.63	44.25204	-110.43969
Abandoned segment of Trail Creek Trail - West	5.78	9.30	16.08	25.88	44.25238	-110.41887
Campsite 8O2	5.98	9.62	15.88	25.56	44.25344	-110.41537
Abandoned segment of Trail Creek Trail - East	6.66	10.72	15.20	24.46	44.25744	-110.40569
Outlet Lake	7.80	12.55	14.06	22.63	4.269427	-110.39194
Spur trail to campsites 7G1 (.03 mi) & 7G2 (.56 mi)	10.47	16.85	11.39	18.33	44.27279	-110.34926
Grouse Creek crossing (15')	10.52	16.93	11.34	18.25	44.27284	-110.34838
Spur trail to campsite 5L2 (0.12 miles)	12.95	20.84	8.91	14.34	44.27802	-110.30703
Jct w/ Trail Creek-Two Ocean Cutoff Trail	13.24	21.31	8.62	13.87	44.27698	-110.30189
Chipmunk Creek crossing (40 to 50')	14.78	23.79	7.08	11.39	44.28727	-110.27957
Jct w/ Two Ocean Plateau Trail	15.74	25.33	6.12	9.85	44.29262	-110.26376
Spur trail to campsite 6A2 (0.57 miles)	16.29	26.22	5.57	8.96	44.29662	-110.25427
Spur trail to campsite 6A3 (0.47 miles)	17.34	27.91	4.52	7.27	44.29727	-110.23469
Alternate/Cabin Bypass Trail - West	17.36	27.94	4.50	7.24	44.29718	-110.23438
Trail Creek Patrol Cabin	17.42	28.03	4.44	7.15	44.29628	-110.23303
Alternate/Cabin Bypass Trail - East	17.59	28.31	4.27	6.87	44.29503	-110.23053
Spur trail to campsite 6A4 (0.04 miles)	18.03	29.02	3.83	6.16	44.29413	-110.22156
Trail Creek crossing (10 to 15')	20.05	32.27	1.81	2.91	44.28918	-110.18723
Jct w/ Upper Ford & Lower Ford Trails	21.86	35.18	0.00	0.00	44.28978	-110.15594

The Trail Creek Trail is one of the longest in the park, running from the Heart Lake Patrol Cabin around the north side of the lake, up Outlet Creek to Outlet Lake, along Grouse Creek, and then along the South and Southeast Arms of Yellowstone Lake before terminating at the junction with the two trails that ford the Yellowstone River in the Thorofare region. Despite its name, however, it only crosses Trail Creek one time on its far east end.

This trail passes through several bear management areas and does not open until July 15. Once it is open, you will need to ford several creeks, streams, and the Yellowstone River to hike from end to end. Generally speaking, many of these are not (safely) crossable until well into August. Even at that point, the water may be three feet or higher and only experienced hikers should consider crossing it. By the beginning of September, it is usually much safer to undertake a crossing of the Yellowstone.

As you approach the Trail Creek Patrol Cabin, there is an alternative trail that takes you up the hill a bit and south of the cabin complex. If you wish to bypass the development, the side trail will not add substantially to your travel distance.

The western end of this trail, between the Heart River and the Heart Lake Trails, is a part of the Continental Divide Trail.

Two Waterfalls Trail — MAP 8-3

TYPE:	O&B	CAT:	BC	CLASS:	U	SURF:	TRAIL	DIST:	8	STATUS:	U
DIFF:	3	TRAF:	1	CHILD:	N	HACC:	N	USE:	H	LENGTH:	1.31
ELEV A:	7772	ELEV B:	8209	ELEV G:	587	ELEV L:	-99	NET:	488	BMA:	- -
MIN:	7720	MAX:	8211	AVG:	7829	AVG +:	4.5%	AVG -:	3.9%	OPEN:	YR

Reference Point	A-B Mi	A-B Km	B-A Mi	B-A Km	Latitude	Longitude
Suspicion Creek Trailhead (9.0 mi N of SE)	0.00	0.00	1.31	2.11	44.25358	-110.64382
Junction Meadow	0.51	0.82	0.80	1.29	44.25791	-110.64883
Cross unnamed tributary (to the left)	0.85	1.37	0.46	0.74	44.25769	-110.65547
Premonition Falls	1.20	1.93	0.11	0.18	44.25914	-110.66193
Confirmation Falls	1.31	2.11	0.00	0.00	44.25955	-110.66401

This unmaintained trail takes you back to two gorgeous waterfalls on "Suspicion Creek." The creek was given this name by the authors of the book, *The Guide to Yellowstone Waterfalls and Their Discovery*, as was the name of the two waterfalls, Premonition Falls and Confirmation Falls. The trail begins at an unmarked pullout just less than a mile north of the Pitchstone Plateau

Trail on the South Entrance Road (where the creek crosses under the roadway). You will follow the creek back into the wilderness and will need to bushwhack part of the way. This trail is lightly used and will therefore not be worn into the ground. It will also pass through some rather marshy areas, so plan your footwear accordingly. Though the average incline is listed as 4.5%, the last quarter mile climbs up a small canyon wall (with a 11% incline).

Premonition Falls is a 20-foot, plunge type permanent waterfall on a tributary of Suspicion Creek, on a stream fed by cold springs emanating from the Pitchstone Plateau. Confirmation Falls is a 75-foot plunge type seasonal waterfall that reaches its peak during the spring snow melt, lasting into July. After that, the waterfall disappears until the following season.

The creek was given its name by former park historian, Lee Whittlesey, because he harbored some suspicion that it was the home of at least one waterfall from the time he first noticed it in 1969. While they were working on their book, the three authors hiked back to discover the two waterfalls. Premonition Falls was given its name because of the premonition Whittlesey had that there were waterfalls along the stream, and Confirmation Falls got its name, as you might imagine, from the fact that their discovery did indeed confirm the waterfalls existed.

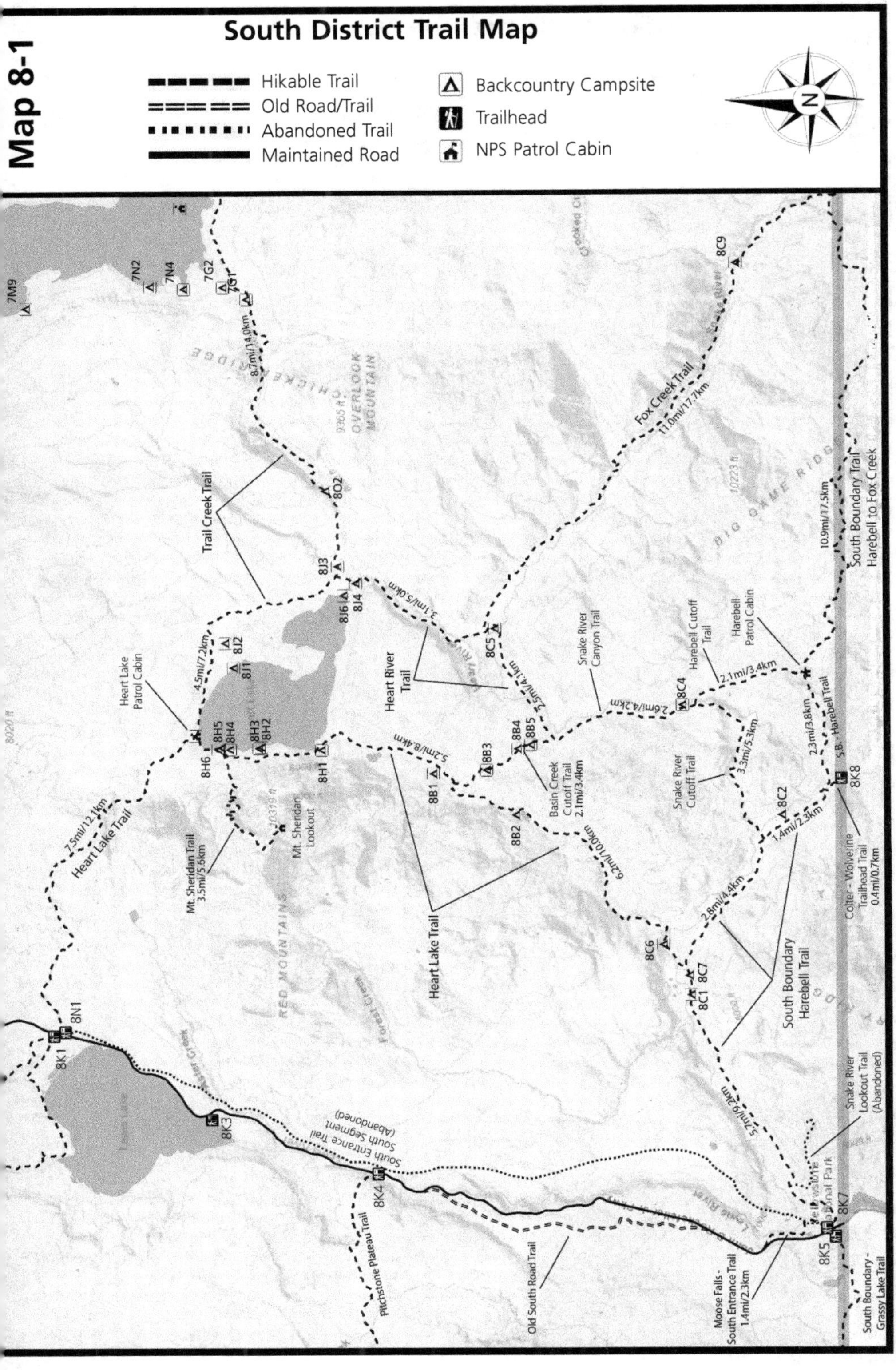

Map 8-1

South District Trail Map

Hikable Trail
Old Road/Trail
Abandoned Trail
Maintained Road

Backcountry Campsite
Trailhead
NPS Patrol Cabin

Trail Creek Trail
8.7mi/14.0km
Chicken Ridge
9365 ft
Overlook Mountain
7M9
7N2
7N4
7G2
7G1
8O2
8J3
8J4
8J6
3.1mi/5.0km
Heart River Trail
Fox Creek Trail
11.0mi/17.7km
Snake River
8C9
Crooked Cr
10223 ft
Big Game Ridge
South Boundary Trail
Harebell to Fox Creek
10.9mi/17.5km
4.5mi/7.2km
8J2
8J1
Heart Lake Patrol Cabin
8H6
8H5
8H4
8H3
8H2
8H1
8020 ft
5.2mi/8.4km
8C5
2.5mi/4.1km
Snake River Canyon Trail
2.6mi/4.2km
8C4
Harebell Cutoff Trail
2.1mi/3.4km
Harebell Patrol Cabin
8B1
8B3
8B4
8B5
Basin Creek Cutoff Trail
2.1mi/3.4km
Snake River Cutoff Trail
3.3mi/5.3km
2.3mi/3.8km
S.B. - Harebell Trail
8K8
8C2
1.4mi/2.3km
7.5mi/12.1km
Heart Lake Trail
10319 ft
Mt. Sheridan Lookout
Mt. Sheridan Trail
3.5mi/5.6km
8B2
6.2mi/10.0km
Red Mountains
Heart Lake Trail
8C6
8C7
8C1
2.8mi/4.4km
South Boundary Harebell Trail
Colter - Wolverine Trailhead Trail
0.4mi/0.7km
8N1
8K1
Lewis Lake
Forest Creek
8K3
South Entrance Trail
South Segment
(Abandoned)
5.7mi/9.2km
Snake River Lookout Trail
(Abandoned)
8K4
Pitchstone Plateau Trail
Old South Road Trail
Lewis River
Yellowstone National Park
8K5
8K7
Moose Falls - South Entrance Trail
1.4mi/2.3km
South Boundary - Grassy Lake Trail

Map 8-2

South District Trail Map

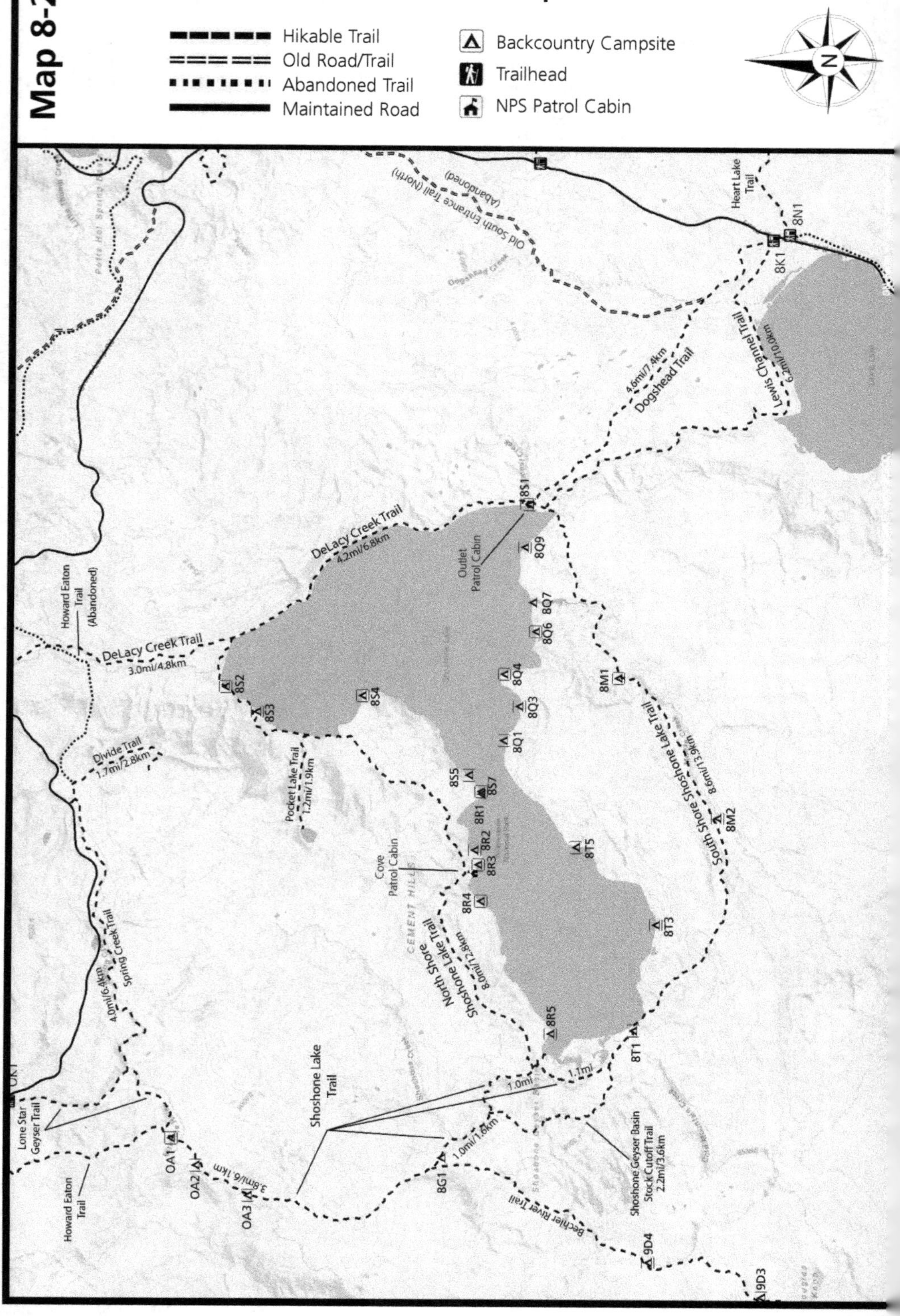

Hikable Trail
Old Road/Trail
Abandoned Trail
Maintained Road

NPS Patrol Cabin

Map 8-3

South District Trail Map

Hikable Trail
Old Road/Trail
Abandoned Trail
Maintained Road

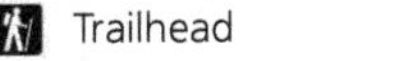

Backcountry Campsite
Trailhead
NPS Patrol Cabin

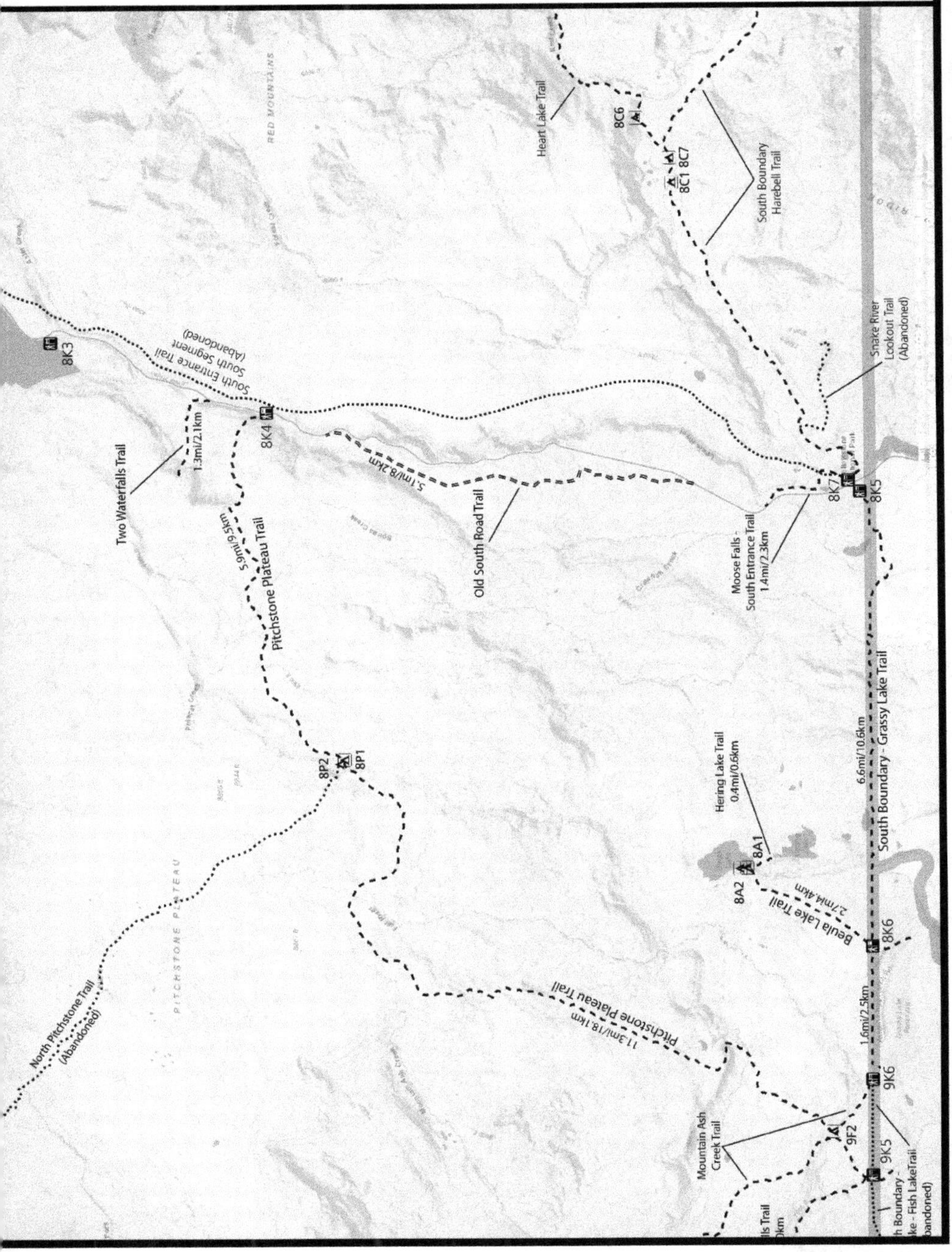

RED MOUNTAINS
Heart Lake Trail
8C6
8C1 8C7
South Boundary Harebell Trail
8K3
South Entrance Trail South Segment (Abandoned)
8K4
Two Waterfalls Trail
1.3mi/2.1km
5.1mi/8.2km
Old South Road Trail
Snake River Lookout Trail (Abandoned)
8K7
8K5
Moose Falls - South Entrance Trail 1.4mi/2.3km
5.9mi/9.5km
Pitchstone Plateau Trail
8P2
8P1
Hering Lake Trail 0.4mi/0.6km
6.6mi/10.6km
South Boundary - Grassy Lake Trail
8A1
8A2
2.7mi/4.4km
Beula Lake Trail
8K6
PITCHSTONE PLATEAU
Pitchstone Plateau Trail
11.3mi/18.1km
1.6mi/2.5km
North Pitchstone Trail (Abandoned)
9K6
Mountain Ash Creek Trail
9F2
9K5

Bechler District Trails

Bechler Meadows Cutoff Trail — MAP 9-1,9-2

Type:	PTP	Cat:	BC	Class:	B	Surf:	Trail	Dist:	9	Status:	E
Diff:	1	Traf:	2	Child:	N	HAcc:	N	Use:	H S	Length:	1.96
Elev A:	6407	Elev B:	6390	Elev G:	155	Elev L:	-172	Net:	-17	BMA:	- -
Min:	6388	Max:	6425	Avg:	6406	Avg +:	2.9%	Avg -:	2.9%	Open:	YR

Reference Point	A-B Mi	A-B Km	B-A Mi	B-A Km	Latitude	Longitude
Trailhead @ jct with Boundary Creek Trail	0.00	0.00	1.96	3.15	44.22616	-111.01589
Bechler Meadows	1.18	1.90	0.78	1.26	44.21453	-111.00623
Jct w/ social/secondary trail - North	1.26	2.03	0.70	1.13	44.21350	-111.00557
Jct w/ social/secondary trail - South	1.54	2.48	0.42	0.68	44.21005	-111.00280
Trailhead @ jct w/ Bechler Meadows Trail	1.96	3.15	0.00	0.00	44.20599	-110.99743

The Bechler Meadows Cutoff is primarily a path designed to allow you to access the Boundary Creek Trail from the Bechler Meadows area or to get to the Bechler Meadows area from the Boundary Creek Trail.

The only important note on this trail is that in the middle, there is an alternate trail that takes you a bit south of the main trail. As is the case in much of the Bechler area during the early part of the season, it can be quite marshy and muddy in places. In some cases, the alternate trail may be a bit more conducive to travel than the main trail.

Bechler Meadows Trail — MAP 9-1

Type:	PTP	Cat:	BC	Class:	B	Surf:	Trail	Dist:	9	Status:	E
Diff:	2	Traf:	2	Child:	N	HAcc:	N	Use:	H S	Length:	5.86
Elev A:	6425	Elev B:	6406	Elev G:	475	Elev L:	-494	Net:	-19	BMA:	- -
Min:	6386	Max:	6481	Avg:	6423	Avg +:	2.3%	Avg -:	2.6%	Open:	YR

Reference Point	A-B Mi	A-B Km	B-A Mi	B-A Km	Latitude	Longitude
Trailhead @ Bechler Ranger Station	0.00	0.00	5.86	9.43	44.14986	-111.04547
Wyoming Creek crossing	0.05	0.08	5.81	9.35	44.15043	-111.04486
Jct w/ Bechler River Cutoff Trail	0.06	0.10	5.80	9.33	44.15053	-111.04474
Jct w/ Boundary Creek Trail	1.61	2.59	4.25	6.84	44.16782	-111.03204
Jct w/ Rocky Ford Cutoff Trail	3.33	5.36	2.53	4.07	44.18267	-111.00780
Spur trail to campsite 9B1	3.57	5.75	2.29	3.69	44.18527	-111.00500
Boundary Creek crossing/South spur to 9M1	3.69	5.94	2.17	3.49	44.18678	-111.00467
North spur trail to campsite 9M1 (stock)	3.80	6.12	2.06	3.32	44.18795	-111.00358
Crossing over unnamed creek (may be dry)	4.42	7.11	1.44	2.32	44.19577	-110.99854
Jct w/ Bechler Meadows Cutoff Trail	5.19	8.35	0.67	1.08	44.20599	-110.99743
Spur trail to campsite 9M2	5.70	9.17	0.16	0.26	44.20979	-110.99175
Bechler River crossing (80')	5.78	9.30	0.08	0.13	44.21072	-110.99133
Spur trail to campsite 9B2	5.79	9.32	0.07	0.11	44.21088	-110.99137
Jct w/ Bechler River Trail	5.86	9.43	0.00	0.00	44.21098	-110.98989

The Bechler Meadows Trail is known as the "middle trail" of the three that depart from the north end of the Bechler Ranger Station. This is the easiest and shortest way to reach the Bechler River Trail if you are planning on following the river trail north to the Old Faithful area. You can use this trail to access the Boundary Creek and Rocky Ford Cutoff as well, creating a loop that will take you back toward the ranger station, but most hikers use it as a straight shot into the upper Bechler area while leaving their vehicles at the ranger station (which affords a bit more security).

s with most other trails in this part of the park, it usually will not be hikable until at least nid-July, and sometimes well into August. Bechler Meadows is known as Bechler Lake for nuch of the season before that because it is always inundated with snowmelt. And even if he water is not deep, it will be marshy and muddy until it has had time to dry out. Always heck the Situation Reports issued by the NPS to determine conditions prior to leaving for he park. To be sure you will not get stuck, plan your trips for well into August or later.

)ne good thing about this trail is that it is almost entirely flat, with very little elevation hange in either direction. There are a couple of creek/river crossings to deal with. There is suspension bridge over Boundary Creek, so that will not be a problem. At the north end ou will have to ford Bechler River in the area of 9B2 and by the time the trails are open, the iver should be calf- to knee-deep and fordable without any issues.

Bechler River Cutoff Trail — MAP 9-1

TYPE:	PTP	CAT:	BC	CLASS:	B	SURF:	TRAIL	DIST:	9	STATUS:	E
DIFF:	1	TRAF:	2	CHILD:	N	HACC:	N	USE:	H S	LENGTH:	1.66
ELEV A:	6408	ELEV B:	6364	ELEV G:	207	ELEV L:	-251	NET:	-44	BMA:	- -
MIN:	6363	MAX:	6493	AVG:	6411	AVG +:	4.8%	AVG -:	5.1%	OPEN:	YR

Reference Point	A-B Mi	A-B Km	B-A Mi	B-A Km	Latitude	Longitude
Trailhead @ jct w/ Bechler Meadows Trail	0.00	0.00	1.66	2.67	44.15053	-111.04474
Trailhead @ jct w/ Bechler River Trail	1.66	2.67	0.00	0.00	44.15624	-111.01423

The Bechler River Cutoff is the "right hand trail" departing from the ranger station. It ffords a quick cutover from the ranger station to the lower end of the Bechler River Trail nd vice versa for those who would rather park at the ranger station and take as much of the ctual Bechler River Trail as possible.

Bechler Ranger Station, 2011. Photo by the author

Bechler River Trail MAP 9-1,9-2,9-3

TYPE:	PTP	CAT:	BC	CLASS:	A	SURF:	TRAIL	DIST:	9	STATUS:	E
DIFF:	4	TRAF:	2	CHILD:	N	HACC:	N	USE:	H S	LENGTH:	25.72
ELEV A:	6229	ELEV B:	7904	ELEV G:	3741	ELEV L:	-2065	NET:	1675	BMA:	- -
MIN:	6210	MAX:	8572	AVG:	7118	AVG +:	3.8%	AVG -:	3.3%	OPEN:	YR

Reference Point	A-B Mi	A-B Km	B-A Mi	B-A Km	Latitude	Longitude
Trailhead @ Cave Falls Trailhead	0.00	0.00	25.72	41.39	44.13667	-111.01015
Cave Falls Parking Lot/Cave Falls	0.85	1.37	24.87	40.02	44.14455	-110.99790
Confluence of the Falls and Bechler Rivers	1.24	2.00	24.48	39.40	44.14774	-110.99589
Bechler Falls	2.18	3.51	23.54	37.88	44.14920	-111.01188
Jct w/ Bechler River Cutoff Trail	2.97	4.78	22.75	36.61	44.15624	-111.01423
Jct w/ Rocky Ford Cutoff Trail	4.94	7.95	20.78	33.44	44.17475	-110.99829
Bechler River crossing (Rocky Ford) (150')	4.97	8.00	20.75	33.39	44.17491	-110.99780
Jct w/ Mountain Ash Trail	5.92	9.53	19.80	31.86	44.17855	-110.98155
Jct w/ Bechler Meadows Trail	8.99	14.47	16.73	26.92	44.21098	-110.98989
Small section of the Bechler Meadows Thermal Area	9.27	14.92	16.45	26.47	44.21241	-110.98485
Spur trail to campsite 9B3	9.65	15.53	16.07	25.86	44.21672	-110.98065
Spur trail to campsite 9B4/West end Bechler Can	10.43	16.79	15.29	24.61	44.22613	-110.97465
Colonnade Falls	12.25	19.71	13.47	21.68	44.23904	-110.94661
Spur trail to campsite 9B5/East end Bechler Can	12.27	19.75	13.45	21.65	44.23928	-110.94617
Iris Falls/Treasure Island	12.49	20.10	13.23	21.29	44.24139	-110.94246
Treasure Island Falls	12.78	20.57	12.94	20.82	44.24397	-110.93814
Spur trail to campsite 9B6	13.44	21.63	12.28	19.76	44.25099	-110.93243
Bechler River crossing (cross at markers) (70')	13.64	21.95	12.08	19.44	44.25346	-110.93245
Spur trail to campsite 9B7	14.15	22.77	11.57	18.62	44.25947	-110.92764
Bechler River crossing (60')	15.07	24.25	10.65	17.14	44.27088	-110.91944
Spur trail to campsite 9B8	15.09	24.28	10.63	17.11	44.27099	-110.91866
Spur trail to campsite 9B9 (0.15 mi)	16.09	25.89	9.63	15.50	44.28047	-110.90610
Three Rivers Junction Thermal Area (South end)	16.20	26.07	9.52	15.32	44.28182	-110.90543
Spur trail to campsite 9B0/Three Rivers Patrol Cabin	16.30	26.23	9.42	15.16	44.28281	-110.90397
Three Rivers Junction Thermal Area (North end)	16.80	27.04	8.92	14.36	44.28726	-110.89726
Three Rivers Junction	17.02	27.39	8.70	14.00	44.28857	-110.89335
Ferris Fork (Bechler River) crossing (20')	17.06	27.46	8.66	13.94	44.28858	-110.89196
Spur trail to campsite 9D1/Phillips Fork Falls	17.09	27.50	8.63	13.89	44.28901	-110.89161
Three Forks Thermal Area/Forlorn Falls	17.20	27.68	8.52	13.71	44.28916	-110.89036
Forlorn Falls	17.28	27.81	8.44	13.58	44.28876	-110.88963
Spur trail to Three Rivers Thermal Area	17.38	27.97	8.34	13.42	44.28922	-110.88796
Spur trail to Twister Falls	18.58	29.90	7.14	11.49	44.29783	-110.86871
Gregg Fork (Bechler River) crossing (20')	18.76	30.19	6.96	11.20	44.29737	-110.86537
Campsite 9D2	18.79	30.24	6.93	11.15	44.29752	-110.86501
Jct w/ North Pitchstone Plateau Trail	19.49	31.37	6.23	10.03	44.30151	-110.85468
Douglas Knob Meadow (South end)	20.65	33.23	5.07	8.16	44.31527	-110.85133
Spur trail to campsite 9D3/D.K. Meadow (North end)	21.04	33.86	4.68	7.53	44.32095	-110.85036
Spur trail to campsite 9D4	22.69	36.52	3.03	4.88	44.33989	-110.84203
Continental Divide	22.91	36.87	2.81	4.52	44.34232	-110.83943
Continental Divide	23.20	37.34	2.52	4.06	44.34621	-110.83783
Trailhead @ jct w/ Shoshone Lake Trail	25.72	41.39	0.00	0.00	44.37513	-110.81948

The Bechler River Trail is perhaps the most iconic trail in Yellowstone, and the one trail that will provide the hiker with access to just about every kind of scenery and feature the park has to offer. If I could recommend one trail for multi-day hiking, this would be it.

The trail technically begins at the junction with the South Boundary Trail almost a mile south of the Cave Falls parking lot. But most people elect to begin from either that lot or to join it from the Bechler Meadows Trail that begins at the ranger station (see above). If you are using stock or are pulling an RV and wish to hike this trail, note that you cannot park those kinds of vehicles at Cave Falls. They must be parked at the ranger station. A driver can drop you and your stock off at Cave Falls, but the vehicle will have to be relocated to the ranger station if it is going to be left in the area overnight.

If you are planning a multi-day hike along the entire route, it is critical that you spend some time pre-planning your route based on how far you wish to hike on any given day and the features and areas you wish to explore. Once you have determined your trip plan, I highly recommend trying to reserve the appropriate campsites for your trip, regardless of the time of year you plan to go. This will ensure you do not have to spend a lot of time playing with your schedule if you get to the Backcountry Office and find out that one or two of your desired sites are not available on the days you want them. The Bechler area is very popular with hikers and given the relatively short season the area experiences, it can be difficult to obtain certain sites on any given day, especially 9D1 and 9B2, two of the most popular campsites in the entire park.

There are several river crossings you will have to deal with along this trail, all of which should be easily fordable by the time the trails have dried out enough for people to start using them. Typically, at the end of July, most of the river crossings will be 2-3 feet deep and will get lower as the season progresses. Of particular note is the crossing at a location known as Rocky Ford. An old road that once passed through this area (known as the Marysville Road) crossed the river here over the rocky bottom. This crossing became known during that time as Rocky Ford and it is known by that moniker even today. This trail follows that old road northeast for a bit until it connects with the Mountain Ash Creek Trail, which follows the road down to the Grassy Lake area. This crossing will be too high until the middle of July in most seasons.

Among the highlights of this hike are numerous canyons, waterfalls, and thermal areas. There is one area near campsite 9D1 where you can get into runoff from one of the thermal features known as Mr. Bubbles (which explains why it is the most popular site in the park).

Once you get to the northern half of the trail, you will get into some elevation changes, most notably climbing up to cross over the Continental Divide twice. You will have about a 2,000-foot (610m) climb over the course of about 10 miles once you've passed campsite 9B5.

This area got its name from Gustavus Bechler, a topographer who accompanied the second Hayden Expedition. He was the first to map the Shoshone Geyser Basin and also prepared accurate maps of the Lower, Middle, and Upper Geyser Basins.[1] The Bechler area is also known as Cascade Corner, for its wide variety of waterfalls and cascades. On many of the original maps drawn of Yellowstone, this area was shown as a large swamp. As a result of farming interests, there were proposals put forth in Congress in 1920 to dam the area and flood it with water from the Bechler and Falls Rivers and provide irrigation to the farms in Idaho, specifically. W. C. Gregg explored the area later that year and documented the vast array of waterfalls and other features, and thus saved this area from being destroyed. The Gregg Fork of the Bechler River is named in his honor.[2]

Boundary Creek Trail

Boundary Creek Trail										MAP 9-2,9-	
TYPE:	PTP	CAT:	BC	CLASS:	C	SURF:	TRAIL	DIST:	9	STATUS:	E
DIFF:	3	TRAF:	1	CHILD:	N	HACC:	N	USE:	H S	LENGTH:	15.35
ELEV A:	6459	ELEV B:	7725	ELEV G:	2212	ELEV L:	-946	NET:	1266	BMA:	- -
MIN:	6388	MAX:	7787	AVG:	6982	AVG +:	3.9%	AVG -:	2.3%	OPEN:	YR

Reference Point	A-B Mi	A-B Km	B-A Mi	B-A Km	Latitude	Longitude
Trailhead @ jct w/ Bechler Meadows Trail	0.00	0.00	15.35	24.70	44.16782	-111.03204
Bartlett Slough	2.27	3.65	13.08	21.05	44.19161	-111.01683
Campsite 9A1	3.56	5.73	11.79	18.97	44.20785	-111.01244
Boundary Creek crossing (40')	3.58	5.76	11.77	18.94	44.20801	-111.01218
Jct w/ Bechler Meadows Cutoff Trail	5.10	8.21	10.25	16.50	44.22616	-111.01589
Spur trail to campsite 9A0 (0.02 miles)	5.25	8.45	10.10	16.25	44.22848	-111.01788
Spur trail to campsite 9A2 (0.11 miles)	5.47	8.80	9.88	15.90	44.23122	-111.01622
Cross unnamed creek (10')	6.12	9.85	9.23	14.85	44.23854	-111.02355
Spur trail to campsite 9A3 (0.16 miles)	6.64	10.69	8.71	14.02	44.24562	-111.02319
Dunanda Falls (150 ft north)	6.76	10.88	8.59	13.82	44.24710	-111.02234
Silver Scarf Falls (100 ft south)	6.79	10.93	8.56	13.78	44.24728	-111.02164
Boundary Creek crossing (40')	8.68	13.97	6.67	10.73	44.27030	-111.03678
Paintbrush Cascade (200 feet east)	9.09	14.63	6.26	10.07	44.27475	-111.03462
Horseshoe Cascade/Boundary Creek Thermal Area	9.18	14.77	6.17	9.93	44.27649	-111.03500
Boundary Creek crossing (30')	9.50	15.29	5.85	9.41	44.28031	-111.03794
Spur trail to campsite 9A4 (0.02 miles)	9.62	15.48	5.73	9.22	44.28170	-111.03950
Upper Boundary Creek Thermal Area (South end)	10.83	17.43	4.52	7.27	44.29678	-111.04554
Boundary Creek crossing (30')	10.88	17.51	4.47	7.19	44.29768	-111.04503
Upper Boundary Creek Thermal Area (North end)	11.35	18.27	4.00	6.44	44.30345	-111.04095
Deep Pool Falls (100 feet NE)	11.83	19.04	3.52	5.66	44.30987	-111.03937
Buffalo Lake/Spur trail to campsite 9A5 (0.36 miles)	14.08	22.66	1.27	2.04	44.32771	-111.07481
Buffalo Lake Patrol Cabin	14.27	22.97	1.08	1.74	44.32813	-111.07757
Park boundary TH 9K8 (cont. into unmaintained area)	15.35	24.70	0.00	0.00	44.32807	-111.09744

Boundary Creek gets its name due to its proximity to the park's western boundary. And though most people hike out to 9A3 specifically to see Dunanda Falls and then return to the ranger station, there are a variety of other waterfalls along the upper reaches of this trail and/or just a few hundred yards off the trail. Both 9A2 and 9A3 make an excellent base from which to explore the dozen or so falls along tributaries of both Boundary Creek and the Bechler River.

This hike does require fording Bartlett Slough, Boundary Creek, and several other streams over the course of its 15-mile length. None of these should present any problem for you, however, by the time you are able to get into the area. Like most other areas of Bechler, during the July and early August time frames, much of this area will still be soggy and marshy, so be sure you bring the appropriate footwear.

Along the upper half of the trail is the Boundary Creek Thermal Area, which contains roughly a hundred or so unnamed thermal features. At the end of the trail is a campsite located on Buffalo Lake (which is fishless).

On the opposite side of the lake is the old Buffalo Patrol Cabin. While there you may be able to see the remnants of the old West Boundary Trail running north and south from the cabin. You can continue out of the park on the trail into the Targhee National Forest.

Cascade Creek-Mountain Ash Cutoff Trail — MAP 9-4

Type:	PTP	**Cat:**	BC	**Class:**	C	**Surf:**	Trail	**Dist:**	9	**Status:**	E
Diff:	1	**Traf:**	1	**Child:**	N	**HAcc:**	N	**Use:**	H S	**Length:**	0.74
Elev A:	7141	**Elev B:**	7060	**Elev G:**	70	**Elev L:**	-150	**Net:**	-81	**BMA:**	- -
Min:	7060	**Max:**	7167	**Avg:**	7117	**Avg +:**	5.3%	**Avg -:**	5.7%	**Open:**	YR

Reference Point	A-B Mi	A-B Km	B-A Mi	B-A Km	Latitude	Longitude
Trailhead @ jct w/ Terraced Falls Trail	0.00	0.00	0.74	1.19	44.13382	-110.84924
Cascade Creek crossing (20')	0.02	0.03	0.72	1.16	44.13406	-110.84939
Trailhead @ jct w/ Mountain Ash Trail	0.74	1.19	0.00	0.00	44.14012	-110.83882

This short cutoff trail serves to allow quicker access to the Mountain Ash Creek Trail from the west. Rather than having to drive another two miles to Grassy Lake (which can be a pain on the bumpy and rutted Grassy Lake Road), you can park at the Cascade Creek/Terraced Falls trailhead and begin your hike there. There are times when the entrance road to the Grassy Lake parking area is muddy and rangers recommend that non-4WD vehicles avoid using it, so this can also serve as an alternative in those cases as well. It meets the main trail just before the Falls River crossing.

Fish Lake-Mountain Ash Cutoff Trail — MAP 9-4,9-1

Type:	PTP	**Cat:**	BC	**Class:**	C	**Surf:**	Trail	**Dist:**	9	**Status:**	E
Diff:	1	**Traf:**	1	**Child:**	N	**HAcc:**	N	**Use:**	H S	**Length:**	1.88
Elev A:	6455	**Elev B:**	6451	**Elev G:**	261	**Elev L:**	-266	**Net:**	-4	**BMA:**	- -
Min:	6441	**Max:**	6501	**Avg:**	6473	**Avg +:**	4.7%	**Avg -:**	5.4%	**Open:**	YR

Reference Point	A-B Mi	A-B Km	B-A Mi	B-A Km	Latitude	Longitude
Trailhead @ jct w/ South Boundary Trail	0.00	0.00	1.88	3.03	44.13716	-110.93958
Falls River crossing (120')	0.03	0.05	1.85	2.98	44.13748	-110.93983
Mountain Ash Creek crossing (100')	1.72	2.77	0.16	0.26	44.16003	-110.93887
Campsite 9U1	1.76	2.83	0.12	0.19	44.16014	-110.93958
Trail split NB or SB	1.81	2.91	0.07	0.11	44.16074	-110.94013
Trailhead @ jct w/ Mountain Ash Trail	1.88	3.03	0.00	0.00	44.16157	-110.94103

This cutoff trail allows access between the South Boundary Trail and the Mountain Ash Creek Trail. This allows hikers to make a loop hiking from the Bechler Ranger Station or the Bechler River Trail towards the east then heading north and returning on the Mountain Ash Creek Trail (or vice versa).

This trail has river fords at both its north and south terminus points. You will have to ford the Falls River at the south (2–3 feet deep in mid-July) and Mountain Ash Creek on the north. Both should be safe to cross by the time you can get into the area.

There is a short, southern segment of this cutoff as well (not shown in chart above) that provides access to areas outside the park (including Fish Lake and Grassy Lake Road).

Mountain Ash Creek Trail — MAP 9-4

Type:	PTP	**Cat:**	BC	**Class:**	B	**Surf:**	Trail	**Dist:**	9	**Status:**	E
Diff:	3	**Traf:**	2	**Child:**	N	**HAcc:**	N	**Use:**	H S	**Length:**	11.38
Elev A:	6409	**Elev B:**	7114	**Elev G:**	1765	**Elev L:**	-1060	**Net:**	705	**BMA:**	- -
Min:	6398	**Max:**	7282	**Avg:**	6744	**Avg +:**	4.2%	**Avg -:**	3.6%	**Open:**	YR

Reference Point	A-B Mi	A-B Km	B-A Mi	B-A Km	Latitude	Longitude
Trailhead @ jct w/ Bechler River Trail	0.00	0.00	11.38	18.31	44.17855	-110.98155
Jct w/ Fish Lake - Mountain Ash Cutoff Trail	2.74	4.41	8.64	13.90	44.16157	-110.94103
Spur trail to Fish Lake-Mountain Ash Cutoff for SB	2.81	4.52	8.57	13.79	44.16213	-110.93978
Spur trail to campsite 9U2 (0.03 miles)	3.87	6.23	7.51	12.09	44.17169	-110.92470
Campsite 9U3	4.00	6.44	7.38	11.88	44.17292	-110.92290
Mountain Ash Creek crossing (70')	4.05	6.52	7.33	11.80	44.17278	-110.92216
Jct w/ Union Falls Trail	5.62	9.04	5.76	9.27	44.17458	-110.89521
Jct w/ Pitchstone Plateau Trail	10.09	16.24	1.29	2.08	44.14126	-110.83969
Falls River crossing (3'+ in July, swift) (70')	10.18	16.38	1.20	1.93	44.14063	-110.83923
Jct w/ Cascade Creek - Mountain Ash Cutoff Trail	10.22	16.45	1.16	1.87	44.14012	-110.83882
Park boundary (TH 9K6)	11.16	17.96	0.22	0.35	44.13264	-110.82364
Trailhead @ Grassy Lake Reservoir	11.38	18.31	0.00	0.00	44.13159	-110.82023

The Mountain Ash Creek Trail (or Mountain Ash Trail) follows the Falls River for a bit, then picks up Proposition Creek, and finally, Mountain Ash Creek. This trail is perhaps most popular for providing access to Union Falls. In fact, the eastern portion of this trail from the reservoir to the falls is often erroneously referred to in many other books as the "Union Falls Trail." Of course, that is what the vast majority of its hikers use it for.

Note that in the reference point chart above, the A trailhead is on the western end of the trail where it begins at the Bechler River Trail. If you are just interested in hiking to Union Falls, you will want to start at the B end for your calculations.

On the east end of the trail as you hike toward Union Falls, you will do a bit of climbing, and then head down about 700 feet (213m) to Proposition Creek. You will then climb another ridge of about 150 feet (46m), then head back down to level ground for the balance of your trip to the junction with the trail to the falls. On the way back, you will have to climb that 700 feet in about a mile and a half to get back to the trailhead.

Most of the trail to the west of the Union Falls area is rather unremarkable and primarily in forested canopy. There is a ford of Mountain Ash Creek, but it will be easy. There are a couple of decent, lightly used campsites on the west side of that creek. Of the two, I would recommend 9U2 since 9U3 is right on the trail (and therefore has no privacy).

This trail follows what was an old (1880s) road that passed through this area. It was known as the Marysville Road and was used by Mormons to travel north and west out of the Jackson area into Idaho. You can still see the occasional wagon trail rut embedded in the ground in some places. At the junction with the Bechler River Trail, the road turned south and west (along today's Rocky Ford Cutoff Trail) and then south through the Bechler area and west into the Marysville, Idaho, area (just east of Ashton).

North Fork (Scout Pool) Trail — MAP 9-4,9-2

Type:	O&B	**Cat:**	BC	**Class:**	U	**Surf:**	Trail	**Dist:**	9	**Status:**	E
Diff:	2	**Traf:**	1	**Child:**	N	**HAcc:**	N	**Use:**	H S	**Length:**	0.32
Elev A:	6630	**Elev B:**	6632	**Elev G:**	220	**Elev L:**	-219	**Net:**	2	**BMA:**	- -
Min:	6609	**Max:**	6748	**Avg:**	6647	**Avg +:**	0.0%	**Avg -:**	0.0%	**Open:**	YR

Reference Point	A-B Mi	A-B Km	B-A Mi	B-A Km	Latitude	Longitude
Trailhead @ jct w/ Union Falls Trail	0.00	0.00	0.32	0.51	44.19170	-110.87816
Ouzel/Scout Pool	0.32	0.51	0.00	0.00	44.19559	-110.87889

This is a little social/side trail that takes you to an area known as Scout Pool, where hikers like to soak. When you arrive at the top of the ridge on the Union Falls Trail and you get to the "hitching post," the trail to the right continues on to Union Falls. The trail to the left goes down the hill to Scout Pool. The pool gets its name from an old Boy Scout camp that was located not too far from the area. The pool is formed by water heated by thermal runoff from a thermal field approximately 1.5 miles (2.4km) upstream.

If you continue up the creek for about a quarter mile, you will find Early Morning Falls, so named because many people believe it is Morning Falls, which is actually an additional mile up the creek. Riverwalk Falls and the Dawn Cascades are located even further up the creek.

Note that this trail is not officially maintained by the NPS. As such, it may be in bad shape in places (even washed out from time to time). Exercise caution when hiking in this area.

North Pitchstone Plateau Trail — MAP 9-3,8-3

Type:	PTP	Cat:	BC	Class:	U	Surf:	Trail	Dist:	9	Status:	A
Diff:	4	Traf:	1	Child:	N	HAcc:	N	Use:	H	Length:	8.44
Elev A:	8156	Elev B:	8537	Elev G:	1224	Elev L:	-843	Net:	381	BMA:	- -
Min:	8143	Max:	8733	Avg:	8967	Avg +:	4.6%	Avg -:	3.6%	Open:	YR

Reference Point	A-B Mi	A-B Km	B-A Mi	B-A Km	Latitude	Longitude
Trailhead @ Jct w/ Bechler River Trail	0.00	0.00	8.44	13.58	44.30151	-110.85468
Gregg Fork crossing (15')	0.15	0.24	8.29	13.34	44.30048	-110.85228
Arrive on top of plateau	2.43	3.91	6.01	9.67	44.28500	-110.81968
Central Pitchstone Plateau Thermal Area (north)	4.29	6.90	4.15	6.68	44.27355	-110.78931
Central Pitchstone Plateau Thermal Area (south)	5.47	8.80	2.97	4.78	44.26094	-110.77595
Campsite 8P2	8.44	13.58	0.00	0.00	44.23025	-110.74001

Though this is listed as an 8.5-mile trail, the first two and a half miles of it (to the top of the plateau) was the only portion that was ever "officially" maintained, and that portion was abandoned in the early 2000s. Travel across the plateau to the campsites is possible, however. Many have likened this landscape to the surface of the moon, and you can certainly get that sense when you are on this trail.

If you are coming up onto the plateau from the north, be prepared for an 800-foot (244m) climb over the course of about three miles. If you are doing it from the south, you will want to depart from campsite 8P2, and you will have a quick 200-foot (61m) scramble up the hill. Once you are up on the plateau, there is no marked trail or path across its surface—no markings, no cairns, no posts, etc. My suggestion would be to put in the GPS coordinates of the thermal area in the reference point list and navigate your way to it. And then do the same for the next point of reference. This will allow you to cross the plateau without getting lost.

There is a USGS seismic station atop the plateau. It is several hundred feet off the trail, but you could encounter it if your calculations are off a bit. If you do, please do not disturb it.

Robinson Creek Trail — MAP 9-1

Type:	PTP	Cat:	BC	Class:	C	Surf:	Trail	Dist:	9	Status:	E
Diff:	2	Traf:	1	Child:	N	HAcc:	N	Use:	H S	Length:	8.70
Elev A:	6425	Elev B:	6743	Elev G:	1329	Elev L:	-1011	Net:	318	BMA:	- -
Min:	6341	Max:	6844	Avg:	6517	Avg +:	4.0%	Avg -:	4.0%	Open:	YR

Reference Point	A-B Mi	A-B Km	B-A Mi	B-A Km	Latitude	Longitude
Trailhead 9K1 @ Bechler Ranger Station	0.00	0.00	8.70	14.00	44.14986	-111.04547
Robinson Lake	1.97	3.17	6.73	10.83	44.16534	-111.07018
Campsite 9A7	4.19	6.74	4.51	7.26	44.19069	-111.08093
Little Robinson Creek crossing	4.21	6.78	4.49	7.23	44.19097	-111.08092
Robinson Creek crossing (25′)	7.18	11.56	1.52	2.45	44.22405	-111.08134
Robinson Creek crossing (25′)	7.28	11.72	1.42	2.29	44.22518	-111.08254
Robinson Canyon Falls	7.35	11.83	1.35	2.17	44.22523	-111.08372
Campsite 9A6	8.10	13.04	0.60	0.97	44.23166	-111.09187
Park boundary TH 9K7 (cont into unmaintained area)	8.70	14.00	0.00	0.00	44.23677	-111.09767

Robinson Creek (and the lake of the same name) is one of the few places in the park that i named after a criminal. Jim Robinson was a rustler from Idaho who, along with two othe men, spent their time stealing cattle in Teton Valley, Idaho. The creek was given its name b U.S. Army scouts who patrolled this part of the park, presumably due to their encounter with the man.[3] This is the "left hand trail" that departs from the Bechler Ranger Station an was once part of the original West Boundary Trail until the majority of it was abandone in the 1960s. This trail ends at the park's boundary with the national forest, but you ca continue onward on the old West Boundary Trail for some time before it becomes to difficult to find.

This is one of the least-traveled trails in the park and is used almost exclusively by ranger on patrols. There are two campsites on the trail. The first is located at Little Robinson Creek but it is used on average just one or two nights per season. The second is located just insid the park's boundary. Surprisingly, it is used about twice as much as the other one. Bot sites are in poor condition owing in large part to their lack of use. Robinson Lake is abou 42 acres in size and averages about four feet deep but is fishless. Robinson Canyon extend for about ⅔rd of a mile near the north end of the trail and is the site of a gorgeous, 30-foo cascade-type waterfall (the only Yellowstone waterfall known to exist in Idaho).

Rocky Ford Cutoff Trail — MAP 9-1,9-2

Type:	PTP	Cat:	BC	Class:	B	Surf:	Trail	Dist:	9	Status:	E
Diff:	1	Traf:	2	Child:	N	HAcc:	N	Use:	H S	Length:	0.82
Elev A:	6404	Elev B:	6412	Elev G:	113	Elev L:	-105	Net:	8	BMA:	- -
Min:	6387	Max:	6418	Avg:	6397	Avg +:	4.9%	Avg -:	4.8%	Open:	YR

Reference Point	A-B Mi	A-B Km	B-A Mi	B-A Km	Latitude	Longitude
Trailhead @ jct w/ Bechler Meadows Trail	0.00	0.00	0.82	1.32	44.18267	-111.00780
Campsite 9C1	0.57	0.92	0.25	0.40	44.17721	-111.00087
Trailhead @ jct w/ Bechler River Trail	0.82	1.32	0.00	0.00	44.17475	-110.99829

This trail serves as a shortcut between the Bechler Meadows and the Bechler River Trails south of Rocky Ford, the crossing of the Bechler River. It was once a part of the old Marysville Road (see the entry above for the Mountain Ash Creek Trail for more details).

South Boundary: Bechler-Mountain Ash Creek — MAP 9-1

Type:	PTP	Cat:	BC	Class:	A	Surf:	Trail	Dist:	9	Status:	E
Diff:	3	Traf:	1	Child:	N	HAcc:	N	Use:	H S	Length:	6.81
Elev A:	6426	Elev B:	6474	Elev G:	929	Elev L:	-881	Net:	48	BMA:	- -
Min:	6190	Max:	6510	Avg:	6376	Avg +:	4.4%	Avg -:	4.0%	Open:	YR

Reference Point	A-B Mi	A-B Km	B-A Mi	B-A Km	Latitude	Longitude
Trailhead 9K1 (S of Bechler Ranger Station Barn)	0.00	0.00	6.81	10.96	44.14919	-111.04619
Wyoming Creek crossing	1.15	1.85	5.66	9.11	44.13431	-111.03864
Jct w/ Bechler River Trail @ Cave Falls	2.77	4.46	4.04	6.50	44.13667	-111.01015
Falls River crossing (225')	2.86	4.60	3.95	6.36	44.13659	-111.00877
Unnamed creek (follow S to Winegar Lake)	5.63	9.06	1.18	1.90	44.13999	-110.95581
Junco Lake (to the south)	6.24	10.04	0.57	0.92	44.13482	-110.94710
Jct w/ Fish Lake-Mountain Ash Cutoff Trail NB	6.66	10.72	0.15	0.24	44.13716	-110.93958
Jct w/ Fish Lk/M. A. C/O SB & Spur to 9F1 (9C6)	6.81	10.96	0.00	0.00	44.13734	-110.93652

This segment of trail got its name back when the trail ran all the way from the Bechler Ranger Station to the Mountain Ash Creek Trail just north of the reservoir. Due to lack of use, the segment between the cutoff trail and the reservoir was abandoned, however. This trail, too, is used more extensively by rangers than hikers, but it does allow people to make a circuit out of the lower half of the Bechler area in combination with the cutoff and the Bechler River Trail.

This trail begins on the west side of the corral at the ranger station, not at the north trailhead where all the other trails depart. It crosses the Falls River (which can be thigh deep here well into July and early August). From that point it passes through dense forest until you get to the terminus of the trail. If you are planning on hiking up the cutoff to the Mountain Ash Creek Trail, the cutoff is a quarter mile before the end of the trail.

There is a single campsite located at the end of the trail, 9F1 (which is shown on older maps and in older books as 9C6). This is a lightly used site, but has excellent privacy and an outstanding view of Calf Creek Meadow to the east.

Terraced Falls Trail — MAP 9-4,8-3

Type:	O&B	**Cat:**	BC	**Class:**	B	**Surf:**	Trail	**Dist:**	9	**Status:**	E
Diff:	2	**Traf:**	1	**Child:**	N	**HAcc:**	N	**Use:**	H S	**Length:**	1.87
Elev A:	7294	**Elev B:**	6923	**Elev G:**	194	**Elev L:**	-565	**Net:**	-371	**BMA:**	- -
Min:	6923	**Max:**	7294	**Avg:**	7070	**Avg +:**	5.9%	**Avg -:**	7.7%	**Open:**	YR

Reference Point	A-B Mi	A-B Km	B-A Mi	B-A Km	Latitude	Longitude
Trailhead 9K5 (off Grassy Lake Road)	0.00	0.00	1.87	3.01	44.12906	-110.84763
Park boundary (TH 9K5)	0.34	0.55	1.53	2.46	44.13267	-110.84878
Jct w/ Cascade Creek-Mountain Ash Cutoff Trail	0.43	0.69	1.44	2.32	44.13382	-110.84924
Pothole Cascades	0.67	1.08	1.20	1.93	44.13642	-110.85197
Diamond Cascade	0.99	1.59	0.88	1.42	44.14032	-110.85385
Humpback Cascade	1.00	1.61	0.87	1.40	44.14060	-110.85417
Cleft Cascades (Upper and Lower)	1.13	1.82	0.74	1.19	44.14208	-110.85491
Confluence of Falls River & Cascade Creek	1.15	1.85	0.72	1.16	44.14232	-110.85495
Cascade Acres	1.41	2.27	0.46	0.74	44.14475	-110.85785
Terraced Falls (Upper)	1.79	2.88	0.08	0.13	44.14692	-110.86437
Terraced Falls (Lower)	1.87	3.01	0.00	0.00	44.14730	-110.86589

The Terraced Falls Trail is one of the hidden gems of Yellowstone. It would be far more popular if it were easier to get to, so the fact that you have to want to be here and have to expend the effort to drive down Grassy Lake Road for so many miles to get to the trailhead makes it even more special. When people would stop into the Backcountry Office and ask me where they could go to see something special, this is where I would send them. It is even more spectacular in the fall when the leaves are changing colors.

The trail follows Cascade Creek for the middle third of its distance, and you can easily se why this creek has its name. You will pass several gorgeous cascades, Pothole, Diamonc Humpback, and the Cleft are all beautiful and do not disappoint. You will then pick up th Falls River at its confluence with Cascade Creek and follow it until you reach your ultimat destination.

Terraced Falls is a six-tiered, two section waterfall on the Falls River. There are severa vantage points along the river from which to view the falls, but be extra careful as the canyo walls here are sheer and the dropoffs are rather precipitous.

There is another waterfall approximately one mile further down the Falls River fron this location. Rainbow Falls is a gorgeous 55-foot high waterfall that can only be reache through some serious off-trail travel to the north and west of where this trail ends.[4]

Three Rivers Thermal Area Spur — MAP 9-2

TYPE:	O&B	CAT:	BC	CLASS:	U	SURF:	TRAIL	DIST:	9	STATUS:	E
DIFF:	2	TRAF:	1	CHILD:	N	HACC:	N	USE:	H S	LENGTH:	0.56
ELEV A:	7377	ELEV B:	7426	ELEV G:	158	ELEV L:	-109	NET:	49	BMA:	- -
MIN:	7376	MAX:	7454	AVG:	7412	AVG +:	7.8%	AVG -:	8.5%	OPEN:	YR

Reference Point	A-B Mi	A-B Km	B-A Mi	B-A Km	Latitude	Longitude
Trailhead @ jct w/ Bechler River Trail	0.00	0.00	0.56	0.90	44.28922	-110.88796
Three Rivers Thermal Area	0.32	0.51	0.24	0.39	44.28879	-110.88228
Social trail to river & thermal features	0.48	0.77	0.08	0.13	44.28809	-110.87948
Trail terminus @ Ferris Fork (Bechler River)	0.56	0.90	0.00	0.00	44.28736	-110.87873

This is the social/unmaintained trail that leads up to the Mr. Bubbles soaking area that is sc popular with those who hike up the Bechler River Trail. Though this is a commonly usec trail, it does pass through a thermal area, so be careful to stay on the actual trail.

Twister Falls Trail — MAP 9-2

TYPE:	O&B	CAT:	BC	CLASS:	U	SURF:	TRAIL	DIST:	9	STATUS:	E
DIFF:	1	TRAF:	1	CHILD:	N	HACC:	N	USE:	H	LENGTH:	0.10
ELEV A:	8003	ELEV B:	7922	ELEV G:	6	ELEV L:	-87	NET:	-81	BMA:	- -
MIN:		MAX:		AVG:		AVG +:	0.0%	AVG -:	0.0%	OPEN:	YR

Reference Point	A-B Mi	A-B Km	B-A Mi	B-A Km	Latitude	Longitude
Trailhead @ jct w/ Bechler River Trail	0.00	0.00	0.10	0.16	44.29783	-110.86871
Twister Falls/Gregg Fork (Bechler River)	0.10	0.16	0.00	0.00	44.29858	-110.86832

This is a short, unofficial/unmaintained trail down to the base of Twister Falls, given its name because of its appearance. Though you can get a decent look at the waterfall from here, the view is better on the other side. Instead of taking this side trail from the Bechler River Trail, continue up the main trail for another few hundred feet, cross over the river, and then follow the bank around to the other side.

If you have the time, once you are at the base of the falls, hike downstream to view Littlesmouth Cascade (named because it is at the mouth of Little's Fork), then continue south to see Ethereal Falls (a 200-foot waterfall). When you are done there, hike back north of the cascade (take the left fork of the creek) about 2/10th of a mile to see the Tempe Cascade, a series of five cascades that has a total drop of over 100 feet.

Union Falls Trail

MAP 9-4,9-2

TYPE:	O&B	CAT:	BC	CLASS:	B	SURF:	TRAIL	DIST:	9	STATUS:	E
DIFF:	2	TRAF:	2	CHILD:	N	HACC:	N	USE:	H S	LENGTH:	2.10
ELEV A:	6550	ELEV B:	6760	ELEV G:	423	ELEV L:	-212	NET:	210	BMA:	- -
MIN:	6545	MAX:	6785	AVG:	6608	AVG +:	5.6%	AVG -:	5.4%	OPEN:	YR

Reference Point	A-B Mi	A-B Km	B-A Mi	B-A Km	Latitude	Longitude
Trailhead @ jct w/ Mountain Ash Trail	0.00	0.00	2.10	3.38	44.17458	-110.89521
Spur trail to campsite 9U4 (0.05 miles)	0.59	0.95	1.51	2.43	44.18012	-110.88785
Mountain Ash Creek crossing (30')	0.61	0.98	1.49	2.40	44.18035	-110.88780
Spur trail to campsite 9U5 (0.13 miles)	0.73	1.17	1.37	2.20	44.18187	-110.88666
Jct w/ North Fork Trail	1.60	2.57	0.50	0.80	44.19170	-110.87816
Union Falls/Trail terminus	2.10	3.38	0.00	0.00	44.19261	-110.87187

This is the spur trail from the Mountain Ash Creek Trail that takes you to Union Falls, one of the most impressive waterfalls in Yellowstone. The waterfall is 250 feet (76m) tall and is named because it is the union of two streams of water, Mountain Ash Creek and an unnamed tributary of that creek. Though it takes some effort to get here, there are often more than a dozen people here at any given time during the height of the summer.

There are two excellent campsites located along this trail. 9U1 has the better view, but is located not too far off the trail and has little privacy. 9U2 is located further from the trail and has a decent view of the river and has more privacy.

If you have the time, you can continue up along Mountain Ash Creek to see a handful of other waterfalls. They are about a mile and a half of off-trail travel (read: considerable bushwhacking), but collectively are worth seeing if you are spending the night in the area and would like to do some exploring. Spritely Falls, Spiral Staircase Falls, Dance of the Seven Veils Falls, Demure Falls, and the Chamber of Rhapsody Falls are all unofficially named and have not been described, even in the popular *Yellowstone Waterfalls and Their Discovery* book. The authors of that book had planned a second edition, and these newly discovered waterfalls were to have been described in it, but a series of issues has thus far prevented a second edition from being developed.

Map 9-1

Bechler District Trail Map

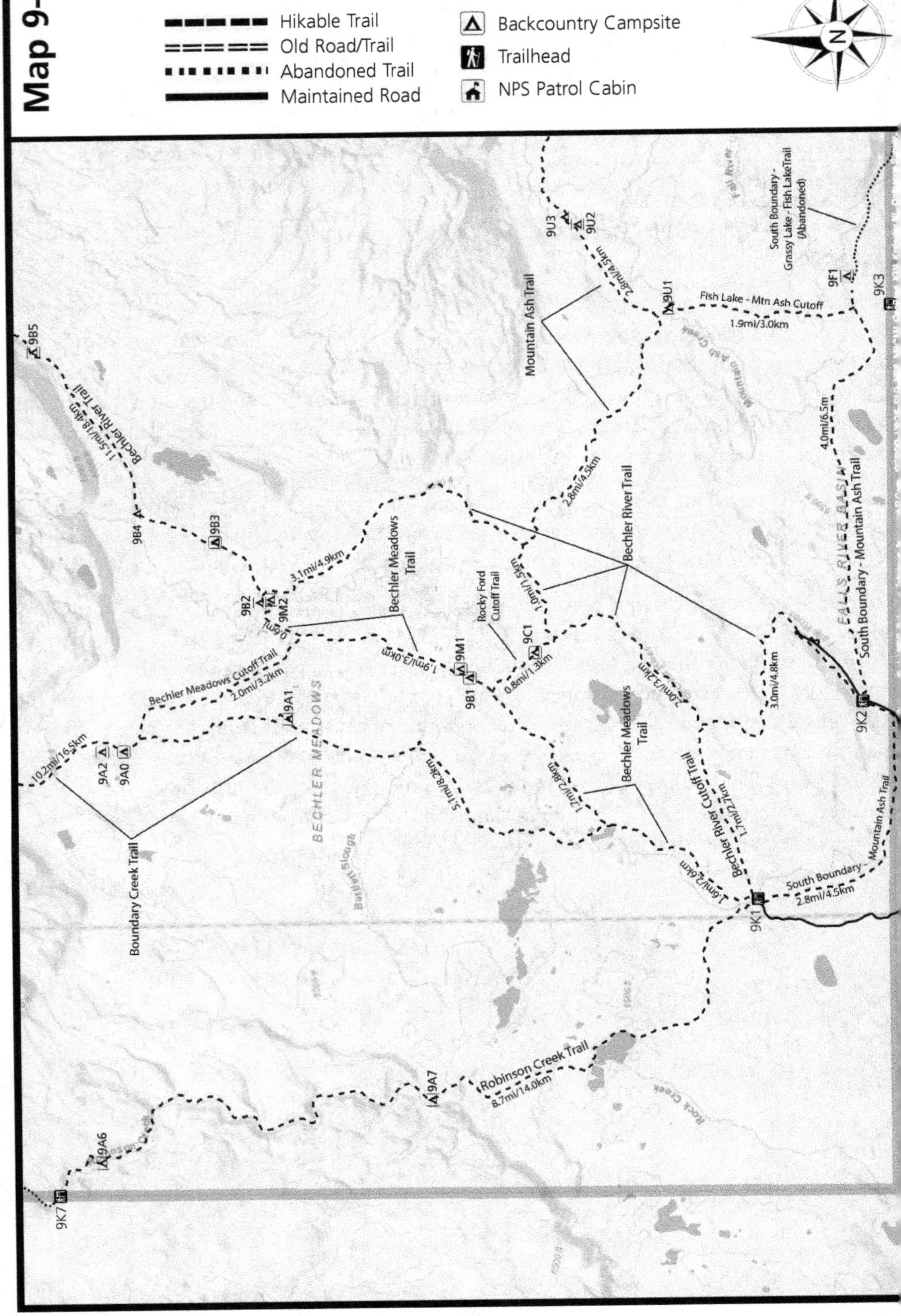

Hikable Trail
Old Road/Trail
Abandoned Trail
Maintained Road

Backcountry Campsite
Trailhead
NPS Patrol Cabin

Bechler River Trail
11.5mi/18.4km
9B5
9B4
9B3
9B2
9M2
3.1mi/4.9km
0.6mi
Bechler Meadows Trail
Bechler Meadows Cutoff Trail
2.0mi/3.2km
9A1
9A2
9A0
10.2mi/16.5km
Boundary Creek Trail
BECHLER MEADOWS
Bartlett Slough
1.9mi/3.0km
9M1
9B1
Rocky Ford Cutoff Trail
9C1
0.8mi/1.3km
1.0mi/1.5km
Bechler River Trail
Mountain Ash Trail
2.8mi/4.5km
9U3
9U2
9U1
Fish Lake - Mtn Ash Cutoff
1.9mi/3.0km
Mountain Ash Creek
Fall River
South Boundary - Grassy Lake - Fish Lake Trail (Abandoned)
9F1
9K3
4.0mi/6.5m
South Boundary - Mountain Ash Trail
FALLS RIVER BASIN
3.0mi/4.8km
9K2
2.0mi/3.2km
Bechler Meadows Trail
5.1mi/8.3km
1.7mi/2.8km
Bechler River Cutoff Trail
1.7mi/2.7km
1.6mi/2.6km
9K1
South Boundary
2.8mi/4.5km
Mountain Ash Trail
Robinson Creek Trail
8.7mi/14.0km
9A7
Rock Creek
9A6
9K7

Map 9-2

Bechler District Trail Map

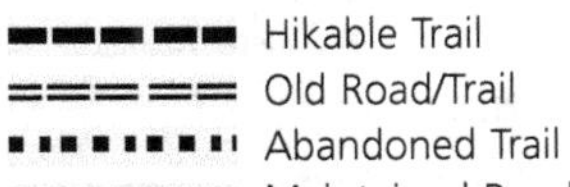

North Pitchstone Trail (Abandoned)
Pitchstone Plateau Trail 17.2mi/27.6km
9D3
6.2mi/10.0km
9D2
2.1mi/3.4km
Three Rivers Thermal Spur 0.6mi/0.9km
Bechler River Trail
Twister Falls Trail
9D1
9B0
9B9
Three Rivers Patrol Cabin
9B8
9B7
9B6
9B5
11.5mi/18.4km
North Fork Trail 0.3mi/0.5km
Union Falls Trail 2.1mi/3.4km
Union Falls Patrol Cabin
9U5
9U4
4.5mi/7.2km
Mountain Ash Trail
2.8mi/4.5km
9U3
9U2
Mountain Ash Trail
9U1
Bechler River Trail
9B4
9B3
9B2
9M2
3.1mi/4.9km
2.8mi/4.5km
Bechler River Trail
Bechler Meadows Cutoff Trail
2.0mi/3.2km
1.7mi/2.8km
9M1
9B1
9C1
2.0mi/3.2km
Bechler Meadows Trail
1.6mi/2.6km
Rocky Ford Cutoff Trail 0.8mi/1.3km
9A2
9A0
9A1
5.1mi/8.2km
10.2mi/16.5km
9A3
9A4
Boundary Creek Trail
9A5
Buffalo Lake Patrol Cabin
9A7
Robinson Creek Trail 8.7mi/14.0km
9A6
9K8
9K7
West Boundary Trail (Abandoned)

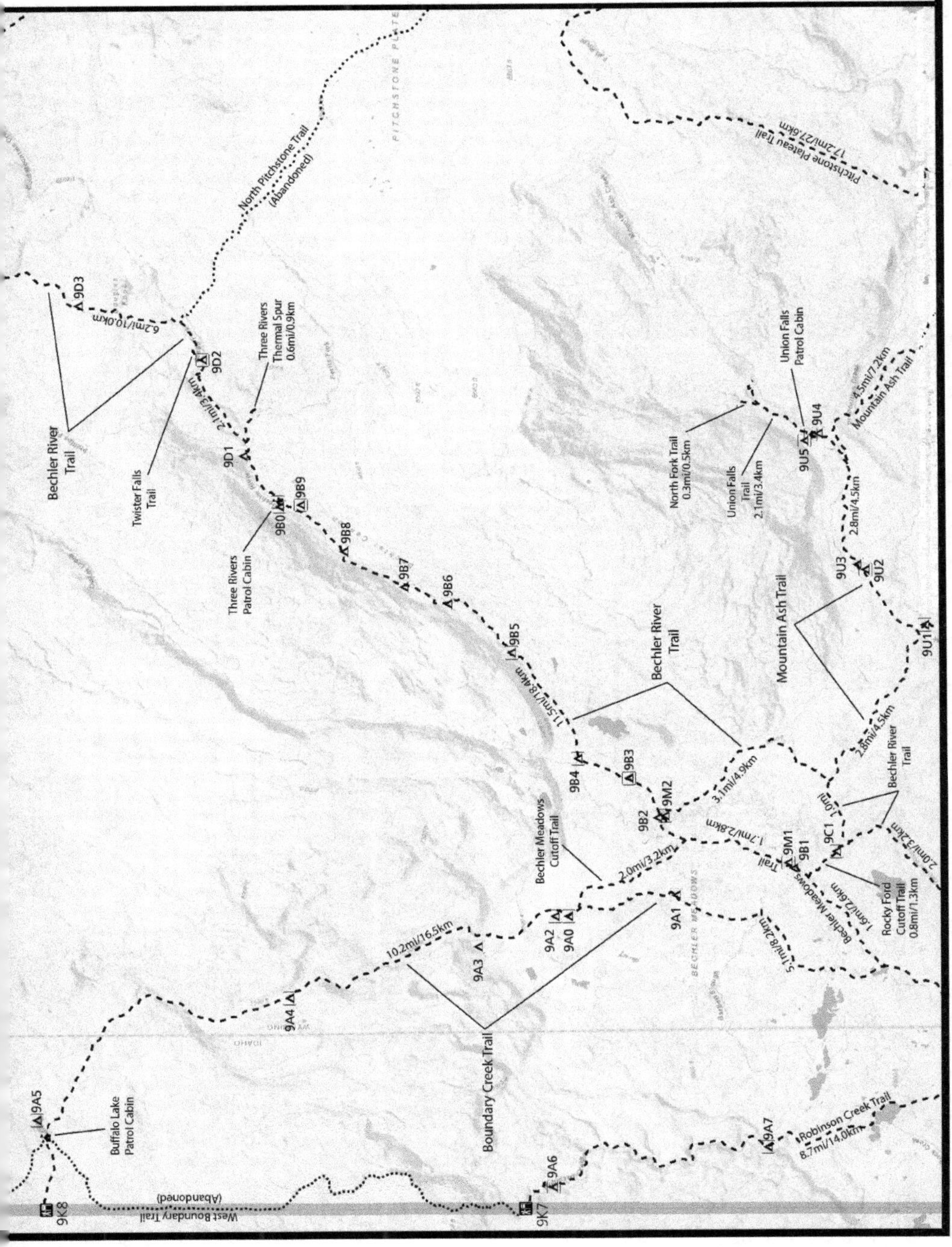

Map 9-3

Bechler District Trail Map

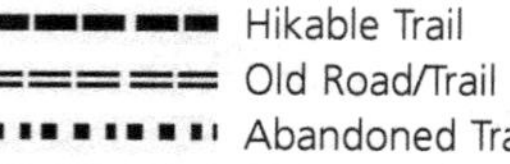

Hikable Trail

Old Road/Trail

Abandoned Trail

Maintained Road

Backcountry Campsite

Trailhead

NPS Patrol Cabin

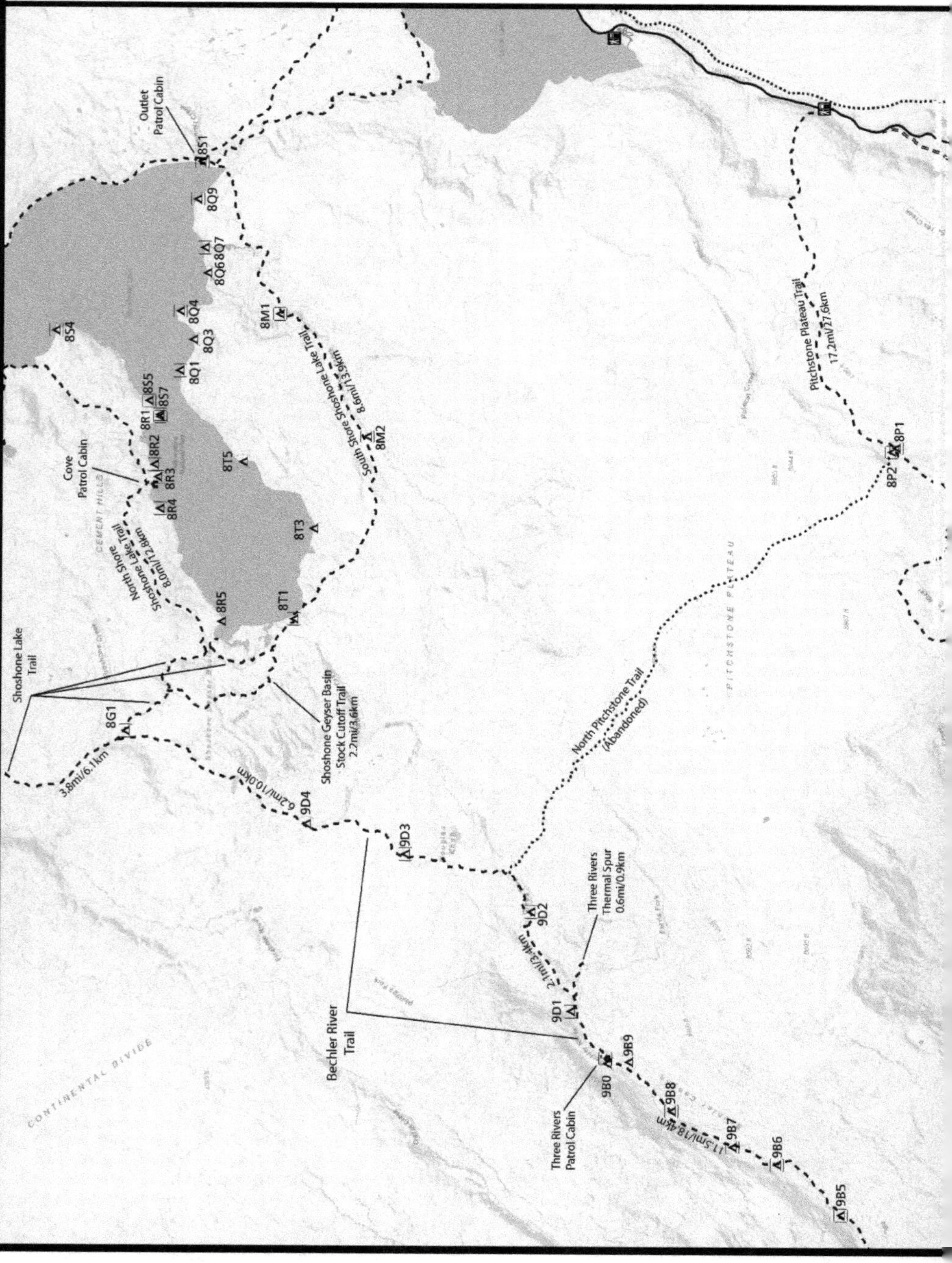

Outlet Patrol Cabin

8S1

8Q9

8Q6 8Q7

8Q4

8Q3

8Q1

8S4

8M1

8R1 8S5

8S7

8R2

8R3

8R4

8T5

8M2

Cove Patrol Cabin

CEMENT HILLS

North Shore Shoshone Lake Trail 8.0mi/12.8km

South Shore Shoshone Lake Trail 8.6mi/13.9km

8T3

8T1

8R5

Shoshone Lake Trail

8G1

3.8mi/6.1km

Shoshone Geyser Basin Stock Cutoff Trail 2.2mi/3.6km

6.2mi/10.0km

9D4

9D3

9D2

2.1mi/3.4km

Three Rivers Thermal Spur 0.6mi/0.9km

9D1

Bechler River Trail

9B9

9B0

Three Rivers Patrol Cabin

9B8

11.5mi/18.4km

9B7

9B6

9B5

CONTINENTAL DIVIDE

North Pitchstone Trail (Abandoned)

PITCHSTONE PLATEAU

Pitchstone Plateau Trail 17.2mi/27.6km

8P1

8P2

Map 9-4

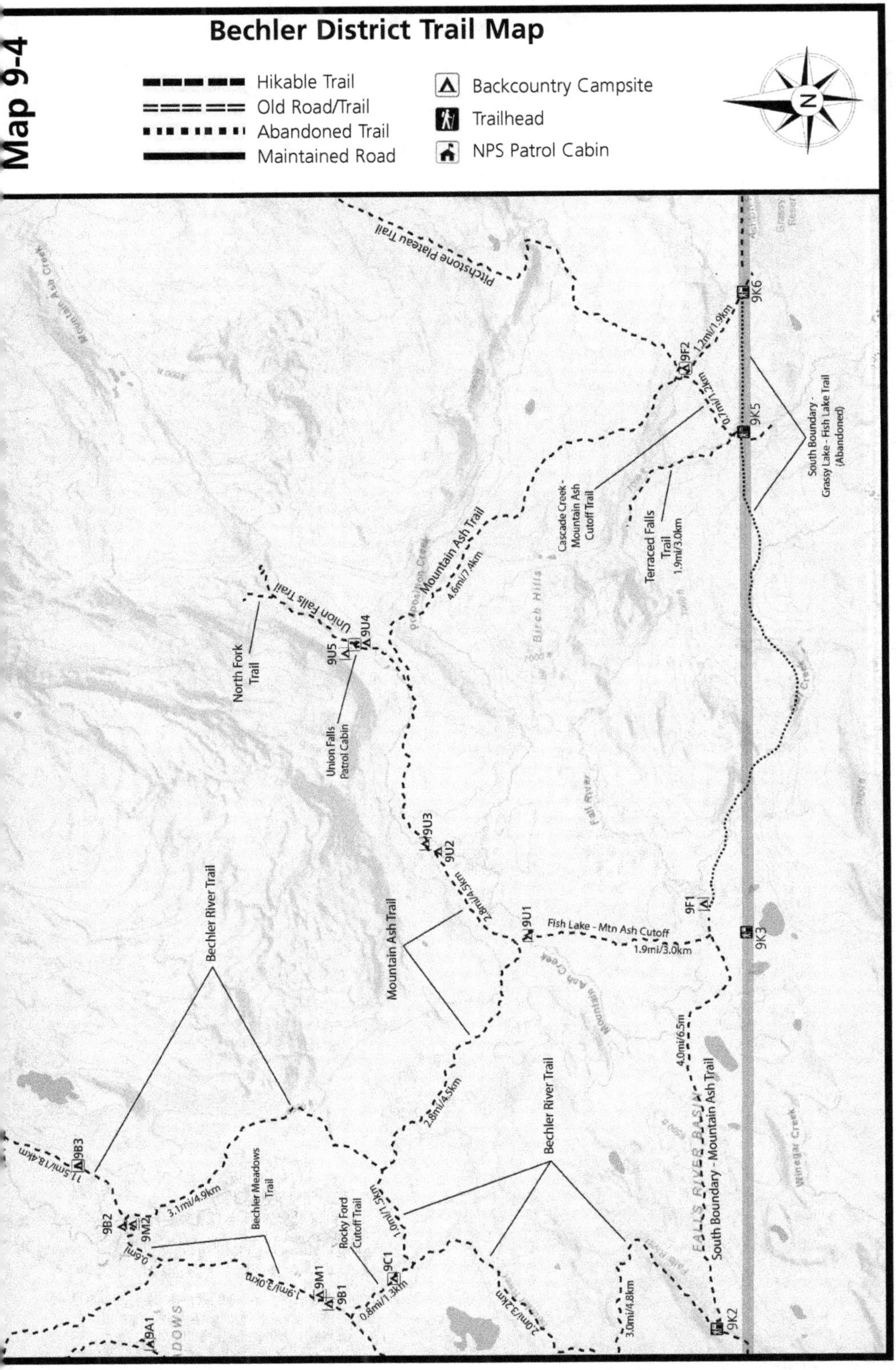

Bechler District Trail Map

- Hikable Trail
- Old Road/Trail
- Abandoned Trail
- Maintained Road
- Backcountry Campsite
- Trailhead
- NPS Patrol Cabin

Pitchstone Plateau Trail
Mountain Ash Creek
9K6
9F2
1.2mi/1.9km
0.7mi/1.1km
9K5
South Boundary - Grassy Lake - Fish Lake Trail (Abandoned)
Cascade Creek - Mountain Ash Cutoff Trail
Terraced Falls Trail 1.9mi/3.0km
Mountain Ash Trail
4.6mi/7.4km
Proposition Creek
Birch Hills
Union Falls Trail
North Fork Trail
9U5
9U4
Union Falls Patrol Cabin
Fall River
9U3
9U2
2.8mi/4.5km
9U1
Fish Lake - Mtn Ash Cutoff
1.9mi/3.0km
9F1
9K3
Mountain Ash Trail
Mountain Ash Creek
Bechler River Trail
4.0mi/6.5m
South Boundary - Mountain Ash Trail
Falls River Basin
Winegar Creek
9B3
11.5mi/18.4km
9B2
9M2
3.1mi/4.9km
Bechler Meadows Trail
0.6mi
1.9mi/3.0km
9M1
9B1
9A1
Rocky Ford Cutoff Trail
9C1
0.8mi/1.3km
1.0mi/1.5km
2.8mi/4.5km
Bechler River Trail
2.0mi/3.2km
3.0mi/4.8km
9K2

Old Faithful District Trails

Biscuit Basin Trail — MAP O-4

Type:	Loop	Cat:	FC	Class:	B	Surf:	Bdwlk	Dist:	O	Status:	E
Diff:	1	Traf:	5	Child:	Y	HAcc:	Y	Use:	H K	Length:	0.61
Elev A:	7273	Elev B:	7273	Elev G:	42	Elev L:	-42	Net:	0	BMA:	- -
Min:	7272	Max:	7303	Avg:	7292	Avg +:	3.2%	Avg -:	2.1%	Open:	YR

Reference Point	A-B Mi	A-B Km	B-A Mi	B-A Km	Latitude	Longitude
Trailhead OK4 (Biscuit Basin parking lot)	0.00	0.00	0.44	0.71	44.48503	-110.85254
Wall Pool/Black Opal Pool	0.12	0.19	0.32	0.51	44.48499	-110.85375
Sapphire Pool	0.14	0.23	0.30	0.48	44.48491	-110.85526
Loop split	0.17	0.27	0.27	0.43	44.48482	-110.85580
Jewel Geyser	0.19	0.31	0.25	0.40	44.48479	-110.85621
Shell Spring	0.21	0.34	0.23	0.37	44.48487	-110.85654
Silver Globe Complex	0.26	0.42	0.18	0.29	44.48522	-110.85735
Avoca Spring/Spur trail to Mystic Falls/Summit	0.28	0.45	0.16	0.26	44.48544	-110.85734
Seaweed Pool	0.29	0.47	0.15	0.24	44.48562	-110.85715
West Mustard Spring	0.33	0.53	0.11	0.18	44.48597	-110.85643
Mustard Spring	0.35	0.56	0.09	0.14	44.48598	-110.85609
Coral Geyser/Black Pearl Geyser	0.38	0.61	0.06	0.10	44.48569	-110.85590
Return to loop split	0.44	0.71	0.00	0.00	44.48482	-110.85580

Biscuit Basin gets its name from the unique "biscuit"-shaped geyserite formations that used to encircle Sapphire Pool (see NPS photo below). While vandalism destroyed many of these little formations, the 1959 Hebgen Lake earthquake cast the final blow to them. After the seismic event, Sapphire went into geyser mode and the force of its eruptions destroyed the remaining biscuits.

Despite the loss of its namesake feature, this area remains worthy of a quick side trip when you are exploring the Upper Geyser Basin. Sapphire Pool is still regarded as one of the most beautiful in the park. Jewel Geyser erupts every 8-10 minutes or so to heights of 20 feet. Coral Geyser remains in a steady state of eruption, and several other features erupt, gurgle, bubble up, and otherwise entertain visitors. The entire trail is boardwalked and accessible.

Black Sand Basin Trail — MAP O-5

Type:	Loop	Cat:	FC	Class:	B	Surf:	Bdwlk	Dist:	O	Status:	E
Diff:	1	Traf:	5	Child:	Y	HAcc:	Y	Use:	H K	Length:	0.18
Elev A:	7299	Elev B:	7290	Elev G:	25	Elev L:	-25	Net:	-9	BMA:	- -
Min:	7286	Max:	7301	Avg:	7291	Avg +:	4.2%	Avg -:	3.8%	Open:	YR

Reference Point	A-B Mi	A-B Km	B-A Mi	B-A Km	Latitude	Longitude
Trailhead @ parking lot/Opalescent Pool spur	0.00	0.00	0.18	0.29	44.46276	-110.85307
Spouter Geyser/Coral Geyser	0.01	0.02	0.17	0.27	44.46265	-110.85317
Spur to Cliff Geyser, Jagged Geyser, Ragged Spring	0.02	0.03	0.16	0.26	44.46212	-110.85356
Green Spring	0.09	0.14	0.09	0.14	44.46181	-110.85410
Iron Spring Creek crossing (footbridge)	0.11	0.18	0.07	0.11	44.46184	-110.85447
Spur trail to Emerald Pool	0.12	0.19	0.06	0.10	44.46198	-110.85471
Handkerchief Pool & Geyser	0.14	0.23	0.04	0.06	44.46217	-110.85487
Rainbow Pool	0.16	0.26	0.02	0.03	44.46251	-110.85503
Terminus/Sunset Pool	0.18	0.29	0.00	0.00	44.46274	-110.85499

Black Sand Basin gets its name from the obsidian gravel found in and among some of the features here. It is home to several gorgeous, interesting, and unique features. Chief among these is Handkerchief Pool, perhaps the second most famous thermal feature in the park after Old Faithful from a historical perspective. For many years early in the park's history, this pool was accessible by a walkway and visitors could dip their handkerchiefs in it (see NPS photo below). The water would be sucked down into the underground plumbing and then regurgitated a short time later. It was said if you put your handkerchief in the pool, the cloth would come back clean. Over time, the various things people put into the feature clogged it up and it no longer works that way. It is no longer accessible by walkway.

Cliff Geyser is one of the more entertaining features in this area, erupting every few minutes for several seconds to several minutes, with heights of 20-40 feet. Sunset Pool, Rainbow Pool, Green Spring, and Emerald Pool are located here and each is worthy of a visit. The boardwalk crosses Iron Spring Creek, which gets its name from the red algae that can be found growing in its thermally-heated waters.

Divide Trail

MAP O-7,7-1

TYPE:	O&B	CAT:	TH	CLASS:	C	SURF:	TRAIL	DIST:	O	STATUS:	E
DIFF:	3	TRAF:	2	CHILD:	N	HACC:	N	USE:	H S	LENGTH:	1.72
ELEV A:	8056	ELEV B:	8778	ELEV G:	815	ELEV L:	-94	NET:	722	BMA:	- -
MIN:	8048	MAX:	8778	AVG:	8408	AVG +:	10.4%	AVG -:	6.0%	OPEN:	YR

Reference Point	A-B Mi	A-B Km	B-A Mi	B-A Km	Latitude	Longitude
Trailhead (11.0 miles W of West Thumb Junction)	0.00	0.00	1.72	2.77	44.43478	-110.73460
Jct w/ Spring Creek Trail	0.08	0.13	1.64	2.64	44.43409	-110.73340
Continental Divide	1.29	2.08	0.43	0.69	44.42174	-110.72143
Continental Divide	1.55	2.49	0.17	0.27	44.42073	-110.72392
Terminus near summit	1.72	2.77	0.00	0.00	44.42188	-110.72656

The Divide Trail is a short, forested trail that takes you to the top of Divide Hill, the site o an old fire lookout tower that was here until the early 1990s. The hill's name comes from th fact that it is located on the Continental Divide. And though there are a couple of spots alon the trail where you will get a decent view of Shoshone Lake and DeLacy Park (meadow) the thick forest canopy prevents you from being able to see much along most of it, even a the top. For this reason, many consider this one of the least worthwhile hikes in the park.

Fairy Creek Trail

MAP O-2

TYPE:	PTP	CAT:	BC	CLASS:	C	SURF:	TRAIL	DIST:	O	STATUS:	E
DIFF:	3	TRAF:	1	CHILD:	N	HACC:	N	USE:	H S	LENGTH:	13.30
ELEV A:	7329	ELEV B:	7223	ELEV G:	1896	ELEV L:	-2002	NET:	-106	BMA:	A
MIN:	7221	MAX:	8236	AVG:	7796	AVG +:	5.1%	AVG -:	4.6%	OPEN:	MDW

Reference Point	A-B Mi	A-B Km	B-A Mi	B-A Km	Latitude	Longitude
Trailhead @ lower jct w/ Mystic Falls Trail	0.00	0.00	13.30	21.40	44.48553	-110.8634
Upper Geyser Basin Overlook	0.65	1.05	12.65	20.36	44.48706	-110.8662
Jct w/ Mystic Falls Trail (Upper)	1.13	1.82	12.17	19.59	44.48695	-110.8751
Spur trail to campsite OD3 (.05 miles)/Lovely Falls	4.49	7.23	8.81	14.18	44.48652	-110.9175
Spur trail to campsite OD2 (.02 mi)/Little FH Meadow	5.10	8.21	8.20	13.20	44.48502	-110.9281
Imperial Geyser/Trail to Crater Lakes	10.86	17.48	2.44	3.93	44.53134	-110.8766
Social trail to Spray Geyser	11.05	17.78	2.25	3.62	44.53043	-110.8728
Jct w/ Fairy Falls Trail	11.25	18.11	2.05	3.30	44.53005	-110.8704
Fairy Creek crossing (footbridge)	11.68	18.80	1.62	2.61	44.53139	-110.8628
Spur trail to campsite OD4 (.21 miles)	11.88	19.12	1.42	2.29	44.53222	-110.8591
Trailhead @ jct w/ Imperial Meadows Trail	13.30	21.40	0.00	0.00	44.54900	-110.8471

This trail takes you from the Biscuit Basin area (after a short hike out on the Mystic Fal Trail) up to a fantastic overlook of the Upper Geyser Basin, on to Little Firehole Meadow up through the Twin Buttes and Imperial Geyser area, ending in Imperial Meadows. Th trail gets its name from the fact it crosses Fairy Creek, on which Fairy Falls is located.

The lower end of this trail is very busy, as it helps form a loop from Mystic Falls to the Upp Geyser Basin Overlook, both extremely popular with those looking for a quick hike. On you get out of that immediate area, though, you will have the trail to yourself for the mo part. There are three decent campsites located along this route, two of which (OD2 ar OD3) afford a good bit of privacy and are near small waterfalls. OD4 is located on the nor end of the trail and has more traffic going past it.

n the north end of this trail is access to some rather interesting thermal and geological atures. Though Imperial Geyser was an impressive sight for many years after its birth in 27, it is less so today. It is still a gorgeous pool and the runoff channel from it is almost ways colored bright red from the algae that grow in its warm waters. Nearby Spray Geyser upts to heights of 30 feet every one to two minutes.

ou can also hike around Imperial to the summit of South Twin Butte (elev 7,923ft/2,416m). his hill, along with its northern twin (elev 7,866ft/2,398m), is a glacial moraine, a pile of ebris accumulated during glacier movement through this area many centuries ago. These ills are easily visible from the Grand Loop Road, and have a variety of monikers, many f which refer to the female chest in one manner or another. These two moraines form an mphitheater-shaped "crater" within which you will find five or six small lakes known as the rater Lakes (all fishless). These are seasonal in nature and the number will vary from time time based on how much snow melt and thermal runoff flows through the area. Exercise aution as you hike in and around this area as there are a number of thermal vents around e buttes.

s you continue past those hills you will pass the Fairy Falls Trail junction. From here, it is ist a quick third of a mile hike south to the falls. Continuing north, you will pass through e Fairy Springs and the Fairy Meadows groups of thermal features. These areas contain ostly unnamed thermal pools, though there are a couple of note. Locomotive Spring on e western hillside of the springs group is in an almost continuous state of eruption to a eight of about six feet. Column Spouter, a large pool just east of the trail in the meadows roup, erupts every 30 minutes or so to heights of up to 10 feet. The northern end of this trail vill also be busy as it is close to the parking area at the end of Fountain Flats Drive.

airy Falls Trail — MAP O-2

YPE:	PTP	CAT:	TH	CLASS:	B	SURF:	TRAIL	DIST:	O	STATUS:	E
IFF:	2	TRAF:	4	CHILD:	N	HACC:	N	USE:	HSKB*	LENGTH:	2.87
LEV A:	7251	ELEV B:	7269	ELEV G:	266	ELEV L:	-247	NET:	18	BMA:	A
IIN:	7243	MAX:	7301	AVG:	7266	AVG +:	3.1%	AVG -:	2.8%	OPEN:	MDW

eference Point	A-B Mi	A-B Km	B-A Mi	B-A Km	Latitude	Longitude
railhead OK5 (4.4 miles N of Old Faithful)	0.00	0.00	2.87	4.62	44.51554	-110.83253
irehole River Bridge	0.04	0.06	2.83	4.55	44.51615	-110.83279
rand Prismatic Overlook	0.72	1.16	2.15	3.46	44.52386	-110.83942
ct w/ Goose Lake/North Spur	1.01	1.63	1.86	2.99	44.52714	-110.84235
ower line crossing	1.11	1.79	1.76	2.83	44.52673	-110.84367
pur trail to campsite OD1 (0.07 miles)	1.72	2.77	1.15	1.85	44.52501	-110.85548
airy Falls	2.48	3.99	0.39	0.63	44.52545	-110.86979
railhead @ jct w/ Fairy Creek Trail	2.87	4.62	0.00	0.00	44.53005	-110.87040

he Fairy Falls Trail is by far the most popular trail in the Old Faithful area away from the oardwalks. Prior to 2017, traffic around this area was frequently at a standstill because of he lack of sufficient parking. And although the NPS tried to remediate this situation with he construction of a new satellite parking area, traffic has only marginally improved. So ack your patience as you head into this area, especially later in the afternoon.

y far the best time to do this hike is early in the season right after it opens (on the Friday f Memorial Day weekend). This is when the snow melt is at full tilt and the runoff causes the creek upon which the falls is located to be running near its peak. The waterfall is mos stunning at this time of year (though some people do prefer it a little later in the seaso when the water flow is less and the falls appears more "fairyish").

The first half of this trail is on an old road and is mostly asphalt. Bicycles are allowed o this part of the trail, but you must park your bike and walk once the trail turns and gets o the road surface. Just before you get to this turnoff you will come across Grand Prismati Hill, upon which you will find a viewing platform from which you can take some incredibl photos of Grand Prismatic Spring in the Midway Geyser Basin. For decades there wer social trails to the top of this hill, and the NPS discouraged people from hiking up to i (largely due to public safety issues; one man doing that was killed by a falling tree in 2014) The NPS finally relented and built an official trail in 2017. It is definitely worth the side tri if you have the time.

When you reach the waterfall, you have the option to turn back and return to the trailhead or you can hike another third of a mile to see Imperial Geyser, Spray Geyser, and Twi Buttes (see the Fairy Creek Trail entry above).

Fern Cascade Loop Trail — MAP O-6

TYPE:	LOOP	CAT:	TH	CLASS:	B	SURF:	TRAIL	DIST:	O	STATUS:	E
DIFF:	2	TRAF:	2	CHILD:	N	HACC:	N	USE:	H S K	LENGTH:	2.35
ELEV A:	7387	ELEV B:	7387	ELEV G:	386	ELEV L:	-386	NET:	0	BMA:	- -
MIN:	7358	MAX:	7603	AVG:	7505	AVG +:	5.9%	AVG -:	6.0%	OPEN:	YR

Reference Point	A-B Mi	A-B Km	B-A Mi	B-A Km	Latitude	Longitude
Trailhead @ Old Faithful Gov't Area	0.00	0.00	2.35	3.78	44.45387	-110.82966
Service Road to Cell Tower/Reservoir	0.22	0.35	2.13	3.43	44.45094	-110.83102
Spur trail to Fern Cascades	1.29	2.08	1.06	1.71	44.44676	-110.84285
Spur trail to OF Housing Area	1.78	2.86	0.57	0.92	44.45250	-110.84039
North Service Road to OF Reservoir/Cell Tower	2.17	3.49	0.18	0.29	44.45402	-110.83342
Terminus at OF Trailhead	2.35	3.78	0.00	0.00	44.45401	-110.82984

This loop hike is accessed via the Howard Eaton trailhead located just south of Old Faithful The entire loop is just over two miles. However, you can get up quickly to the cascades by taking a shortcut. Drive into the Government Area (it is okay to do this) and back toward the mobile home part of the housing area. Park in an out-of-the-way spot and walk along the hillside. You will see a trail going up into the woods at the end of the first "street" of the housing area. Hike about a half mile up the hill and you will come to the cascades. If you are staying in the Old Faithful area, you can walk over to the Government Area as well. Follow the road beside the Ranger Station/Clinic over to the area and then angle back toward the aforementioned housing area.

The cascades are named for the ferns growing along them. It may be difficult to see the water without getting into the woods a bit (use caution).

Fountain Paint Pots Trail — MAP O-2

TYPE:	LOOP	CAT:	FC	CLASS:	B	SURF:	BDWLK	DIST:	O	STATUS:	E
DIFF:	1	TRAF:	5	CHILD:	Y	HACC:	Y	USE:	H	LENGTH:	0.62
ELEV A:	7289	ELEV B:	7289	ELEV G:	75	ELEV L:	-75	NET:	0	BMA:	- -
MIN:	7287	MAX:	7320	AVG:	7301	AVG +:	4.9%	AVG -:	4.1%	OPEN:	YR

Reference Point	A-B Mi	A-B Km	B-A Mi	B-A Km	Latitude	Longitude
Trailhead (7.8 miles N of Old Faithful)	0.00	0.00	0.51	0.82	44.54852	-110.80722
Celestine Pool	0.10	0.16	0.41	0.66	44.54963	-110.80636
Loop split	0.11	0.18	0.40	0.64	44.54986	-110.80630
Silex Spring	0.14	0.23	0.37	0.60	44.55028	-110.80602
Trail split - use east side/Fountain Paint Pot	0.15	0.24	0.36	0.58	44.55043	-110.80622
Trail split - use east side/Fumarole	0.19	0.31	0.32	0.51	44.55089	-110.80629
Red Spouter	0.20	0.32	0.31	0.50	44.55099	-110.80614
Leather Pool	0.21	0.34	0.30	0.48	44.55108	-110.80604
Trail split - turn right	0.24	0.39	0.27	0.43	44.55096	-110.80651
Spur trail for Jet Geyser viewing platform	0.30	0.48	0.21	0.34	44.55093	-110.80769
Bear Claw & Twig Geysers	0.31	0.50	0.20	0.32	44.55097	-110.80783
Fountain Geyser, Morning Geyser, Morning's Thief	0.33	0.53	0.18	0.29	44.55102	-110.80819
Super Frying Pan & Jet Geysers	0.34	0.55	0.17	0.27	44.55100	-110.80839
Clepsydra & Spasm Geysers, Jelly Spring	0.35	0.56	0.16	0.26	44.55094	-110.80858
(Old) Bellefontaine Geyser (way off to the west)	0.38	0.61	0.13	0.21	44.55052	-110.80851
Return to main loop split	0.51	0.82	0.00	0.00	44.54986	-110.80630

Fountain Paint Pots is one of the most interesting thermal areas in the park. Its namesake mudpot looks like boiling paint during the early part of the season when the runoff is high, and Fountain Geyser can occasionally put on a wild show. Silex Spring, also found here, is among the most beautiful and mesmerizing pools in the park.

This area is also home to Celestine Pool. This hot spring gained notoriety in 1981 when a dog got loose from its owner and ran to the pool, jumping into it at full speed. The near boiling temperature caused the dog to begin yelping. For some reason, the friend of the owner, despite pleas by onlookers, jumped in to try to save the dog. He immediately suffered third degree burns over his entire body. Though he would get out of the pool, he died the next day at a burn center in Salt Lake City. Former park historian Lee Whittlesey opens his popular book, *Death in Yellowstone*, with a vivid recounting of that harrowing event, and I think of it every single time I visit this area.[1] This kind of event is one of the primary reasons why Yellowstone does not permit dogs and other pets in the thermal basins.

This area is also home to Leather Pool. This pool was used to supply hot water for baths to the old Fountain Hotel, which was located on the small forested hill across the road from the thermal area. On most days, you can still see the path of the leather-clad pipeline that transported the water in the meadow between Fountain Paint Pots and the old hotel site. The pool gets its name from the brown algae that grow in its warm waters (which are said to give it a leather-like appearance).

One of the most entertaining features here is Clepsydra Geyser. A Clepsydra is a mythical Greek water clock, and the feature received its name due to its supposed eruption regularity. The 1959 Hebgen Lake earthquake destroyed any regularity it might have had, however. Today the geyser is in a state of nearly constant eruption and when the sun is at just the right angle in the sky, it can make for some stunning photographs.

Given its location adjacent to the road, this is one of the busier areas of the park. The rather large parking lot can be filled to capacity on most days during the height of the summer.

The entire trail is boardwalked and is easily accessible to those with mobility impairments and younger children and is well worth the effort if you have the time.

Goose Lake/Feather Lake Trail MAP O-2,O-

TYPE:	PTP	CAT:	TH	CLASS:	B	SURF:	GRVL	DIST:	O	STATUS:	E
DIFF:	1	TRAF:	2	CHILD:	Y	HACC:	Y	USE:	HSBKR	LENGTH:	2.58
ELEV A:	7182	ELEV B:	7258	ELEV G:	155	ELEV L:	-79	NET:	76	BMA:	A
MIN:	7182	MAX:	7259	AVG:	7225	AVG +:	1.7%	AVG -:	1.3%	OPEN:	MDW

Reference Point	A-B Mi	A-B Km	B-A Mi	B-A Km	Latitude	Longitude
Trailhead @ jct w/ Sentinel Meadows Trail	0.00	0.00	2.58	4.15	44.56211	-110.83863
Unnamed Lake	0.51	0.82	2.07	3.33	44.55515	-110.83971
Jct w/ Imperial Meadows Trail	1.00	1.61	1.58	2.54	44.54840	-110.84383
Gosling Lake/Feather Lake (behind Gosling)	1.17	1.88	1.41	2.27	44.54649	-110.84500
Goose Lake/Spur trail to campsite OD5 (0.10 miles)	1.32	2.12	1.26	2.03	44.54441	-110.84619
Old roadbed off to the east	1.85	2.98	0.73	1.17	44.53767	-110.84163
Terminus @ jct w/ Fairy Falls Trail	2.58	4.15	0.00	0.00	44.52714	-110.84235

This trail is listed on most other maps and in other books as a northern access to Fairy Fall from the Fountain Flats Drive parking lot. And it can certainly be used for that (though it i longer to go this way). However, the primary purpose of this trail to provide access to Goos Lake and Feather Lake (and Gosling Lakes, the two smaller ones).

In the not too distant past (until 1995), this old road was open to public travel and you coul drive to the lakes, each of which had its own picnic area. Today it is open only to hikers an bicyclists, however. This trail is gravel for much of its length, and traveling by bicycle can b rough at times.

Goose Lake is home to one of the two campsites in the park designated for handicap wheelchair access, OD5. However, given that the shortest approach is covered in gravel again, this can be rather tiresome for anyone trying to get to it in a wheelchair.

The trail ends at its intersection with the "south" Fairy Falls Trail.

Howard Eaton: Old Faithful to Lone Star MAP O-6

TYPE:	PTP	CAT:	BC	CLASS:	B	SURF:	TRAIL	DIST:	O	STATUS:	E
DIFF:	2	TRAF:	1	CHILD:	N	HACC:	N	USE:	HSK	LENGTH:	2.93
ELEV A:	7387	ELEV B:	7659	ELEV G:	654	ELEV L:	-381	NET:	272	BMA:	- -
MIN:	7387	MAX:	7875	AVG:	7701	AVG +:	7.1%	AVG -:	5.4%	OPEN:	YR

Reference Point	A-B Mi	A-B Km	B-A Mi	B-A Km	Latitude	Longitude
Trailhead OK2 (S end of Old Faithful Gov't Area)	0.00	0.00	2.93	4.72	44.45387	-110.82966
Myriad Creek crossing	0.10	0.16	2.83	4.55	44.45326	-110.82898
Old roadbed	2.82	4.54	0.11	0.18	44.42103	-110.81053
Terminus @ jct w/ Lone Star & Shoshone Lake Trails	2.93	4.72	0.00	0.00	44.41948	-110.81047

This section of the Howard Eaton Trail is one of only a handful that remain in use. It is used primarily to access the Lone Star Geyser area by hikers from Old Faithful who are not in vehicles, or as a cross-country ski trail during the winter.

The entire path of this trail is forested and there is literally nothing along the trail of interest. The trail itself ends at the junction with the Lone Star Trail and the Shoshone Lake Trail. Once you reach this point, you still have a quarter of a mile hike (straight ahead) to get to the geyser.

Imperial Meadows Trail

MAP O-2,O-1

TYPE:	PTP	CAT:	BC	CLASS:	B	SURF:	TRAIL	DIST:	O	STATUS:	E
DIFF:	1	TRAF:	2	CHILD:	Y	HACC:	N	USE:	H S	LENGTH:	1.65
ELEV A:	7229	ELEV B:	7228	ELEV G:	79	ELEV L:	-80	NET:	-1	BMA:	A
MIN:	7224	MAX:	7263	AVG:	7235	AVG +:	1.8%	AVG -:	1.7%	OPEN:	MDW

Reference Point	A-B Mi	A-B Km	B-A Mi	B-A Km	Latitude	Longitude
Trailhead @ jct w/ Fairy Falls Trail - North Spur	0.00	0.00	1.65	2.66	44.54840	-110.84383
Power line crossing	0.05	0.08	1.60	2.57	44.54873	-110.84477
Jct w/ Fairy Creek Trail	0.17	0.27	1.48	2.38	44.54900	-110.84714
Fairy Creek crossing (footbridge)	0.34	0.55	1.31	2.11	44.55063	-110.84937
Social trail intersection	0.83	1.34	0.82	1.32	44.55517	-110.85550
Terminus @ jct w/ Sentinel Meadows Trail	1.65	2.66	0.00	0.00	44.56058	-110.86673

The Imperial Meadows Trail is a part of a confusing mix of trails in this area. If you look at both the Imperial Meadows and Sentinel Meadows Trails, they look like a “U” turned on its side, 90 degrees to the right. Of that shape, the bottom “leg” is the Imperial Meadows Trail while the top “leg” is the Sentinel Meadows Trail. Why the entire thing is not given one name is not known. Most people, of course, will hike in via one trailhead and continue all the way around to the other, thus hiking both trails.

This particular trail passes through the Fairy Meadows Group of thermal features. Most of these are unnamed hot springs with no distinguishing features.

Kepler Cascade Ski Trail

MAP O-6

TYPE:	PTP	CAT:	FC	CLASS:	TH	SURF:	TRAIL	DIST:	O	STATUS:	E
DIFF:	2	TRAF:	1	CHILD:	N	HACC:	N	USE:	H K	LENGTH:	1.12
ELEV A:	7358	ELEV B:	7580	ELEV G:	308	ELEV L:	-86	NET:	222	BMA:	- -
MIN:	7358	MAX:	7601	AVG:	7499	AVG +:	6.9%	AVG -:	5.4%	OPEN:	YR

Reference Point	A-B Mi	A-B Km	B-A Mi	B-A Km	Latitude	Longitude
Trailhead OK3 (E of Old Faithful Lodge Cabin area)	0.00	0.00	1.12	1.80	44.45814	-110.82137
Service road crossing	0.56	0.90	0.56	0.90	44.45354	-110.81299
Trailhead @ Kepler Cascade Parking Lot	1.12	1.80	0.00	0.00	44.44773	-110.80625

This trail passes along what was once the original road into the Old Faithful area from West Thumb. Up until 1972, the road passed right through the center of the complex. However, in the early 1970s, the bypass road was built, the new “modern” interchange was constructed, and the road system around the complex was completely redesigned to better facilitate traffic flow (whether it actually did that or not remains the subject of considerable debate to those who have worked in or visited the park for the past 45 years).

Today, the old road is a hiking trail that will take you up to Kepler Cascade. If you are visiting in the winter, the trail is also maintained as a cross-country skiing trail for the same purpose.

There is some modest elevation gain headed up to Kepler, but overall it is an easy hike/ski. When you get to the end of the trail, you will have to cross the highway. Use caution as vehicles speed through here despite the posted 35 mph limit.

You will cross a service road on this trail. It leads back to the Old Faithful Water Treatment Plant. You are welcome to go back and have a look if you are so inclined.

Lone Star Trail — MAP O-6,O-7

Type:	PTP	Cat:	TH	Class:	B	Surf:	Pv/Trl	Dist:	O	Status:	E
Diff:	2	Traf:	3	Child:	Y	HAcc:	Y	Use:	HBSKR	Length:	2.67
Elev A:	7608	Elev B:	7659	Elev G:	381	Elev L:	-330	Net:	51	BMA:	- -
Min:	7608	Max:	7672	Avg:	7638	Avg +:	4.6%	Avg -:	4.3%	Open:	YR

Reference Point	A-B Mi	A-B Km	B-A Mi	B-A Km	Latitude	Longitude
Trailhead OK1 (2.6 miles S of Old Faithful)	0.00	0.00	2.67	4.30	44.44446	-110.80453
Spur to water impoundment dam	0.11	0.18	2.56	4.12	44.44293	-110.80449
Firehole River crossing (footbridge)	0.50	0.80	2.17	3.49	44.43764	-110.80431
Small thermal area (satellite of Lone Star TA)	0.75	1.21	1.92	3.09	44.43425	-110.80550
Jct w/ Spring Creek Trail	1.60	2.57	1.07	1.72	44.42556	-110.79752
Bicycle path ends	2.33	3.75	0.34	0.55	44.41878	-110.80509
Lone Star Geyser	2.41	3.88	0.26	0.42	44.41820	-110.80646
Jct w/ Shoshone Lake & Howard Eaton OF Trails	2.67	4.30	0.00	0.00	44.41948	-110.81047

The trail to Lone Star Geyser is the second most popular trail in the Old Faithful area after the Fairy Falls Trail. The trail itself is a service road, and was once part of the original road between Old Faithful and West Thumb (up to the late 1930s). It is paved for almost the entire route, though in bad need of repair. It is an excellent bike trail, and is accessible to both those in wheelchairs and those with small children who can hike the five-mile round trip Though most use this to get to the geyser and back, it ends at the junction of two other trails

Just after you begin your hike, you will pass a short side road that takes you to an impoundment dam. This is the water source for the Old Faithful area. The water is captured by this dam and is fed through underground pipes to the water treatment plant located off the Kepler Cascade Ski Trail (see above). Do not climb on or interfere with the operation of the equipment found here.

Just before you get to the geyser itself, the paved road will end, and you will need to leave your bicycles at that point. Lone Star is a tall (9 ft/3m) cone-type geyser that has major eruptions every 3 hours or so, with jets shooting up to 45 feet (14m) in the air. It gets its name from the fact that it sits out by itself. Black Hole Geyser and Perforated Cone Geyser can also be found here, as can about three dozen other minor, unnamed thermal features.

Lower Basin Lake Trail — MAP O-2,O-1

Type:	PTP	Cat:	TH	Class:	N	Surf:	Trail	Dist:	O	Status:	A
Diff:	2	Traf:	1	Child:	N	HAcc:	N	Use:	H	Length:	1.16
Elev A:	7285	Elev B:	7250	Elev G:	132	Elev L:	-167	Net:	35	BMA:	- -
Min:	7217	Max:	7246	Avg:	7285	Avg +:	4.3%	Avg -:	5.1%	Open:	YR

Reference Point	A-B Mi	A-B Km	B-A Mi	B-A Km	Latitude	Longitude
Unmarked trailhead across from Firehole Lake Drive	0.00	0.00	1.16	1.87	44.53450	-110.81936
Lower Basin Lake	0.21	0.34	0.95	1.53	44.53608	-110.82290
Trailhead @ Midway Geyser Basin	1.16	1.87	0.00	0.00	44.53038	-110.83479

This short, abandoned segment of the Howard Eaton Trail takes you to Lower Basin Lake, a small lake named for its location. Though most people hike to the lake and back, you can continue south to Midway Geyser Basin parking lot (though it may require some bushwhacking).

Mallard Creek - Fairy Falls Cutoff Trail — MAP O-3,O-2

Type:	PTP	Cat:	TH	Class:	B	Surf:	Trail	Dist:	O	Status:	E
Diff:	1	Traf:	1	Child:	Y	HAcc:	N	Use:	H S K	Length:	0.79
Elev A:	7335	Elev B:	7247	Elev G:	91	Elev L:	-179	Net:	-88	BMA:	A
Min:	7247	Max:	7379	Avg:	7311	Avg +:	5.8%	Avg -:	6.4%	Open:	MDW

Reference Point	A-B Mi	A-B Km	B-A Mi	B-A Km	Latitude	Longitude
Trailhead @ jct w/ Mallard Creek Trail	0.00	0.00	0.79	1.27	44.50692	-110.82917
Grizzly Pool (colloq)	0.45	0.72	0.34	0.55	44.51236	-110.82943
Till/Rabbit Geyser	0.59	0.95	0.20	0.32	44.51324	-110.83153
Old Faithful to Madison Junction Road	0.64	1.03	0.15	0.24	44.51360	-110.83234
Unnamed hot pool	0.73	1.17	0.06	0.10	44.51477	-110.83260
Terminus @ Fairy Falls Trailhead OK5	0.79	1.27	0.00	0.00	44.51554	-110.83253

This short piece of trail is designed primarily to allow someone to hike from Old Faithful to Mallard Lake, and then out along the Mallard Creek Trail to Fairy Falls. This specific trail will facilitate your travel from Mallard Creek to Fairy Falls.

The trail does have one interesting feature: It passes above Till Geyser (aka Rabbit Geyser). Till has infrequent eruptions of about 30 minutes in duration every 5-11 hours. They can be as high as 20 feet. When you use this trail, you will have to cross the main highway. Be extra careful here as people are watching other vehicles and may not see a random person or two wandering across the road. Note that this trail is in a bear management area.

Mallard Creek Trail — MAP O-3,O-2

Type:	O&B	Cat:	BC	Class:	B	Surf:	Trail	Dist:	O	Status:	E
Diff:	2	Traf:	2	Child:	N	HAcc:	N	Use:	H S K	Length:	4.38
Elev A:	7270	Elev B:	8099	Elev G:	1436	Elev L:	-607	Net:	829	BMA:	- -
Min:	7270	Max:	8271	Avg:	7922	Avg +:	8.7%	Avg -:	7.3%	Open:	YR

Reference Point	A-B Mi	A-B Km	B-A Mi	B-A Km	Latitude	Longitude
Trailhead OK9 (3.8 miles N of Old Faithful)	0.00	0.00	4.38	7.05	44.50697	-110.83314
Jct w/ Powerline Trail	0.08	0.13	4.30	6.92	44.50712	-110.83224
Jct w/ Mallard Creek - Fairy Falls Cutoff Trail	0.22	0.35	4.16	6.69	44.50692	-110.82917
Mallard Creek crossing (often dry in late season)	1.27	2.04	3.11	5.01	44.50005	-110.81329
Jct w/ Mallard Lake Trail	4.38	7.05	0.00	0.00	44.47404	-110.77567

The Mallard Creek Trail is one of two paths to Mallard Lake (the other is named, oddly enough, the Mallard Lake Trail; see below). This one is the longer of the two (by roughly 3/10th of a mile) and though almost entirely in the trees, there is one place where you get a great view of Grand Prismatic Spring off in the distance. You will pass along Mallard Creek Canyon just prior to reaching the Mallard Lake Trail. Turn left here and you have just a few hundred feet to go to reach the lake. The lake itself averages about 30 feet deep and is fishless.

There are three campsites at the lake, with the two on the east side being more popular. This is largely because the one on the west (OB4) does not permit wood fires. These campsites are good for quick, one-night stays for those looking for a short hike to a site. Many people use this trail in conjunction with the Mallard Lake Trail and the Powerline Trail to create a loop from Old Faithful and back.

Mallard Lake Trail — MAP O-3

TYPE:	O&B	CAT:	BC	CLASS:	A	SURF:	TRAIL	DIST:	O	STATUS:	E
DIFF:	2	TRAF:	2	CHILD:	N	HACC:	N	USE:	H S K	LENGTH:	3.53
ELEV A:	7362	ELEV B:	8040	ELEV G:	1108	ELEV L:	-430	NET:	678	BMA:	- -
MIN:	7350	MAX:	8151	AVG:	7787	AVG +:	8.2%	AVG -:	6.4%	OPEN:	YR

Reference Point	A-B Mi	A-B Km	B-A Mi	B-A Km	Latitude	Longitude
Trailhead OK3 (E end of OF Lodge Cabin Complex)	0.00	0.00	3.53	5.68	44.45841	-110.82274
Firehole River crossing (bridge)	0.04	0.06	3.49	5.62	44.45845	-110.82201
Jct w/ Kepler Cascade Ski Trail	0.10	0.16	3.43	5.52	44.45814	-110.82137
Thermal Area (100 ft NW)	0.37	0.60	3.16	5.09	44.45842	-110.81642
Jct w/ Mallard Creek Trail	3.27	5.26	0.26	0.42	44.47404	-110.77567
Mallard Lake/Spur trail to campsite OB4	3.42	5.50	0.11	0.18	44.47597	-110.77560
Spur trails to campsites OB2 & OB3/Terminus	3.53	5.68	0.00	0.00	44.47646	-110.77400

Of the two trails to Mallard Lake, this is the shorter and by far the more popular one (th other is the Mallard Creek Trail; see above). The trailhead for this one can be kind of toug to find if you are new to the Old Faithful area. Go to the Old Faithful Lodge (not the In or the Snow Lodge), and at the main intersection where you can turn left to check in o turn right to head into the cabins area, turn right. Along that little stretch of road, there ar parking spaces on the right-hand side. You can park in any of these. Then, continuing i the same direction, walk around the outer edge of the lodge area, and just as you make th left-hand turn, you will see a sign for the trailhead. Do not park at any of the cabins in thi area unless you are staying in them. This is a relatively easy hike, and the trail is maintaine for cross-country skiers in the winter as well.

Mary Mountain-Nez Perce Creek Trail — MAP O-1,4-

TYPE:	PTP	CAT:	BC	CLASS:	B	SURF:	TRAIL	DIST:	O	STATUS:	E
DIFF:	3	TRAF:	2	CHILD:	N	HACC:	N	USE:	H S	LENGTH:	20.06
ELEV A:	7311	ELEV B:	7871	ELEV G:	2014	ELEV L:	-1454	NET:	560	BMA:	A1
MIN:	7227	MAX:	8351	AVG:	7702	AVG +:	3.4%	AVG -:	2.7%	OPEN:	6/15

Reference Point	A-B Mi	A-B Km	B-A Mi	B-A Km	Latitude	Longitude
Trailhead OK7 (9.4 miles N of Old Faithful)	0.00	0.00	20.06	32.28	44.56992	-110.8161
Culex Thermal Basin (west)	0.22	0.35	19.84	31.93	44.57074	-110.8117
Nez Perce Creek crossing/Culex Thermal Basin (east)	2.19	3.52	17.87	28.76	44.58432	-110.7790
Nez Perce Creek crossing (50 to 60′)	3.14	5.05	16.92	27.23	44.59021	-110.7637
Nez Perce Creek crossing (90′)	3.59	5.78	16.47	26.51	44.59060	-110.7550
Magpie Creek crossing	4.82	7.76	15.24	24.53	44.59598	-110.7327
Cowan Creek crossing	7.00	11.27	13.06	21.02	44.59859	-110.6934
Mary Lake/Mary Lake Patrol Cabin	10.34	16.64	9.72	15.64	44.60433	-110.6405
Old Plateau Trail (A)	10.49	16.88	9.57	15.40	44.60516	-110.6377
Highland Hot Springs (west)	11.46	18.44	8.60	13.84	44.61018	-110.6203
Old Trout Creek Service Road	12.35	19.88	7.71	12.41	44.61540	-110.6047
Highland Hot Springs (east)	12.74	20.50	7.32	11.78	44.61670	-110.5974
Social (U) trail to Violet Springs Thermal Area	16.00	25.75	4.06	6.53	44.64992	-110.5499
Violet Creek crossing (10 to 15′)	16.13	25.96	3.93	6.32	44.64923	-110.5504
Old trail to Otter Creek/Canyon area	18.50	29.77	1.56	2.51	44.66942	-110.5152
Power line crossing	19.48	31.35	0.58	0.93	44.67528	-110.4990
Trailhead 4N1 (4.2 miles S of Canyon Junction)	20.06	32.28	0.00	0.00	44.68333	-110.4937

The Mary Mountain Trail is a 20-mile long trail that connects the west side of the park with the east side of the park. Many people consider it to be two separate trails. The west side, which leads from the trailhead to Mary Lake, is also known as the Nez Perce Creek Trail. This particular segment does not open to the public until June 15 each year due to the heavy presence of grizzly bears in the area. The eastern half, from Mary Lake to the trailhead just north of Alum Creek in Hayden Valley, is typically open all year. This trail is one of the more historic in the park in that much of it was once the road over which visitors traveled from the Old Faithful area to the Canyon and Lake areas in the park's early days, and it is part of the Nez Perce Historic Trail, the path its namesake Native American tribe traversed at they fled from the U.S. Army in 1877.

Note that it is not uncommon at all for either or both sides of this trail to be closed intermittently during the season due to the presence of carcasses near the trail. This path is heavily used by the park's bison, especially before and immediately after the rut in August. It is not uncommon for bison to die as they travel this way and this will attract bears. As a result, the park closes the trail to prevent conflicts between hikers and the big bruins. This trail has one of the highest bear-human contact rates in the park, and several people have been killed by bears in this area (one as recently as 2011). Note that, as a result of heavy bear presence, no overnight camping is allowed in the area.

Given that this trail is so heavily used by bison, there are numerous wildlife trails in the area as well. Be sure you keep your eyes on the trail markers, especially on the eastern four miles, lest you end up on the wrong path. Much of the trail stays marshy year-round as well, so wear shoes suitable for hiking through wet or muddy ground.

The most interesting sights along this trail occur on each end of it. Both have access to some of the park's lesser visited thermal areas. On the west, the Porcupine Hills Group (known as the Morning Mist Springs Group in Scott Bryan's book) is home to about 16 mostly unnamed features. The exception is Porcupine Hill Geyser, located along the trail about ¼ mile east of the trailhead (and which rarely, if ever, erupts these days). Next you will pass through Culex Basin, home to almost 300 mostly unnamed features, while the Nez Perce Thermal Area (south of the trail just before reaching Mary Lake) is home to around 30 unnamed features spread out over several hundred acres.

On the east side, as you head west from the Alum Creek trailhead, you will pass by a small field known as the Alum Creek Group (a dozen unnamed features), and then come to a short social trail that takes you back to the Violet Springs Group. See the separate trail entry for this area in the Canyon District section of this book. Continuing toward the west, you will pass north of Glen Africa Basin (150+ unnamed features) and then enter Highland Hot Springs, an area of less than 80 unnamed features, just before reaching the lake.

Mary Lake itself is an 18-acre body of water that is fishless. One of the park's patrol cabins is located on the north side of the lake. If you arrive at the lake from the west, you will have no doubt encountered the significant hill you had to climb to get there (1,000 feet over 2.5 miles). This hill was known as the "Devil's Stairway" (or Staircase) in the early days of the park when this was a road. Passengers had to get out of their coaches and walk up this hill because the horses could not pull them up fully loaded. In 1890, one visitor died from a heart attack when the park's transportation concessioner forced him to walk up the hill.[2]

Midway Geyser Basin Trail — MAP O-2,O-1

Type:	Loop	Cat:	FC	Class:	B	Surf:	Bdwlk	Dist:	O	Status:	E
Diff:	2	Traf:	5	Child:	Y	HAcc:	Y	Use:	H	Length:	0.64
Elev A:	7230	Elev B:	7230	Elev G:	68	Elev L:	-68	Net:	0	BMA:	- -
Min:	7221	Max:	7272	Avg:	7256	Avg +:	4.7%	Avg -:	3.4%	Open:	YR

Reference Point	A-B Mi	A-B Km	B-A Mi	B-A Km	Latitude	Longitude
Trailhead @ parking lot (5.8 mi N of Old Faithful)	0.00	0.00	0.47	0.76	44.52784	-110.83583
Firehole River crossing (footbridge)	0.02	0.03	0.45	0.72	44.52765	-110.83608
Loop split	0.17	0.27	0.30	0.48	44.52649	-110.83732
Excelsior Geyser	0.22	0.35	0.25	0.40	44.52599	-110.83682
Grand Prismatic Spring	0.34	0.55	0.13	0.21	44.52575	-110.83826
Opal Pool	0.41	0.66	0.06	0.10	44.52656	-110.83861
Turquoise Pool	0.45	0.72	0.02	0.03	44.52651	-110.83769
Return to loop split	0.47	0.76	0.00	0.00	44.52649	-110.83732

Midway Geyser Basin is another one of those areas that is almost always tremendously busy and for which the parking situation is significantly less than adequate. The best time to visit this area from a traffic standpoint is in the early morning or late evening. Doing that, though means the features are considerably less visible and vivid. Early in the morning, steam will obscure the colors of the features, while in the evening the hue of dusk will mute the colors substantially.

Midway is home to two of the most impressive thermal features in Yellowstone. The first Excelsior Geyser, is the blown out crater of what was once the largest geyser in the world. It blew itself apart during an eruption in the late 1800s and has not even remotely approached that grandness since. Today it is a large crater discharging over 4,000 gallons of hot water per minute into the Firehole River (that is two billion gallons per year).

The other feature, of course, is Grand Prismatic. It is the third largest hot spring on the planet and the largest in the United States. The vivid colors in the bacterial and algae mats that surround it have made it one of the most iconic national park features in the world It, too, generates massive quantities of water, discharging some six million gallons per day.

Opal Pool and Turquoise Pool round out the collection. This trail is handicap-accessible and suitable for smaller children. Note that, for much better photographs of Grand Prismatic, there is an observation platform off the Fairy Falls Trail that is worth a visit.

Mystic Falls Trail — MAP O-4,O-8

Type:	PTP	Cat:	TH	Class:	B	Surf:	Trail	Dist:	O	Status:	E
Diff:	2	Traf:	4	Child:	Y*	HAcc:	N	Use:	H S K*	Length:	1.36
Elev A:	7301	Elev B:	7819	Elev G:	696	Elev L:	-178	Net:	518	BMA:	A
Min:	7296	Max:	7819	Avg:	7443	Avg +:	13.2%	Avg -:	7.5%	Open:	MDW

Reference Point	A-B Mi	A-B Km	B-A Mi	B-A Km	Latitude	Longitude
Trailhead @ rear of Biscuit Basin (TH OK4)	0.00	0.00	1.36	2.19	44.48554	-110.85798
Jct w/ Fairy Creek Trail (lower)	0.29	0.47	1.07	1.72	44.48553	-110.86341
Jct w/ Summit Lake Trail	0.34	0.55	1.02	1.64	44.48498	-110.86402
Mystic Falls	0.82	1.32	0.54	0.87	44.48430	-110.87253
Jct w/ Fairy Creek Trail (upper)	1.36	2.19	0.00	0.00	44.48695	-110.87510

The trail to Mystic Falls is another one of the busiest in the Old Faithful area, perhaps third in terms of traffic behind the Fairy Falls and Lone Star Geyser trails. This trail, too, is closed until the Friday of Memorial Day weekend due to the presence of bears in the area. The trail to the falls itself is a little less than a mile and is relatively flat, making it suitable for smaller children. It is not, however, designed for wheelchair access. It is maintained during the winter as a cross-country ski trail.

Though many people just hike to the waterfall and back, consider making the loop that takes you up onto the hill to the north of the falls. This is part of the Fairy Creek Trail, but it will take you to an incredible overlook of the entire Upper Geyser Basin. The view from here, especially in the mornings when the cold air causes all the thermal features to produce steam clouds, is absolutely stunning and other-worldly.

During the summer, the NPS typically offers ranger-led tours to this waterfall. Check at the Old Faithful Visitor Education Center for a schedule of the dates and times.

Mystic Falls Stock Trail — MAP O-4,O-3

TYPE:	PTP	CAT:	TH	CLASS:	B	SURF:	TRAIL	DIST:	O	STATUS:	E
DIFF:	1	TRAF:	1	CHILD:	Y	HACC:	N	USE:	H S	LENGTH:	0.47
ELEV A:	7285	ELEV B:	7300	ELEV G:	66	ELEV L:	-50	NET:	15	BMA:	A
MIN:	7267	MAX:	7304	AVG:	7286	AVG +:	4.8%	AVG -:	4.1%	OPEN:	MDW

Reference Point	A-B Mi	A-B Km	B-A Mi	B-A Km	Latitude	Longitude
Trailhead (pullout 1.7 miles N of Old Faithful)	0.00	0.00	0.43	0.69	44.48100	-110.85392
Little Firehole River footbridge	0.10	0.16	0.33	0.53	44.48190	-110.85511
Jct w/ Mystic Falls Trail	0.43	0.69	0.00	0.00	44.48554	-110.85798

This is a short access trail for those using horses and other stock to get to the Mystic Falls, Fairy Creek, and Summit Lake trails without having to get their animals through the boardwalks at Biscuit Basin. It was once a part of the old Howard Eaton Trail system.

Observation Point Trail — MAP O-5,O-3

TYPE:	O&B	CAT:	TH	CLASS:	B	SURF:	TRAIL	DIST:	O	STATUS:	E
DIFF:	2	TRAF:	3	CHILD:	Y*	HACC:	N	USE:	H	LENGTH:	0.60
ELEV A:	7354	ELEV B:	7579	ELEV G:	318	ELEV L:	-94	NET:	225	BMA:	- -
MIN:	7347	MAX:	7614	AVG:	7463	AVG +:	11.9%	AVG -:	6.7%	OPEN:	YR

Reference Point	A-B Mi	A-B Km	B-A Mi	B-A Km	Latitude	Longitude
Trailhead @ jct w/ Upper Geyser Hill Trail	0.00	0.00	0.60	0.97	44.46236	-110.82764
Jct w/ Solitary Geyser Trail	0.28	0.45	0.32	0.51	44.46416	-110.82568
Terminus @ Observation Point	0.60	0.97	0.00	0.00	44.46454	-110.82452

This is a short but rather steep trail that takes you up to an overlook of the Old Faithful Geyser, the Old Faithful Inn, and the Old Faithful Lodge complexes. While the view of Old Faithful erupting from ground level is incredible in and of itself, the aerial view one gets from this vantage point is absolutely stunning, especially on a sunny day when the sparkling water shooting out of the geyser contrasts with the dark colors of the Inn behind it.

One of the best trips to take here is to go up to the overlook, and then on the way down take the side trail to Solitary Geyser, and finishing it off by taking the circuit around Geyser Hill, upon which you will find a number of unique and interesting thermal features (see below).

Powerline Trail — MAP O-3

TYPE:	PTP	CAT:	TH	CLASS:	B	SURF:	TRAIL	DIST:	O	STATUS:	E
DIFF:	1	TRAF:	1	CHILD:	Y	HACC:	N	USE:	H S K	LENGTH:	1.95
ELEV A:	7282	ELEV B:	7296	ELEV G:	297	ELEV L:	-283	NET:	14	BMA:	- -
MIN:	7272	MAX:	7355	AVG:	7304	AVG +:	5.2%	AVG -:	5.5%	OPEN:	YR

Reference Point	A-B Mi	A-B Km	B-A Mi	B-A Km	Latitude	Longitude
Trailhead @ jct w/ Mallard Creek Trail	0.00	0.00	1.95	3.14	44.50712	-110.83224
Pick up the power lines	0.17	0.27	1.78	2.86	44.50511	-110.83352
Trailhead @ jct w/ Artemisia-Morning Glory Pool Trail	1.95	3.14	0.00	0.00	44.48382	-110.84998

The Powerline Trail is basically designed to facilitate hiking from the Old Faithful area to the trails north of Old Faithful (and back), including the Fairy Falls and the Mallard Creek trails. This trail replaced the segment of the old Howard Eaton Trail that was located on the opposite side of the Firehole River, which was abandoned because it traveled directly through thermal areas and was considered both a safety risk and a potential damage risk to the resources.

The trail follows the powerline easement (and thus the name), and there is little if anything of interest along the trail itself. Access to the south end can be had by hiking to the end of the trail that passes Artemisia Geyser or across from the Biscuit Basin parking lot.

Punch Bowl-Black Sand Basin Trail — MAP O-5,O-3

TYPE:	PTP	CAT:	FC	CLASS:	B	SURF:	TRAIL	DIST:	O	STATUS:	E
DIFF:	1	TRAF:	2	CHILD:	Y	HACC:	Y	USE:	H K	LENGTH:	0.81
ELEV A:	7327	ELEV B:	7300	ELEV G:	80	ELEV L:	-107	NET:	-27	BMA:	- -
MIN:	7308	MAX:	7369	AVG:	7338	AVG +:	4.2%	AVG -:	4.1%	OPEN:	YR

Reference Point	A-B Mi	A-B Km	B-A Mi	B-A Km	Latitude	Longitude
Trailhead @ jct w/ Upper Geyser Basin Trail	0.00	0.00	0.81	1.30	44.46967	-110.84184
Daisy Group/Daisy Geyser	0.11	0.18	0.70	1.13	44.46995	-110.84369
Jct w/ north spur trail	0.21	0.34	0.60	0.97	44.46961	-110.84591
Punchbowl Spring/Group	0.35	0.56	0.46	0.74	44.46910	-110.84844
Power line crossing	0.48	0.77	0.33	0.53	44.46792	-110.85053
Black Sand Pool/Group	0.54	0.87	0.27	0.43	44.46723	-110.85116
Demon's Cave	0.56	0.90	0.25	0.40	44.46686	-110.85100
Trailhead (0.4 miles S of O.F. Interchange)	0.81	1.30	0.00	0.00	44.46367	-110.85214

The Punch Bowl-Black Sand Basin Trail provides access to some interesting thermal features that are off the beaten path in the Old Faithful Area, and provides hiking access to the Black Sand Basin from the trail to Morning Glory Pool.

Daisy Geyser is one of the more entertaining thermal features here, though its eruptions are irregular. The interval between eruptions is between one and seven hours, with the eruptions lasting three to four minutes. The jets of water will typically be between 75 and 150 feet high, though, so if you manage to catch it, it is well worth hanging around for. There are several other geysers here as well, Radiator, Comet, and Splendid to name a few.

Punch Bowl Spring, located on the little side boardwalk just west of Daisy, has a fascinating history. Water from it was piped to the old Wylie Permanent Camping Company tent complex that was located on the hill behind it (still known as Wylie Hill) during the 1910s.

Purple Mountain Trail

MAP O-1

Type:	O&B	**Cat:**	TH	**Class:**	B	**Surf:**	Trail	**Dist:**	O	**Status:**	E
Diff:	3	**Traf:**	1	**Child:**	N	**HAcc:**	N	**Use:**	H S	**Length:**	3.47
Elev A:	6856	**Elev B:**	8414	**Elev G:**	1855	**Elev L:**	-279	**Net:**	1558	**BMA:**	- -
Min:	6856	**Max:**	8442	**Avg:**	7659	**Avg +:**	11.9%	**Avg -:**	7.7%	**Open:**	YR

Reference Point	A-B Mi	A-B Km	B-A Mi	B-A Km	Latitude	Longitude
Trailhead MK1 (just N of Madison Junction)	0.00	0.00	3.47	5.58	44.64653	-110.85503
Terminus @ summit	3.47	5.58	0.00	0.00	44.65937	-110.85818

This trail is a CCC-era trail constructed specifically to allow the park to build and staff a fire lookout tower on the mountain. It, too, was to have been built by the CCC, but before that could happen, the war broke out and the CCC program was abandoned. The tower was finally constructed as a part of the original Mission 66 projects in the late 1950s, but was removed ten years later (as were many of the other lesser-used towers).

The trail itself, however, remains in place, and though lightly used, affords a great view of the Madison Junction & Lower Geyser Basin areas once you get to the top and out of the trees.

Queen's Laundry Spur Trail

MAP O-2

Type:	O&B	**Cat:**	TH	**Class:**	C	**Surf:**	Trail	**Dist:**	O	**Status:**	U
Diff:	1	**Traf:**	2	**Child:**	N	**HAcc:**	N	**Use:**	H S	**Length:**	0.23
Elev A:	7226	**Elev B:**	7225	**Elev G:**	13	**Elev L:**	12	**Net:**	-1	**BMA:**	A
Min:	7213	**Max:**	7227	**Avg:**	7223	**Avg +:**	2.0%	**Avg -:**	2.2%	**Open:**	MDW

Reference Point	A-B Mi	A-B Km	B-A Mi	B-A Km	Latitude	Longitude
Trailhead @ jct w/ Sentinel & Imperial Meadows	0.00	0.00	0.23	0.37	44.56058	-110.86673
Boardwalk/Footbridge	0.13	0.21	0.10	0.16	44.56141	-110.86887
Queen's Laundry/Dumbbell Spring	0.23	0.37	0.00	0.00	44.56265	-110.87005

This short little spur takes you out to the site of one of the most unique structures in the park, the old Norris Bathhouse (NPS photo below). The building itself sits behind a thermal spring known as Queen's Laundry, or Red Terrace Spring. In 1881, park superintendent Philetus W. Norris initiated construction of it to allow visitors to bathe in the warm waters of the Queen's Laundry. However, he was replaced before the structure was completed, and it has sat here since that time in its unfinished condition. It is listed as the oldest structure in a national park intended for public use, and was declared a National Historic Site in 2001.

Sentinel Meadows Trail MAP O-2,O-

TYPE:	PTP	CAT:	BC	CLASS:	B	SURF:	TRAIL	DIST:	O	STATUS:	E
DIFF:	1	TRAF:	2	CHILD:	Y	HACC:	N	USE:	HSRB*	LENGTH:	1.99
ELEV A:	7185	ELEV B:	7217	ELEV G:	198	ELEV L:	-166	NET:	32	BMA:	A
MIN:	7175	MAX:	7248	AVG:	7202	AVG +:	3.5%	AVG -:	3.0%	OPEN:	MDW

Reference Point	A-B Mi	A-B Km	B-A Mi	B-A Km	Latitude	Longitude
Trailhead @ Fountain Flats Parking Area	0.00	0.00	1.99	3.20	44.56713	-110.83522
Ojo Caliente Hot Spring	0.34	0.55	1.65	2.66	44.56272	-110.83823
Firehole River Bridge	0.37	0.60	1.62	2.61	44.56233	-110.83849
Jct w/ Goose Lake/Feather Lake (Fairy Falls) Trail	0.39	0.63	1.60	2.57	44.56211	-110.83863
Fairy Creek crossing (footbridge)	0.52	0.84	1.47	2.37	44.56247	-110.84109
Power line crossing	0.78	1.26	1.21	1.95	44.56327	-110.84609
Spur trail to campsite OG1 (0.05 miles)	1.14	1.83	0.85	1.37	44.56421	-110.85285
Terminus @ jct w/ Imperial Meadows Trail	1.99	3.20	0.00	0.00	44.56058	-110.86673

The Sentinel Meadows Trail is the main trail into this area; it brings you across th bridge from the parking lot and then turns immediately right into its namesake meadow Continuing straight at this point puts you on the Goose Lake/Feather Lake Trail (and wil also take you to the Fairy Falls Trail). The meadow was named after nearby Sentinel Creek which in turn was named because several of the thermal features in this area resemble "sentinels" guarding the area.

Just before you cross the bridge over the Firehole River, you will pass by Ojo Caliente Ho Spring, one of the prettier hot springs in the area, but one with a checkered past. In 1958, young boy who was playing in the area while his father was fishing fell into the pool and late died from the burns he received as a result. The spring's name means "hot eye" in Spanish and the name is fitting. It is one of the hottest thermal pools in Yellowstone.

Once you turn right and head down the trail, you will enter a thermal area known as th Sentinel Group. This is an area of about two dozen features, many of which are named including the aforementioned Red Terrace Spring/Queen's Laundry. Others include Steep Cone, Flat Cone Spring, Rosette Geyser, and Iron Pot. Steep Cone, Mound Spring, and Fla Cone are the "sentinels" that gave this area its name.

This trail has a campsite located on it. OG1 has limited shade, but has excellent views of the thermal field and makes for a great launching point from which to explore this part of the park. The trail ends at the junction with the Imperial Meadows Trail and the spur trail to Queen's Laundry.

Solitary Geyser Trail MAP O-5,O-3

TYPE:	PTP	CAT:	TH	CLASS:	B	SURF:	TRAIL	DIST:	O	STATUS:	E
DIFF:	1	TRAF:	2	CHILD:	Y	HACC:	N	USE:	H	LENGTH:	0.60
ELEV A:	7371	ELEV B:	7445	ELEV G:	154	ELEV L:	-80	NET:	74	BMA:	- -
MIN:	7367	MAX:	7470	AVG:	7432	AVG +:	7.3%	AVG -:	6.2%	OPEN:	YR

Reference Point	A-B Mi	A-B Km	B-A Mi	B-A Km	Latitude	Longitude
Trailhead @ jct w/ Upper Geyser Hill Trail	0.00	0.00	0.60	0.97	44.46468	-110.82978
Solitary Geyser	0.26	0.42	0.34	0.55	44.46816	-110.82933
Trailhead @ jct w/ Observation Point Trail	0.60	0.97	0.00	0.00	44.46416	-110.82568

Solitary Geyser sits off in its own little pocket in the hill north of Geyser Hill (thus, its name). This remote feature was originally a hot spring, but in 1915 its waters were tapped to be the source of warm water for the new pool and bathhouse built by the Henry Brothers across the river from the Old Faithful Inn. Once they started draining the water from it, it took on the nature of a geyser and has performed as such ever since. The bathhouse shut down in 1948 and was destroyed in 1950. Water is no longer being shunted from Solitary but it retains its geyser form these days.

Solitary erupts every four to eight minutes to heights of roughly three feet or so. It will occasionally have a larger eruption of up to 25 feet. The eruptions last for about a minute. This unique feature's historical relationship to the park make it worth seeing if you have the time for the quick side trip.

Spring Creek Trail — MAP O-7,8-2

Type:	PTP	Cat:	TH	Class:	B	Surf:	Trail	Dist:	O	Status:	E
Diff:	2	Traf:	1	Child:	N	HAcc:	N	Use:	H S K	Length:	4.00
Elev A:	7640	Elev B:	8070	Elev G:	1020	Elev L:	-591	Net:	430	BMA:	- -
Min:	7629	Max:	8070	Avg:	7852	Avg +:	7.3%	Avg -:	5.8%	Open:	YR

Reference Point	A-B Mi	A-B Km	B-A Mi	B-A Km	Latitude	Longitude
Trailhead @ jct w/ Lone Star Trail	0.00	0.00	4.00	6.44	44.42556	-110.79752
Firehole River crossing (footbridge)	0.04	0.06	3.96	6.37	44.42549	-110.79694
Turtle Rock/Spring Creek Canyon	1.76	2.83	2.24	3.60	44.42718	-110.77253
Congress Lake Trailhead	2.48	3.99	1.52	2.45	44.43084	-110.76022
Spring Creek Picnic Area Trailhead	2.83	4.55	1.17	1.88	44.42981	-110.75340
Trailhead @ jct w/ Divide Trail	4.00	6.44	0.00	0.00	44.43409	-110.73340

The Spring Creek Trail exists along one of the old park roads. From the early 1890s up until the road was realigned in the 1930s, this was the main road between Old Faithful and West Thumb. You can still find bits of asphalt and rebar along the trail today. Once its time as a road was over, it became part of the Howard Eaton Trail system. And although it is generally only maintained during the winter as a ski trail these days, it makes an excellent hiking trail in the summer for those who want to see an area that not many others get to see.

Along the trail you will pass through Spring Creek Canyon, which is a small but picturesque canyon, and in the author's opinion is one of the prettiest out-of-the-way places in the park. The creek that flows through it gets its name from the fact it is fed by a number of cold springs along its path.

One unique feature along this trail is Turtle Rock (GPS 44.42719, -11077253). The 20-foot-tall rock formation gets its name from its appearance as a snapping turtle rearing its head up into the air. This was the scene of one of the park's five (known) stagecoach robberies. In 1908, a lone robber stood in wait for a train of stagecoaches to come by. One by one, over the course of several hours, the man stopped and robbed 17 stagecoaches and over 150 passengers of their valuables. The thief was never apprehended.

You can access this trail from any one of several locations. It technically starts at the Divide Trail on its eastern end, but you can also access it from the Spring Creek Picnic Area and a couple of unsigned pullouts located to the east of the picnic area. Prior to the middle of July, much of the western portion of this trail is rather muddy and marshy.

Summit Lake Trail — MAP O-8

Type:	PTP	Cat:	BC	Class:	C	Surf:	Trail	Dist:	O	Status:	E
Diff:	3	Traf:	1	Child:	N	HAcc:	N	Use:	H S	Length:	15.95
Elev A:	7619	Elev B:	8052	Elev G:	1426	Elev L:	-993	Net:	433	BMA:	A
Min:	7414	Max:	8611	Avg:	8344	Avg +:	3.4%	Avg -:	2.2%	Open:	MDW

Reference Point	A-B Mi	A-B Km	B-A Mi	B-A Km	Latitude	Longitude
Trailhead (OK4) @ jct w/ Mystic Falls Trail	0.00	0.00	15.95	25.67	44.48498	-110.86402
Little Firehole River crossing (35')	0.05	0.08	15.90	25.59	44.48429	-110.86437
Spur trail to campsite OE1/Summit Lake (0.02 miles)	6.98	11.23	8.97	14.44	44.41541	-110.93695
Smoke Jumper Hot Springs	7.96	12.81	7.99	12.86	44.41202	-110.95399
Park boundary TH 9K9 (continues into CTNF)	15.95	25.67	0.00	0.00	44.39448	-111.09714

The Summit Lake Trail dates to 1910, when it was built to afford access from the western boundary to the Upper Geyser Basin for U.S. Army patrols. The trail is lightly used today mostly by those who wish to explore the Smoke Jumper Hot Springs Thermal Area.

The lake itself gets its name from its location atop the Continental Divide in this area. It is about 30 acres in size, roughly eight feet deep, and is fishless. There is a very small lake located adjacent to Summit, just north of the lone campsite found there. It is informally known as Little Summit Lake for its location next to its larger brother.

The trail to the lake from the Old Faithful area involves a 1,400-foot (427m) climb, much of it in the first two miles of your trek. And keep in mind that, though the western half of the trail is technically open all year, the eastern access does not open until the Friday of Memorial Day weekend (prior to which time the trail will likely still be snowed in anyway).

Smoke Jumper Hot Springs is a large thermal field containing well over 100 known features, none of which are officially named. Continuing westward from the lake, you will reach the old West Boundary Trail running north and south. You can also head out into National Forest land on the USFS trail system.

Terrace Springs Trail — MAP O-1

Type:	Loop	Cat:	FC	Class:	B	Surf:	Bdwlk	Dist:	O	Status:	E
Diff:	1	Traf:	3	Child:	Y	HAcc:	Y	Use:	H	Length:	0.19
Elev A:	6910	Elev B:	6910	Elev G:	50	Elev L:	-50	Net:	0	BMA:	- -
Min:	6902	Max:	6936	Avg:	6914	Avg +:	2.2%	Avg -:	22.9%	Open:	YR

Reference Point	A-B Mi	A-B Km	B-A Mi	B-A Km	Latitude	Longitude
Trailhead (0.8 miles N of Madison Junction)	0.00	0.00		0.00	44.65000	-110.84543
Loop split	0.03	0.05		0.00	44.65005	-110.84595
Terrace Spring	0.10	0.16		0.00	44.65013	-110.84657
Return to loop split	0.16	0.26		0.00	44.65005	-110.84595

Terrace Springs is a small thermal area located just east of Madison Junction. The name comes from the terraces the runoff forms on the other side of the road. The short trail takes hikers along a half dozen of the 13 thermal features in this area, a few of which are named. These pools are rather cool, relatively speaking (most in the 140F range). So the bubbling and gurgling that occurs in the pools is the result of carbon dioxide or other gases. This is a boardwalked trail and is suitable for both younger children and those in wheelchairs.

UGB-Biscuit Basin Bike Trail — MAP O-4,O-5

Type:	PTP	Cat:	FC	Class:	B	Surf:	Trail	Dist:	O	Status:	E
Diff:	1	Traf:	2	Child:	Y	HAcc:	N	Use:	H B K	Length:	0.98
Elev A:	7329	Elev B:	7288	Elev G:	67	Elev L:	-108	Net:	-41	BMA:	- -
Min:	7284	Max:	7352	Avg:	7315	Avg +:	3.0%	Avg -:	3.5%	Open:	YR

Reference Point	A-B Mi	A-B Km	B-A Mi	B-A Km	Latitude	Longitude
Trailhead @ jct w/ UGB Trail	0.00	0.00	0.98	1.58	44.47114	-110.84198
Jct w/ spur trail to Punchbowl/Daisy Trail	0.07	0.11	0.91	1.46	44.47094	-110.84336
Cyclops Spring	0.34	0.55	0.64	1.03	44.47345	-110.84699
Power line crossing	0.49	0.79	0.49	0.79	44.37527	-110.84851
Trailhead @ Biscuit Basin	0.98	1.58	0.00	0.00	44.48060	-110.85380

This short, one-mile trail is basically intended as a path for bicyclists to go from the Morning Glory area to Biscuit Basin, though it is certainly open to hikers as well. It provides access to Cyclops Spring, though you really cannot see much of it other than its runoff field. Note that this trail makes a 90-degree, right hand turn just after you depart from the paved road of the original trail. If you continue straight, you will end up on the Punch Bowl - Daisy Trail.

Along the lower end of the trail (near Biscuit Basin), the trail does afford views of the huge number of geysers and pools located in the Cascade Group (i.e., Artemisia Geyser, Seismic Geyser, Atomizer, etc., across the river) and the Westside Group (on the near side of the river).

UGB-Biscuit Basin to Morning Glory Pool — MAP O-4

Type:	PTP	Cat:	FC	Class:	B	Surf:	Trail	Dist:	O	Status:	E
Diff:	1	Traf:	3	Child:	Y	HAcc:	N	Use:	H K	Length:	0.82
Elev A:	7283	Elev B:	7312	Elev G:	166	Elev L:	-137	Net:	29	BMA:	- -
Min:	7283	Max:	7351	Avg:	7315	Avg +:	5.3%	Avg -:	6.2%	Open:	YR

Reference Point	A-B Mi	A-B Km	B-A Mi	B-A Km	Latitude	Longitude
Trailhead (across from Biscuit Basin parking lot)	0.00	0.00	0.82	1.32	44.48414	-110.85132
Jct w/ Powerline Trail	0.10	0.16	0.72	1.16	44.48382	-110.84998
Cauliflower Geyser	0.11	0.18	0.71	1.14	44.48346	-110.85003
Mirror Pool	0.12	0.19	0.70	1.13	44.48310	-110.85004
Baby Daisy Geyser	0.21	0.34	0.61	0.98	44.48183	-110.85000
Sprite Spring/Cathos Spring	0.36	0.58	0.46	0.74	44.47979	-110.84889
Pinto Spring/Gem Pool	0.38	0.61	0.44	0.71	44.47957	-110.84882
Artemisia Geyser/Atomizer Geyser	0.46	0.74	0.36	0.58	44.47842	-110.84824
Morning Glory Pool/Trail jct w/ UGB Trail	0.82	1.32	0.00	0.00	44.47506	-110.84321

This is one of the more fascinating trails in the Old Faithful area, despite its not being visited by very many people. Most folks venture as far out as Morning Glory Pool and then turn around and head back to Old Faithful, missing out on some of the unique features that can be found within just another mile. This trail follows the path of the original road into Old Faithful; you used to be able to drive right by these pools to see them back in the day. To access this trail from the B end, park in the Biscuit Basin lot and cross the road (carefully).

This trail is home to Artemisia (ar-tuh-MEEZ-ya) Geyser, which is named after the scientific name for sagebrush, the color of which gives the pool its name. It erupts every 19-40 hours for about an hour, with eruptions reaching as high as 60 feet. Seismic Geyser is als located here. It was given its name because it formed in the aftermath of the 1959 Hebge Lake earthquake. Atomizer Geyser, Satellite Geyser, Restless Geyser, Hillside Geyser, an Aftershock Geyser can be found here as well.

Upper Geyser Basin Trail — MAP O-5,O-3

Type:	Loop	**Cat:**	FC	**Class:**	A	**Surf:**	Bdw/Pv	**Dist:**	O	**Status:**	E
Diff:	1	**Traf:**	5	**Child:**	Y	**HAcc:**	Y	**Use:**	H B*	**Length:**	2.98
Elev A:	7363	**Elev B:**	7365	**Elev G:**	157	**Elev L:**	-155	**Net:**	2	**BMA:**	- -
Min:	7319	**Max:**	7371	**Avg:**	7339	**Avg +:**	2.2%	**Avg -:**	2.4%	**Open:**	YR

Reference Point	A-B Mi	A-B Km	B-A Mi	B-A Km	Latitude	Longitude
Trailhead @ jct w/ Upper Geyser Hill Trail	0.00	0.00	2.44	3.93	44.46424	-110.83063
Oxbow bend - site of original Supt Cabin/OFRS	0.11	0.18	2.33	3.75	44.46481	-110.83270
Rubber Pool (south side)	0.22	0.35	2.22	3.57	44.46494	-110.83474
Liberty Pool (south)	0.25	0.40	2.19	3.52	44.46505	-110.83542
Tardy Geyser	0.31	0.50	2.13	3.43	44.46542	-110.83641
Spasmodic Geyser Loop East	0.32	0.51	2.12	3.41	44.46560	-110.83655
Cutoff trail to Crested Pool/Churn Geyser	0.33	0.53	2.11	3.40	44.46569	-110.83659
Spasmodic Geyser Loop West/Belgian Pool	0.36	0.58	2.08	3.35	44.46611	-110.83677
Rift Geyser	0.37	0.60	2.07	3.33	44.46623	-110.83687
Triplet Geysers (N, E, & W)	0.38	0.61	2.06	3.32	44.46632	-110.83708
Grand, Percolator, Vent, & Turban Geysers	0.39	0.63	2.05	3.30	44.46641	-110.83724
Key Spring (north)	0.47	0.76	1.97	3.17	44.46740	-110.83766
Economic & East Economic Geysers	0.50	0.80	1.94	3.12	44.46782	-110.83799
Wave Spring	0.51	0.82	1.93	3.11	44.46803	-110.83802
Crack Geyser (north)	0.52	0.84	1.92	3.09	44.46810	-110.83810
Beauty Pool	0.56	0.90	1.88	3.03	44.46829	-110.83884
Chromatic Pool	0.59	0.95	1.85	2.98	44.46849	-110.83939
Firehole River Crossing (footbridge)	0.67	1.08	1.77	2.85	44.46888	-110.84048
Inkwell Spring	0.68	1.09	1.76	2.83	44.46898	-110.84057
Oblong Geyser	0.71	1.14	1.73	2.78	44.46940	-110.84073
Giant Group/Purple Pools (across river)	0.79	1.27	1.65	2.66	44.47064	-110.84103
Grotto Geyser	0.88	1.42	1.56	2.51	44.47168	-110.84173
Jct w/ spur trail to Morning Glory Pool/Riverside	0.89	1.43	1.55	2.49	44.47167	-110.84203
Jct w/ UGB-Biscuit Basin Bicycle Trail	0.93	1.50	1.51	2.43	44.47114	-110.84198
Jct w/ Punch Bowl-Black Sand Basin Trail	1.05	1.69	1.39	2.24	44.46967	-110.84184
Round Spring Group	1.10	1.77	1.34	2.16	44.46884	-110.84176
Witches Caldron/Crater of the Moon	1.35	2.17	1.09	1.75	44.46543	-110.84059
Orange Spring Group (south)	1.42	2.29	1.02	1.64	44.46480	-110.83944
South Orange Spring Group	1.51	2.43	0.93	1.50	44.46400	-110.83792
Cutoff trail to Crested Pool/Churn Geyser	1.56	2.51	0.88	1.42	44.46360	-110.83714
Castle Geyser, Tortoise Shell Spring, Gizmo Geyser	1.58	2.54	0.86	1.38	44.46341	-110.83679
Gravel trail to Lower Service Station/Gen Store	1.64	2.64	0.80	1.29	44.46288	-110.83588
Myriad Creek/Gravel trail to Lower Gen Store	1.73	2.78	0.71	1.14	44.46192	-110.83451
Site of old Swimming Pool/Bath House	1.88	3.03	0.56	0.90	44.46106	-110.83182
Old Faithful Group boardwalk (turn left/north)	1.92	3.09	0.52	0.84	44.46093	-110.83106
Chinese Spring	2.09	3.36	0.35	0.56	44.46197	-110.82906
Blue Star Spring	2.10	3.38	0.34	0.55	44.46188	-110.82864
Jct w/ Upper Geyser Hill Trail	2.20	3.54	0.24	0.39	44.46101	-110.82696
Old Faithful Geyser	2.38	3.83	0.06	0.10	44.45963	-110.82865
Old Faithful Visitor Education Center	2.44	3.93	0.00	0.00	44.45893	-110.82905

The beginning point for this trail is at its junction with the Geyser Hill Trail (see below), right next to the "Goggles" group of thermal features. As you begin, you will walk downhill into the forested area. The oxbow bend of the Firehole River to your left was the site of the first structures here in the Old Faithful area. It was home to the superintendent's cabin and the original Old Faithful Ranger Station, along with a variety of support structures over time. They were all removed as new facilities were built by the Inn and the Lodge, but you can still see the footprints of some of these old buildings in Google Earth.

Since there are several available guides to the features in this area, this book will not go into descriptions about them. The trail is boardwalked all the way out to the point where it intersects with the old road at Grotto Geyser. There is a quarter mile spur that takes you to Morning Glory Pool, and then you can return back to the Old Faithful Visitor Education Center via the paved trail.

Note that you can ride bicycles on the paved portion of this trail, up to Morning Glory. The boardwalks and non-paved trail surfaces are off-limits to bikes, however.

Upper Geyser Hill Trail — MAP O-5,O-3

Type:	Loop	**Cat:**	FC	**Class:**	A	**Surf:**	Bdwlk	**Dist:**	O	**Status:**	E
Diff:	1	**Traf:**	5	**Child:**	Y	**HAcc:**	Y	**Use:**	H	**Length:**	0.82
Elev A:	7368	**Elev B:**	7368	**Elev G:**	84	**Elev L:**	-84	**Net:**	0	**BMA:**	- -
Min:	7334	**Max:**	7378	**Avg:**	7360	**Avg +:**	4.5%	**Avg -:**	4.6%	**Open:**	YR

Reference Point	A-B Mi	A-B Km	B-A Mi	B-A Km	Latitude	Longitude
Trailhead @ jct w/ UGB Trail (near lodge)	0.00	0.00	0.67	1.08	44.46101	-110.82696
Firehole River crossing (footbridge)	0.10	0.16	0.57	0.92	44.46183	-110.82715
Jct w/ Observation Point Trail	0.12	0.19	0.55	0.89	44.46236	-110.82764
Loop split	0.15	0.24	0.52	0.84	44.46271	-110.82790
Dome Geyser [E}	0.21	0.34	0.46	0.74	44.46358	-110.82831
Infant Geyser [W], Mottled Pool, Butterfly Spring	0.22	0.35	0.45	0.72	44.46372	-110.82834
Vault Geyser; Giantess Geyser	0.26	0.42	0.41	0.66	44.46382	-110.82899
Topaz Spring; Teakettle Spring	0.27	0.43	0.40	0.64	44.46379	-110.82927
Sponge Geyser, Pump Geyser	0.30	0.48	0.37	0.60	44.46376	-110.82975
Doublet Pool	0.34	0.55	0.33	0.53	44.46431	-110.82957
Beach Spring, Aurum Geyser	0.36	0.58	0.31	0.50	44.46461	-110.82958
Jct w/ Solitary Geyser Trail	0.37	0.60	0.30	0.48	44.46468	-110.82978
Pendant Spring	0.39	0.63	0.28	0.45	44.46470	-110.83012
Ear Spring	0.41	0.66	0.26	0.42	44.46453	-110.83041
Jct w/ Upper Geyser Basin Trail	0.43	0.69	0.24	0.39	44.46424	-110.83063
Goggle Spring, North Goggle Spring	0.43	0.69	0.24	0.39	44.46416	-110.83069
Lion Group	0.45	0.72	0.22	0.35	44.46402	-110.83073
Heart Spring, Pot of Gold	0.47	0.76	0.20	0.32	44.46375	-110.83056
Arrowhead Spring, Inverted Geyser	0.49	0.79	0.18	0.29	44.46344	-110.83071
Depression Geyser	0.52	0.84	0.15	0.24	44.46303	-110.83052
Scissor Springs	0.53	0.85	0.14	0.23	44.46293	-110.83035
Beehive Geyser, Beehive Indicator, Copper Kettle	0.55	0.89	0.12	0.19	44.46279	-110.53009
Ballcap Geyser, Plume Geyser	0.58	0.93	0.09	0.14	44.46267	-110.82948
Midget, Surge, & South Anemone Geysers	0.61	0.98	0.06	0.10	44.46280	-110.82911
Bronze Spring, Little Squirt Geyser	0.63	1.01	0.04	0.06	44.46274	-110.52853
Sulphide Spring	0.66	1.06	0.01	0.02	44.46271	-110.82809
Return to loop split	0.67	1.08	0.00	0.00	44.46271	-110.82790

Geyser Hill (or Upper Geyser Hill to some people) is the hill across the Firehole River fro the Old Faithful Geyser. The quickest way to access it is to walk around the Old Faithfu Geyser viewing boardwalk toward the Lodge, and then go down the hill and cross th bridge over the Firehole River. Geyser Hill is home to some of the most popular therma features in the area, including Beehive Geyser.

Immediately after crossing the bridge, hikers have the option of climbing up to Observatio Point. If time permits, the view from atop this hill is incredible, especially on a clea sunny day. You can also access Solitary Geyser from a trail on the opposite side of the hil Regardless, if you have only a limited amount of time for a short hike in the Old Faithfu area, you should definitely consider taking in the sights on Geyser Hill.

White Creek Trail — MAP O-2,O-

TYPE:	O&B	CAT:	TH	CLASS:	N	SURF:	TRAIL	DIST:	O	STATUS:	A
DIFF:	1	TRAF:	1	CHILD:	Y	HACC:	N	USE:	H	LENGTH:	0.35
ELEV A:	7329	ELEV B:	7348	ELEV G:	59	ELEV L:	-39	NET:	19	BMA:	A
MIN:	7328	MAX:	7352	AVG:	7340	AVG +:	5.8%	AVG -:	4.4%	OPEN:	MDW

Reference Point	A-B Mi	A-B Km	B-A Mi	B-A Km	Latitude	Longitude
Trailhead @ Great Fountain Geyser	0.00	0.00	0.35	0.56	44.53633	-110.79928
A-0, A-1, and A-2 Geysers (W)	0.08	0.13	0.27	0.43	44.53519	-110.79919
Botryoidal Spring	0.10	0.16	0.25	0.40	44.53489	-110.79910
Verdant Spring (across river)	0.14	0.23	0.21	0.34	44.53433	-110.79867
Octopus Spring, Diamond Spring	0.19	0.31	0.16	0.26	44.53112	-110.79778
Electric Socket Pool	0.26	0.42	0.09	0.14	44.53330	-110.79746
Tuft Geyser (S), Eclipse Geyser (N)	0.27	0.43	0.08	0.13	44.53313	-110.79727
Five Sisters Springs (across creek)	0.31	0.50	0.04	0.06	44.53277	-110.79667
Spindle Geyser/Trail terminus	0.35	0.56	0.00	0.00	44.53238	-110.79622

The White Creek Trail is a now-closed trail that took you along White Creek from th parking spots at Great Fountain Geyser on the Firehole Lake Drive. This was an informa and largely unmaintained trail that hikers could use to see some additional, unique therma features back along the creek, known collectively as the White Creek Group. However vandalism and public safety concerns (allegedly) led to the closing of this area by the NPS few years ago. The trail detail here in case they elect to open the area back up one day.

The thermal field continues way back up into the woods past Spindle Geyser, and you coul bushwhack through the area to view the thermal features and White Creek Falls, but th "trail" ended at Spindle for the most part. Hopefully, one day the NPS will build an actua trail back up in this area and re-open it to the public.

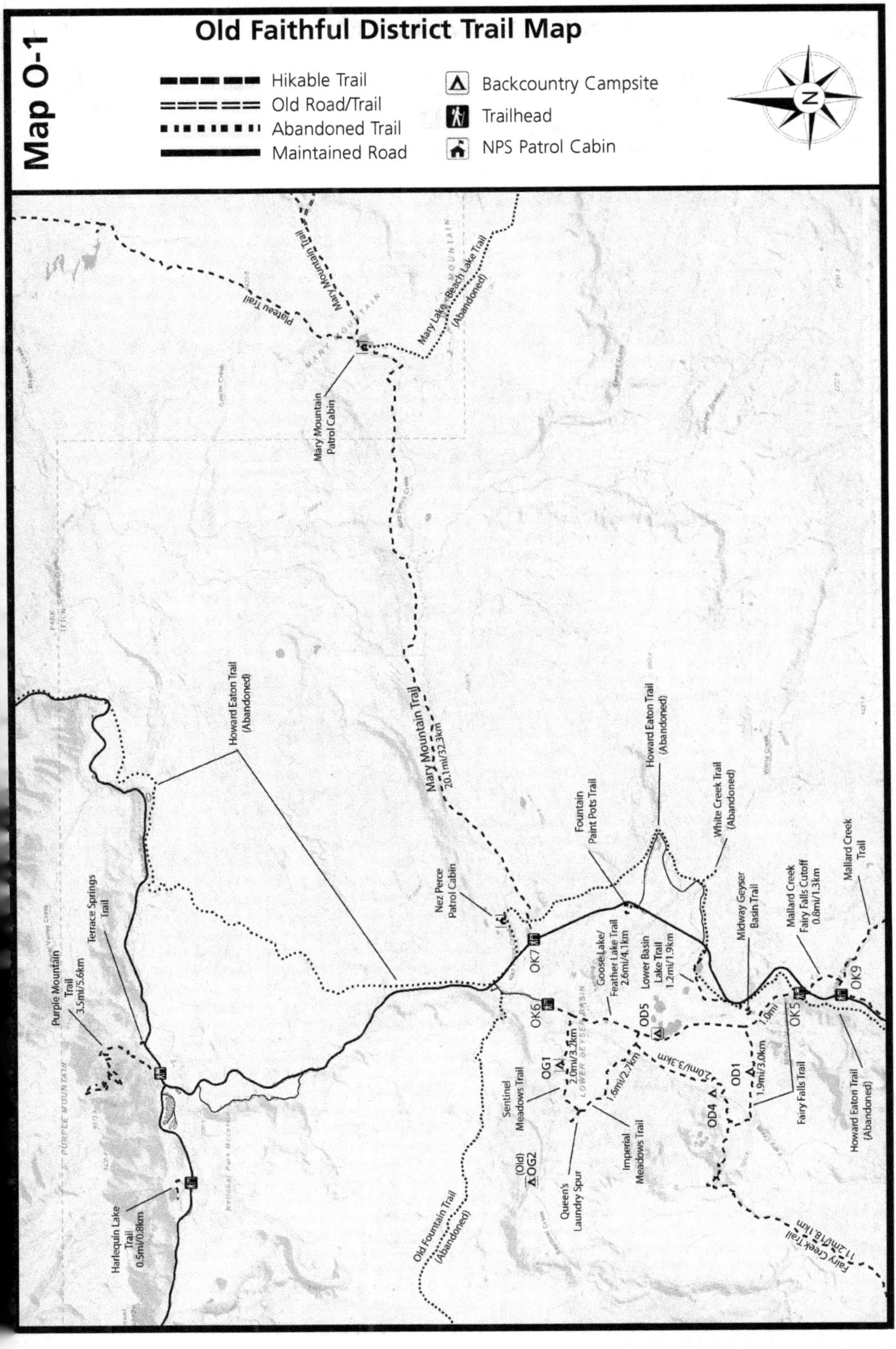

Map O-1

Old Faithful District Trail Map

Hikable Trail
Old Road/Trail
Abandoned Trail
Maintained Road
Backcountry Campsite
Trailhead
NPS Patrol Cabin

Plateau Trail
Mary Mountain Trail
Mary Lake - Beach Lake Trail (Abandoned)
Mary Mountain Patrol Cabin
Howard Eaton Trail (Abandoned)
Mary Mountain Trail 20.1mi/32.3km
Nez Perce Patrol Cabin
Fountain Paint Pots Trail
Howard Eaton Trail (Abandoned)
White Creek Trail (Abandoned)
Midway Geyser Basin Trail
Mallard Creek Fairy Falls Cutoff 0.8mi/1.3km
Mallard Creek Trail
Purple Mountain Trail 3.5mi/5.6km
Terrace Springs Trail
OK7
Goose Lake/ Feather Lake Trail 2.6mi/4.1km
Lower Basin Lake Trail 1.2mi/1.9km
OK6
OD5
1.0mi
OK5
OK9
OG1
2.0mi/3.2km
1.6mi/2.7km
2.0mi/3.3km
OD1
1.9mi/3.0km
OD4
Sentinel Meadows Trail
Imperial Meadows Trail
Fairy Falls Trail
Howard Eaton Trail (Abandoned)
(Old) OG2
Queen's Laundry Spur
Harlequin Lake Trail 0.5mi/0.8km
Old Fountain Trail (Abandoned)
Fairy Creek Trail 11.2mi/18.1km

Map O-2

Old Faithful District Trail Map

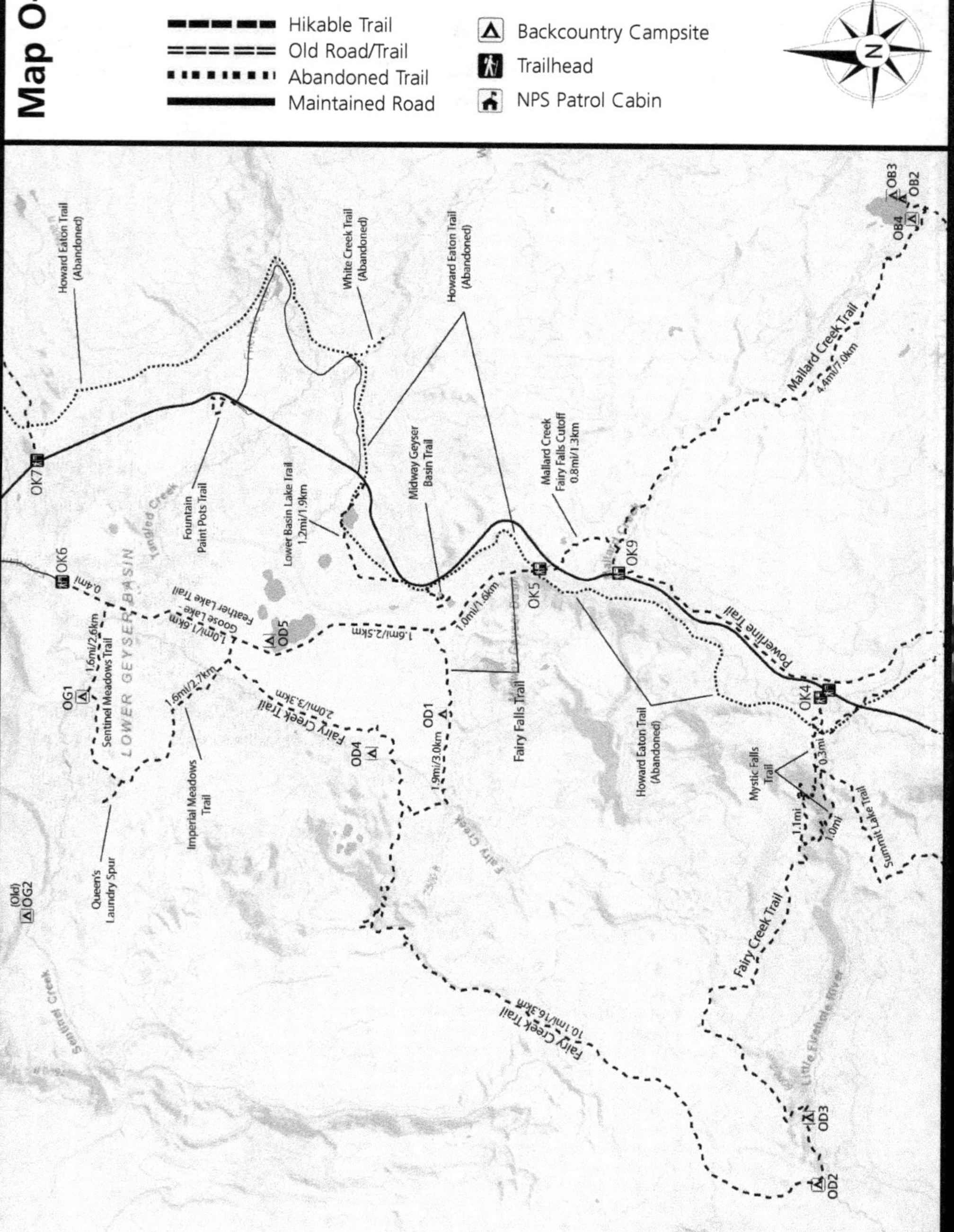

Hikable Trail
Old Road/Trail
Abandoned Trail
Maintained Road

Backcountry Campsite

Trailhead

NPS Patrol Cabin

Map O-3

Old Faithful District Trail Map

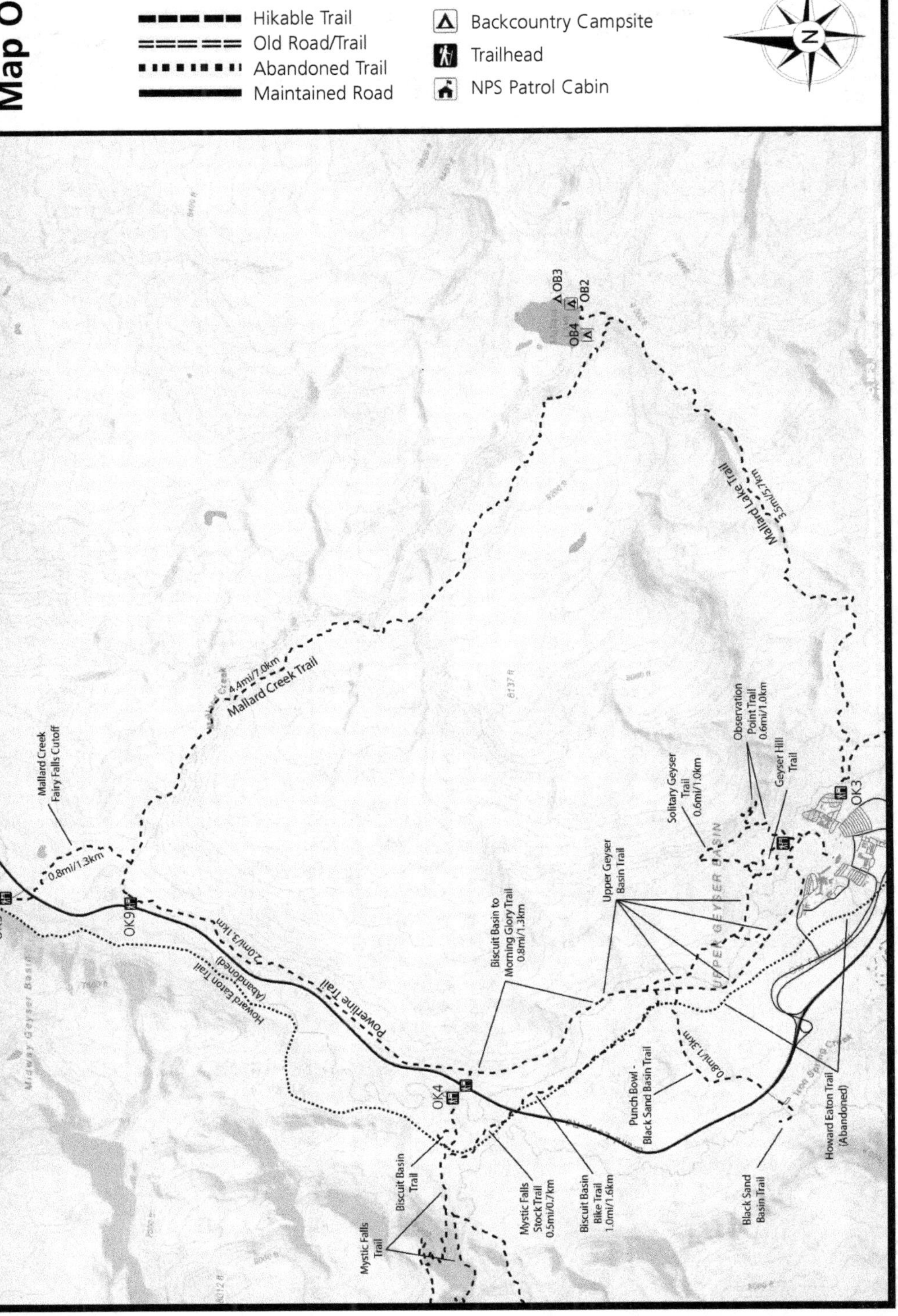

Hikable Trail
Old Road/Trail
Abandoned Trail
Maintained Road

Backcountry Campsite
Trailhead
NPS Patrol Cabin

Map O-4

Old Faithful District Trail Map

Hikable Trail
Old Road/Trail
Abandoned Trail
Maintained Road

Backcountry Campsite
Trailhead
NPS Patrol Cabin

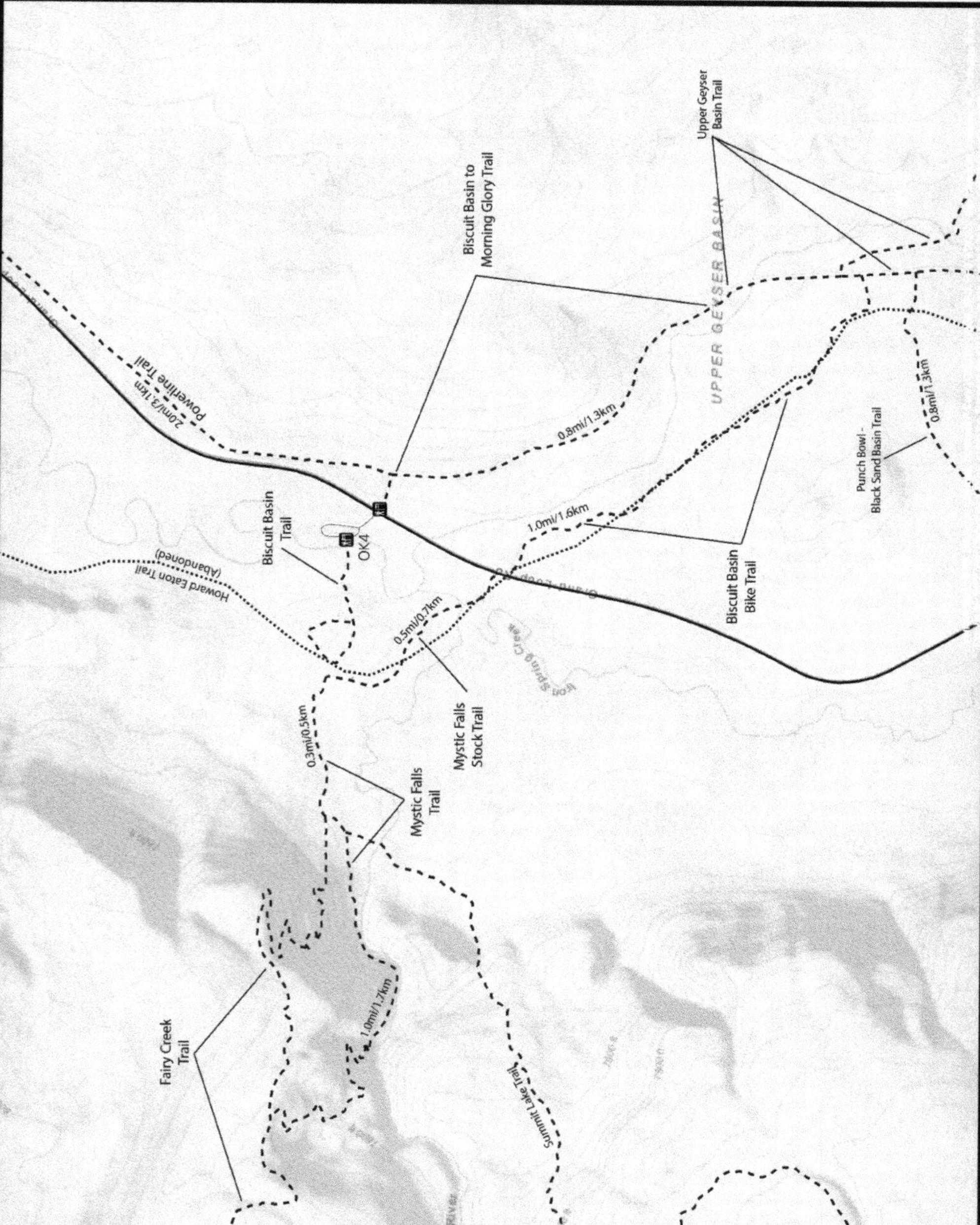

Upper Geyser Basin Trail
Biscuit Basin to Morning Glory Trail
UPPER GEYSER BASIN
Powerline Trail
2.0mi/3.1km
0.8mi/1.3km
0.8mi/1.3km
Punch Bowl - Black Sand Basin Trail
Biscuit Basin Trail
OK4
1.0mi/1.6km
Howard Eaton Trail (Abandoned)
Grand Loop Road
Biscuit Basin Bike Trail
0.5mi/0.7km
Iron Spring Creek
Mystic Falls Stock Trail
0.3mi/0.5km
Mystic Falls Trail
1.0mi/1.7km
Fairy Creek Trail
Summit Lake Trail
Firehole River

Map O-5

Old Faithful District Trail Map

Hikable Trail
Old Road/Trail
Abandoned Trail
Maintained Road

Backcountry Campsite
Trailhead
NPS Patrol Cabin

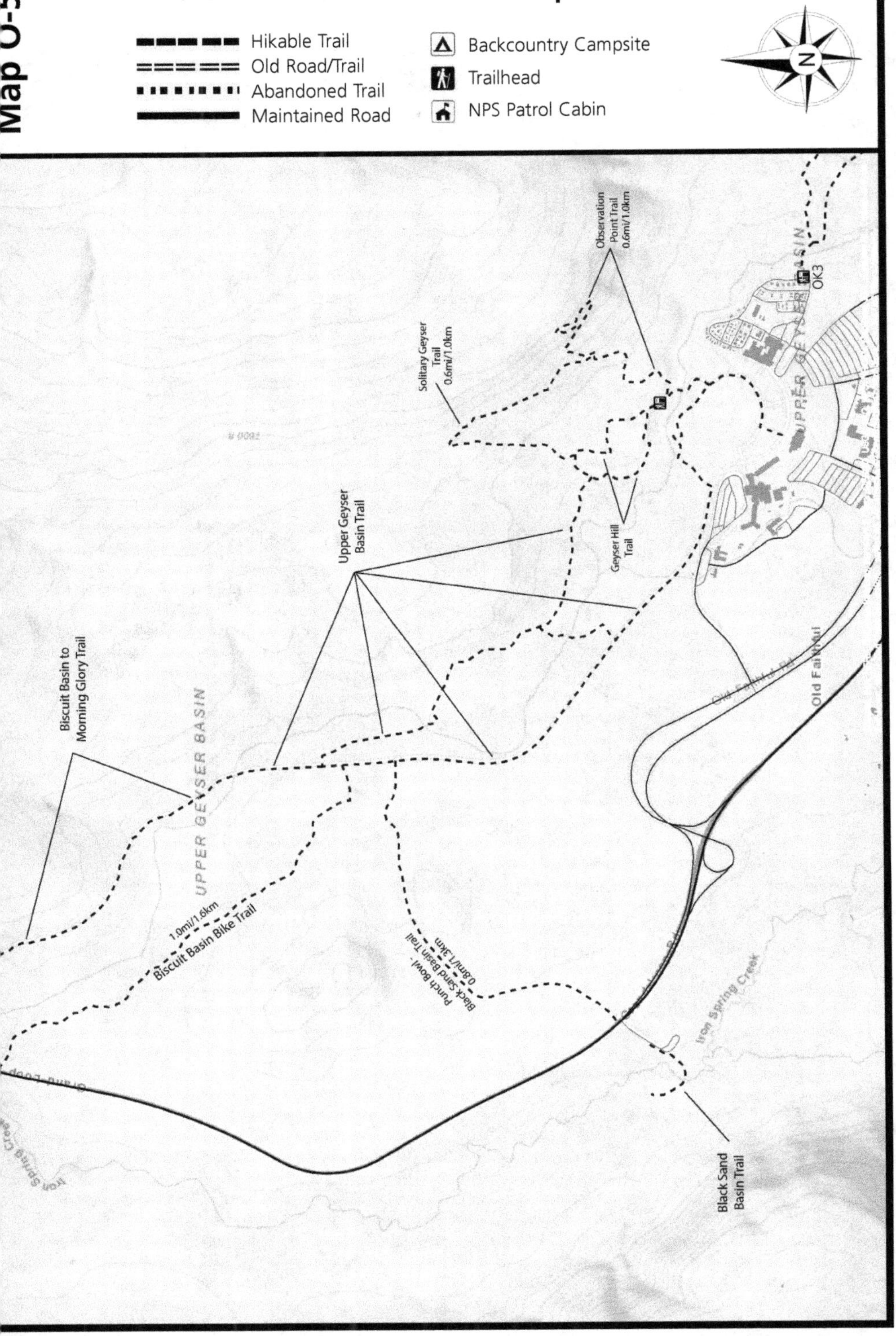

Observation Point Trail 0.6mi/1.0km

UPPER GEYSER BASIN

OK3

Solitary Geyser Trail 0.6mi/1.0km

Upper Geyser Basin Trail

Geyser Hill Trail

Biscuit Basin to Morning Glory Trail

UPPER GEYSER BASIN

Old Faithful Rd

Old Faithful

1.0mi/1.6km
Biscuit Basin Bike Trail

Punch Bowl - Black Sand Basin Trail
0.8mi/1.3km

Iron Spring Creek

Grand Loop

Iron Spring Creek

Black Sand Basin Trail

Map O-6

Old Faithful District Trail Map

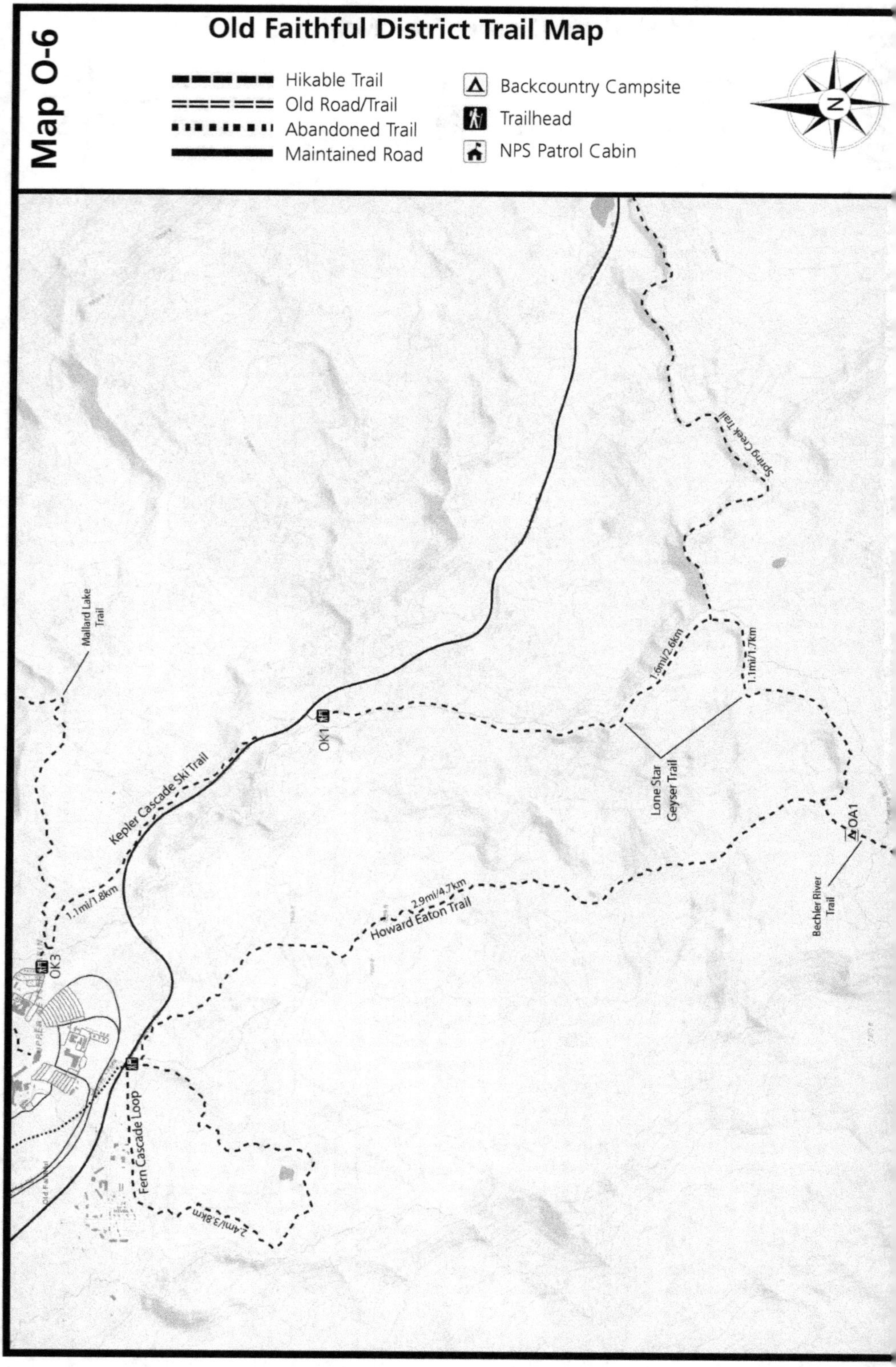

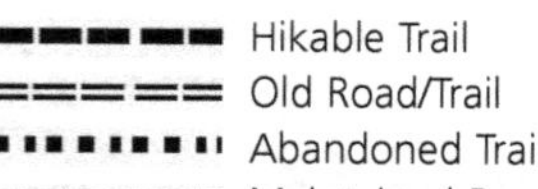

Map O-7

Old Faithful District Trail Map

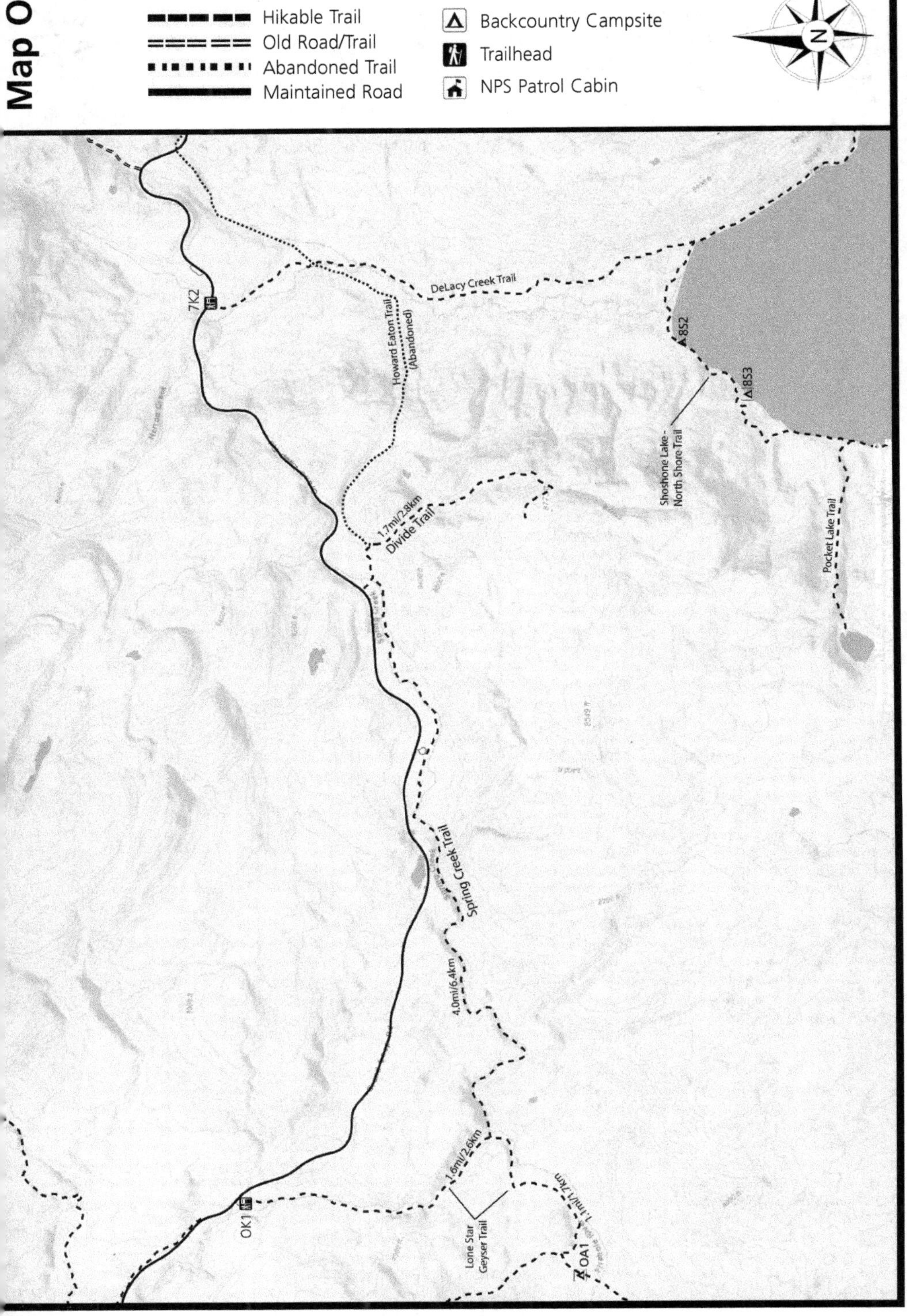

Hikable Trail
Old Road/Trail
Abandoned Trail
Maintained Road

Backcountry Campsite
Trailhead
NPS Patrol Cabin

7K2
DeLacy Creek Trail
Howard Eaton Trail (Abandoned)
852
853
Shoshone Lake - North Shore Trail
Pocket Lake Trail
1.7mi/2.8km
Divide Trail
Spring Creek Trail
4.0mi/6.4km
1.6mi/2.6km
1.1mi/1.7km
OK1
Lone Star Geyser Trail
OA1

Map O-8

Old Faithful District Trail Map

Hikable Trail
Old Road/Trail
Abandoned Trail
Maintained Road

Backcountry Campsite

Trailhead

NPS Patrol Cabin

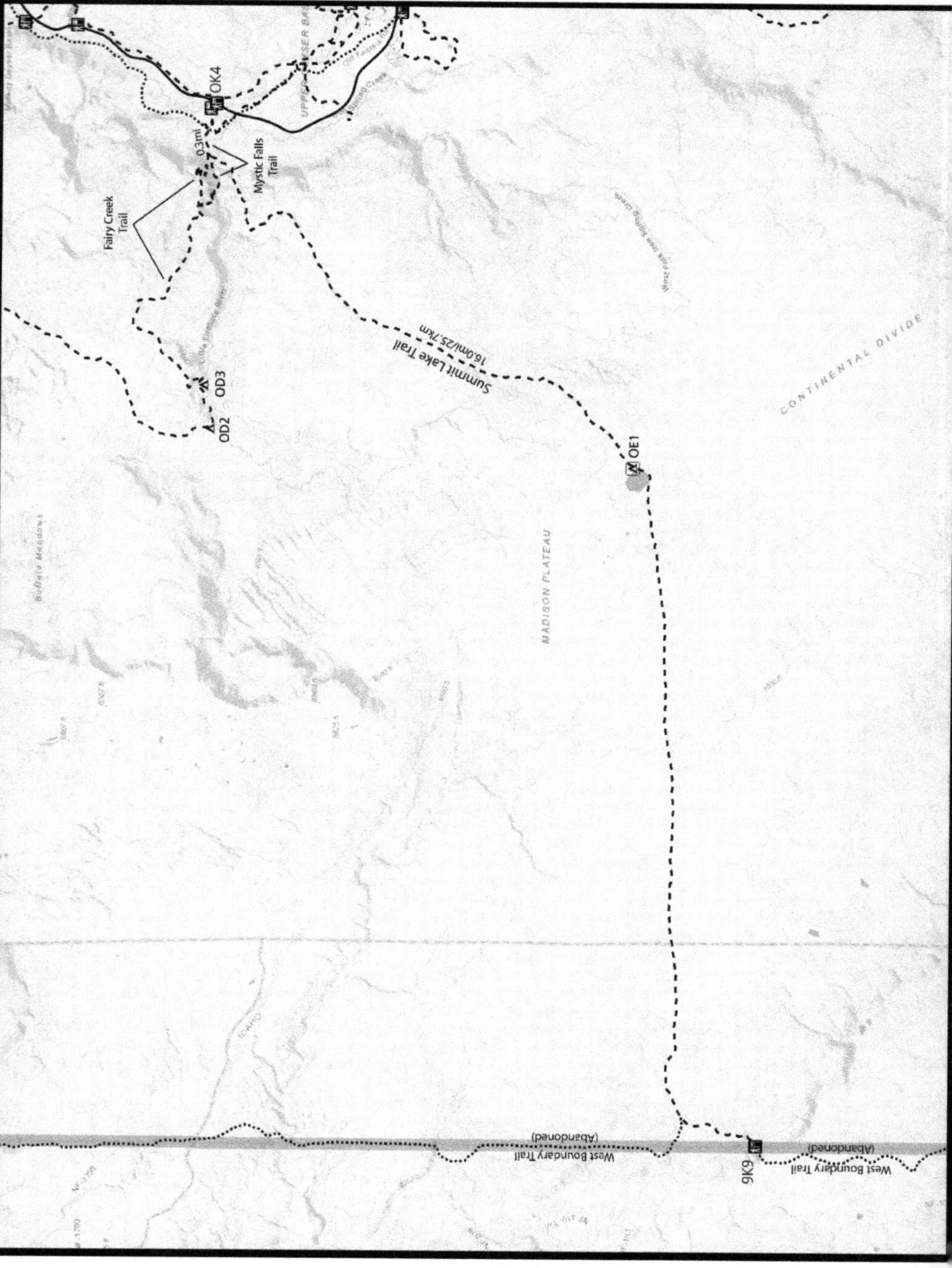

OK4
0.3mi
Mystic Falls Trail
Fairy Creek Trail
OD3
OD2
Summit Lake Trail
16.0mi/25.7km
OE1
MADISON PLATEAU
CONTINENTAL DIVIDE
West Boundary Trail
(Abandoned)
9K9

West/Gallatin District Trails

Bacon Rind Creek Trail MAP W-

TYPE:	PTP	CAT:	BC	CLASS:	B	SURF:	TRAIL	DIST:	W	STATUS:	E
DIFF:	1	TRAF:	1	CHILD:	N	HACC:	N	USE:	H S	LENGTH:	2.14
ELEV A:	7127	ELEV B:	7310	ELEV G:	382	ELEV L:	-199	NET:	183	BMA:	- -
MIN:	7127	MAX:	7314	AVG:	7244	AVG +:	4.7%	AVG -:	5.3%	OPEN:	YR

Reference Point	A-B Mi	A-B Km	B-A Mi	B-A Km	Latitude	Longitude
Trailhead WK4 (8.7 miles S of north boundary)	0.00	0.00	2.14	3.44	44.95520	-111.0706
Park boundary	2.14	3.44	0.00	0.00	44.93716	-111.0971

The Bacon Rind Creek Trail is generally ignored by many Yellowstone visitors, large because many books and trail guides do not address much beyond the first two miles of th trail that are in the park. The trail follows its namesake creek and enters the Lee Metca Wilderness (managed by the Gallatin National Forest). If you stop at the park boundary an turn around, you are missing out. If you travel another three miles or so into the wildernes you will come to a pass with an incredible view of Skyline Ridge, including Redstreak Pea From here you can access many other trails within this area. Visit the Hebgen Lake Range Station (USFS) in West Yellowstone for maps and other details.

Bighorn Pass Trail MAP W-

TYPE:	PTP	CAT:	BC	CLASS:	B	SURF:	TRAIL	DIST:	W	STATUS:	E
DIFF:	4	TRAF:	2	CHILD:	N	HACC:	N	USE:	H S	LENGTH:	19.49
ELEV A:	7217	ELEV B:	7282	ELEV G:	2290	ELEV L:	-2225	NET:	65	BMA:	D
MIN:	7217	MAX:	9094	AVG:	7751	AVG +:	4.3%	AVG -:	4.1%	OPEN:	YR

Reference Point	A-B Mi	A-B Km	B-A Mi	B-A Km	Latitude	Longitude
Trailhead WK6 (9.3 miles N of south boundary)	0.00	0.00	19.49	31.37	44.92811	-111.04912
Gallatin River crossing (footbridge)	0.40	0.64	19.09	30.72	44.92525	-111.04268
Jct w/ Fawn Pass - Bighorn Pass Cutoff Trail	4.29	6.90	15.20	24.46	44.92424	-110.97106
Spur trail to campsite WB1 (0.06 miles)/Landslide	4.33	6.97	15.16	24.40	44.92444	-110.97030
Spur trail to campsite WB3 (0.12 miles)	4.99	8.03	14.50	23.34	44.92600	-110.95805
Spur trail to campsite WB4 (0.02 miles)	5.67	9.12	13.82	22.24	44.92311	-110.94540
Spur trail to campsite WB6 (0.20 miles)	6.53	10.51	12.96	20.86	44.91524	-110.93448
Big Horn Pass	10.97	17.65	8.52	13.71	44.87218	-110.88029
Panther Creek crossing (20')	15.93	25.64	3.56	5.73	44.88370	-110.79506
Indian Creek crossing (35 to 40')	17.27	27.79	2.22	3.57	44.88447	-110.77285
Spur trail to campsite 1B1	18.37	29.56	1.12	1.80	44.88744	-110.75064
Power line crossing	18.58	29.90	0.91	1.46	44.88814	-110.74648
Indian Creek Campground Amphitheater	19.07	30.69	0.42	0.68	44.88649	-110.73895
Indian Creek Campground	19.09	30.72	0.40	0.64	44.88608	-110.73836
Jct w/ Indian Creek Loop Ski Trail	19.35	31.14	0.14	0.23	44.88327	-110.73809
Trailhead @ Indian Creek Campground	19.49	31.37	0.00	0.00	44.88268	-110.73527

The Bighorn Pass Trail is perhaps one of the oldest pathways in the park, having bee used by wildlife and Native Americans (including the Bannock) for quite some time befor Europeans arrived and "discovered" it. This trail is so well-known and well-worn that, a one time, park managers considered building a "northwest entrance" to the park via thi route. It was to have connected to the Grand Loop Road at Seven Mile Bridge south o Indian Creek. This trail is fairly popular and can be hiked from either end with the sam degree of difficulty.

The middle section of this trail, over the pass and through the Gallatin Mountain Range is located inside a bear management area (BMA). As a result, off-trail travel is prohibited from May 1 through November 10 each year. Hikers are also encouraged to hike in groups. Check in with a ranger station or backcountry office to ascertain the status of this trail before setting out earlier in the season. The pass can remain snow-covered until well into July in some seasons.

The hike itself is not that difficult. It gets a slightly high rating because of its length and the fact there are no quick exits from it once you get started. Once you are on it, you are in for the long haul.

There are campsites along the trail, but, with the exception of one just west of the Indian Creek Campground (1B1), they are all on the west side of the pass itself. So if you begin your hike at the east trailhead, you have a 13-mile to 15-mile hike to your campsite. Just after you pass the spur trail to campsite WB3, you will notice the trail diverts around a huge mound. This is the remnant of a landslide that occurred in 1996, which buried a section of the original trail. On the east end, the trail parallels Panther Creek from just below the pass on the east to the Gardner River near the Indian Creek Campground.

This is one of the most wildlife-rich hikes in the park. You will almost certainly see elk and bison, and may see moose, bears (black and grizzly), bighorn sheep, and perhaps the occasional mountain goat on the slopes of Bannock Peak. The area east of the pass is home to a couple of interesting geological features known as cirques, amphitheater-like valleys formed by glacial erosion. There is a small one on the east side of Bannock Peak and a large one (known as The Pocket) northeast of Quadrant Mountain.

Black Butte Trail — MAP W-1

Type:	PTP	**Cat:**	BC	**Class:**	B	**Surf:**	Trail	**Dist:**	W	**Status:**	E
Diff:	2	**Traf:**	2	**Child:**	N	**HAcc:**	N	**Use:**	H S	**Length:**	5.99
Elev A:	6819	**Elev B:**	9890	**Elev G:**	3264	**Elev L:**	-193	**Net:**	3071	**BMA:**	- -
Min:	6819	**Max:**	9890	**Avg:**	8046	**Avg +:**	11.0%	**Avg -:**	4.8%	**Open:**	YR

Reference Point	A-B Mi	A-B Km	B-A Mi	B-A Km	Latitude	Longitude
Trailhead WK2 (2.5 miles S of north boundary)	0.00	0.00	5.99	9.64	45.03491	-111.11408
Jct w/ Black Butte - Dailey Creek Cutoff Trail	1.90	3.06	4.09	6.58	45.05464	-111.09474
Spur trail to campsite WF1 (0.16 miles)	2.06	3.32	3.93	6.32	45.05476	-111.09231
Trailhead @ jct w/ Sky Rim Trail	5.99	9.64	0.00	0.00	45.06644	-111.05620

The Black Butte Trail provides the shortest (and steepest) direct route to Big Horn Peak along the Sky Rim Trail, and as such, many people refer to it (incorrectly) as the Big Horn Peak Trail. The trail has been known in the past as the Lava Butte Trail, however. Black Butte is the large mound to the south of the trail, while Lava Butte is the large one to the north.

The 12-mile out and back trip is doable in a single day, but the 3,000+ (914m) foot climb, 2,200 (671m) of which are within the last half of the trail, is not for the timid. The view from the top of Big Horn Peak, however, is impressive and well worth the effort.

The upper end of the trail near the summit takes you through some of what is left of the white bark pine forest in the park. This is a critical food source for the park's grizzly bears and is in danger of going away completely (due to mountain pine beetle infestation here).

You will also note many examples of petrified trees along the eastern half of this trail. It wa these forests that caused the federal government to annex this section of the park in 1929.

Shortly before you begin the "serious" climb up to the peak, you will cross over Black Butt Creek. If you are low on water, you will want to fill up here, as this will be the last wate source until you get back to this point on the way down if you are doing the out and back Once you get above the tree line, the trail becomes faint and often hard to discern. Kee your eyes open for the rock cairns and the occasional orange markers that will help yo remain on the correct path.

At the end of this trail, you will reach the junction with the Sky Rim Trail (see below). Tur right and go another 3/10 of a mile to the summit of the peak. You will want to be ver careful as you head up to the peak. The trail is very narrow and has precipitous dropoffs o both sides.

Black Butte-Dailey Creek Cutoff Trail — MAP W-

TYPE:	PTP	CAT:	BC	CLASS:	B	SURF:	TRAIL	DIST:	W	STATUS:	E
DIFF:	2	TRAF:	1	CHILD:	N	HACC:	N	USE:	H S	LENGTH:	2.20
ELEV A:	7060	ELEV B:	7428	ELEV G:	720	ELEV L:	-352	NET:	368	BMA:	- -
MIN:	7060	MAX:	7763	AVG:	7474	AVG +:	8.7%	AVG -:	10.1%	OPEN:	YR

Reference Point	A-B Mi	A-B Km	B-A Mi	B-A Km	Latitude	Longitude
Trailhead @ jct w/ Dailey Creek Trail	0.00	0.00	2.20	3.54	45.06883	-111.12147
Trailhead @ jct w/ Black Butte Trail	2.20	3.54	0.00	0.00	45.05464	-111.09474

This trail serves little function other than to connect the Black Butte and Dailey Creek trails and is for all intents and purposes unremarkable, though you do pass between Lava Butt and King Butte. This trail can be used to create a loop between those two trailheads.

Cache Lake Trail — MAP W-2

TYPE:	O&B	CAT:	BC	CLASS:	C	SURF:	TRAIL	DIST:	W	STATUS:	E
DIFF:	2	TRAF:	1	CHILD:	N	HACC:	N	USE:	H S	LENGTH:	0.73
ELEV A:	7844	ELEV B:	8043	ELEV G:	243	ELEV L:	-36	NET:	199	BMA:	D
MIN:	7840	MAX:	8043	AVG:	7951	AVG +:	7.8%	AVG -:	3.7%	OPEN:	YR

Reference Point	A-B Mi	A-B Km	B-A Mi	B-A Km	Latitude	Longitude
Trailhead @ jct w/ Sportsman Lake Trail	0.00	0.00	0.73	1.17	44.98045	-110.79218
Cache Lake	0.73	1.17	0.00	0.00	44.98652	-110.80320

Cache Lake is a small lake that sits at the foot of Electric Peak. It is the headwater for Rees Creek, which wraps around between Electric Peak and Sepulcher Mountain, and emptie into the Yellowstone River at the park's northern boundary near Gardiner.

There are no fish in this lake and no campsites at the lake, though it does make for ar interesting side trip to/from 1G3 or 1G4 if you are heading into or out of that area.

Crescent Lake-High Lake Trail — MAP W-2

TYPE:	PTP	CAT:	BC	CLASS:	B	SURF:	TRAIL	DIST:	W	STATUS:	E
DIFF:	4	TRAF:	1	CHILD:	N	HACC:	N	USE:	H S	LENGTH:	9.34
ELEV A:	8068	ELEV B:	7761	ELEV G:	1950	ELEV L:	-2258	NET:	-307	BMA:	- -
MIN:	7759	MAX:	9404	AVG:	8677	AVG +:	7.5%	AVG -:	9.0%	OPEN:	YR

Reference Point	A-B Mi	A-B Km	B-A Mi	B-A Km	Latitude	Longitude
Trailhead @ jct w/ Sportsman Lake Trail	0.00	0.00	9.34	15.03	45.02561	-110.96512
Specimen Creek, East Fork, crossing	1.40	2.25	7.94	12.78	45.04140	-110.95641
Jct w/ Mill Creek Trail (USFS)	2.98	4.80	6.36	10.24	45.05269	-110.93255
Spur trail to campsite WD4 (0.04 miles)	3.30	5.31	6.04	9.72	45.05528	-110.93722
High Lake	3.37	5.42	5.97	9.61	45.05629	-110.93721
Spur trail to campsite WD5 (0.18 miles)	3.43	5.52	5.91	9.51	45.05715	-110.93750
Jct w/ trail to Sedge & Crag Lakes	7.72	12.42	1.62	2.61	45.06262	-110.99207
Crescent Lake/Campsite WE6	7.92	12.75	1.42	2.29	45.06174	-110.99564
Trailhead @ jct w/ Specimen Creek Trail	9.34	15.03	0.00	0.00	45.07123	-111.01128

This trail takes you to two beautiful, high-altitude lakes. High Lake in particular is very secluded and, if there is no one in the other campsite, you will have the area completely to yourself (notwithstanding the indigenous wildlife population, of course). Crescent Lake sits at the northern foot of Meldrum Mountain.

The trail from High Lake to Crescent follows the park boundary for a while, and then the south face of Shooting Star Mountain before arriving at Crescent Lake. The view from these trails is spectacular, but be careful along these as many of them are quite narrow.

High Lake is the headwater for the East Fork of Specimen Creek, and has a population of cutthroat trout, while Crescent Lake is fishless. Just east of the WE6 campsite is an old, abandoned trail that takes you to Sedge Lake and Crag Lake, both of which are also fishless.

There is an unnamed lake to the west/southwest of the campsite, easily accessible via a social trail. The campsite at Crescent Lake makes an excellent base camp for exploring the entire area.

The trail segment between High Lake and Crescent Lake is not well maintained and it may be tough to follow for much of the year (including climbing over a lot of deadfall).

Dailey Creek Trail — MAP W-1

Type:	PTP	**Cat:**	BC	**Class:**	B	**Surf:**	Trail	**Dist:**	W	**Status:**	E
Diff:	4	**Traf:**	1	**Child:**	N	**HAcc:**	N	**Use:**	H S	**Length:**	4.88
Elev A:	6748	**Elev B:**	8372	**Elev G:**	1750	**Elev L:**	-126	**Net:**	1624	**BMA:**	- -
Min:	6748	**Max:**	8402	**Avg:**	7308	**Avg +:**	7.5%	**Avg -:**	4.2%	**Open:**	YR

Reference Point	A-B Mi	A-B Km	B-A Mi	B-A Km	Latitude	Longitude
Trailhead WK1 (0.9 miles S of north boundary)	0.00	0.00	4.88	7.85	45.04846	-111.13950
Dailey Creek crossing (footbridge)	0.29	0.47	4.59	7.39	45.05070	-111.13493
Jct w/ Black Butte - Dailey Creek Cutoff Trail	1.85	2.98	3.03	4.88	45.06883	-111.12147
Dailey Creek Spur Trail (Teepee Creek Cutoff Trail)	2.67	4.30	2.21	3.56	45.07986	-111.11714
Dailey Creek crossing	3.11	5.01	1.77	2.85	45.08374	-111.11194
Spur trail to campsite WF2 (0.11 miles)	3.57	5.75	1.31	2.11	45.09049	-111.10827
Dailey Pass/Jct w/ Sky Rim Trail/Park Boundary	4.88	7.85	0.00	0.00	45.10513	-111.11446

The Dailey Creek Trail is named for the creek, which in turn is named for an early settler of the Paradise Valley area, Andrew Dailey.[1] This trail affords the quickest access to the Sky Rim Trail from US191. And while this trail does allow some hikers to get into other parts of the trail system, it is most commonly used by hikers on day trips to the Sky Rim area. After crossing over its namesake creek on a small footbridge, you will follow the creek along the base of Crown Butte and begin a slow, gentle climb up to campsite WF2 (700 feet/213m over four miles). The trail is often poorly marked, especially in the open areas during the early part of the season. From the campsite to the Sky Rim Trail, however, you have a significant climb of almost 1,000 feet (305m) in just over a mile. Many hikers elect to stay at WF2 and use it as a jumping-off point for an exploration of the full Sky Rim Trail.

The Dailey Creek Trail intersects with Sky Rim Trail on Dailey Pass. Many books and websites state that the Sky Rim Trail starts to the east on the next ridge. In reality, that trail starts about one mile to the west along One Day Ridge when the Tepee Creek Trail from the USFS enters the park. You can follow this trail back to the Tepee Creek Cutoff Trail (which becomes the Dailey Creek Spur Trail when it enters Yellowstone) to make a loop out of it adding about seven more miles to your five mile excursion to Dailey Pass, the first and last miles of which are inside the park.

You can use the Black Butte-Dailey Creek Cutoff Trail to Black Butte Trail and then follow that trail back to its trailhead for a semi-loop with a short shuttle.

Dailey Creek Spur Trail — MAP W-1

Type:	PTP	**Cat:**	BC	**Class:**	C	**Surf:**	Trail	**Dist:**	W	**Status:**	E
Diff:	1	**Traf:**	1	**Child:**	N	**HAcc:**	N	**Use:**	H S	**Length:**	1.19
Elev A:	7218	**Elev B:**	7319	**Elev G:**	184	**Elev L:**	-83	**Net:**	101	**BMA:**	- -
Min:	7218	**Max:**	7319	**Avg:**	7258	**Avg +:**	4.5%	**Avg -:**	3.5%	**Open:**	YR

Reference Point	A-B Mi	A-B Km	B-A Mi	B-A Km	Latitude	Longitude
Trailhead @ jct w/ Dailey Creek Trail	0.00	0.00	1.19	1.92	45.07986	-111.11714
Park boundary	1.19	1.92	0.00	0.00	45.08051	-111.13797

The Dailey Creek Spur Trail, referred to by some as the Tepee Creek Cutoff Trail, is designed primarily to facilitate access to the USFS Tepee Creek Trail from the Dailey Creek trailhead or to provide access to the Dailey Creek Trail from Tepee Creek. This can also be used to close out a loop for those who hiked up to Dailey Pass and came back down via One Day Ridge.

Electric Peak - Southeast Ridge Trail — MAP W-2

Type:	O&B	**Cat:**	BC	**Class:**	N	**Surf:**	Trail	**Dist:**	W	**Status:**	E
Diff:	5	**Traf:**	2	**Child:**	N	**HAcc:**	N	**Use:**	H S	**Length:**	3.29
Elev A:	8086	**Elev B:**	10932	**Elev G:**	3118	**Elev L:**	-273	**Net:**	2846	**BMA:**	D
Min:	8086	**Max:**	10970	**Avg:**	9069	**Avg +:**	19.5%	**Avg -:**	10.6%	**Open:**	YR

Reference Point	A-B Mi	A-B Km	B-A Mi	B-A Km	Latitude	Longitude
Trailhead @ jct w/ Sportsman Lake Trail	0.00	0.00	3.33	5.36	44.97245	-110.80389
Trail split (take either trail)	0.10	0.16	3.23	5.20	44.97304	-110.80566
Summit of peak	3.33	5.36	0.00	0.00	45.00536	-110.83849

There are three routes to the summit of Electric Peak, the southeast ridge, the southwest ridge (see below), and the north ridge (which requires access to private land and is not covered in this book). The Southeast Ridge trail is by far the most popular (and is the only "official" route), largely because it is the first one people come to as they hike out from Mammoth either on a long day hike or after they have spent the night at one of the nearby campsites (1G3 or 1G4). While it is possible to do this in a single day, the 20-mile, strenuous hike is not recommended for anyone other than the most fit hikers.

ne first half of the trail is pretty easy, climbing only 700 (213m) feet over a mile and a half. ne last half, however, is a different story. You will climb over 2,000 feet (610m) in another ile and a half, much of which is over ill-defined trail and loose rock. This is categorized a severe climb. The suggested itinerary for this is to reach camp the first night, spend day vo on the mountain, and then hike out on the third day.

nce at the summit, you will be rewarded with one of the most spectacular views in the ark, certainly the best in the northwest quadrant. Keep your eyes on the weather, however. his mountain got its name from the fact that it is susceptible to lightning strikes from coming storms, which are quite common in the afternoons during the summers.

lectric Peak - Southwest Ridge Trail — MAP W-2

YPE:	O&B	**CAT:**	BC	**CLASS:**	U	**SURF:**	TRAIL	**DIST:**	W	**STATUS:**	U
FF:	5	**TRAF:**	1	**CHILD:**	N	**HACC:**	N	**USE:**	H S	**LENGTH:**	2.50
LEV A:	9828	**ELEV B:**	10930	**ELEV G:**	2015	**ELEV L:**	-912	**NET:**	1102	**BMA:**	D
IN:	9699	**MAX:**	10930	**AVG:**	10159	**AVG +:**	23.4%	**AVG -:**	15.8%	**OPEN:**	YR

eference Point	A-B Mi	A-B Km	B-A Mi	B-A Km	Latitude	Longitude
ailhead @ Sportsman Lake Trail	0.00	0.00	2.50	4.02	44.98873	-110.87562
ımmit of peak	2.50	4.02	0.00	0.00	45.00536	-110.83849

he hike up the southwest ridge of Electric Peak is actually technically easier than that up e main/official route (the Southeast Ridge). You start out at a higher elevation, the climb more gradual, and there is less loose rock to deal with by going up this way. The primary eason it is not the more popular hike is that it is significantly further from the trailhead at unsen Peak.

he only downside is that the trail is less defined in some areas (because of its relative lack f use). There are also no nearby campsites, so you will have to hike in from one direction r another, climb up the mountain, come back down, and then return to your campsite. The ailhead for this is about four miles west of sites 1G3 and 1G4, or three miles east of sites VD1 and WD2 at Sportsman Lake.

s with the other paths up to the summit, however, there is no water source once the snow ıelts. So ensure you have an adequate supply before you start your way up.

an Creek Trail — MAP W-2,W-3

YPE:	PTP	**CAT:**	BC	**CLASS:**	B	**SURF:**	TRAIL	**DIST:**	W	**STATUS:**	E
IFF:	2	**TRAF:**	2	**CHILD:**	N	**HACC:**	N	**USE:**	H S	**LENGTH:**	7.06
LEV A:	7239	**ELEV B:**	7875	**ELEV G:**	1116	**ELEV L:**	-480	**NET:**	636	**BMA:**	- -
IIN:	7205	**MAX:**	7875	**AVG:**	7470	**AVG +:**	4.3%	**AVG -:**	3.6%	**OPEN:**	YR

eference Point	A-B Mi	A-B Km	B-A Mi	B-A Km	Latitude	Longitude
railhead @ jct w/ Fawn Pass Trail	0.00	0.00	7.06	11.36	44.95305	-111.03357
pur trail to campsite WC2 (0.58 miles)	1.23	1.98	5.83	9.38	44.96426	-111.01772
an Creek crossing (20+')	1.62	2.61	5.44	8.75	44.96833	-111.01998
ct w/ old segment of trail	2.73	4.39	4.33	6.97	44.97781	-111.00556
pur trail to campsite WC3 (0.12 miles)	3.57	5.75	3.49	5.62	44.98487	-110.99365
ampsite WC4	5.16	8.30	1.90	3.06	44.99288	-110.96695
an Creek, North Fork, crossing	6.58	10.59	0.48	0.77	45.00858	-110.95660
railhead @ jct w/ Sportsman Lake Trail	7.06	11.36	0.00	0.00	45.01264	-110.95081

The Fan Creek Trail connects the Fawn Pass Trail with the Sportsman Lake Trail, and is ofte used to complete a loop from the Specimen Creek Trail to the Fawn Pass trailhead, or as connector between the Glen Creek/Bunsen Peak trailheads to the Fawn Pass trailhead. Fa Creek is fairly popular with fishermen and stock/outfitter parties, and the trail is relativel new in terms of park trails.

Note that the crossing of Fan Creek at the mile and a half point can be quite difficult early i the season (until mid-July). The snow melt and resulting runoff make this stream quite higl in high snow years it can be waist-deep.

The three campsites along this trail are among the best in the park. Note, however, that WC and WC4 are stock only campsites. The spur trail to WC2 was at one time the route of th main trail, however the trail itself has since been rerouted.

Many trail guidebooks state that this trail is in a bear management area and may requir restrictions. In actuality, only the easternmost half mile is inside the BMA, and off-trail trave is prohibited until November 10 each year. Off-trail travel is also prohibited from the eas fork of Fan Creek southward during this period.

Fawn Pass Spur/Bacon Rind Cutoff Trail — MAP W-2

Type:	PTP	**Cat:**	BC	**Class:**	B	**Surf:**	Trail	**Dist:**	W	**Status:**	E
Diff:	2	**Traf:**	1	**Child:**	N	**HAcc:**	N	**Use:**	H S	**Length:**	1.45
Elev A:	7188	**Elev B:**	7127	**Elev G:**	70	**Elev L:**	-131	**Net:**	-61	**BMA:**	- -
Min:	7097	**Max:**	7188	**Avg:**	7133	**Avg +:**	2.2%	**Avg -:**	2.8%	**Open:**	YR

Reference Point	A-B Mi	A-B Km	B-A Mi	B-A Km	Latitude	Longitude
Trailhead @ jct w/ Fawn Pass Trail	0.00	0.00	1.45	2.33	44.95349	-111.04395
Fan Creek crossing (25′)	0.30	0.48	1.15	1.85	44.95411	-111.04941
Gallatin River crossing (60 to 70′)	0.79	1.27	0.66	1.06	44.95548	-111.05826
U.S. 191 crossing	1.11	1.79	0.34	0.55	44.95662	-111.06447
Bacon Rind Creek crossing (15′)	1.32	2.12	0.13	0.21	44.95585	-111.06844
Bacon Rind Creek Trailhead WK4	1.45	2.33	0.00	0.00	44.95520	-111.07067

This short, lightly-used trail is merely a connector between the Fawn Pass Trail and the trailhead for the Bacon Rind Creek Trail. It is used primarily by hikers and stock parties entering the area from (or headed into) the Lee Metcalf Wilderness. It is also used by stock parties to access the Fawn Pass Trail (see below). Use caution when crossing US191, as mos drivers do not expect to see people crossing the roadway here.

This trail requires three fords. Two of them, those of Fan Creek and the Gallatin River, car be quite challenging early in the season.

Fawn Pass Trail — MAP W-3,W-2

Type:	PTP	**Cat:**	BC	**Class:**	A	**Surf:**	Trail	**Dist:**	W	**Status:**	E
Diff:	4	**Traf:**	2	**Child:**	N	**HAcc:**	N	**Use:**	H S K	**Length:**	20.83
Elev A:	7128	**Elev B:**	7279	**Elev G:**	2846	**Elev L:**	-2695	**Net:**	151	**BMA:**	D
Min:	7110	**Max:**	9136	**Avg:**	7935	**Avg +:**	4.8%	**Avg -:**	4.6%	**Open:**	YR

Reference Point	A-B Mi	A-B Km	B-A Mi	B-A Km	Latitude	Longitude
Trailhead WK5 (9.4 miles S of north boundary)	0.00	0.00	20.83	33.52	44.95065	-111.05902
West Gallatin River crossing (footbridge)	0.10	0.16	20.73	33.36	44.95074	-111.05786

ference Point	A-B Mi	A-B Km	B-A Mi	B-A Km	Latitude	Longitude
st Gallatin River crossing (footbridge)	0.12	0.19	20.71	33.33	44.95090	-111.05688
: w/ Fawn Pass-Bacon Rind Cutoff Trail	0.80	1.29	20.03	32.24	44.95349	-111.04395
: w/ Fan Creek Trail	1.32	2.12	19.51	31.40	44.95305	-111.03357
: w/ Fawn Pass - Bighorn Pass Cutoff Trail	5.00	8.05	15.83	25.48	44.93436	-110.97140
wn Pass	9.14	14.71	11.69	18.81	44.92961	-110.90469
nall Lake	9.32	15.00	11.51	18.52	44.93091	-110.90176
llow dry creek bed north to Snowshoe Pass	9.74	15.67	11.09	17.85	44.93268	-110.89491
wn Pass Cabin Trail	10.18	16.38	10.65	17.14	44.93017	-110.88799
e Pocket (cirque to the south)	12.88	20.73	7.95	12.79	44.93661	-110.83854
wn Creek crossing (15 to 25')	14.26	22.95	6.57	10.57	44.94877	-110.81712
ur trail to campsite 1F2 (0.05 miles)	15.40	24.78	5.43	8.74	44.95650	-110.79823
ur trail to campsite 1F1 (0.16 miles)	15.91	25.60	4.92	7.92	44.95279	-110.78996
wn Creek crossing (10 to 20')	16.02	25.78	4.81	7.74	44.95271	-110.78767
ardner River crossing (30')	16.38	26.36	4.45	7.16	44.94985	-110.78218
ur trail to campsite 1G2 (0.05 miles)	16.47	26.51	4.36	7.02	44.94927	-110.78125
ur trail to campsite 1G5 (0.23 miles)	16.50	26.55	4.33	6.97	44.94882	-110.78051
en Creek crossing	18.56	29.87	2.27	3.65	44.95576	-110.74829
t w/ Sportsman Lake/Sepulcher Mountain Trails	18.71	30.11	2.12	3.41	44.95757	-110.74639
wer line crossing	18.80	30.26	2.03	3.27	44.95661	-110.74548
ck up old Snow Pass Road	18.85	30.34	1.98	3.19	44.95599	-110.74494
t w/ Howard Eaton-Mammoth Trail	20.61	33.17	0.22	0.35	44.93358	-110.73181
en Creek crossing	20.76	33.41	0.07	0.11	44.93294	-110.72969
t w/ Glen Creek Stock Trail	20.77	33.43	0.06	0.10	44.93285	-110.72953
ailhead 1K3 (Bunsen Peak Parking Area)	20.83	33.52	0.00	0.00	44.93231	-110.72827

he Fawn Pass Trail is typically the first in the Gallatin area to open each spring, usually mid- to late June or sometimes early July in heavy snow years. This trail requires several rds of Fawn Creek and the Gardner River. Early in the season these might be kind of igh, but after mid-July, you should have little problem with them. On the east side, the trail llows Fawn Creek until it turns south to join the Gardiner River. The trail is roughly the ame difficulty regardless of which direction you choose, though the eastern approach to e pass is more gradual.

he only campsites along this trail are on the east side, outside the bear management area, hough on the west side you can cut over to the Bighorn Pass Trail to get to sites there. If you re hiking from the west, then the eastern sites make good stopover places, especially if you lan to return via the Sportsman Lake Trail to the US191 area. If you are headed east to west, is possible to do the entire 21 miles on a single summer day if you get an early start. If you re using horses or other stock to head out onto this trail from the west side, you will need enter via the Fawn Pass Spur/Bacon Rind Cutoff Trail to the north (see above). Instead f using the first section of the Fawn Pass Trail and the bridges over the wetlands here, you ill need to turn north, go about one-half mile and then turn onto the cutoff trail and head outh. The reverse is true if you are headed to the trailhead from the east. The horses will ear up the wetlands area.

you are doing an out and back from either end, the small lake just below the pass on s east side (at the base of Gray Peak) is an excellent place for a picnic meal. The lake is amed...wait for it...Small Lake.[2] The lake is about nine feet deep and is fishless. During the arly part of the season during the spring runoff, the outlet stream (Fawn Creek) has a 12-15 oot (unnamed) waterfall that is quite enchanting.

Fawn Pass-Bighorn Pass Cutoff Trail — MAP W-3,W-

TYPE:	PTP	**CAT:**	BC	**CLASS:**	B	**SURF:**	TRAIL	**DIST:**	W	**STATUS:**	E
DIFF:	1	**TRAF:**	1	**CHILD:**	N	**HACC:**	N	**USE:**	H S	**LENGTH:**	0.95
ELEV A:	7821	**ELEV B:**	7425	**ELEV G:**	40	**ELEV L:**	-436	**NET:**	-396	**BMA:**	- -
MIN:	7425	**MAX:**	7838	**AVG:**	7640	**AVG +:**	3.5%	**AVG -:**	10.5%	**OPEN:**	YR

Reference Point	A-B Mi	A-B Km	B-A Mi	B-A Km	Latitude	Longitude
Trailhead @ jct w/ Fawn Pass Trail	0.00	0.00	0.95	1.53	44.93436	-110.9714
Trailhead @ jct w/ Big Horn Pass Trail	0.95	1.53	0.00	0.00	44.92424	-110.9710

The Fawn Pass - Bighorn Pass Cutoff Trail is basically a utility trail that facilitates movemen from one trail to the other for those who are configuring their own routes through th section of the park. The trail itself is rather unremarkable. If you are traveling north t south, it is a very easy and quick downhill trek of about a mile. If you are heading nort however, you have a rather steep incline to deal with.

Gneiss Creek Trail — MAP W-

TYPE:	PTP	**CAT:**	BC	**CLASS:**	B	**SURF:**	TRAIL	**DIST:**	W	**STATUS:**	E
DIFF:	3	**TRAF:**	1	**CHILD:**	N	**HACC:**	N	**USE:**	H S	**LENGTH:**	14.06
ELEV A:	6885	**ELEV B:**	6774	**ELEV G:**	875	**ELEV L:**	-985	**NET:**	-111	**BMA:**	C
MIN:	6631	**MAX:**	6908	**AVG:**	6766	**AVG +:**	2.0%	**AVG -:**	2.5%	**OPEN:**	7/1

Reference Point	A-B Mi	A-B Km	B-A Mi	B-A Km	Latitude	Longitude
Trailhead WK7 (Fir Ridge Cemetery (outside park))	0.00	0.00	14.06	22.63	44.79621	-111.1032
Park boundary/ NPS Trailhead	0.43	0.69	13.63	21.94	44.79316	-111.0971
Campanula Creek crossing	1.97	3.17	12.09	19.46	44.79283	-111.0691
Spur trail to campsite WA1 (0.09 miles)	4.32	6.95	9.74	15.67	44.77764	-111.0310
Gneiss Creek crossing (10 to 15')	4.94	7.95	9.12	14.68	44.77193	-111.0226
Maple Creek crossing (30')	6.90	11.10	7.16	11.52	44.74901	-111.0037
Cougar Creek crossing	10.18	16.38	3.88	6.24	44.70566	-110.9892
Spur trail to Cougar Cabin (2.57 miles)	12.66	20.37	1.40	2.25	44.67828	-110.9741
Trailhead WK8 (7.7 miles E of West Entrance)	14.06	22.63	0.00	0.00	44.66380	-110.9649

The Gneiss Creek Trail passes through the gorgeous Madison Valley, south of the Gallati Mountain Range. It is a very easy trail, almost flat the entire way, complete with a campsit located about four miles in from the west. This makes it attractive for those who show up late in the day and want access to an overnight site that does not require considerabl hiking. Much of this trail is through forested area that was burned badly in the 1988 fires however, and for the first half of the season it is often covered in downfall.

Since much of the vegetation along this trail is deciduous, it is an outstanding trail during th fall. The Madison Valley is also a favorite hangout for the park's western bison herds, so yo are almost assured of encountering small groups of these huge beasts along your trek. Th hike requires fording several creeks, but they should all be passable regardless of the time o year. Keep in mind, however, that the western half (park boundary to Maple Creek) of thi trail is closed from March 10 until July 1 for bear management purposes. And from then unti November 10, off-trail travel is prohibited.

The western trailhead for this trail is located adjacent to a cemetery outside the park. I fact, you will not enter the park for almost a half mile when you begin from the west. Th eastern trailhead is located in a little turnoff just on the east side of Seven Mile Bridge. From the east side, you skirt around the western ridge of Mt. Jackson and come to a split. The right fork will take you to the Cougar Creek Patrol Cabin (and an abandoned trail that traveled to Winter Creek), while the left fork is the trail. From there it is pretty much flat, indistinguishable land until you get to the seven mile point where you start having to cross creeks. Given that, it is a good idea to have a compass and map or a GPS device with you to ensure you can find your way out of there.

Harlequin Lake Trail — MAP W-4

Type:	O&B	**Cat:**	TH	**Class:**	C	**Surf:**	Trail	**Dist:**	W	**Status:**	E
Diff:	1	**Traf:**	2	**Child:**	Y	**HAcc:**	N	**Use:**	H	**Length:**	0.50
Elev A:	6797	**Elev B:**	6906	**Elev G:**	154	**Elev L:**	-46	**Net:**	109	**BMA:**	- -
Min:	6797	**Max:**	6929	**Avg:**	6877	**Avg +:**	7.6%	**Avg -:**	5.7%	**Open:**	YR

Reference Point	A-B Mi	A-B Km	B-A Mi	B-A Km	Latitude	Longitude
Trailhead HQL (1.7 miles W of Madison Junction)	0.00	0.00	0.50	0.80	44.64032	-110.88741
Harlequin Lake	0.40	0.64	0.10	0.16	44.64319	-110.89030
Terminus	0.50	0.80	0.00	0.00	44.64297	-110.89221

This is a quick hike that is suitable for families with smaller children. It is only a half mile in and a half mile out. The trail itself is through thick forested area, so there is not much of a view, per se. The lake is rather large and full early in the season (around 11 feet max depth), but as the summer progresses and the water begins to evaporate, the lake gets choked with lily pads and often becomes more of a marsh than an actual lake. There are no fish in Harlequin Lake and, believe it or not, you are not likely to find any harlequin ducks here, either (though there are often other waterfowl).

Old Fountain Trail — MAP W-4

Type:	PTP	**Cat:**	BC	**Class:**	N	**Surf:**	Trail	**Dist:**	W	**Status:**	A
Diff:	3	**Traf:**	1	**Child:**	N	**HAcc:**	N	**Use:**	H S K	**Length:**	12.66
Elev A:	6719	**Elev B:**	7169	**Elev G:**	2089	**Elev L:**	-1640	**Net:**	450	**BMA:**	- -
Min:	6719	**Max:**	8094	**Avg:**	7590	**Avg +:**	5.5%	**Avg -:**	4.5%	**Open:**	YR

Reference Point	A-B Mi	A-B Km	B-A Mi	B-A Km	Latitude	Longitude
Trailhead (4.0 miles E of West Entrance)	0.00	0.00	12.66	20.37	44.64974	-111.01827
Power line crossing	12.27	19.75	0.39	0.63	44.57670	-110.83725
Site of old Marshall Hotel (S)	12.36	19.89	0.30	0.48	44.57664	-110.83518
Nez Perce Creek crossing (75′)	12.48	20.08	0.18	0.29	44.57604	-110.83314
Trailhead @ Nez Perce Picnic Area	12.66	20.37	0.00	0.00	44.57774	-110.82068

The Old Fountain Trail is the remnant of one of the early stagecoach roads into the park.[3] The very first road through the west side passed generally along that of the current road. However, it spent much of the year soggy and/or under water. So the park's superintendent at the time (1880) built this road to take traffic from what became West Yellowstone (and the Riverside Mail Station and Ranger Station) to the area near what was at the time the only hotel on this side of the park, the Marshall Hotel, located adjacent to today's Nez Perce Picnic Area. The road through Madison Canyon was rebuilt in 1900, and this road was largely abandoned to traffic. It remained in use as a patrol trail (known as the Madison Trail) for many years thereafter. The current name comes from the fact that the trail brought visitors into the Fountain Flats area.

In its later years it was maintained as a hiking and ski trail, but its relative lack of use led to it being abandoned altogether in the 1990s. The old trail is still passable for the most part, requiring considerable bushwhacking or circumnavigation of downed trees in many places. Its main attraction lies primarily in the fact that it was one of the first roads into the park.

Old Madison River Fire Lookout Trail — MAP W-4

Type:	O&B	**Cat:**	BC	**Class:**	N	**Surf:**	Trail	**Dist:**	W	**Status:**	A
Diff:	2	**Traf:**	1	**Child:**	N	**HAcc:**	N	**Use:**	H	**Length:**	0.40
Elev A:	6700	**Elev B:**	6783	**Elev G:**	125	**Elev L:**	-42	**Net:**	83	**BMA:**	- -
Min:	6699	**Max:**	6789	**Avg:**	6724	**Avg +:**	9.7%	**Avg -:**	4.6%	**Open:**	YR

Reference Point	A-B Mi	A-B Km	B-A Mi	B-A Km	Latitude	Longitude
Trailhead TRW (3.0 miles E of West Entrance)	0.00	0.00	0.40	0.64	44.65214	-111.05045
Summit/Site of old lookout	0.40	0.64	0.00	0.00	44.65172	-111.04463

From 1933 until 1942, the Civilian Conservation Corps did a great deal of work inside our national parks, to include Yellowstone. One of their projects was the construction of fire lookout towers around the park. In 1935, they completed one at the top of this hill just inside the park's western boundary. The towers were fairly frequently used during the 1930s, but after World War II, they saw little use except in extreme conditions. As a result, most fell into disrepair and were removed. The Madison River Fire Lookout was torn down and removed in 1969.

This trail is what is left of the old service road that was used to supply the tower. It is barely discernible until you get into the woods (and as time goes by, even this will get more difficult). Still, it is fun to go to the top of the hill and take in the wide view that the fire lookouts of the 1930s would have had as they kept watch.

Old Mol Heron Creek Trail — MAP W-2

Type:	PTP	**Cat:**	BC	**Class:**	N	**Surf:**	Trail	**Dist:**	W	**Status:**	A
Diff:	2	**Traf:**	1	**Child:**	N	**HAcc:**	N	**Use:**	H S	**Length:**	1.89
Elev A:	7701	**Elev B:**	7120	**Elev G:**	143	**Elev L:**	-724	**Net:**	-581	**BMA:**	D
Min:	7120	**Max:**	7730	**Avg:**	7482	**Avg +:**	4.9%	**Avg -:**	9.6%	**Open:**	YR

Reference Point	A-B Mi	A-B Km	B-A Mi	B-A Km	Latitude	Longitude
Trailhead @ jct w/ WD3 camp spur trail	0.00	0.00	1.89	3.04	45.01455	-110.89890
Park boundary TH WZ3 (cont into CGNF)	1.89	3.04	0.00	0.00	45.02951	-110.88278

The Mol Heron Creek Trail, named for the creek it follows as it heads north into U.S. Forest Service territory, was designed to take hikers to the Mulherin Trail in Gallatin National Forest (where it reached an old dirt service road about six miles out). The NPS portion of the trail has long been abandoned and remains unmaintained, but is passable for the most part to the park's boundary.

No doubt you noticed the disparity between the two trail names. Lee Whittlesey tells us in his manuscript, *Wonderland Nomenclature*, that the name in use within Yellowstone, Mol Heron, is a bastardization (one among many) of the name of the gentleman for whom the creek and the trail are named, John H. Mulherin.[4] The misspelling was officially approved as the creek's name in 1932, and thus, at least within the park, the trail retains this name. Mulherin was a local resident who lived at the mouth of the creek that bears his name.

Riverside Loop Ski Trail — MAP W-4

TYPE:	LOOP	CAT:	TH	CLASS:	B	SURF:	TRAIL	DIST:	W	STATUS:	E
DIFF:	3	TRAF:	2	CHILD:	N	HACC:	N	USE:	H K	LENGTH:	6.98
ELEV A:	6673	ELEV B:	6673	ELEV G:	73	ELEV L:	-73	NET:	0	BMA:	- -
MIN:	6595	MAX:	6693	AVG:	6650	AVG +:	2.8%	AVG -:	2.5%	OPEN:	YR

Reference Point	A-B Mi	A-B Km	B-A Mi	B-A Km	Latitude	Longitude
Trailhead @ West Yellowstone	0.00	0.00	6.41	10.32	44.65930	-111.09716
Connector Service Trail to West Entrance Station	0.29	0.47	6.12	9.85	44.65924	-111.09133
Fourway Junction	1.10	1.77	5.31	8.55	44.66078	-111.07510
Return to Fourway Jct	2.70	4.35	3.71	5.97	44.66078	-111.07510
Fishing Hole	3.54	5.70	2.87	4.62	44.66999	-111.07100
East Jct w/ Down River Cutoff	3.98	6.41	2.43	3.91	44.67242	-111.07770
West Jct w/ Down River Cutoff	5.41	8.71	1.00	1.61	44.67365	-111.07941
Return to Fourway Jct	6.41	10.32	0.00	0.00	44.66078	-111.07510

The Riverside Ski Loop, while intended primarily as a ski trail, can be hiked on foot as well, though during the summer it may be impossible to discern. You can actually ski into this trail from its trailhead just north of the West Entrance without having to pay the entrance fee to get into the park.

The eastern half/loop of this trail traverses an area that was once a large stagecoach and transportation staging complex. Beginning in 1907, the Monida and Western Stagecoach Company brought tourists in via this route after they had arrived on the train at West Yellowstone. In 1916, after the park allowed automobiles to begin using the park's roads, the stagecoach companies switched to using multi-passenger coaches and buses, and the complex became a hub for that operation until the 1960s. The complex was mostly demolished in the 1960s, with a couple of buildings remaining until 1974.

Sedge Lake - Crag Lake Spur Trail — MAP W-2,W-1

TYPE:	O&B	CAT:	BC	CLASS:	N	SURF:	TRAIL	DIST:	W	STATUS:	A
DIFF:	3	TRAF:	1	CHILD:	N	HACC:	N	USE:	H S	LENGTH:	0.93
ELEV A:	8741	ELEV B:	8809	ELEV G:	374	ELEV L:	-305	NET:	68	BMA:	- -
MIN:	8741	MAX:	9027	AVG:	8887	AVG +:	11.6%	AVG -:	13.5%	OPEN:	YR

Reference Point	A-B Mi	A-B Km	B-A Mi	B-A Km	Latitude	Longitude
Trailhead @ jct w/ Crescent Lake/High Lake Trail	0.00	0.00	0.93	1.50	45.06262	-110.99207
Sedge Lake	0.29	0.47	0.64	1.03	45.06401	-110.98623
Crag Lake/Trail terminus	0.93	1.50	0.00	0.00	45.05815	-110.97776

This trail, or what is left of it, is part of the original trail between Crescent Lake and High Lake. At some point, probably in the 1930s during the CCC's trail work programs, the trail was rerouted to its current path, and this segment was for all practical purposes abandoned.[5]

Of course, curiosity gets the best of hikers who show up and find the old path is still passable, and its continued use keeps it in at least a minimally-usable condition. Such is the case today. So while the trail is no longer maintained, it remains a viable path for those who want to do a little bushwhacking and exploring off the beaten path. Neither lake contains fish.

Both lakes were given their names in the 1930s: Sedge Lake from the grasslike plants that grow around it and Crag Lake from the craggy mountains in that area.

Sky Rim Trail

MAP W-1

Type:	PTP	**Cat:**	BC	**Class:**	B	**Surf:**	Trail	**Dist:**	W	**Status:**	E
Diff:	5	**Traf:**	1	**Child:**	N	**HAcc:**	N	**Use:**	H S	**Length:**	10.68
Elev A:	8401	**Elev B:**	10074	**Elev G:**	4907	**Elev L:**	-3234	**Net:**	1673	**BMA:**	- -
Min:	8165	**Max:**	10074	**Avg:**	9289	**Avg +:**	13.8%	**Avg -:**	11.0%	**Open:**	YR

Reference Point	A-B Mi	A-B Km	B-A Mi	B-A Km	Latitude	Longitude
Trailhead @ park boundary (Jct w/ USFS Trail 100)	0.00	0.00	10.68	17.19	45.10108	-111.12974
Dailey Pass/Jct w/ Dailey Creek Trail	1.08	1.74	9.60	15.45	45.10513	-111.11446
Intersection w/ Gallatin Crest Trail (USFS 296)	1.78	2.86	8.90	14.32	45.10885	-111.10318
Jct w/ Black Butte Trail	6.30	10.14	4.38	7.05	45.06644	-111.05620
Summit of Big Horn Peak	6.69	10.77	3.99	6.42	45.06699	-111.04972
Jct w/ Specimen Creek Trail	9.39	15.11	1.29	2.08	45.08813	-111.01573
Park boundary/Sheep Mountain Summit	10.68	17.19	0.00	0.00	45.09802	-111.00077

The Sky Rim Trail (referred to in some early guides as the Skyline Trail) offers what many people consider the pre-eminent and most spectacular views of any trail in the park. If you ask a group of experienced Yellowstone hikers what "the" premier hike in the park would be, many would say this was it. It was constructed in the late 1920s by the U.S. Forest Service.

And while this one will provide you with a true "top of the world" experience, please keep in mind that it is one of the more dangerous trails in the park. In 1969, a park employee was killed when he fell from one of the more narrow stretches of trail. Many others have been injured and had to be evacuated out by rescue personnel.

You will also want to ensure you keep enough water on you (especially after the snow melts in July), as there are no water sources above the tree lines. Weather can also play a big factor in the success of your hike. Storms are very common in the early afternoons during the summer. Enjoy the hike, but be safe about it.

There is a lot of confusion about how long this trail is, where it starts, where it ends, etc. For example, while many guidebooks state that the trail begins at the junction with the Dailey Creek Trail, it actually starts about one mile to the west where USFS Trail #100 crosses the park boundary. This trail is named the Daly Creek Trail by the USFS. This only adds to the confusion, of course. Nevertheless, insofar as the National Park Service is concerned, the Sky Rim Trail starts at the point identified above. The quickest route to access the entire trail is to approach via the Dailey Creek Trail if you are inside the park, or via the Teepee Creek and Daly Creek trails if you want to come in via the USFS trail system.

There are four ways to get to this trail from inside Yellowstone. From the west, you can get to it via the Dailey Creek (recommended), the Black Butte, or the Specimen Creek Trails. From the east, you can get to it via the Crescent Lake-High Lake Trail from the Sportsman Lake Trail. And while it is possible to get up to the trail and see a few things, then head back down in one day, this is truly a part of the park you should plan on spending at least one night in.

There are several campsites in the area that are feasible as jumping off points for a day's hike along the Sky Rim Trail. You just need to decide which path you wish to take into and out of the area and plan accordingly; there are certainly several ways to configure loops suitable for the length of time you wish to be in the area.

ı the early parts of the season, the trail may be hard to find, as the grasses can cover the acks left by hikers from the year before. Stay high - the trail follows the ridge.

n the first of September, sheep hunting season commences in the Forest Service areas ımediately outside the park. If you are going to hike in this area during this period, wear range so that you are easily identifiable as non-wildlife.

ne interesting note, the large movie-screen like intrusion you see mounted on top of ıeep Mountain at the far east end of the trail is what is known as a passive reflector. It is art of a radio relay system used by the USFS.

pecimen Creek Trail — MAP W-1,W-2

YPE:	PTP	CAT:	BC	CLASS:	B	SURF:	TRAIL	DIST:	W	STATUS:	E
IFF:	4	TRAF:	1	CHILD:	N	HACC:	N	USE:	H S	LENGTH:	8.17
LEV A:	6912	ELEV B:	9302	ELEV G:	2591	ELEV L:	-201	NET:	2390	BMA:	- -
IN:	6912	MAX:	9302	AVG:	7609	AVG +:	6.9%	AVG -:	2.2%	OPEN:	YR

eference Point	A-B Mi	A-B Km	B-A Mi	B-A Km	Latitude	Longitude
ailhead WK3 (4.7 miles S of north boundary)	0.00	0.00	8.17	13.15	45.01261	-111.08074
t w/ Sportsman Lake Trail	2.00	3.22	6.17	9.93	45.02808	-111.04777
ampsite WE1	2.12	3.41	6.05	9.74	45.02870	-111.04563
onfluence of North & East Fork/Lightning Hill	2.29	3.69	5.88	9.46	45.02969	-111.04243
pecimen Creek (North Fork) crossing (20 to 30')	4.10	6.60	4.07	6.55	45.05103	-111.02699
our trail to campsite WE4 (0.02 miles)	5.10	8.21	3.07	4.94	45.06373	-111.02226
pecimen Creek (North Fork) crossing (10')	5.57	8.96	2.60	4.18	45.06934	-111.01773
t w/ Crescent Lake/High Lake Trail	5.96	9.59	2.21	3.56	45.07123	-111.01128
our trail to campsite WE5/Shelf Lake (0.11 miles)	7.91	12.73	0.26	0.42	45.09096	-111.01357
our trail to campsite WE7 (0.04 miles)	7.95	12.79	0.22	0.35	45.09087	-111.01416
t w/ Sky Rim Trail	8.17	13.15	0.00	0.00	45.08813	-111.01573

he Specimen Creek Trail gets its name from the petrified tree specimens near the upper ast half of the trail. It is one of the three primary routes to the Sky Rim Trail from the west ide of the park. A lot of hikers will use this trail in combination with others to form a loop ıto and out of the Sky Rim Trail. You can easily come in via the Dailey Creek or Black Butte rails, camp at one of the sites along the way, and then come out via the Specimen Creek rail (or do it backwards). It can also be used to form an end-to-end trail for those coming rom the Mammoth area by way of the Sportsman Lake and Crescent-High Lake Trails.

pecimen Creek is very popular with fly fishermen, with a population of cutbows (hybrids f the cutthroat and rainbow trout).

he first six miles of this trip have a slight incline, but once you are past the junction with he Crescent Lake/High Lake Trail, you begin a 1,600-foot (488m) climb over the next two ıiles, almost straight up with no switchbacks. When you arrive near the top, you will come pon Shelf Lake, a gorgeous (though fishless) five-acre lake that is situated at the foot of the vestern ridge of Sheep Mountain.

he two campsites here are among the best in the park. And though there is not an official rail directly to the top of Sheep Mountain from the lake, it is a fairly easy climb from the ast side of the lake; it is not any more or less difficult than taking the official trail back to the vest and then following that trail up.

One interesting aspect of this hike has to do with the first campsite, WE1. In 2007, the Ov Fire burned through this area, including right through the campsite. A stay here allows yo to see the power of nature as it rebuilds the ecosystem. Immediately south of the campsit which is located at the confluence of the East and North Forks of Specimen Creek is a 8,975-foot (2736m) hill known as Lightning Hill. The hill got its name from the fact th rangers from the Gallatin Ranger Station (which at the time was located just off US19 would travel to this site to check for any lightning-caused wildfires. The hill was the talle in this area that was immediately accessible and was used for this purpose for many years.

Sportsman Lake Trail — MAP W-

TYPE:	PTP	CAT:	BC	CLASS:	A	SURF:	TRAIL	DIST:	W	STATUS:	E
DIFF:	4	TRAF:	1	CHILD:	N	HACC:	N	USE:	H S	LENGTH:	19.91
ELEV A:	7434	ELEV B:	7147	ELEV G:	3958	ELEV L:	-4245	NET:	-287	BMA:	D
MIN:	7147	MAX:	9828	AVG:	8130	AVG +:	7.4%	AVG -:	7.8%	OPEN:	YR

Reference Point	A-B Mi	A-B Km	B-A Mi	B-A Km	Latitude	Longitude
Trailhead @ jct w/ Fawn Pass & Snow Pass C/O Tr	0.00	0.00	19.91	32.04	44.95757	-110.74639
Trailhead @ jct w/ Snow Pass & Fawn Pass Trails	0.16	0.26	19.75	31.78	44.95960	-110.74791
Jct w/ Sepulcher Mountain Trail	0.86	1.38	19.05	30.66	44.96755	-110.75577
Jct w/ Cache Lake Trail	2.99	4.81	16.92	27.23	44.98045	-110.79218
Jct w/ Electric Peak (SE Ridge) Trail	3.96	6.37	15.95	25.67	44.97245	-110.80389
Gardner River crossing (15-20′)	4.28	6.89	15.63	25.15	44.97331	-110.80952
Spur trail to campsite 1G3 (0.10 miles)	4.31	6.94	15.60	25.11	44.97320	-110.81012
Spur trail to campsite 1G4 (0.07 miles)	4.40	7.08	15.51	24.96	44.97342	-110.81185
Gardner River crossing (25′)	5.49	8.84	14.42	23.21	44.98087	-110.82888
Electric Divide(Pass) /Electric Peak SW Ridge Trail	8.15	13.12	11.76	18.93	44.98873	-110.87562
Spur trails to campsite WD3 (0.28 miles)	10.94	17.61	8.97	14.44	45.01315	-110.90066
Social trail to Sportsman Lake	11.05	17.78	8.86	14.26	45.01372	-110.90236
Spur trails to campsite WD2/S.L. Patrol Cabin	11.10	17.86	8.81	14.18	45.01347	-110.90332
Jct w/ Fan Creek Trail	14.05	22.61	5.86	9.43	45.01264	-110.95081
Jct w/ Crescent Lake - High Lake Trail	15.23	24.51	4.68	7.53	45.02561	-110.96512
Spur trail to campsite WD6	15.27	24.57	4.64	7.47	45.02572	-110.96662
Specimen Creek, East Fork, crossing (15′)	16.01	25.77	3.90	6.28	45.02640	-110.97883
Specimen Creek, East Fork, crossing (15′)	17.90	28.81	2.01	3.23	45.02860	-111.01151
Specimen Creek crossing (footbridge)	19.84	31.93	0.07	0.11	45.02761	-111.04653
Trailhead @ jct w/ Specimen Creek Trail	19.91	32.04	0.00	0.00	45.02808	-111.04777

The Sportsman Lake Trail is a fairly strenuous, 20-mile-long trail. Though it can be don from either end, the grades on the western side are more steep, so it is a bit easier to do it eas to west. This trail dates to 1912 when it was built by the U.S. Army to facilitate patrols in th area and to provide a route between the Gallatin area and park headquarters at Mammoth

This trail is used to reach both the southeast and the southwest trails to the summit o Electric Peak. If you are wanting to make the journey up the summit a two-day affai you have two overnight campsites available near the southeast trail (1G3 and 1G4). Th traffic rating for this trail is a 1, though from the Glen Creek Trailhead to the Electric Pea southeastern trail, you are likely to find it a bit busier than that on most days.

Most people begin their journey along this trail via the Specimen Creek Trail on the wes or the Fawn Lake/Glen Creek trailhead on the east, and the mileage for those sections o trail are usually included in the other guides. That is not the case here, however, so kee that in mind when you are planning. With the exception of the extreme east and west ends of this trail, it lies entirely within the Gallatin BMA, so off-trail travel is prohibited through November 10.

If you happen to find yourself in the WD3 campsite area, find the large boulder on the east side of the lake. It is known colloquially as Yahoo Rock, and affords an excellent vantage point from which to view the lake.

At the point where the WD3 trail makes a hard left turn, you may be able to discern the Old Mol Heron Creek Trail heading off to the north. Though this trail was technically abandoned by NPS trail crews some time ago, it is still passable, although you will likely have to crawl over some downed trees every now and again. This trail takes you to the Mulherin Trail in Gallatin National Forest (much of which passes through private land).

Just past the WD2 campsite (heading west), you will see the Sportsman Lake Patrol Cabin. This is one of the newest cabins in the system, having been rebuilt after the original one was destroyed in the 1988 fires (the only patrol cabin lost to the fires).

Note that Electric Pass is typically still snowed in until mid-July, as are Sportsman Lake, Shelf, High, and Crescent lakes. There is only one river crossing that is likely to give you pause. The Gardner River near campsite 1G3 can be rather deep and fast until late June. Sportsman Lake does host a rather robust population of cutthroat trout.

Two Ribbons Trail

MAP W-4

Type:	PTP	**Cat:**	FC	**Class:**	B	**Surf:**	Bdwlk	**Dist:**	W	**Status:**	E
Diff:	1	**Traf:**	2	**Child:**	Y	**HAcc:**	Y	**Use:**	H	**Length:**	0.70
Elev A:	6696	**Elev B:**	6696	**Elev G:**	57	**Elev L:**	-57	**Net:**	0	**BMA:**	- -
Min:	6688	**Max:**	6705	**Avg:**	6692	**Avg +:**	3.1%	**Avg -:**	3.5%	**Open:**	YR

Reference Point	A-B Mi	A-B Km	B-A Mi	B-A Km	Latitude	Longitude
East Trailhead TRE (3.4 miles E of West Entrance)	0.00	0.00	0.59	0.95	44.65163	-111.03081
East loop split	0.11	0.18	0.48	0.77	44.65219	-111.03248
Jct w/ west trailhead spur	0.32	0.51	0.27	0.43	44.65248	-111.03648
Return to east loop split	0.59	0.95	0.00	0.00	44.65219	-111.03248

The Two Ribbons Trail is a very easy, wheelchair-accessible and child-friendly boardwalk that takes you through an area that was partially burned in the 1988 fires. Burned, dead trees (known as snags) co-exist alongside healthy, vibrant, green trees that were left untouched by the fires. Thus, the trail's name.

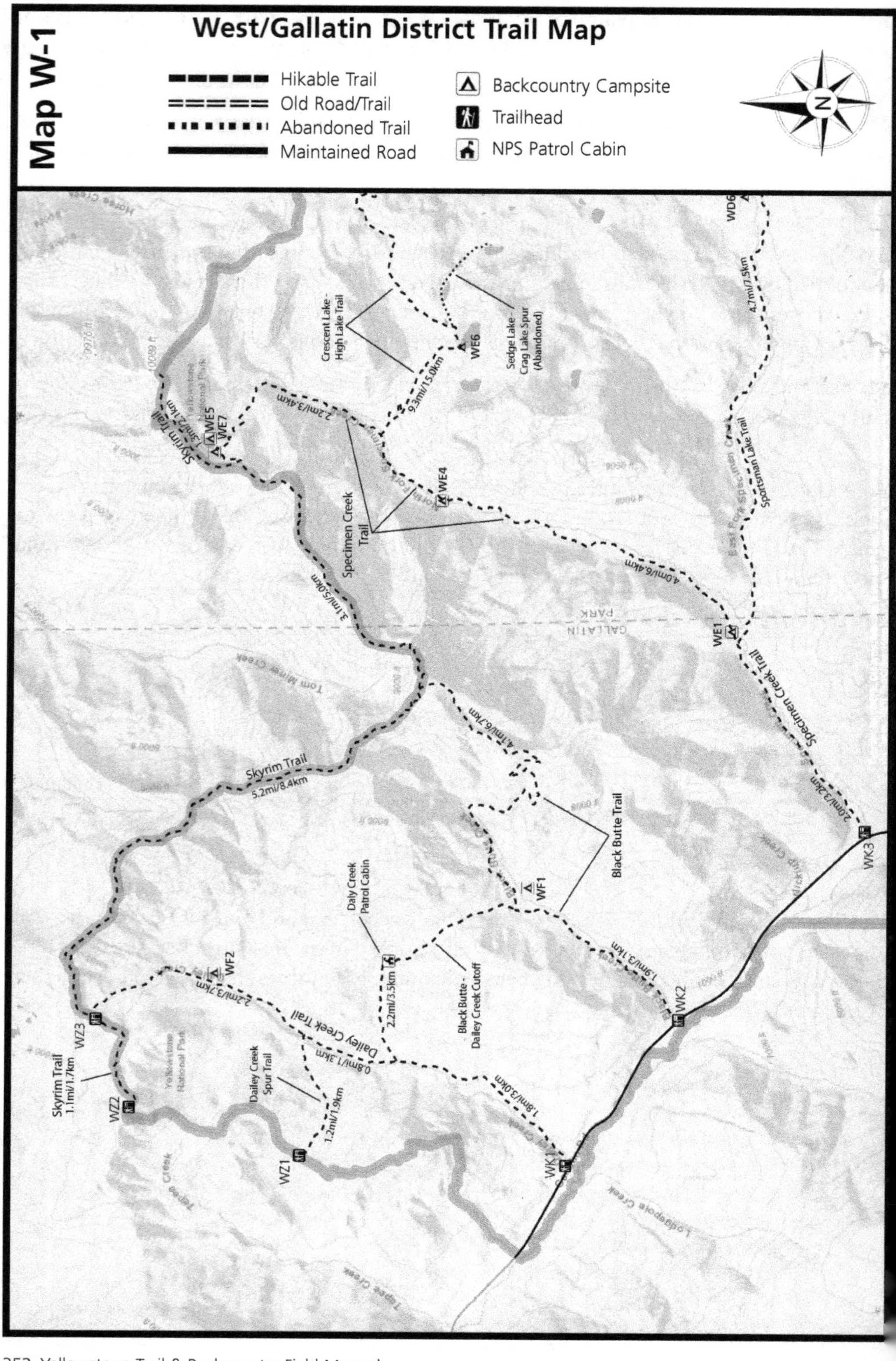

Map W-1

West/Gallatin District Trail Map

Hikable Trail
Old Road/Trail
Abandoned Trail
Maintained Road

Backcountry Campsite
Trailhead
NPS Patrol Cabin

Crescent Lake - High Lake Trail
9.3mi/15.0km
WE6
Sedge Lake - Crag Lake Spur (Abandoned)
WD6
4.7mi/7.5km
2.2mi/3.4km
Skyrim Trail
1.3mi/2.1km
WE5
WE7
WE4
Specimen Creek Trail
3.1mi/5.0km
4.0mi/6.4km
East Fork Specimen Creek
Sportsman Lake Trail
GALLATIN
PARK
WE1
Specimen Creek Trail
Tom Miner Creek
4.1mi/6.7km
Skyrim Trail
5.2mi/8.4km
Black Butte Trail
2.0mi/3.2km
WK3
WF1
Daly Creek Patrol Cabin
WF2
2.2mi/3.7km
Dailey Creek Trail
2.2mi/3.5km
Black Butte - Dailey Creek Cutoff
1.9mi/3.1km
WK2
WZ3
Skyrim Trail
1.1mi/1.7km
Yellowstone National Park
WZ2
Dailey Creek Spur Trail
0.8mi/1.3km
1.2mi/1.9km
1.8mi/3.0km
WZ1
WK1
Tepee Creek
Lodgepole Creek

Map W-2

West/Gallatin District Trail Map

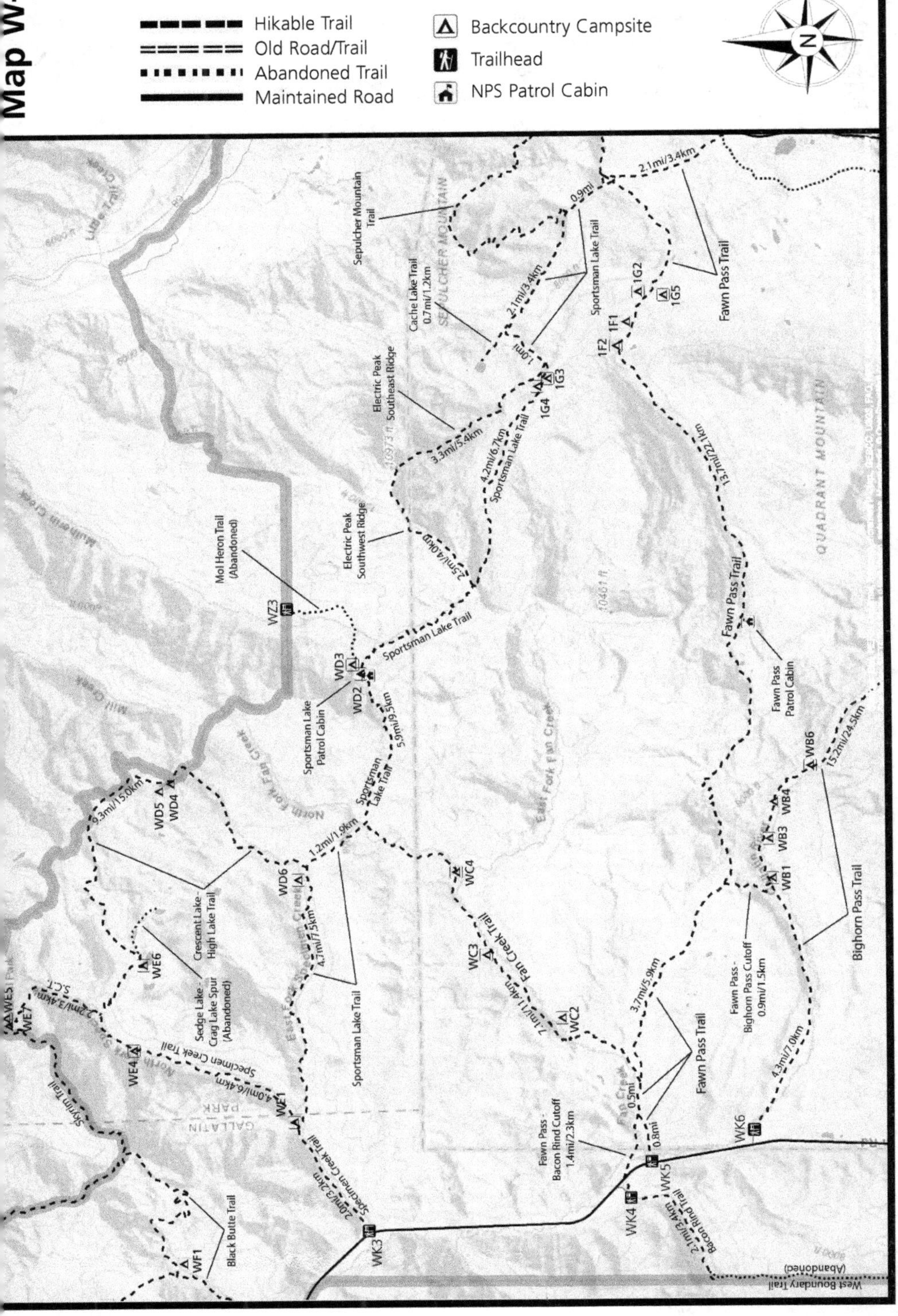

Hikable Trail
Old Road/Trail
Abandoned Trail
Maintained Road

Backcountry Campsite
Trailhead
NPS Patrol Cabin

Sepulcher Mountain Trail
SEPULCHER MOUNTAIN
2.1mi/3.4km
0.9mi
Cache Lake Trail 0.7mi/1.2km
2.1mi/3.4km
Sportsman Lake Trail
1G2
1G5
Fawn Pass Trail
1F2
1F1
1.0mi
Electric Peak Southeast Ridge
1G4
1G3
3.3mi/5.4km
4.2mi/6.7km
Sportsman Lake Trail
13.7mi/22.1km
QUADRANT MOUNTAIN
Electric Peak Southwest Ridge
2.5mi/4.0km
Mol Heron Trail (Abandoned)
WZ3
Fawn Pass Trail
Sportsman Lake Trail
WD3
WD2
Sportsman Lake Patrol Cabin
5.9mi/9.5km
Fawn Pass Patrol Cabin
North Fork Fan Creek
East Fork Fan Creek
Sportsman Lake Trail
WB6
15.2mi/24.5km
9.3mi/15.0km
WD5
WD4
1.2mi/1.9km
WB4
WB3
WB1
WC4
WD6
Crescent Lake - High Lake Trail
4.7mi/7.5km
Fan Creek Trail
WC3
Bighorn Pass Trail
WE6
Sedge Lake - Crag Lake Spur (Abandoned)
Sportsman Lake Trail
1.1mi/1.4km
WC2
3.7mi/5.9km
Fawn Pass - Bighorn Pass Cutoff 0.9mi/1.5km
4.3mi/7.0km
WE7
2.2mi/3.4km
WE4
Specimen Creek Trail
4.0mi/6.4km
WE1
Fawn Pass Trail
0.5mi
0.8mi
Fawn Pass - Bacon Rind Cutoff 1.4mi/2.3km
WK6
GALLATIN PARK
Sprim Trail
Specimen Creek Trail
2.0mi/3.2km
WK5
WK4
Bacon Rind Trail
2.1mi/3.4km
Black Butte Trail
WF1
WK3
West Boundary Trail (Abandoned)

Map W-3

West/Gallatin District Trail Map

Hikable Trail
Old Road/Trail
Abandoned Trail
Maintained Road

Backcountry Campsite
Trailhead
NPS Patrol Cabin

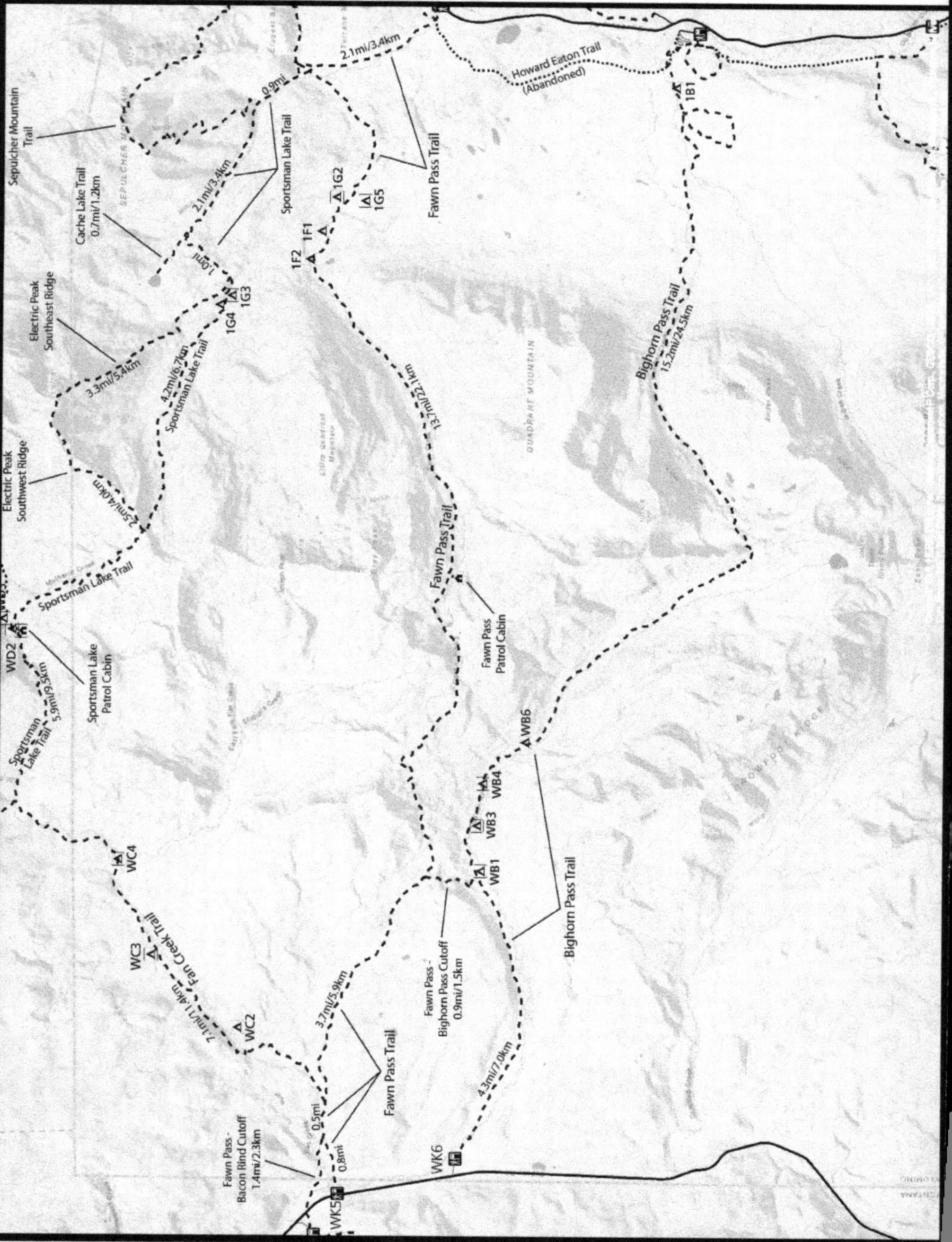

Sepulcher Mountain Trail
Cache Lake Trail 0.7mi/1.2km
2.1mi/3.4km
0.9mi
Sportsman Lake Trail
2.1mi/3.4km
Howard Eaton Trail (Abandoned)
Fawn Pass Trail
1G2
1G5
1F1
1F2
1.0mi
1G3
1G4
1B1
Electric Peak Southeast Ridge
3.3mi/5.4km
4.2mi/6.7km Sportsman Lake Trail
13.7mi/22.1km
Bighorn Pass Trail 15.2mi/24.5km
Quadrant Mountain
Electric Peak Southwest Ridge
2.5mi/4.0km
Sportsman Lake Trail
WD2
Sportsman Lake Patrol Cabin
Fawn Pass Trail
Fawn Pass Patrol Cabin
Sportsman Lake Trail 5.9mi/9.5km
WB6
WB4
WB3
WB1
WC4
Bighorn Pass Trail
WC3
Fan Creek Trail 7.1mi/11.4km
WC2
3.7mi/5.9km
Fawn Pass - Bighorn Pass Cutoff 0.9mi/1.5km
Fawn Pass Trail
4.3mi/7.0km
0.5mi
0.8mi
Fawn Pass - Bacon Rind Cutoff 1.4mi/2.3km
WK6
WK5

Map W-4

West/Gallatin District Trail Map

Hikable Trail
Old Road/Trail
Abandoned Trail
Maintained Road

Backcountry Campsite
Trailhead
NPS Patrol Cabin

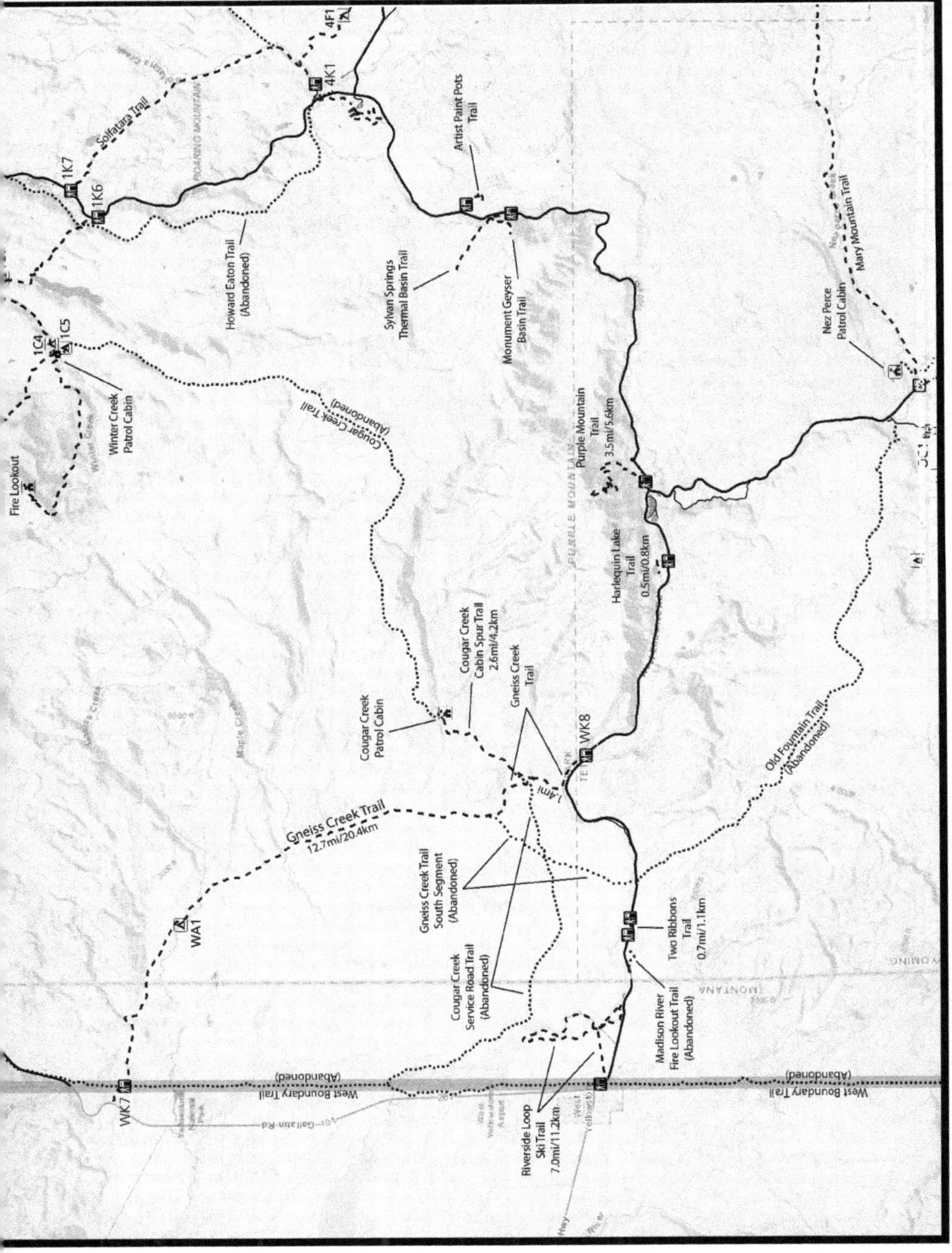

4F1
4K1
Solfatara Trail
Roaring Mountain
1K7
1K6
Artist Paint Pots Trail
Howard Eaton Trail (Abandoned)
Sylvan Springs Thermal Basin Trail
Monument Geyser Basin Trail
Nez Perce Patrol Cabin
Mary Mountain Trail
1C4
1C5
Winter Creek Patrol Cabin
Fire Lookout
Cougar Creek Trail (Abandoned)
Purple Mountain Trail 3.5mi/5.6km
Purple Mountain
Harlequin Lake Trail 0.5mi/0.8km
Cougar Creek Cabin Spur Trail 2.6mi/4.2km
Gneiss Creek Trail
Cougar Creek Patrol Cabin
WK8
Old Fountain Trail (Abandoned)
Gneiss Creek Trail 12.7mi/20.4km
Gneiss Creek Trail South Segment (Abandoned)
WA1
Two Ribbons Trail 0.7mi/1.1km
Cougar Creek Service Road Trail (Abandoned)
Madison River Fire Lookout Trail (Abandoned)
Montana
Wyoming
West Boundary Trail (Abandoned)
WK7
Riverside Loop Ski Trail 7.0mi/11.2km
West Yellowstone

The Lost and Forgotten Trails

Yellowstone is more than 145 years old. And though the park contains over 220 maintained trails today, there are literally dozens of trails that used to exist but have been abandoned or are no longer maintained. There are a variety of reasons for this.

- The trails originally served as patrol paths for U.S. Army soldiers prior to the NPS assuming control of the park, and once the soldiers were gone, the trails no longer served any purpose.
- The trails may have passed through sensitive thermal areas or wildlife habitat.
- The trails may have been abandoned in favor of a newer trail that provided a more favorable hiking route.
- The trails were originally designed for horse travel from one place to another and once that mode of travel was no longer popular inside the park, the trails were no longer necessary.
- The trails simply fell into disuse and were abandoned because the NPS did not believe the resources (money and staff effort) to keep them open was worth it any longer.

And while these trails no longer officially exist, it is perhaps important to reflect on their role within the park while they were around.

The following pages list almost two dozen of the more well-known trails, some of which technically never actually existed as official trails but were used by park visitors to one extent or another, nonetheless. There are a handful of abandoned trails that are still navigable today without a huge amount of bushwhacking. Those trails are listed in the relevant district chapters that precede this chapter.

At the end of this chapter is a pair of maps that show the abandoned trails from this chapter without the clutter of all the other existing trails surrounding them. Each trail/segment below has a bolded number beside it that corresponds with its location on these maps. All of the maps of the existing trails in the previous chapters also show all of these abandoned trails within the context of the overall trail system as it exists today.

The Howard Eaton Trail (1-12)

The Howard Eaton Trail is, arguably, the most storied trail in the park. At over 157 mile (253km) in length, it was by far the longest contiguous trail in the park (though, in th truest sense of the word, it was not entirely contiguous). The trail was originally develope in the early 1920s to serve as a path for pack horses/mules to take groups of campers on circuitous, multi-day tour of the park (the specific number of days was dependent upon th tour guides and the wishes of the group).

This was in the days shortly after Yellowstone managers allowed automobiles on its road and horseback was still a popular way to visit the park. Since horses could not occupy th roads at the same time as the vehicles, it was necessary to have a separate trail system fro which the outfitters could conduct their tours.

One outfit that conducted such tours was headed by a gentleman named Howard Eato (and his two brothers), the namesake of the trail. Sadly, Mr. Eaton passed away in 192 shortly before the trail was completed, and the company's tours would never get to mak use of the fully-completed trail.[1]

The Howard Eaton Trail (HET) underwent several modifications throughout its life spar The original one, completed in 1923 (which was constructed largely out of pre-existin wagon trails and paths); one in the 1930s that was developed in the aftermath of the roa building program adopted by the Bureau of Public Roads in the late 1920s (built almos exclusively by the Civilian Conservation Corps); and one that evolved through the 1950s an 1960s that came about as the result of several major road realignments undertaken durin the Mission 66 program. At some point in the early 1970s, NPS decided to abandon much o the old trail, largely because sections of it were rarely used or they passed through sensitiv wildlife habitat or thermal fields. Map A-3 shows the trail as it existed in the late 1950s.[2]

Many segments of what was the HET have been subsumed into other trails, however. Fo example, the "Chain of Lakes Trail" that links Ice Lake, Wolf Lake, Grebe Lake, and Cascad Lake north of the road between Canyon and Norris is a segment of the trail as it existed i the 1930s. There are sections between Fishing Bridge and Canyon, between Mammoth an Glen Creek, and between Old Faithful and Lone Star Geyser that also remain in place.

Though it no longer officially exists, many enthusiasts continue to hike and explore the ol sections of this trail to this day, and in 2014 a project was begun to document certain feature and sections of the old trail.[3] The Yellowstone Forever organization occasionally offers course during the summer related to the trail as well. See their website for details.

Many of the individual sections of this trail have a rather unique history as well. Som highlights include:

- Blacktail to Tower Fall: This segment ran across the Northern Range, roughly paralleling the existing road from the current Blacktail/Lava Creek area to Tower Junction. Though there are a handful of areas where this trail is still discernible, most of it traversed grassland and the continuous grass growth has erased much of it. (13.5 miles; 21.7km) **(1)**
- Tower Junction to Washburn Spur Trail: This section of the trail is located within one of the most bear-rich sections of the park. It was abandoned because of this, and the area is all but impossible to get permission to be in. The 10-mile segment

At the dedication of the trail, July 19, 1923. Individuals are, from left to right, Horace Albright, the park's Superintendent, Steven Mather, NPS Director, Willis Eaton and Alder Eaton, Howard's brothers, and Jack E. Haynes, the park's official photographer. This dedication board was located at the site of today's Sheepeater Cliff Parking Area. Photo courtesy NPS.

links the Tower area to the Washburn Spur Trail to the summit of Mt. Washburn. This section was originally built by the park's second superintendent, Philetus W. Norris, in 1878 as a wagon trail to facilitate access to the top of Mt. Washburn. Recall that this was long before the present road (and its predecessor) was constructed. The section between Tower and where the trail crossed Antelope Creek is outside the bear management area, but no sign of the old trail exists any longer. (10.0 miles; 16.1km) **(2)**

- The section between the existing Chittenden Bridge and Glacial Boulder was cut through the woods before the current roads and trails along the Canyon wall were constructed. (4.3 miles; 6.9km) **(3)**
- There was a small segment that departed southward from the existing Cascade Creek Trailhead across Cascade Meadow and down to where the old Canyon Village used to be located (site of the present day Brink of the Upper Falls parking lot). This trail is still visible and hikable. (1.6 miles; 2.5km) **(4)**
- Fountain Flats to Lower Basin Lake: This section of trail is closed to public access due to its passing through sensitive thermal areas. (5.0 miles; 8.0km) **(5)**
- Lower Geyser Basin Lake to Old Faithful: The north end of this section of the trail remains navigable and will take you to Lower Geyser Basin Lake from the pullout just south of the entrance to Firehole Lake Drive to the parking area at Midway Geyser Basin. From that point south, the trail no longer exists (and is in a closed area). (8.0 miles; 12.9km) **(6)**
- Duck Lake to Natural Bridge: This section of the trail remains largely navigable and is even marked in some locations. Much of the north end follows an old roadway (known as the Arnica Bypass). However, part of it is closed for most of the summer due to the presence of a carcass dump along its northern end. Check with the Grant Backcountry Office for its status. (5.0 miles; 8.1km) **(7)**

- A segment that ran from what is today the termination of the Spring Creek Trail (which itself was once part of the HET) at the Divide Trail to the DeLacy Creek Trail is shrouded in old growth forest and is discernible in certain places. On some of the treks through the park, the parties would proceed south on the DeLacy Creek Trail to the old South Entrance Trail (see below) to spend some time in the Tetons before returning via the same route. (2.1 miles; 3.4km) **(8)**
- From DeLacy Creek the old trail picked up Dry Creek and followed it across the existing road, and then paralleled the original road built to West Thumb from Old Faithful. It terminated northeast of Duck Lake, where it picked up the segment heading north to Natural Bridge. This was a segment of the original Howard Eaton Trail and I have never been able to find any sign of it. The trail was abandoned once the existing road was constructed in the late 1930s in favor of the old road just to the north of this particular segment (which is still visible on satellite imagery). (7.5 miles; 12.0km) **(9)**
- A segment of the old HET ran between the south end of the current Howard Eaton Trail from Mammoth at Glen Creek, through Swan Lake Flat (to the west of the lake), down to the current Indian Creek Campground, and then along the west side of Obsidian Creek where it intersected with the current Mt. Holmes Trail. Given the significant marshiness and verdant growth of grass and bushes along this route, it should be no surprise that this section of the trail is no longer discernible. (6.6 miles; 10.7km) **(10)**
- Another major segment of the Howard Eaton Trail ran from the current Mt. Holmes Trail, paralleling the existing road to Norris, where it came to an end just south of the existing campground. This section has been abandoned so long that it, too, is almost impossible to locate any longer. (10.2 miles; 16.4km) **(11)**
- The final major segment of the HET ran from the Norris Campground, through the thermal basin (parallel to the original road that ran through the basin at that time), then paralleled the road to Gibbon Canyon. From there it climbed up onto the little plateau on the east side of the current road, passing just east of the (current) Mesa Maintenance Complex, and then paralleling the road southbound to the Nez Perce Patrol Cabin, whereupon travelers would cross the creek and continue on through the Fountain Flat portion of the trail to Old Faithful. Portions of this section of trail can still be found, especially along the stretch just north and east of Madison Junction. The fact that it travels through so many thermal fields, however, makes traveling along the entire route impossible today. (17.4 miles;28.0km) **(12)**

Arrow Canyon Trail (13)

This is an old trail that existed for a short time in the early days of the park (and was an old Native American trail), but has been abandoned for about a century. It shows up on some ancient park maps and in some trail maintenance logs, as well as "recommended trail" on some early Master Plans. It departed from the existing Solfatara Trail and crossed Solfatara Creek just north of its southernmost bend, climbed up the hills, and then roughly paralleled Arrow Canyon Creek and its canyon to the junction with Lava Creek, and then paralleled that stream northward to Thompson's Peak. It then bent to the northwest and descended to the main road just east of the bridge that crosses over Gardner River east of Mammoth.

A search of archive records found no indication of why this trail was abandoned. It would have been one of the more scenic trails in the park even today, especially along the southern half near Arrow Canyon. Any attempt to follow this trail today would require some heavy duty bushwhacking. (15.9 miles/25.6 km)

ach Lake to Dryad Lake (14)

his is another trail that does not appear on many (if any) maps produced by the park. here are, however, trail markers along the route, so it was maintained by local ranger staff r some time. This trail is 2.6 miles long from shoreline to shoreline.

he specific source of the lake's name is not known, but there is a species of flower known a dryad that grows in the park. Dryads were also mythological forest fairies that protected e trees. The heavily forested area could have also been the source of the name. (2.6 miles; 1 km)

son Peak Ridge Trail (15)

he Bison Peak Ridge Trail was primarily a path rangers used to get from the Lamar Ranger ation/Buffalo Ranch to the Slough Creek Patrol Cabin/Ranger Station. It crossed Rose reek just west of the old service road running north from the ranch, and then paralleled e road until it got to the Lamar River Overlook. From there it traveled northward along a asonal creek on the west flank of Bison Peak, and then through the woods to the Slough reek Patrol Cabin. With the construction of the barns on the entrance road to the Slough reek Campground, backcountry rangers no longer operate from the Lamar Station, and so is trail is no longer used. (5.7 miles; 9.2 km)

acktail Trail (16)

his old trail was apparently only used by the U.S. Army for horse-mounted patrols and r traveling to Mammoth from the Canyon and Lake areas. It departed from the Blacktail idge Trail (see below) on the north shoulder of Cook Peak, and then followed Blacktail eer Creek all the way to the (still extant) Upper Blacktail Creek Patrol Cabin.

hile the NPS rangers used horses for backcountry patrol, they were more focused on reventing poaching along the borders and did not invest any time patrolling inside the igure-8 road network. Since the trail contained nothing most tourists would want to see, was abandoned altogether.

the early 1920s, there were plans to cut a trail from Lava Creek to join up with this trail st south of the current patrol cabin and provide a complete trail from Lava Creek to the anyon area. For unknown reasons (though likely financial), it was never completed. (6.8 iles; 11.0 km)

acktail Ridge Trail (17)

his was an old patrol trail that traversed the "Blacktail Ridge," the spine consisting of the wer peaks on the western side of the Washburn Range. It began at Observation Peak, ent down the saddle between that peak and Cook Peak, up to near the summit of Cook eak, and then began a northeastward bend that took it along the eastern flanks of Folsom eak and Prospect Peak before descending to meet the current Lost Lake Trail just south f Petrified Tree.

s with the Arrow Canyon Trail, this one was abandoned in the park's early days. ocumentation regarding this trail and the Blacktail Trail (see above) ceases after the Army urned over the park to the newly created National Park Service in 1916. So it appears as if had been used by the Army as a patrol trail and the NPS elected not to use it. (15.4 miles; 4.8 km)

Clear Creek Trail (18)

The Clear Creek Trail, constructed in 1926, picked up off the East Entrance Road at th first pullout west of Sylvan Lake, and generally followed Clear Creek all the way down t Yellowstone Lake where it joined the Thorofare Trail. In its early days, it, along with the ol roadbed that used to form the original East Entrance Road (the current one was constructe in the 1930s, leaving the old one abandoned), served as a primary route for stock parties t enter the park from the east side. The trail remains marked and fairly navigable.

Though it was never considered a part of the old Howard Eaton Trail system, it did exi and was used contemporaneously with that trail. The decline of the horse parties and th lack of use of it for foot hiking, plus the area being prime grizzly bear habitat, led to its bein abandoned in the 1960s as well. (6.9 miles; 11.0 km)

Cougar Creek Trail (19)

This trail was also known as the Cougar Creek-Winter Creek Trail. Originally part of a fir patrol trail (constructed in 1914) that linked the (former) Crystal Springs and (still extant Cougar Creek patrol cabins, this old trail fell into disuse with the reduction in backcountr horse patrols over time. There is nothing of any real consequence to see and no points c interest along the trail, so it was deleted from the trail maintenance program. This area wa heavily burned in the 1988 fires and the growth of new trees and grasses has pretty muc eradicated any sign of the trail. (14.2 miles; 22.8 km)

Cougar Creek Service Road (20)

This was an old fire road designed to facilitate access into the Gneiss Creek/Maple Cree area to fight wildfires (including in 1988). It was never maintained as an actual trail, but doe show up on many trail maps even today as either a trail or an old road. (8.7 miles; 14.1km)

Crow Creek Pass Trail/Crow Creek Cutoff (21)

Like the Jones Pass Trail (see below), the Crow Creek Trail was both a historic Nativ American pathway through the eastern side of the park and a victim of the restrictions o usage of the trail system on the east side of the park implemented in the 1980s. The trai began at the rear of the old road camp/picnic area that was once located in the hairpin curv on the East Entrance Road where Cub Creek crosses. It continued up to Crow Creek Pass located on the north side of Avalanche Peak. The trail was very lightly used, however, an it, too, was abandoned.

Just before one got to the pass itself, a spur trail took off to the north. Known as the Crov Creek Cutoff, it climbed up to the ridgeline and proceeded northwest along that ridgelin until it connected to the Jones Pass Trail. It was then possible to do a (shuttle) loop fron the Turbid Lake area to the Cub Creek area. Trying to follow this trail would require a lot o bushwhacking and you'd need to be out of the area by 7 p.m. (2.8 miles; 4.6 km)

Gneiss Creek Trail (South End) (22)

In its original configuration, the Gneiss Creek Trail led from the park's West Boundary Trai down to the Madison River across from the Old Fountain Trail. These two trails provide the original path into the west side of the park (for those who had been traveling along th Madison River). As most people came in on horseback or carriage in those days, it wa relatively easy to cross the river here and continue on down toward the Old Faithful area

Obviously, over time this trail was used less and less after the current (more or less) West Entrance Road was constructed. After the road was realigned and the new bridge built at Seven Mile (1958), the trail was rerouted to its current eastern trailhead just above the bridge, and this segment was abandoned. The trail is no longer navigable. (3.4 miles; 5.4km)

Jones Pass Trail (23)

The Jones Pass Trail is, with the exception of the various sections of the Howard Eaton Trail, the most historic trail in the park to have been abandoned. This trail followed an old Native American path through the park and out eastward to Cody. It was one of two paths park engineer Hiram Chittenden surveyed for a possible East Entrance Road back in the early 1900s. Chittenden ended up selecting the (current) Sylvan Pass path because it was prettier, in his opinion. Once the Army elected not to use it, it remained largely unused until 1920 when an actual trail along its path was constructed.

This was a moderately popular trail in its day, as its terminus at Jones Pass (south of Mt. Chittenden) afforded breathtaking views of this section of the Absaroka Range. Former park historian Lee Whittlesey wrote an impassioned plea to continue maintaining the trail in 2000 when the trail system parkwide was re-evaluated in the aftermath of the production of the draft Backcountry Management Plan. It was his belief that the trail would be eligible for historic designation (as a National Historic Trail) based on its use by both Native Americans and the U.S. Army in the days before the road existed.[4]

A modification of the usage of the Pelican Valley and adjacent areas with regard to bear management resulted in this area becoming day-use only, and it was pretty much impossible to get to Jones Pass and back in a single day and comply with the new usage requirements. As a result, in 2001 this trail was officially abandoned with the Crow Creek Pass Trail and the spur that linked the two together (see above).

Attempting to hike this trail would likely involve a considerable amount of bushwhacking. And you will need to keep in mind that you will have to be out of the area no later than 7 p.m. due to current usage restrictions. (5.0 miles; 8.1 km)

Lakeshore Trail (24)

This trail (aka Lake Lodge-Fishing Bridge Trail) went from the west side of Fishing Bridge down to the Lake Ranger Station across Lodge Meadow, along the shore of Yellowstone Lake. It was closed in the 1990s due to erosion and public safety concerns associated with its trailhead being right at the edge of the road. Much of this area is closed until well into July each season, but the trail remains largely hikable otherwise. (1.3 miles; 2.2km)

Lamar Valley Trail (25)

This was never an actual maintained trail, but it had been proposed as one in several iterations throughout the 1930s and 1940s. However, many people have traced this path from the westernmost access to Specimen Ridge (at Crystal Creek) to the junction with the existing Lamar River Trail on the eastern end at the river's bend toward the mountains.

Though it does not exist as an official trail, this path is out in the open and remains hikable by anyone wishing to do it. Do keep in mind that this is an area where a huge number of bison hang out and so your travels may be interrupted by wandering herds from time to time (and you will surely need to watch where you are stepping). (9.0 miles; 14.4km)

Little Buffalo Pack Trail (26)

Named for its proximity to the Little Buffalo Creek on its west end, this trail was a vestige of the old "fire lane" built between Gardiner and Slough Creek in 1918 by the U.S. Army. It originally served to allow fire crews to gain quicker access to the areas of the park north of the Yellowstone River. In its later life it served as a means for rangers to get to the Hellroaring Patrol Cabin and the upper Buffalo Plateau areas from the Buffalo Ranch, and then the barns at Slough Creek. It is no longer an officially maintained trail, and it is tough to follow most of the year. (7.4 miles; 11.9km)

Mary Lake to Beach Lake Trail (27)

Though this trail does not show up on any trail maintenance logs or on any of the maps produced by the park, it must have been at least informally an official trail at some point, as there are numerous accounts of people hiking from one lake to the other along a prepared path. There are even orange blazes along the entire trail, which takes you over the Central Plateau and down to Beach Lake. This suggests some level of maintenance by rangers.

Approximately a third of a mile south of the trailhead you will come across a section of Highland Hot Springs. This area consists of about a half dozen mostly defunct fumaroles. Another mile south of this, you will come into another section of the springs. It, too, consists of about a half dozen quiet features, though it covers a much larger area. Beach Lake itself is a little over five miles south of the Mary Mountain Trail; the lake is fishless. (6.6 mi; 10.6km)

McBride Trail (28)

This old trail took hikers up onto Anderson Ridge from the Slough Creek Trail west to (what is now the) Buffalo Fork Trail. It basically followed what is today the spur trail to campsite 2S8 and continued up the drainage up to the ridge, and then north to the old Poacher's Trail that parallels the park boundary. From there you could head west back down to connect with the BFT, or east to the Silver Tip Ranch just outside the park's boundary on the Slough Creek Trail. This trail was abandoned in the early 1960s during the re-imagining of the trail system that occurred with the Mission 66 cleanup era. This is not to be confused with the (unofficial) trail that takes you up to McBride Lake. Both trails and the lake get their name from James McBride, the park's first Chief Ranger. (2.5 miles; 4.0km)

Opal Creek - Raven Creek Trail (29)

This trail shows up on early USGS maps of the park (ca. late 1800s) as a path from the Specimen Ridge Trail just after it crosses the Lamar River. It runs southeast paralleling the river until it gets to Opal Creek, then follows the drainage up onto Mirror Plateau to the site of present day backcountry campsite 3O1. From there it followed an almost straight southeast path to Mirror Lake, and then followed the Mirror Fork drainage all the way down to Timothy Creek.

In later days, a trail was constructed along Timothy Creek to connect this (by then abandoned) trail to the Lamar River Trail (see below). After crossing Timothy Creek, however, the trail turned southwest and paralleled an unnamed creek until it got into the Raven Creek drainage. It then followed Raven Creek all the way into Pelican Valley, terminating somewhere near the present day Raven Creek Cutoff Trail. This would have been a path of more than 20 miles. Much of this trail still exists on the Mirror Plateau and in Pelican Valley because it is (and probably always has been) a migration route for bison between the Pelican Valley and the Lamar Valley. It was also the route the Hayden Expedition took on their sojourn through the park in 1871.

This trail is almost entirely within the Mirror Plateau Bear Management Area, and therefore any attempt to hike it must be in accordance with the restrictions in place (which provides for day use only, except for a narrow window of time each season where camping at 3O1 is permitted). (22.5 miles; 36.2km)

Otter Creek - Mary Mountain Trail (30)

This short stretch of trail was the original eastern trailhead for the Mary Mountain Trail back when the original Canyon Village existed south of its present location. And, though technically it was not considered part of the Howard Eaton Trail system, it was used to allow stock parties to get from the Mary Mountain Trail up to the Howard Eaton Trail that ran from Canyon up to northern areas of the park, as well as allowing tourists who rented horses from the concession corral at the old Canyon Hotel (located where the current concession corrals are) to head south into Hayden Valley and into the Mary Mountain Trail. The trail itself is not too hard to find and is still used by rangers on horseback patrolling the Central Plateau from the NPS corrals located at its northern end. (3.4 miles; 5.4km)

Pelican Creek Trail (31)

This trail was constructed in 1927, and went from Fishing Bridge to Indian Pond (formerly Squaw Lake). It passed along the lake shore near where the present day museum is located, moved into the woods where the old campground used to be, and then traveled east to the old group camp located on the south side of what is today Indian Pond.[5] This trail was probably intended to provide access to the Pelican Valley area from the Howard Eaton Trail, but it ceased being maintained sometime after World War II (though it continued to be used as a "party trail" by park employees well into the 1970s). This trail is not to be confused with the existing Pelican Creek Trail which passes through Pelican Valley. (3.0 miles; 4.8km)

South Boundary Trail: Grassy Lake to Fish Lake (32)

This old segment of the South Boundary Trail was abandoned many years ago and is likely tough to navigate these days. There were two primary factors in its demise. First, the vast majority of hikers who hiked in this area preferred to take the more northern path which afforded them access to the rivers and several waterfalls (most notably Union Falls). Second, the trail passed through a heavily wooded area and therefore it required a substantial tree-clearing effort each spring. For a trail that was so lightly used, this effort seemed inefficient. Therefore, the trail was abandoned. (6.0 miles; 9.6km)

South Entrance Trail (South Segment) (33)

The old South Entrance Trail had two segments to it. The northernmost was largely part of the original South Entrance Road, leading from what is today a maintenance area near West Thumb to the current Dogshead/Lewis Channel trailhead. That trail is described in the section for the Grant District Trails.

The second and much longer segment, constructed in 1929 to complete a single trail from the Snake River Ranger Station to the West Thumb Ranger Station, traveled up along the east side of the Lewis River Canyon and the Lewis River, along the east side of the existing South Entrance Road, and up to the current Heart Lake trailhead.

Similar to the Clear Creek Trail referenced above, this trail existed primarily as a path fo stock parties to enter the park from the Flagg Ranch area. However, once people cease coming in via this method, this trail, too, was abandoned (ca. 1960s). Very little evidence o it exists today, and any attempt to travel along this route would be fraught with a great dea of bushwhacking. (13.8 miles; 22.2km)

Three Senses Nature Trail (Not Shown)
The Three Senses Nature Trail was a short, boardwalk trail that encircled Firehole Lak on the Firehole Lake Drive north of Old Faithful. It was designed to allow the hiker t experience one of the thermal features in the senses of hearing, smell, and touch. You coul feel the heat emanating from the lake, you could smell the sulfurous odors issuing fort from the waters, and you could hear the bubbling of the water as it rose to the surface o the lake. Though you can still walk on what is left of the trail on the south end of the lake the remainder of the boardwalk was removed because of continuous shifts in the groun around the lake. (0.2 miles; 0.3km)

Timothy Creek Trail (34)
This was a four-mile long trail that paralleled Timothy Creek. It took off from the Lama River Trail about ten miles south of its north trailhead. The trail was largely nondescript an had no features other than the creek, and its lack of use caused it to be abandoned. At th western end of this trail, it was possible to travel along Mirror Fork (Creek) up to Mirro Lake (about three and a half miles of bushwhacking), one of the most remote lakes in th park. (4.1 miles; 6.6km)

West Boundary Trail (35-37)
The West Boundary Trail, like the South Boundary Trail, paralleled the park boundary for great many miles. It originally departed from the Bechler Ranger Station along the present day Robinson Creek Trail, traveled along the park's western boundary, detoured eastwar to Buffalo Lake, then continued northward for a great many miles. It then passed throug Dry Canyon and continued north to West Yellowstone. From there it continued to paralle the park's western boundary, alternating between being inside the park and outside it boundaries, until it reached what is today the end of the NPS segment of the Bacon Rin Creek Trail. The southern half was constructed in 1911-1912, while the portion north of Wes Yellowstone was built in 1913.

Much of this trail passed through clear-cut spaces carved out of the woods by the USFS as a way to delineate the park boundary from the USFS property, and it served primarily a a patrol route for U.S. Army soldiers and NPS backcountry rangers looking for poachers etc. The section most often used by civilians was from the little town of West Yellowston southward to explore Jack Straw Basin, Dry Canyon, and Echo Canyon. Much of this trai remains passable today (due in large part to its continued use by NPS rangers to access th South Riverside Patrol Cabin), though some sections will have considerable downfall to dea with. (Three abandoned segments totaling 51.9 miles; 83.5km)

Map A-1

Abandoned Trail Map - North

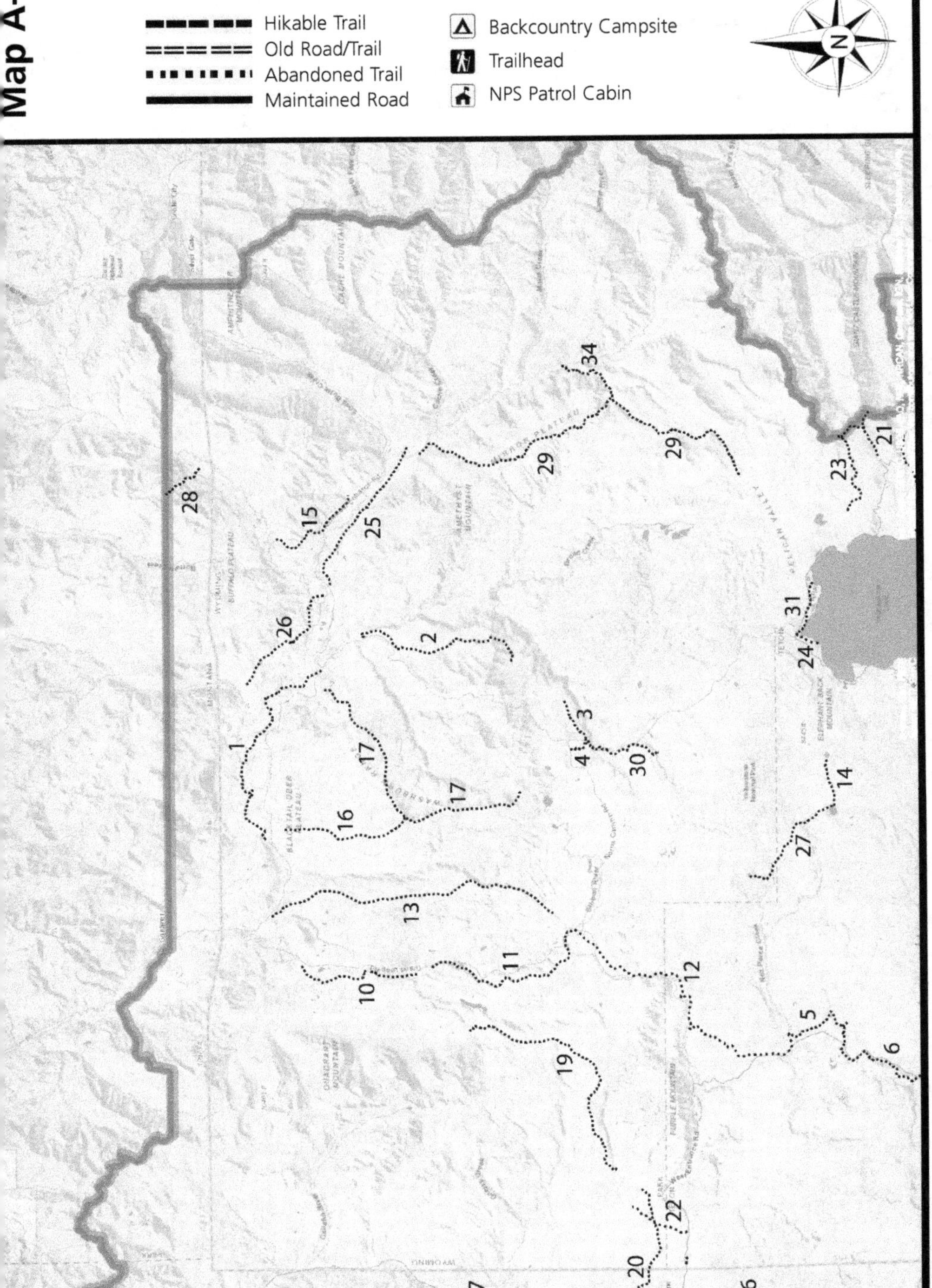

- Hikable Trail
- Old Road/Trail
- Abandoned Trail
- Maintained Road
- Backcountry Campsite
- Trailhead
- NPS Patrol Cabin

1 2 3 4 5 6 10 11 12 13 14 15 16 17 19 20 21 22 23 24 25 26 27 28 29 30 31 34 36 37

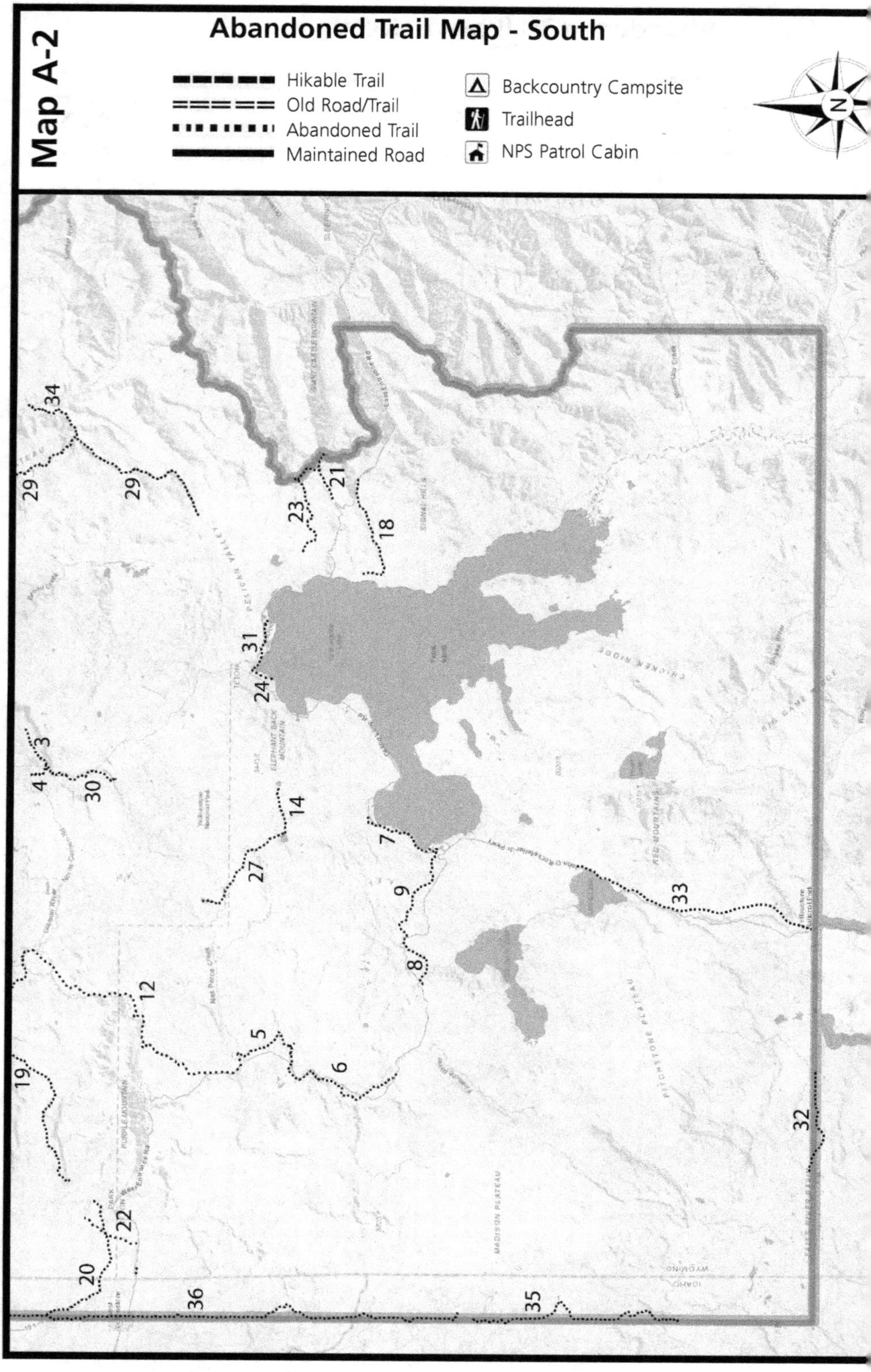
Map A-2
Abandoned Trail Map - South
Hikable Trail
Old Road/Trail
Abandoned Trail
Maintained Road
Backcountry Campsite
Trailhead
NPS Patrol Cabin
N
34
29
29
23
21
18
31
24
3
4
30
14
27
7
9
8
33
12
5
6
19
32
22
20
36
35

Map A-3

Howard Eaton Trail System - Late 1950s

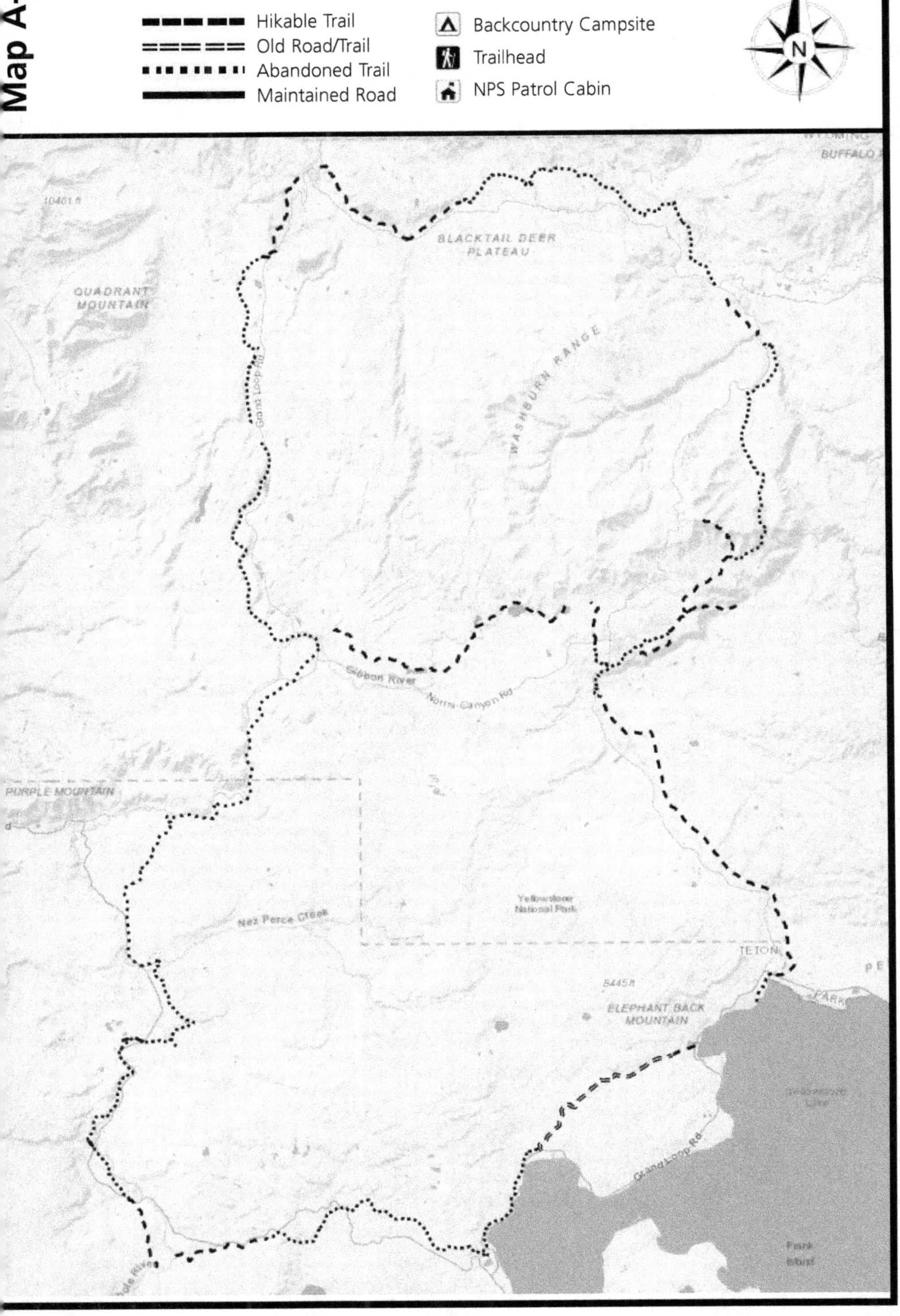

Hikable Trail
Old Road/Trail
Abandoned Trail
Maintained Road

Backcountry Campsite
Trailhead
NPS Patrol Cabin

BUFFALO
10401 ft
QUADRANT MOUNTAIN
BLACKTAIL DEER PLATEAU
WASHBURN RANGE
Grand Loop Rd
Gibbon River
Norris-Canyon Rd
PURPLE MOUNTAIN
Nez Perce Creek
Yellowstone National Park
TETON
8445 ft
ELEPHANT BACK MOUNTAIN
Grand Loop Rd

Backcountry Campsite Profiles

The following table lists all of the park's backcountry campsites (as of the summer of 2018), along with detailed information about each. Be sure to consult the latest edition of the Backcountry Trip Planner on the park's website to confirm locations and features. This information will help you determine which campsite(s) you may wish to stay in on your hikes.

Setting up camp

There are no proscribed tent sites at many of the camps. You can set up your tent anywhere you can find suitable flat ground to do so, subject to the recommendation that you don't camp within 100 yards of your food pole/box. You want to be far enough away from it such that, if a bear should wander into your camp after having smelled your food, it will be far enough away that it doesn't associate you with the food.

Some camp sites will have large spaces suitable for deploying numerous tents, while others may not have space for more than a single tent. I try to point out the latter by indicating that they are "small sites" in the profiles that follow.

Each campsite has a detailed set of descriptors for it in the tables below. The followin explains how to interpret the information contained within those tables.

Campsite Attribute Nomenclature

TYPE: Each site is one of several types:

- F: Hiker only
- S: Stock parties only
- F/S: Foot (hiker) and/or Stock
- B: Boat parties only
- F/B: Foot (hiker) or Boat parties

LAT/LONG: This is the geographic coordinates for the campsite in decimal degrees.

ELEV: Elevation of the site above sea level (ASL).

TRAILHD: Trailhead from which most hikers typically hike or boat to the campsite. Thi does not mean that you have to depart from this trailhead, but it is the shortest distanc from the site if you do. When you check in to get your backcountry permit, the ranger wi verify which trailhead you plan to start from. This will provide a sense of what your hik will look like distance-wise, and will allow your parking permit to reflect where you'll b leaving your vehicle. Note that the three-character trailhead designator (e.g., 1K5) doe not appear on the trailhead signs around the park. These are primarily for administrativ recordkeeping. The name of the trailhead will appear on your permit.

PEOPLE: This the maximum number of people you can have at your campsite. Thes limitations are set based on potential resource impact at the site itself. You're not allowe to have more than this number of people staying at your site, and you can be fined if backcountry ranger finds more than the maximum.

STOCK: Similar to the limitations for the number of people you can have at any given site sites suitable for stock use have a limitation on the maximum number of animals (includin any pack animals) you can have.

USE RAT: This number tells you approximately how popular the site is. It is derived from a algorithm that measures three separate years of usage statistics from the park's backcountr office. The higher the number, the more popular the site. Numbers can range from zero t almost 400. A site with a Use Rat of "15" will be a very seldom used site, while a site with Use Rat of "366" will be among the most popular in the park. Having these numbers wil allow you to make a decision about whether or not to reserve a particular site in the cas that your travel plans are not flexible.

DIST TH: This is the distance of the campsite from the main trail, measured in miles (mi) generally. Some measurements are provided in feet (ft) for sites very close to the trail.

DIST WTR: This is the distance from the main body of the campsite to water suitable fo use as drinking water (after being treated, of course). These measurements are provided i feet.

PRIVACY: This is a subjective analysis of the relative privacy of the campsite. This take into consideration how close the site is to the main trail, how visible it is from the trail (a site in the trees is much less visible than one out in the open), how close it is to other, nearby campsites, how dense the trees and other foliage are around the site, and so forth. The sites are categorized as one of three types:

- C: Complete privacy - sites that are far enough from the trail and/or shielded from view of other sites such that you could walk around naked and not have to worry about other hikers seeing you.
- P: Partial privacy - sites that are somewhat private, but that may be visible from the trail or another campsite.
- N: No privacy - sites that are located on or adjacent to the trails or that are out in the open and visible from nearby trails and sites.

SHADE: This is a measure of how much shade you'll have at the main body of the campsite. These fall into one of four categories:

- C: Complete shade: campsites that are located in forest with a canopy dense enough to provide good shade for most/much of the site.
- P: Partial shade - campsites that are located in areas where the foliage provides good shade for at least part of the campsite (may be either the food prep/eating area or the tent area(s)).
- L: Limited shade - campsites that have little foliage or foliage that provides comparatively little shade for most or all of the site.
- N: No shade - campsites that are out in the open, exposed, and have very little to no places where you can find protection from the sun.

FIRE PIT: This will indicate if the campsite has a fire pit. Sites that are listed as "No Wood Fires" almost invariably will not have a fire pit and will be listed as "NWF."

TOILET: Some of the busier sites have toilets of one form or another (almost invariably pit toilets). If the site has access to a toilet, it will be indicated with a "Y."

STAY: Any stay limitations for the site will be provided here. Many of the campsites have a limit of a certain number of nights, and these limitations may only apply to certain kinds of campers.

WTR SRC: The closest, suitable water source for the site is listed here. You can, of course, use any water source you can find.

BMA: If the site is located inside one of the park's Bear Management Areas (BMA), it will be indicated here. You can use the information about each BMA found on pages 62-63 to see what, if any, limitations there may be on your travel, stay, or use of the area.

EASY: If the campsite can be reached via a relatively short, easy hike, you'll find a "Y" in this box. These sites are suitable for those who show up late in the day and have little time to hike out to a campsite for the night, or for those with smaller children who may not wish to hike long distances in order to enjoy Yellowstone's backcountry.

NOTES: This box will list the reference notes for the site. These notes can be found at the end of the profiles. These notes often contain very important information about accessing or using the site, so be sure to refer to these prior to making your decision about getting it.

ANALYSIS: This is a quick analysis of the site that contains subjective qualitative information about the site's views, location, availability of wood for fires, and so forth.

1A1 Lower Blacktail Creek

TYPE:	F/S	LAT/LONG:	44.979707 -110.593446			ELEV:	6338	TRAILHD:	1N5
PEOPLE:	10	STOCK:	6	USE RAT:	215	DIST TH:	0.16 mi	DIST WTR:	157
PRIVACY:	C	SHADE:	P	FIRE PIT:	Y	TOILET:	N	STAY:	
WTR SRC:	Blacktail Deer Creek					BMA:	N	EASY:	Y
NOTES:									

ANALYSIS: Good water source, limited views. Site has pretty good privacy from the trail. Easy access.

1A2 Rescue Creek

TYPE:	F	LAT/LONG:	44.982207 -110.624337			ELEV:	6721	TRAILHD:	1N5
PEOPLE:	10	STOCK:	0	USE RAT:	165	DIST TH:	0.10 mi	DIST WTR:	35
PRIVACY:	N	SHADE:	P	FIRE PIT:	Y	TOILET:	N	STAY:	
WTR SRC:	Rescue Creek (or seasonal unnamed creek)					BMA:	N	EASY:	Y
NOTES:									

ANALYSIS: One of the better campsites (though little/no privacy from trail) in the park and easy to get to.

1A3 Lava Creek

TYPE:	F	LAT/LONG:	44.950174 -110.655685			ELEV:	6097	TRAILHD:	1N3
PEOPLE:	6	STOCK:	0	USE RAT:	122	DIST TH:	0.04 mi	DIST WTR:	36
PRIVACY:	N	SHADE:	P	FIRE PIT:	NWF	TOILET:	N	STAY:	
WTR SRC:	Lava Creek					BMA:	N	EASY:	Y
NOTES:									

ANALYSIS: Easy access site, partial shade and little privacy from the trail.

1B1 Bighorn Pass Trail

TYPE:	F	LAT/LONG:	44.887221 -110.750526			ELEV:	7396	TRAILHD:	1K5
PEOPLE:	10	STOCK:	0	USE RAT:	161	DIST TH:	0.02 mi	DIST WTR:	250
PRIVACY:	N	SHADE:	P	FIRE PIT:	Y	TOILET:	N	STAY:	
WTR SRC:	Indian Creek					BMA:	N	EASY:	Y
NOTES:									

ANALYSIS: Easy site to get to, no privacy, limited shade. Water source distance away on other side of main trail.

1C1 Straight Creek South

TYPE:	F	LAT/LONG:	44.825831 -110.769566			ELEV:	7490	TRAILHD:	1K8
PEOPLE:	10	STOCK:	0	USE RAT:	129	DIST TH:	0.02 mi	DIST WTR:	290
PRIVACY:	N	SHADE:	N	FIRE PIT:	Y	TOILET:	N	STAY:	
WTR SRC:	Straight Creek					BMA:	N	EASY:	
NOTES:									

ANALYSIS: Site is right off the trail; no privacy. Very limited shade. May be marshy w/ limited tent sites early

1C2 Straight Creek North

TYPE:	F/S	LAT/LONG:	44.834268 -110.766170			ELEV:	7476	TRAILHD:	1K8
PEOPLE:	10	STOCK:	6L	USE RAT:	102	DIST TH:	0.03 mi	DIST WTR:	50
PRIVACY:	P	SHADE:	N	FIRE PIT:	Y	TOILET:	N	STAY:	
WTR SRC:	Unnamed lake on Straight Creek					BMA:	N	EASY:	
NOTES:	37								

ANALYSIS: Stock use limited to llamas only. Limited privacy. Good jumping off point for hike to Mt. Holmes summit

1C4 Winter Creek

TYPE:	F/S	LAT/LONG:	44.812145 -110.796903			ELEV:	7696	TRAILHD:	1K6
PEOPLE:	10	STOCK:	6	USE RAT:	144	DIST TH:	0.01 mi	DIST WTR:	28
PRIVACY:	P	SHADE:	P	FIRE PIT:	Y	TOILET:	N	STAY:	
WTR SRC:	Winter Creek/Unnamed seasonal creek					BMA:	N	EASY:	
NOTES:	AH								

ANALYSIS: Limited privacy from trail. Good view of meadow along Winter Creek

C5 Winter Creek Southwest

YPE:	F/S	**LAT/LONG:**	44.808403 -110.798553			**ELEV:**	7701	**TRAILHD:**	1K6
EOPLE:	10	**STOCK:**	6	**USE RAT:**	81	**DIST TH:**	0.26 mi	**DIST WTR:**	237
RIVACY:	C	**SHADE:**	F	**FIRE PIT:**	Y	**TOILET:**	N	**STAY:**	
/TR SRC:			Winter Creek			**BMA:**	N	**EASY:**	
OTES:	AH								

NALYSIS: Site is private, but may be difficult to find, marshy. Water is considerable distance away

F1 Fawn Creek/Gardner's Hole

YPE:	S	**LAT/LONG:**	44.954957 -110.791061			**ELEV:**	7746	**TRAILHD:**	1K3
EOPLE:	12	**STOCK:**	20	**USE RAT:**	58	**DIST TH:**	0.16 mi	**DIST WTR:**	202
RIVACY:	P	**SHADE:**	L	**FIRE PIT:**	Y	**TOILET:**	N	**STAY:**	
/TR SRC:			Fawn Creek			**BMA:**	N	**EASY:**	
OTES:	81, AD								

NALYSIS: Site has limited shade; firewood is limited in the area

F2 Fawn Lake

YPE:	F	**LAT/LONG:**	44.957172 -110.798719			**ELEV:**	7860	**TRAILHD:**	1K3
EOPLE:	10	**STOCK:**	0	**USE RAT:**	120	**DIST TH:**	0.05 mi	**DIST WTR:**	112
RIVACY:	C	**SHADE:**	P	**FIRE PIT:**	Y	**TOILET:**	N	**STAY:**	
VTR SRC:			Fawn Creek			**BMA:**	D	**EASY:**	
OTES:	15, AE								

NALYSIS: Lake is 1/4 mile south of site. Private site. Limited firewood nearby. Site is in BMA (travel restrictions)

G2 Gardner's Hole

YPE:	F	**LAT/LONG:**	44.952149 -110.781557			**ELEV:**	7745	**TRAILHD:**	1K3
EOPLE:	10	**STOCK:**	0	**USE RAT:**	177	**DIST TH:**	0.22 mi	**DIST WTR:**	100
RIVACY:	C	**SHADE:**	F	**FIRE PIT:**	Y	**TOILET:**	N	**STAY:**	
VTR SRC:			Gardner River			**BMA:**	N	**EASY:**	
OTES:									

NALYSIS: Limited wood availability. Good privacy and great views.

G3 Gardner River

YPE:	F	**LAT/LONG:**	44.972093 -110.808910			**ELEV:**	8044	**TRAILHD:**	1K3
EOPLE:	10	**STOCK:**	0	**USE RAT:**	219	**DIST TH:**	0.10 mi	**DIST WTR:**	140
RIVACY:	C	**SHADE:**	P	**FIRE PIT:**	Y	**TOILET:**	N	**STAY:**	
VTR SRC:			Gardner River			**BMA:**	D	**EASY:**	
OTES:	15, AD								

NALYSIS: Old trail to 1F1 & 1G5 goes through campsite (may impact privacy)

G4 Upper Gardner River

YPE:	F	**LAT/LONG:**	44.974424 -110.811493			**ELEV:**	8065	**TRAILHD:**	1K3
EOPLE:	10	**STOCK:**	0	**USE RAT:**	263	**DIST TH:**	0.07 mi	**DIST WTR:**	120
RIVACY:	P	**SHADE:**	L	**FIRE PIT:**	Y	**TOILET:**	N	**STAY:**	
VTR SRC:			Gardner River			**BMA:**	D	**EASY:**	
OTES:	15								

NALYSIS: Site has better tent sites than 1G3, only partial privacy, however.

G5 Soldier's Corral

YPE:	S	**LAT/LONG:**	44.946660 -110.782603			**ELEV:**	7697	**TRAILHD:**	1K3
EOPLE:	12	**STOCK:**	25	**USE RAT:**	188	**DIST TH:**	0.23 mi	**DIST WTR:**	275
RIVACY:	P	**SHADE:**	P	**FIRE PIT:**	Y	**TOILET:**	Y	**STAY:**	
VTR SRC:			Gardner River			**BMA:**	N	**EASY:**	
OTES:	81								

NALYSIS: Site is private and has great views. Considerable evidence of stock use. Has toilet.

1R1 West Cottonwood Creek

TYPE:	F/S	LAT/LONG:	44.992748 -110.516502		ELEV:	5604	TRAILHD:	2K8
PEOPLE:	12	STOCK:	6	USE RAT: 176	DIST TH:	0.07 mi	DIST WTR:	50
PRIVACY:	N	SHADE:	N	FIRE PIT: NWF	TOILET:	N	STAY:	2N/S
WTR SRC:		Yellowstone River			BMA:	N	EASY:	
NOTES:								

ANALYSIS: No shade, no privacy. Site situated alongside river & Cottonwood Creek. No wood fires permitted.

1R2 East Cottonwood Creek

TYPE:	F	LAT/LONG:	44.992021 -110.513859		ELEV:	5599	TRAILHD:	1N5
PEOPLE:	6	STOCK:	0	USE RAT: 112	DIST TH:	0.11 mi	DIST WTR:	165
PRIVACY:	N	SHADE:	P	FIRE PIT: NWF	TOILET:	N	STAY:	
WTR SRC:		Yellowstone River			BMA:	N	EASY:	
NOTES:								

ANALYSIS: Limited shade, no privacy. No wood fires permitted.

1R3 Little Cottonwood Creek

TYPE:	F/S	LAT/LONG:	44.990287 -110.483736		ELEV:	6184	TRAILHD:	2K8
PEOPLE:	10	STOCK:	10	USE RAT: 139	DIST TH:	0.07 mi	DIST WTR:	150
PRIVACY:	P	SHADE:	P	FIRE PIT: NWF	TOILET:	N	STAY:	2N/S
WTR SRC:		Seasonal creek or Little Cottonwood Creek			BMA:	N	EASY:	
NOTES:	A							

ANALYSIS: On bench above Yell River. Water source is seasonal creek (150 ft) or Little Cottonwood Ck (0.23 mi)

1Y1 Yellowstone River Trail West

TYPE:	F	LAT/LONG:	45.013875 -110.626693		ELEV:	5417	TRAILHD:	1N5
PEOPLE:	10	STOCK:	0	USE RAT: 236	DIST TH:	0.04 mi	DIST WTR:	104
PRIVACY:	N	SHADE:	L	FIRE PIT: NWF	TOILET:	N	STAY:	
WTR SRC:		Yellowstone River			BMA:	N	EASY:	
NOTES:	90							

ANALYSIS: Excellent site at base of Buffalo Mtn; food storage too close to tent sites; excellent river view.

1Y2 Yellowstone River Trail East

TYPE:	F	LAT/LONG:	45.015641 -110.609712		ELEV:	5525	TRAILHD:	1N5
PEOPLE:	10	STOCK:	0	USE RAT: 101	DIST TH:	0.05 mi	DIST WTR:	25
PRIVACY:	N	SHADE:	L	FIRE PIT: NWF	TOILET:	N	STAY:	
WTR SRC:		Yellowstone River			BMA:	N	EASY:	
NOTES:	90							

ANALYSIS: Food pole/cooking area across trail from tent sites. Soft tent sites. No privacy. Close to Knowles Falls.

1Y4 Crevice Lake

TYPE:	F	LAT/LONG:	45.004066 -110.581034		ELEV:	5594	TRAILHD:	1N5
PEOPLE:	6	STOCK:	0	USE RAT: 186	DIST TH:	0.04 mi	DIST WTR:	72
PRIVACY:	P	SHADE:	P	FIRE PIT: NWF	TOILET:	N	STAY:	
WTR SRC:		Yellowstone River			BMA:	N	EASY:	
NOTES:								

ANALYSIS: Excellent site with fairly good privacy. Close to Crevice Lake & Knowles Falls. No wood fires permitted.

1Y5 Yellowstone River Bridge

TYPE:	F	LAT/LONG:	44.996287 -110.574401		ELEV:	5573	TRAILHD:	1N5
PEOPLE:	6	STOCK:	0	USE RAT: 127	DIST TH:	0.11 mi	DIST WTR:	70
PRIVACY:	C	SHADE:	P	FIRE PIT: NWF	TOILET:	N	STAY:	
WTR SRC:		Yellowstone River			BMA:	N	EASY:	
NOTES:								

ANALYSIS: Great site with good privacy (may be hard to find, in fact). Close to Crevice Lake.

Y6 East Blacktail Cabin

YPE:	F	LAT/LONG:	44.993812 -110.570868			ELEV:	5568	TRAILHD:	1N5
EOPLE:	6	STOCK:	0	USE RAT:	113	DIST TH:	0.46 mi	DIST WTR:	150
RIVACY:	N	SHADE:	F	FIRE PIT:	NWF	TOILET:	N	STAY:	
WTR SRC:			Yellowstone River			BMA:	N	EASY:	
OTES:	90								

NALYSIS: Site has bear box. Site is private but lies along trail to campsite 1Y8.

Y7 Yellowstone River Trail

YPE:	F/S	LAT/LONG:	44.992102 -110.556961			ELEV:	5589	TRAILHD:	1N5
EOPLE:	10	STOCK:	6	USE RAT:	277	DIST TH:	0.14 mi	DIST WTR:	210
RIVACY:	P	SHADE:	L	FIRE PIT:	NWF	TOILET:	N	STAY:	2N/S
WTR SRC:			Yellowstone River			BMA:	N	EASY:	
OTES:									

NALYSIS: Excellent site with great views to the east; limited privacy

Y8 Oxbow Creek

YPE:	F	LAT/LONG:	44.992033 -110.564885			ELEV:	5570	TRAILHD:	1N5
EOPLE:	6	STOCK:	0	USE RAT:	106	DIST TH:	0.82 mi	DIST WTR:	76
RIVACY:	C	SHADE:	P	FIRE PIT:	NWF	TOILET:	N	STAY:	
WTR SRC:			Yellowstone River			BMA:	N	EASY:	
OTES:	90								

NALYSIS: Site is considerable distance from trail; excellent privacy, w/ great views

Y9 Yellowstone River Trail

YPE:	F	LAT/LONG:	44.993580 -110.547012			ELEV:	5607	TRAILHD:	1N5
EOPLE:	8	STOCK:	0	USE RAT:	166	DIST TH:	0.14 mi	DIST WTR:	85
RIVACY:	C	SHADE:	L	FIRE PIT:	NWF	TOILET:	N	STAY:	
WTR SRC:			Yellowstone River			BMA:	N	EASY:	
OTES:									

NALYSIS: Excellent privacy; great views.

B1 Buffalo Plateau

YPE:	F/S	LAT/LONG:	45.016747 -110.377847			ELEV:	8404	TRAILHD:	2K8
EOPLE:	10	STOCK:	16	USE RAT:	91	DIST TH:	0.68 mi	DIST WTR:	500
RIVACY:	C	SHADE:	L	FIRE PIT:	Y	TOILET:	N	STAY:	
WTR SRC:			Unnamed tributary of Coyote Creek			BMA:	N	EASY:	
OTES:	8, A								

NALYSIS: Very private site. Water source may be seasonal. Closes after 9/14 each season.

C1 Coyote Creek

YPE:	F	LAT/LONG:	45.000665 -110.417111			ELEV:	6755	TRAILHD:	2K8
EOPLE:	8	STOCK:	0	USE RAT:	112	DIST TH:	0.09 mi	DIST WTR:	90
RIVACY:	C	SHADE:	L	FIRE PIT:	Y	TOILET:	N	STAY:	
WTR SRC:			Coyote Creek			BMA:	N	EASY:	
OTES:	A								

NALYSIS: Decent, private site with limited view. Tempestuous Falls 1/3 miles downstream.

C2 Coyote Creek

YPE:	F	LAT/LONG:	45.008944 -110.407947			ELEV:	7161	TRAILHD:	2K8
EOPLE:	8	STOCK:	0	USE RAT:	169	DIST TH:	0.01 mi	DIST WTR:	220
RIVACY:	P	SHADE:	P	FIRE PIT:	Y	TOILET:	N	STAY:	
WTR SRC:			Coyote Creek			BMA:	N	EASY:	
OTES:	A								

NALYSIS: Site is located adjacent to trail, limited privacy.

2C3 **Coyote Creek**

TYPE:	S	LAT/LONG:	45.016087 -110.408672		ELEV:	7177	TRAILHD:	2K
PEOPLE:	10	STOCK:	16	USE RAT: 84	DIST TH:	0.14 mi	DIST WTR:	27
PRIVACY:	C	SHADE:	P	FIRE PIT: Y	TOILET:	N	STAY:	
WTR SRC:			Coyote Creek		BMA:	N	EASY:	
NOTES:	31, A							

ANALYSIS: Site is for stock parties only. Good privacy

2H1 **North Yellowstone/Hellroaring Confluence**

TYPE:	F	LAT/LONG:	44.974602 -110.475112		ELEV:	5772	TRAILHD:	2K
PEOPLE:	8	STOCK:	0	USE RAT: 125	DIST TH:	1.14 mi	DIST WTR:	17
PRIVACY:	P	SHADE:	L	FIRE PIT: NWF	TOILET:	N	STAY:	
WTR SRC:			Hellroaring Creek or Yellowstone River		BMA:	N	EASY:	
NOTES:	A							

ANALYSIS: Outstanding campsite (one of the best in the park). Limited privacy if site 2H2 is occupied.

2H2 **South Yellowstone/Hellroaring Confluence**

TYPE:	F	LAT/LONG:	44.973608 -110.475287		ELEV:	5730	TRAILHD:	2K
PEOPLE:	6	STOCK:	0	USE RAT: 135	DIST TH:	1.33 mi	DIST WTR:	25
PRIVACY:	P	SHADE:	P	FIRE PIT: NWF	TOILET:	N	STAY:	
WTR SRC:			Hellroaring Creek or Yellowstone River		BMA:	N	EASY:	
NOTES:	A							

ANALYSIS: Outstanding campsite (one of the best in the park). Limited privacy if site 2H1 is occupied.

2H3 **Hellroaring Creek**

TYPE:	F	LAT/LONG:	44.972131 -110.458743		ELEV:	5815	TRAILHD:	2K
PEOPLE:	10	STOCK:	0	USE RAT: 122	DIST TH:	0.20 mi	DIST WTR:	48
PRIVACY:	N	SHADE:	L	FIRE PIT: NWF	TOILET:	N	STAY:	
WTR SRC:			Hellroaring Creek		BMA:	N	EASY:	
NOTES:	A							

ANALYSIS: Located right on the creek. Excellent site. Limited privacy from spur to 2H1 & visible from across cree

2H4 **Hellroaring Creek**

TYPE:	F	LAT/LONG:	44.975025 -110.463480		ELEV:	5817	TRAILHD:	2K8
PEOPLE:	6	STOCK:	0	USE RAT: 105	DIST TH:	0.74 mi	DIST WTR:	12
PRIVACY:	C	SHADE:	L	FIRE PIT: NWF	TOILET:	N	STAY:	
WTR SRC:			Hellroaring Creek		BMA:	N	EASY:	
NOTES:	A							

ANALYSIS: Located right on creek. Very limited shade. Limited privacy from hikers going to 2H2 or across creek,

2H5 **Hellroaring Creek**

TYPE:	F	LAT/LONG:	44.977681 -110.442828		ELEV:	5935	TRAILHD:	2K8
PEOPLE:	8	STOCK:	0	USE RAT: 77	DIST TH:	0.07 mi	DIST WTR:	53
PRIVACY:	P	SHADE:	L	FIRE PIT: NWF	TOILET:	N	STAY:	
WTR SRC:			Hellroaring Creek		BMA:	N	EASY:	
NOTES:	A							

ANALYSIS: Requires descent of steep incline to get to site. Limited shade.

2H6 **Hellroaring Creek**

TYPE:	F	LAT/LONG:	44.976690 -110.443727		ELEV:	5901	TRAILHD:	2K8
PEOPLE:	8	STOCK:	0	USE RAT: 159	DIST TH:	0.06 mi	DIST WTR:	72
PRIVACY:	P	SHADE:	L	FIRE PIT: NWF	TOILET:	N	STAY:	
WTR SRC:			Hellroaring Creek		BMA:	N	EASY:	
NOTES:	A							

ANALYSIS: Limited shade and privacy (can be seen from trails on both sides of creek), but decent site.

7 Hellroaring Creek

PE:	F	LAT/LONG:	44.983511 -110.433004		ELEV:	5992	TRAILHD:	2K8
OPLE:	10	STOCK:	0	USE RAT: 177	DIST TH:	0.07 mi	DIST WTR:	106
IVACY:	N	SHADE:	L	FIRE PIT: NWF	TOILET:	N	STAY:	
TR SRC:		Hellroaring Creek			BMA:	N	EASY:	
TES:	A							

ALYSIS: Decent site, with limited shade. Site is visible from trail on both sides of creek.

8 Hellroaring Creek

PE:	F	LAT/LONG:	44.994288 -110.427932		ELEV:	6142	TRAILHD:	2K8
OPLE:	8	STOCK:	0	USE RAT: 108	DIST TH:	0.54 mi	DIST WTR:	260
IVACY:	C	SHADE:	L	FIRE PIT: NWF	TOILET:	N	STAY:	
TR SRC:		Hellroaring Creek (or Coyote Creek)			BMA:	N	EASY:	
TES:	A							

NALYSIS: Limited shade, but nice site (good privacy) at confluence of Hellroaring & Coyote Creeks.

9 Hellroaring Creek

PE:	F	LAT/LONG:	45.008784 -110.434041		ELEV:	6239	TRAILHD:	2K8
OPLE:	8	STOCK:	0	USE RAT: 243	DIST TH:	0.05 mi	DIST WTR:	232
IVACY:	P	SHADE:	L	FIRE PIT: Y	TOILET:	N	STAY:	
TR SRC:		Hellroaring Creek			BMA:	N	EASY:	
OTES:	A							

NALYSIS: Decent site, but limited privacy (visible from trail).

1 Lower Slough Creek

PE:	F/S	LAT/LONG:	44.970015 -110.236467		ELEV:	6674	TRAILHD:	2K5
OPLE:	8	STOCK:	12	USE RAT: 372	DIST TH:	0.60 mi	DIST WTR:	130
IVACY:	C	SHADE:	L	FIRE PIT: Y	TOILET:	N	STAY:	3N
TR SRC:		Slough Creek			BMA:	N	EASY:	
OTES:	21, C							

NALYSIS: Excellent site, and is one of the most popular in the park. Limited shade. McBride Lake 3/4 mile south

2 Lower Slough Creek

YPE:	F	LAT/LONG:	44.965760 -110.228162		ELEV:	6650	TRAILHD:	2K5
EOPLE:	6	STOCK:	0	USE RAT: 269	DIST TH:	0.05 mi	DIST WTR:	84
RIVACY:	P	SHADE:	L	FIRE PIT: Y	TOILET:	N	STAY:	3N
TR SRC:		Hornaday Creek			BMA:	N	EASY:	
OTES:	21, 90, C							

NALYSIS: Limited privacy & shade. Site has a bear box.

S3 Slough Creek

YPE:	F	LAT/LONG:	44.976381 -110.212223		ELEV:	6719	TRAILHD:	2K5
EOPLE:	8	STOCK:	0	USE RAT: 281	DIST TH:	0.13 mi	DIST WTR:	65
RIVACY:	P	SHADE:	L	FIRE PIT: Y	TOILET:	N	STAY:	3N
TR SRC:		Unnamed creek/tributary of Slough Creek			BMA:	N	EASY:	
OTES:	21, 90, C							

NALYSIS: Nice, mostly private site. Site has a bear box.

S4 Slough Creek

YPE:	F	LAT/LONG:	44.990012 -110.203962		ELEV:	6659	TRAILHD:	2K5
EOPLE:	8	STOCK:	0	USE RAT: 337	DIST TH:	0.11 mi	DIST WTR:	160
RIVACY:	C	SHADE:	C	FIRE PIT: Y	TOILET:	N	STAY:	3N
TR SRC:		Slough Creek			BMA:	N	EASY:	
OTES:	21, C							

NALYSIS: Good, very private site. Another very popular site.

2S6 **Upper Slough Creek**

TYPE:	F	**LAT/LONG:**	45.002649 -110.185271			**ELEV:**	6891	**TRAILHD:**	2K5
PEOPLE:	8	**STOCK:**	0	**USE RAT:**	315	**DIST TH:**	0.03 mi	**DIST WTR:**	46
PRIVACY:	P	**SHADE:**	L	**FIRE PIT:**	Y	**TOILET:**	N	**STAY:**	3N
WTR SRC:		Slough Creek (See analysis)				**BMA:**	N	**EASY:**	
NOTES:	21, C								

ANALYSIS: Limited privacy (right off the trail). Getting to water requires traversing marshy area early in season.

2S7 **Upper Slough Creek**

TYPE:	S	**LAT/LONG:**	44.993308 -110.214020			**ELEV:**	6874	**TRAILHD:**	2K5
PEOPLE:	12	**STOCK:**	20	**USE RAT:**	227	**DIST TH:**	0.81 mi	**DIST WTR:**	604
PRIVACY:	C	**SHADE:**	P	**FIRE PIT:**	Y	**TOILET:**	N	**STAY:**	3N
WTR SRC:		Unnamed tributary of Slough Creek				**BMA:**	N	**EASY:**	
NOTES:	21, 83, C								

ANALYSIS: Good site, complete privacy. Access requires fording Slough Creek.

2S8 **Upper Slough Creek**

TYPE:	S	**LAT/LONG:**	45.006078 -110.199225			**ELEV:**	6796	**TRAILHD:**	2K5
PEOPLE:	12	**STOCK:**	20	**USE RAT:**	195	**DIST TH:**	1.42 mi	**DIST WTR:**	59
PRIVACY:	C	**SHADE:**	L	**FIRE PIT:**	Y	**TOILET:**	N	**STAY:**	3N
WTR SRC:		Unnamed tributary of Slough Creek				**BMA:**	N	**EASY:**	
NOTES:	21, 83, C								

ANALYSIS: Very private site; great views. Access requires fording Slough Creek.

2Y1 **Agate Creek**

TYPE:	F	**LAT/LONG:**	44.852000 -110.358219			**ELEV:**	6468	**TRAILHD:**	2K4
PEOPLE:	8	**STOCK:**	0	**USE RAT:**	148	**DIST TH:**	25 ft	**DIST WTR:**	800
PRIVACY:	N	**SHADE:**	P	**FIRE PIT:**	Y	**TOILET:**	N	**STAY:**	
WTR SRC:		Agate Creek (seasonal)/Yellowstone River				**BMA:**	N	**EASY:**	
NOTES:	7								

ANALYSIS: Trail goes through campsite (though trail is lightly used); water source considerable distance away.

3C2 **Lower Cache Creek**

TYPE:	F/S	**LAT/LONG:**	44.853959 -110.066627			**ELEV:**	7274	**TRAILHD:**	3K1
PEOPLE:	12	**STOCK:**	20	**USE RAT:**	152	**DIST TH:**	0.13 mi	**DIST WTR:**	170
PRIVACY:	N	**SHADE:**	L	**FIRE PIT:**	Y	**TOILET:**	N	**STAY:**	2N/S
WTR SRC:		Cache Creek				**BMA:**	N	**EASY:**	
NOTES:	H, K								

ANALYSIS: Site is visible from the trail (no privacy); Great views

3C3 **Upper Cache Creek**

TYPE:	F/S	**LAT/LONG:**	44.874226 -110.047970			**ELEV:**	7561	**TRAILHD:**	3K3
PEOPLE:	12	**STOCK:**	25	**USE RAT:**	131	**DIST TH:**	0.22 mi	**DIST WTR:**	250
PRIVACY:	P	**SHADE:**	N	**FIRE PIT:**	Y	**TOILET:**	N	**STAY:**	
WTR SRC:		Cache Creek				**BMA:**	N	**EASY:**	
NOTES:	H, I, J, K								

ANALYSIS: No shade at all for this site, but it does have great views.

3C4 **Upper Cache Creek**

TYPE:	F	**LAT/LONG:**	44.923179 -110.004633			**ELEV:**	7876	**TRAILHD:**	3K3
PEOPLE:	12	**STOCK:**	0	**USE RAT:**	102	**DIST TH:**	0.13 mi	**DIST WTR:**	53
PRIVACY:	C	**SHADE:**	N	**FIRE PIT:**	Y	**TOILET:**	N	**STAY:**	
WTR SRC:		Unnamed tributary of Cache Creek				**BMA:**	N	**EASY:**	
NOTES:	H, I, J, K								

ANALYSIS: Water source may be seasonal in dry years. Excellent view of The Thunderer. No shade, however.

3F1 Cold Creek

TYPE:	F	**LAT/LONG:**	44.679324 -110.052419			**ELEV:**	7347	**TRAILHD:**	5K3
PEOPLE:	6	**STOCK:**	0	**USE RAT:**	65	**DIST TH:**	0.07 mi	**DIST WTR:**	84
PRIVACY:	C	**SHADE:**	L	**FIRE PIT:**	Y	**TOILET:**	N	**STAY:**	
WTR SRC:	Unnamed tributary of Lamar River/Lamar River					**BMA:**	N	**EASY:**	
NOTES:	67, N (from 5K3)								

ANALYSIS: Primary water source is seasonal. Abandoned trail passes through site. Limited shade.

3F2 Lemon City

TYPE:	F/S	**LAT/LONG:**	44.669533 -110.041566			**ELEV:**	7373	**TRAILHD:**	5K3
PEOPLE:	12	**STOCK:**	25	**USE RAT:**	61	**DIST TH:**	0.03 mi	**DIST WTR:**	129
PRIVACY:	P	**SHADE:**	C	**FIRE PIT:**	Y	**TOILET:**	N	**STAY:**	
WTR SRC:	Unnamed tributary of Lamar River					**BMA:**	N	**EASY:**	
NOTES:	N (from 5K3)								

ANALYSIS: Site is partially visible from trail, but is shaded. Views not that great.

3L1 North Lower Cache Creek

TYPE:	F/S	**LAT/LONG:**	44.831262 -110.143287			**ELEV:**	6959	**TRAILHD:**	3K1
PEOPLE:	12	**STOCK:**	8L	**USE RAT:**	347	**DIST TH:**	0.17 mi	**DIST WTR:**	210
PRIVACY:	P	**SHADE:**	L	**FIRE PIT:**	Y	**TOILET:**	N	**STAY:**	
WTR SRC:	Cache Creek					**BMA:**	N	**EASY:**	
NOTES:	37, G, L								

ANALYSIS: Stock use limited to llamas. Very popular site & area is popular for fishing.

3L2 South Lower Cache Creek

TYPE:	F	**LAT/LONG:**	44.831091 -110.149236			**ELEV:**	6934	**TRAILHD:**	3K1
PEOPLE:	12	**STOCK:**	0	**USE RAT:**	226	**DIST TH:**	0.14 mi	**DIST WTR:**	180
PRIVACY:	C	**SHADE:**	L	**FIRE PIT:**	Y	**TOILET:**	N	**STAY:**	
WTR SRC:	Cache Creek					**BMA:**	N	**EASY:**	
NOTES:	G, H, L								

ANALYSIS: Site is private, but fishermen in the area might reduce that. Gravel in tent areas.

3L3 Lower Lamar

TYPE:	F	**LAT/LONG:**	44.813342 -110.142526			**ELEV:**	6792	**TRAILHD:**	3K1
PEOPLE:	12	**STOCK:**	0	**USE RAT:**	169	**DIST TH:**	0.10 mi	**DIST WTR:**	80
PRIVACY:	C	**SHADE:**	P	**FIRE PIT:**	Y	**TOILET:**	N	**STAY:**	
WTR SRC:	Lamar River					**BMA:**	N	**EASY:**	
NOTES:	G								

ANALYSIS: Good, though well-worn site. Good privacy, shade, water source.

3L4 Lower Lamar

TYPE:	F	**LAT/LONG:**	44.807549 -110.135322			**ELEV:**	6804	**TRAILHD:**	3K1
PEOPLE:	12	**STOCK:**	0	**USE RAT:**	213	**DIST TH:**	0.08 mi	**DIST WTR:**	140
PRIVACY:	N	**SHADE:**	L	**FIRE PIT:**	Y	**TOILET:**	N	**STAY:**	
WTR SRC:	Lamar River					**BMA:**	N	**EASY:**	
NOTES:	G								

ANALYSIS: Exposed site - no shade, no privacy.

3L6 Middle Lamar

TYPE:	S	**LAT/LONG:**	44.755438 -110.097871			**ELEV:**	7030	**TRAILHD:**	3K1
PEOPLE:	12	**STOCK:**	20	**USE RAT:**	44	**DIST TH:**	0.16 mi	**DIST WTR:**	98
PRIVACY:	P	**SHADE:**	L	**FIRE PIT:**	Y	**TOILET:**	N	**STAY:**	2N/S
WTR SRC:	Lamar River					**BMA:**	N	**EASY:**	
NOTES:	61, G								

ANALYSIS: Access to site requires ford of Lamar River.

3L7 Middle Lamar

TYPE:	F	LAT/LONG:	44.753473 -110.097057			ELEV:	7049	TRAILHD:	3K1
PEOPLE:	12	STOCK:	0	USE RAT:	185	DIST TH:	0.10 mi	DIST WTR:	100
PRIVACY:	P	SHADE:	L	FIRE PIT:	Y	TOILET:	N	STAY:	
WTR SRC:			Lamar River			BMA:	N	EASY:	

NOTES: G

ANALYSIS: Excellent site, limited shade, however.

3L8 Timothy Creek

TYPE:	F	LAT/LONG:	44.734090 -110.089494			ELEV:	7069	TRAILHD:	3K1
PEOPLE:	12	STOCK:	0	USE RAT:	54	DIST TH:	0.14 mi	DIST WTR:	240
PRIVACY:	N	SHADE:	L	FIRE PIT:	Y	TOILET:	N	STAY:	
WTR SRC:			Lamar River			BMA:	N	EASY:	

NOTES: G (this site may be shown on some old maps as 3L9 - used to be that site before washout years ago)

ANALYSIS: Though site is named for Timothy Creek, it is a good distance away. Lightly used, exposed site.

3L9 Warm Spring Meadow

TYPE:	F/S	LAT/LONG:	44.729959 -110.087929			ELEV:	7073	TRAILHD:	3K1
PEOPLE:	12	STOCK:	20	USE RAT:	133	DIST TH:	0.14 mi	DIST WTR:	188
PRIVACY:	P	SHADE:	L	FIRE PIT:	Y	TOILET:	N	STAY:	
WTR SRC:			Lamar River			BMA:	N	EASY:	

NOTES: G (this is the "new" 3L9 site - may not appear on older maps)

ANALYSIS: Good site, good privacy. Finding wood for campfires may be difficult.

3M1 Appaloosa Meadows

TYPE:	F/S	LAT/LONG:	44.761723 -110.075037			ELEV:	7134	TRAILHD:	3K1
PEOPLE:	12	STOCK:	25	USE RAT:	133	DIST TH:	0.27 mi	DIST WTR:	154
PRIVACY:	C	SHADE:	L	FIRE PIT:	Y	TOILET:	N	STAY:	2N/S >15
WTR SRC:			Miller Creek			BMA:	N	EASY:	

NOTES: 61, G

ANALYSIS: Requires ford of Miller Creek. Very private site. Considerable evidence of stock use, however.

3M2 Lower Miller Creek

TYPE:	F	LAT/LONG:	44.755620 -110.044490			ELEV:	7294	TRAILHD:	3K1
PEOPLE:	12	STOCK:	0	USE RAT:	49	DIST TH:	0.18 mi	DIST WTR:	64
PRIVACY:	C	SHADE:	L	FIRE PIT:	Y	TOILET:	N	STAY:	
WTR SRC:			Miller Creek			BMA:	N	EASY:	

NOTES: 74, G

ANALYSIS: Site is in floodplain and may be flooded/inaccessible early in season. Good privacy.

3M3 Lower Miller Creek

TYPE:	F/S	LAT/LONG:	44.751539 -110.031269			ELEV:	7262	TRAILHD:	3K1
PEOPLE:	12	STOCK:	20	USE RAT:	75	DIST TH:	0.06 mi	DIST WTR:	78
PRIVACY:	N	SHADE:	C	FIRE PIT:	Y	TOILET:	N	STAY:	
WTR SRC:			Miller Creek			BMA:	N	EASY:	

NOTES: 61, G

ANALYSIS: Access requires ford of Miller Creek. Good site, good shade & privacy.

3M4 Upper Miller Creek

TYPE:	F	LAT/LONG:	44.751102 -109.978114			ELEV:	7480	TRAILHD:	3K1
PEOPLE:	6	STOCK:	0	USE RAT:	3	DIST TH:	0.03 mi	DIST WTR:	150
PRIVACY:	N	SHADE:	P	FIRE PIT:	Y	TOILET:	N	STAY:	
WTR SRC:			Miller Creek			BMA:	N	EASY:	

NOTES: G

ANALYSIS: Fairly poor campsite, very rarely used. No privacy, limited shade.

3M5 Upper Miller Creek

TYPE:	F	**LAT/LONG:**	44.750086 -109.970680			**ELEV:**	7550	**TRAILHD:**	3K1
PEOPLE:	12	**STOCK:**	0	**USE RAT:**	65	**DIST TH:**	0.23 mi	**DIST WTR:**	100
PRIVACY:	C	**SHADE:**	P	**FIRE PIT:**	Y	**TOILET:**	N	**STAY:**	
WTR SRC:			Miller Creek			**BMA:**	N	**EASY:**	
NOTES:	G								

ANALYSIS: Private site, many downed trees in the area (be cautious of snags & hazard trees in area)

3M6 Hoodoo Basin

TYPE:	F	**LAT/LONG:**	44.727671 -109.884509			**ELEV:**	9360	**TRAILHD:**	3K1
PEOPLE:	12	**STOCK:**	0	**USE RAT:**	63	**DIST TH:**	0.06 mi	**DIST WTR:**	83
PRIVACY:	P	**SHADE:**	L	**FIRE PIT:**	Y	**TOILET:**	N	**STAY:**	
WTR SRC:			Unnamed tributary of the Lamar River			**BMA:**	N	**EASY:**	
NOTES:	G								

ANALYSIS: Site is fairly private, w/ limited shade. Water source may be seasonal in dry years. Great views.

3M7 Boundary

TYPE:	F/S	**LAT/LONG:**	44.727546 -109.866337			**ELEV:**	9680	**TRAILHD:**	3K1
PEOPLE:	12	**STOCK:**	20	**USE RAT:**	36	**DIST TH:**	0.05 mi	**DIST WTR:**	104
PRIVACY:	N	**SHADE:**	L	**FIRE PIT:**	Y	**TOILET:**	N	**STAY:**	1N/S
WTR SRC:			Unnamed tributary of the Lamar River			**BMA:**	N	**EASY:**	
NOTES:	18, 68, G								

ANALYSIS: Outstanding view of the Hoodoos. Lightly used site. Water source may be seasonal in dry years.

3O1 Opal Creek

TYPE:	F/S	**LAT/LONG:**	44.799265 -110.199280			**ELEV:**	8773	**TRAILHD:**	3K1
PEOPLE:	12	**STOCK:**	20	**USE RAT:**	50	**DIST TH:**	3.75 mi	**DIST WTR:**	350
PRIVACY:	C	**SHADE:**	L	**FIRE PIT:**	N	**TOILET:**	N	**STAY:**	
WTR SRC:			Opal Creek			**BMA:**	H	**EASY:**	
NOTES:	16, 22, 63								

ANALYSIS: Requires off trail travel along Opal Creek. Must have compass/GPS & map skills. Leave No Trace rules.

3P1 Pebble Creek

TYPE:	F	**LAT/LONG:**	44.958985 -110.118588			**ELEV:**	7500	**TRAILHD:**	3K2
PEOPLE:	12	**STOCK:**	0	**USE RAT:**	164	**DIST TH:**	0.09 mi	**DIST WTR:**	300
PRIVACY:	C	**SHADE:**	P	**FIRE PIT:**	Y	**TOILET:**	N	**STAY:**	
WTR SRC:			Pebble Creek			**BMA:**	N	**EASY:**	
NOTES:	D, E								

ANALYSIS: Great site, with good views, good privacy, partial shading. Firewood supply may be limited.

3P2 Bliss Pass Jct

TYPE:	F	**LAT/LONG:**	44.994793 -110.110268			**ELEV:**	7760	**TRAILHD:**	3K2
PEOPLE:	12	**STOCK:**	0	**USE RAT:**	175	**DIST TH:**	0.04 mi	**DIST WTR:**	170
PRIVACY:	C	**SHADE:**	P	**FIRE PIT:**	Y	**TOILET:**	N	**STAY:**	
WTR SRC:			Pebble Creek			**BMA:**	N	**EASY:**	
NOTES:	D, E, F								

ANALYSIS: Decent site, good privacy. Limited views. Firewood supply may be limited.

3P3 Bliss Pass Jct

TYPE:	F	**LAT/LONG:**	45.001204 -110.107003			**ELEV:**	7780	**TRAILHD:**	3K4
PEOPLE:	6	**STOCK:**	0	**USE RAT:**	193	**DIST TH:**	0.02 mi	**DIST WTR:**	364
PRIVACY:	C	**SHADE:**	C	**FIRE PIT:**	Y	**TOILET:**	N	**STAY:**	
WTR SRC:			Pebble Creek			**BMA:**	N	**EASY:**	
NOTES:	E, F								

ANALYSIS: Good site, good privacy, good shading. Firewood supply may be limited.

3P4 Upper Pebble Creek

TYPE:	F/S	LAT/LONG:	45.021258 -110.077817		ELEV:	7960	TRAILHD:	3K4
PEOPLE:	12	STOCK:	20	USE RAT: 129	DIST TH:	0.06 mi	DIST WTR:	576
PRIVACY:	N	SHADE:	N	FIRE PIT: Y	TOILET:	N	STAY:	
WTR SRC:			Pebble Creek		BMA:	N	EASY:	
NOTES:	E							

ANALYSIS: Not exactly the best site. No shade, little privacy. Water source on other side of main trail.

3P5 Upper Pebble Creek

TYPE:	F	LAT/LONG:	45.019008 -110.056459		ELEV:	8060	TRAILHD:	3K4
PEOPLE:	12	STOCK:	0	USE RAT: 115	DIST TH:	0.07 mi	DIST WTR:	159
PRIVACY:	P	SHADE:	L	FIRE PIT: Y	TOILET:	N	STAY:	
WTR SRC:			Pebble Creek		BMA:	N	EASY:	Y
NOTES:	E							

ANALYSIS: Decent site (best of the two between 3P4 & 3P5). Firewood supply may be limited. Limited shade.

3T2 Mist Creek Meadows

TYPE:	F/S	LAT/LONG:	44.621727 -110.118320		ELEV:	8080	TRAILHD:	5K3
PEOPLE:	12	STOCK:	12	USE RAT: 123	DIST TH:	0.06 mi	DIST WTR:	179
PRIVACY:	P	SHADE:	P	FIRE PIT: Y	TOILET:	N	STAY:	2N/S
WTR SRC:			Mist Creek		BMA:	N	EASY:	
NOTES:	82, N							

ANALYSIS: Requires fording Mist Creek. Excellent view, w/ good privacy and shade.

3T3 Mist Creek Pass

TYPE:	F/S	LAT/LONG:	44.613676 -110.133846		ELEV:	8140	TRAILHD:	5K3
PEOPLE:	12	STOCK:	25	USE RAT: 162	DIST TH:	0.21 mi	DIST WTR:	55
PRIVACY:	C	SHADE:	P	FIRE PIT: Y	TOILET:	N	STAY:	2N/S
WTR SRC:			Mist Creek		BMA:	N	EASY:	
NOTES:	82, N							

ANALYSIS: Requires fording Mist Creek. Good site w/ complete privacy and good shade.

3U1 Lower Willow Creek

TYPE:	F/S	LAT/LONG:	44.718114 -110.086051		ELEV:	7100	TRAILHD:	3K1
PEOPLE:	12	STOCK:	25	USE RAT: 152	DIST TH:	0.27 mi	DIST WTR:	384
PRIVACY:	P	SHADE:	L	FIRE PIT: Y	TOILET:	N	STAY:	
WTR SRC:			Lamar River		BMA:	N	EASY:	
NOTES:	61, 62 (mid-July), G							

ANALYSIS: Requires ford of Lamar River (see notes). Large site, w/ decent views. Great privacy, but limited shade

3U2 Lower Willow Creek

TYPE:	F	LAT/LONG:	44.702323 -110.080271		ELEV:	7170	TRAILHD:	5K3
PEOPLE:	12	STOCK:	0	USE RAT: 79	DIST TH:	0.12 mi	DIST WTR:	50
PRIVACY:	C	SHADE:	L	FIRE PIT: Y	TOILET:	N	STAY:	
WTR SRC:			Lamar River		BMA:	N	EASY:	
NOTES:	N							

ANALYSIS: Great site along the Lamar River. Good privacy, but limited shade.

3U3 Little Saddle Creek

TYPE:	F	LAT/LONG:	44.689905 -110.068205		ELEV:	7240	TRAILHD:	5K3
PEOPLE:	12	STOCK:	0	USE RAT: 77	DIST TH:	0.16 mi	DIST WTR:	280
PRIVACY:	C	SHADE:	P	FIRE PIT: Y	TOILET:	N	STAY:	
WTR SRC:			Lamar River		BMA:	N	EASY:	
NOTES:	61, N							

ANALYSIS: Requires crossing good-sized creek. Very private, good shading.

J4 Cold Creek Jct

'PE:	S	**LAT/LONG:**	44.679070 -110.057661			**ELEV:**	7320	**TRAILHD:**	5K3
:OPLE:	12	**STOCK:**	25	**USE RAT:**	97	**DIST TH:**	0.21 mi	**DIST WTR:**	150
RIVACY:	C	**SHADE:**	P	**FIRE PIT:**	Y	**TOILET:**	N	**STAY:**	
TR SRC:		Lamar River				**BMA:**	N	**EASY:**	

OTES: N

NALYSIS: Good site w/ decent views. Good privacy and shade. Firewood supply may be limited.

31 Joseph Coat Springs

'PE:	F	**LAT/LONG:**	44.735264 -110.322467			**ELEV:**	8100	**TRAILHD:**	4K9
EOPLE:	6	**STOCK:**	0	**USE RAT:**	80	**DIST TH:**	4.00 mi	**DIST WTR:**	125
RIVACY:	C	**SHADE:**	L	**FIRE PIT:**	Y	**TOILET:**	N	**STAY:**	2N/E
'TR SRC:		Broad Creek				**BMA:**	N	**EASY:**	

OTES: 63, R (Must have good map & compass/GPS skills)

NALYSIS: Requires bushwacking from Wapiti Lake Trail (no defined trail). Located in thermal area. Limited shade.

B2 Broad Creek

YPE:	F/S	**LAT/LONG:**	44.730183 -110.303174			**ELEV:**	8140	**TRAILHD:**	4K9
EOPLE:	6	**STOCK:**	0	**USE RAT:**	19	**DIST TH:**	2.45 mi	**DIST WTR:**	72
RIVACY:	C	**SHADE:**	L	**FIRE PIT:**	Y	**TOILET:**	N	**STAY:**	
/TR SRC:		Broad Creek				**BMA:**	N	**EASY:**	

OTES: 63, R (Must have good map & compass/GPS skills)

NALYSIS: Requires bushwacking from Wapiti Lake Trail (no defined trail). Limited shade. Traffic to 4B1 passes by.

B3 Broad Creek

YPE:	F/S	**LAT/LONG:**	44.710769 -110.282056			**ELEV:**	8160	**TRAILHD:**	4K9
EOPLE:	12	**STOCK:**	6	**USE RAT:**	18	**DIST TH:**	0.21 mi	**DIST WTR:**	39
RIVACY:	P	**SHADE:**	L	**FIRE PIT:**	Y	**TOILET:**	N	**STAY:**	
VTR SRC:		Unnamed tributary of Broad Creek/Broad Creek				**BMA:**	N	**EASY:**	

IOTES: 63, R

NALYSIS: Short bushwack/off-trail hike to access. Limited shade.

B4 Broad Creek

YPE:	F/S	**LAT/LONG:**	44.711610 -110.273416			**ELEV:**	8160	**TRAILHD:**	4K9
EOPLE:	12	**STOCK:**	10	**USE RAT:**	24	**DIST TH:**	0.03 mi	**DIST WTR:**	500
RIVACY:	N	**SHADE:**	N	**FIRE PIT:**	Y	**TOILET:**	N	**STAY:**	
VTR SRC:		Broad Creek (across main trail)				**BMA:**	N	**EASY:**	

IOTES: This site is listed on pre-1988 maps/books as 4B5.

NALYSIS: Poor quality site. No shade, no privacy. Out in open, water some distance away.

C1 Old Seven Mile Hole

YPE:	F	**LAT/LONG:**	44.748269 -110.413875			**ELEV:**	6760	**TRAILHD:**	4K6
EOPLE:	8	**STOCK:**	0	**USE RAT:**	173	**DIST TH:**	0.27 mi	**DIST WTR:**	280
RIVACY:	C	**SHADE:**	L	**FIRE PIT:**	NWF	**TOILET:**	N	**STAY:**	
VTR SRC:		Yellowstone River (do not use Sulphur Creek)				**BMA:**	N	**EASY:**	

IOTES: 54, O, P

NALYSIS: Getting water is a bit tough here (incline). Private site, but limited shade. View is decent. Dusty at times.

C2 Seven Mile Hole

YPE:	F	**LAT/LONG:**	44.753325 -110.405384			**ELEV:**	6740	**TRAILHD:**	4K6
EOPLE:	8	**STOCK:**	0	**USE RAT:**	136	**DIST TH:**	0	**DIST WTR:**	220
RIVACY:	N	**SHADE:**	L	**FIRE PIT:**	NWF	**TOILET:**	N	**STAY:**	
VTR SRC:		Yellowstone River (do not use Sulphur Creek)				**BMA:**	N	**EASY:**	

IOTES: 54, O, P

NALYSIS: Site is located along trail, so no privacy from those exploring. Limited shade.

4C3 Seven Mile Hole

TYPE:	F	**LAT/LONG:**	44.755042 -110.401381			**ELEV:**	6740	**TRAILHD:**	4K6
PEOPLE:	8	**STOCK:**	0	**USE RAT:**	145	**DIST TH:**	0	**DIST WTR:**	156
PRIVACY:	L	**SHADE:**	C	**FIRE PIT:**	NWF	**TOILET:**	N	**STAY:**	
WTR SRC:	Yellowstone River (do not use Sulphur Creek)					**BMA:**	N	**EASY:**	
NOTES:	54, O, P								

ANALYSIS: Most private of the 3, but hikers will enter since it is at end of trail.

4D1 Ice Lake North

TYPE:	F	**LAT/LONG:**	44.722475 -110.631943			**ELEV:**	7900	**TRAILHD:**	4K2
PEOPLE:	6	**STOCK:**	0	**USE RAT:**	186	**DIST TH:**	0.01 mi	**DIST WTR:**	39
PRIVACY:	N	**SHADE:**	P	**FIRE PIT:**	Y	**TOILET:**	N	**STAY:**	
WTR SRC:	Ice Lake					**BMA:**	N	**EASY:**	Y
NOTES:	V								

ANALYSIS: Site is on a spur, but spur is often mistaken for trail, so no privacy. Small site.

4D2 Ice Lake East

TYPE:	F	**LAT/LONG:**	44.722036 -110.620315			**ELEV:**	7900	**TRAILHD:**	4K2
PEOPLE:	8	**STOCK:**	0	**USE RAT:**	225	**DIST TH:**	0.05 mi	**DIST WTR:**	40
PRIVACY:	P	**SHADE:**	C	**FIRE PIT:**	Y	**TOILET:**	N	**STAY:**	
WTR SRC:	Ice Lake					**BMA:**	N	**EASY:**	Y
NOTES:	V								

ANALYSIS: Great view of the lake. Private site, with good shade.

4D3 Ice Lake South

TYPE:	F	**LAT/LONG:**	44.720124 -110.633046			**ELEV:**	7900	**TRAILHD:**	4K2
PEOPLE:	4	**STOCK:**	0	**USE RAT:**	74	**DIST TH:**	0.14 mi	**DIST WTR:**	85
PRIVACY:	P	**SHADE:**	L	**FIRE PIT:**	Y	**TOILET:**	Y	**STAY:**	
WTR SRC:	Ice Lake					**BMA:**	N	**EASY:**	Y
NOTES:	64, 73, V								

ANALYSIS: Small, HC-accessible site. Limited privacy as hikers mistake spur as part of main trail. Has pit toilet.

4E1 Washburn Meadows

TYPE:	F	**LAT/LONG:**	44.777540 -110.411171			**ELEV:**	8190	**TRAILHD:**	4K6
PEOPLE:	8	**STOCK:**	0	**USE RAT:**	114	**DIST TH:**	0.03 mi	**DIST WTR:**	291
PRIVACY:	P	**SHADE:**	P	**FIRE PIT:**	Y	**TOILET:**	N	**STAY:**	
WTR SRC:	Unnamed tributary of Glade Creek (seasonal)					**BMA:**	N	**EASY:**	
NOTES:	54, 67								

ANALYSIS: Good base camp for exploring area thermals and waterfalls. Seasonal water source.

4E2 Cascade Lake

TYPE:	F	**LAT/LONG:**	44.749770 -110.527951			**ELEV:**	8000	**TRAILHD:**	4K4
PEOPLE:	4	**STOCK:**	0	**USE RAT:**	130	**DIST TH:**	0.04 mi	**DIST WTR:**	1000
PRIVACY:	P	**SHADE:**	C	**FIRE PIT:**	Y	**TOILET:**	N	**STAY:**	
WTR SRC:	Cascade Lake (or Cascade Creek, which may be seasonal)					**BMA:**	N	**EASY:**	
NOTES:									

ANALYSIS: Very small site (one tent, basically). Water may be some distance away. No view.

4E3 Cascade Lake

TYPE:	F	**LAT/LONG:**	44.756209 -110.524256			**ELEV:**	8010	**TRAILHD:**	4K4
PEOPLE:	8	**STOCK:**	0	**USE RAT:**	196	**DIST TH:**	0.03 mi	**DIST WTR:**	1000
PRIVACY:	P	**SHADE:**	C	**FIRE PIT:**	Y	**TOILET:**	N	**STAY:**	
WTR SRC:	Cascade Lake					**BMA:**	N	**EASY:**	
NOTES:									

ANALYSIS: Great view of the lake, but distance to lake (water source) is considerable. Good shade, limited privacy.

4E4 **Cascade Lake**

TYPE:	F/S	**LAT/LONG:**	44.755085 -110.517012			**ELEV:**	7990	**TRAILHD:**	4K4
PEOPLE:	8	**STOCK:**	12	**USE RAT:**	188	**DIST TH:**	0.09 mi	**DIST WTR:**	84
PRIVACY:	P	**SHADE:**	C	**FIRE PIT:**	Y	**TOILET:**	N	**STAY:**	
WTR SRC:	Cascade Creek (poss seasonal)/Cascade Lake					**BMA:**	N	**EASY:**	Y
NOTES:									

ANALYSIS: May be marshy early in the season/after heavy rains. Good privacy/shade.

4F1 **Norris Meadows**

TYPE:	F	**LAT/LONG:**	44.730042 -110.664205			**ELEV:**	7550	**TRAILHD:**	4K2
PEOPLE:	8	**STOCK:**	0	**USE RAT:**	70	**DIST TH:**	0.02 mi	**DIST WTR:**	75
PRIVACY:	P	**SHADE:**	C	**FIRE PIT:**	Y	**TOILET:**	N	**STAY:**	
WTR SRC:	Unnamed tributary of Solfatara Creek					**BMA:**	N	**EASY:**	Y
NOTES:	U								

ANALYSIS: Great views of meadow/potential wildlife. See note U. Water source may be seasonal (1000 ft to next)

4G2 **Grebe Lake South**

TYPE:	F	**LAT/LONG:**	44.749242 -110.555708			**ELEV:**	8030	**TRAILHD:**	4K3
PEOPLE:	8	**STOCK:**	0	**USE RAT:**	220	**DIST TH:**	0.14 mi	**DIST WTR:**	20
PRIVACY:	P	**SHADE:**	C	**FIRE PIT:**	Y	**TOILET:**	N	**STAY:**	
WTR SRC:	Grebe Lake					**BMA:**	N	**EASY:**	
NOTES:	64								

ANALYSIS: Right on edge of lake (excellent wildlife viewing). Private, but may have hikers wandering in.

4G3 **Grebe Lake Northeast**

TYPE:	F/S	**LAT/LONG:**	44.754103 -110.552253			**ELEV:**	8050	**TRAILHD:**	4K3
PEOPLE:	8	**STOCK:**	6	**USE RAT:**	177	**DIST TH:**	0.02 mi	**DIST WTR:**	135
PRIVACY:	N	**SHADE:**	C	**FIRE PIT:**	NWF	**TOILET:**	N	**STAY:**	
WTR SRC:	Grebe Lake					**BMA:**	N	**EASY:**	
NOTES:									

ANALYSIS: Wood fires not permitted. No privacy (too close to trail). Great views of the lake.

4G4 **Grebe Lake North**

TYPE:	F/S	**LAT/LONG:**	44.755299 -110.559898			**ELEV:**	8040	**TRAILHD:**	4K3
PEOPLE:	8	**STOCK:**	6	**USE RAT:**	258	**DIST TH:**	0.06 mi	**DIST WTR:**	145
PRIVACY:	P	**SHADE:**	C	**FIRE PIT:**	Y	**TOILET:**	N	**STAY:**	
WTR SRC:	Grebe Lake					**BMA:**	N	**EASY:**	
NOTES:									

ANALYSIS: Two entrances to this site (hikers may use one to cut across to lake and back). Great lake view.

4G5 **Grebe Lake Northwest**

TYPE:	F/S	**LAT/LONG:**	44.753651 -110.564345			**ELEV:**	8050	**TRAILHD:**	4K3
PEOPLE:	8	**STOCK:**	6	**USE RAT:**	159	**DIST TH:**	0.03 mi	**DIST WTR:**	225
PRIVACY:	P	**SHADE:**	C	**FIRE PIT:**	Y	**TOILET:**	N	**STAY:**	
WTR SRC:	Grebe Lake					**BMA:**	N	**EASY:**	
NOTES:									

ANALYSIS: Site is close to main trail & has limited privacy.

4G6 **Wolf Lake**

TYPE:	F/S	**LAT/LONG:**	44.745565 -110.580744			**ELEV:**	7980	**TRAILHD:**	4K3
PEOPLE:	8	**STOCK:**	12	**USE RAT:**	163	**DIST TH:**	0.05 mi	**DIST WTR:**	250
PRIVACY:	P	**SHADE:**	C	**FIRE PIT:**	Y	**TOILET:**	N	**STAY:**	
WTR SRC:	Gibbon River					**BMA:**	N	**EASY:**	
NOTES:	V, W								

ANALYSIS: Good view of the lake and meadows. Fairly close to trail, so privacy is a bit limited.

4G7 Wolf Lake

TYPE: F **LAT/LONG:** 44.743414 -110.585902 **ELEV:** 7980 **TRAILHD:** 4K3
PEOPLE: 8 **STOCK:** 0 **USE RAT:** 100 **DIST TH:** 30 ft **DIST WTR:** 160
PRIVACY: N **SHADE:** C **FIRE PIT:** Y **TOILET:** N **STAY:**
WTR SRC: Wolf Lake or Gibbon River **BMA:** N **EASY:**
NOTES: V, W
ANALYSIS: Site is located right off the trail, so no privacy. Great lake view.

4M2 Moss Creek

TYPE: F/S **LAT/LONG:** 44.726767 -110.362585 **ELEV:** 8480 **TRAILHD:** 4K7
PEOPLE: 12 **STOCK:** 6 **USE RAT:** 169 **DIST TH:** 0.06 mi **DIST WTR:** 200
PRIVACY: P **SHADE:** L **FIRE PIT:** Y **TOILET:** N **STAY:**
WTR SRC: Moss Creek **BMA:** N **EASY:**
NOTES: Q
ANALYSIS: Fairly private site, but with limited shade. May have limited access early in the season.

4P1 Observation Peak

TYPE: F **LAT/LONG:** 44.771558 -110.546315 **ELEV:** 9397 **TRAILHD:** 4K5
PEOPLE: 8 **STOCK:** 0 **USE RAT:** 51 **DIST TH:** 0.02 mi **DIST WTR:** 3.0 mi
PRIVACY: P **SHADE:** L **FIRE PIT:** NWF **TOILET:** N **STAY:**
WTR SRC: Snow melt (early in season) or Cascade Lake **BMA:** N **EASY:**
NOTES: 67 (3+ miles after), T
ANALYSIS: No water source after snow melts. Interesting site/location. Great views from summit nearby.

4R1 Ribbon Lake

TYPE: F **LAT/LONG:** 44.724362 -110.449848 **ELEV:** 7820 **TRAILHD:** 4K8
PEOPLE: 8 **STOCK:** 0 **USE RAT:** 192 **DIST TH:** 0.06 mi **DIST WTR:** 135
PRIVACY: P **SHADE:** C **FIRE PIT:** Y **TOILET:** N **STAY:**
WTR SRC: Ribbon lake **BMA:** N **EASY:** Y
NOTES:
ANALYSIS: Good view of the lake. Hikers often wander into campsite to view lake.

4R2 Ribbon Lake

TYPE: F **LAT/LONG:** 44.726120 -110.447550 **ELEV:** 7820 **TRAILHD:** 4K7
PEOPLE: 8 **STOCK:** 0 **USE RAT:** 183 **DIST TH:** 0.16 mi **DIST WTR:** 300
PRIVACY: C **SHADE:** C **FIRE PIT:** Y **TOILET:** N **STAY:**
WTR SRC: Ribbon Lake **BMA:** N **EASY:** Y
NOTES: 64
ANALYSIS: Good view of the lake. Can be marshy early in season. Occasional hiker wandering into the site.

4W1 Wrangler Lake

TYPE: F/S **LAT/LONG:** 44.685114 -110.436325 **ELEV:** 7850 **TRAILHD:** 4K7
PEOPLE: 12 **STOCK:** 6 **USE RAT:** 69 **DIST TH:** 0.04 mi **DIST WTR:** 200
PRIVACY: C **SHADE:** C **FIRE PIT:** Y **TOILET:** N **STAY:**
WTR SRC: Wrangler Lake **BMA:** N **EASY:**
NOTES: S
ANALYSIS: Access early in season may be difficult (see note). Good shade, but view of lake is marginal.

4W2 Wapiti Lake

TYPE: F **LAT/LONG:** 44.720200 -110.255544 **ELEV:** 8450 **TRAILHD:** 5K3
PEOPLE: 8 **STOCK:** 0 **USE RAT:** 47 **DIST TH:** 0.02 mi **DIST WTR:** 55
PRIVACY: P **SHADE:** C **FIRE PIT:** Y **TOILET:** N **STAY:**
WTR SRC: Wapiti Lake **BMA:** N **EASY:**
NOTES:
ANALYSIS: Visible from campsite 4W3, so limited privacy. Best of the two sites on the lake.

4W3 Wapiti Lake

TYPE:	F	**LAT/LONG:**	44.721185 -110.254758			**ELEV:**	8450	**TRAILHD:**	5K3
PEOPLE:	8	**STOCK:**	0	**USE RAT:**	32	**DIST TH:**	0.02 mi	**DIST WTR:**	110
PRIVACY:	P	**SHADE:**	C	**FIRE PIT:**	Y	**TOILET:**	N	**STAY:**	
WTR SRC:	Wapiti Lake					**BMA:**	N	**EASY:**	
NOTES:									

ANALYSIS: Visible from campsite 4W2, so limited privacy. Least desirable of the two Wapiti Lake sites.

5B1 Broad Creek

TYPE:	F/S	**LAT/LONG:**	44.686335 -110.266237			**ELEV:**	8180	**TRAILHD:**	5K3
PEOPLE:	12	**STOCK:**	25	**USE RAT:**	144	**DIST TH:**	0.08 mi	**DIST WTR:**	250
PRIVACY:	C	**SHADE:**	C	**FIRE PIT:**	Y	**TOILET:**	N	**STAY:**	
WTR SRC:	Unnamed creek next to site or Broad Creek					**BMA:**	N	**EASY:**	
NOTES:									

ANALYSIS: Access requires fording Broad Creek. Good views of area.

5B2 Broad View

TYPE:	F/S	**LAT/LONG:**	44.697650 -110.261179			**ELEV:**	8170	**TRAILHD:**	5K3
PEOPLE:	12	**STOCK:**	15	**USE RAT:**	45	**DIST TH:**	0.05 mi	**DIST WTR:**	250
PRIVACY:	P	**SHADE:**	C	**FIRE PIT:**	Y	**TOILET:**	N	**STAY:**	
WTR SRC:	Unnamed tributary of Broad Creek or Broad Creek					**BMA:**	N	**EASY:**	
NOTES:									

ANALYSIS: Good views; limited privacy. Evidence of stock use throughout the area.

5E1 Beaverdam Trail

TYPE:	F	**LAT/LONG:**	44.324325 -110.182302			**ELEV:**	7810	**TRAILHD:**	5K5
PEOPLE:	12	**STOCK:**	0	**USE RAT:**	78	**DIST TH:**	0.02	**DIST WTR:**	157
PRIVACY:	P	**SHADE:**	L	**FIRE PIT:**	Y	**TOILET:**	N	**STAY:**	
WTR SRC:	Beaverdam Creek (steep access)					**BMA:**	J2	**EASY:**	
NOTES:	4, 30, AA, HH								

ANALYSIS: Closed until 7/14. Some older maps/books may list access in wrong place/trail has been relocated.

5E2 Terrace Point

TYPE:	B	**LAT/LONG:**	44.334212 -110.221840			**ELEV:**	7930	**TRAILHD:**	5K4
PEOPLE:	12	**STOCK:**	0	**USE RAT:**	95	**DIST TH:**	0.12 mi	**DIST WTR:**	73
PRIVACY:	P	**SHADE:**	P	**FIRE PIT:**	Y	**TOILET:**	N	**STAY:**	
WTR SRC:	Yellowstone Lake					**BMA:**	J2	**EASY:**	
NOTES:	10, 32, 43, AA								

ANALYSIS: Closed until 7/14. Camping access by boat only (hiking in not permitted).

5E3 Brimstone Point

TYPE:	F/B	**LAT/LONG:**	44.351903 -110.226582			**ELEV:**	7770	**TRAILHD:**	5K5
PEOPLE:	12	**STOCK:**	0	**USE RAT:**	85	**DIST TH:**	0.11 mi	**DIST WTR:**	50
PRIVACY:	C	**SHADE:**	P	**FIRE PIT:**	Y	**TOILET:**	N	**STAY:**	
WTR SRC:	Yellowstone Lake					**BMA:**	J2	**EASY:**	
NOTES:	10, 32, 43, AA								

ANALYSIS: Great views, good privacy.

5E4 Brimstone Bay

TYPE:	F/B	**LAT/LONG:**	44.374247 -110.228356			**ELEV:**	7770	**TRAILHD:**	5K5
PEOPLE:	12	**STOCK:**	0	**USE RAT:**	81	**DIST TH:**	0.10 mi	**DIST WTR:**	55
PRIVACY:	C	**SHADE:**	P	**FIRE PIT:**	Y	**TOILET:**	N	**STAY:**	
WTR SRC:	Yellowstone Lake					**BMA:**	J2	**EASY:**	
NOTES:	10, 32, 43, AA								

ANALYSIS: Great view of Promontory Point. Good privacy; frequently windy.

5E6 Columbine Meadow

TYPE:	F/S/B	**LAT/LONG:**	44.405825 -110.255600			**ELEV:**	7770	**TRAILHD:**	5K5
PEOPLE:	12	**STOCK:**	25	**USE RAT:**	202	**DIST TH:**	0.05 mi	**DIST WTR:**	90
PRIVACY:	P	**SHADE:**	P	**FIRE PIT:**	Y	**TOILET:**	Y	**STAY:**	1N/E
WTR SRC:		Yellowstone Lake				**BMA:**	J2	**EASY:**	
NOTES:	51, AA								

ANALYSIS: Decent site, with great views. Limitations on stock use - see notes.

5E7 Meadow Creek

TYPE:	F/S	**LAT/LONG:**	44.427038 -110.286200			**ELEV:**	7790	**TRAILHD:**	5K5
PEOPLE:	12	**STOCK:**	25	**USE RAT:**	87	**DIST TH:**	0.05 mi	**DIST WTR:**	100
PRIVACY:	N	**SHADE:**	P	**FIRE PIT:**	Y	**TOILET:**	N	**STAY:**	
WTR SRC:		Meadow Creek				**BMA:**	J2	**EASY:**	
NOTES:	4, 30, AA								

ANALYSIS: Closed until 7/14. Poor site; area usually marshy, lack of good view. Two spurs (from S = 0.26 mi)

5E8 Park Point South

TYPE:	F/B	**LAT/LONG:**	44.424253 -110.288667			**ELEV:**	7770	**TRAILHD:**	5K5
PEOPLE:	12	**STOCK:**	0	**USE RAT:**	162	**DIST TH:**	0.15 mi	**DIST WTR:**	80
PRIVACY:	C	**SHADE:**	L	**FIRE PIT:**	Y	**TOILET:**	N	**STAY:**	
WTR SRC:		Yellowstone Lake				**BMA:**	J2	**EASY:**	
NOTES:	10, 33, 43, AA								

ANALYSIS: Considered one of the best sites in the park. Travel from site limited until 7/14.

5E9 Park Point North

TYPE:	F/B	**LAT/LONG:**	44.428493 -110.293651			**ELEV:**	7770	**TRAILHD:**	5K5
PEOPLE:	12	**STOCK:**	0	**USE RAT:**	206	**DIST TH:**	0.15 mi	**DIST WTR:**	252
PRIVACY:	C	**SHADE:**	C	**FIRE PIT:**	Y	**TOILET:**	N	**STAY:**	
WTR SRC:		Yellowstone Lake				**BMA:**	J1	**EASY:**	
NOTES:	10, 33, 43, AA								

ANALYSIS: Great site, but with travel from site limited until 7/14.

5H1 Midshore

TYPE:	B	**LAT/LONG:**	44.458312 -110.288932			**ELEV:**	7770	**TRAILHD:**	5K5
PEOPLE:	6	**STOCK:**	0	**USE RAT:**	17	**DIST TH:**	B/O	**DIST WTR:**	121
PRIVACY:	C	**SHADE:**	L	**FIRE PIT:**	Y	**TOILET:**	N	**STAY:**	FLNO
WTR SRC:		Yellowstone Lake				**BMA:**	J1	**EASY:**	
NOTES:	23, 25, 32, 43								

ANALYSIS: Boat access only. Poor site. Travel from site limited until 8/10.

5L2 Monument Camp

TYPE:	F/B	**LAT/LONG:**	44.276473 -110.308227			**ELEV:**	7760	**TRAILHD:**	8N1
PEOPLE:	8	**STOCK:**	0	**USE RAT:**	39	**DIST TH:**	0.12 mi	**DIST WTR:**	225
PRIVACY:	P	**SHADE:**	N	**FIRE PIT:**	Y	**TOILET:**	N	**STAY:**	
WTR SRC:		Unnamed tributary of Yellowstone River				**BMA:**	K	**EASY:**	
NOTES:	6, 33								

ANALYSIS: Closed until 7/14. May be marshy early in the season. Views not that great, no shade.

5L3 Chipmunk Creek Outlet

TYPE:	B	**LAT/LONG:**	44.298454 -110.304524			**ELEV:**	7801	**TRAILHD:**	7K1
PEOPLE:	12	**STOCK:**	0	**USE RAT:**	52	**DIST TH:**	B/O	**DIST WTR:**	99
PRIVACY:	C	**SHADE:**	C	**FIRE PIT:**	Y	**TOILET:**	Y	**STAY:**	
WTR SRC:		Yellowstone Lake				**BMA:**	K	**EASY:**	
NOTES:	6, 35, 47, Y								

ANALYSIS: Boat access only. Closed until 7/14. Great views of the southern end of the South Arm.

4 South Arm Cove

YPE:	B	LAT/LONG:	44.304104 -110.311279		ELEV:	7751	TRAILHD:	7K1
EOPLE:	8	STOCK:	0	USE RAT: 20	DIST TH:	B/O	DIST WTR:	71
RIVACY:	C	SHADE:	P	FIRE PIT: Y	TOILET:	N	STAY:	
VTR SRC:			Yellowstone Lake		BMA:	N	EASY:	
OTES:	6, 35, 47, Y							

NALYSIS: Boat access only. Closed until 7/14.

L5 Promontory Point

YPE:	B	LAT/LONG:	44.350068 -110.328608		ELEV:	7745	TRAILHD:	7K1
EOPLE:	12	STOCK:	0	USE RAT: 16	DIST TH:	B/O	DIST WTR:	146
RIVACY:	C	SHADE:	N	FIRE PIT: Y	TOILET:	N	STAY:	
VTR SRC:			Yellowstone Lake		BMA:	N	EASY:	
OTES:	32, 43, Y							

NALYSIS: Boat access only. Site was burned through some years ago & no shade available.

L6 Promontory Shore

YPE:	B	LAT/LONG:	44.363984 -110.318963		ELEV:	7772	TRAILHD:	7K1
EOPLE:	12	STOCK:	0	USE RAT: 19	DIST TH:	B/O	DIST WTR:	137
RIVACY:	C	SHADE:	L	FIRE PIT: Y	TOILET:	N	STAY:	
VTR SRC:			Yellowstone Lake		BMA:	N	EASY:	
OTES:	32, 43, Y							

NALYSIS: Boat access only. Much of area was burned through a few years ago. Shade is limited.

L7 Promontory Bay

YPE:	B	LAT/LONG:	44.376420 -110.298699		ELEV:	7839	TRAILHD:	7K1
EOPLE:	12	STOCK:	0	USE RAT: 20	DIST TH:	B/O	DIST WTR:	84
RIVACY:	C	SHADE:	C	FIRE PIT: Y	TOILET:	N	STAY:	
VTR SRC:			Yellowstone Lake		BMA:	N	EASY:	
OTES:	32, 43, Y							

NALYSIS: Boat access only. This area escaped the burn & thus campsite has plenty of shade.

L8 Promontory Tip

YPE:	B	LAT/LONG:	44.392629 -110.284840		ELEV:	7760	TRAILHD:	5K4
EOPLE:	8	STOCK:	0	USE RAT: 34	DIST TH:	B/O	DIST WTR:	112
RIVACY:	C	SHADE:	L	FIRE PIT: Y	TOILET:	Y	STAY:	
VTR SRC:			Yellowstone Lake		BMA:	N	EASY:	
OTES:	32, 40, 44, Y							

NALYSIS: Boat access only. Limited shade, but with great views of the lake.

L9 Promontory Saddle

YPE:	B	LAT/LONG:	44.358414 -110.272758		ELEV:	7751	TRAILHD:	5K4
EOPLE:	12	STOCK:	0	USE RAT: 73	DIST TH:	B/O	DIST WTR:	138
RIVACY:	C	SHADE:	L	FIRE PIT: Y	TOILET:	Y	STAY:	
VTR SRC:			Yellowstone Lake		BMA:	N	EASY:	
OTES:	32, 40, 44, Y							

NALYSIS: Boat access only. Good view of Southeast Arm, but with limited shade.

P7 Pelican Creek

YPE:	F/S	LAT/LONG:	44.709298 -110.207363		ELEV:	8442	TRAILHD:	4K7
EOPLE:	6	STOCK:	12	USE RAT: 21	DIST TH:	2.17 mi	DIST WTR:	100
RIVACY:	P	SHADE:	C	FIRE PIT: N	TOILET:	N	STAY:	
VTR SRC:			Unnamed tributary of Pelican Creek		BMA:	H	EASY:	
OTES:	22							

NALYSIS: Limited availability (see note 22); Leave No Trace protocols required.

6A1 Promontory Southeast

TYPE:	B	**LAT/LONG:**	44.327571 -110.277131			**ELEV:**	7747	**TRAILHD:**	5K4
PEOPLE:	12	**STOCK:**	0	**USE RAT:**	65	**DIST TH:**	B/O	**DIST WTR:**	126
PRIVACY:	C	**SHADE:**	C	**FIRE PIT:**	Y	**TOILET:**	N	**STAY:**	
WTR SRC:		Yellowstone Lake				**BMA:**	N	**EASY:**	

NOTES: 35

ANALYSIS: Boat access only. Good shade; nice views.

6A2 Southeast Arm Inlet

TYPE:	B	**LAT/LONG:**	44.302886 -110.252898			**ELEV:**	7821	**TRAILHD:**	5K4
PEOPLE:	10	**STOCK:**	0	**USE RAT:**	66	**DIST TH:**	0.57 mi	**DIST WTR:**	56
PRIVACY:	C	**SHADE:**	L	**FIRE PIT:**	Y	**TOILET:**	N	**STAY:**	
WTR SRC:		Yellowstone Lake				**BMA:**	K	**EASY:**	

NOTES: 6, 35, X

ANALYSIS: Closed until 7/15. Excellent views of the lake & Molly Islands. Limited shade.

6A3 Trail Point

TYPE:	F/B	**LAT/LONG:**	44.303036 -110.233426			**ELEV:**	7750	**TRAILHD:**	5K4
PEOPLE:	12	**STOCK:**	0	**USE RAT:**	114	**DIST TH:**	0.47 mi	**DIST WTR:**	180
PRIVACY:	C	**SHADE:**	L	**FIRE PIT:**	Y	**TOILET:**	N	**STAY:**	
WTR SRC:		Yellowstone Lake				**BMA:**	K	**EASY:**	

NOTES: 11, 33, 35, X

ANALYSIS: No off-trail travel allowed until 7/15. Limited shade, but great views.

6A4 Trail Bay

TYPE:	F/B	**LAT/LONG:**	44.294647 -110.221734			**ELEV:**	7770	**TRAILHD:**	5K4
PEOPLE:	12	**STOCK:**	0	**USE RAT:**	83	**DIST TH:**	0.04 mi	**DIST WTR:**	209
PRIVACY:	N	**SHADE:**	L	**FIRE PIT:**	Y	**TOILET:**	N	**STAY:**	
WTR SRC:		Yellowstone Lake				**BMA:**	K	**EASY:**	

NOTES: 33, 35, X

ANALYSIS: No off-trail travel allowed until 7/15. Site may be marshy early in the season. Limited shade.

6B1 Lower Ford

TYPE:	F/S	**LAT/LONG:**	44.296585 -110.155422			**ELEV:**	7793	**TRAILHD:**	6K1
PEOPLE:	20	**STOCK:**	20	**USE RAT:**	81	**DIST TH:**	44 ft	**DIST WTR:**	599
PRIVACY:	N	**SHADE:**	P	**FIRE PIT:**	Y	**TOILET:**	N	**STAY:**	1N/S
WTR SRC:		Yellowstone River (or Cabin Creek early in season)				**BMA:**	K	**EASY:**	

NOTES: 11, X, DD, FF, GG, HH

ANALYSIS: Site is located right off trail (no privacy). No off-trail travel before 7/15. See access notes.

6B2 Upper Ford

TYPE:	F	**LAT/LONG:**	44.290045 -110.150654			**ELEV:**	7772	**TRAILHD:**	5K5
PEOPLE:	8	**STOCK:**	0	**USE RAT:**	41	**DIST TH:**	0.05 mi	**DIST WTR:**	28
PRIVACY:	P	**SHADE:**	C	**FIRE PIT:**	Y	**TOILET:**	N	**STAY:**	
WTR SRC:		Yellowstone River				**BMA:**	K	**EASY:**	

NOTES: 6, 61, X, FF, GG, HH

ANALYSIS: Closed until 7/15. See access notes. Excellent view of Colter Peak & Turret Mt.

6B4 Beaverdam Meadow

TYPE:	F/S	**LAT/LONG:**	44.323884 -110.177993			**ELEV:**	7918	**TRAILHD:**	5K5
PEOPLE:	20	**STOCK:**	20	**USE RAT:**	55	**DIST TH:**	0.33 mi	**DIST WTR:**	308
PRIVACY:	C	**SHADE:**	C	**FIRE PIT:**	Y	**TOILET:**	N	**STAY:**	
WTR SRC:		Beaverdam Creek				**BMA:**	J2	**EASY:**	

NOTES: 4, X, FF, GG, HH

ANALYSIS: Closed until 7/15. See access notes. Good privacy.

C1 Colter Meadows

YPE:	F/S	**LAT/LONG:**	44.269697 -110.128514			**ELEV:**	7873	**TRAILHD:**	6K1
EOPLE:	12	**STOCK:**	15	**USE RAT:**	34	**DIST TH:**	0.04 mi	**DIST WTR:**	204
RIVACY:	P	**SHADE:**	P	**FIRE PIT:**	Y	**TOILET:**	N	**STAY:**	
VTR SRC:	Nearby cold spring					**BMA:**	N	**EASY:**	
OTES:	52, X, FF, GG, HH								

NALYSIS: Water supply may be limited. Great view of Colter Peak.

C2 Rivers Edge

YPE:	F/S	**LAT/LONG:**	44.251013 -110.134080			**ELEV:**	7813	**TRAILHD:**	6K1
EOPLE:	20	**STOCK:**	25	**USE RAT:**	133	**DIST TH:**	1.10 mi	**DIST WTR:**	30
RIVACY:	C	**SHADE:**	L	**FIRE PIT:**	Y	**TOILET:**	N	**STAY:**	
VTR SRC:	Yellowstone River					**BMA:**	N	**EASY:**	
OTES:	X, FF, GG, HH								

NALYSIS: See access notes. Very private site.

C3 Turret View

YPE:	F	**LAT/LONG:**	44.259361 -110.114907			**ELEV:**	7922	**TRAILHD:**	5K5
EOPLE:	10	**STOCK:**	0	**USE RAT:**	44	**DIST TH:**	0.13 mi	**DIST WTR:**	365
RIVACY:	P	**SHADE:**	P	**FIRE PIT:**	Y	**TOILET:**	N	**STAY:**	
VTR SRC:	Unnamed tributary of Yellowstone River					**BMA:**	N	**EASY:**	
OTES:	X, FF, GG, HH								

NALYSIS: See access notes. Great views of Turret Mountain.

D1 Mountain Creek

YPE:	F/S	**LAT/LONG:**	44.224370 -110.128901			**ELEV:**	7820	**TRAILHD:**	6K1
EOPLE:	20	**STOCK:**	10	**USE RAT:**	20	**DIST TH:**	1.15 mi	**DIST WTR:**	155
RIVACY:	C	**SHADE:**	C	**FIRE PIT:**	Y	**TOILET:**	N	**STAY:**	
VTR SRC:	Yellowstone River or Mountain Creek					**BMA:**	N	**EASY:**	
OTES:	FF, GG, HH								

NALYSIS: See access notes. Interesting contrast between forested site vs. burned area across river. Long hike.

D2 Mountain Creek Ford

YPE:	F	**LAT/LONG:**	44.230460 -110.106756			**ELEV:**	7873	**TRAILHD:**	6K1
EOPLE:	20	**STOCK:**	0	**USE RAT:**	48	**DIST TH:**	50 ft	**DIST WTR:**	10
RIVACY:	N	**SHADE:**	P	**FIRE PIT:**	Y	**TOILET:**	N	**STAY:**	
VTR SRC:	Mountain Creek					**BMA:**	N	**EASY:**	
OTES:	65, FF, GG, HH								

NALYSIS: See access notes. Campsite is right off trail (no privacy), & stock trail to 6D3 goes through site.

D3 Mountain Creek

YPE:	S	**LAT/LONG:**	44.231002 -110.101821			**ELEV:**	7885	**TRAILHD:**	6K1
EOPLE:	20	**STOCK:**	25	**USE RAT:**	68	**DIST TH:**	0.30 mi	**DIST WTR:**	200
RIVACY:	C	**SHADE:**	C	**FIRE PIT:**	Y	**TOILET:**	N	**STAY:**	
VTR SRC:	Mountain Creek					**BMA:**	N	**EASY:**	
OTES:	31, FF, GG, HH								

NALYSIS: Stock parties only. Great views, good privacy.

D5 Upper Mountain Creek

YPE:	F/S	**LAT/LONG:**	44.243685 -110.058456			**ELEV:**	8065	**TRAILHD:**	6K1
EOPLE:	20	**STOCK:**	20	**USE RAT:**	10	**DIST TH:**	0.10 mi	**DIST WTR:**	34
RIVACY:	C	**SHADE:**	P	**FIRE PIT:**	Y	**TOILET:**	N	**STAY:**	
VTR SRC:	Unnamed tributary of Mountain Creek					**BMA:**	N	**EASY:**	
OTES:	FF, GG, HH								

NALYSIS: See access notes. Water source may be seasonal (alt use Mountain Creek - 700 ft away).

6D6 Howell Creek

TYPE:	F/S	LAT/LONG:	44.267086 -110.025874		ELEV:	8320	TRAILHD:	6K1
PEOPLE:	20	STOCK:	25	USE RAT: 40	DIST TH:	0.15 mi	DIST WTR:	100
PRIVACY:	P	SHADE:	C	FIRE PIT: Y	TOILET:	N	STAY:	
WTR SRC:		Howell Creek			BMA:	N	EASY:	
NOTES:	FF, GG, HH							

ANALYSIS: See access notes. Great views of Turret, Table, and Eagle Peaks/Mountains.

6D7 Howell Creek

TYPE:	F	LAT/LONG:	44.277143 -110.018631		ELEV:	8540	TRAILHD:	6K1
PEOPLE:	20	STOCK:	0	USE RAT: 23	DIST TH:	0.07 mi	DIST WTR:	55
PRIVACY:	C	SHADE:	C	FIRE PIT: Y	TOILET:	N	STAY:	
WTR SRC:		Unnamed tributary of Howell Creek			BMA:	N	EASY:	
NOTES:	FF, GG, HH							

ANALYSIS: See access notes. Great site nestled between feet of Turret Mountain and Eagle Peak.

6D8 Howell Creek

TYPE:	F/S	LAT/LONG:	44.304315 -110.003085		ELEV:	9500	TRAILHD:	6K1
PEOPLE:	20	STOCK:	10	USE RAT: 17	DIST TH:	0.09 mi	DIST WTR:	117
PRIVACY:	C	SHADE:	P	FIRE PIT: Y	TOILET:	N	STAY:	
WTR SRC:		Howell Creek			BMA:	N	EASY:	
NOTES:	19, FF, GG, HH							

ANALYSIS: See access notes. High elevation site. Great base for exploration of Eagle Peak area. No stock after 9/1.

6M3 Mariposa Lake

TYPE:	F	LAT/LONG:	44.15254 -110.245744		ELEV:	8997	TRAILHD:	6K3
PEOPLE:	8	STOCK:	0	USE RAT: 43	DIST TH:	0.03 mi	DIST WTR:	216
PRIVACY:	P	SHADE:	L	FIRE PIT: NWF	TOILET:	N	STAY:	
WTR SRC:		Mariposa Lake (or feeder stream if available)			BMA:	L	EASY:	
NOTES:	12, 60, BB, CC, EE, FF, GG, HH. Campsite is unmarked (no sign)							

ANALYSIS: See access and use limitation notes. Requires Leave No Trace protocols. Plateau Falls 0.4 mi away.

6M4 Two Ocean Trail Jct

TYPE:	F/S	LAT/LONG:	44.152146 -110.261088		ELEV:	8577	TRAILHD:	6K3
PEOPLE:	12	STOCK:	25	USE RAT: 63	DIST TH:	0.06 mi	DIST WTR:	34
PRIVACY:	P	SHADE:	P	FIRE PIT: Y	TOILET:	N	STAY:	
WTR SRC:		Plateau Creek			BMA:	L	EASY:	
NOTES:	12, CC, FF, GG, HH							

ANALYSIS: See access and use limitation notes. Great base camp for exploring Two Ocean Plateau area.

6M5 Upper Passage Creek

TYPE:	F/S	LAT/LONG:	44.203144 -110.259558		ELEV:	8688	TRAILHD:	6K3
PEOPLE:	12	STOCK:	25	USE RAT: 42	DIST TH:	0.10 mi	DIST WTR:	110
PRIVACY:	C	SHADE:	P	FIRE PIT: Y	TOILET:	N	STAY:	
WTR SRC:		Passage Creek			BMA:	N	EASY:	
NOTES:	12, CC, EE, FF, GG, HH							

ANALYSIS: See access and use limitation notes.

6M7 Fox Creek

TYPE:	F	LAT/LONG:	44.134697 -110.297443		ELEV:	8242	TRAILHD:	6K3
PEOPLE:	12	STOCK:	0	USE RAT: 35	DIST TH:	0.09 mi	DIST WTR:	378
PRIVACY:	P	SHADE:	L	FIRE PIT: Y	TOILET:	N	STAY:	
WTR SRC:		Unnamed tributary of the Snake River			BMA:	L	EASY:	
NOTES:	66, CC, EE, FF, GG, HH							

ANALYSIS: See access and use limitation notes. Site can be seen/heard from nearby patrol cabin (no privacy)

'1 South Thorofare

'PE:	F/S	LAT/LONG:	44.139869 -110.103701			ELEV:	7869	TRAILHD:	6K4
OPLE:	20	STOCK:	20	USE RAT:	66	DIST TH:	0.03 mi	DIST WTR:	34
IVACY:	P	SHADE:	P	FIRE PIT:	Y	TOILET:	N	STAY:	
TR SRC:			Thorofare Creek			BMA:	N	EASY:	
OTES:	61, FF, GG, HH								

NALYSIS: See access notes. One of the most remote campsites in the park. Limited privacy.

T2 North Thorofare

'PE:	F	LAT/LONG:	44.142358 -110.106003			ELEV:	7863	TRAILHD:	6K4
EOPLE:	20	STOCK:	0	USE RAT:	52	DIST TH:	0.22 mi	DIST WTR:	150
RIVACY:	C	SHADE:	C	FIRE PIT:	Y	TOILET:	N	STAY:	
'TR SRC:			Thorofare Creek			BMA:	N	EASY:	
OTES:	FF, GG, HH								

NALYSIS: See access notes. Excellent site w/ great views, good privacy & shade. Very remote.

Y2 South Yellowstone River

YPE:	F	LAT/LONG:	44.143923 -110.126096			ELEV:	7845	TRAILHD:	6K4
EOPLE:	12	STOCK:	0	USE RAT:	5	DIST TH:	40 ft	DIST WTR:	150
RIVACY:	N	SHADE:	N	FIRE PIT:	Y	TOILET:	N	STAY:	
/TR SRC:			Yellowstone River			BMA:	N	EASY:	
OTES:	FF, GG, HH								

NALYSIS: See access notes. No privacy (right off side of trail), no shade, but great views.

Y4 East Confluence

YPE:	F/S	LAT/LONG:	44.161089 -110.118630			ELEV:	7838	TRAILHD:	6K4
EOPLE:	20	STOCK:	25	USE RAT:	46	DIST TH:	0.62 mi	DIST WTR:	177
RIVACY:	C	SHADE:	C	FIRE PIT:	Y	TOILET:	N	STAY:	
/TR SRC:			Thorofare Creek			BMA:	N	EASY:	
OTES:	53, FF, GG, HH								

NALYSIS: See access notes. West approach is usually marshy. Use east (1.63 mi) if possible. Poor stock site.

Y5 Cliff Creek

YPE:	F	LAT/LONG:	44.168970 -110.101105			ELEV:	7874	TRAILHD:	6K5
EOPLE:	20	STOCK:	0	USE RAT:	29	DIST TH:	0.31 mi	DIST WTR:	100
RIVACY:	C	SHADE:	P	FIRE PIT:	Y	TOILET:	N	STAY:	
VTR SRC:			Cliff Creek			BMA:	N	EASY:	
OTES:	FF, GG, HH								

NALYSIS: See access notes. Great views of the meadows along the creek west of the site.

Y6 Three Mile Bend

YPE:	F/S	LAT/LONG:	44.186029 -110.110090			ELEV:	7835	TRAILHD:	6K5
EOPLE:	20	STOCK:	25	USE RAT:	73	DIST TH:	0.27 mi	DIST WTR:	30
RIVACY:	C	SHADE:	P	FIRE PIT:	Y	TOILET:	N	STAY:	
VTR SRC:			Yellowstone River			BMA:	N	EASY:	
OTES:	FF, GG, HH								

NALYSIS: See access notes. Private site, great views.

Y7 Yellowstone Meadows

YPE:	S	LAT/LONG:	44.211812 -110.110361			ELEV:	7843	TRAILHD:	6K5
EOPLE:	20	STOCK:	25	USE RAT:	17	DIST TH:	0.03 mi	DIST WTR:	263
RIVACY:	N	SHADE:	L	FIRE PIT:	Y	TOILET:	N	STAY:	
VTR SRC:			Yellowstone River			BMA:	N	EASY:	
OTES:	FF, GG, HH								

NALYSIS: See access notes. Site is visible from the trail and has little privacy.

7F1 Frank Island Bay North

TYPE:	B	LAT/LONG:	44.422798 -110.354325			ELEV:	7745	TRAILHD:	7K1
PEOPLE:	8	STOCK:	0	USE RAT:	34	DIST TH:	N/A	DIST WTR:	N/A
PRIVACY:	N/A	SHADE:	N/A	FIRE PIT:	N/A	TOILET:	N/A	STAY:	
WTR SRC:			Yellowstone Lake			BMA:	N	EASY:	

NOTES: 45, 46, 48, 49

ANALYSIS: Boat anchorage site only. See access restriction notes.

7F2 Frank Island Bay South

TYPE:	B	LAT/LONG:	44.416376 -110.354685			ELEV:	7745	TRAILHD:	7K1
PEOPLE:	8	STOCK:	0	USE RAT:	20	DIST TH:	N/A	DIST WTR:	N/A
PRIVACY:	N/A	SHADE:	N/A	FIRE PIT:	N/A	TOILET:	N/A	STAY:	
WTR SRC:			Yellowstone Lake			BMA:	N/A	EASY:	

NOTES: 45, 46, 48, 49

ANALYSIS: Boat anchorage site only. See access restriction notes.

7G1 Grouse Creek

TYPE:	F/S	LAT/LONG:	44.273707 -110.347609			ELEV:	7807	TRAILHD:	8N1
PEOPLE:	12	STOCK:	20	USE RAT:	26	DIST TH:	0.14 mi	DIST WTR:	75
PRIVACY:	N	SHADE:	L	FIRE PIT:	Y	TOILET:	N	STAY:	
WTR SRC:			Grouse Creek			BMA:	K	EASY:	

NOTES: 6, 65, 80

ANALYSIS: Limited privacy. See stock limitation notes. Closed until 7/15. Decent views.

7G2 Grouse Creek

TYPE:	F/S	LAT/LONG:	44.279256 -110.343491			ELEV:	7875	TRAILHD:	8N1
PEOPLE:	12	STOCK:	20	USE RAT:	42	DIST TH:	0.56 mi	DIST WTR:	44
PRIVACY:	C	SHADE:	L	FIRE PIT:	Y	TOILET:	N	STAY:	
WTR SRC:			Grouse Creek			BMA:	K	EASY:	

NOTES: 6, 80

ANALYSIS: Very private site, with good views of South Arm. See stock limitation notes. Closed until 7/15.

7L1 Breeze Bay North

TYPE:	B	LAT/LONG:	44.433661 -110.462314			ELEV:	7779	TRAILHD:	7K1
PEOPLE:	12	STOCK:	0	USE RAT:	221	DIST TH:	B/O	DIST WTR:	50
PRIVACY:	C	SHADE:	L	FIRE PIT:	Y	TOILET:	N	STAY:	FLNO
WTR SRC:			Yellowstone Lake			BMA:	N	EASY:	

NOTES: 23, 42, 43

ANALYSIS: Great views. Water may be shallow. Check with Grant BCO for updates.

7L2 Breeze Bay

TYPE:	B	LAT/LONG:	44.424476 -110.443223			ELEV:	7761	TRAILHD:	7K1
PEOPLE:	12	STOCK:	0	USE RAT:	130	DIST TH:	B/O	DIST WTR:	50
PRIVACY:	C	SHADE:	L	FIRE PIT:	Y	TOILET:	N	STAY:	FLNO
WTR SRC:			Yellowstone Lake			BMA:	N	EASY:	

NOTES: 23, 43

ANALYSIS: Views are decent, but not as good as 7L1.

7L3 Breeze Bay South

TYPE:	B	LAT/LONG:	44.430125 -110.431267			ELEV:	7745	TRAILHD:	7K1
PEOPLE:	12	STOCK:	0	USE RAT:	76	DIST TH:	B/O	DIST WTR:	185
PRIVACY:	P	SHADE:	L	FIRE PIT:	Y	TOILET:	N	STAY:	
WTR SRC:			Yellowstone Lake			BMA:	N	EASY:	

NOTES: 5

ANALYSIS: Closed until 7/10. Site is very close to 7L4 (if occupied, less privacy). Good views.

7L4 **Ravine**

TYPE:	B	LAT/LONG:	44.427037 -110.422293			ELEV:	7745	TRAILHD:	7K1
PEOPLE:	12	STOCK:	0	USE RAT:	70	DIST TH:	B/O	DIST WTR:	176
PRIVACY:	P	SHADE:	L	FIRE PIT:	Y	TOILET:	N	STAY:	
WTR SRC:			Yellowstone Lake			BMA:	N	EASY:	
NOTES:									

ANALYSIS: Great views. If site 7L3 is occupied, you'll have less privacy.

7L5 **Wolf Bay**

TYPE:	B	LAT/LONG:	44.418091 -110.418279			ELEV:	7772	TRAILHD:	7K1
PEOPLE:	8	STOCK:	0	USE RAT:	357	DIST TH:	B/O	DIST WTR:	162
PRIVACY:	P	SHADE:	L	FIRE PIT:	Y	TOILET:	Y	STAY:	
WTR SRC:			Yellowstone Lake			BMA:	K	EASY:	
NOTES:	13, 46, 50, 70, 90, X, Y								

ANALYSIS: Excellent 3-party dock site. See access & use restriction notes. Has bear box, fire grate & picnic table.

7L6 **Eagle Bay**

TYPE:	B	LAT/LONG:	44.402308 -110.396528			ELEV:	7745	TRAILHD:	7K1
PEOPLE:	8	STOCK:	0	USE RAT:	337	DIST TH:	B/O	DIST WTR:	252
PRIVACY:	P	SHADE:	L	FIRE PIT:	Y	TOILET:	Y	STAY:	
WTR SRC:			Yellowstone Lake			BMA:	K	EASY:	
NOTES:	13, 46, 50, 70, X, Y								

ANALYSIS: Great 3-party dock site. See access & use restrictions. Has bear box, fire grate, & picnic table.

7L7 **Bodego Bay**

TYPE:	B	LAT/LONG:	44.381838 -110.393564			ELEV:	7752	TRAILHD:	7K1
PEOPLE:	12	STOCK:	0	USE RAT:	133	DIST TH:	B/O	DIST WTR:	253
PRIVACY:	C	SHADE:	P	FIRE PIT:	Y	TOILET:	Y	STAY:	
WTR SRC:			Yellowstone Lake			BMA:	K	EASY:	
NOTES:	13, 42, 43, X, Y								

ANALYSIS: See access/use restrictions. Water may be shallow (check w/ Grant BCO). Great views.

7L8 **Flat Mountain Arm North**

TYPE:	B	LAT/LONG:	44.376488 -110.404293			ELEV:	7778	TRAILHD:	7K1
PEOPLE:	12	STOCK:	0	USE RAT:	80	DIST TH:	B/O	DIST WTR:	98
PRIVACY:	C	SHADE:	P	FIRE PIT:	Y	TOILET:	N	STAY:	
WTR SRC:			Yellowstone Lake			BMA:	K	EASY:	
NOTES:	13, X, Y								

ANALYSIS: See access/use restrictions.

7L9 **Flat Mountain Arm South**

TYPE:	B	LAT/LONG:	44.370315 -110.421357			ELEV:	7864	TRAILHD:	7K1
PEOPLE:	8	STOCK:	0	USE RAT:	43	DIST TH:	B/O	DIST WTR:	150
PRIVACY:	C	SHADE:	C	FIRE PIT:	Y	TOILET:	N	STAY:	
WTR SRC:			Yellowstone Lake			BMA:	K	EASY:	
NOTES:	13, 35, 43, X, Y								

ANALYSIS: See access/use restrictions. Small site w/ limited tent space.

7M1 **Grizzly Bay**

TYPE:	B	LAT/LONG:	44.369695 -110.417157			ELEV:	7841	TRAILHD:	5K1
PEOPLE:	8	STOCK:	0	USE RAT:	43	DIST TH:	N/A	DIST WTR:	N/A
PRIVACY:	N/A	SHADE:	N/A	FIRE PIT:	N/A	TOILET:	N/A	STAY:	
WTR SRC:			Yellowstone Lake			BMA:	K	EASY:	
NOTES:	6, 46, 69, X, Y								

ANALYSIS: 2-party boat anchorage site only. Closed until 7/15.

7M3 Flat Mountain Bay

TYPE:	B	**LAT/LONG:**	44.374180 -110.370102			**ELEV:**	7909	**TRAILHD:**	7K1
PEOPLE:	12	**STOCK:**	0	**USE RAT:**	121	**DIST TH:**	B/O	**DIST WTR:**	121
PRIVACY:	C	**SHADE:**	P	**FIRE PIT:**	Y	**TOILET:**	Y	**STAY:**	
WTR SRC:			Yellowstone Lake			**BMA:**	K	**EASY:**	
NOTES:	13, X, Y								

ANALYSIS: No travel from site until 7/15. Good view of Flat Mountain.

7M4 Plover Point

TYPE:	B	**LAT/LONG:**	44.383409 -110.351669			**ELEV:**	7745	**TRAILHD:**	7K1
PEOPLE:	8	**STOCK:**	0	**USE RAT:**	230	**DIST TH:**	B/O	**DIST WTR:**	146
PRIVACY:	C	**SHADE:**	L	**FIRE PIT:**	Y	**TOILET:**	Y	**STAY:**	
WTR SRC:			Yellowstone Lake			**BMA:**	K	**EASY:**	
NOTES:	13, 46, 50, 70, 90, X, Y, Z								

ANALYSIS: Good 3-party dock site. See access/use restrictions. Has bear box. May be marshy at times.

7M5 Plover Bay

TYPE:	B	**LAT/LONG:**	44.369525 -110.358729			**ELEV:**	7837	**TRAILHD:**	7K1
PEOPLE:	12	**STOCK:**	0	**USE RAT:**	92	**DIST TH:**	B/O	**DIST WTR:**	56
PRIVACY:	C	**SHADE:**	C	**FIRE PIT:**	Y	**TOILET:**	Y	**STAY:**	
WTR SRC:			Yellowstone Lake			**BMA:**	K	**EASY:**	
NOTES:	13, 43, X, Y								

ANALYSIS: No travel from site until 7/15. Landing may be tough; beach is rocky.

7M6 South Arm

TYPE:	B	**LAT/LONG:**	44.346284 -110.358718			**ELEV:**	7805	**TRAILHD:**	7K1
PEOPLE:	12	**STOCK:**	0	**USE RAT:**	103	**DIST TH:**	B/O	**DIST WTR:**	58
PRIVACY:	C	**SHADE:**	C	**FIRE PIT:**	Y	**TOILET:**	Y	**STAY:**	
WTR SRC:			Yellowstone Lake			**BMA:**	K	**EASY:**	
NOTES:	6, 43, X, Y								

ANALYSIS: Site closed until 7/15. Toilet may be in bad shape (unusable, in fact).

7M7 South Arm

TYPE:	B	**LAT/LONG:**	44.337654 -110.355251			**ELEV:**	7768	**TRAILHD:**	7K1
PEOPLE:	12	**STOCK:**	0	**USE RAT:**	71	**DIST TH:**	B/O	**DIST WTR:**	67
PRIVACY:	C	**SHADE:**	P	**FIRE PIT:**	Y	**TOILET:**	Y	**STAY:**	
WTR SRC:			Yellowstone Lake			**BMA:**	K	**EASY:**	
NOTES:	6, 43, X, Y								

ANALYSIS: Site closed until 7/15. Great view of South Arm.

7M9 South Arm

TYPE:	B	**LAT/LONG:**	44.326022 -110.350527			**ELEV:**	7776	**TRAILHD:**	7K1
PEOPLE:	12	**STOCK:**	0	**USE RAT:**	42	**DIST TH:**	B/O	**DIST WTR:**	43
PRIVACY:	C	**SHADE:**	L	**FIRE PIT:**	Y	**TOILET:**	Y	**STAY:**	
WTR SRC:			Yellowstone Lake			**BMA:**	K	**EASY:**	
NOTES:	6, 43, X, Y								

ANALYSIS: Site closed until 7/15. Great view of South Arm.

7N2 Gowdy Camp

TYPE:	F/B	**LAT/LONG:**	44.296509 -110.343289			**ELEV:**	7786	**TRAILHD:**	7K1
PEOPLE:	12	**STOCK:**	0	**USE RAT:**	108	**DIST TH:**	1.33 mi*	**DIST WTR:**	72
PRIVACY:	C	**SHADE:**	L	**FIRE PIT:**	Y	**TOILET:**	Y	**STAY:**	
WTR SRC:			Yellowstone Lake			**BMA:**	K	**EASY:**	
NOTES:	6, 34, X, Y								

ANALYSIS: Site closed until 7/15. *Accessible via off-trail bushwacking (1.33 mi from site 7G2)

7N4 **Southwest Bay**

TYPE:	F/B	**LAT/LONG:**	44.288537 -110.344056			**ELEV:**	7767	**TRAILHD:**	7K1
PEOPLE:	12	**STOCK:**	0	**USE RAT:**	76	**DIST TH:**	0.77 mi*	**DIST WTR:**	71
PRIVACY:	C	**SHADE:**	C	**FIRE PIT:**	Y	**TOILET:**	Y	**STAY:**	
WTR SRC:			Yellowstone Lake			**BMA:**	K	**EASY:**	
NOTES:	6, 34								

ANALYSIS: Site closed until 7/15. *Accessible via off-trail bushwacking (0.77 mi from site 7G2)

8A1 **Beula Lake**

TYPE:	F	**LAT/LONG:**	44.155560 -110.767638			**ELEV:**	7413	**TRAILHD:**	8K6
PEOPLE:	8	**STOCK:**	0	**USE RAT:**	62	**DIST TH:**	40 ft	**DIST WTR:**	120
PRIVACY:	N	**SHADE:**	P	**FIRE PIT:**	Y	**TOILET:**	Y	**STAY:**	
WTR SRC:			Beula Lake			**BMA:**	N	**EASY:**	Y
NOTES:	71								

ANALYSIS: Site is located right alongside trail, so no privacy. Great views of the lake.

8A2 **Beula Lake**

TYPE:	F	**LAT/LONG:**	44.156807 -110.767832			**ELEV:**	7412	**TRAILHD:**	8K6
PEOPLE:	6	**STOCK:**	0	**USE RAT:**	53	**DIST TH:**	40 ft	**DIST WTR:**	80
PRIVACY:	N	**SHADE:**	P	**FIRE PIT:**	Y	**TOILET:**	Y	**STAY:**	
WTR SRC:			Beula Lake			**BMA:**	N	**EASY:**	Y
NOTES:	71								

ANALYSIS: Site is located alongside trail. Has more privacy than 8A1, but hikers pass right by. Great views.

8B1 **Basin Creek**

TYPE:	F	**LAT/LONG:**	44.229648 -110.511201			**ELEV:**	7378	**TRAILHD:**	8K7
PEOPLE:	4	**STOCK:**	0	**USE RAT:**	56	**DIST TH:**	0.15 mi	**DIST WTR:**	35
PRIVACY:	C	**SHADE:**	C	**FIRE PIT:**	Y	**TOILET:**	N	**STAY:**	
WTR SRC:			Basin Creek			**BMA:**	O	**EASY:**	
NOTES:	3, II								

ANALYSIS: Closed until 7/1. Old maps may not show correct trail location. Small site, w/ good view.

8B2 **Basin Creek Lake**

TYPE:	F/S	**LAT/LONG:**	44.210130 -110.525243			**ELEV:**	7419	**TRAILHD:**	8K7
PEOPLE:	12	**STOCK:**	6	**USE RAT:**	91	**DIST TH:**	0.08 mi	**DIST WTR:**	550
PRIVACY:	C	**SHADE:**	C	**FIRE PIT:**	Y	**TOILET:**	N	**STAY:**	
WTR SRC:			Basin Creek Lake			**BMA:**	O	**EASY:**	
NOTES:	3, II								

ANALYSIS: Closed until 7/1. Private site, but no view to speak of (other than the lake).

8B3 **Basin Creek**

TYPE:	S	**LAT/LONG:**	44.217034 -110.510078			**ELEV:**	7321	**TRAILHD:**	8K7
PEOPLE:	12	**STOCK:**	20	**USE RAT:**	71	**DIST TH:**	75 ft	**DIST WTR:**	50
PRIVACY:	N	**SHADE:**	C	**FIRE PIT:**	Y	**TOILET:**	N	**STAY:**	
WTR SRC:			Basin Creek			**BMA:**	O	**EASY:**	
NOTES:	3, 31, 84, II								

ANALYSIS: Closed until 7/1. Stock parties only. Located right along trail (no privacy).

8B4 **Basin Creek**

TYPE:	S	**LAT/LONG:**	44.209557 -110.502762			**ELEV:**	7279	**TRAILHD:**	8K7
PEOPLE:	12	**STOCK:**	20	**USE RAT:**	116	**DIST TH:**	0.03 mi	**DIST WTR:**	84
PRIVACY:	P	**SHADE:**	C	**FIRE PIT:**	Y	**TOILET:**	N	**STAY:**	
WTR SRC:			Basin Creek			**BMA:**	O	**EASY:**	
NOTES:	3, 31, 84, II								

ANALYSIS: Closed until 7/1. Stock parties only. Close to trail (limited privacy).

8B5 **Basin Creek**

TYPE:	F	**LAT/LONG:**	44.206436 -110.501396			**ELEV:**	7261	**TRAILHD:**	8K7
PEOPLE:	8	**STOCK:**	0	**USE RAT:**	65	**DIST TH:**	0.02 mi	**DIST WTR:**	195
PRIVACY:	P	**SHADE:**	C	**FIRE PIT:**	Y	**TOILET:**	N	**STAY:**	
WTR SRC:			Basin Creek			**BMA:**	O	**EASY:**	
NOTES:	3, II								

ANALYSIS: Closed until 7/1. Decent privacy, but no views.

8C1 **Snake River**

TYPE:	F	**LAT/LONG:**	44.168562 -110.586553			**ELEV:**	6963	**TRAILHD:**	8K7
PEOPLE:	8	**STOCK:**	0	**USE RAT:**	148	**DIST TH:**	50 ft	**DIST WTR:**	140
PRIVACY:	N	**SHADE:**	C	**FIRE PIT:**	Y	**TOILET:**	N	**STAY:**	
WTR SRC:			Snake River			**BMA:**	N	**EASY:**	
NOTES:	II								

ANALYSIS: Site is located along the trail, so little privacy. Good view of the river and valley.

8C2 **Snake River**

TYPE:	F/S	**LAT/LONG:**	44.146776 -110.525621			**ELEV:**	7060	**TRAILHD:**	8K7
PEOPLE:	12	**STOCK:**	25	**USE RAT:**	114	**DIST TH:**	0.19 mi	**DIST WTR:**	50
PRIVACY:	P	**SHADE:**	L	**FIRE PIT:**	Y	**TOILET:**	N	**STAY:**	
WTR SRC:			Snake River			**BMA:**	N	**EASY:**	
NOTES:	II								

ANALYSIS: Excellent site located right alongside the river. Firewood may be difficult to find.

8C4 **Snake River**

TYPE:	F/S	**LAT/LONG:**	44.170328 -110.488094			**ELEV:**	7212	**TRAILHD:**	8K7
PEOPLE:	12	**STOCK:**	6	**USE RAT:**	57	**DIST TH:**	0.05 mi	**DIST WTR:**	100
PRIVACY:	C	**SHADE:**	L	**FIRE PIT:**	Y	**TOILET:**	N	**STAY:**	
WTR SRC:			Snake River			**BMA:**	N	**EASY:**	
NOTES:	II								

ANALYSIS: Located alongside river, but with limited shade.

8C5 **Snake River**

TYPE:	F/S	**LAT/LONG:**	44.214924 -110.461396			**ELEV:**	7416	**TRAILHD:**	8K7
PEOPLE:	12	**STOCK:**	10	**USE RAT:**	105	**DIST TH:**	0.05 mi	**DIST WTR:**	290
PRIVACY:	P	**SHADE:**	L	**FIRE PIT:**	Y	**TOILET:**	N	**STAY:**	
WTR SRC:			Snake River			**BMA:**	O	**EASY:**	
NOTES:	3, II								

ANALYSIS: Closed until 7/1. Great view of the area, but with limited shade. Firewood may be hard to find.

8C6 **Snake River Ford**

TYPE:	F	**LAT/LONG:**	44.175066 -110.569361			**ELEV:**	7014	**TRAILHD:**	8K7
PEOPLE:	8	**STOCK:**	0	**USE RAT:**	107	**DIST TH:**	0.02 mi	**DIST WTR:**	756
PRIVACY:	N	**SHADE:**	L	**FIRE PIT:**	Y	**TOILET:**	N	**STAY:**	
WTR SRC:			Snake River			**BMA:**	N	**EASY:**	
NOTES:	II								

ANALYSIS: Site just north of main trail, w/ no privacy and limited shade. Good views. Water a good distance away.

8C7 **Snake River**

TYPE:	S	**LAT/LONG:**	44.168956 -110.579980			**ELEV:**	6979	**TRAILHD:**	8K7
PEOPLE:	12	**STOCK:**	25	**USE RAT:**	122	**DIST TH:**	50 ft	**DIST WTR:**	336
PRIVACY:	N	**SHADE:**	P	**FIRE PIT:**	Y	**TOILET:**	N	**STAY:**	
WTR SRC:			Snake River			**BMA:**	N	**EASY:**	
NOTES:	31, II								

ANALYSIS: Site is located along the trail, so no privacy. Stock site only.

8C9 Crooked Creek

TYPE:	F/S	LAT/LONG:	44.157301 -110.335943			ELEV:	7963	TRAILHD:	6K3
PEOPLE:	12	STOCK:	20	USE RAT:	90	DIST TH:	0.04 mi	DIST WTR:	100
PRIVACY:	P	SHADE:	P	FIRE PIT:	Y	TOILET:	N	STAY:	
WTR SRC:		Unnamed tributary of the Snake River				BMA:	L	EASY:	
NOTES:	EE, II								

ANALYSIS: Limited views, limited shade. Close to trail (less privacy).

8G1 Shoshone Meadows

TYPE:	F	LAT/LONG:	44.373637 -110.817210			ELEV:	7903	TRAILHD:	OK1
PEOPLE:	12	STOCK:	8L	USE RAT:	399	DIST TH:	0.02 mi	DIST WTR:	150
PRIVACY:	P	SHADE:	C	FIRE PIT:	NWF	TOILET:	Y	STAY:	
WTR SRC:		Unnamed tributary of Shoshone Creek				BMA:	N	EASY:	
NOTES:	37								

ANALYSIS: Stock limited to llamas. Most popular backcountry camp site in park. Limited views.

8H1 South Bay

TYPE:	F	LAT/LONG:	44.256208 -110.502997			ELEV:	7511	TRAILHD:	8N1
PEOPLE:	8	STOCK:	0	USE RAT:	182	DIST TH:	0.07 mi	DIST WTR:	501
PRIVACY:	C	SHADE:	C	FIRE PIT:	NWF	TOILET:	Y	STAY:	2N/E*
WTR SRC:		Heart Lake				BMA:	O	EASY:	
NOTES:	3, 20, JJ								

ANALYSIS: Closed until 7/1. Small site, not so close to the lake. Good privacy, shade, and has pit toilet.

8H2 Sheridan Creek

TYPE:	F	LAT/LONG:	44.270540 -110.501829			ELEV:	7508	TRAILHD:	8N1
PEOPLE:	6	STOCK:	0	USE RAT:	242	DIST TH:	0.17 mi	DIST WTR:	39
PRIVACY:	P	SHADE:	P	FIRE PIT:	Y	TOILET:	Y	STAY:	2N/E*
WTR SRC:		Heart Lake				BMA:	O	EASY:	
NOTES:	3, 20, JJ								

ANALYSIS: Closed until 7/1. Private site if 8H3 is not occupied. Great view of the lake. Access trail may be marshy.

8H3 Hideaway

TYPE:	F	LAT/LONG:	44.271122 -110.502125			ELEV:	7517	TRAILHD:	8N1
PEOPLE:	4	STOCK:	0	USE RAT:	224	DIST TH:	0.19 mi	DIST WTR:	160
PRIVACY:	P	SHADE:	C	FIRE PIT:	Y	TOILET:	Y	STAY:	2N/E*
WTR SRC:		Heart Lake				BMA:	O	EASY:	
NOTES:	3, 20, JJ								

ANALYSIS: Closed until 7/1. Private site if 8H2 is not occupied. Same notes as 8H2.

8H4 West Shore

TYPE:	F	LAT/LONG:	44.277975 -110.502552			ELEV:	7474	TRAILHD:	8N1
PEOPLE:	8	STOCK:	0	USE RAT:	243	DIST TH:	0.11 mi	DIST WTR:	84
PRIVACY:	C	SHADE:	C	FIRE PIT:	NWF	TOILET:	Y	STAY:	2N/E*
WTR SRC:		Heart Lake				BMA:	O	EASY:	
NOTES:	3, 20, JJ								

ANALYSIS: Closed until 7/1. Excellent, private site. Great site to base for ascent of Mt. Sheridan.

8H5 Sheridan Trail

TYPE:	F	LAT/LONG:	44.279967 -110.501908			ELEV:	7471	TRAILHD:	8N1
PEOPLE:	6	STOCK:	0	USE RAT:	236	DIST TH:	0.07 mi	DIST WTR:	123
PRIVACY:	P	SHADE:	C	FIRE PIT:	NWF	TOILET:	Y	STAY:	2N/E*
WTR SRC:		Heart Lake				BMA:	O	EASY:	
NOTES:	3, 20, 71, JJ								

ANALYSIS: Closed until 7/1. Privacy reduced if site 8H6 is occupied. Decent view of the lake.

8H6 Rustic

TYPE:	F	**LAT/LONG:**	44.280761 -110.502401			**ELEV:**	7476	**TRAILHD:**	8N1
PEOPLE:	6	**STOCK:**	0	**USE RAT:**	204	**DIST TH:**	0.02 mi	**DIST WTR:**	99
PRIVACY:	N	**SHADE:**	C	**FIRE PIT:**	NWF	**TOILET:**	Y	**STAY:**	2N/E*
WTR SRC:			Heart Lake			**BMA:**	O	**EASY:**	
NOTES:	3, 20, 71, JJ								

ANALYSIS: Closed until 7/1. Privacy reduced if site 8H5 is occupied. Decent view of the lake.

8J1 Beaver Creek

TYPE:	F	**LAT/LONG:**	44.277026 -110.474536			**ELEV:**	7468	**TRAILHD:**	8N1
PEOPLE:	8	**STOCK:**	0	**USE RAT:**	235	**DIST TH:**	0.43 mi	**DIST WTR:**	184
PRIVACY:	C	**SHADE:**	C	**FIRE PIT:**	Y	**TOILET:**	Y	**STAY:**	2N/E*
WTR SRC:			Heart Lake			**BMA:**	O	**EASY:**	
NOTES:	3, 20, JJ								

ANALYSIS: Closed until 7/1. Great, private site. Stay limitations in July & Aug.

8J2 Beaver Creek Meadow

TYPE:	S	**LAT/LONG:**	44.279070 -110.465963			**ELEV:**	7527	**TRAILHD:**	8N1
PEOPLE:	12	**STOCK:**	25	**USE RAT:**	124	**DIST TH:**	0.21 mi	**DIST WTR:**	196
PRIVACY:	C	**SHADE:**	C	**FIRE PIT:**	Y	**TOILET:**	Y	**STAY:**	2N/E
WTR SRC:			Heart Lake			**BMA:**	O	**EASY:**	
NOTES:	31, 90, JJ								

ANALYSIS: Closed until 7/1. Great, private site. Limited view of the lake. Stock parties only. Has bear boxes.

8J3 Surprise Creek

TYPE:	F	**LAT/LONG:**	44.252219 -110.439613			**ELEV:**	7511	**TRAILHD:**	8N1
PEOPLE:	8	**STOCK:**	0	**USE RAT:**	56	**DIST TH:**	0.01 mi	**DIST WTR:**	75
PRIVACY:	N	**SHADE:**	L	**FIRE PIT:**	Y	**TOILET:**	N	**STAY:**	
WTR SRC:			Surprise Creek			**BMA:**	O	**EASY:**	
NOTES:	3, JJ								

ANALYSIS: Closed until 7/1. Not much of a view. Main trail passes through the site (no privacy)

8J4 Heart River

TYPE:	F	**LAT/LONG:**	44.247917 -110.445547			**ELEV:**	7609	**TRAILHD:**	8N1
PEOPLE:	8	**STOCK:**	0	**USE RAT:**	103	**DIST TH:**	0.02 mi	**DIST WTR:**	39
PRIVACY:	P	**SHADE:**	L	**FIRE PIT:**	Y	**TOILET:**	N	**STAY:**	
WTR SRC:			Heart River			**BMA:**	O	**EASY:**	
NOTES:	3, JJ								

ANALYSIS: Closed until 7/1. Little privacy (too close to trail); limited views.

8J6 East Shore

TYPE:	F	**LAT/LONG:**	44.250864 -110.449823			**ELEV:**	7522	**TRAILHD:**	8N1
PEOPLE:	4	**STOCK:**	0	**USE RAT:**	118	**DIST TH:**	0.37 mi	**DIST WTR:**	47
PRIVACY:	C	**SHADE:**	C	**FIRE PIT:**	Y	**TOILET:**	Y	**STAY:**	
WTR SRC:			Heart Lake			**BMA:**	O	**EASY:**	
NOTES:	3, JJ								

ANALYSIS: Closed until 7/1. Outstanding view of the lake & Mt. Sheridan (esp in the mornings). Very private.

8M1 Moose Creek

TYPE:	F/S	**LAT/LONG:**	44.345108 -110.703800			**ELEV:**	7957	**TRAILHD:**	8K1
PEOPLE:	8	**STOCK:**	15	**USE RAT:**	115	**DIST TH:**	0.04 mi	**DIST WTR:**	155
PRIVACY:	P	**SHADE:**	C	**FIRE PIT:**	NWF	**TOILET:**	Y	**STAY:**	
WTR SRC:			Moose Creek			**BMA:**	N	**EASY:**	
NOTES:									

ANALYSIS: Site is fairly close to trail (limited privacy). Marginal views.

8M2 **Moose Creek Meadow**

TYPE:	F/S	LAT/LONG:	44.328673 -110.736868			ELEV:	8003	TRAILHD:	8K1
PEOPLE:	8	STOCK:	15	USE RAT:	115	DIST TH:	0.04 mi	DIST WTR:	280
PRIVACY:	C	SHADE:	C	FIRE PIT:	Y	TOILET:	Y	STAY:	2N/E
WTR SRC:			Moose Creek			BMA:	N	EASY:	
NOTES:									

ANALYSIS: Fairly private site with decent views of Moose Creek area.

8O2 **Outlet Creek**

TYPE:	F	LAT/LONG:	44.253440 -110.415368			ELEV:	7899	TRAILHD:	8N1
PEOPLE:	6	STOCK:	0	USE RAT:	26	DIST TH:	0.15 mi	DIST WTR:	134
PRIVACY:	N	SHADE:	Y	FIRE PIT:	Y	TOILET:	N	STAY:	
WTR SRC:			Outlet Creek			BMA:	O	EASY:	
NOTES:	3, 14, DD (Maps/Books older than 2016 may show this site by lake. It's been relocated)								

ANALYSIS: Closed until 7/1. Travel east of site prohibited until 7/15. Site alongside trail (no privacy).

8P1 **Phantom Campsite**

TYPE:	F/S	LAT/LONG:	44.229342 -110.738956			ELEV:	8542	TRAILHD:	8K4
PEOPLE:	8	STOCK:	6	USE RAT:	26	DIST TH:	0.03 mi	DIST WTR:	130
PRIVACY:	P	SHADE:	P	FIRE PIT:	Y	TOILET:	N	STAY:	
WTR SRC:	Nearby cold spring or seasonal tributary of Polecat Creek					BMA:	N	EASY:	
NOTES:	36, 68								

ANALYSIS: Check w/ BCO for status of water. Stock use not recommended. 8P1 is best of the two sites.

8P2 **Phantom Campsite**

TYPE:	F	LAT/LONG:	44.230209 -110.740083			ELEV:	8548	TRAILHD:	8K4
PEOPLE:	8	STOCK:	0	USE RAT:	45	DIST TH:	0.06 mi	DIST WTR:	130
PRIVACY:	P	SHADE:	P	FIRE PIT:	Y	TOILET:	N	STAY:	
WTR SRC:	Nearby cold spring or seasonal tributary of Polecat Creek					BMA:	N	EASY:	
NOTES:	36, 68								

ANALYSIS: Check w/ BCO for status of water. Stock use not recommended. 8P1 is best of the two sites.

8Q1 **South Narrow Point**

TYPE:	B	LAT/LONG:	44.363863 -110.718947			ELEV:	7801	TRAILHD:	8K3
PEOPLE:	8	STOCK:	0	USE RAT:	276	DIST TH:	B/O	DIST WTR:	56
PRIVACY:	C	SHADE:	L	FIRE PIT:	NWF	TOILET:	Y	STAY:	2N/E
WTR SRC:			Shoshone Lake			BMA:	N	EASY:	
NOTES:	OO, PP, SS								

ANALYSIS: Check conditions/status at BCO. Limited shade, but great view of the lake. First & last nights only.

8Q3 **South Narrow Beach**

TYPE:	B	LAT/LONG:	44.361326 -110.710686			ELEV:	7804	TRAILHD:	8K3
PEOPLE:	8	STOCK:	0	USE RAT:	268	DIST TH:	B/O	DIST WTR:	109
PRIVACY:	C	SHADE:	C	FIRE PIT:	NWF	TOILET:	Y	STAY:	2N/E
WTR SRC:			Shoshone Lake			BMA:	N	EASY:	
NOTES:	PP, SS								

ANALYSIS: Check conditions/status at BCO. Site may be marshy. Good shade, great views. First & last nights only.

8Q4 **Moose Creek Point**

TYPE:	B	LAT/LONG:	44.363805 -110.703068			ELEV:	7817	TRAILHD:	8K3
PEOPLE:	8	STOCK:	0	USE RAT:	283	DIST TH:	B/O	DIST WTR:	126
PRIVACY:	C	SHADE:	C	FIRE PIT:	NWF	TOILET:	Y	STAY:	2N/E
WTR SRC:			Shoshone Lake			BMA:	N	EASY:	
NOTES:	PP, SS								

ANALYSIS: Check condition/status at BCO. Good panoramic views of the lake. First & last nights only.

8Q6 Moose Creek Outlet

TYPE:	B	**LAT/LONG:**	44.358745 -110.692761			**ELEV:**	7805	**TRAILHD:**	8K3
PEOPLE:	8	**STOCK:**	0	**USE RAT:**	248	**DIST TH:**	B/O	**DIST WTR:**	185
PRIVACY:	C	**SHADE:**	P	**FIRE PIT:**	NWF	**TOILET:**	Y	**STAY:**	2N/E
WTR SRC:			Shoshone Lake			**BMA:**	N	**EASY:**	
NOTES:	OO, PP, SS								

ANALYSIS: Check conditions/status at BCO. Site may be marshy. Great views. First & last night only.

8Q7 Moose Creek Beach

TYPE:	B	**LAT/LONG:**	44.359257 -110.685848			**ELEV:**	7812	**TRAILHD:**	8K3
PEOPLE:	8	**STOCK:**	0	**USE RAT:**	195	**DIST TH:**	B/O	**DIST WTR:**	25
PRIVACY:	C	**SHADE:**	P	**FIRE PIT:**	NWF	**TOILET:**	Y	**STAY:**	2N/E
WTR SRC:			Shoshone Lake			**BMA:**	N	**EASY:**	
NOTES:	OO, PP, SS								

ANALYSIS: Check conditions/status at BCO. Site may be marshy. Great views. First & last night only.

8Q9 Channel

TYPE:	B	**LAT/LONG:**	44.360639 -110.672803			**ELEV:**	7801	**TRAILHD:**	8K3
PEOPLE:	8	**STOCK:**	0	**USE RAT:**	334	**DIST TH:**	B/O	**DIST WTR:**	58
PRIVACY:	P	**SHADE:**	C	**FIRE PIT:**	NWF	**TOILET:**	Y	**STAY:**	2N/E
WTR SRC:			Shoshone Lake			**BMA:**	N	**EASY:**	
NOTES:	PP, SS								

ANALYSIS: Privacy limited due to other boats passing along shore. Great views. First & last nights only.

8R1 Windy Point

TYPE:	B	**LAT/LONG:**	44.367504 -110.731567			**ELEV:**	7845	**TRAILHD:**	8K3
PEOPLE:	8	**STOCK:**	0	**USE RAT:**	228	**DIST TH:**	B/O	**DIST WTR:**	330
PRIVACY:	C	**SHADE:**	C	**FIRE PIT:**	NWF	**TOILET:**	Y	**STAY:**	
WTR SRC:			Shoshone Lake			**BMA:**	N	**EASY:**	
NOTES:	39, 41, PP, SS								

ANALYSIS: See use limitations. Privacy limited if 8S7 occupied. Great views of the neck of the lake.

8R2 Bluff Top

TYPE:	F/B	**LAT/LONG:**	44.368506 -110.744816			**ELEV:**	7821	**TRAILHD:**	8K3
PEOPLE:	8	**STOCK:**	0	**USE RAT:**	257	**DIST TH:**	0.17 mi	**DIST WTR:**	340
PRIVACY:	C	**SHADE:**	C	**FIRE PIT:**	NWF	**TOILET:**	Y	**STAY:**	
WTR SRC:			Shoshone Lake			**BMA:**	N	**EASY:**	
NOTES:	33, OO, PP, SS								

ANALYSIS: Nice views from a cliff overlooking the lake.

8R3 Cove

TYPE:	F	**LAT/LONG:**	44.367888 -110.748210			**ELEV:**	7842	**TRAILHD:**	OK1
PEOPLE:	8	**STOCK:**	0	**USE RAT:**	203	**DIST TH:**	0.17 mi	**DIST WTR:**	55
PRIVACY:	C	**SHADE:**	C	**FIRE PIT:**	NWF	**TOILET:**	Y	**STAY:**	
WTR SRC:			Shoshone Lake			**BMA:**	N	**EASY:**	
NOTES:	30, PP, SS, UU								

ANALYSIS: Trail access only. Site is hilly, but has great views.

8R4 Flat Top

TYPE:	B	**LAT/LONG:**	44.367452 -110.756687			**ELEV:**	7814	**TRAILHD:**	8K1
PEOPLE:	8	**STOCK:**	0	**USE RAT:**	227	**DIST TH:**	B/O	**DIST WTR:**	182
PRIVACY:	C	**SHADE:**	P	**FIRE PIT:**	NWF	**TOILET:**	Y	**STAY:**	
WTR SRC:			Shoshone Lake			**BMA:**	N	**EASY:**	
NOTES:	39, 41, PP, SS								

ANALYSIS: Check conditions/status at BCO. Good lake views.

R5 Basin Bay Point

YPE:	F	**LAT/LONG:**	44.355819 -110.787617			**ELEV:**	7836	**TRAILHD:**	OK1
EOPLE:	8	**STOCK:**	0	**USE RAT:**	336	**DIST TH:**	0.40 mi	**DIST WTR:**	145
RIVACY:	C	**SHADE:**	C	**FIRE PIT:**	NWF	**TOILET:**	Y	**STAY:**	
TR SRC:			Shoshone Lake			**BMA:**	N	**EASY:**	
OTES:	PP, SS, UU								

NALYSIS: Probably the best hiker site on the lake. Excellent base from which to explore thermal areas.

S0 Outlet (Foot)

YPE:	F	**LAT/LONG:**	44.359857 -110.662605			**ELEV:**	7818	**TRAILHD:**	8K1
EOPLE:	8	**STOCK:**	0	**USE RAT:**	215	**DIST TH:**	0.08 mi	**DIST WTR:**	168
RIVACY:	N	**SHADE:**	C	**FIRE PIT:**	NWF	**TOILET:**	Y	**STAY:**	2N/3
TR SRC:			Shoshone Lake			**BMA:**	N	**EASY:**	
OTES:	66, 69, PP, SS								

NALYSIS: 2-party site (one by boat, one by foot). Next to patrol cabin - no privacy, and can be noisy.

S1 Outlet (Boat)

YPE:	B	**LAT/LONG:**	44.359857 -110.662605			**ELEV:**	7818	**TRAILHD:**	8K3
EOPLE:	8	**STOCK:**	0	**USE RAT:**	202	**DIST TH:**	B/O	**DIST WTR:**	168
RIVACY:	N	**SHADE:**	C	**FIRE PIT:**	NWF	**TOILET:**	Y	**STAY:**	2N/3
TR SRC:			Shoshone Lake			**BMA:**	N	**EASY:**	
OTES:	66, 69, PP, SS								

NALYSIS: 2-party site (one by boat, one by foot). Next to patrol cabin - no privacy, and can be noisy.

S2 Delacy Creek

YPE:	F/B	**LAT/LONG:**	44.409490 -110.706517			**ELEV:**	7820	**TRAILHD:**	7K2
EOPLE:	8	**STOCK:**	0	**USE RAT:**	234	**DIST TH:**	20 ft	**DIST WTR:**	84
RIVACY:	N	**SHADE:**	C	**FIRE PIT:**	NWF	**TOILET:**	Y	**STAY:**	
TR SRC:			Shoshone Lake			**BMA:**	N	**EASY:**	
OTES:	65, PP, SS								

NALYSIS: Busy main trail passes right through campsite - no privacy. Decent views of the lake.

S3 Coyote

YPE:	F	**LAT/LONG:**	44.404270 -110.712448			**ELEV:**	7840	**TRAILHD:**	7K2
EOPLE:	8	**STOCK:**	0	**USE RAT:**	251	**DIST TH:**	0.04 mi	**DIST WTR:**	42
RIVACY:	C	**SHADE:**	C	**FIRE PIT:**	NWF	**TOILET:**	Y	**STAY:**	
TR SRC:			Shoshone Lake			**BMA:**	N	**EASY:**	
OTES:	PP, SS								

NALYSIS: Decent privacy and shade. Good views of the lake.

S4 North Grizzly Beach

YPE:	B	**LAT/LONG:**	44.387055 -110.708383			**ELEV:**	7802	**TRAILHD:**	8K3
EOPLE:	8	**STOCK:**	0	**USE RAT:**	187	**DIST TH:**	B/O	**DIST WTR:**	56
RIVACY:	C	**SHADE:**	L	**FIRE PIT:**	NWF	**TOILET:**	Y	**STAY:**	
TR SRC:			Shoshone Lake			**BMA:**	N	**EASY:**	
OTES:	OO, PP, SS								

NALYSIS: Check conditions/status at BCO. Decent views of the lake.

S5 South Grizzly Beach

YPE:	B	**LAT/LONG:**	44.379142 -110.712335			**ELEV:**	7801	**TRAILHD:**	8K3
EOPLE:	8	**STOCK:**	0	**USE RAT:**	138	**DIST TH:**	N/A	**DIST WTR:**	86
RIVACY:	C	**SHADE:**	C	**FIRE PIT:**	NWF	**TOILET:**	Y	**STAY:**	
TR SRC:			Shoshone Lake			**BMA:**	N	**EASY:**	
OTES:	OO, PP, SS								

NALYSIS: Check conditions/status at BCO. Good views of the lake.

8S7 North Narrows

TYPE:	B	LAT/LONG:	44.369546 -110.727162			ELEV:	7827	TRAILHD:	8K3
PEOPLE:	8	STOCK:	0	USE RAT:	218	DIST TH:	B/O	DIST WTR:	92
PRIVACY:	C	SHADE:	C	FIRE PIT:	NWF	TOILET:	Y	STAY:	
WTR SRC:			Shoshone Lake			BMA:	N	EASY:	
NOTES:	OO, PP, SS								
ANALYSIS:	Limited privacy if site 8R1 is occupied.								

8T1 Basin Beach

TYPE:	F	LAT/LONG:	44.342214 -110.786828			ELEV:	7812	TRAILHD:	OK1
PEOPLE:	4	STOCK:	0	USE RAT:	147	DIST TH:	50 ft	DIST WTR:	33
PRIVACY:	N	SHADE:	P	FIRE PIT:	NWF	TOILET:	Y	STAY:	
WTR SRC:			Shoshone Lake			BMA:	N	EASY:	
NOTES:	1 tent, OO, PP, SS, TT, UU								
ANALYSIS:	Nice but very small site (one tent only). Seasonal creek between camp & toilet. Good base for exploring								

8T3 Hillside

TYPE:	B	LAT/LONG:	44.338608 -110.761950			ELEV:	7806	TRAILHD:	8K3
PEOPLE:	8	STOCK:	0	USE RAT:	190	DIST TH:	B/O	DIST WTR:	175
PRIVACY:	C	SHADE:	C	FIRE PIT:	NWF	TOILET:	Y	STAY:	
WTR SRC:			Shoshone Lake			BMA:	N	EASY:	
NOTES:	39, 41, OO, PP, SS								
ANALYSIS:	Check conditions/status at BCO. Good views of the lake. Lots of downfall in the area.								

8T5 Tranquility

TYPE:	B	LAT/LONG:	44.351908 -110.744025			ELEV:	7801	TRAILHD:	8K3
PEOPLE:	8	STOCK:	0	USE RAT:	165	DIST TH:	B/O	DIST WTR:	137
PRIVACY:	C	SHADE:	C	FIRE PIT:	NWF	TOILET:	Y	STAY:	
WTR SRC:			Shoshone Lake			BMA:	N	EASY:	
NOTES:	39, 41, OO, PP, SS								
ANALYSIS:	Check conditions/status at BCO. Poor quality site, w/ decent views of the lake. Lots of downfall.								

9A0 Upper Boundary Creek-Stock

TYPE:	S	LAT/LONG:	44.228342 -111.018055			ELEV:	6436	TRAILHD:	9K1
PEOPLE:	12	STOCK:	25	USE RAT:	128	DIST TH:	0.02 mi	DIST WTR:	31
PRIVACY:	N	SHADE:	L	FIRE PIT:	Y	TOILET:	N	STAY:	
WTR SRC:			Boundary Creek			BMA:	N	EASY:	
NOTES:	KK, LL, MM								
ANALYSIS:	Small stock site bisected by the trail. No privacy.								

9A1 Boundary Creek Meadows

TYPE:	F/S	LAT/LONG:	44.207847 -111.012431			ELEV:	6405	TRAILHD:	9K1
PEOPLE:	12	STOCK:	20	USE RAT:	147	DIST TH:	20 ft	DIST WTR:	50
PRIVACY:	N	SHADE:	N	FIRE PIT:	Y	TOILET:	N	STAY:	
WTR SRC:			Boundary Creek			BMA:	N	EASY:	
NOTES:	KK, LL Maps/books published prior to 1994 show incorrect location for this site.								
ANALYSIS:	Site is right off the trail - no privacy. Good views of meadows, but site may be marshy.								

9A2 Upper Boundary Creek

TYPE:	F	LAT/LONG:	44.230994 -111.018062			ELEV:	6442	TRAILHD:	9K1
PEOPLE:	12	STOCK:	0	USE RAT:	295	DIST TH:	0.11 mi	DIST WTR:	143
PRIVACY:	C	SHADE:	L	FIRE PIT:	Y	TOILET:	Y	STAY:	
WTR SRC:			Unnamed tributary of Boundary Creek			BMA:	N	EASY:	
NOTES:	KK, LL								
ANALYSIS:	Good privacy. Nice site with good views, but shade is limited.								

9A3 Dunanda Falls

TYPE:	F	LAT/LONG:	44.245631 -111.026177	ELEV:	6783	TRAILHD:	9K1
PEOPLE:	12	STOCK:	0	USE RAT: 393		DIST TH:	0.16 mi	DIST WTR: 280
PRIVACY:	C	SHADE:	L	FIRE PIT: Y		TOILET:	Y	STAY:
WTR SRC:		Boundary Creek				BMA:	N	EASY:
NOTES:	KK, LL							

ANALYSIS: Excellent, private, popular site near Dunanda Falls. Excellent view from the toilet, even!

9A4 Talus Terrace

TYPE:	F/S	LAT/LONG:	44.281613 -111.039802	ELEV:	7384	TRAILHD:	9K1
PEOPLE:	12	STOCK:	25	USE RAT: 29		DIST TH:	0.02 mi	DIST WTR: 84
PRIVACY:	N	SHADE:	L	FIRE PIT: Y		TOILET:	N	STAY:
WTR SRC:		Boundary Creek				BMA:	N	EASY:
NOTES:	KK, LL							

ANALYSIS: Fair quality site, with no privacy from the trail, and limited shade.

9A5 Buffalo Lake

TYPE:	F/S	LAT/LONG:	44.329835 -111.072716	ELEV:	7799	TRAILHD:	9K1
PEOPLE:	12	STOCK:	25	USE RAT: 17		DIST TH:	0.36 mi	DIST WTR: 180
PRIVACY:	P	SHADE:	P	FIRE PIT: Y		TOILET:	N	STAY:
WTR SRC:		Buffalo Lake				BMA:	N	EASY:
NOTES:	66, KK, LL Hikers can use toilet at the patrol cabin.							

ANALYSIS: Campsite is visible from nearby patrol cabin. Good views of lake, but limited tent sites.

9A6 Robinson Creek

TYPE:	F/S	LAT/LONG:	44.231494 -111.091876	ELEV:	6723	TRAILHD:	9K1
PEOPLE:	12	STOCK:	25	USE RAT: 11		DIST TH:	50 ft	DIST WTR: 77
PRIVACY:	P	SHADE:	P	FIRE PIT: N		TOILET:	N	STAY:
WTR SRC:		Robinson Creek				BMA:		EASY:
NOTES:	63 (Fires OK), KK, LL							

ANALYSIS: Site is in poor condition/location, and is rarely used. Site may be marshy. Views not that great.

9A7 Little Robinson Creek

TYPE:	F	LAT/LONG:	44.190551 -111.081146	ELEV:	6370	TRAILHD:	9K1
PEOPLE:	12	STOCK:	0	USE RAT: 7		DIST TH:	50 ft	DIST WTR: 125
PRIVACY:	P	SHADE:	L	FIRE PIT: Y		TOILET:	N	STAY:
WTR SRC:		Robinson Creek/Little Robinson Creek				BMA:	N	EASY:
NOTES:	KK, LL							

ANALYSIS: Fairly poor site adjacent to confluence of LRC & Robinson Creek. Little privacy and little shade.

9B0 Three River Meadow-Stock

TYPE:	S	LAT/LONG:	44.282918 -110.905834	ELEV:	7289	TRAILHD:	9K1
PEOPLE:	12	STOCK:	25	USE RAT: 142		DIST TH:	0.13 mi	DIST WTR: 39
PRIVACY:	C	SHADE:	P	FIRE PIT: NWF		TOILET:	Y	STAY: 2N/E
WTR SRC:		Bechler River				BMA:	N	EASY:
NOTES:	KK, LL							

ANALYSIS: Heavily worn stock site near patrol cabin (privacy may suffer). Limited shade.

9B1 Lower Boundary Creek

TYPE:	F	LAT/LONG:	44.185408 -111.005282	ELEV:	6405	TRAILHD:	9K1
PEOPLE:	12	STOCK:	0	USE RAT: 205		DIST TH:	0.02 mi	DIST WTR: 252
PRIVACY:	P	SHADE:	P	FIRE PIT: NWF		TOILET:	Y	STAY: 2N/E
WTR SRC:		Boundary Creek				BMA:	N	EASY:
NOTES:	KK, LL							

ANALYSIS: Good site, but near enough to trail that privacy is impacted.

9B2 Bechler Ford

TYPE:	F	LAT/LONG:	44.211301 -110.991270			ELEV:	6408	TRAILHD:	9K1
PEOPLE:	12	STOCK:	0	USE RAT:	334	DIST TH:	0.02 mi	DIST WTR:	182
PRIVACY:	P	SHADE:	C	FIRE PIT:	NWF	TOILET:	Y	STAY:	2N/E
WTR SRC:			Bechler River			BMA:	N	EASY:	
NOTES:	KK, LL, MM								

ANALYSIS: Popular, good site. Close to busy trail so privacy is limited.

9B3 Trail Spring

TYPE:	S	LAT/LONG:	44.216746 -110.980296			ELEV:	6483	TRAILHD:	9K1
PEOPLE:	20	STOCK:	25	USE RAT:	133	DIST TH:	0.03 mi	DIST WTR:	64
PRIVACY:	P	SHADE:	C	FIRE PIT:	Y	TOILET:	Y	STAY:	2N/E
WTR SRC:			Unnamed tributary of the Bechler River			BMA:	N	EASY:	
NOTES:	KK, LL								

ANALYSIS: Good view of the meadows. Decent site, but close enough to trail to impact privacy.

9B4 Ouzel Falls

TYPE:	F	LAT/LONG:	44.226374 -110.974921			ELEV:	6464	TRAILHD:	9K1
PEOPLE:	12	STOCK:	0	USE RAT:	287	DIST TH:	0.02 mi	DIST WTR:	154
PRIVACY:	P	SHADE:	C	FIRE PIT:	Y	TOILET:	Y	STAY:	1N/E
WTR SRC:			Bechler River			BMA:	N	EASY:	
NOTES:	KK, LL								

ANALYSIS: Nice, popular site w/ good views. Close enough to trail for privacy impact. Near falls & Bechler Canyon.

9B5 Colonnade Falls

TYPE:	F	LAT/LONG:	44.238941 -110.946055			ELEV:	6691	TRAILHD:	9K1
PEOPLE:	12	STOCK:	0	USE RAT:	283	DIST TH:	0.02 mi	DIST WTR:	42
PRIVACY:	P	SHADE:	C	FIRE PIT:	Y	TOILET:	Y	STAY:	1N/E
WTR SRC:			Bechler River			BMA:	N	EASY:	
NOTES:	KK, LL								

ANALYSIS: Site too close to trail (no privacy), but sound of waterfall in the distance makes it excellent site.

9B6 Lower Ford

TYPE:	F	LAT/LONG:	44.250940 -110.932768			ELEV:	6901	TRAILHD:	9K1
PEOPLE:	12	STOCK:	0	USE RAT:	166	DIST TH:	0.02 mi	DIST WTR:	56
PRIVACY:	P	SHADE:	L	FIRE PIT:	Y	TOILET:	Y	STAY:	1N/E
WTR SRC:			Bechler River			BMA:	N	EASY:	
NOTES:	KK, LL, MM								

ANALYSIS: Site is close to trail (privacy issues) and has limited shade.

9B7 Talus Spring

TYPE:	F	LAT/LONG:	44.259350 -110.928044			ELEV:	7126	TRAILHD:	9K1
PEOPLE:	12	STOCK:	0	USE RAT:	119	DIST TH:	0.02 mi	DIST WTR:	236
PRIVACY:	P	SHADE:	C	FIRE PIT:	Y	TOILET:	Y	STAY:	1N/E
WTR SRC:			Bechler River			BMA:	N	EASY:	
NOTES:	KK, LL								

ANALYSIS: Site doesn't have good view (opposite side of trail from river). Toilet has been in bad shape.

9B8 Upper Ford

TYPE:	F	LAT/LONG:	44.270746 -110.918420			ELEV:	7059	TRAILHD:	9K1
PEOPLE:	12	STOCK:	0	USE RAT:	188	DIST TH:	0.02 mi	DIST WTR:	81
PRIVACY:	P	SHADE:	C	FIRE PIT:	Y	TOILET:	Y	STAY:	1N/E
WTR SRC:			Bechler River			BMA:	N	EASY:	
NOTES:	KK, LL, MM								

ANALYSIS: Limited privacy due to site being close to trail. Small seasonal waterfall nearby.

9 Albright Falls

PE:	F	LAT/LONG:	44.278862 -110.905391			ELEV:	7274	TRAILHD:	9K1
OPLE:	12	STOCK:	0	USE RAT:	273	DIST TH:	0.15 mi	DIST WTR:	112
IVACY:	C	SHADE:	P	FIRE PIT:	NWF	TOILET:	Y	STAY:	2N/E
TR SRC:	Unnamed tributary of the Bechler River					BMA:	N	EASY:	

OTES: KK, LL. Books/maps published before 1990s may show incorrect site location.

NALYSIS: Excellent private site w/ view of the waterfall (sound is awesome, too).

1 Rocky Ford

PE:	F	LAT/LONG:	44.177206 -111.000837			ELEV:	6401	TRAILHD:	9K1
OPLE:	12	STOCK:	0	USE RAT:	220	DIST TH:	50 ft	DIST WTR:	252
IVACY:	N	SHADE:	L	FIRE PIT:	Y	TOILET:	Y	STAY:	2N/E
TR SRC:	Bechler River					BMA:	N	EASY:	

OTES: KK, LL

NALYSIS: Campsite lies along trail (little privacy). Marginal views of a bend in the river.

1 Ferris Fork

PE:	F	LAT/LONG:	44.289842 -110.891722			ELEV:	7454	TRAILHD:	9K1
OPLE:	12	STOCK:	0	USE RAT:	331	DIST TH:	0.07 mi	DIST WTR:	156
IVACY:	C	SHADE:	P	FIRE PIT:	NWF	TOILET:	Y	STAY:	1N/E
TR SRC:	Gregg Fork (Bechler River)					BMA:	N	EASY:	

OTES: KK, LL

NALYSIS: Probably best site in Bechler area for launching exploration. Near Mr. Bubbles hot pool.

2 Gregg Fork

PE:	F	LAT/LONG:	44.297399 -110.865017			ELEV:	8011	TRAILHD:	OK1
OPLE:	12	STOCK:	0	USE RAT:	212	DIST TH:	50 ft	DIST WTR:	67
IVACY:	P	SHADE:	P	FIRE PIT:	Y	TOILET:	Y	STAY:	1N/E
TR SRC:	Gregg Fork (Bechler River)					BMA:	N	EASY:	

OTES: 72, KK, LL

NALYSIS: Site is off side of trail (limited privacy). Views not that great. Site has poor runoff during rainstorms.

D3 Douglas Knob Meadow

YPE:	F/S	LAT/LONG:	44.320986 -110.849650			ELEV:	8375	TRAILHD:	OK1
EOPLE:	12	STOCK:	25	USE RAT:	202	DIST TH:	0.02 mi	DIST WTR:	313
RIVACY:	P	SHADE:	L	FIRE PIT:	NWF	TOILET:	N	STAY:	1N/E
TR SRC:	Unnamed tributary of LIttles Fork					BMA:	N	EASY:	

OTES: KK, LL

NALYSIS: Limited privacy & shade. Good views of Douglas Knob/Meadows & Trischman Knob.

D4 Continental Divide

YPE:	F	LAT/LONG:	44.339611 -110.841639			ELEV:	8536	TRAILHD:	OK1
EOPLE:	12	STOCK:	0	USE RAT:	199	DIST TH:	0.03 mi	DIST WTR:	179
RIVACY:	P	SHADE:	P	FIRE PIT:	NWF	TOILET:	Y	STAY:	1N/E
TR SRC:	Unnamed creek					BMA:	N	EASY:	

OTES: KK, LL

NALYSIS: Marginal site with marginal views near one of the crossings of the Continental Divide.

F1 Lower Falls River

YPE:	F	LAT/LONG:	44.138018 -110.933991			ELEV:	6477	TRAILHD:	9K3
EOPLE:	12	STOCK:	0	USE RAT:	43	DIST TH:	0.16 mi	DIST WTR:	80
RIVACY:	C	SHADE:	L	FIRE PIT:	Y	TOILET:	N	STAY:	
TR SRC:	Falls River					BMA:	N	EASY:	

OTES: KK, LL, MM (Site is listed as 9C6 on older maps/books)

NALYSIS: Good, private site with good views of this part of river and Calf Creek Meadow.

9F2 Upper Falls River

TYPE:	F	**LAT/LONG:**	44.139920 -110.837343			**ELEV:**	7073	**TRAILHD:**	9K6
PEOPLE:	12	**STOCK:**	0	**USE RAT:**	69	**DIST TH:**	0.04 mi	**DIST WTR:**	112
PRIVACY:	P	**SHADE:**	P	**FIRE PIT:**	Y	**TOILET:**	N	**STAY:**	1N/E
WTR SRC:			Falls River			**BMA:**	N	**EASY:**	Y

NOTES: KK, LL, MM (This site used to be 9U6 and 9C5 in the past - some older maps/books still reflect that)

ANALYSIS: Easy to get to site, with good views of the river, good privacy.

9M1 Lower Boundary Creek-Stock

TYPE:	S	**LAT/LONG:**	44.186484 -111.003745			**ELEV:**	6394	**TRAILHD:**	9K1
PEOPLE:	12	**STOCK:**	25	**USE RAT:**	38	**DIST TH:**	0.06 mi	**DIST WTR:**	190
PRIVACY:	N	**SHADE:**	P	**FIRE PIT:**	NWF	**TOILET:**	N	**STAY:**	2N/E
WTR SRC:			Boundary Creek			**BMA:**	N	**EASY:**	

NOTES: KK, LL

ANALYSIS: Limited privacy. Stock site for 9B1. Old maps may list this as 9B1. North access trail is 0.11 mi long.

9M2 Bechler Ford-Stock

TYPE:	S	**LAT/LONG:**	44.209910 -110.990780			**ELEV:**	6405	**TRAILHD:**	9K1
PEOPLE:	12	**STOCK:**	25	**USE RAT:**	93	**DIST TH:**	0.09 mi	**DIST WTR:**	140
PRIVACY:	P	**SHADE:**	L	**FIRE PIT:**	NWF	**TOILET:**	Y	**STAY:**	2N/E
WTR SRC:			Bechler River			**BMA:**	N	**EASY:**	

NOTES: KK, LL

ANALYSIS: Large stock site for 9B2 (old maps may list this as 9B2). Limited privacy and shade.

9U1 Falls River Cutoff

TYPE:	F/S	**LAT/LONG:**	44.160142 -110.939400			**ELEV:**	6459	**TRAILHD:**	9K3
PEOPLE:	12	**STOCK:**	25	**USE RAT:**	175	**DIST TH:**	50 ft	**DIST WTR:**	230
PRIVACY:	N	**SHADE:**	P	**FIRE PIT:**	Y	**TOILET:**	N	**STAY:**	
WTR SRC:			Mountain Ash Creek			**BMA:**	N	**EASY:**	

NOTES: KK, LL, MM

ANALYSIS: Site is located right along trail (no privacy). Great view of the river and the meadows.

9U2 Mountain Ash Creek

TYPE:	F	**LAT/LONG:**	44.171374 -110.924237			**ELEV:**	6478	**TRAILHD:**	9K3
PEOPLE:	12	**STOCK:**	0	**USE RAT:**	117	**DIST TH:**	0.03 mi	**DIST WTR:**	45
PRIVACY:	P	**SHADE:**	C	**FIRE PIT:**	Y	**TOILET:**	N	**STAY:**	
WTR SRC:			Mountain Ash Creek			**BMA:**	N	**EASY:**	

NOTES: KK, LL, MM

ANALYSIS: Marginal site with decent view of the river. Close to trail (limited privacy).

9U3 Mountain Ash Creek

TYPE:	F	**LAT/LONG:**	44.172948 -110.922865			**ELEV:**	6478	**TRAILHD:**	9K3
PEOPLE:	12	**STOCK:**	0	**USE RAT:**	93	**DIST TH:**	50 ft	**DIST WTR:**	185
PRIVACY:	N	**SHADE:**	P	**FIRE PIT:**	NWF	**TOILET:**	Y	**STAY:**	
WTR SRC:			Mountain Ash Creek			**BMA:**	N	**EASY:**	

NOTES: KK, LL, MM

ANALYSIS: Site is located along trail (no privacy). Decent view of the river.

9U4 Union Falls

TYPE:	F	**LAT/LONG:**	44.180166 -110.886734			**ELEV:**	6593	**TRAILHD:**	9K6
PEOPLE:	12	**STOCK:**	0	**USE RAT:**	292	**DIST TH:**	0.05 mi	**DIST WTR:**	85
PRIVACY:	C	**SHADE:**	C	**FIRE PIT:**	Y	**TOILET:**	Y	**STAY:**	2N/E
WTR SRC:			Mountain Ash Creek			**BMA:**	N	**EASY:**	

NOTES: KK, LL

ANALYSIS: Good, private site, but views are limited. This site allows wood fires.

5 Union Falls

'PE:	F/S	LAT/LONG:	44.182842 -110.888676	ELEV:	6605	TRAILHD:	9K3
OPLE:	12	STOCK:	12 USE RAT: 198	DIST TH:	0.13 mi	DIST WTR:	70
IVACY:	C	SHADE:	P FIRE PIT: NWF	TOILET:	N	STAY:	2N/E
TR SRC:		Warm Fork (Mountain Ash Creek)		BMA:	N	EASY:	
OTES:	KK, LL, MM						

NALYSIS: Campsite is close enough to patrol cabin to hear/be heard. No wood fires allowed here.

A1 Lone Star

PE:	F/S	LAT/LONG:	44.417924 -110.812903	ELEV:	7719	TRAILHD:	OK1
OPLE:	12	STOCK:	10 USE RAT: 359	DIST TH:	0.02 mi	DIST WTR:	480
IVACY:	N	SHADE:	P FIRE PIT: Y	TOILET:	Y	STAY:	
TR SRC:		Firehole River		BMA:	N	EASY:	Y
OTES:	WW, XX						

NALYSIS: Site is very close to trail (no privacy), with limited views. Good first site for Bechler hike from the north.

A2 Upper Firehole

PE:	F	LAT/LONG:	44.413910 -110.819216	ELEV:	7697	TRAILHD:	OK1
EOPLE:	6	STOCK:	0 USE RAT: 277	DIST TH:	0.02 mi	DIST WTR:	90
RIVACY:	P	SHADE:	L FIRE PIT: Y	TOILET:	Y	STAY:	
TR SRC:		Firehole River		BMA:	N	EASY:	
OTES:	XX						

NALYSIS: Decent site w/ limited privacy and shade. Located in a thermal area (use caution outside campsite)

A3 Firehole Springs

YPE:	F	LAT/LONG:	44.405288 -110.826339	ELEV:	7703	TRAILHD:	OK1
EOPLE:	6	STOCK:	0 USE RAT: 187	DIST TH:	0.03 mi	DIST WTR:	100
RIVACY:	P	SHADE:	L FIRE PIT: Y	TOILET:	N	STAY:	
TR SRC:		Firehole River		BMA:	N	EASY:	
OTES:	XX						

NALYSIS: Campsite is located next to trail (limited privacy) w/ no real view. Hard ground

B2 Mallard Lake Southeast

YPE:	F	LAT/LONG:	44.476616 -110.774137	ELEV:	8044	TRAILHD:	OK3
EOPLE:	6	STOCK:	0 USE RAT: 166	DIST TH:	0.01 mi	DIST WTR:	45
RIVACY:	P	SHADE:	C FIRE PIT: Y	TOILET:	N	STAY:	
VTR SRC:		Mallard Lake		BMA:	N	EASY:	
IOTES:	64, ZZ						

NALYSIS: Site is on peninsula w/ great views. Hikers often mistake access trail as main trail (privacy issue).

B3 Mallard Lake East

YPE:	F	LAT/LONG:	44.477573 -110.773612	ELEV:	8047	TRAILHD:	OK3
EOPLE:	6	STOCK:	0 USE RAT: 184	DIST TH:	0.09 mi	DIST WTR:	85
RIVACY:	P	SHADE:	C FIRE PIT: Y	TOILET:	N	STAY:	
VTR SRC:		Mallard Lake		BMA:	N	EASY:	
IOTES:	64, ZZ						

NALYSIS: Site has good view of lake, but hikers often mistake access trail as part of main trail (erodes privacy)

B4 Mallard Lake Outlet

YPE:	F	LAT/LONG:	44.475514 -110.777228	ELEV:	8073	TRAILHD:	OK3
EOPLE:	6	STOCK:	0 USE RAT: 88	DIST TH:	0.11 mi	DIST WTR:	45
RIVACY:	P	SHADE:	C FIRE PIT: NWF	TOILET:	N	STAY:	
VTR SRC:		Mallard Lake		BMA:	N	EASY:	
IOTES:	64, ZZ						

NALYSIS: Good site on west side of lake. No wood fires permitted at this one, however.

OD1 Fairy Meadows

TYPE:	F	LAT/LONG:	44.525957 -110.855682			ELEV:	7286	TRAILHD:	OK5
PEOPLE:	6	STOCK:	0	USE RAT:	158	DIST TH:	0.07 mi	DIST WTR:	1500
PRIVACY:	C	SHADE:	C	FIRE PIT:	NWF	TOILET:	N	STAY:	
WTR SRC:		None				BMA:	A	EASY:	Y
NOTES:	1 (Small site), XX, YY								

ANALYSIS: Closed until Friday before Memorial Day. No water source. No views. Not a good site, but private.

OD2 Firehole Meadows

TYPE:	F	LAT/LONG:	44.484869 -110.928610			ELEV:	7901	TRAILHD:	OK4
PEOPLE:	10	STOCK:	0	USE RAT:	168	DIST TH:	0.02 mi	DIST WTR:	460
PRIVACY:	C	SHADE:	C	FIRE PIT:	Y	TOILET:	N	STAY:	
WTR SRC:		Little Firehole River				BMA:	A	EASY:	
NOTES:	1, XX, YY								

ANALYSIS: Closed until Friday before Memorial Day. Great view of Little Firehole Meadows. Private site.

OD3 Firehole Falls

TYPE:	F	LAT/LONG:	44.485929 -110.918102			ELEV:	7909	TRAILHD:	OK4
PEOPLE:	6	STOCK:	0	USE RAT:	187	DIST TH:	0.05 mi	DIST WTR:	70
PRIVACY:	C	SHADE:	C	FIRE PIT:	Y	TOILET:	N	STAY:	
WTR SRC:		Little Firehole River				BMA:	A	EASY:	
NOTES:	1, XX, YY								

ANALYSIS: Closed until Friday before Memorial Day. Waterfall next to campsite. Private, good setting.

OD4 Imperial Meadows

TYPE:	F	LAT/LONG:	44.533581 -110.861945			ELEV:	7246	TRAILHD:	OK5
PEOPLE:	12	STOCK:	0	USE RAT:	230	DIST TH:	0.21 mi	DIST WTR:	210
PRIVACY:	C	SHADE:	L	FIRE PIT:	Y	TOILET:	N	STAY:	
WTR SRC:		Fairy Creek				BMA:	A	EASY:	
NOTES:	1, XX, YY								

ANALYSIS: Closed until Friday before Memorial Day. Good view of Imperial Meadows, but little shade.

OD5 Goose Lake

TYPE:	F	LAT/LONG:	44.544689 -110.844181			ELEV:	7229	TRAILHD:	OK5
PEOPLE:	6	STOCK:	0	USE RAT:	96	DIST TH:	0.10 mi	DIST WTR:	58
PRIVACY:	P	SHADE:	P	FIRE PIT:	Y	TOILET:	N	STAY:	1N/E
WTR SRC:		Goose Lake				BMA:	A	EASY:	Y
NOTES:	1, 73, WW, XX, YY								

ANALYSIS: Closed until Friday before Memorial Day. HC/Bike accessible site. Good view of lake, but limited privacy.

OE1 Summit Lake

TYPE:	F/S	LAT/LONG:	44.415504 -110.937231			ELEV:	8574	TRAILHD:	OK4
PEOPLE:	6	STOCK:	6	USE RAT:	94	DIST TH:	0.02 mi	DIST WTR:	84
PRIVACY:	N	SHADE:	L	FIRE PIT:	Y	TOILET:	N	STAY:	
WTR SRC:		Summit Lake				BMA:	N	EASY:	
NOTES:	9, VV, XX								

ANALYSIS: Site is near trail, but low use means decent privacy. Not accessible via OK4 until Mem Day weekend.

OG1 Sentinel Meadows East

TYPE:	F	LAT/LONG:	44.564886 -110.853365			ELEV:	7209	TRAILHD:	OK6
PEOPLE:	8	STOCK:	0	USE RAT:	194	DIST TH:	0.05 mi	DIST WTR:	18
PRIVACY:	P	SHADE:	L	FIRE PIT:	N	TOILET:	N	STAY:	
WTR SRC:		Sentinel Creek				BMA:	A	EASY:	Y
NOTES:	1, XX, YY								

ANALYSIS: Closed until Friday of Memorial Day weekend. Limited shade, but good views of thermal fields.

A1 Gneiss Creek

YPE:	F/S	**LAT/LONG:**	44.777248 -111.032542	**ELEV:**	6651	**TRAILHD:**	WK7
OPLE:	10	**STOCK:**	20 **USE RAT:** 19	**DIST TH:**	0.09 mi	**DIST WTR:**	207
IVACY:	N	**SHADE:**	L **FIRE PIT:** Y	**TOILET:**	N	**STAY:**	
TR SRC:			Gneiss Creek	**BMA:**	B	**EASY:**	
OTES:	2, 15, AG						

NALYSIS: Closed until 7/1. Exposed site with little privacy. Good views of the area, though.

B1 Gallatin River

YPE:	F	**LAT/LONG:**	44.923701 -110.969557	**ELEV:**	7521	**TRAILHD:**	WK6
EOPLE:	10	**STOCK:**	0 **USE RAT:** 115	**DIST TH:**	0.06 mi	**DIST WTR:**	196
RIVACY:	P	**SHADE:**	P **FIRE PIT:** Y	**TOILET:**	N	**STAY:**	
TR SRC:			Gallatin River	**BMA:**	N	**EASY:**	
OTES:	AE, AF						

NALYSIS: Great site with great views. Firewood supply may be limited.

B3 Gallatin River

YPE:	S	**LAT/LONG:**	44.924426 -110.956933	**ELEV:**	7508	**TRAILHD:**	WK6
EOPLE:	12	**STOCK:**	25 **USE RAT:** 98	**DIST TH:**	0.12 mi	**DIST WTR:**	168
RIVACY:	N	**SHADE:**	P **FIRE PIT:** Y	**TOILET:**	N	**STAY:**	
TR SRC:			Gallatin River	**BMA:**	N	**EASY:**	
OTES:	15, 85, AE, AF						

NALYSIS: Though site is good distance from trail, it is still visible from trail.

B4 Gallatin River

YPE:	S	**LAT/LONG:**	44.923358 -110.945213	**ELEV:**	7575	**TRAILHD:**	WK6
EOPLE:	12	**STOCK:**	25 **USE RAT:** 88	**DIST TH:**	0.02 mi	**DIST WTR:**	212
RIVACY:	P	**SHADE:**	C **FIRE PIT:** Y	**TOILET:**	Y	**STAY:**	
TR SRC:			Gallatin River	**BMA:**	N	**EASY:**	
OTES:	15, 85, AE, AF, AJ						

NALYSIS: Decent site, with good views, but is visible from the main trail.

B6 Gallatin River

YPE:	F	**LAT/LONG:**	44.915300 -110.933727	**ELEV:**	7598	**TRAILHD:**	WK6
EOPLE:	10	**STOCK:**	0 **USE RAT:** 61	**DIST TH:**	0.06 mi	**DIST WTR:**	56
RIVACY:	P	**SHADE:**	C **FIRE PIT:** Y	**TOILET:**	N	**STAY:**	
TR SRC:			Unnamed tributary of Gallatin River	**BMA:**	D	**EASY:**	
OTES:	15, AE, AF						

NALYSIS: Decent privacy, good shading, with great views up the Gallatin River.

C2 Fan Creek

YPE:	F	**LAT/LONG:**	44.970010 -111.013145	**ELEV:**	7370	**TRAILHD:**	WK5
EOPLE:	10	**STOCK:**	0 **USE RAT:** 113	**DIST TH:**	0.58 mi	**DIST WTR:**	394
RIVACY:	C	**SHADE:**	C **FIRE PIT:** Y	**TOILET:**	N	**STAY:**	
TR SRC:			Fan Creek	**BMA:**	D	**EASY:**	
OTES:							

NALYSIS: Very private site (lies on closed section of original trail). Good views. Access to water is marshy.

C3 Fan Creek

YPE:	S	**LAT/LONG:**	44.986574 -110.993345	**ELEV:**	7475	**TRAILHD:**	WK5
EOPLE:	12	**STOCK:**	25 **USE RAT:** 98	**DIST TH:**	0.12 mi	**DIST WTR:**	199
RIVACY:	C	**SHADE:**	C **FIRE PIT:** Y	**TOILET:**	Y	**STAY:**	
TR SRC:			Unnamed tributary of Fan Creek	**BMA:**	D	**EASY:**	
OTES:							

NALYSIS: Good site, far enough away from trail to be private.

WC4 Fan Creek Junction/Northeast Fork

TYPE:	S	**LAT/LONG:**	44.993042 -110.966859			**ELEV:**	7651	**TRAILHD:**	WK5
PEOPLE:	12	**STOCK:**	25	**USE RAT:**	95	**DIST TH:**	50 ft	**DIST WTR:**	129
PRIVACY:	N	**SHADE:**	P	**FIRE PIT:**	Y	**TOILET:**	Y	**STAY:**	
WTR SRC:	North Fork of Fan Creek					**BMA:**	D	**EASY:**	
NOTES:	AJ								

ANALYSIS: Campsite is right along trail, so no privacy. Good views.

WD1 East Fork Specimen Creek

TYPE:	F	**LAT/LONG:**	45.028341 -110.978751			**ELEV:**	7960	**TRAILHD:**	WK3
PEOPLE:	10	**STOCK:**	0	**USE RAT:**	105	**DIST TH:**	0.12 mi	**DIST WTR:**	660
PRIVACY:	C	**SHADE:**	C	**FIRE PIT:**	Y	**TOILET:**	N	**STAY:**	
WTR SRC:	Unnamed tributary of East Fork, Specimen Creek					**BMA:**	D	**EASY:**	
NOTES:									

ANALYSIS: Old maps may show this campsite in wrong location. Good site, private, but limited views.

WD2 Sportsman Lake

TYPE:	F/S	**LAT/LONG:**	45.013661 -110.903466			**ELEV:**	7740	**TRAILHD:**	WK3
PEOPLE:	12	**STOCK:**	20	**USE RAT:**	159	**DIST TH:**	0.02 mi	**DIST WTR:**	450
PRIVACY:	P	**SHADE:**	P	**FIRE PIT:**	Y	**TOILET:**	Y	**STAY:**	
WTR SRC:	Sportsman Lake					**BMA:**	D	**EASY:**	
NOTES:	15, 16, AB, AC								

ANALYSIS: No stock before 7/15. Decent view, but not as good as WD3. Visible from nearby patrol cabin.

WD3 Sportsman Lake

TYPE:	F	**LAT/LONG:**	45.015364 -110.900539			**ELEV:**	7788	**TRAILHD:**	WK3
PEOPLE:	10	**STOCK:**	0	**USE RAT:**	136	**DIST TH:**	0.28 mi	**DIST WTR:**	367
PRIVACY:	P	**SHADE:**	C	**FIRE PIT:**	Y	**TOILET:**	N	**STAY:**	
WTR SRC:	Sportsman Lake					**BMA:**	D	**EASY:**	
NOTES:	15, AB, AC								

ANALYSIS: Good, private site with great views of the lake. Bypass old site right after creek crossing.

WD4 High Lake

TYPE:	F	**LAT/LONG:**	45.055476 -110.937922			**ELEV:**	8819	**TRAILHD:**	WK3
PEOPLE:	10	**STOCK:**	0	**USE RAT:**	133	**DIST TH:**	0.04 mi	**DIST WTR:**	156
PRIVACY:	P	**SHADE:**	P	**FIRE PIT:**	NWF	**TOILET:**	N	**STAY:**	
WTR SRC:	High Lake					**BMA:**	D	**EASY:**	
NOTES:	AB								

ANALYSIS: Excellent site with great view of the lake. Close enough to trail to limit privacy.

WD5 High Lake

TYPE:	F/S	**LAT/LONG:**	45.057962 -110.940361			**ELEV:**	8924	**TRAILHD:**	WK3
PEOPLE:	10	**STOCK:**	5	**USE RAT:**	102	**DIST TH:**	0.18 mi	**DIST WTR:**	32
PRIVACY:	C	**SHADE:**	P	**FIRE PIT:**	NWF	**TOILET:**	N	**STAY:**	
WTR SRC:	High Lake					**BMA:**	D	**EASY:**	
NOTES:	38, AB								

ANALYSIS: Stock reservations limited to llama parties. Great view of the lake, good privacy.

WD6 High Lake / Sportsman Jct

TYPE:	S	**LAT/LONG:**	45.027615 -110.968958			**ELEV:**	8229	**TRAILHD:**	WK3
PEOPLE:	12	**STOCK:**	25	**USE RAT:**	108	**DIST TH:**	0.20 mi	**DIST WTR:**	336
PRIVACY:	C	**SHADE:**	C	**FIRE PIT:**	Y	**TOILET:**	Y	**STAY:**	
WTR SRC:	East Fork of Specimen Creek					**BMA:**	D	**EASY:**	
NOTES:	16, AB, AJ								

ANALYSIS: No stock before 7/15. Decent site, limited view. Good for base for exploring High Lake, etc.

E1 Specimen Creek Jct

PE:	F/S	**LAT/LONG:**	45.028834 -111.045743			**ELEV:**	7178	**TRAILHD:**	WK3
OPLE:	12	**STOCK:**	10	**USE RAT:**	140	**DIST TH:**	50 ft	**DIST WTR:**	160
IVACY:	N	**SHADE:**	L	**FIRE PIT:**	Y	**TOILET:**	N	**STAY:**	2N/E
TR SRC:			Specimen Creek			**BMA:**	D	**EASY:**	Y
OTES:	AB								

NALYSIS: Located right along trail, so no privacy. Great views of area, including Meldrum Mountain.

E4 Specimen Creek

PE:	F	**LAT/LONG:**	45.063844 -111.022535			**ELEV:**	7587	**TRAILHD:**	WK3
OPLE:	12	**STOCK:**	0	**USE RAT:**	106	**DIST TH:**	0.02 mi	**DIST WTR:**	56
IVACY:	N	**SHADE:**	P	**FIRE PIT:**	Y	**TOILET:**	N	**STAY:**	
TR SRC:			North Fork of Specimen Creel			**BMA:**	D	**EASY:**	
OTES:	AB								

NALYSIS: Just off the trail, so little privacy. Decent views, esp of Meldrum Mountain.

E5 Shelf Lake

PE:	F	**LAT/LONG:**	45.091801 -111.011969			**ELEV:**	9249	**TRAILHD:**	WK2
OPLE:	8	**STOCK:**	0	**USE RAT:**	162	**DIST TH:**	0.11 mi	**DIST WTR:**	84
IVACY:	C	**SHADE:**	L	**FIRE PIT:**	NWF	**TOILET:**	N	**STAY:**	
TR SRC:			Shelf Lake			**BMA:**	D	**EASY:**	
OTES:	AB								

NALYSIS: High altitude site. One of the best sites in the park, but wood fires not permitted (prepare for cold)

E6 Crescent Lake

YPE:	F	**LAT/LONG:**	45.061659 -110.995694			**ELEV:**	8631	**TRAILHD:**	WK3
EOPLE:	8	**STOCK:**	0	**USE RAT:**	111	**DIST TH:**	25 ft	**DIST WTR:**	30
RIVACY:	N	**SHADE:**	C	**FIRE PIT:**	Y	**TOILET:**	N	**STAY:**	
TR SRC:			Crescent Lake			**BMA:**	D	**EASY:**	
OTES:	AB								

NALYSIS: Good site, but located on the trail (limited privacy). Use tent sites on the hill away from food pole.

E7 Shelf Lake

YPE:	F	**LAT/LONG:**	45.091292 -111.014314			**ELEV:**	9323	**TRAILHD:**	WK2
EOPLE:	8	**STOCK:**	0	**USE RAT:**	88	**DIST TH:**	0.04 mi	**DIST WTR:**	218
RIVACY:	P	**SHADE:**		**FIRE PIT:**	NWF	**TOILET:**	N	**STAY:**	
TR SRC:			Shelf Lake			**BMA:**	D	**EASY:**	
OTES:	AB								

NALYSIS: High altitude site. Another excellent site, but as with WE5, wood fires not permitted, so prep for cold.

F1 Black Butte Creek

YPE:	F/S	**LAT/LONG:**	45.053184 -111.090966			**ELEV:**	9160	**TRAILHD:**	WK2
EOPLE:	10	**STOCK:**	10	**USE RAT:**	105	**DIST TH:**	0.16 mi	**DIST WTR:**	56
RIVACY:	C	**SHADE:**	C	**FIRE PIT:**	Y	**TOILET:**	N	**STAY:**	
TR SRC:			Black Butte Creek (or unnamed tributary if wet)			**BMA:**	D	**EASY:**	Y
OTES:									

NALYSIS: Requires ford of Black Butte Creek to access. Good, private site, with limited views.

F2 Upper Dailey Creek

YPE:	F/S	**LAT/LONG:**	45.090879 -111.106281			**ELEV:**	7532	**TRAILHD:**	WK1
EOPLE:	10	**STOCK:**	10	**USE RAT:**	103	**DIST TH:**	0.11 mi	**DIST WTR:**	179
RIVACY:	C	**SHADE:**		**FIRE PIT:**	Y	**TOILET:**	N	**STAY:**	
TR SRC:			Unnamed tributary of Dailey Creek			**BMA:**	D	**EASY:**	Y
OTES:	67								

NALYSIS: Older maps may show wrong location for this site. Seasonal water source. Good views, privacy.

Campsite Notes

(1) Closed 3/10 to Friday of Memorial Day weekend

(2) Closed 3/10 to 6/30

(3) Closed 4/1 to 6/30

(4) Closed 4/1 to 7/14

(5) Closed 5/15 - 7/10

(6) Closed 5/15 - 7/14

(7) Closed Friday of Memorial Day weekend until 7/15

(8) Closes on 9/14

(9) No access from OK4 trailhead from 3/10 to Friday of Memorial Day weekend

(10) No off-trail travel from 4/1 through 7/14

(11) No off-trail travel from 5/15 through 7/14

(12) No off-trail travel from 3/10 through 7/14 AND from 8/22 through 11/10; Off-trail travel by permit only from 7/15 to 8/21

(13) No travel from campsite from 5/15 through 7/14

(14) No travel east of campsite before 7/14

(15) No off-trail travel permitted at all

(16) No stock use before 7/15

(17) No stock use before 7/20

(18) No stock use before 8/1

(19) No stock use after 9/1

(20) Two-night limit between 7/1 and 8/31

(21) Only three (3) nights allowed for all 2S sites from 6/15 to 9/15

(22) Located in Mirror Plateau BMA; open only from 7/1 to 8/14 for 14 nights @ 3O1 and 5P7

(23) First and/or last night only

(24) Access may be difficult prior to mid-July

(25) No off-trail travel from 4/1 through 8/10

(30) Trail access only

(31) Stock access only

(32) Boat access only

(33) Trail or boat access only

(34) Off-trail or non-motorized boat access only

(35) Non-motorized boat access only

(36) Stock use not recommended

(37) Llamas only

(38) Only llama parties can reserve campsite in advance

(39) No more than 2 boats permitted

(40) Not advised for boats over 20 feet in length

(41) Limited landing area early in the season

(42) Shallow water at/near landing

(43) Boat must be completely removed from the water

(44) Boat must be completely removed from the water or anchored off shore

(45) Anchorage site only

(46) Boat must be self-contained (self-contained means campers may go ashore to use toilet & exercise; must cook, eat, and sleep on the boat).

(47) Shore use only; no overnight anchoring

(48) Boat must be further than 100 feet from shore, 300 feet from dock and within land points that define double cove of Frank Island

(49) No shore landing prior to 8/15 except at dock and picnic area. No camping on shore

(50) Only two parties may sleep on shore (sites A&B); one party must be self-contained; no more than one canoe or non-motorized boat

(51) No stock west of site except to load/unload

(52) Keep stock away from natural spring

(53) Due to excessive willow growth, picketing stock in adjacent meadow not feasible

(54) No stock on trail

(60) Leave No Trace camping procedures must be followed; camp 100 yards from shore

(61) Requires ford of stream or river; Check SITREP @ online or at nearest Backcountry Office

(62) No hikers before water recedes

(63) Site is off-trail and may be difficult to find

(64) Hikers often mistake camp site spur trail as main trail, resulting in interrupted privacy

(65) Main trail passes through campsite

(66) Site can be seen/heard from nearby patrol cabin

(67) Seasonal water source

(68) Unpredictable water source

(69) 2-party site

(70) 3-party site

(71) Shared toilet facilities

(72) Water runs through campsite when it rains

(73) Reserved for handicap use only

(74) Site is located in a floodplain and prone to flooding

(80) 7G1 and 7G2 cannot be occupied by stock at the same time

(81) 1F1 and 1G5 cannot be occupied by stock at the same time

(82) 3T2 and 3T3 cannot be occupied by stock at the same time

(83) 1 party per night at either 2S7 or 2S8

(84) 8B3 and 8B4 cannot be occupied at the same time

(85) WB3 and WB4 cannot be occupied at the same time

(90) Bear box (for food storage) located at camp site

General Area/Trail Notes

A	Hellroaring Creek & Coyote Creek sites (1R3, 2B1, 2C#, 2H#) - several loops hikes are possible by exiting and re-entering northern boundary of the park into Gallatin National Forest. Hikers must know how to use a compass and map or GPS device as there are numerous unmarked trail junctions. These trails are at higher elevations and receive a lot of stock use. Not recommended for fall use as hunting begins in September.
B	Hellroaring Creek is too high and swift to ford before late July and often it's not fordable until mid-August. Hikers should cross via the bridge north of site 2H7 during high water. See the BCO situation report for the latest information.
C	Trailhead 2K5 is located on the Slough Creek Campground access road. It is accessible by vehicle only when the campground is open. Otherwise, you'll have to hike from the main road to the trailhead before then (about 3 miles).
D	Trailhead 3K2 (Pebble Creek) has two parking areas, one of which is along the highway.
E	Site 3P1 is the only site accessible along Pebble Creek in the early season before high water recedes. There are four fords of the creek which are quite high and therefore sites 3P2-3P5 may not be accessible until late June.
F	Bliss Pass Trail is 7.2 miles between Slough Creek & Pebble Creek trails with an elevation gain of around 3,000 feet in 4.5 miles on Slough Creek side & 1,700 feet on the Pebble Creek side. Snow likely at the top into July & the trail is not accessible from the Pebble Creek side until the creek is fordable. Trail not recommended for pack strings due to numerous switchbacks & steep terrain.
G	3K1 has two trailheads. The western one is for stock, the eastern for hikers. Hikers must not park at the stock trailhead.
H	Cache Creek ford - sites 3L1 and the 3C# sites are only accessible in the early season. Cache Creek is typically too swift and high to ford until mid-June (and sometimes early July).
I	Trailhead 3K3 requires fording Soda Butte Creek. In early season it is recommended that hikers ford the creek in the vicinity of Round Prairie (across from Pebble Creek campground) and hike back to access the trail on the east side of the creek. Hikers should not cross at the logjam near 3K3 because of dangerous conditions.
J	The trail up Thunderer from the 3K3 trailhead climbs 2,400 feet in 3.7 miles. From Cache Creek side, climbs 1,100 feet in 1.3 miles. Snow may be present near summit until early July.
K	Republic Pass: Snow may be present on the upper end of the pass until July. Trail near top of pass can be difficult to follow; look for cairns and blazes and carry a map/compass or GPS. From the pass at the park boundary, it is 4.5 miles to the Shoshone National Forest trailhead (which is about 1 mile from Cooke City).
L	Lamar River ford: There is a ford of the Lamar River at the east end of the Specimen Ridge Trail. This is typically not crossable until July. It is easier to cross at beginning of hike rather than near end of it (16 miles in). For some it may be more prudent to begin hike at east end to accomplish ford early in the hike.
M	Trailheads 3N2, 3N3, and 3N4 are high-elevation passes (above 9K) and may be snow-covered until mid- or late July.
N	Pelican Valley and trailhead 5K3 is closed (BMA) from April 1 to July 4. Between 7/4 and 11/10 area is day use only between 9 a.m. and 7 p.m.
O	7-Mile Hole - Campsite 4C3 is not accessible in early season because Sulphur Creek is too high. Once water recedes in late June/early July, creek is crossable via rock hopping. Sulphur Creek is located between sites 4C2 & 4C3. Hikers advised not to drink water from Sulphur Creek, even if purified (due to chemicals in the water). Hikers should get water from Yellowstone River (upstream, away from confluence). Elevation gain is 1,250 feet in 2 miles. Caution advised when traveling through thermal area, as it can be tough to distinguish trail.
P	Stock not allowed on 7-Mile Hole trail or Washburn spur.
Q	Wapiti Lake Trail is one of the last in the area to be cleared each season. Hikers should expect significant downfall, especially east of 4M2. Trail remains snowbound well into June each year.
R	4B1 and 4B2 - access to these sites is via off-trail hiking. Hikers will need map/compass or GPS. Suggestion is to travel east off trail from 4M2 or by following Broad Creek downstream from where trail crosses the stream near 4B3.
S	4W1 may be inaccessible in early spring due to Sour Creek ford (which can be up to 4 feet deep).

T	Observation Peak (4P1) trail climbs 1,500 feet in 2.5 miles. Closest reliable water source once the snow melts in early summer is Cascade Lake, which is about 3 miles away.
U	The Solfatara Trail and Howard Eaton Trail west of Ice Lake are infrequently maintained. Hikers should expect to encounter downfall, especially through the burned areas between 4F1 and Ice Lake and between trailheads 4K1 and 1K7.
V	Virginia Meadows Trailhead: This is not a designated trailhead, but this trail provides an alternate access route to Ice and Wolf Lakes. The parking area is 1/2 mile east of trailhead 4K2 and is on the south side of the road. The trail begins on the north side of the road and has blazes, but no trail marker or sign.
W	Little Gibbon River ford, between 4G6 and 4G7, slow moving, soft bottom, can be 3-4 feet in early season.
X	Lake Spawn BMA: From May 15 through July 14, no off trail travel is allowed and the trail between Cabin Creek and Outlet Creek is closed. Open campsites are 7L5, 7L6, 7L7, 7L8, 7M3, 7M4, 7M5, 6A3, 6A4, and 6B1 (with no travel away from campsites). On July 15 all campsites open and off-trail travel is permitted.
Y	Lake area campsites: Designated anchor sites with shore camping: 5L8, 5L9, 7L5, 7L6, 7M4, 7M5; Recommended shore sites for parties with large powerboats: 7L5, 7L6, 7L8, 7M3, 7M4; Anchor sites for self-contained boats only (no camping onshore): 7F1, 7F2, 7M1; Sites with docks for self-sufficient boats or shore camping: 7L5, 7L6, 7M4
Z	7M4 shore sites are subject to early season flooding and may possibly be closed through mid-July. Advance reservations are not allowed for dates prior to 7/15.
AA	Clear Creek BMA (J2): From 4/1 through 7/14, travel is only allowed on the east shore trail from Park Point to Beaverdam Creek. All other trails are closed and off-trail travel is prohibited. Open campsites are 5E2, 5E3, 5E4, and 5E6 (with no travel away from campsite). All others are closed. On July 15, all campsites open and off-trail travel is permitted.
BB	Mariposa Lake 6M3: Hikers must follow Leave No Trace camping practices. There is no trail sign or maker for this site. Hikers should choose a suitable spot at least 100 yds from lake shore. Campfires are not allowed. There is no food pole at the site. Hikers are required to hang their food and odorous items and must find a suitable tree for this purpose.
CC	Two Ocean Plateau BMA (L): March 10 through July 14, and from Aug 22 through Nov 10, travel is allowed only on designated trails (off-trail travel is prohibited). From July 15 through August 21, a permit is required for persons wishing to travel away from designated trails. Contact the BCO or the Snake River Ranger Station for permit information.
DD	Trail Creek Trail between Outlet Creek (site 8O2) and Cabin Creek (site 6B1) is closed from May 15 through July 14 as part of the Lake Spawn BMA.
EE	South Boundary Trail: It is permissible for hikers to camp in the national forest south of Yellowstone boundary west of trailhead 6K3. Contact Bridger-Teton National Forest at 307-739-5500 for more info.
FF	Yellowstone River fords on the Trail Creek Trail: On average these fords are not open and safe to cross until mid-August. When the fords are first opened, the water is typically a little over 3 feet deep and recommended only for experienced hikers. By September, water is <2.5 feet. LOWER FORD of the Yellowstone River is the northernmost ford, between 6B1 and 6B2. The ford is actually two separate fords each around 15 feet wide and separated by an island. The UPPER FORD of the Yellowstone south of site 6B2 is around 25 yards wide and is marked with an orange blaze on the east side and a rock cairn on the west. The crossing follows the shallowest portion of the river along a gravel bar.
GG	Thorofare/South Boundary fords: On average, these fords open and are safe to cross around late July or early August. Confluence Ford near site 6Y4 is around 25 yards wide in relatively slow moving water. The trail is marked from both sides, but hikers will need to scout around to find the obviously shallow riffles just downstream of the confluence. - Yellowstone River ford on the South Boundary Trail, located near site 6Y2, is around 25 yards wide. - Thorofare Ford on the South Boundary Trail, located between sites 6T1 and 6T2 is around 20 yards wide. - Thorofare Ford on the Hawk's Rest Trail is located just north of the boundary and trailhead 6K5. - Bridge across Yellowstone River south of Bridger Lake near the Hawks Rest Patrol Cabin in the national forest. Hikers can cross on this bridge, but getting back to the South Boundary Trail would require a lot of marshy off-trail travel. Plus hikers still must ford Thorofare Creek.

HH	Thorofare trail fords of Beaverdam Creek and Mountain Creek are typically too high to cross before early July.
II	Snake River Ford at the South Entrance is usually not safe to ford until mid-July. Hikers wishing to access the SBT w/o fording the Snake can use the Sheffield Creek TH in Teton NF 3 miles south of the park. All other Snake River and Heart River fords are usually crossable in early to mid-July.
JJ	Heart Lake does not open until July 1. Sites 8H3 and 8J2 typically remain closed until mid-July due to seasonal flooding. All Heart Lake campsites (8H and 8J) are NWF except 8H2, 8H3, and 8J1.
KK	All Bechler sites are not reservable for trips starting prior to July 15. Walk-up permits are allowed prior to August as conditions permit. The Bechler area is typically wet & buggy in July and early August.
LL	Typical ford conditions in Bechler area: All Bechler fords are usually too high to safely cross until mid- to late July. Most fords are 2-3 ft in July and 1-2 feet in August. - Rocky Ford (Bechler River) @ 9C1 - high water before mid-July, tricky footing with slippery rock bottom, cross 30-feet down river from trail
MM	- Bechler Ford @ 9B2, good footing, slow-moving water - Upper Canyon Ford @ 9B8, cross at trail - Lower Canyon Ford @ 9B6, swift water and slippery rock bottom can be difficult, cross down river 30 feet from trail, marked on both sides with orange diamonds. - Boundary Creek @ 9A1, slow-moving, but 2-3 feet in July - Falls River @ 9K2, very wide and swift, don't attempt until August - Falls River @ 9K3, 2-3 ft by mid-July, tricky footing, swift water - Falls River @ 9F2, wide and swift, 3 ft+ before mid-July, 2-2.5 ft by August
NN	Ashton to Bechler is 26 miles. Grassy Lake Rd is closed to motorized vehicles from April 1- June 1, but open to bicyclists, hikers, and skiers.
OO	Many Shoshone Lake sites are subject to flooding, lingering snowpack and lack of a landing area due to high water. Advance reservations not available for trips starting prior to dates listed, however they may be available on a walk-up basis depending on conditions.
PP	All boat access to Shoshone Lake requires paddling up the Lewis River from Lewis Lake. Total length of river is 3 miles. It is possible to paddle the first two miles, but the river becomes too swift to paddle the last mile. You'll have to pull your boat up river while wading in the river. In the early season the river can be swift, cold and deep; a wetsuit is recommended. Also recommend using a suitable length rope attached to the boat so that it can be ferried out and around downfall in the river channel.
QQ	Launching from northeast shore of Lewis Lake is not recommended. The prevailing winds are from the southeast and large waves traveling across the lake are not uncommon.
RR	Ice is usually off Lewis Lake by first week of June and off Shoshone soon afterward.
SS	Motor boats are allowed on Lewis Lake, but not Shoshone or the Lewis River. Motor boaters wishing to travel up the Lewis River to Shoshone Lake must remove their motors from the boat before entering the Lewis River Channel and store them on shore. Most boaters leave their motors chained to the advisory sign at the entrance to the channel.
TT	Cold Mountain Creek north of 8T1 often overflows its banks in the early season (June - early July). Hikers may need to hike 1/2 mile in 2 feet of cold water.
UU	Stock parties must bypass the Shoshone thermal basin.
VV	The trail west of Summit Lake is infrequently maintained. Hikers may encounter significant amount of downfall. Water sources are unreliable to non-existent.
WW	Bikes: OD5 is the only bike-accessible site in the park. OD5 is located along Fountain Flat Road on a mostly level dirt/gravel road between trailheads OK6 and OK5. Bicyclists may also travel to Lone Star via trailhead OK1 to access site OA1. Bikes aren't allowed beyond the end of the old road just before the geyser, but it is less than 1/2 mile to site OA1 from that point.
XX	Thermal areas: Off-trail hiking is discouraged in much of the Old Faithful area due to danger of thermal features and thin crust. Swimming and bathing in thermal pools is prohibited.
YY	Firehole BMA (A): Includes Fountain Freight Rd and Firehole Lake Drive. It is closed 3/10 through the Friday of Memorial Day weekend. The Mary Mountain Trail from the Nez Perce trailhead OK7 to Mary Lake is closed from 3/10 to June 15. Through travel from the east side is not allowed, though you can hike to Mary Lake and back. Streamside use is allowed from the point where the Nez Perce crosses the main road to a point one mile upstream along the creek.

ZZ	Trailhead OK3 is located between the Old Faithful Lodge and the Firehole River in the developed area. Take the first right as you enter the lodge parking area and continue approx 330 yds down the road to get to the trailhead.
AB	Shelf, High, Sportsman, and Crescent Lakes are usually snow-bound and inaccessible until mid-July. The trail between Crescent Lake and High Lake is difficult to follow. Hikers should carry maps/compass or GPS.
AC	Electric Pass remains snow-covered and impassable until early to mid June.
AD	There is an unmaintained trail between 1F1 and 1G3. Direct off-trail travel (following the Gardner River) is allowed between these sites only.
AE	Fawn Pass is usually snow-free by late June to early July.
AF	Bighorn Pass may be snow-covered into early or mid-July. Foot parties will be able to cross this before stock parties will.
AG	Trailhead WK7 is outside the park at milepost 10. The trail is accessed near the cemetery where hikers need to follow the well-worn trail for about 1/3 mile before they cross into the park.
AH	The Trail to Trilobite Lake receives minimal maintenance and can be difficult to follow.
AI	The Solfatara Trail is infrequently maintained and hikers can expect to encounter downfall.
AJ	Campsites are at or near Gallatin Bear Management Area. No off-trail travel to the east of these campsites.

Appendix 1: Yellowstone Lakes

How to Use This Table

This table provides a listing of all of the named lakes in Yellowstone. Of the more than 2,100 lakes and ponds identified in the park, just less than 200 have been named (officially). Of those, 164 whose size exceeds two acres are found in this list (with a handful of exceptions for popular smaller lakes and ponds).

- **NAME**: Official or commonly accepted name of each lake
- **RANK**: Rank in size (in terms of surface acreage) among size among all lakes (not just those named)
- **ACRES**: Size of lake in surface acreage
- **PERIM**: Lake perimeter in feet
- **LAT**: Latitude
- **LONG**: Longitude
- **ELEV**: Elevation (in feet ASL)
- **DEPTH**: Depth of lake in feet. Depth is provided in terms of average, if known. "M=##" is the maximum depth of the lake in feet, if known. "Seasonal" indicates lake contains water early in the season, usually during spring snow melt, but is usually/often dry by later in the season.
- **FISH**: Species of fish that can be found in the lake, if any. This is subject to change, and is based on the best information available at the time the book was printed. There are other minor species that may also be found in some areas that aren't included in this list. See table below for fish type codes.[1]
- **NOTES**: Any relevant notes about the lake, especially with regard to closures, late openings, etc.

Code	Fish	Code	Fish
AG	Arctic Grayling*	LT	Lake Trout
BrnT	Brown Trout	MW	Mountain Whitefish*
BrkT	Brook Trout	R/C	Hybrid Rainbow/Cutthroat
CT	Cutthroat Trout*	RS	Redside Shiner*
LC	Lake Chub	RT	Rainbow Trout
LND	Long-nosed Dace*	UC	Utah Chub*
LNS	Long-nosed Sucker	US	Utah Sucker*

LAKE/POND	RANK	ACRES	PERIM	LAT	LONG	ELEV	DEPTH	FISH	NOTES
Ace Of Hearts Lake	123	5.9	2616	44.84147	-110.65501	8101	Unk	None	
Africa Lake	189	1.7	1157	44.94976	-110.71334	6813	Unk	None	
Alder Lake	12	120.2	9349	44.33681	-110.31194	7742	12/M=20	CT, LNS, RS	
Aldridge Lake	49	24.2	5551	45.09105	-110.81160	5873	Unk	None	
Aster Lake	65	14.6	2956	44.30105	-110.55876	8208	Unk	None	
Basin Creek Lake	85	10.5	3241	44.20798	-110.52560	7420	M=17	CT, RS?	
Beach Lake	14	91.6	8383	44.54149	-110.57061	8146	M=30	None	
Beach Springs Lake	24	38.8	6902	44.55066	-110.29666	7735	2/M=41	LC	
Beaver Lake	50	23.8	5967	44.81600	-110.73110	7385	Marsh	None	
Beula Lake	11	130.9	10845	44.15976	-110.76588	7406	M=36	CT	
Big Bear Lake (East)	163	3.2	2161	44.55843	-111.01477	7998	Unk	None	
Big Bear Lake (West)	157	3.7	3983	44.55659	-111.01734	8026	Unk	None	
Big Beaver Pond	159	3.5	1896	44.99829	-110.71842	6369	6/M=13	None	
Black Warrior Lake	198	1.2	974	44.54421	-110.78711	7372	Unk	None	
Blacktail Pond (Center)	209	0.3	425	44.95514	-110.60273	6610	Seasonal	None	Closed until 7/1
Blacktail Pond (East)	152	4.0	1796	44.95606	-110.60121	6610	11/M=26	CT, BrkT	Closed until 7/1
Blacktail Pond (West)	184	2.0	1726	44.95413	-110.60395	6610	Seasonal	None	Closed until 7/1
Buck Lake	126	5.7	2340	44.90438	-110.12559	6983	M=37	None	
Buffalo Lake	77	12.7	3528	44.32916	-111.07416	7687	6/M=16	None	
Cache Lake	76	12.9	2734	44.98679	-110.80527	8038	4/M=12	None	
Canoe Lake	192	1.5	1405	44.79119	-109.93901	9151	Unk	None	
Cascade Lake	36	29.9	4573	44.75162	-110.52285	7990	M=27	CT, AG	
Chickadee Lake	46	25.0	5165	44.46798	-110.61623	8334	Unk	None	
Clear Lake	172	2.6	1402	44.71360	-110.47972	7780	Unk	None	
Crag Lake	118	6.3	2199	45.05788	-110.97868	8776	M=21	None	
Crater Lake #1	146	4.5	1752	44.53578	-110.87690	7523	Seasonal	None	
Crater Lake #2	186	1.9	1151	44.53695	-110.87689	7535	Seasonal	None	
Crater Lake #3	208	0.5	595	44.53750	-110.87452	7511	Seasonal	None	
Crater Lake #4	160	3.4	1476	44.53607	-110.87405	7475	Seasonal	None	
Crater Lake #5	190	1.7	991	44.53477	-110.87528	7489	Seasonal	None	

LAKE/POND	RANK	ACRES	PERIM	LAT	LONG	ELEV	DEPTH	FISH	NOTES
Crescent Lake	64	14.7	3550	45.06049	-110.99380	8577	M=48	None	
Crevice Lake	55	18.7	3426	45.00064	-110.57813	5555	58/M=98	None	
Cygnet Lake #1	121	5.9	3367	44.66829	-110.61770	8291	M=11	None	
Cygnet Lake #2	137	4.8	2941	44.66672	-110.61500	8291	M=7	None	
Cygnet Lake #3	105	7.0	3315	44.66539	-110.61450	8291	M=11	None	
Cygnet Lake #4	133	5.3	4056	44.66268	-110.61734	8291	M=9	None	
Cygnet Lake #5	43	26.2	8990	44.65949	-110.61334	8291	M=17	None	
DeLacy Lake (East)	45	25.2	6693	44.47780	-110.70596	8550	M=42	None	
DeLacy Lake (West)	33	32.7	8151	44.47834	-110.71391	8550	M=50	None	
Delusion Lake	5	567.9	32253	44.39956	-110.45763	7819	M=30	None	
Dewdrop Lake	112	6.6	2551	44.67730	-110.36942	8180	12/M=25	None	
Divide Lake	95	8.7	2584	44.91198	-111.05119	7300	3/M=7	None	
Dryad Lake	26	38.3	5130	44.54584	-110.51155	8301	8/M=25	None	
Duck Lake	27	36.2	5074	44.42074	-110.58027	7787	M=60	None	
Echo Lake (Arvid Lake)	147	4.3	1595	44.82709	-110.87576	8881	Unk	Unknown	
Eleanor Lake	181	2.2	1594	44.46985	-110.14021	8530	M=13	CT	
Ephemeral Pond	167	2.9	1443	44.97144	-110.45267	5873	Seasonal	None	
Fawn Lake	162	3.3	1584	44.95330	-110.79939	7820	8/M=18	BrkT	
Feather Lake	61	16.4	3787	44.54429	-110.83586	7200	M=30	None	
Fern Lake (Was 2nd Wapiti Lake)	13	96.6	8983	44.67795	-110.27582	8241	13/M=25	CT	
Firehole Lake	203	0.6	736	44.54420	-110.78471	7388	Unk	None	
Fish Lake (Outside The Park)	34	30.8	4433	44.12946	-110.93704	6460	Unk	Unknown	
Floating Island Lake	129	5.6	2034	44.94191	-110.45035	6600	M=10	None	
Forest Lake	94	8.8	2398	44.16351	-110.63831	7419	4/M=8	None	
Foster Lake	155	3.7	1955	44.87371	-110.16771	6686	9/M=19	None	
Frost Lake	62	15.5	4446	44.61849	-110.03330	9530	Unk	None	
Gallatin Lake	48	24.5	4011	44.85560	-110.88276	8834	M=47	None	
Geode Lake	81	10.8	3433	44.97743	-110.48936	5980	4/M=11	None	
Glade Lake	98	8.0	2346	44.34962	-110.08807	9700	9/M=15	None	
Goose Lake	28	35.2	6492	44.54239	-110.84287	7212	M=31	RT, BrkT?	

LAKE/POND	RANK	ACRES	PERIM	LAT	LONG	ELEV	DEPTH	FISH	NOTES
Gooseneck Lake	130	5.6	2939	44.52032	-110.84763	7356	Unk	RT	
Gosling Lake	148	4.3	1627	44.54545	-110.83984	7217	Unk	None	
Grebe Lake	10	131.3	9593	44.75194	-110.55796	8023	M=32	RT, AG	
Grizzly Lake	9	148.2	18026	44.80745	-110.77477	7507	M=36	BrkT	
Hals Lake	156	3.7	1706	44.91940	-110.79178	7684	Unk	None	
Harlequin Lake	84	10.6	2942	44.64407	-110.89109	7290	4/M=11	None	
Heart Lake	4	2186	57781	44.26644	-110.48251	7466	M=180	CT, LT, MW, UC, US, RS, BrnT, RT	
Hering Lake	18	75.9	11216	44.14577	-110.76203	7405	11/M=44	CT	
Hicks Lake	128	5.7	1820	44.53879	-110.83159	7222	Unk	None	
Hidden Lake	21	58.7	14588	44.38164	-110.46050	7835	Unk	None	
Hidden Lake (Outside The Park)	96	8.7	3143	45.06413	-110.27382	7723	Unk	Unknown	
High Lake	100	7.8	2521	45.05646	-110.93840	8788	M=180	CT	
Hot Lake	153	3.9	2380	44.54407	-110.78914	7367	Unk	Unknown	
Ice Lake	20	62.6	9542	44.72121	-110.62760	7950	22/M=53	None	
Ice Reservoir	174	2.5	1360	45.03170	-110.75044	5470	Unk	None	
Indian Pond	42	26.8	3988	44.55797	-110.32462	7775	M=72	CT, LC, LNS	
Isa Lake	206	0.5	926	44.44056	-110.71980	8262	Unk	None	
Joffe Lake	177	2.4	1623	44.94760	-110.70130	6483	M=9	BrkT	
Junction Lake	89	9.5	3316	44.93457	-110.38411	6314	Unk	Unknown	
Lake Of The Woods	40	27.3	4470	44.80045	-110.71438	7762	6/M=23	None	
Lake Wyodaho	74	13.2	3088	44.23263	-110.98627	6820	14/M=33	None	
Leech Lake	113	6.6	2219	45.04783	-111.00105	8704	Unk	Unknown	
Lewis Lake	3	2773	53196	44.30412	-110.62867	7779	M=108	LT, BrnT, UC, RS, LND	
Lily Pad Lake (Canyon, colloq)	182	2.2	1501	44.71835	-110.47091	7795	Unk	Unknown	
Lilypad Lake	19	66.5	9431	44.16733	-111.01007	6420	9/M=26	None	
Little Beaver Pond	193	1.5	976	44.99665	-110.72392	6551	9/M=18	None	
Little Robinson Lake	90	9.4	2817	44.23554	-111.03357	6535	Unk	BrkT	
Little Slide Lake	200	1.1	879	45.00251	-110.70077	5730	M=9	None	
Little Trumpeter Lake	92	9.2	2356	44.91728	-110.37398	6106	7/M=10	None	
Lost Lake (Mammoth)	205	0.5	732	44.96855	-110.69347	6076	Seasonal	None	

LAKE/POND	RANK	ACRES	PERIM	LAT	LONG	ELEV	DEPTH	FISH	NOTES
Lost Lake (Roosevelt)	103	7.3	3297	44.90947	-110.43007	6770	18/M=40	None	
Lower Basin Lake	97	8.6	2424	44.53610	-110.82470	7250	Unk	None	
Madison Lake	149	4.1	1684	44.34856	-110.86485	8211	Seasonal	None	
Mallard Lake	30	34.4	5615	44.47783	-110.77595	8030	M=30	None	
Mammoth Reservoir	171	2.7	1420	44.94920	-110.70467	6636	Unk	BrkT	
Mariposa Lake	69	14.0	3802	44.15175	-110.24128	9200	4/M=7	CT, R/C	
Mary Lake	57	18.1	4533	44.60342	-110.63853	8280	17/M=35	None	
McBride Lake	41	27.0	7110	44.96339	-110.25363	6645	M=22	CT, LC	
Middle Trilobite Lake	102	7.3	2226	44.82926	-110.84386	8798	Unk	None	
Mirror Lake	68	14.2	4345	44.73530	-110.16372	8960	6/M=13	None	
North Twin Lake	83	10.6	2819	44.77481	-110.73761	7850	M=11	None	
Nuphar Lake	202	0.9	779	44.72777	-110.69951	7527	Unk	None	
Nuthatch Lake	73	13.2	2892	44.45902	-110.61787	8437	Unk	None	
Nymph Lake	71	13.4	3856	44.75175	-110.72725	7499	2/M=70	None	
Obsidian Lake	56	18.7	4794	44.83829	-110.71671	7743	4/M=25	None	
Old Mammoth Reservoir	199	1.2	951	44.96661	-110.70306	6376	Unk	None	
Outlet Lake	67	14.4	3712	44.27160	-110.39286	7778	3/M=5	CT, R/C?	
Phantom Lake	194	1.5	981	44.95548	-110.52736	6800	Seasonal	None	
Phoneline Lake	47	24.7	4080	44.14171	-111.05875	6374	Unk	None	
Plateau Lake	201	1.0	1092	44.46086	-110.99933	8830	Seasonal	None	
Pocket Lake	66	14.4	3246	44.39571	-110.74166	8150	M=24	CT, BrkT	
Rainbow Lake	143	4.6	1967	45.02217	-110.74069	5876	3/M=9	None	
Rainbow Lake	180	2.2	1473	45.02349	-110.74272	5863	Unk	None	
Rainbow Lake	187	1.8	1204	45.02131	-110.73824	5891	Unk	None	
Rainy Lake	195	1.5	1141	44.90914	-110.40221	6380	Unk	None	
Ranger Lake	22	55.8	9016	44.22037	-110.96622	6992	38/M=98	RT	
Ribbon Lake	106	6.9	2266	44.72435	-110.44792	7821	M=19	RT	
Riddle Lake	6	178.5	14036	44.35697	-110.54827	7926	M=27	CT, LNS, RS	
Robinson Lake	23	41.7	6622	44.16774	-111.07225	6500	4/M=8	None	
Rosa Lake	173	2.5	1352	44.81812	-110.87039	9190	Unk	None	

LAKE/POND	RANK	ACRES	PERIM	LAT	LONG	ELEV	DEPTH	FISH	NOTES
Ruddy Duck Pond	185	2.0	1414	44.91431	-110.39280	6264	Seasonal	None	
Rush Lake	170	2.9	1316	44.56167	-110.82662	7226	Seasonal	None	
Rye Pond	204	0.6	624	44.95991	-110.69329	6206	Seasonal	None	
Scaup Lake	125	5.9	2312	44.43058	-110.76704	7930	M=10	None	
Sedge Lake	161	3.4	1956	45.06349	-110.98590	8873	Unk	None	
Shelf Lake	135	5.0	1955	45.09219	-111.01260	8700	M=40	None	
Sheridan Lake	59	17.3	3625	44.24382	-110.50547	7395	2/M=5	CT, RS	
Shoshone Lake	2	7067	127127	44.37070	-110.71891	7790	M=205	LT, BrnT, BrkT, UC, RS	
Shrimp Lake	183	2.0	1122	44.90555	-110.13094	7078	M=19	None	
Sieve Lake	196	1.4	1022	44.73071	-110.70067	7522	Unk	None	
Slide Lake	117	6.3	2289	45.00394	-110.69911	5691	M=17	None	
Small Lake	175	2.5	1269	44.92992	-110.90125	9078	M=9	None	
Solfatara Lake	122	5.9	1960	44.69570	-110.58484	8211	Unk	None	
South Boundary Lake	60	16.5	3736	44.13354	-110.75583	7400	Unk	None	
South Twin Lake	58	17.4	4067	44.77079	-110.73472	8000	M=29	None	
Sportsman Lake	141	4.6	1712	45.01577	-110.90281	7750	5/M=26	CT	
Summit Lake (Mammoth)	207	0.5	612	44.95915	-110.73562	7474	Seasonal	None	
Summit Lake (Old Faithful)	35	30.4	4300	44.41468	-110.94026	8630	8/M=21	None	
Swan Lake	25	38.3	5098	44.91957	-110.73578	7268	M=3	None	
Sylvan Lake	39	29.2	8147	44.47950	-110.16082	8460	7/M=21	CT, LNS	
Tanager Lake	51	23.7	5051	44.13495	-110.68453	6971	M=11	RS	
Teal Lake	99	7.9	4035	44.46065	-110.75434	8446	Unk	None	
Tern Lake (Was "Turn Lakes")	17	78.2	20123	44.66595	-110.26593	8260	E=1/W=5	None	
The Reservoir	197	1.3	1093	44.73150	-110.70963	7491	Unk	None	
Trail Lake	15	86.9	8684	44.27842	-110.17389	7776	M=12	CT, LNS, RS	
Trilobite Lake	86	10.0	2587	44.82935	-110.83546	8362	21/M=43	BrkT	
Trout Lake	75	13.0	2982	44.90055	-110.12972	6957	M=17	RT, R/C	
Trumpeter Lake	53	22.2	4922	44.91591	-110.36816	6126	5/M=10	None	
Turbid Lake	8	157.4	12078	44.54938	-110.26017	7835	17/M=125	None	
Unnamed Lake On Canyon Hill	63	15.4	4065	44.72959	-110.53589	8153	Unk	None	

LAKE/POND	RANK	ACRES	PERIM	LAT	LONG	ELEV	DEPTH	FISH	NOTES
Unnamed Lake On Mt. Everts	54	20.5	4099	44.96042	-110.62494	7280	Unk	Unknown	
Unnamed Lake SE Of 9A7	44	25.9	8021	44.18124	-111.06417	6520	Unk	Unknown	
Unnamed Lake S Of Delusion Lake	37	29.5	5610	44.37431	-110.45300	7833	Unk	None	
Unnamed Lake SSW Of 5E1	52	22.9	8210	44.30626	-110.19009	7738	Unk	Unknown	
Unnamed Lake SW of Delusion Lake	72	13.3	3342	44.37695	-110.48174	7898	Unk	None	
Unnamed Lake West Of 9C1	16	84.0	15960	44.17940	-111.04454	6510	Unk	Unknown	
Upper Trilobite Lake	176	2.4	1383	44.82486	-110.84510	8881	Unk	None	
Wapiti Lake	70	13.9	5125	44.71875	-110.25762	8437	6/M=15	None	
West Tern Lake	32	33.2	4848	44.66245	-110.27207	8267	Unk	None	
White Lake	7	167.0	21565	44.65236	-110.27482	8250	N=22/S=7	CT	
Winegar Lake	38	29.5	4927	44.13600	-110.96080	6460	12/M=26	RS?	
Wolf Lake	31	33.6	5355	44.74723	-110.58508	7999	M=32	RT, AG	
Wrangler Lake	29	34.6	4598	44.68336	-110.43551	7890	16/M=33	None	
Yellowstone Lake	1	84353	756893	44.43366	-110.36599	7745	140/M=407	CT, LT, RS, LC, LNS	

Appendix 2: Rivers, Streams, and Creeks

ow to Use This Table

here are well over 10,000 identified river, stream, and creek segments within Yellowstone ational Park. The vast majority of these have not been named or are (unnamed) tributaries named rivers, streams, and creeks. The following table provides data on 268 named vers, streams, and creeks.[1]

- **STREAM/RIVER NAME:** Officially recognized name of the stream, river, or creek (as recognized by the USGS Board of Geographic Names)
- **ORIG LAT:** Headwater latitude (where the body of water begins)
- **ORIG LONG:** Headwater longitude
- **TERM LAT:** Termination point latitude (where the body of water ends)
- **TERM LONG:** Termination point longitude
- **FISH:** List of fish species believed to be present in the body of water, according to the best information available at the time the book was printed. There may be other types in these waters as well. Use the table below to determine fish type.

CODE	FISH	CODE	FISH
AG	Arctic Grayling*	LT	Lake Trout
BrnT	Brown Trout	MW	Mountain Whitefish*
BrkT	Brook Trout	R/C	Hybrid Rainbow/Cutthroat
CT	Cutthroat Trout*	RS	Redside Shiner*
LC	Lake Chub	RT	Rainbow Trout
LND	Long-nosed Dace*	UC	Utah Chub*
LNS	Long-nosed Sucker	US	Utah Sucker*

ome people might be asking the question, "What good is the origination and termination titude and longitude information to me?" This information allows you to determine here the river, etc., begins and ends. You can almost invariably trace the body of water on satellite image or a topographic map if you know where it starts and where it ends, so this formation is provided to allow you to have some basic idea of where these streams are ocated. There's really no other way to provide any meaningful information about these in nis kind of format.

STREAM/RIVER NAME	ORIG LAT	ORIG LONG	TERM LAT	TERM LONG	FISH
Agate Creek	44.87403	-110.30698	44.85021	-110.36023	CT, R/C
Aldridge Creek	45.08087	-110.82176	45.10176	-110.82120	None
Alluvium Creek	44.38082	-110.21615	44.38540	-110.24158	CT
Alum Creek	44.66959	-110.49832	44.66951	-110.49877	CT, RS
Amethyst Creek	44.89284	-110.24948	44.87464	-110.26152	CT
Amphitheater Creek	44.97451	-110.00515	44.92089	-110.09527	CT
Antelope Creek	44.89435	-110.38231	44.79557	-110.41103	BrkT
Arnica Creek	44.48005	-110.60306	44.47250	-110.53500	CT, LNS
Arrow Canyon Creek	44.83796	-110.62191	44.78732	-110.63367	BrkT
Aster Creek	44.26751	-110.63363	44.26824	-110.56210	BrkT, BrnT
Astringent Creek	44.58706	-110.24139	44.63084	-110.27279	None
Bacon Rind Creek	44.96109	-111.06701	44.93007	-111.12523	CT, RT, R/C
Badger Creek	44.20976	-110.18941	44.24822	-110.13099	CT
Bartlett Slough	44.18120	-111.05913	44.19075	-111.01281	None
Basin Creek	44.21970	-110.51255	44.21951	-110.51191	CT, RS
Bassett Creek	45.12249	-110.70574	45.11017	-110.79076	None
Bear Creek	45.03074	-110.66575	44.55029	-110.26177	CT
Bear Creek, North Fork	45.12497	-110.65892	45.07367	-110.63118	CT
Beaver Creek	45.08422	-110.40213	44.34227	-110.48147	CT, US, MS, RS
Beaverdam Creek	44.32939	-110.17373	44.32842	-110.17680	CT
Bechler River	44.28920	-110.89356	44.14817	-110.99580	CT, RT, R/C
Big Spring Creek	44.71906	-110.48753	44.73185	-110.48809	None
Big Thumb Creek	44.40466	-110.56681	44.41983	-110.66249	CT
Black Butte Creek	45.03370	-111.11428	45.07118	-111.06727	CT
Black Canyon Thirsty Creek	44.47122	-111.12416	44.41880	-110.96023	
Blacktail Deer Creek	44.85986	-110.57529	44.99624	-110.57606	CT, BrkT
Bluff Creek	44.62296	-110.32358	44.66780	-110.37198	CT?
Bog Creek	44.70449	-110.33303	44.68183	-110.40352	CT?
Boundary Creek	44.40106	-111.04916	44.18076	-111.00066	CT, R/C
Bridge Creek	44.53020	-110.43377	44.53238	-110.49383	CT
Broad Creek	44.79058	-110.35399	44.64276	-110.26438	CT
Brundage Creek	45.07704	-110.42421	45.12493	-110.44324	
Buffalo Creek	45.17526	-110.25448	44.94937	-110.30709	
Buffalo Fork	44.63768	-110.14275	44.70665	-110.10924	RT
Burnt Creek	44.77860	-110.26275	44.83337	-110.34332	None
Cabin Creek	44.30776	-110.11188	44.30228	-110.17212	
Cache Creek	44.83076	-110.13985	44.82828	-110.13319	CT
Calf Creek	44.12490	-110.89742	44.12507	-110.88946	CT, RT, R/C
Calfee Creek	44.79326	-109.97028	44.78106	-110.11540	CT
Campanula Creek	44.82382	-110.96250	44.78015	-111.06306	BrkT, RT
Canyon Creek	44.66507	-110.69640	44.64778	-110.77241	MG, BrnT, BrkT, RT
Carnelian Creek	44.85638	-110.45549	44.77569	-110.48847	BrkT, RT
Cascade Creek	44.74564	-110.53509	44.12474	-110.84206	CT, MG
Castle Creek	44.68990	-110.65727	44.71995	-110.68185	None
Chalcedony Creek	44.86723	-110.20419	44.82156	-110.23928	CT
Chipmunk Creek	44.19541	-110.19712	44.28748	-110.28815	CT, LNS
Cinnabar Creek	45.09554	-110.88590	45.10995	-110.82045	

REAM/RIVER NAME	ORIG LAT	ORIG LONG	TERM LAT	TERM LONG	FISH
ear Creek	44.45914	-110.14025	44.47497	-110.28212	CT, LNS
ematis Creek	44.97512	-110.70232	44.98687	-110.76088	None
ff Creek	44.16975	-110.11165	44.20050	-110.00852	CT
over Creek	44.74680	-110.09701	44.73161	-110.13587	CT
ld Creek	44.56468	-110.14411	44.67734	-110.05701	CT
ld Mountain Creek	44.33107	-110.82184	44.34550	-110.78777	
lumbine Creek	44.41983	-110.13305	44.40034	-110.25444	CT, LNS
ttongrass Creek	44.63680	-110.38207	44.68102	-110.47699	CT
ttonwood Creek	45.12497	-110.87930	44.99331	-110.51765	CT?
ugar Creek	44.69152	-110.81389	44.70905	-111.00141	CT, MS
ulter Creek	44.13527	-110.51865	44.12424	-110.50640	
wan Creek	44.62475	-110.63906	44.59503	-110.69421	BrkT, BrnT, RT
yote Creek	44.99479	-110.42869	44.15165	-110.04429	CT
awfish Creek	44.16513	-110.69118	44.15039	-110.66804	CT
evice Creek	45.08714	-110.52614	45.01032	-110.58777	CT
ooked Creek	44.18019	-110.25018	44.15958	-110.33821	
ystal Creek	44.87787	-110.31705	44.91472	-110.32319	CT
ub Creek	44.48939	-110.28339	44.51454	-110.14515	CT
utoff Creek	45.02577	-110.11908	45.02649	-110.18080	CT
aly Creek	45.07144	-111.08275	45.04735	-111.14202	CT?
arroch Creek	45.12497	-110.55484	45.10876	-110.60027	
eaf Jim Creek	45.05524	-110.83800	45.07633	-110.85415	
eep Creek	44.84326	-110.35751	44.78871	-110.21331	CT
eLacy Creek	44.47284	-110.68830	44.42516	-110.70122	BrkT, BrnT
elusion Creek	44.36022	-110.48938	44.40958	-110.41771	
xon Creek	45.11114	-110.92070	45.11225	-110.85594	
ogshead Creek	44.31513	-110.60547	44.38304	-110.61476	None
y Creek	44.43497	-110.69767	44.42639	-110.65676	None
uck Creek	44.78067	-111.09305	44.77424	-111.12578	BrkT, BrnT, RT, MW
agle Creek	45.02938	-110.69363	45.06580	-110.67821	None
ectric Creek	45.01348	-110.84013	45.03825	-110.79455	CT?
k Antler Creek	44.57599	-110.46403	44.64059	-110.45477	CT
k Creek	45.10009	-110.32597	44.90883	-110.48730	BrkT
k Tongue Creek	44.99350	-110.13773	44.99126	-110.20118	CT
scarpment Creek	44.18449	-110.00074	44.16669	-110.11198	CT
xplorers Creek	44.44218	-110.24968	44.47252	-110.27882	CT
airy Creek	44.49591	-110.89447	44.56292	-110.84107	BrnT, RT, BrkT
alcon Creek	44.11843	-110.15933	44.13831	-110.12134	CT
all Creek	44.35138	-110.80035	44.34160	-110.82493	BrkT
alls River	44.22270	-110.74536	44.12494	-111.02086	RT, CT, R/C, RS
an Creek	44.95380	-111.05779	44.99207	-110.97056	CT, MW
an Creek, East Fork	44.98154	-110.96171	44.98127	-110.96183	
an Creek, North Fork	45.04011	-110.91560	44.99207	-110.97056	
awn Creek	44.92883	-110.88733	44.92919	-110.88840	BrkT
erris Fork	44.28893	-110.89304	44.27324	-110.80866	None
rehole River	44.63650	-110.86561	44.34050	-110.87642	RT, BrkT, MW
int Creek	44.78748	-110.11889	44.75542	-110.16527	CT

STREAM/RIVER NAME	ORIG LAT	ORIG LONG	TERM LAT	TERM LONG	FISH
Flood Creek	44.72987	-110.72303	44.77392	-110.73601	None
Forest Creek	44.26006	-110.56347	44.16835	-110.59910	CT
Gallatin River	45.03891	-111.12198	44.91815	-110.93894	CT, MW, RT, BrnT, R/C, MG
Gardner River	44.97075	-110.68189	44.89341	-110.74922	RT, BrnT, BrkT, CT, MW
Garnet Creek	44.96359	-110.47531	44.96341	-110.47507	None
Geode Creek	44.98673	-110.49486	44.95086	-110.48716	None
Geyser Creek	44.68587	-110.69907	44.69742	-110.74435	None
Gibbon River	44.71772	-110.72668	44.64145	-110.86455	BrkT, BrnT, RT, CT, MW, MG
Glade Creek	44.75768	-110.39492	44.13648	-110.75922	CT
Glen Creek	44.97101	-110.79507	44.95121	-110.68160	BrkT
Gneiss Creek	44.78015	-111.06306	44.77844	-110.93673	BrkT, BrnT
Grassy Creek	45.05544	-110.24015	44.13453	-110.82393	RT, CT, BrkT
Grayling Creek	44.86676	-110.96258	44.80548	-111.12578	CT, RT, R/C, BrnT, MW
Gregg Fork	44.31819	-110.81945	44.28920	-110.89356	CT
Grizzly Creek	45.12496	-110.39551	44.60373	-110.32887	None
Grouse Creek	44.28336	-110.33647	44.22442	-110.34230	CT, LNS?
Harebell Creek	44.13444	-110.51344	44.13209	-110.41542	CT
Hatchery Creek (Lake)	44.75987	-110.53686	44.54878	-110.40471	CT
Heart River	44.21202	-110.48557	44.24956	-110.44783	CT, MW, RS, UC, US
Hellroaring Creek	45.12239	-110.38536	44.97404	-110.47632	CT
Hellroaring Creek, East Fork	45.11273	-110.31679	45.12239	-110.38536	CT
Herron Creek	44.47538	-110.72792	44.44615	-110.70357	BrkT?
Hoppe Creek	45.08927	-110.83570	45.05865	-110.82931	
Hornaday Creek (Plateau Crk)	44.96543	-110.22763	44.96543	-110.22763	
Horse Creek	45.06883	-110.42122	45.12497	-110.49014	
Horse Creek, West Fork	45.12311	-110.51607	45.11316	-110.48516	
Hotel Creek	44.55791	-110.41229	44.54886	-110.40182	None
Howell Creek	44.24242	-110.04754	44.32171	-110.00223	CT
Indian Creek	44.89006	-110.74274	44.83140	-110.86494	BrkT
Iron Spring Creek	44.48146	-110.85607	44.48146	-110.85607	
Iron Spring Creek, West Fork	44.46102	-110.85344	44.40849	-110.89942	
Jasper Creek	44.89539	-110.25484	44.87540	-110.29565	CT
Juniper Creek	44.50754	-110.63999	44.57771	-110.68200	None
Lamar River	44.89417	-110.24657	44.67035	-110.02937	CT, RT, R/C, LNS, MS
Landslide Creek	45.00978	-110.74068	45.04571	-110.74562	None
Lava Creek	44.78572	-110.58572	44.96109	-110.67431	BrkT, BrnT, RT
Lemonade Creek	44.78946	-110.72030	44.81011	-110.73616	None
Lewis River	44.34463	-110.65208	44.21409	-110.65409	BrkT, BrnT, LT, CT, RS
Lion Creek	45.08055	-110.94713	45.09554	-110.88590	
Little Arnica Creek	44.47264	-110.54556	44.46341	-110.60659	
Little Blacktail Deer Creek	44.88590	-110.51527	44.95398	-110.58981	
Little Buffalo Creek	44.99483	-110.35301	44.96141	-110.43360	CT?
Little Cottonwood Creek	45.02706	-110.47494	44.98850	-110.48774	None
Little Firehole River	44.48299	-110.85458	44.42617	-110.94180	BrkT, BrnT, CT, RT
Little Lamar River	44.65775	-109.90935	44.65571	-109.91268	CT
Little Robinson Creek	44.19073	-111.08166	44.29059	-111.05887	BrkT
Little Tepee Creek	44.83124	-111.11756	44.83321	-111.12578	

TREAM/RIVER NAME	ORIG LAT	ORIG LONG	TERM LAT	TERM LONG	FISH
ttle Thumb Creek	44.43666	-110.57937	44.44179	-110.62857	CT
ttle Trail Creek	45.08463	-110.72014	45.07034	-110.77116	
ttles Fork	44.34452	-110.84766	44.29989	-110.87074	None
odge Creek	44.55975	-110.40292	44.55626	-110.38858	CT
ost Creek (Tower)	44.97120	-110.68209	44.88328	-110.49263	BrkT
upine Creek	44.84882	-110.58591	44.94016	-110.62817	BrkT
nx Creek	44.17080	-110.12006	44.17598	-110.17397	CT
adison River	44.72465	-111.11931	44.63733	-110.88969	RT, BrnT, BrkT, MW, MS, CT, MG
adison River, South Fork	44.48569	-111.02305	44.51389	-111.12578	
agpie Creek	44.62189	-110.70660	44.59179	-110.73253	BrnT, BrkT, RT
allard Creek	44.50682	-110.83503	44.47657	-110.77876	None
aple Creek	44.77343	-111.12554	44.73731	-111.03304	BrkT, BrnT, MS
eadow Creek	44.42560	-110.28968	44.43579	-110.21030	CT
iddle Creek	44.48916	-110.00124	44.48794	-110.00556	CT, RT, R/C
igration Creek	44.93817	-111.12555	44.93514	-111.09624	CT
ill Creek	45.09401	-110.88698	45.05254	-110.92430	
iller Creek	44.76505	-110.08234	44.75142	-109.98301	CT
irror Fork (Timothy Creek)	44.70234	-110.12248	44.75371	-110.15344	None
ist Creek	44.64541	-110.07224	44.59429	-110.15480	CT?
ol Heron Creek	44.99427	-110.88390	45.12784	-110.80515	CT
loose Creek	44.31249	-110.75762	44.35925	-110.69718	BrkT, BrnT?
loss Creek	44.71194	-110.34576	44.75714	-110.39641	None
lountain Ash Creek	44.19114	-110.87504	44.18925	-110.87814	RT, CT, R/C
lountain Creek	44.24151	-110.01352	44.22572	-110.12027	CT
lyriad Creek	44.44640	-110.82520	44.46397	-110.83456	None
ez Perce Creek	44.58091	-110.83215	44.57780	-110.62214	BrnT, RT, BrkT
o Name Creek	44.35091	-110.40642	44.36846	-110.40565	CT
bsidian Creek	44.88590	-110.73168	44.78581	-110.74015	BrkT
pal Creek	44.78786	-110.19534	44.83639	-110.17151	CT?
tter Creek	44.66420	-110.58944	44.70168	-110.50593	None
utlet Creek	44.26946	-110.39473	44.24739	-110.44539	CT
uzel Creek	44.22677	-110.97679	44.35177	-110.88912	RT, CT, R/C
xbow Creek	44.90393	-110.49956	44.99087	-110.56160	BrkT
almer Creek	45.05263	-110.58709	45.04881	-110.65547	
anther Creek	44.88512	-110.79195	44.88512	-110.79195	BrkT
ark Creek	44.70712	-110.69940	44.71951	-110.72198	None
assage Creek	44.19762	-110.25882	44.24527	-110.27641	CT
ebble Creek	45.05002	-110.02382	44.91074	-110.10968	CT, RT, R/C
elican Creek	44.69743	-110.18772	44.55629	-110.36094	CT, LNS, RS
helps Creek	45.05254	-110.70378	45.07053	-110.69913	
hillips Fork	44.28920	-110.89356	44.32961	-110.88053	None
hlox Creek	44.18302	-110.16518	44.21180	-110.12399	CT
ine Creek	45.06610	-110.57729	45.07834	-110.62833	
lateau Creek (Snake River)	44.15851	-110.22529	44.15993	-110.23659	CT?
ole Creek	45.06496	-110.63825	45.08212	-110.65804	
olecat Creek	44.12494	-110.71092	44.25726	-110.73871	CT? Poss others
rimrose Creek	44.97702	-110.70320	44.97992	-110.71385	None

STREAM/RIVER NAME	ORIG LAT	ORIG LONG	TERM LAT	TERM LONG	FISH
Proposition Creek	44.17754	-110.80933	44.16543	-110.92728	RT, CT, R/C
Quartz Creek	44.88470	-110.33010	44.87211	-110.36410	None
Rabbit Creek	44.52137	-110.81176	44.51627	-110.83257	None
Raven Creek	44.59772	-110.21903	44.68982	-110.18118	CT, LNS
Red Creek	44.17336	-110.56360	44.24063	-110.54655	CT?
Reese Creek	45.06683	-110.77220	44.98659	-110.80346	CT?
Rescue Creek	44.98170	-110.64004	44.97171	-110.58899	BrkT?
Richards Creek	44.76970	-111.07352	44.76324	-111.00279	BrkT, BrnT?
Robinson Creek	44.16566	-111.12538	44.28661	-111.08766	BrkT, BrnT?
Rock Creek	44.12489	-111.10652	44.16696	-111.07511	BrkT
Rocky Creek	44.37140	-110.15736	44.37122	-110.15740	CT
Rocky Draw Creek	44.57693	-111.10330	44.62366	-111.10038	
Rose Creek	44.92714	-110.15948	44.89267	-110.23841	CT, RT, R/C
Sage Creek	44.54780	-110.17455	44.58846	-110.23532	CT
Sandy Creek	44.39382	-110.55859	44.37571	-110.57947	CT
Scully Creek	44.24604	-110.79758	44.21032	-110.87772	
Secret Valley Creek	44.66988	-110.84802	44.65822	-110.76984	None
Sedge Creek	44.52404	-110.28299	44.54203	-110.17405	CT
Sentinel Creek	44.50835	-110.91865	44.56697	-110.84326	BrnT, RT, BrkT
Sewer Creek	44.36393	-110.53548	44.39136	-110.52877	
Shaft House Creek	45.06580	-110.71181	45.05473	-110.71487	
Shallow Creek	44.72763	-110.23333	44.78259	-110.32589	None
Sheridan Creek	44.26720	-110.52601	44.27106	-110.50134	None
Shoshone Creek	44.34731	-110.79472	44.40091	-110.76099	BrnT, BrkT, Minnows?
Sickle Creek	44.18508	-110.40730	44.22314	-110.33792	CT?
Signal Creek	44.39912	-110.24623	44.41995	-110.22508	CT?
Slime Creek	44.64541	-110.20306	44.64361	-110.22948	None
Slough Creek	45.06637	-110.15631	44.91783	-110.34720	CT, RT, R/C, LNS, LC
Snake River	44.21542	-110.46282	44.12497	-110.65875	CT, MW, BrnT, BrkT, LT, US MS, MS, RS, UC
Snowslide Creek	44.99214	-111.08133	44.97247	-111.12416	
Soda Butte Creek	45.00229	-110.00074	44.86520	-110.17124	CT, R/C, BrkT
Solfatara Creek	44.81775	-110.66519	44.73564	-110.69341	
Solution Creek	44.35703	-110.54320	44.40673	-110.50088	
Sour Creek	44.68255	-110.47654	44.64664	-110.30890	
South Cache Creek	44.83821	-109.93412	44.83856	-110.07818	
Specimen Creek	45.01086	-111.08514	45.02861	-111.04170	
Specimen Creek, East Fork	45.06768	-110.95075	45.02861	-111.04170	
Specimen Creek, North Fork	45.07795	-110.96349	45.02861	-111.04170	
Spirea Creek	44.22424	-110.67713	44.16078	-110.68007	
Spring Creek	45.09133	-110.77944	44.45009	-110.73407	
Spruce Creek	44.57217	-110.58452	44.59290	-110.70745	BrnT, BrkT, RT
Squirrel Creek	44.34377	-110.82938	44.35723	-110.79877	BrkT, BrnT, RT
Stand Alone Stream	45.12075	-110.88948	44.55297	-110.87571	
Stellaria Creek	44.94334	-110.91689	44.94334	-110.91689	CT?
Stephens Creek	45.00022	-110.77448	45.04888	-110.75098	CT?
Straight Creek	44.83762	-110.76321	44.74282	-110.80450	BrkT

STREAM/RIVER NAME	ORIG LAT	ORIG LONG	TERM LAT	TERM LONG	FISH
Sulphur Creek	44.78264	-110.45330	44.75412	-110.40334	None
Sulphur Spring Creek	44.65635	-110.49548	44.67835	-110.48397	None
Summit Creek	44.35510	-110.66134	44.38054	-110.62153	BrkT
Surface Creek	44.71938	-110.44064	44.72942	-110.45121	RT
Surprise Creek	44.34612	-110.42007	44.25205	-110.44024	CT, MS
Tangled Creek	44.55525	-110.83156	44.53503	-110.75303	None
Tantalus Creek	44.71368	-110.69625	44.73408	-110.71721	None
Tepee Creek	44.80785	-111.09422	44.87192	-111.12577	CT, RT, R/C, BrnT
Tepee Creek, East Fork	44.88290	-111.12719	44.86787	-111.12368	
Terminal Monument Creek	44.99413	-111.05132	44.98647	-111.08035	CT?
Thistle Creek	44.60828	-110.38552	44.61974	-110.31112	CT?
Thorofare Creek	44.12021	-110.00031	44.16074	-110.12276	CT
Timothy Creek	44.73802	-110.09075	44.72153	-110.18442	CT
Tower Creek	44.89517	-110.38327	44.78116	-110.50400	BrkT, RT
Trail Creek	44.25179	-110.17528	44.29010	-110.20785	CT, LNS, RSU
Trappers Creek	44.33420	-110.08444	44.26988	-110.15013	CT
Trout Creek	44.55960	-110.50111	44.64645	-110.45733	CT
Trout Creek, North Fork	44.64253	-110.52635	44.63960	-110.47462	
Tucker Creek	45.03618	-110.17555	45.06136	-110.19790	
Twin Creek	44.81332	-110.14382	44.78015	-110.19922	CT?
Violet Creek	44.65856	-110.57314	44.64910	-110.54901	None
Warm Fork	44.24824	-110.82696	44.18026	-110.88794	CT, RT, R/C
Weasel Creek	44.51355	-110.41698	44.48652	-110.48755	CT
Wells Creek	44.54372	-110.41859	44.53571	-110.47549	CT
White Creek	44.54372	-110.83001	44.48769	-110.72128	BrnT
Wickiup Creek	45.01985	-111.09461	45.04057	-111.07350	CT?
Willow Creek	44.64523	-110.11706	44.70914	-110.08163	CT?
Winter Creek	44.80771	-110.85848	44.85125	-110.73665	BrkT
Witch Creek	44.29463	-110.54019	44.28474	-110.50115	CT, US, UC, RS
Wrong Creek	44.74614	-110.16478	44.76818	-110.28065	None
Wyoming Creek	44.12493	-111.05266	44.16959	-111.04374	BrkT?
Yancey Creek	44.93144	-110.43397	44.90824	-110.43878	BrkT?
Yellowstone River	45.12495	-110.79917	44.12444	-110.12090	CT, MW, LNS, MSU, BrnT BrkT, RT, R/C, MS

Appendix 3: Yellowstone Waterfalls

ow to Use This Table

he following table lists 265 of the park's almost 300 identified waterfalls. Those that are left f the table are ones that have not been tentatively named or detailed in any of the current ark literature, or in either Charles Maynard's 1996 book, *Waterfalls of Yellowstone Park*, or *e Guide to Yellowstone Waterfalls and Their Discovery*, published in 2000, by co-authors Paul ubinstein, (former park historian) Lee Whittlesey, and Mike Stevens.

ach fall is identified, along with its height in feet (f) and meters(m), its latitude and ngitude, and the closest backcountry campsite(s) to it. For those that do not have a ampsite within a day's walk of it, or for those that are located at the end of a specific trail, r those that are located along the roadside, no campsite is listed (N/A).

hose waterfalls that have (official) names recognized by the USGS Board of Geographic ames (BGN) do not have asterisks by their names. The waterfalls with asterisks are lentified using the "proposed" or "suggested" names provided by Rubinstein, et. al., their book. See earlier chapters for information on how the park goes about naming atures, to include the waterfalls and other bodies of water found within its boundaries.

he type of waterfall is also provided, using the following codes:

- **C - Cascade**: Water descends via a series of "steps"
- **F - Fan**: Water spreads horizontally as it descends while remaining in contact with bedrock.
- **H - Horsetail**: Descending water maintains contact with bedrock most of the time.
- **P - Plunge**: Water descends vertically, losing complete contact with the bedrock surface at/near its spill.
- **S - Segmented**: Distinctly separate flows of water form as it descends (used in conjunction with other types, generally. SP = segmented plunge, for ex.
- **T - Tiered**: The length of the waterfall is broken into two or more distinct falls.

inally, a handful of the falls have unique or special circumstances that require the use of otes following the table.

small handful of these features involve dangerous treks over rough terrain or through angerous ground (such as into or through thermal areas). These are denoted with a (D). lease exercise extreme caution if you attempt to hike to these waterfalls.

WATERFALL	HEIGHT	TYPE	LAT	LONG	NEAREST CAMPSITE(S)
Acheron Falls*	27f/8m	H/F	44.23159	-110.99935	9A2, 9B2, 9M2
Agony Falls*	115f/35m	U	45.00143	-110.76828	N/A
Albright Falls	260f/79m	C	44.27841	-110.90356	9B9 (Base of falls), 9B0
Alder Falls*	23f/7m	U	45.01431	-110.77250	N/A
Alfheim Falls*	30f/9m	P	44.77110	-110.40203	4E1 (D)
Amazon Falls*	59f/18m	SP	44.78418	-110.33905	4C3 (D)
Angled Falls*	30f/9m	TC	44.66141	-110.68396	N/A
Anniversary Falls*	227f/69m	H	44.95060	-110.41078	N/A (Garnet Hill Trail)
Apron Falls*	39f/12m	P/F	44.96701	-110.47761	2H2, 2H1 (See Note 1)
Bastille Falls*	98f/30m	P	44.99681	-110.02136	N/A
Bear Feeding Falls*	25f/8m	C	44.69527	-110.51553	N/A (See Note 2)
Bechler Falls	16f/5m	C	44.14939	-111.01175	N/A (Bechler River Trail)
Bighorn Springs Cascades*	200f/61m	SC	44.91888	-110.93611	WB6, WB4
Birdseye Falls*	100f/30m	C	44.24961	-111.00511	9A2, 9A3
Bonus Falls*	60f/16m	C	44.69210	-110.53285	N/A (See Note 2)
Boulder Falls	20f/6m	P	44.89406	-110.38733	Located behind Tower Fall
Bradley Falls*	12f/4m	P	44.16391	-110.77321	8A1, 8A2
Breathtaking Falls*	330f/100m	U	44.89919	-110.10110	N/A
Bride Falls*	20f/6m	SC	44.28393	-110.88915	9D1
Brimstone Cascades*	100f/30m	C	44.75838	-110.42661	4C2, 4C3, 4E1
Cascade Acres	50f/15m	SC	44.14481	-110.85703	N/A (Terraced Falls Trail)
Cascade Falls	5f/2m	P/C	44.47619	-110.84443	N/A (See Note 3)
Cascades of the Firehole	20f/6m	TC	44.61627	-110.85531	(Roadside)
Castle Ruins Falls*	30f/9m	P	44.72753	-110.46902	N/A (D)
Cave Falls	20f/6m	TP	44.14370	-110.99719	(Cave Falls Parking Area)
Chamber of Rhapsody Falls*	30f/9m	P	44.20650	-110.84486	9U4, 9U5
Chasm Falls*	15f/5m	P	44.27340	-110.96348	9B4
Childhood's Dream Falls*	100f/30m	U	44.24490	-110.96983	9B4
Citadel of Asgard Falls*	600f/183m	SP/C	44.77152	-110.40295	4E1
Cleft Cascade (Lower)	16f/5m	C	44.14194	-110.85452	N/A (Terraced Falls Trail)
Cleft Cascade (Upper)	20f/6m	C	44.14173	-110.85454	N/A (Terraced Falls Trail)
Cloistered Falls*	15f/5m	P	44.69407	-110.61237	N/A
Colonnade Falls	102f/31m	TP	44.23916	-110.94701	9B5
Confederate Falls*	10f/3m	P	44.23583	-111.02677	9A2, 9A3
Confirmation Falls*	90f/27m	P	44.25950	-110.66404	N/A (See Note 4)
Confusion Cascade*	130f/40m	F/C	44.29726	-110.86173	9D2 (See Note 5)
Conjunction Cascade*	100f/30m	C	44.89174	-110.10686	N/A
Consolation Cascade*	25f/8m	C	44.25776	-111.00015	9A2
Crecelius Cascade	75f/23m	TP/C	44.46815	-110.13916	(Roadside)
Crystal Falls	129f/39m	P/F	44.71674	-110.50143	(Uncle Tom's Trailhead)
Dance of the Seven Veils*	10f/3m	F	44.20526	-110.84687	9U4, 9U5
Dancing Water Cascade*	12f/4m	C	44.90433	-110.70974	N/A
Dashing Falls*	25f/8m	F/C	44.40667	-110.83709	OA3
Dawn Cascade #1*	60f/18m	C	44.21935	-110.87066	9U4, 9U5
Dawn Cascade #2*	40f/12m	C	44.21893	-110.86710	9U4, 9U5
Dawn Cascade #3*	80f/24m	C	44.22019	-110.86319	9U4, 9U5
Dawn Cascade #4*	75f/23m	C	44.22345	-110.85919	9U4, 9U5

WATERFALL	HEIGHT	TYPE	LAT	LONG	NEAREST CAMPSITE(S)
ead End Delight Casc #1*	60f/18m	C	44.96964	-110.06043	N/A
ead End Delight Casc #2*	60f/18m	C	44.96935	-110.05834	N/A
eep Pool Falls*	15f/5m	P	44.31042	-111.03912	9A4, 9A5
emure Falls*	40f/12m	P	44.20560	-110.84634	9U4, 9U5
evil's Elbow Cascade*	16f/5m	C	44.71051	-110.65167	N/A
amond Cascade*	15f/5m	C	44.14031	-110.85360	N/A (Terraced Falls Trail)
ouble Grotto Falls*	45f/14m	TP/C	44.68655	-110.55316	N/A
ouglas Knob Falls*	25f/8m	SC	44.31097	-110.85508	9D3
uet Falls*	12+16f/9m	TP/F	44.69291	-110.61965	N/A
unanda Falls	150f/46m	P	44.24809	-111.02446	9A3
arly Morning Falls*	15f/5m	P	44.19798	-110.87822	9U4/9U5
ast Entrance Road Falls*	35f/10m	C	44.46652	-110.09440	(Roadside)
ysian Falls*	125f/38m	C	44.66083	-110.68543	N/A
nbowered Falls*	25f/8m	P	44.79205	-110.44650	N/A
nerald Pool Falls*	15f/5m	P	44.27188	-110.96434	9B4
nchantress Falls*	90f/27m	P	44.99186	-110.01821	N/A
ndless Cascades*	150f/46m	C	44.70377	-110.64503	N/A
nduring Falls*	18f/5m	P	44.96307	-110.30904	Slough Creek CG
thereal Falls*	200f/61m	TH	44.29961	-110.87204	9D1
airies Fall	32f/10m	P	44.88874	-110.24566	(See Note 6)
airy Falls	197f/60m	P	44.52501	-110.87027	OD1, OD4
all of the Elves*	17f/5m	P	44.76835	-110.40246	4E1 (D)
all of the Valkyries*	15f/5m	TP	44.76894	-110.41089	4E1
ern Cascades	100f/30m	C	44.44660	-110.84359	N/A (Fern Cascades Trail)
irehole Falls	40f/12m	P	44.63067	-110.86402	(Roadside)
ume Cascades #1 (Lwr)*	25f/8m	C	44.30148	-110.88392	9D1
ume Cascades #2 (Mid)*	15f/5m	C	44.30362	-110.87946	9D1
ume Cascades #3 (Upr)*	80f/24m	C	44.30381	-110.87879	9D1
orbidding Falls*	40f/12m	TP	44.17660	-110.60232	8C1, 8C7 (D)
order's Cascade*	30f/9m	C	44.16341	-110.98402	N/A
orgotten Falls*	20f/6m	P	44.13834	-110.81564	N/A
orks of Shoshone Falls*	60f/9m	C/P	44.36268	-110.83259	8G1
orlorn Falls*	15f/5m	C	44.28918	-110.88997	9D1
our Springs Cascade #1*	60f/15m	C	44.18761	-110.73605	8P1, 8P2
our Springs Cascade #2*	75f/23m	C	44.18368	-110.73363	8P1, 8P2
our Springs Cascade #3*	100f/30m	C	44.18433	-110.73499	8P1, 8P2
our Springs Cascade #4*	180f/55m	C	44.18275	-110.73680	8P1, 8P2
raternal Falls*	60f/18m	TP	44.98691	-110.01452	N/A
reya's Fall*	38f/12m	P	44.76781	-110.39963	4E1 (D)
ates of Valhalla Falls*	100f/30m	TP	44.76837	-110.40663	4E1 (D)
ibbon Falls	84f/26m	H/F	44.65413	-110.77077	(Roadside)
ibbon River Rapids (Lower)	50f/15m	C	44.71133	-110.73969	(Roadside)
ibbon River Rapids (Upper)	50f/15m	C	44.71157	-110.73857	(Roadside)
ilded Falls*	75f/23m	C/P	44.92193	-110.92724	WB6, WB4
olden Fleece Falls*	100f/30m	P/F	44.78083	-110.32289	N/A (D)
raceful Falls*	25f/8m	F/C	44.25732	-111.00099	9A2, 9A3
ranite Falls*	20f/6m	F	45.02285	-110.30267	(USFS land outside park)

WATERFALL	HEIGHT	TYPE	LAT	LONG	NEAREST CAMPSITE(S)
Grants Pass Cascade*	25f/8m	C	44.38877	-110.83678	8G1, OA3
Grayling Falls	6f/2m	P	44.86022	-111.05331	N/A (Off US191)
Groom Falls*	20f/6m	SC	44.28469	-110.88829	9D1
Guardian Falls*	30f/9m	P	44.74906	-110.32081	N/A (D)
Gwinna Falls	15f/5m	P	44.28174	-110.88019	9D1
Halfway Falls*	30f/6m	P	44.76333	-110.32233	N/A (D)
Hanging Falls*	20f/6m	P	44.53303	-110.69238	N/A
Hidden Falls	20f/6m	C	44.98703	-110.58424	1A1, 1Y6, 1Y8
Hidden Grotto Falls*	62f/19m	U	44.88508	-110.11810	N/A
Horseshoe Cascade*	30f/9m	C	44.27660	-111.03368	9A4
Horsetail Falls*	72f/22m	H	44.88604	-110.12067	N/A
Humpback Cascade*	15f/5m	C	44.14064	-110.85393	N/A (Terraced Falls Trail)
Hundred Step Cascade*	100f/30m	C	44.41603	-110.78479	OA1
Ice Box Falls	18f/5m	C	44.92916	-110.08650	N/A (Northeast Ent Road)
Icicle Falls*	165f/50m	U	45.01151	-110.77795	N/A
Iddings Falls*	22f/7m	SP	44.62466	-110.16658	N/A
Idyllic Falls*	10f/3m	P	44.58942	-110.21030	N/A (Off Pelican Valley Trail,
Impasse Falls*	25f/8m	P	44.77830	-110.32783	N/A (D)
Instant Falls*	25f/8m	P/F	44.79720	-110.12892	3L4
Iris Falls	45f/14m	P	44.24144	-110.94325	9B5
Isolation Falls*	50f/15m	P	44.13544	-110.13181	6Y2
Jordan Falls	40f/12m	C	44.64560	-110.73942	N/A
Kepler Cascades	100f/30m	TC	44.44584	-110.80631	(Roadside)
Knowles Falls	15f/5m	C	45.01196	-110.59462	1Y2, 1Y4
Last Rose Petal Falls*	115f/35m	P	44.99197	-110.02442	N/A
Leaping Falls*	30f/9m	P	44.40309	-110.83470	OA3
LeHardy Rapids	20f/6m	Rapid	44.60728	-110.38389	(Roadside)
Lewis Canyon Falls (Lower)	50f/15m	SC	44.21947	-110.65419	(Roadside)
Lewis Canyon Falls (Upper)	80f/24m	C	44.22658	-110.65350	(Roadside)
Lewis Falls	30f/9m	C	44.26740	-110.63691	(Roadside)
Little Eden Falls (Lower)*	20f/5m	P	44.84204	-110.21601	N/A
Little Eden Falls (Upper)*	16f/6m	P	44.84075	-110.21757	N/A
Little Gibbon Falls	25f/8m	C	44.71660	-110.61579	4D2
Littlesmouth Cascade*	45f/14m	C	44.29990	-110.87074	9D1
Lone Star Cascade*	130f/40m	C	44.42485	-110.82701	OA1, OA2
Looking Glass Falls*	75f/23m	TP	44.43619	-110.09599	N/A
Lost Creek Falls	40f/12m	P	44.90917	-110.42002	N/A (Direct Trail)
Lovely Falls*	10f/3m	P	44.48578	-110.91788	OD3 (Adjacent to falls)
Lower Falls	308f/94m	P	44.71801	-110.49608	N/A (Direct Trail)
Lower Stephens Cascade*	196f/60m	C	45.00907	-110.77400	N/A
Lower Undine Falls	40f/12m	P	44.94408	-110.64016	N/A (D)
Luxuriant Falls *	20f/6m	C	44.96901	-110.47435	2H2 (See Note 1)
Mist Cascade*	40f/12m	C	44.14172	-110.80593	N/A
Mist of the Trident Falls*	140f/43m	P	44.17305	-110.09221	6Y5, 6Y6
Moose Falls	30f/9m	P	44.15182	-110.67271	(Roadside)
Morning Falls	60f/18m	P	44.21178	-110.87755	9U4, 9U5
Mosquito Falls*	15f/5m	TC	44.66141	-110.68373	N/A

WATERFALL	HEIGHT	TYPE	LAT	LONG	NEAREST CAMPSITE(S)
ɔssy Falls*	18f/5m	P/F	44.89992	-110.10577	N/A
ystic Falls	70f/21m	TC/P	44.48398	-110.87325	N/A (Direct Trail)
tural Bridge Cascade	40f/12m	TC	44.52629	-110.45546	N/A (Direct Trail)
in Falls*	130f/40m	P/C	44.76721	-110.39880	4E1 (D)
chid Falls*	100f/30m	C	44.30036	-110.77339	8M2
prey Falls	150f/46m	P	44.92857	-110.68098	N/A (Direct Trail)
uzel Falls	230f/70m	H/F/P	44.23568	-110.97522	9B4
intbrush Cascade*	20f/6m	C	44.27430	-111.03333	9A4
nset Falls*	50f/15m	P	44.13768	-110.70422	N/A
lisade Falls*	50f/15m	TP	44.82496	-110.34322	N/A (D)
terson Falls*	40f/12m	TP/C	44.85115	-110.35811	2Y1 (Just above falls)
trified Falls*	260f/80m	U	44.88893	-110.10038	N/A
illips Fork Fall	6f/2m	SC	44.29021	-110.89268	9D1
cnic Falls*	25f/8m	C	44.71350	-110.68039	(See Note 7)
ateau Falls	80f/24m	P	44.15911	-110.23624	6M3, 6M4
llux Peak Falls*	200f/61m	H	44.66909	-109.91058	N/A
thole Cascades*	40f/12m	C	44.13662	-110.85164	N/A (Terraced Falls Trail)
ecipitous Falls*	25f/8m	P	44.48481	-110.90802	OD3
emonition Falls*	20f/6m	P	44.25910	-110.66199	N/A (See Note 4)
stine Cascades #1*	22f/7m	P	44.27217	-110.84979	9D1
istine Cascades #2*	16f/5m	C	44.27318	-110.84607	9D1
istine Cascades #3*	19f/6m	P	44.27286	-110.84441	9D1
istine Cascades #4*	11f/3m	P	44.27287	-110.84258	9D1
rgatory Falls*	70f/21m	P	44.26921	-110.98045	9A3, 9M2, 9B2
uadruple Cascades #1*	15f/5m	C	44.38816	-110.84964	OA3
uadruple Cascades #2*	15f/5m	C	44.38740	-110.85011	OA3
uadruple Cascades #3*	20f/6m	C	44.38694	-110.85064	OA3
uadruple Cascades #4*	15f/5m	C	44.38678	-110.85140	OA3
uartz Falls*	62f/19m	P	44.89390	-110.10937	N/A
uiver Cascade #1	15f/3m	P	44.29858	-110.88691	9D1
uiver Cascade #2	30f/9m	F/C	44.29944	-110.88635	9D1
uiver Cascade #3	30f/9m	C	44.30039	-110.88559	9D1
uiver Cascade #4	40f/12m	TC	44.30095	-110.88489	9D1
uiver Cascade #5	25f/8m	C	44.30198	-110.88418	9D1
uiver Cascade #6	35f/11m	C	44.30282	-110.88288	9D1
uiver Cascade #7	90f/27m	H/F	44.30400	-110.88158	9D1
uiver Cascade #8	20f/6m	H	44.30523	-110.88117	9D1
agged Falls	45f/14m	SC	44.28840	-110.89031	9D1
ainbow Falls	55f/17m	SP	44.14167	-110.87951	N/A (See Note 8)
apunzel Falls*	500f/152m	TP/H	44.35265	-110.08818	N/A
ealm of the Dead Falls (U)*	40f/12m	P	44.75994	-110.39309	N/A (D)
ealm of the Dead Falls (L)*	20f/6m	P	44.75957	-110.39350	N/A (D)
echerche Falls*	75f/23m	H	44.89694	-110.10045	N/A
eclusive Falls*	80f/25m	U	44.86358	-110.14058	N/A
ed Rock Cascade*	250f/76m	C	44.72128	-110.48856	N/A (Visible from trails)
iverwalk Falls*	40f/12m	TC	44.21161	-110.87284	9U4, 9U5
obinson Canyon Falls*	30f/9m	C	44.22524	-111.08391	9A6

WATERFALL	HEIGHT	TYPE	LAT	LONG	NEAREST CAMPSITE(S)
Rocky Top Falls*	30f/9m	SP	44.20369	-110.70856	8P1, 8P2
Rustic Falls	47f/14m	P/H/F	44.93448	-110.72406	(Roadside)
Sanctuary Falls*	262f/80m	U	44.88199	-110.10884	N/A
Savage Creek Cascades #1*	70f/21m	C	44.17169	-110.78977	8A1, 8A2
Savage Creek Cascades #2*	70f/21m	C	44.17197	-110.79027	8A1, 8A2
Savage Creek Cascades #3*	25f/8m	C	44.17277	-110.79105	8A1, 8A2
Savage Creek Cascades #4*	20f/6m	C	44.17308	-110.79164	8A1, 8A2
Secret Falls*	59f/18m	U	44.18749	-110.84035	N/A
Sentinel Falls*	150f/46m	TC	44.56009	-110.91144	OG1 (See Note 9)
Serendipity Falls*	30f/9m	SP/C	44.21212	-110.70456	8P1, 8P2
Sidedoor Cascade*	80f/24m	SH/C	44.44265	-110.85632	N/A
Silver Cascades*	262f/80m	C	45.01085	-110.77049	N/A
Silver Cord Cascade	1200f/366m	HT	44.72672	-110.45079	N/A (Seven Mile Hole Trail)
Silver Scarf Falls	250f/76m	C	44.24678	-111.02161	9A3
Siren Falls*	20f/6m	C	44.16912	-110.86623	9U4, 9U5
Slide Cascade*	20f/6m	C	44.71077	-110.78123	N/A
Slippery Rock Cascade*	40f/12m	C	44.70495	-110.64761	N/A
Sluiceway Falls	10f/3m	P	44.27886	-110.87911	9D1
Snowy Falls*	50f/15m	U	44.98996	-110.02558	N/A
Sojourner Falls*	50f/15m	C	44.78490	-110.33994	4C3 (D)
Spiral Staircase Falls*	164f/50m	H/P	44.20458	-110.84840	9U4, 9U5
Spritely Falls*	50f/15m	U	44.20350	-110.85012	9U4, 9U5
Stone Hollow Falls*	40f/12m	P	44.91940	-110.93248	WB6, WB4
Sublimity Falls*	20f/6m	P	44.92580	-110.91830	WB6, WB4
Sundial Falls*	15f/5m	C	44.45231	-110.71921	N/A
Sunset Falls*	50f/15m	P	44.13768	-110.70422	N/A
Surprise Falls*	98f/30m	U	44.98335	-110.05515	N/A
Sweetwater Falls*	16f/5m	P	44.70344	-110.66856	N/A (See Note 7)
Swiftwater Cascade*	40f/12m	C	44.89793	-110.10153	N/A
Sylvan Falls*	20f/6m	P	44.46933	-110.06935	(Roadside)
Talus Falls*	100f/30m	H/C	44.46308	-110.12394	(Roadside)
Tawny Falls*	17f/5m	C	44.34561	-110.81382	8R5, 8T1
Tempe Cascade #1	20f/6m	C	44.30152	-110.86962	9D1
Tempe Cascade #2	20f/6m	C/P	44.30177	-110.86988	9D1
Tempe Cascade #3	25f/8m	C/F	44.30208	-110.87006	9D1
Tempe Cascade #4	15f/5m	C	44.30225	-110.87007	9D1
Tempe Cascade #5	30f/9m	C	44.30238	-110.87011	9D1
Tempest Falls*	150f/46m	P	44.91835	-110.14005	Pebble Creek CG
Tempestuous Fall*	75f/23m	C/P	44.99811	-110.42344	2H8, 2C1
Tendoy Falls	33f/10m	P	44.28382	-110.87926	9D1
Terraced Falls	140f/43m	TP	44.14753	-110.86635	N/A (Direct trail)
The Falls of Hayden Valley*	15f/5m	SC	44.69153	-110.46489	N/A (Adjacent to trail)
Thermal Falls*	35f/11m	SP	44.62388	-110.26488	N/A (Pelican Valley BMA)
Thimbleberry Falls	39f/12m	U	44.87544	-110.12198	N/A
Thistle Falls*	15f/5m	C	44.54478	-110.20367	N/A (Pelican Valley BMA)
Threshold Falls*	56f/17m	U	44.89274	-110.10764	N/A
Tower Fall	132f/40m	P	44.89366	-110.38722	N/A (Direct trail)

WATERFALL	HEIGHT	TYPE	LAT	LONG	NEAREST CAMPSITE(S)
Treasure Island Falls*	25f/8m	SP	44.24304	-110.93952	9B5, 9B6
Tukuarika Falls*	25f/8m	C	44.88920	-110.71807	Indian Creek CG
Twin Falls (North)	150f/46m	P/C	44.74512	-110.41042	4C1, 4C2 (See Note 10)
Twin Falls (South)	200f/61m	SH/F	44.74812	-110.41089	4C1, 4C2 (See Note 10)
Twister Falls	55f/17m	C	44.29853	-110.86809	9D1
Two-Lane Cascade*	60f/18m	SC	44.89922	-110.10363	N/A
Undine Falls	60f/18m	TP/F	44.94398	-110.63863	(Roadside)
Unfaithful Falls*	100+f/30m	P/C	44.47462	-110.87108	(Roadside)
Union Falls	250f/76m	P/F	44.19241	-110.87065	9U4, 9U5
Upper Fairy Falls	20f/6m	F	44.52443	-110.87027	OD1
Upper Falls	109f/33m	P	44.71289	-110.49955	N/A (Direct Trail)
Upper Stephens Cascade*	197f/60m	C	45.00991	-110.77279	N/A
Velvet Falls*	60f/18m	U	44.89488	-110.11199	N/A
Verdant Falls*	15f/5m	TC	44.24659	-111.00660	9A2, 9A0, 9A3
Verdure Falls*	46f/14m	U	44.88389	-110.11496	N/A
Vest Falls*	150f/46m	H/P/C	44.76487	-110.27733	N/A
Virginia Cascade	60f/18m	C	44.71318	-110.64813	(Roadside)
Wahhi Falls (Lower)	18f/5m	P	44.27663	-110.87776	9D1
Wahhi Falls (Upper)	28f/9m	P	44.27511	-110.87724	9D1
Weeping Falls*	20f/6m	P	44.23419	-110.97504	9B4
White Angel Falls*	16f/5m	C	44.16268	-110.97040	9U1
White Creek Falls	6f/2m	P	44.52976	-110.79044	(Area is closed to public)
Whortleberry Falls*	40f/12m	TF	44.26941	-110.51152	8H2, 8H3
Wild Rose Falls*	70f/21m	TP	44.83594	-110.19551	N/A
Woodland Falls*	18f/5m	C	44.25114	-111.00591	9A2, 9A3
Wraith Falls	100f/30m	C	44.93692	-110.62180	N/A (Direct trail)
Xanadu Falls*	150f/46m	H/C	44.76035	-110.42445	4E1
Zephyr Falls*	400f/122m	P	44.91817	-110.14173	Pebble Creek CG

Notes

1. Apron Falls is located on the opposite side of the Yellowstone River from these campsites, so you'd need to ford the river, which is not recommended. A better approach would be to try to trace the old segment of Howard Eaton Trail that runs just southeast of this waterfall, and bushwhack to the falls itself. This applies to Luxuriant Falls as well.
2. Accessible via the old Otter Creek Service Road/Bear Feeding Area.
3. This waterfall can be found approximately 1/10th of a mile north of Morning Glory Pool on the trail between Artemisia Geyser and The Upper Geyser Basin Trail.
4. These waterfalls are accessible via an easy hike from the South Entrance Road.
5. This is labeled on older USGS maps as "Twister Falls." This is inaccurate and was a mistake on the part of the USGS. The confusion over the name is actually the source of the suggested name for this particular waterfall.
6. Fairies Fall can often be seen from the Northeast Entrance Road if you are just west of the entrance to the Lamar/Buffalo Ranch entrance drive. It is located across the Lamar River valley where Amethyst Creek empties into the river.
7. This one is fairly easy to get to if you hike up the old service road. However, at times, the NPS has this area closed to the public due to the presence of an itinerant carcass dump along this road (which means it's a high-traffic area for bears and other predators).
8. Rainbow Falls can be reached by continuing to hike one mile past Terrace Falls (requires considerable bushwhacking)
9. There is a closer campsite, OG2, but that was closed by NPS a few years ago. If it reopens, use OG2 rather than OG1.
10. The Seven Mile Hole Trail was originally built by Superintendent Philetus Norris in the late 1870s specifically to take people to see these waterfalls. Its original name was the Twin Falls Trail, in fact.[1]

Appendix 4: Mountains and Passes

How to Use These Tables

There are two tables in this section. The first table lists the 145 highest named mountains and peaks within Yellowstone National Park. They are ranked in order from tallest to the lowest in terms of elevation.[1]

The second table lists the named mountain passes within the park. They are listed in alphabetical order.

Each provides geographical coordinates along with their elevations in both feet and meters. The names of those features denoted with an asterisk(*) are unofficial and mostly of localized use (i.e., they have not been approved by the USGS Board of Geographic Names). Both tables are presented with maps showing the location of all features for user reference.

Yellowstone's Named Mountains, Peaks, and Hills

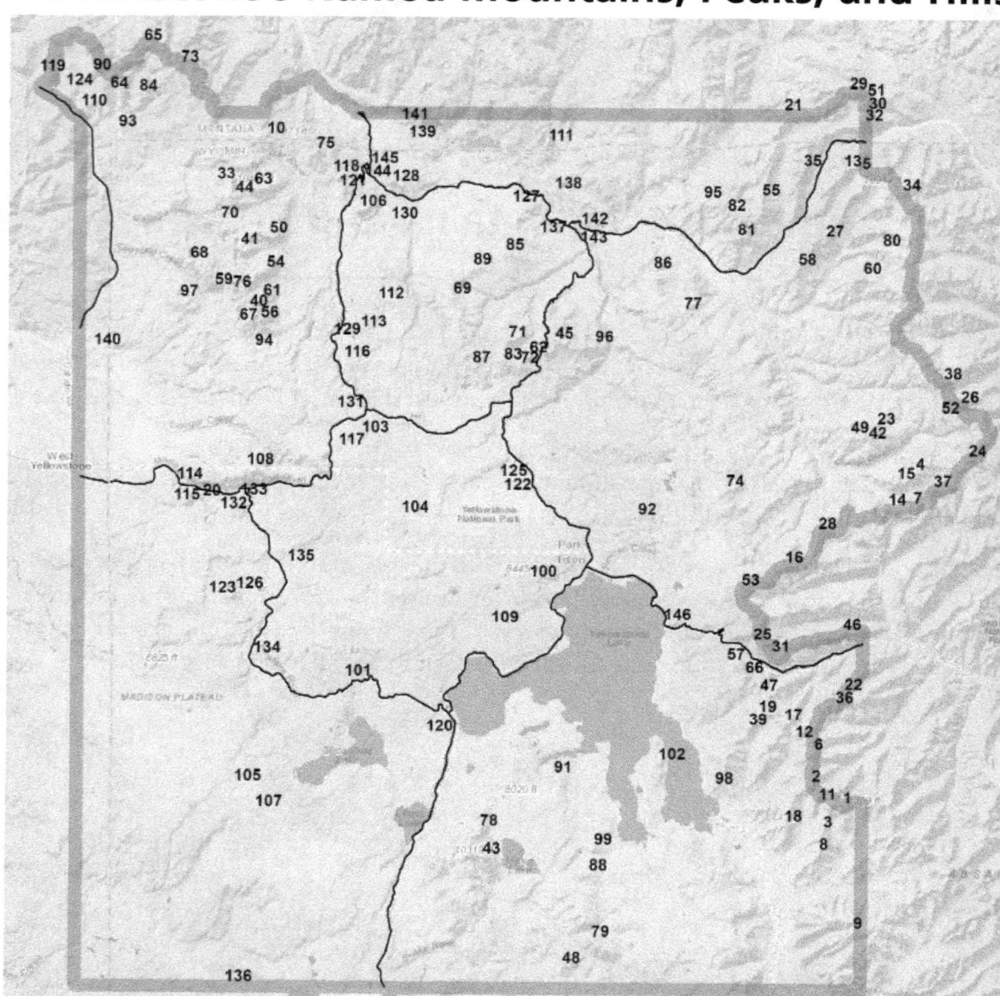

PEAK	MAP ID	RANGE	HT FEET	HT METERS	LATITUDE	LONGITUDE
Eagle Peak	1	Absaroka	11361	3464	44.320833	-110.027778
Mount Schurz	2	Absaroka	11161	3403	44.342500	-110.071944
Table Mountain	3	Absaroka	11060	3372	44.295805	-110.055346
Pollux Peak	4	Absaroka	11043	3367	44.666667	-109.929167
Amphitheater Mountain	5	Absaroka	11020	3360	44.972500	-110.006944
Atkins Peak	6	Absaroka	11017	3359	44.375833	-110.068889
Notch Mountain	7	Absaroka	10992	3351	44.630740	-109.936188
Turret Mountain	8	Absaroka	10987	3350	44.272778	-110.060556
The Trident	9	Absaroka	10981	3348	44.193333	-110.011944
Electric Peak	10	Gallatin	10961	3342	45.005278	-110.836667
Mount Humphreys	11	Absaroka	10951	3339	44.332701	-110.061965
Plenty Coups Peak	12	Absaroka	10932	3333	44.390270	-110.069770
Abiathar Peak	13	Absaroka	10919	3329	44.975278	-110.032222

PEAK	MAP ID	RANGE	HT FEET	HT METERS	LATITUDE	LONGITUDE
ant Peak	14	Absaroka	10863	3312	44.630278	-109.947222
stor Peak	15	Absaroka	10850	3308	44.656944	-109.955278
thedral Peak	16	Absaroka	10784	3288	44.570556	-110.110833
ount Langford	17	Absaroka	10781	3287	44.406944	-110.110278
lter Peak	18	Absaroka	10692	3260	44.301667	-110.110000
ount Doane	19	Absaroka	10649	3247	44.413611	-110.148056
toff Mountain	21	Absaroka	10636	3243	45.031498	-110.115842
servation Peak	22	Absaroka	10620	3238	44.431667	-110.026944
ddle Mountain	23	Absaroka	10613	3236	44.710833	-109.983611
mar Mountain	24	Absaroka	10581	3226	44.680372	-109.855744
alanche Peak	25	Absaroka	10574	3224	44.489722	-110.141111
odoo Peak	26	Absaroka	10571	3223	44.734580	-109.866864
e Thunderer	27	Absaroka	10535	3212	44.903333	-110.056667
ramid Peak	28	Absaroka	10499	3201	44.605405	-110.064680
olverine Peak	29	Absaroka	10495	3200	45.053403	-110.009533
ineral Mountain	30	Absaroka	10495	3200	45.031024	-109.997822
oyt Peak	31	Absaroka	10485	3197	44.477222	-110.128611
eridian Peak	32	Absaroka	10479	3195	45.027222	-110.002500
seph Peak	33	Gallatin	10459	3189	44.958611	-110.884722
public Peak	34	Absaroka	10426	3179	44.950833	-109.949722
rronette Peak	35	Absaroka	10426	3179	44.975278	-110.088611
thur Peak	36	Absaroka	10417	3176	44.424722	-110.039167
andlestick Mountain	37	Absaroka	10371	3162	44.649075	-109.903974
ively Peak	38	Absaroka	10365	3160	44.758161	-109.890587
ount Stevenson	39	Absaroka	10344	3154	44.401667	-110.159444
ount Holmes	40	Gallatin	10331	3150	44.818889	-110.855833
annock Peak	41	Gallatin	10331	3150	44.891667	-110.872500
ague Mountain	42	Absaroka	10321	3147	44.705833	-110.000556
ount Sheridan	43	Red	10318	3146	44.266111	-110.529444
ray Peak	44	Gallatin	10302	3141	44.944722	-110.880278
ount Washburn	45	Washburn	10259	3128	44.797500	-110.433333
ody Peak	46	Absaroka	10249	3125	44.500833	-110.029167
op Notch Peak	47	Absaroka	10243	3123	44.452222	-110.144444
ount Hancock	48	Isolated	10220	3116	44.155278	-110.417500
ttle Saddle Mountain	49	Absaroka	10220	3116	44.701911	-110.016435
uadrant Mountain	50	Gallatin	10216	3115	44.903889	-110.832222
unset Peak	51	Absaroka	10197	3109	45.045405	-109.999756
arker Peak	52	Absaroka	10177	3103	44.723333	-109.894167
ount Chittenden	53	Absaroka	10174	3102	44.546667	-110.171111
ntler Peak	54	Gallatin	10056	3066	44.868611	-110.836389
ount Hornaday	55	Absaroka	10033	3059	44.945000	-110.146111
ilobite Point	56	Gallatin	9993	3047	44.816944	-110.843889
rizzly Peak	57	Absaroka	9974	3041	44.468611	-110.176111
ount Norris	58	Absaroka	9938	3030	44.874444	-110.094722
hree Rivers Peak	59	Gallatin	9938	3030	44.850278	-110.883333
he Needle	60	Absaroka	9901	3019	44.865556	-110.003611
ome Mountain	61	Gallatin	9898	3018	44.839444	-110.840833

PEAK	MAP ID	RANGE	HT FEET	HT METERS	LATITUDE	LONGITUDE
Dunraven Peak	62	Washburn	9898	3018	44.782778	-110.469444
Little Quadrant Mountain	63	Gallatin	9885	3014	44.953559	-110.853897
Big Horn Peak	64	Gallatin	9885	3014	45.066156	-111.056349
Sheep Mountain	65	Gallatin	9839	3000	45.098101	-111.009889
Signal Hills	66	Absaroka	9836	2999	44.454915	-110.165077
White Peaks	67	Gallatin	9803	2989	44.814444	-110.873611
Crowfoot Ridge	68	Gallatin	9793	2986	44.877530	-110.942577
Cook Peak	69	Washburn	9754	2974	44.842778	-110.575278
Monument Peak*	70	Gallatin	9687	2953	44.918633	-110.900875
Inside Mountain*	71	Washburn	9681	2952	44.798254	-110.498035
Hedges Peak	72	Washburn	9669	2948	44.777500	-110.479722
Shooting Star Mountain	73	Gallatin	9662	2946	45.076551	-110.957507
Pelican Cone	74	Isolated	9649	2942	44.648104	-110.193129
Sepulcher Mountain	75	Gallatin	9642	2940	44.990278	-110.766944
Echo Peak	76	Gallatin	9639	2939	44.847778	-110.883056
Amethyst Mountain	77	Washburn	9619	2933	44.828611	-110.254167
Factory Hill	78	Red	9616	2932	44.295000	-110.533611
Barlow Peak	79	Isolated	9616	2932	44.182778	-110.377222
Cache Mountain	80	Absaroka	9606	2929	44.894444	-109.976389
Druid Peak	81	Absaroka	9580	2921	44.904444	-110.179167
Frederick Peak	82	Absaroka	9573	2919	44.929167	-110.193333
Stone Mountain*	83	Washburn	9548	2911	44.775737	-110.504495
Meldrum Mountain	84	Gallatin	9534	2907	45.047500	-111.015833
Prospect Peak	85	Washburn	9531	2906	44.888056	-110.502778
Specimen Ridge	86	Washburn	9495	2895	44.870278	-110.296667
Observation Peak	87	Washburn	9406	2868	44.771944	-110.548056
Overlook Mountain	88	Isolated	9363	2855	44.250215	-110.381469
Folsom Peak	89	Washburn	9334	2846	44.872778	-110.547500
King Butte	90	Isolated	9301	2836	45.067979	-111.080212
Flat Mountain	91	Isolated	9170	2796	44.349934	-110.431175
Stonetop Mountain	92	Isolated	9052	2760	44.618930	-110.315923
Lightning Hill*	93	Gallatin	8975	2736	45.011376	-111.043744
South End Hills*	94	Gallatin	8945	2727	44.788181	-110.851798
Bison Peak	95	Absaroka	8940	2726	44.942500	-110.226944
Phelps Peak*	96	Washburn	8855	2700	44.794100	-110.377250
The Crags	97	Gallatin	8845	2697	44.838221	-110.956164
Langford Cairn	98	Isolated	8819	2689	44.339705	-110.206164
Channel Mountain	99	Isolated	8750	2668	44.276389	-110.374722
Lake Butte	146	Isolated	8733	2663	44.512467	-110.262962
Elephant Back Mountain	100	Isolated	8724	2660	44.554167	-110.467222
Corkscrew Hill	101	Isolated	8651	2638	44.449224	-110.724110
The Promentory	102	Isolated	8645	2636	44.364399	-110.285781
Gibbon Hill	103	Isolated	8609	2625	44.700811	-110.702179
Mary Mountain	104	Isolated	8606	2624	44.619989	-110.645821
Trischman Knob	105	Isolated	8586	2618	44.339444	-110.877500
Bunsen Peak	106	Gallatin	8563	2611	44.931667	-110.706944
Douglas Knob	107	Isolated	8550	2607	44.313333	-110.847500

PEAK	MAP ID	RANGE	HT FEET	HT METERS	LATITUDE	LONGITUDE
rple Mountain	108	Gallatin	8514	2596	44.667222	-110.862222
otted Woods Hill*	109	Isolated	8451	2577	44.506010	-110.519411
ack Butte	110	Isolated	8412	2565	45.032110	-111.096707
llroaring Mountain	111	Absaroka	8364	2550	44.999556	-110.445066
rseshoe Hill	112	Isolated	8314	2535	44.837222	-110.680556
e Landmark	113	Isolated	8291	2528	44.808445	-110.704534
ount Jackson	114	Gallatin	8274	2523	44.652500	-110.929444
ount Haynes	115	Gallatin	8235	2511	44.632778	-110.946111
aring Mountain	116	Isolated	8156	2487	44.777222	-110.727500
intpot Hill	117	Isolated	8054	2455	44.688044	-110.734417
agett Butte	118	Gallatin	8045	2453	44.964444	-110.735000
own Butte	119	Gallatin	8045	2453	45.066877	-111.136152
vage Hill*	120	Isolated	8043	2452	44.811545	-110.587304
rrace Mountain	121	Gallatin	8005	2441	44.955556	-110.735556
lphur Mountain	122	Isolated	7946	2423	44.648947	-110.469557
uth Twin Butte	123	Isolated	7923	2416	44.535404	-110.881867
va Butte	124	Isolated	7900	2409	45.053059	-111.105362
ater Hills	125	Isolated	7867	2398	44.656884	-110.473537
orth Twin Butte	126	Isolated	7866	2398	44.540303	-110.875792
escent Hill	127	Isolated	7861	2397	44.937511	-110.470469
ount Everts	128	Gallatin	7848	2393	44.975000	-110.661389
ickyard Hill*	129	Isolated	7720	2354	44.800380	-110.742424
ompson's Peak*	130	Isolated	7717	2353	44.919425	-110.662786
at Top Mountain*	131	Isolated	7622	2324	44.723415	-110.700735
ree Brothers Mountains	132	Gallatin	7618	2323	44.633056	-110.887778
ational Park Mountain	133	Gallatin	7549	2302	44.636672	-110.871139
ylie Hill*	134	Isolated	7476	2279	44.472276	-110.851304
orcupine Hills	135	Isolated	7458	2274	44.569013	-110.804441
alf Creek Hill	136	Isolated	7415	2261	44.133881	-110.888048
ancey Hill*	137	Isolated	7249	2210	44.921041	-110.456018
arnet Hill	138	Isolated	7054	2151	44.950996	-110.435207
rkey Pen Peak	139	Isolated	6985	2130	45.011813	-110.639363
andy Butte	140	Isolated	6961	2122	44.788045	-111.076711
attlesnake Butte	141	Isolated	6719	2048	45.020253	-110.649747
nction Butte	142	Isolated	6604	2013	44.917548	-110.390601
umpus Butte	143	Isolated	6588	2009	44.908244	-110.399273
apitol Hill	144	Isolated	6414	1955	44.971980	-110.700903
ude Hill*	145	Isolated	6144	1873	44.975601	-110.691314

Yellowstone's Named Passes

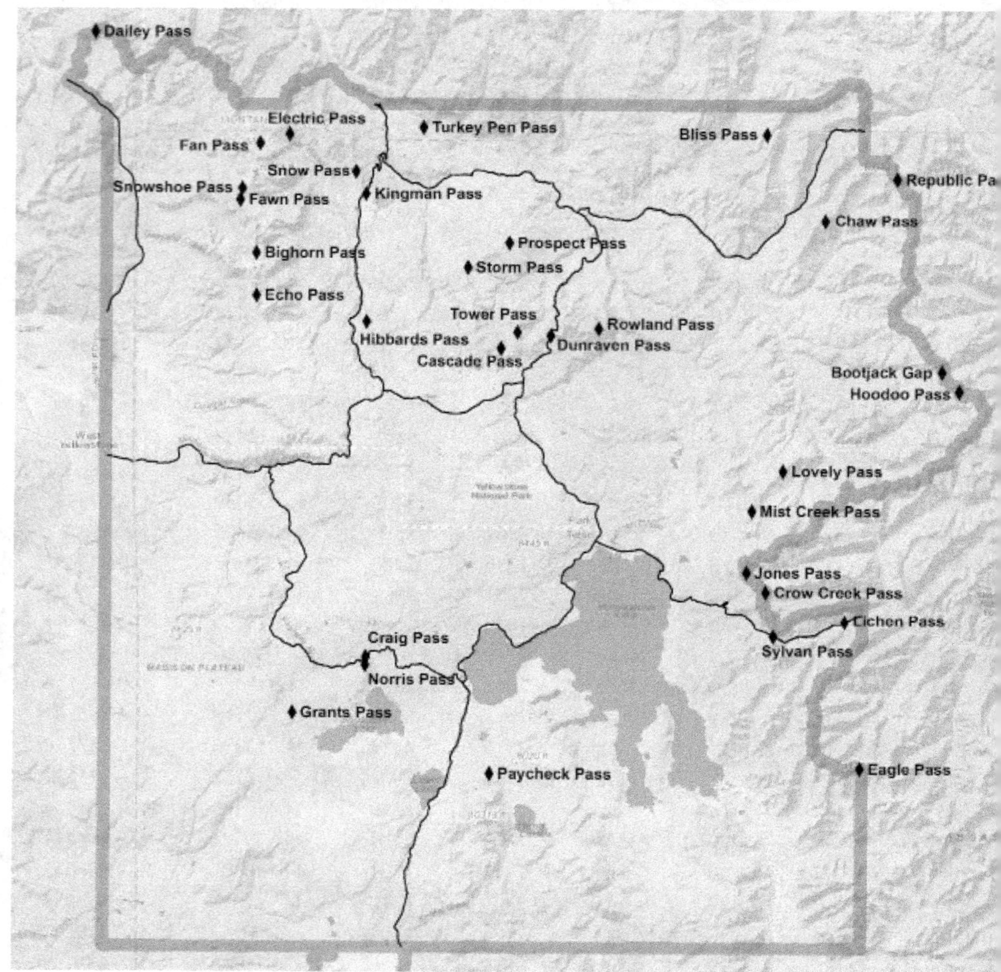

PASS	ELEV FT	ELEV M	LATITUDE	LONGITUDE
Bighorn Pass	9088	2771	44.872432	-110.880771
Bliss Pass	9111	2778	44.999105	-110.142412
Bootjack Gap	9147	2789	44.748277	-109.887960
Cascade Pass	8520	2598	44.772151	-110.525486
Chaw Pass	8834	2693	44.917450	-110.043370
Craig Pass	8323	2538	44.441603	-110.719654
Crow Creek Pass	9872	3010	44.514388	-110.141302
Dailey Pass	8350	2546	45.105207	-111.114670
Dunraven Pass	8842	2696	44.785494	-110.454091
Eagle Pass	9498	2896	44.323835	-110.004075
Echo Pass	9125	2782	44.827342	-110.880112
Electric Pass (Electric Divide)	9813	2992	44.988734	-110.875620
Fan Pass	9839	3000	44.988736	-110.875652
Fawn Pass	9104	2776	44.928543	-110.903828

PASS	ELEV FT	ELEV M	LATITUDE	LONGITUDE
Grants Pass	8028	2448	44.381877	-110.825212
Hibbards Pass	7835	2389	44.799860	-110.720357
Hoodoo Pass	9750	2973	44.727918	-109.863082
Jones Pass	9655	2944	44.535222	-110.169358
Kingman Pass	7103	2166	44.935412	-110.721944
Lichen Pass	7050	2149	44.481649	-110.026921
Lovely Pass	8766	2673	44.643554	-110.116579
Mist Creek Pass	8658	2640	44.601332	-110.162136
Norris Pass	8241	2513	44.433547	-110.720210
Paycheck Pass	8112	2473	44.317396	-110.539731
Prospect Pass	8730	2662	44.883472	-110.514392
Republic Pass	9993	3047	44.952163	-109.953517
Rowland Pass	8757	2670	44.792971	-110.384530
Snow Pass	7467	2277	44.959102	-110.736323
Snowshoe Pass	9606	2929	44.940765	-110.901050
Storm Pass	9400	2866	44.857363	-110.574117
Sylvan Pass	8524	2599	44.465500	-110.130190
Tower Pass	9388	2862	44.789028	-110.502308
Turkey Pen Pass	6463	1970	45.005738	-110.639063

Appendix 5: Yellowstone Thermal Areas

ow to Use This Table

nis table provides a listing of all of the major thermal fields in Yellowstone. The park is ome to over 10,000 identified thermal features - hot springs, geysers, mudpots, fumaroles, nd terraces. It contains by far the largest concentration of these kinds of natural nenomena on the planet.

he table is listed alphabetically. Those with an asterisk(*) at the end of their names e locally-named and the names are not officially recognized by the USGS Board of eographic Names.[1]

- **MAP ID**: The number for the thermal field that corresponds to its location on the provided map.
- **LAT**: Latitude of the centroid of the thermal field or the group of thermal fields.
- **LONG**: Longitude of the centroid of the thermal field or the group of thermal fields.
- **PERIM**: Perimeter of the field or grouping of fields expressed in meters
- **AREA**: Area of the field or group of fields expressed in square meters
- **FEATURES**: Number of unique thermal features that have been identified in this particular area. These surveys were done in the late 1990s and early 2000s, and the figures represent the number of features found at that time. As these features can disappear and new ones can appear, this number is to be used as a guide only. Note that some of these fields are list as DOR (dormant), EXT (extinct), or UNK (unknown, meaning an inventory of the area has not been undertaken)
- **ACCESS NOTES**: Basic instructions on the location of the thermal field and the best way to gain access to it.

afety in the Thermal Fields

Many of these areas are in the park's frontcountry and have boardwalks and trails built nrough them to carry foot traffic (stock traffic is not permitted in thermal areas). In other reas, especially in the remote areas of the backcountry, there may not be any trails. Please se extreme caution when traveling through and exploring these areas. Note that, under ederal law, if a trail is provided through a thermal area, it is against the law to travel off that rail. Damaging, defacing, or destroying any feature in the park, including the bacterial and lgal mats surrounding the park's thermal features, is a federal crime.

Yellowstone Thermal Fields

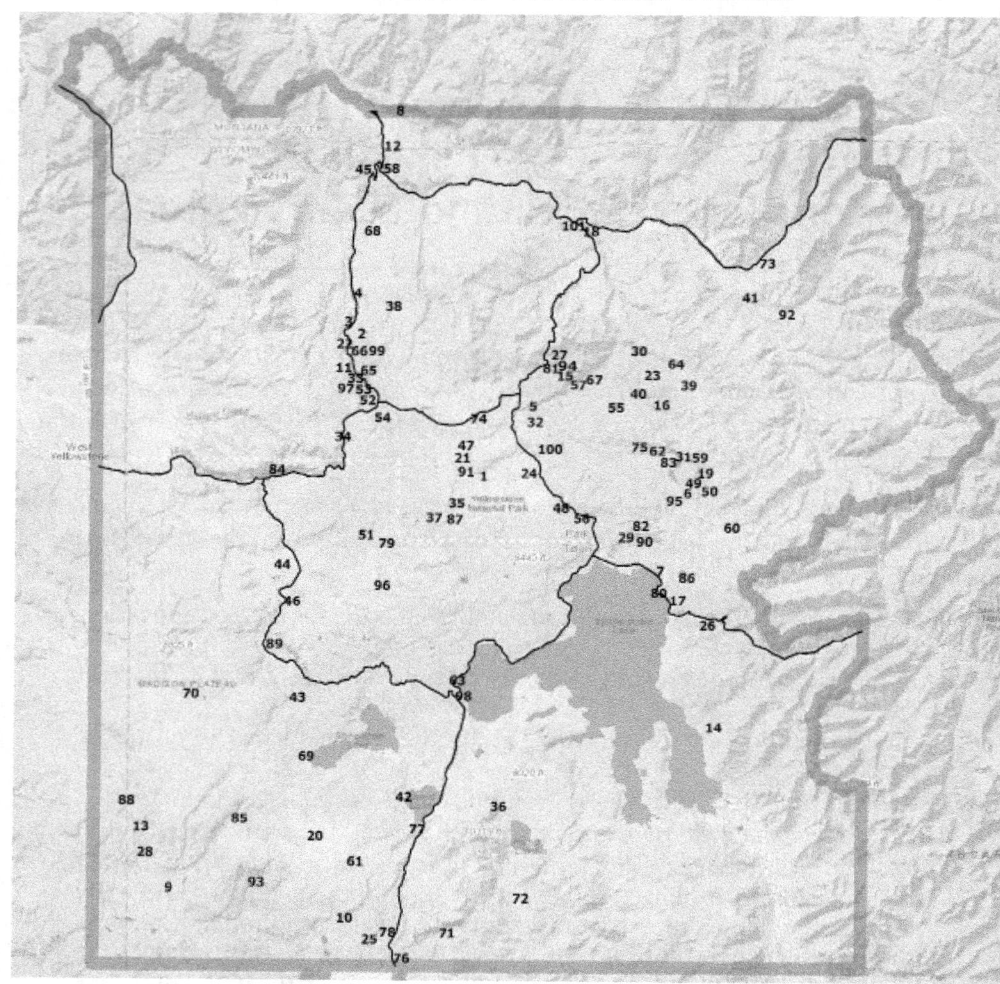

THERMAL AREA NAME	MAP ID	LAT	LONG	PERIM	AREA	FEATURES	ACCESS NOTES
Alum Creek Springs*	1	44.651258	-110.545631	2497	249121	18	Along Mary Mountain Trail W of E trailhead
Amphitheater Springs	2	44.799373	-110.725372	4518	353125	36	North end of Solfatara Trail
Amphitheater Springs North	3	44.810151	-110.732185	1020	19896	8	Near Beaver Lake Picnic Area
Apollinaris Spring	4	44.841732	-110.726832	1032	29232	UNK	Above Apollinaris Spring
Artist Point Thermal Area*	5	44.724011	-110.474960	9003	998042	UNK	Canyon walls/base near Artist Point
Astringent Creek Thermal Area*	6	44.634491	-110.253680	1649	102255	DOR	Dormant area - Astringent Creek Trail
Beach Springs	7	44.550447	-110.299551	2780	146582	16	Roadside - East Entrance Road
Bear Creek Thermal Area*	8	45.031527	-110.668470	1284	47699	4	North end of Yellowstone River Trail
Bechler Meadows Thermal Area*	9	44.213414	-110.990289	1859	51392	30	Bechler River Trail near 9B2/9M2
Beula Lake Thermal Area*	10	44.183367	-110.739597	5057	649990	32	Remote - NE of Beula Lake
Bijah Spring	11	44.761137	-110.732014	1134	46530	10	Roadside - North of Norris
Boiling River	12	44.985041	-110.688875	556	6059	3	North of Mammoth on North Entrance Road
Boundary Creek Thermal Area*	13	44.277182	-111.031164	1535	54271	24	Boundary Creek Trail
Brimstone Basin	14	44.386467	-110.214737	22955	2477888	EXT	Thorofare Trail near 5E4
Brimstone Cascade Thermal Area*	15	44.758665	-110.430753	3455	153946	21	Washburn Spur Trail N of Sevenmile Hole Trail
Broad Creek Thermal Area*	16	44.726046	-110.292407	11976	529557	10	Wapiti Lake Trail 4B2/4B3/4B4
Butte Springs	17	44.519303	-110.275954	2919	157719	20	Roadside - East Entrance Road
Calcite Springs	18	44.908137	-110.394555	1759	39853	2	Yell River Canyon below The Narrows
Central Pelican Creek Thermal Area*	19	44.659625	-110.229302	3928	297042	48	Pelican Creek Trail
Central Pitchstone Plateau Thermal Area*	20	44.268148	-110.782671	6037	1089709	EXT	North Pitchstone Plateau Trail (A)
Central Plateau Thermal Area*	21	44.669148	-110.571953	4081	452620	50	Central Plateau btwn Violet Springs & the Mud Pots
Clearwater Springs	22	44.788657	-110.738873	884	36338	16	Roadside on Norris to Mammoth Rd
Coffee Pot Springs	23	44.757330	-110.305976	5970	494942	85	Remote Mirror Plateau NE of 4B1
Crater Hills	24	44.654172	-110.481293	4641	330649	70	Direct trail - Hayden Valley
Crawfish Thermal Area*	25	44.161600	-110.690070	7165	221967	>60	Along Crawfish Creek - W of Old South Road Trl
Cub Creek Thermal Area*	26	44.496204	-110.224836	4172	100877	12	South of East Entrance Rd w of Cub Creek Curve
Devil's Inkstand Thermal Area*	27	44.769856	-110.437732	809	35704	EXT	NW of Mt Washburn Spur Trail
Dundunda Falls Thermal Area*	28	44.249989	-111.025116	1464	11584	10	Boundary Creek Trail north of 9A3
Ebro Springs	29	44.587759	-110.341157	532	9676	29	Sulphur Hills NE of Fishing Bridge, Remote
Fairyland Basin	30	44.782506	-110.325303	1488	36564	18	Broad Creek Canyon N of 4B1

THERMAL AREA NAME	MAP ID	LAT	LONG	PERIM	AREA	FEATURES	ACCESS NOTES
Fern Lake Thermal Area*	31	44.672457	-110.269928	1947	60924	108	South of Fern Lake Trail
Forest Springs	32	44.711406	-110.472529	10633	644626	>350	Between Wapiti Lake & Clear Lake Trails
Frying Pan Springs	33	44.752088	-110.722953	670	7351	10	Roadside on Norris to Mammoth Road
Gibbon Geyser Basin	34	44.691217	-110.747506	38877	1874455	>800	Along road near Artist Paint Pots (E & W)
Glen Africa Basin	35	44.616451	-110.584611	2282	225603	>150	South of Mary Mountain Trail in Hayden Valley
Heart Lake Geyser Basin	36	44.300855	-110.521604	13748	769952	>400	Along Heart Lake Trail
Highland Hot Springs	37	44.607228	-110.616697	22265	1268122	50	Along Mary Mountain Trail E of Mary Lake
Horseshoe Hill Thermal Area*	38	44.827980	-110.676590	13579	351979	7	On Horseshoe Hill (W of old Arrow Canyon Trail)
Hot Springs Basin Group	39	44.746800	-110.254178	23567	1320165	>900	On Mirror Plateau N of 4W2/4W3
Joseph's Coat Springs	40	44.737622	-110.325903	17189	904171	200	On Mirror Plateau - Campsite 4B1 located in area
Lamar River Thermal Area*	41	44.839222	-110.166447	5291	410224	3	Lamar River Trail W of Cache Creek Trail junction
Lewis Lake Thermal Area*	42	44.310576	-110.656438	9909	683453	51	West shore of Lewis Lake
Lone Star Geyser Basin	43	44.416567	-110.809496	24052	1113193	>900	Around Lone Star & south along Shoshone Lake Trl
Lower Geyser Basin	44	44.557495	-110.832873	72481	11632723	>1800	Along road south of Madison Junction to OF
Mammoth Hot Springs	45	44.967162	-110.710438	6310	879332	100	At Mammoth Hot Springs
Midway Geyser Basin	46	44.518751	-110.823889	19292	2165098	300	Along roadway between Madison Jct & OF
Mud Pot	47	44.682861	-110.571713	4202	138411	100	North of Violet Springs/E of Cygnet Lake Trail
Mud Volcano Area	48	44.618127	-110.434589	11012	569387	70	Along roadway/river north of Fishing Bridge
Mudkettles, The	49	44.635805	-110.233178	1691	40333	30	W of Pelican Creek N of Pelican Valley
Mushpots, The	50	44.636361	-110.227295	4880	127791	>150	E of Pelican Creek N of Pelican Valley
Nez Perce Thermal Area*	51	44.589245	-110.713034	18439	908366	20	Along Mary Mountain Trail E of West Trailhead
Norris Geyser Basin	52	44.730266	-110.709745	13443	2587045	450	At junction of Canyon-Norris Rd & road to Mammoth
Norris Mammoth Corridor Thermal Area	53	44.741150	-110.715152	6472	611653	80	North of Norris GB/W of main road
NE Gibbon Hill Thermal Area*	54	44.711437	-110.691161	8391	461338	50	NE of Gibbon Hill/SE of Norris Junction
Not Orange Rock Springs*	55	44.723200	-110.357330	91	330	2	Wapiti Lake Trail S of 4M2
Ochre Springs	56	44.607405	-110.405085	1032	31391	<10	On hill above LeHardy Rapids Picnic Area
Painted Cliffs Thermal Area*	57	44.753426	-110.411573	14768	1538103	100	End of Seven mile Hole Trail along canyon walls
Parade Grounds*	58	44.974639	-110.702052	901	41819	EXT	Parade ground at Mammoth
Pelican Creek Mud Volcano*	59	44.671537	-110.237302	6844	143616	80	Pelican Creek Trail S of Pelican Creek Cutoff
Pelican Springs	60	44.598397	-110.190742	198	2180	EXT	NE of Pelican Springs Patrol Cabin

THERMAL AREA NAME	MAP ID	LAT	LONG	PERIM	AREA	FEATURES	ACCESS NOTES
Phantom Fumarole	61	44.241722	-110.725104	2236	175961	5	Pitchstone Plateau NE of 8P1/8P2
Ponuntpa Springs	62	44.672274	-110.295857	3414	297711	26	On Fern Lake Trail W of Fern Lake
Potts Hot Spring Basin	63	44.432129	-110.581128	2357	92129	192	Along roadside north of West Thumb GB
Rainbow Springs	64	44.769059	-110.272119	2863	89256	18	Remote Mirror Plateau NE of 4B1
Roadside Springs	65	44.755374	-110.724387	4464	307956	>20	Roadside along/around Nymph Lake
Roaring Mountain Thermal Area*	66	44.780888	-110.725186	25384	2746743	13	E&W of road & behind Roaring Mountain
Sevenmile Hole Thermal Area*	67	44.752164	-110.392181	3698	142845	EXT	Along Moss Creek mouth on Grand Canyon wall @ 7MH
Sheepeaters Thermal Area*	68	44.907364	-110.707874	544	4748	4	Along Gardiner River above Osprey Falls
Shoshone Geyser Basin	69	44.353142	-110.796229	8211	986698	500	Along west side of Shoshone Lake
Smoke Jumper Hot Springs	70	44.420276	-110.961536	31897	2366743	125	Along Summit Lake Trail W of the lake
Snake River Hot Springs	71	44.167905	-110.593063	6518	354608	26	Along South Boundary Trail @ 8C1/8C7
Snake River Thermal Area*	72	44.204823	-110.487949	1670	84644	EXT	Along Heart River Trail E of west trailhead
Soda Butte Thermal Area*	73	44.877855	-110.152458	136	1358	3	At Soda Butte on Northeast Entrance Road
Solfatara Plateau Thermal Area*	74	44.710952	-110.553689	2350	254790	250	Along roadside on Canyon-Norris Rd W of Grebe Lake TH
Sour Creek Thermal Area*	75	44.682145	-110.323381	14544	859919	37	SW of Fern Lake/Wapiti Lake junction
South Boundary Trail Thermal Area*	76	44.141455	-110.658132	1476	62347	24	NE of Snake River Ranger Station on opp side of river
South Lewis Lake Thermal Area*	77	44.275836	-110.637002	1059	35351	33	South end of lake at Lewis River outlet
Spirea Creek Thermal Area*	78	44.166672	-110.682069	11540	709109	236	Along Spirea Creek W of Old South Road Trail
Spruce - Juniper Thermal Area*	79	44.580371	-110.684174	11429	860337	15	SE of Nez Perce Thermal Area. S of Mary Mtn Trail
Steamboat Springs	80	44.529904	-110.294053	1794	60793	16	Along East Entrance Road @ Steamboat Springs
Sulphur Creek Thermal Area*	81	44.763900	-110.442815	1185	39692	27	Along Mt Washburn Spur Trail N of junction
Sulphur Hills Thermal Area*	82	44.593605	-110.320779	5778	441370	7	N of Pelican Creek, N of Indian Pond
Tern Lake Thermal Area*	83	44.666457	-110.281891	1011	51809	6	NW of W Tern Lake, N of White Lake
Terrace Springs	84	44.646772	-110.847066	3651	351194	13	Along roadside N of Madison Junction
Three Rivers Junction Thermal Area*	85	44.286736	-110.890462	7500	339003	237	Bechler River Trail between 9B9 and 9B1, E of 9B1
Tower Junction Thermal Area*	101	44.913767	-110.409767	387	6311	4	East of rear entrance into Roosevelt Corrals
Turbid Springs	86	44.546251	-110.254681	1660	32758	7	South and east of Turbid Lake
Upper Alum Creek Thermal Area*	87	44.605803	-110.586859	1868	66147	EXT	Along old Trout Creek Service Road Trl S of Glen Africa Basin
Upper Boundary Creek TA*	88	44.305424	-111.052196	10317	464573	100	Along Boundary Creek Trail N of 9A4
Upper Geyser Basin	89	44.469400	-110.846840	38575	2921536	>800	Along roadway at Old Faithful

THERMAL AREA NAME	MAP ID	LAT	LONG	PERIM	AREA	FEATURES	ACCESS NOTES
Vermilion Springs	90	44.583512	-110.315241	2698	137202	12	Along Pelican Creek, due N of Indian Pond
Violet Springs	91	44.655381	-110.571146	7380	247450	84	In Hayden Valley N of Mary Mtn Trail, E of Mary Mtn
Wahb Springs	92	44.821615	-110.115009	3630	132044	5	Along Cache Creek Trail E of W trailhead
Warm Creek Thermal Area	93	44.219687	-110.865832	2490	33268	160	North of Union Falls
Washburn Hot Springs	94	44.766133	-110.429745	1306	78769	17	Along Mt. Washburn Spur Trail S of 4E1
West Astringent Creek TA*	95	44.626061	-110.273091	22554	905088	EXT	West of Astringent Creek Trail S of White Lake
West Juniper Creek Thermal Area*	96	44.536366	-110.689932	19939	1409778	EXT	South of Mary Mountain Trail, S of Juniper Creek TA
West Nymph Creek Thermal Area*	97	44.741564	-110.743901	5702	64021	82	Remote area NW of Norris GB
West Thumb Geyser Basin	98	44.418888	-110.572346	3111	118270	171	At West Thumb Junction
Whiterock Springs	99	44.781264	-110.699748	1575	29931	7	Along Solfatara Trail S of Amphitheater Springs TA
Yellowstone River Thermal Area*	100	44.679228	-110.452115	3055	237054	4	Hayden Valley SE of Sour Creek-Howard Eaton Trl Jct

Appendix 6: Popular Features

How to Use This Table

This table provides a quick reference for finding the closest backcountry campsites to some of the park's more popular backcountry features. Simply locate the feature you wish to explore on your hike and use the chart to determine which campsite(s) is closest to it, and you can make your travel plans based on that. More detailed information regarding the location of some of these may available in the other chapters, maps, and appendices found herein.

FEATURE	NEARBY CAMPSITE(S)
Acheron Falls	9A2
Albright Falls	9B9
Baronette Peak	3P1; 3P2 (both W)
Basin Creek Lake	8B2
Batchelder Column	9B9
Bechler Canyon	9B4
Bechler Meadows Thermal Area	9B2; 9M2
Bechler Rivers Hot Springs	9B0; 9B9
Beula Lake	8A1; 8A2
Bighorn Springs Cascade	WB6; WB4
Black Canyon of the Yellowstone	2H1; 2H2; 1R3
Boundary Creek Thermal Area	9A4
Bradley Falls	8A1; 8A2
Brimstone Basin	5E4
Broad Creek Thermal Area	4B2; 4B3; 4B4
Bride Falls	9D1
Buffalo Lake	9A5
Cache Lake	1G3 (2 miles); 1G4 (2.2 miles)
Cascade Lake	4E2; 4E3; 4E4
Childhood's Dream Falls	9B4
Citadel of Asgard Falls	4E1
Colonnade Falls	9B5
Confederate Falls	9A2
Confusion Cascade	9D2
Cottonwood Creek	1R1; 1R2 (0.25 miles E)
Crescent Lake	WE6
Crevice Lake	1Y4; 1Y5
Death Gulch (Wahb Springs)	3L1; 3L2
Douglas Knob	9D3
Douglas Knob Falls	9D3

FEATURE	NEARBY CAMPSITE(S)
Dunanda Falls	9A3
Dunanda Falls Thermal Area	9A3
Electric Peak	1G3; 1G4 (SE)
Fairy Falls	OD1
Fawn Lake	1F2 (0.25 miles N OT)
Feather Lake	OD5
Fern Lake	5B1
Forlorn Falls	9D1
Gilded Falls	WB6; WB4
Goose Lake	OD5
Grants Pass	8G1
Grebe Lake	4G2; 4G3; 4G4; 4G5
Grizzly Lake	1C1 (0.7 miles N); 1C2 (1.4 miles N)
Groom Falls	9D1
Gwinna Falls	9D1
Heart Lake Geyser Basin	8H4; 8H5; 8H6
Hellroaring Mtn	2H8 ((E); 2H9 (NE); 2H7 (SE)
Hering Lake	8A1; 8A2
Hidden Falls	1A1 (1.1 miles S)
High Lake	WD4; WD5
Hoodoo Basin	3M6; 3M7
Horseshoe Cascade	9A4
Ice Lake	4D1; 4D2; 4D3
Indian Creek	1B1
Instant Falls	3L4
Iris Falls	9B5
Isolation Falls	6Y2
Joseph's Coat Hot Springs	4B1
Knowles Falls	1Y2 (1 mile N); 1Y4 (1.1 miles S)
Little Cottonwood Creek	1R3 (0.25 miles E)

FEATURE	NEARBY CAMPSITE(S)
Lone Star Geyser	OA1
Lone Star Geyser Basin	OA2; OA3
Lovely Falls	OD3
Mallard Lake	OB2; OB3; OB4
Mariposa Lake	6M3
McBride Lake	2S1 E
Mirror Lake	3L6, 3L7
Mist of the Trident Falls	6Y5
Mr. Bubbles (thermal pool)	9D1; 9B9
Mt. Everts	1A2 (north slope); 1A3 (South face)
Mt. Holmes (summit)	1C4; 1C5
Mt. Sheridan	8H4; 8H5; 8H6
Opal Creek Thermal Area	3L2
Outlet Lake	8O2
Ouzel Falls	9B4
Paintbrush Cascade	9A4
Painted Cliffs Thermal Area (7 Mile Hole)	4C1; 4C2; 4C3
Peterson Falls	2Y1
Phantom Fumarole	8P1; 8P2
Phillips Fork Falls	9D1
Plateau Falls	6M3
Precipitous Falls	OD3
Queens Laundry	OG1
Ragged Falls	9D1
Ranger Lake	9B4
Robinson Canyon Falls	9B6

FEATURE	NEARBY CAMPSITE(S)
Rugged Falls	9D1
Sentinel Falls	OG2
Sentinel Meadows	OG1
Shelf Lake	WE5; WE7
Shoshone Geyser Basin	8R5; 8T1
Silver Scarf Falls	9A3
Sluiceway Falls	9D1
Smokejumper Hot Springs	OE1
Snake River Hot Springs	8C1; 8C7
Snake River Thermal Area	8B5
Sportsman Lake	WD2; WD3
Stone Hollow Falls	WB6; WB4
Tempestuous Falls	2C1 (N); 2H8 (S)
Tendoy Falls	9D1
Treasure Island	9B5
Treasure Island Falls	9B5
Trilobite Lake	1C4; 1C5
Twister Falls	9D2
Union Falls	9U4; 9U5
Wahb Springs/Death Gulch	3L1; 3L2
Wahhi Falls	9D1
Wapiti Lake	4W2; 4W3
Weeping Falls	9B4
Whortleberry Falls	8H3; 8H2
Wolf Lake	4G6; 4G7
Wrangler Lake	4W1

Appendix 7: Trail Recommendations

One of the most common question backcountry offices (and, to a somewhat lesser extent, the interpretation rangers at the Visitor Centers and gate rangers at the park's entrances) receive from visitors is, "Which trail would be best for X, Y, or Z?" People want to know which trails are best for families with young children, which trails are best for seeing particular kinds of wildlife, wildflowers, etc., which trails are best for staying one night in the backcountry, and all kinds of other combinations of things they'd like to do while on their trip to Yellowstone.

It's hard to quantify any kind of "best" trail for any given person or group, because everyone's idea of what constitutes "best" is subjective. So the best I can do as the author of this book is to provide a list of trails I usually recommend people consider when they're planning a trip to Yellowstone.

Trails for Families with Small(erish) Children

- Wraith Falls Trail
- Mystic Falls Trail
- Ice Lake Trail
- Storm Point Trail
- Children's Fire Trail/Nature Trail
- Harlequin Lake Trail
- Any of the frontcountry thermal areas (Mammoth, Old Faithful, etc.)

Trails for Quick, Half-Day Hikes

- Mount Washburn (Dunraven Pass) Trail
- Avalanche Peak Trail
- Turbid Lake Trail (Nine-Mile Trailhead to Pelican Valley)

Trails for Day-Long Hikes

- Mary Mountain Trail
- Specimen Ridge Trail
- Howard Eaton Trail: Fishing Bridge to Canyon

Trails for First Time Backcountry Campers

- Mallard Lake Trail
- Fairy Falls Trail
- Lava Creek Trail
- Beula Lake Trail
- Lone Star Trail

Trails for Seeing Backcountry Thermal Features

- Crater Hills/Sulphur Mountain Trail (half day)
- Bechler River Trail (multi-day)
- Seven Mile Hole Trail (half day + or overnight)
- Washburn Spur Trail (day hike or overnight)
- Summit Lake Trail (day hike or overnight)

Trails for Backcountry Waterfalls

- Bechler River Trail (multi-day)
- Union Falls Trail (can be done in a day, but best overnight)
- Terraced Falls Trail (day hike)

Short Trails for Seeing Lakes

- Trout Lake Trail
- Beula Lake Trail
- Lost Lake Trail
- Riddle Lake Trail
- Duck Lake Trail
- Harlequin Lake Trail

Trails for Seeing Wildlife

- Mary Mountain Trail (day hike)
- Lamar River Trail (multi-day)
- Howard Eaton Trail (Fishing Bridge to Canyon)

"Serious" Mountain Climbs

- Avalanche Peak Trail
- Electric Peak, Southeast Ridge Trail
- Electric Peak, Southwest Ridge Trail

Most Picturesque Trails

- Terraced Falls Trail (especially in the fall)
- Elephant Back Trail
- Specimen Ridge Trail
- Yellowstone River Trail
- Sky Rim Trail

Trails for Two-Day/Night Hikes

- Shoshone Lake Trail (any of the three routes in)
- Heart Lake Trail
- Pelican Creek Trail (Campground to Warm Springs Trailhead)

Trails for Three-Day/Night Hikes

- Heart Lake Trail to South Entrance
- Bechler River Trail

Trails for Getting Away From It All

- Thorofare Trail
- Yellowstone River Trail
- Hoodoo Basin Trail
- Bighorn Pass Trail

st All-Around Trails in the Park

- Bechler River Trail
- Sky Rim Trail
- Yellowstone River Trail

e Ultimate Yellowstone Hikes

- Bechler River Trail
- Thorofare Trail
- Yellowstone River Trail

ails for Those with Mobility Issues

- Ice Lake Trail
- Artist Point Trail
- Lone Star Trail
- Any of the boardwalked trails in the thermal basins

Appendix 8: Trailhead Information

ow to Use These Tables

here are two tables included in this section. The first is a list of the trailheads around e park. It includes the backcountry trailheads (identified by a number-letter-number heme) as well as the frontcountry and threshold trail trailheads (designated by three tters).[1] It provides location information along with details about how many vehicles can accommodated at each.

he second table provides distance information between backcountry trailheads for all mbinations of possible hikes you could use to get from one to the other. For example, if u wish to begin at trailhead 5K5 (Nine Mile) and come out at 6K3 (Fox Creek), there are vo possible routes. One is 45.6 miles long and the other is 40.9 miles long. You can use this formation to plan routes based on how much distance you wish to cover (which would low you to determine how long of a trip you'd need based on how many miles you wished hike in your itinerary).

or the first table, the following information is provided:

- **ID**: Trailhead Designator. For backcountry trailheads, the first character is the district the trailhead is in (see the chart in the chapter on the introduction to the trails), the second character is an administrative grouping identifier (always a K, N, or a Z), and the third character is a sequence number. For frontcountry and threshold trails, it's just a three-letter abbreviation for the trail name.
- **NAME**: Trailhead name
- **LAT**: Latitude of the trailhead
- **LONG**: Longitude of the trailhead
- **PARKING**: Description of the numbers and kinds of vehicles that can be accommodated at the trailhead. NPS reconfigures trailheads from time to time, so this information is subject to change.
- **IN PARK**: Indicates whether the trailhead is inside Yellowstone or not. Trailheads that are inside the park are patrolled by NPS law enforcement rangers, whereas those that are outside the park are patrolled by local law enforcement (or USFS law enforcement in some cases).

ID	NAME	LAT	LONG	PARKING	IN PAR
1K1	Sepulcher Mtn	44.97379	-110.70432	Large parking lot	Y
1K2	Snow Pass	44.95897	-110.71212	Small pullout across road; 3 cars	Y
1K3	Glen Creek/Fawn Pass	44.93228	-110.72828	Bunsen Peak Lot; 15 cars	Y
1K4	Bunsen Peak	44.93216	-110.72784	15 cars; small RVs possible	Y
1K5	Indian Creek	44.88268	-110.73527	Approx 10 cars; 2 RVs	Y
1K6	Mt Holmes	44.83825	-110.73273	Approx 10 cars	Y
1K7	Solfatara North	44.80660	-110.73471	8-10 cars	Y
1K8	Grizzly Lake	44.79903	-110.74532	6-7 cars	Y
1N1	Yellowstone River	45.04540	-110.67801	12 cars; 2-3 RVs	N
1N2	Rescue Creek	45.01780	-110.69366	10 cars; 2-3 smaller RVs	Y
1N3	Lava Creek (Boiling River)	44.99236	-110.69133	14 cars; 1-2 smaller RVs	Y
1N3	Lava Creek North	44.97858	-110.69203	6-7 cars; 1-2 RVs	Y
1N4	Beaver Ponds	44.97749	-110.70137	Large parking lot	Y
1N5	Blacktail Creek	44.95566	-110.59385	8 cars; RVs & stock across road	Y
1N6	Lava Creek South	44.94089	-110.63220	4-5 cars in picnic area across street	Y
2K2	Tower Junction	44.91614	-110.41608	8-10 cars; 2-3 RVs	Y
2K4	Specimen Ridge	44.91229	-110.38738	12-15 cars; 2-3 RVs	Y
2K5	Slough Creek	44.94352	-110.30805	16-18 cars; 2-3 RVs	Y
2K6	Chittenden Road	44.82452	-110.44458	Large parking lot	Y
2K7	Yellowstone River Picnic Area	44.91674	-110.40064	6-8 cars; 2-3 smaller RVs	Y
2K8	Hellroaring	44.94895	-110.45058	8-10 cars; 2-3 smaller RVs	Y
2N1	Coyote Creek	45.02984	-110.40309	USFS Entry Point	Y
2N2	Buffalo Plateau	45.02979	-110.34507	USFS Entry Point	Y
2N3	Buffalo Fork	45.02977	-110.29316	USFS Entry Point	Y
2N4	Upper Slough	45.02941	-110.17477	USFS Entry Point	Y
2N5	Upper Hellroaring	45.02971	-110.44023	USFS Entry Point	Y
3K1	Soda Butte	44.86922	-110.16622	20 cars;4-5 RVs	Y
3K1	Soda Butte Stock	44.86840	-110.17449	3-4 cars;4-5 stock trailers (No RVs)	Y
3K2	Pebble Creek	44.91689	-110.11318	4-5 cars in PA; 2-3 in pullout; 1-2 RVs	Y
3K3	Thunderer	44.92144	-110.09559	10-12 cars; 2-3 RVs	Y
3K4	Warm Creek	45.00539	-110.03420	10-12 cars; 2-3 smaller RVs	Y
3N1	Republic Pass	44.95184	-109.95323	USFS Entry Point	Y
3N2	Canoe Lake	44.79324	-109.93584	USFS Entry Point	Y
3N3	Bootjack Gap	44.74819	-109.88654	USFS Entry Point	Y
3N4	Hoodoo	44.70052	-109.82663	USFS Entry Point	Y
3N5	Frost Lake	44.62387	-110.02555	USFS Entry Point	Y
4K1	Solfatara South	44.73814	-110.69214	1-2 cars (add'l lot nearby)	Y
4K2	Ice Lake	44.71683	-110.63397	10-12 cars; 2-3 smaller RVs	Y
4K3	Grebe Lake	44.71793	-110.54974	7-8 cars; 2-3 smaller RVs	Y
4K4	Cascade Creek	44.73527	-110.50339	10 cars; 2-3 smaller RVs	Y
4K5	Cascade Lake	44.75018	-110.49197	22 cars; 2-3 RVs	Y
4K6	Glacial Boulder	44.72964	-110.47277	10-12 cars; 2-3 RVs	Y
4K7	Wapiti Lake	44.70773	-110.50028	44 cars;3-4 RVs	Y
4K8	Artist Point	44.72020	-110.47978	Large parking lot	Y
4K9	Dunraven Pass	44.78500	-110.45344	35-50 cars; 4-6 RVs	Y
4N1	Mary Mountain East	44.68333	-110.49374	10-12 cars; 3-5 RVs	Y
4N2	Clear Lake	44.71458	-110.49539	Large parking lot	Y

ID	NAME	LAT	LONG	PARKING	IN PARK
N3	Cygnet Lakes	44.70586	-110.57299	10-12 cars;2-3 RVs	Y
N4	Wolf Lake Cutoff	44.71284	-110.62732	15-20 cars;4-5 RVs	Y
K1	Bridge Bay Marina	44.53331	-110.43999	Large parking lot	Y
K2	Fishing Bridge	44.56579	-110.37943	20-25 cars;8-10 RVs	Y
K3	Pelican Valley	44.55899	-110.30778	(Trailhead parking being rebuilt)	Y
K4	Sedge Bay	44.51921	-110.27800	Large parking lot	Y
K5	Nine Mile	44.50562	-110.27556	25-30 cars;5-6 RVs/stock	Y
K6	Pumice Point	44.45270	-110.50421	15-20 cars;4-5 RVs	Y
N1	East Entrance	44.48940	-110.00175		Y
N2	Avalanche Peak	44.47072	-110.14258	10 cars; 2-3 smaller RVs in picnic area	Y
Z1	Jones Pass	44.53496	-110.16893	USFS Entry Point	Y
Z2	Crow Creek Pass	44.51406	-110.14086	USFS Entry Point	Y
K1	Eagle Pass	44.32408	-110.00437	USFS Entry Point	Y
K2	Thorofare	44.13264	-110.07231	USFS Entry Point	Y
K3	Fox Creek	44.13263	-110.30061	USFS Entry Point	Y
K4	Bridger Lake	44.13265	-110.10951	USFS Entry Point	Y
K5	Hawks Rest	44.13263	-110.08484	USFS Entry Point	Y
Z1	Dike Creek	44.27876	-110.00114	USFS Entry Point	Y
K1	Grant Village Marina	44.39222	-110.54789	19 long slots (vehicles w/ trailers)	Y
K2	DeLacy Creek	44.44678	-110.70161	20-25 cars;3-5 RVs	Y
K3	Riddle Lake	44.35852	-110.58170	10-15 cars;2-3 RVs	Y
3K1	Lewis Channel / Dogshead	44.32009	-110.59953		Y
3K3	Lewis Lake Dock	44.28272	-110.62854	20-25 cars;Lot for trailers/RVs	Y
3K4	Pitchstone Plateau	44.24324	-110.64732	3 cars;1 RV	Y
3K5	South Boundary West	44.13436	-110.66894	Use South Boundary East	Y
3K6	Beula Lake	44.13260	-110.78836	3 cars; No RVs	N
3K7	South Boundary East	44.13644	-110.66601	15-20 cars;4-5 RVs/stock trailers	Y
3K8	Colter / Wolverine	44.13260	-110.51342	USFS Entry Point	Y
3N1	Heart Lake	44.31744	-110.59825	20-25 cars;6-8 RVs/stock trailers	Y
9K1	Bechler Ranger Station	44.14986	-111.04547	25-30 cars;3-4 RVs	Y
9K2	Cave Falls	44.13675	-111.01006	10-15 cars;2-3 RVs (1/10th mile away)	Y
9K3	Fish Lake	44.13270	-110.93909	8-10 cars; No RVs	N
9K5	Cascade Creek	44.13266	-110.84878	4-5 cars;No RVs	N
9K6	Grassy Lake	44.13264	-110.82364	35-40 cars;No RVs	N
9K7	Robinson Creek	44.23677	-111.09767	USFS Entry Point	Y
9K8	Boundary Creek	44.32807	-111.09744	USFS Entry Point	Y
9K9	Summit Lake	44.39448	-111.09714	USFS Entry Point	Y
APP	Artist Paint Pots	44.69625	-110.74108	Large parking lot	Y
ART	Artemisia	44.48414	-110.85132	Use Biscuit Basin parking lot	Y
HQL	Harlequin Lake	44.64032	-110.88741	Large pullout across road	Y
MGB	Monument Geyser	44.68378	-110.74466	6-8 cars;2-3 smaller RVs	Y
MK1	Purple Mountain	44.64653	-110.85503	5-6 cars;1-2 RVs	Y
OBS	Observation Point	44.46236	-110.82764	Use Old Faithful Lots	Y
OK1	Lone Star	44.44446	-110.80453	10-15 cars;4-6 RVs + Kep Cascade Lot	Y
OK2	Howard Eaton	44.45387	-110.82966	5-6 cars;1 smaller RV	Y
OK3	Mallard Lake	44.45841	-110.82274	25-40 cars;5-6 RVs	Y
OK4	Biscuit Basin	44.48503	-110.85254	Large parking lot	Y

ID	NAME	LAT	LONG	PARKING	IN PAR
OK5	Fairy Falls	44.51554	-110.83253	40-50 cars;RVs use south pullout	Y
OK6	Fountain Flats Dr/Freight Rd	44.56713	-110.83522	Large parking lot	Y
OK7	Nez Perce/Mary Mtn West	44.56992	-110.81611	6-7 cars;1-2 RVs	Y
OK9	Mallard Creek	44.50697	-110.83314	7-10 cars;1-2 smaller RVs	Y
PEL	Pelican Creek Nature Trail	44.55998	-110.36075	8-12 cars;1-2 smaller RVs	Y
STM	Storm Point Trail	44.55937	-110.32771	12 cars in West; 15-18 in East	Y
TRE	Two Ribbons East	44.65163	-111.03081	Large parking lot	Y
TRL	Trout Lake	44.89911	-110.12319	9-10 cars;1-2 smaller RVs	Y
TRW	Two Ribbons West	44.65232	-111.03753	Large parking lot	Y
WK1	Dailey Creek	45.04846	-111.13950	15-20 cars;4-5RVs/stock trailers	Y
WK2	Black Butte	45.03491	-111.11408	8-10 cars;1-2 smaller RVs	Y
WK3	Specimen Creek	45.01261	-111.08074	10-15 cars;2-3 RVs	Y
WK4	Bacon Rind	44.95520	-111.07067	10-15 cars;1-2 smaller RVs	Y
WK5	Fawn Pass	44.95065	-111.05902	15-20 cars;6-8 RVs/stock trailers	Y
WK6	Bighorn Pass	44.92811	-111.04912	8-10 cars;1-2 smaller RVs	Y
WK7	Gneiss Creek	44.79316	-111.09714	15-20 cars;5-8 RVs/stock trailers	N
WK8	Seven Mile Bridge	44.66380	-110.96496	4-5 cars;1 smaller RV	Y
WK9	Riverside Ski Trails	44.66028	-111.09719	Large strip parking along WYS road	N
WN1	Sky Rim	45.10513	-111.11446	USFS Entry Point	Y
WRF	Wraith Falls	44.94225	-110.62343	12-15 cars;1-2 smaller RVs	Y
WZ1	Teepee Creek	45.08051	-111.13797	USFS Entry Point	Y
WZ2	Skyrim West	45.10108	-111.12973	USFS Entry Point	Y
WZ3	Mulherin	45.02958	-110.88276	USFS Entry Point	Y

This second table provides detailed routing information between the park's backcountr trailheads. All possible configurations to get from one point to another are provide (assuming no side trips or other deviations). This information can be used to plan route based on mileage.

- **FROM**: Starting point trailhead
- **TO**: End point trailhead
- **ROUTE**: Provides the route using trail codes. Codes are provided in the second half of the table.
- **DIS-MI**: Distance of each route in U.S. miles
- **DIS-KM**: Distance of each route in kilometers.

An example of how to use this would be as follows:

Say you wish to go in at the Specimen Creek Trailhead (WK3) and come out at the Fawn Pas Trailhead (WK5). There are two possible hiking routes (again, assuming no side trips) you could use to do this. The first, SPCR-SPLA-FACR-FAPA, is a route that takes you along the Specimen Creek Trail, then the Sportsman Lake Trail, then the Fan Creek Trail, and then the Fawn Pass Trail out to its trailhead. The total hiking distance would be 16.24 miles (26.14km) Alternatively, you could take the routing SPCR-CRHI-SPLA-FACR-FAPA, which takes you from the Specimen Creek Trail to the Crescent Lake/High Lake Trail, to the Sportsman Lake Trail, to the Fan Creek Trail, and then to the Fawn Pass Trail where you'd exit at its trailhead The total distance for this hike would be 24.86 miles (40.01km).

FROM	TO	ROUTE	DIS-MI	DIS-KM
1K1	1K2	SEMO-CLBU-SNPA	4.81	7.74
1K1	1K2	SEMO-SPLA-SNPA	10.46	16.83
1K1	1K2	SEMO-HEMA-SNPA	1.72	2.77
1K1	1K3	SEMO-SPLA-FAPA	10.64	17.12
1K1	1K3	SEMO-CLBU-SNPA-FAPA	6.09	9.80
1K1	1K3	SEMO-CLBU-SNPA-HEMA-FAPA	7.66	12.33
1K1	1K3	SEMO-HEMA-FAPA	4.32	6.95
1K1	WN1	SEMO-SPLA-CRHI-SPCR-SKYR	41.89	67.42
1K1	WN1	SEMO-CLBU-SNPA-SPLA-CRHI-SPCR-SKYR	38.74	62.35
1K1	WZ1	SEMO-SPLA-CRHI-SPCR-SKYR-DACR-DCSP	45.29	72.89
1K1	WZ1	SEMO-CLBU-SNPA-SPLA-CRHI-SPCR-SKYR-DACR-DCSP	42.14	67.82
1K1	WZ2	SEMO-SPLA-CRHI-SPCR-SKYR	42.97	69.15
1K1	WZ2	SEMO-CLBU-SNPA-SPLA-CRHI-SPCR-SKYR	39.82	64.08
1K1	WZ3	SEMO-SPLA-WD3S-MOLH	19.78	31.83
1K1	WZ3	SEMO-CLBU-SNPA-SPLA-WD3S-MOLH	16.63	26.76
1K2	1K3	SNPA-HEMA-FAPA	2.92	4.70
1K2	1K3	SNPA-FAPA	4.22	6.79
1K2	WN1	SNPA-SPLA-CRHI-SPCR-SKYR	36.30	58.42
1K2	WZ1	SNPA-SPLA-CRHI-SPCR-SKYR-DACR-DCSP	39.73	63.94
1K2	WZ2	SNPA-SPLA-CRHI-SPCR-SKYR	37.38	60.16
1K2	WZ3	SNPA-SPLA-WD3S-MOLH	14.22	22.88
1K4	WN1	FAPA-SPLA-CRHI-SPCR-SKYR	36.35	58.50
1K4	WZ1	FAPA-SPLA-CRHI-SPCR-SKYR-DACR-DCSP	39.75	63.97
1K4	WZ2	FAPA-SPLA-CRHI-SPCR-SKYR	37.43	60.24
1K4	WZ3	FAPA-SPLA-WD3S-MOLH	14.24	22.92
1K6	1K8	MHWC-GRLA	6.71	10.80
1K7	4K2	SOLF-HECA-ICLA	10.01	16.11
1K7	4K3	SOLF-HECA-GREB	19.16	30.83
1K7	4K4	SOLF-HECA-CASL-CASC	20.20	32.51
1K7	4K5	SOLF-HECA-CASL	19.42	31.25
1K7	4N4	SOLF-HECA-WOLA	12.28	19.76
1N1	1N3	YERI-BLDC-BPLC-LACR	18.93	30.46
1N1	1N5	YERI-BLDC	12.54	20.18
1N1	1N6	YERI-BLDC-BPLC-LACR	14.51	23.35
1N1	2K2	YERI-HECR-GHHC-GHLT(S)	20.60	33.15
1N1	2K2	YERI-HECR-GHHC-GHLT(N)	22.12	35.60
1N1	2K8	YERI-HECR	20.67	33.27
1N1	2N1	YERI-HECR-BUPL-COCR	21.95	35.33
1N1	2N2	YERI-HECR-BUPL	24.35	39.19
1N1	2N5	YERI-HECR	20.67	33.27
1N2	1N1	RECR-BLDC-YERI	19.19	30.88
1N2	1N3	RECR-BLDC-BPLC-LACR	14.42	23.21
1N2	1N5	RECR-BLDC	8.03	12.92
1N2	1N6	RECR-BLDC-BPLC-LACR	10.00	16.09
1N2	2K2	RECR-BLDC-YERI-HECR-GHHC-GHLT(S)	22.71	36.55
1N2	2K2	RECR-BLDC-YERI-HECR-GHHC-GHLT(N)	24.23	38.99
1N2	2K8	RECR-BLDC-YERI-HECR	19.87	31.98

FROM	TO	ROUTE	DIS-MI	DIS-KM
1N2	2N1	RECR-BLDC-YERI-HECR-BUPL-COCR	24.06	38.72
1N2	2N2	RECR-BLDC-YERI-HECR-BUPL	26.46	42.58
1N2	2N5	RECR-BLDC-YERI-HECR	22.78	36.66
1N3	1N5	LACR-BPLC-BLDC	2.81	4.52
1N3	2K2	LACR-BPLC-BLDC-YERI-HECR-GHHC-GHLT(S)	17.30	27.84
1N3	2K2	LACR-BPLC-BLDC-YERI-HECR-GHHC-GHLT(N)	18.82	30.29
1N3	2K8	LACR-BPLC-BLDC-YERI-HECR	15.19	24.45
1N3	2N1	LACR-BPLC-BLDC-YERI-HECR-BUPL-COCR	19.38	31.19
1N3	2N2	LACR-BPLC-BLDC-YERI-HECR-BUPL	21.78	35.05
1N3	2N5	LACR-BPLC-BLDC-YERI-HECR	18.10	29.13
1N4	1K2	BEPO-SEMO-HEMA-SNPA	6.64	10.69
1N4	1K2	BEPO-SEMO-CLBU-SNPA	7.53	12.12
1N4	1K3	BEPO-SEMO-HEMA-FAPA	9.23	14.85
1N4	1K3	BEPO-SEMO-CLBU-SNPA-HEMA-FAPA	11.47	18.46
1N5	2K2	BLDC-YERI-HECR-GHHC-GHLT(S)	16.06	25.85
1N5	2K2	BLDC-YERI-HECR-GHHC-GHLT(N)	17.58	28.29
1N5	2K8	BLDC-YERI-HECR	13.22	21.28
1N5	2N1	BLDC-YERI-HECR-BUPL-COCR	17.41	28.02
1N5	2N2	BLDC-YERI-HECR-BUPL	19.81	31.88
1N5	2N5	BLDC-YERI-HECR	16.13	25.96
2K2	2K8	GHLT(S)-GHHC-HECR	4.32	6.95
2K2	2K8	GHLT(N)-GHHC-HECR	5.84	9.40
2K2	2N1	GHLT(S)-GHHC-HECR-BUPL-COCR	10.05	16.17
2K2	2N1	GHLT(N)-GHHC-HECR-BUPL-COCR	11.57	18.62
2K2	2N2	GHLT(S)-GHHC-HECR-BUPL	12.45	20.04
2K2	2N2	GHLT(N)-GHHC-HECR-BUPL	13.97	22.48
2K2	2N5	GHLT(S)-GHHC-HECR	10.17	16.37
2K2	2N5	GHLT(N)-GHHC-HECR	11.69	18.81
2K5	2N3	SLCR-BUFO	8.14	13.10
2K5	3K2	SLCR-BLPA-PECR	20.42	32.86
2K5	3K4	SLCR-BLPA-PECR	19.31	31.08
2K7	2K4	YEOV-SPRI	3.05	4.91
2K7	3K1	YEOV-SPRI	17.95	28.89
2K8	2K2	HECR-GHHC-GHLT(S)	4.32	6.95
2K8	2K2	HECR-GHHC-GHLT(N)	5.84	9.40
2K8	2N1	HECR-BUPL-COCR	7.21	11.60
2K8	2N2	HECR-BUPL	9.61	15.47
3K1	3K3	SPRI-LARI-CACR-THCU	18.74	30.16
3K1	3N1	SPRI-LARI-CACR-THCU	19.34	31.12
3K1	3N2	SPRI-LARI-MICR-CALA	20.73	33.36
3K1	3N3	SPRI-LARI-MICR-BOGA	21.49	34.58
3K1	3N4	SPRI-LARI-MICR-BOGA-HOBA	27.38	44.06
3K1	3N5	SPRI-LARI-FRLA	22.51	36.23
3K1	4K7	SPRI-LARI-MISC-RACR-PELC-UPCC-ASCR-FELA-WALA	52.25	84.09
3K1	4K7	SPRI-LARI-MISC-RACR-PELC-UPCC-ASCR-WALA	38.68	62.25
3K1	4K7	SPRI-LARI-MISC-RACR-PELC-WALA	38.07	61.27
3K1	4K8	SPRI-LARI-MISC-RACR-PELC-UPCC-ASCR-FELA-WALA-RILA-APPS	52.12	83.88

FROM	TO	ROUTE	DIS-MI	DIS-KM
3K1	4N2	SPRI-LARI-MISC-RACR-PELC-UPCC-ASCR-FELA-WALA-RILA-CLLA-CLLC	52.44	84.39
3K1	5K3	SPRI-LARI-MISC-PEVA	34.19	55.02
3K1	5K3	SPRI-LARI-MISC-RACR-PELC-PEVA	35.80	57.61
3K1	5K5	SPRI-LARI-MISC-PEVA-TULA	38.58	62.09
3K2	2N4	PECR-BLPA-SLCR	16.61	26.73
3K3	3N1	THCU-CACR	10.60	17.06
3K4	2N4	PECR-BLPA-SLCR	15.51	24.96
4K2	4K3	ICLA-HECA-GREB	10.27	16.53
4K2	4K4	ICLA-HECA-CASL-CAS	14.50	23.34
4K2	4K5	ICLA-HECA-CASL	14.05	22.61
4K2	4N4	ICLA-HECA-WOLA	3.39	5.46
4K3	4K4	GREB-HECA-CASL-CAS	8.71	14.02
4K3	4K5	GREB-HECA-CASL	8.26	13.29
4K4	4K5	CASC-CASL	3.84	6.18
4K6	2K6	SEMI-MWST-CHMW	10.98	17.67
4K6	4K9	SEMI-MWST-DUNR	11.36	18.28
4N4	4K3	WOLA-HECA-GREB	9.58	15.42
4N4	4K4	WOLA-HECA-CASL-CASC	10.29	16.56
4N4	4K5	WOLA-HECA-CASL	9.84	15.84
5K2	4K7	HEFC-SOCR-WALA	13.85	22.29
5K2	4K8	HEFC-SOCR-WALA-CLLA-RILA-APPS	15.44	24.85
5K2	4N2	HEFC-SOCR-WALA-CLLA-CLLC	14.52	23.37
5K5	6K1	THOR-MOCR	25.88	41.65
5K5	6K3	THOR-YEMC-SBLC	45.62	73.42
5K5	6K3	THOR-LOFO-TRAC-TWOC-SBLC	40.90	65.82
5K5	6K4	THOR-YEMC	33.39	53.74
5K5	6K5	THOR-HALA	33.29	53.57
5K5	6Z1	THOR-MOCR-DICR	32.07	51.61
5K5	8K7	THOR-YEMC-SBLC-SBHF-SBHB	69.42	111.72
5K5	8K7	THOR-LOFO-TRAC-TWOC-SBLC-SBHF-SBHB	74.40	119.73
5K5	8K7	THOR-LOFO-TRAC-HERI-SNRI-SNRC-SBHB	57.74	92.92
5K5	8K7	THOR-LOFO-TRAC-HELA-SBHB	59.35	95.51
5K5	8K8	THOR-LOFO-TRAC-HERI-SNRI-HACU-SBHF-COWO	49.93	80.35
5K5	8K8	THOR-LOFO-TRAC-TWOC-SBLC-SBHF-COWO	55.21	88.85
7K2	9K1	DECR-NSSL-SHLA-BERI-BEME	39.40	63.41
7K2	OK1	DECR-NSSL-SHLA-LOST	19.48	31.35
7K2	OK2	DECR-NSSL-SHLA-HECR	19.74	31.77
8K1	7K2	DOGS-DECR	11.80	18.99
8K1	7K2	LERI-SSSL-DECR	13.53	21.77
8K1	9K1	DOGS-SSSL-SHLA-BERI-BEME	39.10	62.93
8K1	9K1	LERI-SSSL-SHLA-BERI-BEME	40.35	64.94
8K1	OK1	DOGS-DECR-NSSL-SHLA-LOST	25.34	40.78
8K1	OK1	LERI-SSSL-SHLA-LOST	24.23	38.99
8K1	OK2	DOGS-DECR-NSSL-SHLA-HECR	25.60	41.20
8K1	OK2	LERI-SSSL-SHLA-HECR	24.49	39.41
8K4	9K1	PIPL-MOAS-FLMA-SBBM	33.00	53.11
8K4	9K1	PIPL-MOAS-FLMA-SBBM-BERI-BRCO-BEME	34.92	56.20

FROM	TO	ROUTE	DIS-MI	DIS-KM
8K4	9K2	PIPL-MOAS-FLMA-SBBM	30.23	48.65
8K4	9K3	PIPL-MOAS-FLMA-SBBM-FMS	26.86	43.23
8K4	9K5	PIPL-MOAS-CCMA-TEFA	18.48	29.74
8K4	9K6	PIPL-MOAS	18.47	29.72
8K7	6K2	SBHB-SBHF-SBLC-YEMC-TSBC-THOR	39.00	62.76
8K7	6K3	SBHB-SBHF	23.88	38.43
8K7	6K4	SBHB-SBHF-SBLC-YEMC	37.03	59.59
8K7	6K5	SBHB-SBHF-SBLC-YEMC-TSBC-THOR-HALA	38.90	62.60
8K7	8K8	SBHB-COWO	10.35	16.66
8N1	5K5	HELA-TRAC-LOFO-THOR	49.76	80.08
8N1	6K1	HELA-TRAC-UPFO-THOR-MOCR	44.41	71.47
8N1	6K2	HELA-TRAC-UPFO-THOR	42.90	69.04
8N1	6K3	HELA-TRAC-HERI-FOCR-SBLC	26.85	43.21
8N1	6K4	HELA-TRAC-UPFO-THOR-YEMC	41.25	66.39
8N1	6K4	HELA-TRAC-TCTO-TWOC-SBLC-YEMC	41.81	67.29
8N1	6Z1	HELA-TRAC-UPFO-THOR-MOCR-DICR	41.60	66.95
8N1	8K7	HELA-SBHB	24.67	39.70
8N1	8K7	HELA-TRAC-HERI-SNRI-SNRC-SBHB	32.09	51.64
8N1	8K7	HELA-TRAC-TCTO-TWOC-SBLC-SBHF-SBHB	58.16	93.60
8N1	8K8	HELA-BCCO-SNRI-SNRC-SBHB-COWO	22.59	36.35
9K1	8K5	BEME-BRCO-BERI-SBBM-FLMA-MOAS-SBGL*	27.25	43.85
9K1	9K2	BEME-BRCO-BERI	4.69	7.55
9K1	9K3	BEME-BRCO-BERI-SBBM-FMS	9.10	14.64
9K1	9K5	BEME-BRCO-BERI-SBBM-FLMA-MOAS-CCMA-TEFA	19.11	30.75
9K1	9K6	BEME-BRCO-BERI-SBBM-FLMA-MOAS	19.10	30.74
9K1	9K8	BEME-BOCR	16.96	27.29
9K1	9K8	BEME-BMCO-BOCR	17.40	28.00
9K1	OK1	BEME-BERI-SHLA-LOST	31.12	50.08
9K1	OK2	BEME-BERI-SHLA-HECR	31.38	50.50
9K2	9K3	BERI-MOAS-FLMA-FLMS	11.13	17.91
9K2	9K6	BERI-MOAS	17.30	27.84
9K2	9K7	SBBM-ROCR	11.47	18.46
9K2	9K8	BERI-RFCO-BEME-BMCO-BOCR	19.83	31.91
OK3	OK9	MALA-MACR	7.65	12.31
OK4	9K9	BIBA-MYFA-SULA	16.57	26.67
OK4	OK5	BIBA-MYFA(U)-FAIC-FAIF	14.63	23.54
OK4	OK5	BIBA-MYFA(L)-FAIC-FAIF	14.69	23.64
OK4	OK6	BIBA-MYFA(U)-FAIC-FAIF-GLFL-SEME	16.59	26.70
OK4	OK6	BIBA-MYFA(L)-FAIC-FAIF-GLFL-SEME	16.65	26.80
OK4	OK6	BIBA-MYFA(U)-FAIC-IMME-SEME	17.28	27.81
OK4	OK6	BIBA-MYFA(L)-FAIC-IMME-SEME	17.34	27.91
WK1	1K1	DACR-SKYR-SPCR-CRHI-SPLA-SNPA-CLBU-SEMO	43.62	70.20
WK1	1K1	DACR-BBDC-BLBU-SKYR-SPCR-CRHI-SPLA-SNPA-CLBU-SEMO	47.69	76.75
WK1	1K2	DACR-SKYR-SPCR-CRHI-SPLA-SNPA	42.07	67.70
WK1	1K2	DACR-BBDC-BLBU-SKYR-SPCR-CRHI-SPLA-SNPA	46.14	74.25
WK1	1K3	DACR-SKYR-SPCR-CRHI-SPLA-FAPA	41.93	67.48
WK1	1K3	DACR-BBDC-BLBU-SKYR-SPCR-CRHI-SPLA-FAPA	46.00	74.03

FROM	TO	ROUTE	DIS-MI	DIS-KM
WK1	SHPMTN	DACR-SKYR	14.48	23.30
WK1	SHPMTN	DACR-BBDC-BLBU-SKYR	12.52	20.15
WK1	WK2	DACR-BBDC-BLBU	8.14	13.10
WK1	WK3	DACR-SKYR-SPCR	21.36	34.38
WK1	WK3	DACR-BBDC-BLBU-SKYR-SPCR	19.40	31.22
WK1	WK5	DACR-BBDC-BLBU-SKYR-SPCR-CRHI-SPLA-FACR-FAPA	32.34	52.05
WK1	WZ1	DACR-DCSP	3.04	4.89
WK1	WZ2	DACR-SKYR	5.96	9.59
WK1	WZ3	DACR-SKYR-SPCR-CRHI-SPLA-WD3S-MOLH	31.07	50.00
WK1	WZ3	DACR-BBDC-BLBU-SKYR-SPCR-CRHI-SPLA-WD3S-MOLH	29.11	46.85
WK2	1K1	BLBU-SKYR-SPCR-CRHI-SPLA-SNPA-CLBU-SEMO	39.51	63.59
WK2	1K2	BLBU-SKYR-SPCR-CRHI-SPLA-SNPA	37.80	60.83
WK2	1K3	BLBU-SKYR-SPCR-CRHI-SPLA-FAPA	37.82	60.87
WK2	SHPMTN	BLBU-SKYR	10.37	16.69
WK2	WK3	BLBU-SKYR-SPCR	17.25	27.76
WK2	WK5	BLBU-SKYR-SPCR-CRHI-SPLA-FACR-FAPA	30.19	48.59
WK2	WN1	BLBU-BBDC-DACR	6.31	10.15
WK2	WN1	BLBU-SKYR	11.21	18.04
WK2	WZ1	BLBU-BBDC-DACR-DCSP	6.11	9.83
WK2	WZ2	BLBU-BBDC-DACR-SKYR	7.39	11.89
WK2	WZ2	BLBU-SKYR	12.29	19.78
WK2	WZ3	BLBU-SKYR-SPCR-CRHI-SPLA-WD3S-MOLH	26.96	43.39
WK3	1K1	SPCR-SPLA-SNPA-CLBU-SEMO	25.56	41.13
WK3	1K2	SPCR-SPLA-SNPA	23.85	38.38
WK3	1K3/4	SPCR-SPLA-FAPA	23.87	38.41
WK3	WK5	SPCR-SPLA-FACR-FAPA	16.24	26.14
WK3	WK5	SPCR-CRHI-SPLA-FACR-FAPA	24.86	40.01
WK3	WN1	SPCR-SKYR	16.48	26.52
WK3	WZ1	SPCR-SKYR-DACR-DCSP	19.88	31.99
WK3	WZ2	SPCR-SKYR	17.56	28.26
WK3	WZ3	SPCR-SPLA-WD3S-MOLH	13.01	20.94
WK5	1K1	FAPA-SNPA-CLBU-SEMO	22.52	36.24
WK5	1K2	FAPA-SNPA	20.81	33.49
WK5	1K5	FAPA-FPBP-BIHO	21.15	34.04
WK5	SHPMTN	FAPA-FACR-SPLA-CRHI-SPCR-SKYR	22.40	36.05
WK5	WK6	FAPA-FPBP-BIHO	10.24	16.48
WK5	WN1	FAPA-FACR-SPLA-CRHI-SPCR-SKYR	29.42	47.35
WK5	WZ1	FAPA-FACR-SPLA-CRHI-SPCR-SKYR-DACR-DCSP	32.82	52.82
WK5	WZ2	FAPA-FACR-SPLA-CRHI-SPCR-SKYR	30.50	49.08
WK5	WZ3	FAPA-FACR-SPLA-WD3SS-MOLHH	13.53	21.77
WK6	1K1	BIHO-FPBP-FAPA-SNPA-CLBU-SEMO	21.66	34.86
WK6	1K2	BIHO-FPBP-FAPA-SNPA	21.05	33.88
WK6	1K3/4	BIHO-FPBP-FAPA	21.07	33.91

TRAIL NAME	CODE
Agate Creek Trail	AGCR
Amethyst Fossil Forest Trail	AFFT
Artist Point Trail	ARPO
Artist Point-Point Sublime Trail	APPS
Artists' Paintpots Trail	ARPA
Astringent (Broad) Creek Trail	ASCR
Avalanche Peak Trail	AVPE
Bacon Rind Creek Trail	BARI
Bannock Ski Trail	BAST
Baronette Bridge - Buffalo Ford Trail	BBBF
Baronette Ski Trail	BARS
Basin Creek Cutoff Trail	BCCO
Beach Lake Trail	BELA
Beaver Ponds Trail	BEPO
Bechler Meadows Cutoff Trail	BMCO
Bechler Meadows Trail	BEME
Bechler River Cutoff Trail	BRCO
Bechler River Trail	BERI
Beula Lake Trail	BEUL
Big Horn Ski Loop	BIHO
Bighorn Pass Trail	BIHO
Biscuit Basin Trail	BIBA
Black Butte Trail	BLBU
Black Butte-Dailey Creek Cutoff Trail	BBDC
Black Sand Basin Trail	BLSA
Blacktail Deer Creek Trail	BLDC
Blacktail Plateau Ski Trail	BLPL
Blacktail Ponds - Lava Creek Cutoff Trail	BPLC
Blacktail Ponds Stock Spur	BLSS
Bliss Pass Trail	BLPA
Boiling River Trail - Mammoth Campground	BRMC
Boiling River Trail (Main)	BORI
Bootjack Gap Trail	BOGA
Boundary Creek Trail	BOCR
Bridge Bay-Natural Bridge Trail	BBNB
Buffalo Fork Trail	BUFO
Buffalo Plateau Trail	BUPL
Bunsen Peak Service Road Trail	BPSR
Bunsen Peak Trail	BUPE
Cache Creek Trail	CACR
Cache Lake Trail	CALK
Canoe Lake Trail	CALA
Cascade Creek Trail	CASC
Cascade Creek-Mountain Ash Cutoff Trail	CCMA
Cascade Lake Trail	CASL
Children's Fire Trail	CHFI
Chittenden Road (Road to Parking Area)	CHRD
Chittenden Road-Mount Washburn Trail	CHMW
Clagett Butte Trail	CLBU
Clear Lake Cutoff	CLLC
Clear Lake Trail	CLLA
Colter/Wolverine Trailhead Trail	COWO

TRAIL NAME	COD
Coyote Creek Trail	COC
Crescent Lake-High Lake Trail	CRH
Cygnet Lakes Trail	CYL
Dailey Creek Spur Trail	DCS
Dailey Creek Trail	DAC
Delacy Creek Trail	DEC
Dike Creek Trail	DICR
Divide Trail	DIVI
Dogshead Trail	DOG
Duck Lake Trail	DUL
Electric Peak - Southeast Ridge	EPSE
Electric Peak - Southwest Ridge	EPSW
Elephant Back Trail	ELBA
Fairy Creek Trail	FAIC
Fairy Falls Trail	FAIF
Fan Creek Trail	FACR
Fawn Pass Spur/Bacon Rind TH Trail	FPBR
Fawn Pass Trail	FAPA
Fawn Pass-Bighorn Pass Cutoff Trail	FPBP
Fern Cascade Loop Trail	FELK
Fern Lake Trail	FELA
Fish Lake-Mount Ash Cutoff Trail	FLMA
Fish Lake-Mountain Ash Cutoff South	FLMS
Fountain Paint Pots Trail	FOPA
Fox Creek Trail	FOCR
Frost Lake Trail	FRLA
Garnet Hill Loop Trail	GHLT
Garnett Hill - Hellroaring Cutoff	GHHC
Gneiss Creek Trail	GNCR
Goose Lake/Feather Lake Trail (FF North Spur)	GLFL
Grebe Lake Trail	GREB
Grizzly Lake Trail	GRLA
Harebell Cutoff Trail	HACU
Harlequin Lake Trail	HARL
Hawk's Lake Trail	HALA
Heart Lake Trail	HELA
Heart River Trail	HERI
Hellroaring Creek Trail	HECR
Hellroaring Stock Cutoff Trail	HESC
Hering Lake Spur Trail	HERL
Hoodoo Basin Trail	HOBA
Howard Eaton - Arnica Crk to Natural Bridge	HEAC
Howard Eaton Trail - Old Faithful to Lone Star	HEOL
Howard Eaton Trail, Cascade Lake - Norris	HECA
Howard Eaton Trail, Fishing Bridge - Canyon	HEFC
Howard Eaton Trail, Mammoth - Golden Gate	HEMA
Ice Lake Trail	ICLA
Imperial Meadows Trail	IMME
Indian Creek Ski Loop Trail	ICSL
Kepler Cascade/Ski Trail	KECA
Lake Overlook Trail (West Thumb Overlook)	LAOV
Lamar River Stock Cutoff Trail	LRSC

TRAIL NAME	CODE
mar River Trail	LARI
va Creek Trail	LACR
wis River Channel Trail	LERI
ne Star Trail	LOST
st Lake Horse Spur Trail	LLSS
st Lake Trail	LOLA
wer Basin Lake Trail (Old HET Trail)	LOBA
wer Ford Trail	LOFO
allard Creek - Fairy Falls Cutoff Trail	MCFF
allard Creek Trail	MACR
allard Lake Trail	MALA
ammoth Hot Springs Lower Trail	MHSL
ammoth Hot Springs Upper Trail	MHSU
ary Mountain-Nez Perce Trail	MAMO
cBride Lake Trail	MCLA
idway Geyser Basin Trail	MIDW
iller Creek Trail	MICR
ist Creek Trail	MISC
onument Geyser Basin Trail	MOGB
oose Falls - South Entrance Trail	MFSE
ount Holmes-Winter Creek Trail	MHWC
ount Sheridan Trail	MTSH
ount Washburn (Dunraven) Trail	DUNR
ount Washburn Spur Trail	MWST
ountain Ash Creek Trail	MOAS
ountain Creek Trail	MOCR
ountain Creek Triangle Trail	MOCT
ud Volcano Trail	MUVO
ystic Falls Stock Trail	MFST
ystic Falls Trail	MYFA
atural Bridge Trail	NABR
orris Geyser Back Basin Trail	NGBB
orris Geyser Basin Campground Connector	NGCC
orris Geyser Porcelain Basin Trail	NGPB
orth Fork (Scout Pool) Trail	NOFO
orth Pitchstone Plateau Trail (A)	NOPI
orth Rim Trail	NORI
orth Shore Shoshone Lake Trail	NSSL
bservation Peak Trail	OBPE
bservation Point Trail	OBPO
ld Canyon Road Trail	CARO
ld Dry Creek - West Thumb Road Trail	DCWT
ld Dunraven Road Trail	DURT
ld Dunraven Service Road Trail	DUSR
ld Fountain Trail	OLFO
ld Gardiner Road Trail	OLGA
ld Golden Gate State Coach Road	GGSR
ld Hoodoo Road Segment	HORD
ld Lake Road Trail	LARO
ld Madison River Fire Lookout Trail	MRFL
ld Mol Heron Creek Trail	MOLH
ld South Road Hiking/Bike Trail	SORO

TRAIL NAME	CODE
Old Trout Creek Service Road Trail	TRCR
Old Turbid Lake Trail - West	TULW
Old Undine Falls Road Segment	UNFA
Osprey Falls Trail	OSFA
Otter Creek Bear Feeding Area Trail	OBCF
Pebble Creek Trail	PECR
Pelican Cone Trail	PECO
Pelican Creek Nature Trail	PECN
Pelican Creek Trail	PELC
Pelican Valley Trail	PEVA
Pitchsone Plateau Trail	PIPL
Plateau Trail	PLTR
Pocket Lake Trail	POLA
Powerline Trail	POWR
Punch Bowl-Black Sand Basin Trail	PBBS
Purple Mountain Trail	PUMO
Queen's Laundry Spur Trail	QULA
Raven Creek Cutoff Trail	RACR
Rescue Creek Trail	RECR
Ribbon Lake Trail	RILA
Riddle Lake Trail	RIDL
Riverside Loop Ski Trail	RIVL
Robinson Creek Trail	ROCR
Rocky Ford Cutoff Trail	RFCO
Roosevelt Lodge-Tower Falls Trail	RLTF
Sedge Lake - Crag Lake Spur Trail	SEDG
Sentinel Meadows Trail	SEME
Sepulcher Mountain Trail	SEMO
Seven Mile Hole Trail	SEMI
Sheepeater Ski Trail	SHST
Shoshone Geyser Basin Spur Trail	SGBT
Shoshone Geyser Basin Stock Cutofff Trail	SGBS
Shoshone Lake Trail	SHLA
Silver Cord Cascade Trail	SILA
Sky Rim Trail	SKYR
Slough Creek Trail	SLCR
Snake River Canyon Trail	SNRI
Snake River Cutoff Trail	SNRC
Snake River Lookout Trail	SNRL
Snow Pass Trail	SNPA
Soldier's Trail	SOTR
Solfatara Trail	SOLF
Solitary Geyser Trail	SOGE
Sour Creek Trail	SOCR
South Boundary - Bechler to Mountain Ash Cr	SBBM
South Boundary - Harebell	SBHB
South Boundary - Lynx Creek	SBLC
South Boundary Trail (S Ent to Grassy Lake)	SBGL
South Boundary-Harebell-Fox Creek	SBHF
South Entrance Trail - North Segment	SENS
South Rim Trail	SORI
South Shore Shoshone Lake Trail	SSSL

TRAIL NAME	CODE
Specimen Creek Trail	SPCR
Specimen Forest Trail - East	SFTE
Specimen Forest Trail - West	SFTW
Specimen Ridge Trail	SPRI
Sportsman Lake Trail	SPLA
Spring Creek Trail	SPCR
Stagecoach Road Trail	STRO
Storm Point Trail	STOP
Summit Lake Trail	SULA
Terrace Springs Trail	TESP
Terraced Falls Trail	TEFA
Thorofare - South Boundary Cutoff	TSBC
Thorofare Trail	THOR
Three Rivers Thermal Area Spur	THRI
Thunderer Cutoff Trail	THCU
Tower Creek Trail	TOCR
Tower Falls Trail	TOFA
Trail Creek Cabin Bypass Trail	TCCB
Trail Creek Trail	TRAC
Trail Creek-Two Ocean Cutoff Trail	TCTO
Trilobite Lake Trail	TRLA
Trout Lake Trail	TROU
Turbid Lake Trail	TULA
Twister Falls Trail	TWFA
Two Ocean Plateau Trail	TWOC
Two Ribbons Trail	TWOR
UGB-Biscuit Basin Bike Trail	UGBB
UGB-Morning Glory to Artemisia	MGAR
Uncle Tom's Trail	UNCT
Union Falls Trail	UNFA
Upper Ford Trail	UPFO
Upper Geyser Basin Trail	UGBT
Upper Geyser Hill Trail	UGHT
Upper Lamar River Trail	ULRT
Upper Pelican Creek Cutoff Trail	UPCC
Violet Springs Trail	VISP
Wapiti Lake Trail	WALA
West Thumb Geyser B Trail (Loop & Cutoff)	WTGB
White Creek Trail	WHCR
Wolf Lake Cutoff/Little Gibbon Falls Trail	WOLA
Wraith Falls Trail	WRFA
Wrangler Lake Trail	WRLA
YCC to Snow Pass Connector Trail	YCCC
YCC Trail	YCCT
Yellowstone Meadows Cutoff Trail	YEMC
Yellowstone River Overlook Trail	YEOV
Yellowstone River Picnic Area Outer Spur Trail	YPAS
Yellowstone River Trail	YERI

Appendix 9: Patrol Cabins

ow to Use This Table

ne following table lists the park's 37 backcountry patrol cabins. The accompanying map ows the approximate location of each.

or each cabin, the district is listed (corresponds with the trail districts), as well as the titude and longitude, and a quick description of its location. In parentheses after the cation note is the closest backcountry campsite to the cabin. Those with an "N/A" do not ive a campsite within a day's walking distance.

Yellowstone's Backcountry Patrol Cabins

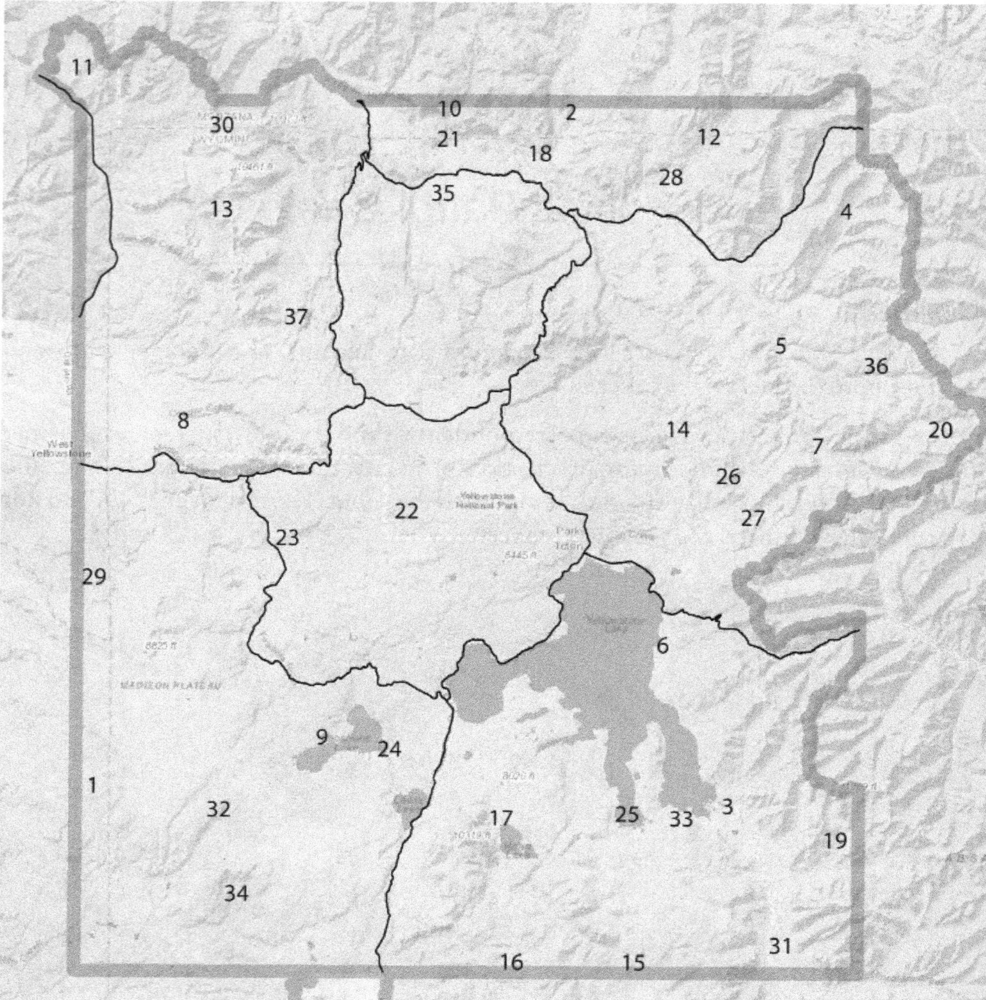

CABIN	MAP ID	DIST	LAT	LONG	LOCATION/NEAREST CAMPSITE
Buffalo Lake Cabin	1	9	44.328189	-111.077547	West side of Buffalo Lake (9A5)
Buffalo Plateau Cabin	2	2	45.024962	-110.359328	Inside north boundary (2B1)
Cabin Creek Cabin	3	6	44.301608	-110.157224	North of Lower Ford Trail (6B1)
Cache Creek Cabin	4	3	44.917575	-110.020163	Jct of Thunderer & Cache Creek Trails (3C4
Calfee Cabin	5	3	44.777523	-110.113175	Lamar River Trl S of Calfee Creek (3L4)
Clear Creek Cabin	6	5	44.474568	-110.282622	Yell Lake @ mouth of Clear Crk (5H1)
Cold Creek Cabin	7	3	44.683403	-110.060799	Lamar River north of Cold Creek (3U4/3F1
Cougar Cabin	8	W	44.702963	-110.947659	Cougar Creek N of Gneiss Creek Trail (N/A
Cove Cabin	9	8	44.368829	-110.750252	N side of Shoshone Lk w of Narrows (8R3)
Crevice Mountain Cabin	10	1	45.029857	-110.588425	Crevice Mtn inside N boundary (1Y4)
Daly Creek Cabin	11	W	45.069885	-111.103939	Daly Creek Trail east of Daly Creek (WF1)
Elk Tongue Cabin	12	2	44.990622	-110.201203	Slough Crk @ mouth Elk Tongue Crk (2S4)
Fawn Pass Cabin	13	W	44.928673	-110.888273	Fawn Pass Trail @ Fawn Pass (N/A)

CABIN	MAP ID	DIST	LAT	LONG	LOCATION/NEAREST CAMPSITE
Fern Lake Cabin	14	5	44.686177	-110.247495	Pellican Creek S of Wapiti Lake Trail (5B1)
Fox Creek Cabin	15	6	44.133869	-110.300304	South Boundary Trl E of Snake River (6M7)
Harebell Cabin	16	8	44.140949	-110.477742	S Boundary Trl @ Harebell Cutoff Trl (8C4)
Heart Lake Cabin	17	8	44.286120	-110.497844	Heart Lake Trail @ Heart Lake (8H6/8H5)
Hellroaring Cabin	18	2	44.979464	-110.438368	Hellroaring Trail E of Yell River Trail (2H5)
Howell Fork Cabin	19	6	44.286793	-110.006048	Mountain Crk Trl W of Eagle Pass (6D7)
Lamar Mountain Cabin	20	3	44.683933	-109.850015	Lamar Mtn @ headwtrs of Lamar Rvr (N/A)
Lower Blacktail Cabin	21	1	44.996321	-110.576443	S of Yell River E of Blacktail Deer Trl (1Y6)
Mary Lake Cabin	22	4	44.604209	-110.640391	Northwest side of Mary Lake (on the trail)
Nez Perce Creek Cabin	23	O	44.576643	-110.810663	Service Road N of Mary Mtn W TH (N/A)
Outlet Cabin	24	8	44.360370	-110.662517	Shoshone Lk N of Lewis Chnl Outlet (8S1)
Peale Island Cabin	25	5	44.289261	-110.316247	N side of Peale Island (N/A)
Pelican Cone Cabin	26	5	44.648181	-110.193288	Atop Pelican Cone (N/A)
Pelican Springs Cabin	27	5	44.596622	-110.193029	Jct of Raven Creek & Mist Creek Trails (3Y3)
Slough Creek Cabin	28	2	44.950168	-110.276908	Slough Creek Trl E of Buffalo Fork Trail (CG)
South Riverside Cabin	29	W	44.527003	-111.090954	Old W Bndary Trl N of Echo Canyon (N/A)
Sportsman Lake Cabin	30	W	45.011929	-110.903965	S of Sportsman Lake (WD2/WD3)
Thorofare Cabin	31	6	44.145490	-110.080316	Foot of Trident Mountain (6Y5)
Three Rivers Cabin	32	9	44.283517	-110.904555	Bechler River S of Philips Fork (9B0)
Trail Creek Cabin	33	6	44.296249	-110.232951	SE Arm of Yell Lake W of Trail Creek (6A3)
Union Falls Cabin	34	9	44.181652	-110.887044	Union Falls Trail S of Union Falls (9U5/9U4)
Upper Blacktail Cabin	35	1	44.947295	-110.586233	End of Blacktail Service Road (N/A)
Upper Miller Creek Cabin	36	3	44.749194	-109.954731	Miller Creek W of Hoodoos Trail (3M5)
Winter Creek Cabin	37	1	44.811270	-110.801175	Jct of Mt Holmes & Trilobite Lk Trails (1C4)

Notes

Introduction

1. If you're interested in the history along the park's road system, I highly recommend my book, *Yellowstone Mileposts.*

2. Fifth Annual Report of the Superintendent of the Yellowstone National Park, 1881. P. W. Norris, p. 67.

Hiking in Yellowstone

1. In June, 2017, a man was hiking alone in the northern part of the park along Turkey Pen Peak. He fell and was unable to call for help. He died of injuries and it was several days before rangers were able to locate his body.

2. You can also obtain permits to camp in "non-designated" areas that are devoid of officially-established campsites. Details on this can be found in the chapter, "The Yellowstone Backcountry."

The Yellowstone Backcountry

1. Backcountry Management Plan. Unpublished document. Yellowstone National Park, July, 1996. p. 8.

2. A complete list of these is provided in Appendix 5.

Trail and Backcountry Etiquette

1. Mr. Bubbles was once known by a more formal name, Ferris Fork Pool.

2. This was current as of the publication date of this book in early 2019. The compendium can be found at: https://www.nps.gov/yell/learn/management/compendium.htm.

Weather in Yellowstone

1. There is some disagreement among park history buffs about the legitimacy of this story and/or its underlying assertions. Regardless, it is a tradition in the park and is celebrated every August 25.

2. There are a variety of sources for these kinds of figures, and I've seen anywhere from a 4–5% increase per 1,000 feet to an 8–10% increase per 100 feet. Therefore I averaged it for the purposes of this book.

3. Their stories are told in former park historian Lee Whittlesey's popular book, *Death in Yellowstone.*

4. This is basically the same policy that was in place when the 1988 fires occurred.

Safety

1. A copy of the detailed report of this encounter is available online at http://www.fws.gov/mountain-prairie/species/mammals/grizzly/September2011MatayoshiInvestigationTeamReport_redacted.pdf.

2. A summary of that study can be found at https://above.nasa.gov/safety/documents/Bear/bearspray_vs_bullets.pdf.

3. In 2014, a man shot a grizzly bear that was attacking him in Glacier National Park (after his bear spray failed to deter the animal). Consistent with the law, park rangers charged the man with the illegal

discharge of a weapon inside a national park. Prosecutors later dismissed the charge. When the 2010 law that allows people to carry firearms was passed, the intent was to prevent people from traveling across the country and otherwise carrying a firearm legally from having to worry about being arrested for illegally carrying their weapons as they traveled through national parks. The law was not passed specifically to allow people to defend themselves. However, only an insane prosecutor would charge someone with a criminal act for an act of self-defense when the victim was otherwise obeying the law. Having said that, from a technically legal perspective, it remains illegal to discharge a firearm inside a national park, even in self-defense. Doing so will almost certainly require you to incur considerable expense to defend yourself, especially if prosecutors elect to charge you with a crime.

4. You can find information about using bear spray on mountain lions at http://fwp.mt.gov/recreation/safety/wildlife/lion/lionBearSpray.html.

5. Former park historian Lee Whittlesey's book, *Death in Yellowstone*, provides rather vivid details about many of these deaths.

6. The study results can be found at: https://www.bearstudy.org/website/images/stories/Publications/Reactions_of_Black_Bears_to_Human_Menstrual_Odors.pdf.

Hiking and Camping Equipment

1. One I highly recommend is *The Backpacker's Field Manual: A Comprehensive Guide to Mastering Backcountry Skills* (Three Rivers Press). It covers not only clothing and equipment selection, but also discusses food, first-aid kits, essential tools, and a wealth of other material that would be relevant to your hikes in Yellowstone.

Winter Hiking and Camping

1. As is the case with all other non-natural fatalities in the park, Lee Whittlesey offers a rather vivid account of this incident in his book, *Death in Yellowstone*.

2. The ranger force in the park during the winter is about one quarter the size of that present during the summer, so assembling a rescue crew during the winter can be a time-consuming and difficult process.

Mammoth District Trails

1. The other is the Firehole Canyon Swimming Area located just above Firehole Cascade on the Firehole River near Madison Junction.

2. Lee Whittlesey recounts the gentleman's story on page 151 of his *Death in Yellowstone* book (2nd ed).

3. If the small pullout across from the trailhead is full or inaccessible, you will need to park at the parking area for the Upper Terrace Drive to the north, and then walk the 0.4 mile south to the trailhead along the side of the highway.

4. Whittlesey, *Wonderland Nomenclature*, p 1122.

Tower District Trails

1. The correct spelling is without the final "e" despite the peak bearing his name being misspelled.

2. Yancey died in 1903 and the hotel was operated by his son from 1903-1906.

3. Whittlesey, *Wonderland Nomenclature*, p 874.

Lamar District Trails

1. The book is *Biography of a Grizzly* by Ernest Thompson Seton (1900). The thermal area itself is named after the bear in the story, Wahb.

2. Whittlesey, *Wonderland Nomenclature*, p. 179.

3. Ibid. p. 440.

4. *The Yellowstone National Park. A Manual for Tourists.*, Henry J. Winser. 1883, p. 84

5. The reason this occurred is that, up until the mid-1980s, there was an extension of the Lamar River Trail that paralleled the river on its south side all the way west to the Crystal Creek Trail (the trail that takes you straight up to the petrified forest on Specimen Ridge's western end, now known as the Specimen Forest Trail - East). The Lamar River Trail thus began at that point and technically crossed what was originally the Specimen Ridge Trail's eastern terminus at its present location. The abandoned section of trail was only lightly used, however (due in large part to its being underwater or marshy almost the entire season), so it was dispensed with and is no longer even discernible on satellite imagery.

6. Whittlesey, *Wonderland Nomenclature*, p. 773-776.

Canyon District Trails

1. The bear was defending her cubs and was not destroyed after the attack. A couple of months later, the same bear and her cubs killed a man in Hayden Valley. The mother was euthanized and her cubs were sent to a bear refuge.

2. Whittlesey, *Wonderland Nomenclature*. p. 1025.

3. That boulder came loose as four employees from Grand Teton National Park were climbing illegally on the walls. Lee Whittlesey shares the story in detail in his book, *Death in Yellowstone*.

Lake District Trails

1. The Beach Lake Trail was never really maintained to any significant degree, but it was officially abandoned in the aftermath of the re-evaluation of trails subsequent to the completion of the Backcountry Management Plan.

2. Whittlesey, *Wonderland Nomenclature*, p. 390

3. Ibid. p. 991.

4. In 2019, the NPS will begin reconstructing a segment of road from Fishing Bridge to just east of the existing Pelican Valley Trailhead. As a part of that, they will be building a new trailhead and parking area. Therefore, from later in 2019 onward, the actual trailhead may be further out from Fishing Bridge Junction than 3.3 miles.

Thorofare District Trails

1. Whittlesey, *Wonderland Nomenclature,* p. 330.

2. While on this trail outside the park's boundaries, you are in USFS territory. The USFS has more relaxed rules about camping so it is usually unnecessary to camp in a specific site or to obtain a permit to camp at all. Contact the Jackson or Blackrock USFS ranger stations for addition details.

3. Ibid. p. 954

Grant District Trails

1. Both the creek and the "park" (meadow) were named after Walter DeLacy, an expedition guide who created the first reasonably accurate map of the Yellowstone area in the 1860s. DeLacy Park was the site of itinerant camps run by the Shaw and Powell Camp Company and by trail guide Howard Eaton as they took their tour groups through this area of the park.

2. For an in-depth discussion of the various features found here, see Scott Bryan's book, *The Geysers of Yellowstone*.

South District Trails

1. Whittlesey, *Wonderland Nomenclature*, p. 265.

2. Ibid, p. 586.

3. Ibid, p. 590

4. The reason this lookout was not enclosed is because it was intended to be used on an itinerant basis by rangers from the Snake River Ranger Station since the station was so close to it. There was no need for

the ranger to "live" in the lookout overnight or for several days as was the case with the other lookouts, so it was built with a minimalistic frame.

5. Paul Rubinstein, et. al., *The Guide to Yellowstone Waterfalls and Their Discovery*, pp. 256-258.

Bechler District Trails

1. Whittlesey, *Wonderland Nomenclature*, p. 92.
2. Ibid, p. 182.
3. Ibid, p. 1047.
4. Paul Rubinstein, et. al., *The Guide to Yellowstone Waterfalls and Their Discovery*, pp. 72-73.

Old Faithful District Trails

1. Whittlesey, *Death in Yellowstone, 2nd ed.*, p. 3
2. Whittlesey, *Wonderland Nomenclature*, p. 312.

West-Gallatin District Trails

1. Whittlesey, *Wonderland Nomenclature*, p. 292. Note that many trail books and maps show this as the "Daly Creek Trail," which is an incorrect (though common) misspelling of the man's name.
2. Small Lake is not an official name, but is rather a colloquial one used by park employees and hikers familiar with the area. The lake is fishless.
3. This trail is shown on some maps as the "Old Fountain Pack Trail."
4. Whittlesey, *Wonderland Nomenclature*, p. 794-795
5. Per park trail maintenance logs.
6. Whittlesey, *Wonderland Nomenclature*, p. 691.

The Lost Trails

1. For an interesting (mostly fictitious, but very realistic) account of what the tourist experience might have been like on these trips, see Don DeJarnett's book, *Cowboy Tales on the Eaton Trail in Yellowstone.*
2. Map A-3 shows what the trail looked like (roughly) in the late 1950s by combining the abandoned segments (light dashes) and the road segment (dashed road) with the current trails (long dashes). The small blank spaces intermingled within these are existing (but not shown) service roads or main roads or small segments of much longer trails.
3. The results of much of that project's work, and an excellent treatment of the historical significance of the Howard Eaton Trail can be found in Judith L. Meyer's paper, Yellowstone's Howard Eaton Trail as Management Tool and Cultural Artifact, published in 2018 by the George Wright Society. It is available online.
4. Whittlesey, Some History of the Jones Pass Trail in Yellowstone National Park, Wyoming. Memo dated May 22, 2000.
5. Up until the early 1970s, there were a handful of "group camps" spread around the park, including the one referenced here, which was located in the trees on the south side of Indian Pond. These camps were used primarily by scouting groups.

Appendix 1: Yellowstone Lakes

1. The fish data is based on information found in the book, *Yellowstone Fishes: Ecology, History, and Angling in the Park*, along with various publications and information compiled by the park's Aquatics Division. All other data is derived from the park's GIS database.

Appendix 2: Rivers, Streams, and Creeks

1. The fish data is based on information found in the book, *Yellowstone Fishes: Ecology, History, and Angling in the Park*, along with various publications and information compiled by the park's Aquatics Division. All other data is derived from the park's GIS database.

Appendix 3: Waterfalls

1. Rubinstein, et. al., pp 180-185.

Appendix 4: Popular Features with Campsites

1. This data comes from the USGS Board of Geographic Names database. The elevation data provided in these tables is provided by the USGS and is the "official" elevation for each mountain/pass listed.

Appendix 5: Thermal Areas

1. The data in this table comes from a variety of public sources, including various studies by the USGS and material published by NPS.

Appendix 8: Trailhead Information

1. Only those trailheads with a "K" or an "N" as the middle letter are "official" trailhead designations used by Yellowstone National Park Backcountry staff. I created the other trailhead designators specifically for this book to allow the references throughout the book to remain consistently formatted.

References

ıderson, Roger, and Carol Shively Anderson. (2000). *A Ranger's Guide to Yellowstone Day Hikes.* Helena, MT: Montana Magazine.

ıch, Jr., Orville. (1973). *Hiking the Yellowstone Backcountry.* San Francisco, CA: Sierra Book Club.

ıch, Jr., Orville. (1998). *Exploring the Yellowstone Backcountry: A Guide to the Hiking Trails of Yellowstone with Additional Sections on Canoeing, Bicycling, and Cross-country Skiing.* San Francisco, CA: Sierra book Club.

evins, Bruce H. (2014). *Mapping Yellowstone: A History of the Mapping of Yellowstone National Park.* Mansfield Centre, CT: Martino Publishing.

ɔhannan, Thomas P. (2014). *Yellowstone Mileposts.* New Castle, DE: Hayden Publishing

'yan, T. Scott. (2018). *The Geysers of Yellowstone, Fifth Edition.* Boulder, CO: University Press of Colorado.

ırter, Thomas B. (1978). *Yellowstone Backcountry Basics and Trail Guide.* Publisher unknown.

aines, Aubrey. (1977). *The Yellowstone Story: A History of Our First National Park, Volume II.* Yellowstone National Park, WY: Yellowstone Library and Museum Association.

ˌarschall, Mark C. (1978). *Yellowstone Trails: A Hiking Guide.* Yellowstone National Park, WY: Yellowstone Library and Museum Association.

ˌarschall, Mark C. (1990). *Yellowstone Trails: A Hiking Guide.* Gardiner, MT: Yellowstone Association.

ˌarschall, Mark C. (1999). *Yellowstone Trails: A Hiking Guide.* Gardiner, MT: Yellowstone Association.

ˌarschall, Mark C., and Joy Sellers Marschall. (2008). *Yellowstone Trails: A Hiking Guide.* Gardiner, MT: Yellowstone Association.

ˌayer, Judith L, and Yolonda Youngs. (2018). Historical Landscape Change in Yellowstone National Park: Demonstrating the Value of Intensive Field Observation and Repeat Photography. *Geographical Review*, American Geographical Society, Vol 108, Issue 3, p. 387-409.

'ational Park Service. (Various dates 1872-1968). Annual Reports of the Superintendent of Yellowstone National Park. Washington, DC: U.S. Government Printing Office.

ˌystrom, Andrew Dean. (2012). *Top Trails: Yellowstone and Grand Teton National Parks: Must-Do Hikes for Everyone.* Birmingham, AL: Wilderness Press.

ˌierce, Steve. 1987. *The Lakes of Yellowstone.* Seattle, WA: The Mountaineers.

Rubinstein, Paul, Lee H. Whittlesey, and Mike Stevens. (2000). *The Guide to Yellowstone Waterfalls and Their Discovery*. Englewood, CO: Westcliffe Publishers, Inc.

Schneider, Bill. 1997. *Hiking Yellowstone National Park*. Helena, MT: Falcon Publishing.

Schneider, Bill. (2003). *Hiking Yellowstone National Park*. Helena, MT: Falcon Publishing.

Schreier, Carl. (1997). *Hiking Yellowstone Trails*. Moose, WY: Homestead Publishing.

Varley, John D., and Paul Schullery. (1998). *Yellowstone Fishes: Ecology, History, and Angling in the Park*. Mechanicsburg, PA: Stackpole Books.

Whittelsey, Lee H. (2014). *Death in Yellowstone: Accidents and Foolhardiness in the First National Park, 2nd Edition*. Lanham, MD: Roberts Rhinehart.

Whittlesey, Lee H. (1988). *Wonderland Nomenclature*. Unpublished manuscript.

Whittlesey, Lee H. (2000). Some History of the Jones Pass Trail in Yellowstone National Park, Wyoming. Unpublished memo, Yellowstone National Park Archives, Accessed July 15, 2016.

Winser, Henry J. (1883). *The Yellowstone National Park. A Manual for Tourists*. New York, NY: Putnams.

Yellowstone National Park. (1996). *Backcountry Management Plan*, "Final" Version. Unpublished document. Mammoth, WY.

Yellowstone National Park. (n.d.). Winter Backcountry Trip Planner. Mammoth, WY.

Trail Index

NAME	STAT	INFO	MAP(S)
ate Creek Trail	E	154	2-1
iethyst Fossil Forest Trail	A	176	2-1
ow Canyon Trail	A	358	A-1
tist Point Trail	E	194	4-9
tist Point-Point Sublime Trail	E	195	4-6
tists' Paintpots Trail	E	194	4-2
tringent (Broad) Creek Trail	E	228	5-1, 4-8
alanche Peak Trail	E	228	5-3
con Rind Creek Trail	E	336	W-2
nnock Ski Trail	E	176	3-1
ronette Bridge - Buffalo Ford	U	154	2-4, 2-1
ronette Ski Trail	E	176	3-1
sin Creek Cutoff Trail	E	266	8-1
ach Lake - Dryad Lake Trail	A	359	5-2, A-2
ach Lake Trail	A	228	5-2
aver Ponds Trail	E	122	1-1
chler Meadows Cutoff Trail	E	286	9-1, 9-2
chler Meadows Trail	E	286	9-1
chler River Cutoff Trail	E	287	9-1
chler River Trail	E	288	9-1,2,3
ula Lake Trail	E	266	8-3
ghorn Ski Loop	E	122	1-2
ghorn Pass Trail	E	336	W-3
scuit Basin Trail	E	304	O-4
son Peak Ridge Trail	A	359	A-1
ack Butte Trail	E	337	W-1
ack Butte-Dailey Creek Cutoff	E	338	W-1
ack Sand Basin Trail	E	305	O-5
acktail Deer Creek Trail	E	123	1-6,1-7
acktail Plateau Ski Trail	E	155	1-8
acktail Ponds - Lava Creek C/O	E	123	1-6,1-7
acktail Ponds Stock Spur	E	124	1-6
acktail Ridge Trail	A	359	A-1
ss Pass Trail	E	177	2-3,3-1
oiling River-Mammoth CG Trail	U	125	1-1
oiling River Trail (Main)	E	124	1-1, 1-7
otjack Gap Trail	E	177	3-4, 3-2
oundary Creek Trail	E	290	9-2, 9-1
idge Bay-Natural Bridge C/O Trl	E	229	5-2
ink of the Upper Falls Trail	E	215	4-9
uffalo Fork Trail	E	155	2-3
uffalo Plateau Trail	E	156	2-2
unsen Peak Service Road Trail	E	126	1-3
unsen Peak Trail	E	125	1-3
ache Creek Trail	E	178	3-3

NAME	STAT	INFO	MAP(S)
Cache Lake Trail	E	338	W-2
Canoe Lake Trail	E	178	3-5, 3-2
Cascade Creek Trail	E	195	4-3
Cascade Crk-Mountain Ash C/O	E	291	9-4
Cascade Lake Trail	E	195	4-3
Children's Fire Trail	E	126	1-6, 1-8
Chittenden Road (Parking Area)	E	196	4-4
Chittenden Rd-Mt Washburn Trl	E	196	4-4
Clagett Butte Trail	E	127	1-4,1-5
Clear Creek Trail	A	360	5-3, A-2
Clear Lake Cutoff	E	197	4-6
Clear Lake Trail	E	197	4-6
Colter/Wolverine Trailhead Trail	E	266	8-1
Cougar Creek Cabin Spur Trail	E	345	W-4
Cougar Creek Trail	A	360	W-4, A-1
Coyote Creek Trail	E	156	2-2
Crater Hills/Sulphur Mtn Trail	U	198	4-7, 4-8
Crescent Lake-High Lake Trail	E	338	W-2
Crow Creek Pass Trail	A	360	5-3, A-2
Cygnet Lakes Trail	E	199	4-7, 4-3
Dailey Creek Spur Trail	E	340	W-1
Dailey Creek Trail	E	339	W-1
Delacy Creek Trail	E	260	7-1
Dike Creek Trail	E	246	6-2
Divide Trail	E	306	O-7, 7-1
Dogshead Trail	E	267	8-2, 7-1
Duck Lake Trail	E	260	7-1
Electric Peak - Southeast Ridge	E	340	W-2
Electric Peak - Southwest Ridge	U	341	W-2
Elephant Back Trail	E	230	5-2
Fairy Creek Trail	E	306	O-2
Fairy Falls Trail	E	307	O-2, O-1
Fan Creek Trail	E	341	W-2, W-3
Fawn Pass Spur/Bacon Rind TH	E	342	W-2
Fawn Pass Trail	E	342	W-3, W-2
Fawn Pass-Bighorn Pass Cutoff	E	344	W-3, W-2
Fern Cascade Loop Trail	E	308	O-6
Fern Lake Trail	E	230	5-1, 4-8
Fish Lake-Mount Ash Cutoff Trail	E	291	9-4, 9-1
Fish Lake-Mountain Ash C/O S	E	291	9-4
Fountain Paint Pots Trail	E	308	O-2
Fox Creek Trail	E	246	6-4
Frost Lake Trail	E	179	3-6, 5-1
Garnet Hill Loop Trail	E	157	2-4
Garnet Hill - Hellroaring Cutoff	E	157	2-4, 2-2

NAME	STAT	INFO	MAP(S)
Gneiss Creek Trail	E	344	W-4
Goose Lake/Feather Lake Trail	E	310	O-2, O-1
Grebe Lake Trail	E	199	4-3
Grizzly Lake Trail	E	127	1-10
Harebell Cutoff Trail	E	268	8-1, 6-4
Harlequin Lake Trail	E	345	O-1, W-4
Hawk's Rest Trail	E	247	6-3
Heart Lake Trail	E	268	8-1
Heart River Trail	E	270	8-1, 6-4
Hellroaring Creek Trail	E	158	2-2
Hellroaring Stock Cutoff Trail	E	159	2-2
Hering Lake Spur Trail	U	270	8-3
Hoodoo Basin Trail	E	179	3-4, 3-2
HET - Arnica Creek to Nat Bridge	R	231	5-2
HET - Blacktail to Tower Fall	A	356	1-9, A-1
HET - Cascade to Canyon	A	357	4-6, A-1
HET - Chain of Lakes Trail	E	200	4-3
HET - Chitt Brdg to Glacial Bould	A	357	4-6, A-1
HET - DeLacy Creek to Duck Lk	A	358	7-1, A-2
HET - Divide to DeLacy Creek	A	358	O-7, 7-1
HET - Duck Lake to Arnica	A	357	7-1, A-2
HET - Fishing Bridge to Canyon	E	231	4-8
HET - Fountain Flats to LGB Lake	A	357	O-1, O-2
HET - Glen Creek to Mt Holmes	A	358	W-3, A-1
HET - LGB Lake to Old Faithful	A	357	O-2, O-3
HET - Mammoth - Golden Gate	E	128	1-3,1-4
HET - Mt Holmes to Norris GB	A	358	A-1
HET - Norris GB to Fountain Flats	A	358	A-2, 4-2
HET - Old Faithful to Lone Star	E	310	O-6
HET - Washburn Spur to Twr Fall	A	356	A-1, 4-4
Ice Lake Trail	E	200	4-3
Imperial Meadows Trail	E	311	O-2, O-1
Indian Creek Ski Loop Trail	E	129	1-2
Jones Pass - Crow Creek Cutoff	A	360	A-2, 5-3
Jones Pass Trail	A	361	A-2, 5-3
Kepler Cascade/Ski Trail	E	311	O-6
Lake Overlook Trail (W Thumb)	E	261	7-1
Lamar River Stock Cutoff Trail	E	182	3-2
Lamar River Trail	E	181	3-2
Lamar Valley Trail	A	361	A-1, 2-1
Lava Creek Trail	E	129	1-7
Lewis Channel Trail	E	271	8-2
Little Buffalo Pack Trail	A	362	A-1, 2-2
Lone Star Trail	E	312	O-6, O-7
Lost Lake Horse Spur Trail	E	160	2-5
Lost Lake Trail	E	159	2-5
Lower Basin Lake Trail	A	312	O-2, O-1
Lower Ford Trail	E	247	6-2
Mallard Creek - Fairy Falls Cutoff	E	313	O-3, O-2
Mallard Creek Trail	E	313	O-3, O-2
Mallard Lake Trail	E	314	O-3
Mammoth Hot Springs Lower Trl	E	130	1-4
Mammoth Hot Springs Upper Trl	E	130	1-4
Mary Lake - Beach Lake Trail	A	362	A-2, 5-2
Mary Mountain-Nez Perce Trail	E	314	O-1, 4-7
McBride Lake Trail	U	160	2-3
McBride Trail	A	364	2-3
Midway Geyser Basin Trail	E	316	O-2, O-1
Miller Creek Trail	E	182	3-5
Mirror Lake Trail	U	232	5-1
Mist Creek Trail	E	183	3-6, 5-
Monument Geyser Basin Trail	E	201	4-2
Moose Falls - South Ent Trail	U	271	8-3
Mount Everts Trail	U	131	1-7
Mount Holmes-Winter Creek Trl	E	131	1-10
Mount Sheridan Trail	E	271	8-1
Mount Washburn (Dunraven) Trl	E	201	4-4
Mount Washburn Spur Trail	E	202	4-4
Mountain Ash Creek Trail	E	289	9-4
Mountain Creek Trail	E	248	6-2
Mountain Creek Triangle Trail	E	248	6-2, 6-
Mud Volcano Trail	E	202	4-8, 4-
Mystic Falls Stock Trail	E	317	O-4, O
Mystic Falls Trail	E	316	O-4, O
Natural Bridge Trail	E	233	5-2
Norris Geyser Back Basin Trail	E	203	4-1
Norris GB - CG Connector Trail	E	N/A	4-1
Norris Geyser Porcelain Basin Trl	E	204	4-1
North Fork (Scout Pool) Trail	E	292	9-4, 9-
North Pitchstone Plateau Trail	A	293	9-3, 8-
North Rim Cutoff Trail	E	205	4-6
North Rim Trail	E	206	4-6
North Shore Shoshone Lake Trail	E	272	8-2
Observation Peak Trail	E	206	4-3
Observation Point Trail	E	317	O-5, O-
Old Blacktrail Trail	A	359	A-1
Old Canyon Road East Trail	R	207	4-3
Old Canyon Road West Trail	R	207	4-3
Old Cougar Crk Service Rd Trail	A	360	W-4, A-
Old Dry Creek - W Thumb Rd Trl	R	261	7-1
Old Dunraven Road Trail	R	207	4-4
Old Dunraven Service Road Trail	R	160	2-7
Old Fountain Trail	A	345	W-4
Old Gardiner Road Trail	E	132	1-7
Old Gneiss Creek South End Trail	A	361	W-4, A-
Old Golden Gate Stg Coach Rd	A	132	1-3
Old Hoodoo Road Segment	A	133	1-3
Old Lake Road Trail	U	233	5-2
Old Lakeshore Trail	A	361	5-2, 5-
Old Madison River Fire Lookout	A	346	W-4
Old Mol Heron Creek Trail	A	346	W-2
Old South Road Hiking/Bike Trail	R	273	8-3, 8-
Old Trout Creek Service Road Trl	R	208	4-7
Old Turbid Lake Trail - West	A	234	5-3
Old Undine Falls Road Segment	A	133	1-6
Opal Creek - Raven Creek Trail	A	364	5-1, 3-
Opal Creek Trail (Access to 301)	U	N/A	2-1
Osprey Falls Trail	E	134	1-3
Otter Creek - Mary Mountain Trl	A	363	4-3, 4-
Otter Crk Bear Feeding Area Trail	A	208	4-3, 4-
Pebble Creek Trail	E	183	3-1
Pelican Cone Trail	E	234	5-1
Pelican Creek (Fishing Bridge) Trl	A	363	5-3, 5-
Pelican Creek Nature Trail	E	234	5-2, 5-
Pelican Creek Trail	E	235	5-1, 4-
Pelican Valley Trail	E	236	5-1
Pitchstone Plateau Trail	E	273	8-3
Plateau Trail	A	209	4-7

NAME	STAT	INFO	MAP(S)
Pocket Lake Trail	E	274	8-2
Powerline Trail	E	318	O-3
Punch Bowl-Black Sand Basin Trl	E	318	O-5, O-3
Purple Mountain Trail	E	319	O-1
Queen's Laundry Spur Trail	E	319	O-2
Raven Creek Cutoff Trail	E	236	5-1
Red Rock Point Trail	E	215	4-9
Rescue Creek Trail	E	134	1-7
Ribbon Lake Trail	E	210	4-6, 4-5
Riddle Lake Trail	E	262	7-1
Riverside Loop Ski Trail	E	347	W-4
Robinson Creek Trail	E	293	9-1
Rocky Ford Cutoff Trail	E	294	9-1, 9-2
Roosevelt Lodge-Tower Falls Trail	E	161	2-6
Sedge Lake - Crag Lake Spur	A	347	W-2, W-1
Sentinel Meadows Trail	E	320	O-2, O-1
Sepulcher Mountain Trail	E	135	1-5
Seven Mile Hole Trail	E	210	4-5
Sheepeater Ski Trail	E	136	1-2
Shoshone Geyser Basin Spur Trail	E	275	8-2
Shoshone GB Stock Cutoff Trail	E	275	8-2, 9-3
Shoshone Lake Trail	E	274	8-2
Silver Cord Cascade Spur Trail	E	211	4-6
Sky Rim Trail	E	348	W-1
Slough Creek Trail	E	161	2-3
Snake River Canyon Trail	E	276	8-1, 6-4
Snake River Cutoff Trail	E	276	8-1, 6-4
Snake River Lookout Trail	A	276	8-3, 8-1
Snow Pass Trail	E	137	1-4, 1-5
Snow Pass - Fawn Pass Cutoff	E	N/A	1-5
Snow Pass - Glen Creek Cutoff	E	N/A	1-5
Soldier's Trail	E	162	2-3
Solfatara Trail	E	137	1-11
Solitary Geyser Trail	E	320	O-5, O-3
Sour Creek Trail	E	211	4-7, 4-8
SBT - Bechler to Mtn Ash Creek	E	294	9-1
SBT - Grassy Lake to Fish lake	A	363	A-2, 9-4
SBT - Harebell	E	277	8-1
SBT - Lynx Creek	E	249	6-3
SBT - South Ent to Grassy Lake	E	277	8-3
SBT - Harebell-Fox Creek	E	249	6-4, 8-1
South Entrance Trail - N Segment	R	260	7-1
South Entrance Trail - S Segment	A	363	8-1, A-2
South Rim Trail	E	212	4-6
South Shore Shoshone Lake Trail	E	278	8-2, 9-3
Specimen Creek Trail	E	349	W-1, W-2
Specimen Forest Trail - East	U	163	2-1
Specimen Forest Trail - West	U	164	2-1
Specimen Ridge Trail	E	162	2-1
Sportsman Lake Trail	E	350	W-2

NAME	STAT	INFO	MAP(S)
Spring Creek Trail	E	321	O-7, 8-2
Stagecoach Road Trail	E	164	2-4
Storm Point Trail	E	237	5-3, 5-2
Summit Lake Trail	E	322	O-8
Sylvan Springs Thermal Area Trail	U	212	4-2
Terrace Springs Trail	E	322	O-1
Terraced Falls Trail	E	295	9-4, 8-3
Thorofare - South Boundary C/O	E	250	6-3
Thorofare Trail	E	237	6-1,2,3
Three Rivers Thermal Area Spur	E	296	9-2
Three Senses Nature Trail	A	364	N/A
Thunderer Cutoff Trail	E	184	3-3, 3-1
Timothy Creek Trail	A	364	3-2, A-1
Tower Creek Trail	E	164	2-7
Tower Falls Trail	E	165	2-7, 2-6
Trail Creek Cabin Bypass Trail	E	251	6-4
Trail Creek Trail	E	279	6-4
Trail Creek-Two Ocean Cutoff	E	251	6-4, 6-3
Trilobite Lake Trail	E	138	1-10
Trout Lake Trail	E	185	3-3
Turbid Lake Trail	E	239	5-3
Twister Falls Trail	E	296	9-2
Two Ocean Plateau Trail	E	251	6-3, 6-4
Two Ribbons Trail	E	351	W-4
Two Waterfalls Trail	U	280	W-3
UGB-Biscuit Basin Bike Trail	E	323	O-4, O-5
UGB-Morning Glory to Bisc Basin	E	323	O-4, O-3
Uncle Tom's Trail	E	215	4-9
Union Falls Trail	E	297	9-4, 9-2
Upper Ford Trail	E	252	6-2
Upper Geyser Basin Trail	E	324	O-5, O-3
Upper Geyser Hill Trail	E	325	O-5, O-3
Upper Lamar River Trail	A	186	3-2
Upper Pelican Creek Cutoff Trail	E	240	5-1, 4-8
Violet Springs Trail	U	213	4-7
Wapiti Lake Trail	E	213	4-8
WBT - Robinson Lk - Summit Lk	A	364	9-2, A-2
WBT - Summit Lake to WYS	A	364	O-8, A-2
WBT - WYS to Bacon Rind	A	364	W-4, A-1
West Thumb Geyser Basin Trail	E	263	7-1
White Creek Trail	A	326	O-2, O-1
Wolf Lake C/O - Little Gibbon Fls	E	214	4-3
Wraith Falls Trail	E	139	1-6
Wrangler Lake Trail	E	214	4-7, 4-8
YCC to Snow Pass Connector Trl	U	139	1-4, 1-5
YCC Trail	E	139	1-4
Yellowstone Meadows Cutoff Trl	E	252	6-3
Yellowstone River Overlook Trail	E	165	2-6
Yell River Picnic Area Outer Spur	U	166	2-6
Yellowstone River Trail	E	140	1-9

Subject Index

ɪis index does not include references to words found in the Points of Reference tables r the individual trails nor the entries found in the various tables in the book's appendices. cluding those would produce an index that would be as thick as the balance of the book.

ɔr the main entries/map locations for the trails, see the Trail Index that precedes this index.

D

E

G

H

M

O

P

Q

R

T

U

V

W

X

Y